DIVIDED
WATERS

DIVIDED WATERS

THE NAVAL HISTORY OF THE CIVIL WAR

IVAN MUSICANT

HarperCollins*Publishers*

HarperCollins books may be purchased for educational, business, or sales promotional use. For information, please write: Special Markets Department, HarperCollins Publishers, Inc., 10 East 53rd Street, New York, NY 10022.

FIRST EDITION

Designed by Alma Orenstein

Library of Congress Cataloging-in-Publication Data
Musicant, Ivan, 1943–
   Divided waters : the naval history of the Civil War / Ivan Musicant.—1st ed.
   p. cm.
   Includes bibliographical references and index.
   ISBN 0–06–016482–4
   1. United States—History—Civil War, 1861–1865—Naval operations.
I. Title.
E591.M87   1995
973.7'5—dc 20   95–8676

95 96 97 98 99 ❖/HC 10 9 8 7 6 5 4 3 2 1

For the women:

Gretchen
Ruth
Diane
and Edna G.

Flaunt out O sea your separate flags of nations!
Flaunt out visible as ever the various ship-signals!
But do you reserve especially for yourself and for the soul of man
    one flag above all the rest,
A spiritual woven signal for all nations, emblem of man elate above
    death,
Token of all brave captains and all intrepid sailors and mates,
And all that went down doing their duty,
Reminiscent of them, twined from all intrepid captains young or old,
A pennant universal, subtly waving all time, o'er all brave sailors,
All seas, all ships.

—WALT WHITMAN

ACKNOWLEDGMENTS

To the staffs of the University of Minnesota's Wilson and Walter libraries, the Minnesota Historical Society, and the U.S. Naval Historical Center, Washington, D.C., my sincerest appreciation for their always conscientious and cheerful attention to my research requirements.

A great deal of thanks must go to Leland and Rae Lien, the excellent and always knowledgeable proprietors of Lien's Old and Rare Books, Minneapolis, Minnesota, without which my own library would consist mostly of bare shelves.

And to Captain James Moffett, of the 1st Minnesota Regiment, and Mr. Bruce Daniel, both of whom happily contributed their enormous knowledge of matters military and explosive.

CONTENTS

Introduction   1

1 Fort Sumter   6

2 The Fires of Norfolk   28

3 Going South   41

4 Shaking Down   50

5 Bricks Without Straw   65

6 Half-Drowned Shores   76

7 Port Royal   90

8 Stone Fleets   102

9 The *Trent* Affair   108

10 Up the Sounds   123

11 "our friends, the enemy"   134

12 Cheese on a Raft   155

13 Stinkpots and Turtles   179

14 "on to Memphis"   205

15 New Orleans   217

16 Vicksburg Rebuff   237

17 Vicksburg Return   256

18 Red River   292

19 Mobile Bay   306

20 On the High Seas   325

21 "On to Charleston!"   368

22 Wilmington, to the End   409

Sources   433

Bibliography   441

Index   453

Maps and illustrations follow page 268.

Introduction

The Civil War caught the United States Navy at the nadir of one of its periodic "dark ages." Less than half of its ninety wooden ships were in commission, and these were spread around the globe in little flag-showing squadrons, more for the sake of national prestige than strategic purpose.

The navy's institutional memory reached to its last great endeavor, the War of 1812, in which several senior captains of 1861 had fought as child midshipmen. The victorious Mexican War of fifteen years past gave some experience in blockade, shore bombardment, and amphibious operations in support of the army. But on the waters there were no contests, for Mexico had no navy.

The two decades prior to the Civil War witnessed revolutionary changes in war at sea with the advent of steam navigation, shell-firing guns, and iron-armored vessels, and the U.S. Navy had participated, more or less, in these new industrial age technologies. The backbone of the fleet lay in six burly, wooden steam frigates, and a half dozen fast screw sloops. The twelve carried forty-four 10-, 9-, and 8-inch Dahlgren "soda bottle" guns. The smaller, fast crew sloops mounted impressively heavy batteries for their size. These ships and their armament were the envy of the world's maritime powers when they began to enter service in the late 1850s. Still, in 1860, fully thirty-four of the navy's serviceable ships were powered by sail only, and tentative experiments in armor plate had borne no fruit.*

If the navy did not spend its time preparing for conflict, it made good as the nation's exploration and diplomatic arm. Scientific expeditions to the North Pacific and Antarctica rivaled those of Charles Darwin. On other fronts, the West African Squadron tirelessly patrolled against the slave trade. In 1853–1854, the navy achieved its greatest foreign success when a powerful steam fleet under Commodore Matthew Calbraith Perry forced open the sealed doors of Japan to the commerce and intercourse of the Western world.

The navy's officer corps was stagnantly somnolent, virtually devoid of promotion opportunities, and it was hardly uncommon to find lieutenants with thirty years' service. There were no admirals, an aristocratic title shunned by a service born in the fire of revolution nearly a century ago. Captain was the highest substantive rank, but when commanding departmental bureaus, stations ashore, or forces afloat, a captain would go by the temporary honorific of commodore or flag officer.†

The service's political leadership, inherent in the office of secretary of the navy, was largely uninspiring, its chief recommendation for appointment being a geographic balance for the national election ticket or outright cronyism.‡ It was said that the nearest to salt water any secretary need go was a barrel of pork. In 1860, the office was held by Isaac Toucy, former Democratic U.S. senator from Connecticut, a man whose object in politics was to avoid all conflict and decisions.

In short, the United States Navy on the very eve of the Civil War was a drowsy, moth-eaten organization. Then the war changed its face, brain, and body completely.

Torn away were one fifth of its officers, to organize and command the new enemy, the navy of the Confederate States of America. With a

---

* Sixteen additional sailing vessels in the Navy List were unserviceable to any degree.

† There was one exception. In 1859 Congress bestowed the permanent rank of flag officer on Charles Stewart, eighty-three years old, in the navy since 1798. He last served at sea commanding the Home Squadron in 1843. In the 1860 Navy Register, Stewart is listed as "waiting orders."

‡ Until the unification of the services in 1947 into the Department of Defense, the secretaries of war (retitled to secretary of the army) and navy were Cabinet-level positions.

handful of talented officers, scratch, indifferent crews, and a penny packet of blacksmithed vessels, this offshoot child delivered some telling blows in defense of its cause, only to disappear as little more than a historical footnote.

By the end of the Civil War, the U.S. Navy had become arguably the most powerful sea force in the world, with a total of 670 ships* led by an impressive fleet of turreted, ironclad monitors, equipped with 8-inch rifles and 15-inch smoothbore cannon, unmatched afloat. The original 1,500 officers and 7,500 enlisted men of 1860 had increased sevenfold, the rank structure had been expanded, and by war's end, eight admirals headed the Navy Register.

Politically, Abraham Lincoln's choice of the ex-Jacksonian Democrat, the wigged fusspot, Gideon Welles, to head the department as secretary of the navy was brilliant. A ruthless administrator, good strategist, and excellent judge of talent, he presided in office for eight years, the longest tenure on record. He was fifty-eight years old in 1860, the quintessential Connecticut Yankee, born in Glastonbury. Descended from the oldest Puritan stock of the colony, Gideon Welles was the son of a merchant farmer, and related on his mother's side to Nathan Hale. Philosophically a Jefferson-Jackson Democrat, Welles served eight years in the state legislature, a stint as state comptroller, and five years as Hartford's postmaster. He was no abolitionist, but he did oppose the divisive Fugitive Slave Law on both constitutional and humanitarian grounds and fought every attempt to extend slavery into the territories.

Gideon Welles' first experience with the Navy Department came in 1845. As a Democratic party warhorse, he had expected the Cabinet seat of postmaster general in the administration of James K. Polk. Instead, he received the minor and distinctly disappointing office of chief of the navy's Bureau of Provisions and Clothing, the only one headed by a civilian. The sleepy office, however, was soon a hive of activity, for war had broken out with Mexico.

To supply a wartime navy, deployed on both sides of the continent, Welles had five clerks crowded into two musty rooms of the Navy Building across the street from the White House. The new chief defied the established custom of buying the cheapest and instead contracted for the best. Irish butter, for example, kept better at sea than the less expensive domestic variety. "It is assumed," Welles informed the secretary of the navy, "that after enjoyment of sweet butter and good cheese, the crews would not relish inferior." For much of the

---

* A number not remotely approached again until the massive building programs of World War I and II.

fleet's provisions, the bureau chief wrote the specifications himself, such as "whiskey in sound, bright, white oak barrels, coopered with four iron hoops."

Welles began the practice of buying comparative samples before disbursing large sums for wholesale lots of clothing. He sent officers to the civilian bakeries to inspect the navy's bread and hardtack. He demoted clerks who could not do their arithmetic, and demanded regular, accurate reports and audits of the bureau.

A less tangible benefit for the navy, though auguring greatly for its future, was Welles' introduction to many junior and mid-ranking officers who would play large roles in the Civil War, among them a commander named David Glasgow Farragut, who had some novel ideas regarding the bombardment of seacoast forts.

A political man to his fingertips, Welles experienced a mounting disaffection with both the Democrats and Whigs, parties that had become "mere hulks in the channel of progress," bound to the personalities of self-serving leaders, bereft of principle, blind to human and national progress. In 1855 Welles broke from the Democrats, and threw his support to a new coalition forming in the north and west calling itself the Republicans.

As a Republican national committeeman, Welles met Abraham Lincoln for the first time in March 1860: "He is in every way large, brain included," he editorialized. But Welles did not commit himself to Lincoln's nomination.

Two months later Welles led the Connecticut delegation to the Republican national convention at the Great Wigwam in Chicago. Initially a backer of Ohio's Governor Salmon Chase, Welles proved a bulwark in denying the nomination to New York Senator William Seward, whom he considered a power-grabbing opportunist. On the third ballot, Welles switched the Connecticut vote to Abraham Lincoln.

In November Lincoln carried Connecticut and all of New England, with the help of Welles' own political organization, the Wide-Awakes. The state's newspapers took up the cause "Welles for the Cabinet." Postmaster General, an office Welles considered entirely suitable, was an important patronage position and was given to Montgomery Blair of the influential Blair family of wavering, border state Maryland. Welles, as an ex-Democrat and New Englander, was given the navy to provide the Cabinet with political and geographic balance. The fact that he had been chief of the Bureau of Provisions and Clothing had hardly anything to do with this appointment. The choice was made on political grounds only.

Once Welles was sworn into office by Chief Justice Roger B. Taney,* the country soon learned of the fussy Puritan moralist who was now secretary of the navy; Gideon Welles wore a long wig parted in the middle, a long white beard, smoked a clay pipe, and had pinched features that made him always look as if he were smelling something unpleasant. "Father Neptune" became a popular nickname; Abraham Lincoln used "Uncle Gideon," but his probity and iron backbone were matched by few politicians then or since. More than once in the Civil War, when all, including Abraham Lincoln, seemed to lose their heads in momentary panic, it was to Gideon Welles they turned.

Gideon Welles' initial disappointment at what was considered a second-rate appointment vanished immediately. The Southern rebellion was in full blow, and the job at hand subsumed any regret at not receiving the prized postmaster generalship. Under his steady, sure hand, the navy would prove an anvil upon which the Confederacy would be crushed and the Union forged and preserved in fire.

---

* The author of the Supreme Court's Dred Scott decision, declaring that slaves had no standing to file suit in Federal court, and thus, in essence, were nonhumans.

1

Fort Sumter

"Seward, see that I don't burn my fingers."

—Abraham Lincoln

T he city of Charleston, South Carolina, cradle of the Confederate rebellion, sits at the tip of a fat finger of land, four miles up a tidal estuary bounded by the Cooper and Ashley rivers. The surrounding shores are a jigsaw puzzle of creeks and swampy bottom. In the center of the harbor, between Sullivan's Island to the north, and Morris Island on the south, loom the fifty-foot-high, six-foot-thick, brick and masonry walls of Fort Sumter, in the last months of 1860 unfinished, unmanned, with just a few old guns lying about on the parade ground.

Other posts ringed the harbor. Given full garrisons, these installations could boast a thousand troops, with over half for Sumter alone. But there were barely enough men to serve a dozen guns. An elderly sergeant filled his time as Sumter's caretaker while the rest, sixty-four gunners and eight musicians of the 1st U.S. Artillery, commanded by Major Robert Anderson, lived in the pleasant green surroundings of Fort Moultrie on Sullivan's Island.

After the November 1860 presidential elections, tensions in Charleston had escalated sharply. With Abraham Lincoln slated to take office the question was no longer "if" South Carolina would secede from the Union, but "when," and the city transformed itself into an armed camp.

In early December, less than two weeks before the state held its secession convention, lame duck President James Buchanan, the wool-gathering "Old Public Functionary," uttered a dangerous, in fact illegal, "implied pledge" not to reinforce the Charleston harbor forts so long as South Carolina made no attempt at seizing Federal property—in other words, to maintain the military status quo.

The soldiers in Fort Moultrie felt abandoned by the outgoing Democratic administration and the citizens of Charleston regarded the mere presence of the garrison as an insulting, "coercive" act. Armed civilians and militia already marched just outside of the fort's embrasures.

For weeks Major Anderson cabled alarms to the War Department about his tiny force, secessionist military preparations, and the utter defenselessness of Fort Sumter. "I would thank you . . . to inform me," ended one report, "whether I would be justified in firing upon an armed body which may be seen approaching our works."

On December 7, in response to Anderson's pleas, Secretary of War John B. Floyd, whom one naval officer termed "an arch traitor," sent Major Don Carlos Buell to Charleston. Buell obediently reiterated the secretary's "anxiety" that Anderson avoid a collision or any measures that might further inflame the "present excited state of the public mind." But Buell went beyond Floyd's instructions. He charged Anderson "to hold possession of the forts . . . and if attacked . . . to defend yourself to the last extremity." He extended Anderson permission to transfer his command to a less exposed position in the harbor than Fort Moultrie. Privately Buell recommended "that you do not allow the opportunity to escape you." Major Buell prepared a copy of Anderson's orders for the President. Following channels, it went first to Secretary Floyd, who deemed the orders "In conformity to my instructions." He passed them on to the White House.

South Carolina authorities were well aware that the removal of Anderson's command from Moultrie to Sumter was sound military logic, and therefore to be prevented at all costs. On December 18, two days prior to South Carolina voting her ordinance of secession, Governor Francis Pickens ordered the state militia to establish a water patrol and prevent at all hazards the transfer of United States troops to Fort Sumter.

On December 21, the day after South Carolina voted to quit the Union, Secretary Floyd wrote to Major Anderson, "you might infer that you are required to make a vain and useless sacrifice of your own life and the lives of the men under your command, upon a mere point of honor." Thus Floyd annulled his own orders and all but ordered Anderson to surrender his posts!

Late in the afternoon of December 26 at Fort Moultrie, the executive officer, Captain Abner Doubleday, received an entirely unexpected order. "Captain," said Major Anderson; "in twenty minutes you will leave this fort with your company for Fort Sumter." Doubleday had no illusions as to the outcome. "I thought of the immediate hostilities of which the movement would be the occasion." But no one interfered when Doubleday embarked his men into three barges. Evening came, and with it a full moon cast its winter light over the harbor as all but the rear guard filed quietly into their boats at Moultrie's wharf. The rear guard spiked the guns, burned their carriages, and just before embarking for Sumter, they cut down the flagstaff.

The next morning the *Charleston Mercury* accused the Federal government of a "gross breach of faith" by altering the military situation in the harbor; and to Anderson, it accorded "the unenviable distinction of opening civil war between American citizens." Governor Pickens demanded that the major return immediately to Fort Moultrie. When Anderson refused, South Carolina militia took possession of every Federal facility within the city: the arsenal, Castle Pinckney, Fort Moultrie, the local branch of the Treasury, the post office, and customs house. Above each, they hoisted the state's red palmetto flag.

When news of Anderson's shift to Fort Sumter reached Washington on the morning of December 27, John B. Floyd simply refused to believe it. "It is impossible," he told stunned South Carolina commissioners in town to negotiate the transfer of Federal property to their newly "independent" state. "It would not be only without orders, but in the face of orders." He rushed off to the War Department and sent a telegram demanding Anderson's immediate explanation.

With equal haste, a trio of eminent Southerners led by Senator Jefferson Davis of Mississippi called on the President. Buchanan listened to the news with "astonishment and regret." Davis maintained the "implied pledge" had been broken. "And now, Mr. President," he said, "you are surrounded with blood and dishonor on all sides." The only thing, Davis pressed, was to order a complete Federal withdrawal from Charleston; after all, it was the chief executive's solemn word that was at stake.

During his whole time in office Buchanan had frugally hewed to a policy of aimless delay. Now an obscure major of artillery had forced the issue, and whichever way it went, half the nation would be outraged. The President recoiled from pulling the garrison out entirely. But he was ready to order Anderson back to Fort Moultrie and wished to consult his Cabinet.

At the Cabinet meeting later that morning, Secretary Floyd, despite documented evidence, insisted Anderson had moved in contravention to orders, thus violating the President's "pledge." The administration's sole avenue to preserve its integrity, he maintained, was to order a complete withdrawal from the harbor. Attorney General Edwin Stanton responded contemptuously that anyone giving such an order equaled the treachery of Benedict Arnold. "A President of the United States who would make such an order would be guilty of treason." "Oh, no!" replied Buchanan, "not so bad as that my friend! Not so bad as that!"

Nothing resolved, Buchanan decided that he needed time to "say my prayers when required to act upon any great State affair." Meanwhile the army's commanding general, seventy-four-year-old Winfield Scott, "Old Fuss and Feathers," in bed, racked with loose bowels and agonizing gout, bestirred himself to dictate a message to the secretary of war. Scott urged that orders not be issued for Sumter's evacuation, and instead that 150 recruits be shipped from New York as reinforcements, and "one or two armed vessels be sent to support said fort."

Backed into a corner, and facing national collapse, Buchanan finally asked the secretary of state, Judge Jeremiah Black, to frame the answer to the rebels. With Stanton furiously copying, Black stiffened the President's spine and charted the administration's course. The Charleston forts, he dictated without equivocation, "belong to the Government, are its own, and cannot be given up." As for the "implied pledge" to maintain the military status quo, the President must personally issue a flat denial of the existence of any such bargain—"The fact that he pledged himself in any such way can not be true." Regarding Major Anderson's decision to evacuate Fort Moultrie, Black challenged, "It is a strange assumption of right . . . to say that United States troops must remain in the weakest position they can find in the harbor." Finally, Black faced the matter of Sumter's reinforcement. The President must order the powerful steam sloop *Brooklyn* and the frigate *Macedonian* to Charleston "without the least delay," with troops to follow immediately. "If this be done at once all may yet not be well, but comparatively safe. If not," he prophesied, "I can see nothing before us but disaster and ruin to the country."

On New Year's Eve, 1860, General Scott ordered the commanding officer at Fort Monroe, Virginia, to prepare four companies of infantry and ninety days' provisions for the Sumter garrison, "as secretly and confidentially as possible. *Look to This*." The same day, twelve miles across Hampton Roads, the commandant of the Norfolk Navy Yard received a confidential order from Navy Secretary Isaac Toucy: "Fill up *Brooklyn* with provisions, water, and coal."

That busy New Year's Eve, while the military and naval services struggled uncertainly with bare means, President Buchanan sealed his reply to the South Carolina commissioners. He absolutely refused to order the troops out of Fort Sumter. "This I cannot do," he penned, "this I will not do." But when all that was wanting was the final order to promptly reinforce Sumter, Buchanan and Scott became possessed of an onslaught of ill-guided chivalry. Had the President and his chief advisers acted immediately, hastening the *Brooklyn* and her reinforcements, the ship could have arrived off the bar in less than three days, and guns run out, swept past the makeshift rebel defenses. It is quite possible Charleston harbor would have been denied to the Confederacy for the course of the war, an enormous advantage for the Union.

But neither Buchanan nor Scott were up to it. The President felt it only right that he delay until the rebel commissioners had the opportunity to read and reply to his letter of the morning. Scott concurred without demur, considering the decision "gentlemanly and proper."

On January 2, the President and Cabinet convened in noisy vituperation. Jacob Thompson of Interior threatened resignation if the *Brooklyn* and the reinforcements were sent. Bowing to the argument, Buchanan agreed to send a messenger to Fort Sumter inquiring whether Major Anderson actually desired reinforcements. Secretary of State Black was stunned. "Does the sending of a messenger," he demanded, "imply that no additional troops are to be sent until his return?" The President sniffed, "Judge Black, it implies nothing."

At that moment a clerk entered with the rebel commissioners' reply. They totally rejected Buchanan's attempts at mollification, charging the President for defaulting on his "pledge." South Carolina, they insisted, posed no threat to Anderson at Fort Sumter, but the fact that he had moved "under cover of night, to a safer position [meant] war."

Denounced as a liar, Buchanan girded his loins and placed himself firmly in the Cabinet's Unionist camp. "It is now all over," he said, "and reinforcements must be sent."

But Winfield Scott flinched instead. Suddenly, he saw major impediments to sending the *Brooklyn* and the four companies of Regulars from Fort Monroe. After conferring with a mysterious person, whom he "believed to possess much knowledge and practical experience in naval affairs," Scott erroneously determined that the *Brooklyn* was incapable of crossing the Charleston bar at anything but high tide.

In addition, Scott determined that Fort Monroe, the nation's premier coastal fortification, gatekeeper to Chesapeake Bay and tidewater Virginia, truly could not afford to be stripped of half its garrison. It would be better to ship 200 "well instructed" recruits from New York, and to assure "secrecy and success," to embark them in an unarmed merchant steamer!

With precious time evaporating, one of Scott's adjutants set off for New York and chartered the steamer *Star of the West* for $1,250 a day.

On January 5, First Lieutenant Charles Woods took command of the relief force, and was advised to mask his intent until the final moment. Major Anderson at Fort Sumter was duly informed of the mission—by ordinary mail! However, by the time he received the letter, which authorized him to return fire gun for gun if the rebel batteries fired on the relief vessel, the *Star of the West* had come and gone.

On January 7, with the *Star of the West* midway on her passage, the New York papers carried the story of the reinforcement. Navy Secretary Toucy dispatched two sets of orders to the *Brooklyn* at Hampton Roads. One set was from Scott to Lieutenant Woods, the other, Toucy's personal instructions to Captain William Walker, skipper of the *Brooklyn*. Their baffling, contrary vagueness is stunning. Woods was told that the *Brooklyn* was on a dual mission, "first to afford aid and succor in case your ship be . . . injured; second to convey this order of recall for your detachment in case it cannot land at Fort Sumter." Walker's orders were equally opaque. He was to "render such aid and assistance" as the *Star of the West* required, but, Toucy cautioned, "It is not considered expedient that you should attempt to cross the [harbor] bar." Given that proscription, it is difficult to see what real assistance the *Brooklyn* could actually have provided.

At Fort Sumter on the evening of January 8, Anderson received the day's edition of the *Charleston Mercury* and read with interest the story of the *Star of the West*. The major was inclined to discount it, the journal was a notorious spreader of rumors and falsehood. Actually, the *Star of the West* was already off the bar, but showing no lights, she was invisible to Sumter's sentries. There were no lights in the harbor either, and prudence dictated the ship's master, John McGowan, wait until dawn to bring the vessel in. At daybreak, January 9, 1861, with the American flag at her peak, and the soldiers hidden below deck, the *Star of the West* crossed the bar and steamed up the main ship channel.

From Sumter's parapets, Abner Doubleday swept the harbor with his long glass. "As I looked seaward I saw a large steamer pass the bar and enter the Morris Island channel. It had the ordinary United States flag up; and as [the ship] evidently did not belong to the navy, I came to the conclusion it must be the *Star of the West*," just as the *Mercury* had predicted.

When abreast of Cummings Point on Morris Island, less than two miles from the fort, the rebel batteries opened fire. One shot struck forward, another hit in the area of the rudder, neither causing any damage. Master McGowan ordered a huge, 36-foot army garrison flag hoisted to the foremast, hoping that "Major Anderson would understand it and protect the ship under the guns of Sumter."

Anderson ordered the drums to beat the long roll, and the men rushed to the guns. The batteries on Cummings Point pounded away, but the *Star* steamed out of range to within gunshot of Fort Moultrie. "We'll catch the devil from Sumter," mused one rebel gunner, expecting the covering fire at any moment. But Anderson refused all entreaties from his officers to shoot. According to one soldier, the major was "excited and uncertain of what to do."

On board the *Star of the West* consternation reigned. Why did Sumter remain silent? Ahead, Master McGowan watched a rebel steamer, flying the red palmetto flag, making straight for his ship. "The battery [at Fort Moultrie] firing on us all the time," he remembered, "and having no cannon to defend ourselves from the attack . . . we concluded that to avoid certain capture or destruction, we would endeavor to get to sea." The first relief of Fort Sumter had ended in abject failure.

News of the firing on the *Star of the West* stirred strong indignant feelings in the North. But the acrimony quickly subsided, as if by unspoken agreement the nation had decided to await the incoming administration of Abraham Lincoln to solve the national crisis. James Buchanan did nothing to stem the yawning rift, and by February 1861, Alabama, Florida, Mississippi, Georgia, Louisiana, and Texas had all passed ordinances of secession.

Within the Cabinet, secretaries Holt and Black continued their pressure for Sumter's relief. The garrison had only two months' provisions remaining, and all the rebels needed to do was wait and starve

Anderson out. "The men will be exhausted," noted Jeremiah Black, "surrender is a question of time only."

During the first week of February, Gustavus Vasa Fox, an astute former naval officer, who had left the dead-end service for the more stimulating life as captain of a mail steamer, presented a sound relief plan to Winfield Scott. Scott was impressed and he introduced the bald, goateed, heavily mustached Fox, to Secretary Holt, who in turn laid the plan before the President that very evening.

Fox proposed to embark the relief force "on board of a large, comfortable [merchant] sea steamer," accompanied by a pair of New York harbor tugs, all to be convoyed by the navy steam sloop *Pawnee* and the big revenue cutter *Harriet Lane,* the only suitable warships available in home waters.* Should any cockleshell rebel craft attempt to interfere, the warships would "destroy or drive them on shore." Anderson would cooperate by firing on any hostile vessels or batteries within his range.

Then, Fox continued, "at night, two hours before high water, with half the force on board each tug . . . I should run in to Fort Sumter." Fox requested he be placed "in charge of everything," except the actual command of the warships.

But Buchanan had other matters to ponder. On February 8, at Montgomery, Alabama, the Provisional Congress of the Confederate States of America voted to accept the constitution for their new "nation," and elected Jefferson Davis president. As for Fort Sumter, Fox received dismal news from the general in chief. The administration had decided to make no further efforts toward relief.

On March 4, 1861, Abraham Lincoln became the sixteenth president of the United States. No chief executive, before or since, faced an ordeal of more horrific proportions: the literal collapse of the nation.

Following his inaugural address, Lincoln entered the White House and was handed a message from Major Anderson, received that day by Secretary of War Holt, in his last hours of office. Fort Sumter, the new President learned, had a month's provisions left—perhaps forty days with careful saving. Anderson waxed pessimistic. "I confess," he lamented, "that I would not be willing to risk my reputation on an attempt to throw reinforcements into this harbor . . . with a force of less than twenty-thousand good and disciplined men."

---

* The Treasury Department's Revenue Marine was the nation's oldest armed service. In 1915 its name was changed to the Coast Guard. The *Harriet Lane,* named for Buchanan's popular niece, was its first steam vessel.

The news forced Lincoln to face an incredible complication. Counting on at least *some* time to sort out the national calamity, he had no ready program for either winning the seceding states back to the Union or going to war; certainly not with an army numbering barely over 16,000 men, a sleepy navy flung to the world's corners, and the officers of both services hemorrhaging South at an alarming rate.

Lincoln inexplicably waited five days before convening his Cabinet, when he put the question: "Assuming it to be possible to now provision Fort Sumter, under all the circumstances, is it wise to attempt it?" The members retired to consult with General Scott, Gustavus V. Fox, and several senior officers, losing another week before submitting their written answers.

Secretary of State William Seward, who thought *he* should be the president, counseled prudence. No, he said, now was not the time to use force. Salmon Chase of the Treasury veered in both directions. Yes, reinforce if the movement might bring a peaceful solution; no if it meant war and million-dollar budgets. "I cannot advise it," said Simon Cameron, the corrupt new secretary of war. "No practical benefit will result to the country." No, said Interior's Caleb Smith. True, he reasoned, a surrender would cause widespread "surprise and complaint" in the North, but it could all be eventually "explained and understood." Attorney General Edward Bates voted against. "I am willing to evacuate Fort Sumter." Navy Secretary Gideon Welles joined the naysayers, "I entertain doubts," he said. Only Postmaster General Montgomery Blair, Gus Fox's brother-in-law, unequivocally voted yes. Buchanan had hesitated, he argued, and he had failed. Blair harkened to Andrew Jackson's decisive action in crushing South Carolina's attempt to unilaterally "nullify" the tariff in 1832. Jackson had reinforced the Federal military presence in Charleston and he had won. To provision Fort Sumter now, Blair concluded, would "vindicate the hardy courage of the North, and the determination of the people and their President to maintain the authority of the Government."

On March 12, Blair ushered Gus Fox into Lincoln's office. After explaining his plan, Fox audaciously suggested he take a personal trip to Charleston to evaluate the situation. Lincoln agreed, provided that General Scott and Secretary Cameron posed no objections. There were none.

Traveling by train through Virginia and the Carolinas, Fox arrived at the city on March 21, and permission to visit the fort was readily granted. On the subject of relief, he found Major Anderson in a dejected mood. He believed naval operations impossible, and nothing short of 10,000 men adequate to force the issue ashore.

Fox thought otherwise, and when investigating the harbor from the parapets, he concluded that given the darkness of night, a vessel remained invisible until she nearly bumped the fort's landing jetty. Fox, nonetheless, confirmed the dire strait of Sumter's larder, and he agreed that unless something were done, the fort could not hold out past April 15, three weeks away. On his return to Washington, Fox met several times with Lincoln and the Cabinet, pushing hard to get going. On March 30, Lincoln sent him to New York with verbal orders to prepare the relief "but to make no binding engagements."

The service secretaries, Gideon Welles and Simon Cameron, alerted their minions. The War Department ordered 200 recruits, with a full year's stores, mustered at New York's Governor's Island. Welles instructed his commandants at the Brooklyn, Washington, and Norfolk navy yards to ready the *Pawnee, Harriet Lane,* and the steam sloops *Powhatan* and *Pocahontas* for service by April 6.

At Brooklyn, the *Powhatan,* on whose guns and boats Fox relied to carry the offensive burden, had just returned from extended service in Mexican waters. Her engines were worn out, and she had gone out of commission for repairs. The officers were scattered on leave and her 200 sailors awaited passage to Norfolk. Welles placed the *Powhatan* back on active service, informing the skipper, Captain Samuel Mercer, that he now commanded the naval portion of the Sumter relief expedition, with all vessels to arrive off Charleston bar by the morning of April 11. Welles briefed Lincoln on the arrangements, and the President, Welles noted in diary, "approved them."

"Telegram just received," wired the Brooklyn Navy Yard's acting commandant, Commander Andrew Foote. "All possible dispatch, night and day, being made to get *Powhatan* off the yard on Friday."

That same day, April 6, in Washington, a disgruntled, black-bearded naval officer, David Dixon Porter, sat at dinner with his family. The son of Commodore David Porter, of War of 1812 fame, he was typical of those old lieutenants grown weary of spending their best years in a doldrumed navy with little hope of promotion. He was nearly forty-eight, number six on the lieutenants' list, and had been in his present rank for twenty years. This family dinner was to be a farewell. Porter was abandoning Washington for California to command the only ship he could obtain, a vessel of the Treasury Department's Coast Survey. From there he planned to leave the navy for the merchant service.

The present national crisis held no attraction for him, and indeed, Porter's request for duty across the continent had raised suspicions about his loyalty. Resignations were coming fast, and Gideon Welles deemed the "officers who at such time sought duties in the Pacific and on foreign stations ... *prima facie,* as in sympathy with the Secessionists." Of Fort Sumter and its portents, Porter showed hardly an interest, even though his neighbor, Captain Montgomery Meigs of the army, had mentioned something about "a small squadron ... being fitted out for the supposed purpose [of its relief].* They had also discussed an audacious plan to retake the Pensacola Navy Yard, already fallen to the rebels without a shot and reinforce Fort Pickens in Pensacola Bay as well.

On January 12, three months back, Florida's Pensacola Navy Yard, little more than a supply and coaling station, but the navy's only permanent base on the Gulf of Mexico, had surrendered to some poorly armed companies of Florida and Alabama militia.

Commanded by Captain Adam Slemmer, a tiny coast artillery garrison, very much like that at Fort Sumter, had taken refuge in Fort Pickens on a sandspit island overlooking the yard in Pensacola Bay. But unlike the situation in Charleston, a small naval squadron comprising the *Brooklyn* with a company of troops aboard, two sailing frigates, and a sloop, already stood offshore, in direct support of the fort. Yet because of ludicrous, outdated orders, the soldiers sat useless, stifling in the ship. In early April, Gideon Welles sent a trusted officer, Lieutenant John L. Worden, to the scene. Though he managed to land the reinforcements, an odd cease-fire, "the truce of Fort Pickens," continued between the rebels, the fort's garrison, and the navy.

Lieutenant Porter never finished the gloomy meal with his family. A coach stopped at the front door bearing a messenger from Secretary of State Seward, requesting the lieutenant to call immediately. Porter threw down his napkin, jumped into the carriage and trotted off to Seward's office. "I found Mr. Seward," he remembered, "lying on his back on a sofa, with his knees up, reading a lengthy document." Without changing his supine position, the secretary asked, "Can you tell me how we can save Fort Pickens from falling into the hands of the rebels?"

Now this was something completely out of the channels of the Navy

---

* At the time, Meigs directed the work completing the new dome and wings of the Capitol building. Within a month, he was promoted to brigadier general, and (replacing Joseph E. Johnston, who had gone South) quartermaster general of the army, a post he ably filled for the duration of the war.

Department, and Seward's motives were nothing if not complex. On the surface, according to Porter's interpretation, the secretary was "anxious to show the Southerners that the [Federal] government had a right to hold its own forts." But it went much deeper than that. In fact, behind Lincoln's back, he was secretly negotiating the evacuation of Fort Sumter.

The Machiavellian Seward had no great admiration for Lincoln's ability to lead the nation. He considered himself a far abler statesman—in fact, the one who should have received the Republican presidential nomination. Seward intended to establish himself as a sort of prime minister, guiding the President along the correct path. Seward also had no faith in the Navy Department's bureaucracy, not with officer resignations increasing every day and confidences likely to be reported South by secessionist-minded clerks. In addition, Seward remained enraged at Gideon Welles for blocking his presidential aspirations and supporting Lincoln's nomination. What better form of revenge than to wrest control of naval operations at this early stage of the conflict?

Hardly in a position to realize the secretary's entangled designs, Lieutenant David Dixon Porter answered Seward's question of Fort Pickens directly:

"I can, sir."

"Then," Seward said, "you are the man I want, if you can do it."

"I can do it."

"Now, come," said Seward, rising from his couch, "tell me how you will save that place."

At that moment, Montgomery Meigs stepped into the room, and it alighted on Lieutenant Porter that the secretary of state had known a bit more than he let on.

What was needed, Porter said, was a "good-sized steamer," packed with 300 or so troops, heavy artillery, and sufficient ammunition. They would land "under the guns of a ship of war, and the fort would soon be made impregnable." Porter had no doubts of the plan's success. "Give me command of the *Powhatan,*" he asked, as if the secretary of state had the authority to appoint captains afloat, "and I will guarantee that everything shall be done without a mistake."

Seward took the two officers to meet the President, and to Lincoln's question as to whether Fort Pickens could be held, Meigs stingingly replied, "Certainly, if the navy would do its duty." Porter had some very definite ideas about that, and he explained to the President "the queer state of things existing in the Navy at this time." Welles, he said, was surrounded by officers and civilian clerks, "some of whom are disloyal at heart." Should the orders for the Pickens expedition emanate from Welles' desk, "and pass through all the department red tape, the news would at once be flashed over the wires, and Fort Pickens would be lost for ever." Boldly he requested that Lincoln personally issue the orders for him to take the *Powhatan* to Pensacola; "I will guarantee their prompt execution to the letter."

Lincoln, however, was decidedly uncomfortable. "But is not this a most irregular mode of proceeding?" "Certainly," Porter replied, "but necessary under the circumstances." For these utterances, Porter was extremely lucky not to spend the remainder of the war as an unemployed officer.

When Lincoln seemed to hesitate, Seward chimed in, "Mr. President, you are the commander-in-chief of the army and navy, and this is a case where it is necessary to issue direct orders without passing them through intermediaries."

Lincoln wavered. "But what will Uncle Gideon say?"

"Oh," Seward answered blithely, "I will make it all right with Mr. Welles. This is the only way, sir, the thing can be done."

Reluctantly, Lincoln agreed. He took no notice of the incompatibility of the Pensacola scheme with the Sumter relief expedition, perhaps simply confusing the name of the ship whose presence was vital to assure success at both places.

Porter immediately wrote the "confidential," *carte blanche* orders for the President's signature. Meigs copied them out in a finer hand, and passed the papers to the President for his signature. Lincoln picked up his pen. "Seward," he said, "see that I don't burn my fingers."

Now that they had their ship, Porter and Meigs needed to find the troops, and not a single private could be issued marching orders without Winfield Scott's concurrence. From the White House they took the short ride to the general in chief's quarters. "Tell Captain Meigs to walk in," the general growled to his aide, "I won't see any naval officer; *he* can't come in." Faced with Lincoln's signed orders, Scott dictated instructions for Colonel Harvey Brown to take four depleted companies of soldiers, 200 men, from Governor's Island by the steamer *Atlantic* to Fort Pickens, and there assume overall authority.

On Thursday, April 4, Gus Fox took command of the Sumter relief expedition. But he and everyone else connected with the mission were unaware the *Powhatan* had been secretly reassigned. Fox, after a last meeting with Lincoln, traveled to New York where he chartered the steamer *Baltic* and three tugs, one of which, the *Yankee,* he equipped with a novel weapon, "fitted to throw hot water." Porter and Meigs were also in New York. While Porter unpacked at the Astor House, Meigs took an East River ferry to the Brooklyn Navy Yard and presented Commander Foote with the orders for the *Powhatan*. Foote had already received instructions from Secretary Welles regarding that ship for the Sumter expedition, yet here were conflicting documents signed by the President himself.

Sidestepping the order's smelly prohibition "that under no circumstances" was he to inform the Navy Department, Foote composed a vaguely worded cable to the secretary, informing him of "certain preparations made and things placed on board of vessels . . . about which you are familiar." But, he added, "as the orders do not come direct [from you], I make this report . . . no time is to be lost, I am preparing what is called for, and report my action."

After a busy day, Welles had retired to his rooms at Willard's Hotel, when sometime before midnight, he was called upon by Secretary Seward and his son, Frederick. Seward was agitated because he had just received a telegram from Meigs in New York complaining the *Powhatan*'s movements were "retarded and embarrassed by conflicting orders from the Secretary of the Navy."

Welles was mystified. He had yet to receive Foote's cryptic message and was ignorant of any cross purposes. Seward explained that it must have something to do with Porter's taking command of the ship. What command? Welles wanted to know; Porter had no command. The *Powhatan* was under orders as flagship for the Sumter relief expedition, and Seward knew this. With a straight face, Seward posed there must be an error somewhere, and suggested "that we had better call on the President."

Although it was nearly midnight, Lincoln was awake and very surprised at his visitors' calling, a surprise, Welles observed, that "was not diminished on learning our errand." There had to be some blunder here, Lincoln said, the *Powhatan* cannot possibly be the flagship of the Sumter relief force. There was no error, Welles insisted, the President had already approved the orders. Lincoln was unsure, and Welles hurried across the street to the Navy Department to fetch them.

Studying the documents, Lincoln remembered and knew he had been duped. Angrily, he rounded on Seward and demanded the *Powhatan* be restored to Captain Mercer, and that on no account must the Sumter relief expedition be interfered with. Seward remonstrated that Fort Pickens was just as important, and might well fall should the *Powhatan* be recalled.

Lincoln would have none of it. Pickens, he rightly exclaimed, could wait. It already had a partly reinforced garrison and a sizable naval force patrolling outside the bay. Seward continued to obstruct. With rising anger, Lincoln cut him off; it was "imperative" and must be done. Beaten at his game, Seward scribbled on a telegraph blank, "Give the *Powhatan* up to Captain Mercer," addressed it to Porter, and handed it to a clerk for transmission.

With that, Lincoln profusely apologized to his secretary of the navy. "He took upon himself the whole blame," Welles wrote, "said it was carelessness, heedlessness on his part, he ought to have been more careful and attentive. President Lincoln never shunned any responsibility."

Porter arrived at the Brooklyn Navy Yard the next morning, Saturday, April 6, and according to him, spent "three hours' earnest conversation" trying to persuade Andrew Foote that "I was not a rebel in disguise plotting with the *Powhatan*'s officers to run away with the ship, and deliver her over to the South."

Foote felt extremely uneasy. He had received no answer from his telegram to Secretary Welles. He read Porter's orders from the President several times, examining the watermark and the "Executive Mansion" stamp. "You see, Porter," he said, "there are so many fellows whom I would have trusted to the death who have deserted the flag that I don't know whom to believe. How do I know *you* are not a traitor?" He thought it best to keep Porter close at hand, and invited him to share his quarters at the navy yard until preparations on the *Powhatan* were complete.

No sooner had Foote agreed, albeit with a very wary eye, to carry out Porter's presidential orders, than the *original* orders arrived from the Navy Department, the ones Lincoln had seen and forgotten, addressed to Captain Mercer of the *Powhatan* to take command of the Sumter relief forces.

Porter scrambled about for a plausible explanation. "We are telegraphing to Mr. Seward," he told the astonished Foote. "Meigs thinks Mr. Welles' telegram is bogus." Lacking definitive instructions from the Department, Foote had no choice but to obey the presidential seal.

That afternoon, the *Powhatan,* her refit hardly complete, especially to her broken-down engineering plant, made ready to cast off her lines. To preserve the aura of secrecy, Porter came aboard unnoticed and hid in a cabin below. The plan was for Mercer to take her out, then hand over command off Staten Island.

Near 3 P.M., the ship's wheezy engines coughed into life, and she headed downriver for the open sea. At virtually that moment came Seward's canceling telegram, "Give the *Powhatan* up to Captain Mercer."

Foote detailed an officer to charter a civilian tug that managed to overhaul the warship just outside the lower bay Narrows. Mercer had already gone ashore, and Porter reading the cable signed by Seward put a fine point to protocol. He again placed his career in the starkest jeopardy and quickly jotted an answer: "I received my [original] orders from the President and shall proceed and execute them."

Perhaps realizing the possible results of his temerity, he also composed a letter to Andrew Foote, "This is an unpleasant position to be in, but I will work out of it." Foote read the notes and shook his head in bewilderment. "He's clean daft—or has run off with the ship to join the rebels ... Well, I'll never trust anyone again. I have lost faith in human nature." And with that, the *Powhatan* thrashed off, useless and needless, to Pensacola.

On Saturday, April 6, Lincoln sent special messengers to South Carolina's Governor Pickens and to the commander of the rebel forces in Charleston, Brigadier General Pierre G. T. Beauregard, informing them that "an attempt will be made to supply Fort Sumter with provisions only." If they saw fit not to interfere, he would make no effort at a military reinforcement, except "in case of an attack."

On its face, this official notification seems absurd; why would Lincoln notify the rebels of his intentions? But it was a political masterstroke. The Union had taken enough slaps in the face already, but none, not even the fiasco of the *Star of the West*, had set the tone for the national determination so necessary for the prosecution of a war, should it come to that. If the rebels opened fire on unarmed ships' boats, laden with food for hungry men, the Confederacy, Lincoln hoped, would stand accused of committing an undeniable, overt act of war.

United determination was also very much on the mind of Confederate President Jefferson Davis. On receiving the text of Lincoln's messages, he hastily summoned his Cabinet to seek a consensus on the issue. The rebel statesmen, mirroring Lincoln's Cabinet, were initially divided. Secretary of War Leroy Walker knew well their complete unreadiness for any sort of protracted conflict. An attack on Fort Sumter, he said, or its relief forces, would commence a bloody civil war. "It is suicide, murder," he told Davis, "and will lose us every friend at the North."

The Cabinet's radical faction, however, carried Davis with them. He was under extreme pressure, as was Lincoln, to "do something." The

border states and the upper South, Virginia chief among them, still hesitated, but a bold strike might shake them into the Confederate camp.
Further, the radicals—indeed, the South as a whole—sincerely
believed the Union possessed more bluster than fight and would
meekly acquiesce in the face of Southern arms.

On the international stage, there was the matter of "King Cotton
diplomacy," the South's only economic lever. The Confederate politicians genuinely accepted that, should war come, Britain and France
would have little choice but to recognize their new nation, on whom
Europe depended for its cotton. And with diplomatic recognition might
well come active military support.

But of all the reasons for attacking Fort Sumter, none were more
compelling than Southern nationalism. The very idea that a Federal
post should be maintained in one of the Confederacy's principal ports,
the very cradle of the rebellion, was anathema. The orders went out to
General Beauregard. If he was convinced the Federal government
would attempt to supply Fort Sumter by force, "you will at once
demand its evacuation, and, if this is refused, proceed, in such manner
as you may determine, to reduce it."

In New York, Gus Fox, having not the slightest notion of the Pensacola expedition, was having a difficult time putting together his own
Sumter relief expedition. The indifference and delay of the senior army
officers at Governor's Island lost many precious hours. Now the best
troops were already at sea, bound for Fort Pickens, and the army allot-
ted Fox the scrapings of the barrel.

Beginning on Monday, April 8, the ships of the Sumter relief force
put to sea from New York and Hampton Roads, and immediately
steamed into a lashing Atlantic gale. In his departing report to the Navy
Department, Commander John Gillis of the *Pocahontas* typified the
statements of his fellow skippers: "detained by thick weather and heavy
gales . . . will exert all diligence and dispatch." Of Fox's three tugs, so
laboriously gathered, only the *Yankee* ever arrived off Charleston Bar—
too late.

While the ships battled the elements, General Beauregard sent his
demand for Anderson's surrender. "The flag," wrote the chivalrous general, "which you have upheld so long and with so much fortitude, under
the most trying circumstances, may be saluted by you on taking it
down." Anderson refused the offer. But unthinkingly he remarked to
the Confederate heralds, "Gentlemen, if you do not batter the fort to
pieces about us, we shall be starved out in a few days."

Beauregard telegraphed this vital news to his chiefs. Jefferson

Davis conferred with his secretary of war, and they agreed it would be folly to needlessly open a bombardment, so long as Anderson stated a specific time for his evacuation, and promised to fire no guns without provocation. If he refused, they authorized Beauregard to "reduce the fort . . . " But Beauregard had just two days' worth of powder for his guns and reports that Federal warships lay off the bar were sweeping the city. In the early minutes of Friday, April 12, the rebels sent new terms of capitulation out to Fort Sumter, demanding immediate surrender. Major Anderson, unaware that a relief force was already off the bar, offered to evacuate the fort by noon, Monday, the day the garrison would run out of food. Unlike the fort's garrison, Beauregard's messengers knew the revenue cutter *Harriet Lane* rode off the bar, and they refused Anderson's counteroffer. Instead, they handed the major their own hastily scribbled note: "We have the honor to notify you that [Brigadier General Beauregard] will open the fire of his batteries on Fort Sumter in one hour from this time."

The storms had not abated, but the waters within the harbor lay calm, under bright stars, now just beginning to fade. At 4:30 A.M., a mortar shell rose high in a steeply arching trajectory—a signal for the rebel batteries to commence firing. Seconds later, its shell burst over Fort Sumter; the Civil War had truly begun.

In the heaving, offshore seas, the steamer *Baltic,* carrying Gustavus Fox, his few hundred recruits, and enough provisions to supply Fort Sumter's garrison for many months, lurched about the rendezvous some miles off Charleston bar. The ship had arrived less than two hours before the bombardment, and Fox might have attempted an entrance right then. But only the *Harriet Lane* was visible from the masthead, and Fox dared not move without a substantially armed vessel to accompany him. Of the fusillade of shot and shell bursting over Fort Sumter, Fox neither saw nor heard a thing.

Sometime before 7 A.M., the steam sloop *Pawnee,** a fast, powerful, twin-screwed vessel mounting eight 9-inch guns, hove up to the rendezvous. Fox requested her commanding officer, Stephen Rowan, to stand in toward the bar as the *Baltic*'s escort. No shrinking violet, Rowan nonetheless refused. His orders, he explained to Fox, required him to remain ten miles out and await the *Powhatan;* he was not "going in there to inaugurate civil war." Rowan, however, armed his boats and readied them for bringing in provisions.

---

* The first vessel in the U.S. Navy fitted with twin propellers.

Tossing prudence to the wind, Fox returned to the *Baltic* and followed by the frail *Harriet Lane,* "who cheerfully accompanied me," steamed toward the bar. Approaching land, the men on deck distinctly heard the booming discharges and watched the rising black smoke. "It was observed," Fox drolly reported, "that war had commenced." The two ships at once went about to inform Commander Rowan. He, too, had seen the smoke. Through a hailing trumpet, he shouted across the rolling swells. "[He] asked for a pilot," Fox said, "declaring his intention of standing in to the harbor and sharing the fate of his brethren of the Army."

The *Pawnee* and the *Harriet Lane,* guns loaded and decks cleared for action, dropped their anchors near the bar, at the edge of the Swash Channel. None of the ships carried boats nor sailors enough to ferry the troops and supplies in anything like a timely manner, but Fox was certain the *Powhatan* must shortly arrive. Still, a couple of boats' worth of provisions might be forced through. Because the heavy seas "crippled the night movement," the attempt would have to be made the following morning.

Saturday, April 13, dawned foggy-thick, with very heavy swells. Resolved that one boat could run the gauntlet of fire and reach Fort Sumter, the army's Lieutenant Robert Tyler, suffering miserably from seasickness, as were most of the troops, organized a boat's crew from among his men.

Off the bar, merchantmen backed and filled, none daring to enter the harbor during the bombardment. Suddenly the *Pawnee* spotted an ice schooner heading inshore. Rowan, "suspecting her to belong to Charleston," fired three shots across her bow, bringing the vessel to anchor. "I at once determined to use her for the purpose of transferring both men and provisions" to Fort Sumter.

Fox lost no time in taking a boat to the *Pawnee.* He immediately agreed with Rowan's plan and took command of the schooner: "Plenty of volunteers agreed to man the vessel and go in with me."

Since the *Baltic*'s arrival the day before, Rowan was well aware of the acute anxiety regarding the *Powhatan.* But for unknown reasons, he kept to himself that he had received a letter from Captain Mercer, dated April 6, notifying him that the ship had been detached on orders "of superior authority ... for another destination." Rowan now produced the note, and Fox was stunned speechless.

At 2 P.M., the *Pocahontas* was finally sighted steaming through the "unpropitious" weather. Commander Gillis boarded the *Pawnee,* and being eight numbers ahead of Rowan in the Navy Register, superseded him as the senior naval officer present. He joined the tactical discussion and agreed to the arrangements "to send provisions and some men to the relief . . . after dark." But the *Pawnee*'s masthead lookouts were shouting down to the deck, and all eyes snapped ashore. "The flagstaff on Fort Sumter was shot away," Gillis said, "and we witnessed the sad spectacle of the fall of our flag, which we were so impotent to assist. In vain we looked for its reappearance . . . instead . . . the firing from Sumter became more and more weak, and at length ceased entirely."

Presuming Sumter's capitulation, Gillis sent a boat to Cummings Point to learn whether the fort had indeed struck its colors, and if so, to arrange "to take off the heroic and patriotic Major Anderson and his command if they had survived the conflagration." It was 4 P.M., and Rowan penned his log, "At the close of this watch a steamer is lying alongside Fort Sumter with the secession flag flying."

Inside Sumter, the last of the bread had long been eaten, and the garrison subsisted on a diet of bad salt pork. Anderson faced the grim truth. The relieving ships had made no attempt to force the bar, and he could not presume an onset of audacity on the navy's part anytime soon. Further resistance to the bombardment was useless, and he agreed to accept Beauregard's terms. At 1:30 P.M., Saturday, April 13, after thirty-three hours of bombardment, a white hospital bedsheet flapped from the parapet.

In response to Gillis' boat, a rebel steamer bearing a white flag and an officer from Fort Sumter came out to the *Pocahontas*. Major Anderson wished to know what transportation the navy could provide for his garrison, which under the terms of capitulation would evacuate the fort the next morning. There was no problem, Gillis said, they could all sail home in the *Baltic*. He boarded the rebel steamer to make the offer in person.

On the fifteenth, the troops were ferried out to the *Baltic*, and Gus Fox experienced the utter humiliation of not only having failed in the relief attempt, but having to carry home the paroled garrison. That evening, he steamed off for New York.

Fox placed the entire blame for the failure of his expedition on the *Powhatan*'s absence. "Yet I was permitted to sail," he bitterly wrote in his report, "without intimation that the main portion, the fighting portion, of our expedition was taken away . . . " But an examination of the means at hand dispels much of that thunder. Once the ice schooner had been taken, it largely mooted the need for the missing tugs and the *Powhatan*'s boats; enough for immediate purposes could have been taken from the vessels present. Further, the *Pawnee*'s armament of eight 9-inch guns provided all the force Fox required. There was no reason that she could not have assumed the *Powhatan*'s role in covering the schooner and boats in their passage over the bar into the harbor. More telling still, the *Pawnee*'s ten-foot draft was much lighter than the *Powhatan*'s, and she could have crossed the bar at anything save low water. For all of Fox's protestations, had he overcome his righteous anger and employed the forces available, the relief of Fort Sumter would have been accomplished.

The attack on Fort Sumter set in train the immediate politico-military events that led to the actual Civil War fighting. The Northern apathy toward the seceding states—"just let the wayward sisters go"—vanished in the thunderclap of Beauregard's artillery. The rebels had given Abraham Lincoln an irrefutable *casus belli,* and he could now forcefully pursue a single-minded policy. The future of the Union, Lincoln wrote, was either "immediate dissolution or blood," and Lincoln chose blood.

The President called the Cabinet on Sunday, April 14. The next day he announced to the nation that South Carolina, Georgia, Alabama, Florida, Mississippi, Louisiana, and Texas were in a state of rebellion. Acting under the authority of the Constitution, Lincoln called for the mobilization of 75,000 militia for three months' service, "to suppress such combinations, and to cause the laws to be duly executed." On the nineteenth, he proclaimed a *de facto* war against the rebels by declaring a blockade of the Confederate coast from South Carolina to the mouth of the Rio Grande.

On Tuesday, April 16, Captain Meigs arrived off Pensacola with the steamer *Atlantic* and Colonel Isaac Brown's 450 troops. Surveying the rebel batteries on the mainland, the two officers determined that it would be folly for Dave Porter, beating his way through the same storms that had delayed the Sumter expedition, to bring the *Powhatan* into the bay. The news of Sumter's bombardment had not yet reached Pensacola, and they "found it desirable that we put off the day of collision as long as possible."

During the voyage, Porter had relentlessly exercised his crew. Those men he considered slow or deficient found chalked sarcasms—"Snail," "Turtle," or "Slow Coach"—marked on their gun barrels. Only when the crew reached Porter's standard of smartness would he erase the scrawls in solemn little ceremonies. One clear day, sailors were hoisted over the side to paint over the conspicuous gunport shutters, disguising the *Powhatan* as a British mail steamer. By this masquerade, Porter hoped to gain precious minutes in running past the rebel batteries.

On April 17, the *Powhatan,* flying British colors, stood into the bay, decks cleared for action. When nearing Fort Pickens, Porter ordered the engines full ahead and steamed over the bar. Suddenly, the navy storeship *Wyandotte,* with Meigs on board, hoisted signals for Porter to heave-to and await instructions, "which I did not answer, but stood on." She thereupon threw herself across the *Powhatan*'s bow. On deck, Porter saw "Captain Meigs ... waving a document ... I felt like running over [him], but obeyed the order ... In twenty minutes more I should have been inside [the navy yard] or sunk."

After all of the impetuous machinations to bring the *Powhatan* to Pensacola, Porter's decision to halt at the final moment is unfathomable. He called it "the great disappointment of my life."

It is quite likely that Porter, dashing into the bay under the cover of night, guns loaded with grape and canister, could have retaken the navy yard. The *Powhatan*'s well-handled guns, seconded by the *Brooklyn,* would have played havoc among the rustic, untrained rebels in the mainland forts, and with troops coming in behind the Union could have held the facility. But the *Powhatan,* stripped from the Sumter relief expedition, was nullified at Pensacola as well.

The Fires of Norfolk

"The Commodore was in a state of complete prostration. He sat in his office immovable, not knowing what to do."

—Engineer in Chief Benjamin Franklin Isherwood, USN

As the lashing Atlantic gales beat down on the Sumter and Pickens relief ships, Gideon Welles, increasingly concerned about wavering Virginia, turned his attention to the Norfolk Navy Yard. The complex actually lay across from Norfolk, by Portsmouth, on the south branch of the Elizabeth River, twenty miles upriver from Hampton Roads, the gateway to Chesapeake Bay and the Atlantic.

Unlike flyblown Pensacola, this yard was a bustling, first-class establishment. Two huge, slat-sided ship houses, with a third under construction, dominated the riverfront. They were completely equipped for building the most up-to-date warships, and five steam vessels had already gone down their ways. The yard was also chockablock with foundries; machine and boiler shops; smithies; timber sheds; spar, sail, and riggers' lofts; a rope walk; and carpentries.

The yard maintained the navy's premier arsenal and reserve store of guns with nearly 2,000 pieces of ordnance, including 300 modern Dahlgren smoothbore cannon, the famed "soda bottles."

Among its most valuable assets was the granite masonry dry dock. One of only two in the nation (Boston's Charlestown Navy Yard had the other), it could berth any ship in the fleet.* Nearby stood the big naval hospital. Opposite the yard, on the Norfolk side of the river, were the powder magazine and the gun carriage works at old forts Norfolk and St. Helena. The whole navy yard held every facility for building and servicing a modern, steam-driven, wooden fleet.

Tied up on the waterfront, in varying degrees of readiness, lay a potentially powerful naval force. Commodore Garrett Pendergrast of the Home Squadron had come on April 1. His flagship, the 24-gun sailing sloop *Cumberland,* had finished minor repairs and replenished her water and stores. Ready and provisioned for sea, but lacking crews, were the smaller sisters *Germantown* and *Plymouth,* plus the little brig *Dolphin.*

The steam frigate *Merrimack,* 4,636 tons, and 40 guns, was by far the most impressive vessel. Commissioned in 1856, she and her four sisters of the *Wabash* class had been the world's envy; the zenith of wooden walls. But now she was laid up "in ordinary," out of commission with guns unshipped and engines dismantled and condemned.

The rest belonged in a nautical museum. In moldering retirement rested three great ships of the line led by the 120-gun *Pennsylvania,* the grandest ever in the United States Navy, serving out her dotage as the yard receiving ship. Other remains included the skeletal hull of the *New York,* rotting on the ways since 1816, and ancient frigates, including the *United States,* which had entered service in 1797.

The yard's commander was as antiquated as some of his charges. Commodore Charles S. McCauley, a Unionist Pennsylvanian was sixty-eight years old with fifty-two years in the service, and epitomized the navy's dark decades of no risk, no blame. When combined with his fondness for hard drink, McCauley turned, as Gideon Welles wrote, "feeble and incompetent," utterly unfit to confront the emergency that burst about his head.

Under him were 22 officers and about 160 sailors and marines. The officers, almost to a man, were Southerners, and most would resign their commissions in the weeks to come. In addition, the yard's 1,000 civilian workers were all Democrats. The navy yards were sinkholes of corrupt patronage, and civilian workmen who received their jobs on the basis of political affiliation were routinely assessed "contributions" by

* On June 17, 1833, the *Delaware* entered its sluice gates, inaugurating the first drydock in the Western Hemisphere. As of this writing the venerable dock is still in use. The original brown brick, white-columned hospital is there, too.

the district congressman. Whenever a new presidential administration took office, the wholesale replacement of navy yard workforces inevitably followed. Lincoln moved cautiously, anxious not to offend wavering Virginia, and ordered Gideon Welles to refrain "from all unnecessary exercise of political party authority." It proved a big mistake.

Robert Danby, the yard's chief engineer, stood loyal to the Union. His principal concern was getting the *Merrimack* to safety. Commodore McCauley, prompted by secessionist officers, began putting impediments in his way. It would take at least one month, he told Danby, to set up the ship's machinery and fire the boilers. This, Danby knew, was ridiculous. In a private letter to the navy's new engineer in chief, Benjamin Franklin Isherwood, he estimated the time at no more than a week.

Isherwood received the letter on April 10 and brought it to Gideon Welles' attention. The secretary dictated a set of confidential instructions, sending them to Norfolk by special courier. "The steamer *Merrimack*," he ordered McCauley, "should be in condition to proceed to Philadelphia . . . in case danger from unlawful attempts to take possession of her." But Welles, in *his* attempts to assure Virginia of the government's trust, inserted a fatal flaw. "It is desirable," he wrote, "there should be no steps taken to give needless alarm."

McCauley ordered the *Merrimack* to the ordnance wharf for mounting her guns. But this movement brought a howling, self-righteous protest from Norfolk secessionists, forcing the commodore to halt the work and order the ship back to her moorings. Welles' "needless alarm" stricture had taken its first toll at the navy yard.

After the rebels opened fire on Fort Sumter, Welles temporized no further. He ordered Isherwood and Commander James Alden to Norfolk. "Without creating a sensation, but in a quiet manner," Isherwood taking charge of the *Merrimack*'s refit, and once done, Alden would take command and bring her safely to Philadelphia.

Welles had to find a crew. Fully manned, the *Merrimack* shipped more than 600 sailors and marines; mustering even a skeleton force would strip the East Coast of every idle bluejacket. The secretary telegraphed the commandant at Brooklyn to dispatch 200 "seamen, ordinary seamen, landsmen, and coal heavers" to Norfolk without delay. Unfortunately, Porter had taken most of the available sailors in the *Powhatan*. There were only 63 left, barely enough to get the *Merrimack* across Hampton Roads, much less to Philadelphia. But recruiting officers were beating up the bushes, and Brooklyn hoped to have at least part of the contingent sailing in about a week.

* * *

At Norfolk on April 13, Commander Alden stepped ashore at the city's commercial docks and was shocked to learn that his "private instructions" from the secretary of the navy had become public knowledge. "To my surprise," he said, "all Norfolk seemed to be full of it." Passing through the city, crossing the river to the yard, Alden was closely watched. Noticing "the attitude of the people was threatening," he destroyed his written orders before reporting. When he arrived at the navy yard, Alden was in for his second big surprise of the day. The civilian yard workers, McCauley blandly informed him, had all quit their jobs and gone home!

Isherwood arrived at the navy yard, on Sunday, April 14, the day of Fort Sumter's surrender, and immediately conducted a thorough inspection of the *Merrimack*'s machinery. It was not an easy task, for not only were her engines dismantled, they were scattered—iron and brass, nuts and bolts, bits and pieces, throughout the shops and forges of the yard. Nonetheless, he estimated it could be patched together for temporary steaming in three days.

Isherwood and Danby scoured the neighborhoods around the yard until they had rousted enough mechanics to begin work in the ship. The chief divided the workmen into three gangs for round-the-clock shifts, with himself and Danby alternating supervision every twelve hours. In a message to Gideon Welles, he reported the *Merrimack* would be ready for sea on Thursday, April 18.

Welles had every confidence in Isherwood's energy, but he placed none with McCauley, and to prod that officer along, he sent one of his senior advisers: wizened, wispy Captain Hiram Paulding, a man with nearly fifty years of service. Captain Paulding landed at Norfolk city on the seventeenth and was not assured by his first impressions. Lincoln's call for 75,000 volunteers had vigorously stoked the fires of secession. Paulding reported "a threatening and hostile spirit seemed to pervade the vicinity of the yard." Six officers, all Southerners, men Paulding "had known and esteemed for their honor from boyhood," painfully assured him "they would defend the public property to the last." Privately, however, one commander pleaded "to say to the Secretary of the Navy that it was very desirable to them to be relieved [of duty]." Paulding returned to Washington the same evening and reported to the secretary and President. With keen foresight, Lincoln put no faith in the pledges of loyalty and ordered all wavering officers replaced by "reliable Northerners."

To no avail, for that day, the Virginia convention, citing the President's call for volunteers as a declaration of war against the South, voted an ordinance of secession. Then, nearly to a man, the navy yard officers resigned their commissions.

At 4 P.M. that busy Wednesday, Isherwood and Danby, exhausted from their labors, presented themselves to the commandant. With strenuous efforts they had managed to put the *Merrimack*'s engines in a fit state for steaming. Isherwood engaged forty-four firemen and coal heavers for the voyage and he requested permission to fire the boilers. McCauley, "seemingly startled by the suddenness of the preparations," refused; "tomorrow," he told the engineers, would be time enough. They returned to the ship, set an engine room watch, and passed the waning hours in teeth-grinding impotence.

That night, "fresh with rain," according to the *Cumberland*'s log, masthead lookouts spotted a steam tug, with small craft in tow, heading downriver. Rightly assuming them to be Norfolk secessionists obstructing the channel, Captain John Marston ordered his ship's boats to investigate. The choke point of the Elizabeth lay four miles downstream at Craney Island, and though the *Cumberland*'s boats rowed the distance, the dark, rainy weather prevented any contact with the rebels.

By dawn, Thursday, the skies cleared. At pierside the *Merrimack* sat thumping with life, a black column of coal smoke rising from her funnel. At midmorning, Isherwood made the short walk to McCauley's quarters and reported the engineer force on board, steam up, and all that was needed was the commandant's order to cast off. But McCauley, desperate for any excuse to delay a decision, shook his head, pointing to the attempt at blocking the channel and the danger this posed to the ship's passage.

Isherwood pleaded in vain. The *Merrimack,* he argued, carried neither guns nor stores, and her light draft would likely pass over any blockage, but every hour's delay increased the danger of her never getting out. Isherwood then called attention to Secretary Welles' peremptory orders. Still McCauley would not budge. "He sat in his office immovable," the engineer in chief said; "not knowing what to do ... I could not get him to do anything."

After loading enough coal for a passage across Hampton Roads to either Newport News or Fort Monroe (without a crew, Philadelphia was no longer an option), Commander Alden reported the *Merrimack* ready, awaiting McCauley's permission to sail. Commodore Pendergrast and Captain Marston both supported Alden's view. But McCauley, probably drunk, remained paralyzed with tortured reasoning that nothing should be done to inflame the locals.

In the strongest terms, both Pendergrast and Marston demanded the *Merrimack,* towing the *Germantown,* be removed straight away to Fort Monroe, and thirty *Cumberland* sailors were detailed as skeleton crews. For a moment McCauley wavered. Alden pressed the advantage and received permission to load a pair of light guns into the ship as a token battery. He sped from the office and ordered one of the *Cumberland*'s officers to offer $1,000 to any civilian pilot willing to take the *Merrimack* across Hampton Roads, "and twice that sum, together with a place in the Navy for life, if we succeeded in getting the *Germantown* out also." With high optimism, Alden ran to the ordnance wharf for his two guns.

Independent of Alden's efforts, Isherwood and Danby managed to scrape up their own crew of sorts. Mustering the mechanics, they asked any with sea experience to step forward. A few did, and these Isherwood detailed to take the wheel and sound the channel with the lead.* With promises of lavish pay, enough firemen, oilers, and coal heavers agreed to work the vessel as far as Newport News. Anticipating a rapid, and possibly hostile departure, Isherwood stationed axmen at the bitts to cut the mooring lines upon his order.

At the ordnance wharf, Alden met with nothing but procrastination, and in disgust he returned to the *Merrimack* to supervise the final preparations for sailing. Alden fell in with Commander Robert Robb, the yard's executive officer, and from him requested a party of seamen to warp the ship into the fairway. Robb, who resigned that day, refused. Anyway, he said, it was no longer necessary, McCauley had just ordered Isherwood to draw the fires. Stunned and "unwilling to believe in the correctness of Commander Robb's statement, whose loyalty I had begun to doubt," Alden burst into McCauley's office, "and found it was too true. The fatal order had been given."

And Alden meekly accepted that decision, although it flew in direct contravention to his own orders from the secretary of the navy. Isherwood had met the preliminary conditions in getting the ship ready for sea, and Alden was totally justified in taking her out then and there. But after thirty-two years of service, he shied from taking the initiative.

Why McCauley issued the "fatal order" also remains unclear. Many years later, Isherwood wrote, "The Commodore was in a state of complete prostration. He sat in his office immovable, not knowing what to

* A lead weight at the end of a measured line, thrown ahead of the ship to determine the depth of water.

do. He was weak, vacillating, hesitating, and overwhelmed by the
responsibilities of his position . . . he behaved as though stupefied."

Isherwood returned to the frigate for the last time and shut down
her plant. "As I witnessed the gradual dying out of the revolutions of
the *Merrimack*'s engines, I was greatly tempted to cut the ropes that
held her, and to bring her out on my own responsibility." But like Alden
before him, his initiative gave way. The rules and traditions of the navy
were too ingrained. He was an engineer, not a line officer, and prohibited from holding command afloat. "With great sorrow, I dismissed my
men, waited until the engines made their last revolution [and] left the
yard."

On Friday, April 19, the day Lincoln proclaimed the blockade of the
rebel coast, Welles finally relieved Commodore McCauley of his command and rushed whatever reinforcements were at hand to Norfolk.
He ordered the Brooklyn Navy Yard to expedite its efforts, sending
"ordinary men" if necessary; the receiving ship, *Allegheny,* at Baltimore, was ordered to enlist and dispatch 50 raw recruits by commercial steamer; the Philadelphia yard directed to charter the fastest available steamer and pack it with 100 marines and sailors, plus artillery,
ammunition, and provisions; and the Washington Navy Yard to march
100 marines aboard Stephen Rowan's *Pawnee.*

With "full powers to command the services of the entire naval
force," Welles sent Hiram Paulding back to Norfolk. He charged him to
"repel force by force," to prevent "anything" from falling into rebel
hands, and "should it finally become necessary," to destroy the navy
yard and everything that could not be gotten out. In case of that catastrophe, the *Pawnee* loaded forty extra barrels of gunpowder and eleven
tanks of turpentine.

That morning Confederate Major General William Taliaferro
arrived from Richmond, carrying orders from Governor Letcher to
"endeavor by a rapid movement, to secure the navy yard." At Norfolk,
he found a motley collection of local militia companies, numbering
about 600 men, most without weapons, and "a few 6-pounder field
pieces" for artillery. Regardless of the size of Taliaferro's forces, so
long as the *Cumberland*'s grape-shotted guns bore on the landward
approaches, storming the yard by regular attack was out of the question. In the meantime, two regiments of South Carolina infantry and
four Georgia companies, in total something less than 1,000 men, were
ordered up by rail.

The *Cumberland*'s lookouts also spotted rebel earthworks being thrown up across the river, commanding the seaward approaches to the yard. Lieutenant Thomas Selfridge suggested he be sent under a flag of truce to Norfolk, to inform the rebels that if work on the batteries continued, the *Cumberland* would open fire on the city. Selfridge landed at the Norfolk commercial piers "under a flag of truce which fortunately," he said, "was respected by the large and excited crowd collected on the waterfront." He confronted Taliaferro and delivered the message "in very forcible terms." Taliaferro took offense. It would be "a terrible thing," he said, to open fire on an undefended city. But Selfridge shot back it would also be "a terrible thing" if the navy yard and its ships were destroyed by rebel artillery.

For the moment Selfridge held the aces, and on Taliaferro's orders, Colonel Henry Heth (who two years later commanded the division that opened the Battle of Gettysburg) crossed over to the yard. The earthen batteries, he told McCauley, were empty, because other than their few popgun 6-pounders, the Virginia militia had no artillery. Still, he gave "effective assurances" that work on the revetments would cease. Taliaferro then moved his militia companies to the unguarded powder magazine at Fort Norfolk and seized it without a shot; 2,800 barrels of Yankee gunpowder passed to the Confederacy.

That Friday evening, the *Pawnee* cast off her lines and headed down the Potomac into Chesapeake Bay. In addition to Hiram Paulding, she carried several key officers to command the valuable ships at Norfolk. Chief among them, slated for the *Merrimack,* was the noted Antarctic explorer, the prickly Captain Charles Wilkes. From the army came Captain Horatio Wright of the engineers, charged with organizing the navy yard's defenses, and—if necessary—its demolition.

Gideon Welles' efforts at reinforcement were having mixed results. Brooklyn could scratch up only "173 recruits, and maybe 50 more" and they could arrive at Norfolk no earlier than Sunday, the twenty-first. At Philadelphia, Commodore Samuel Du Pont had chartered the steamer *Keystone State* at $1,000 per day, but her engine had unaccountably broken down. "By extraordinary exertions" Du Pont reported, she "was towed to the yard, the work on the machinery going on all the time." By sunset, Friday, the sailors, marines, artillery, ammunition, seven days' coal, and two weeks' provisions were loaded on board, and she belched off for Norfolk at first light.

At Baltimore, rife with secessionist passion and killing riots, the local steam packet line refused to give 50 naval recruits passage to Norfolk; "we decline to take them," wrote the president of the firm.

In midafternoon, Saturday, April 20, Stephen Rowan's *Pawnee* rounded Old Point Comfort, steamed into Hampton Roads, and anchored under the great guns of Fort Monroe. Her officer of the watch penned in the log. "At 5:15 p.m., the Third Massachusetts Regiment . . . marched out and embarked on this ship to the number of 349, rank and file." These were fresh recruits, some of the first of Lincoln's 75,000 volunteers, virtually undrilled and armed with obsolete muskets. But they were no worse than anything the rebels mustered at the moment. At dusk, the *Pawnee* set out the final eighteen miles across Hampton Roads and up the Elizabeth River to the navy yard.

As the sloop passed Sewell's Point and entered the river's mouth, Commander Rowan cleared for action, and his eight 9-inch guns were loaded and run out. He passed Craney Island without hindrance, and in the settling night the *Pawnee* glided alongside the navy yard wharf. "With a hurricane of heartiness," said Tom Selfridge, *Cumberland*'s bluejackets scampered up the rigging to cheer her in, the welcome being returned in equal measure.

But the reception might as well have been a funeral dirge. For in a moment, Hiram Paulding learned an awful truth. "To my amazement and chagrin," Paulding said, "I found that all ships [except the *Cumberland*] had been scuttled two or three hours before, and were fast sinking." He at once landed his soldiers and marines and ordered them to defensive positions around the yard. Thousands of armed rebels were said to be in the neighborhood, but strangely, he could see none, "nor any hostile demonstration." Captain Wilkes brought McCauley on board the *Pawnee*. The drunk, pathetic man, he recalled, "was armed like a Brigand—swords and pistols in his belt and revolvers in his hand . . . His condition . . . unabled him to comprehend the situation and [he had] great difficulty in walking steady. He was unfitted for all duty."

The debacle, McCauley tried to explain later, occurred just after Colonel Heth had given his word regarding the unarmed Confederate batteries. Hearing that, said the wretched commodore, "I then commenced scuttling the *Germantown, Plymouth, Dolphin,* and *Merrimack* . . . My officers, with a few exceptions," he continued incredibly, "had all deserted me; even the watchmen had thrown off their allegiance and had taken part with the secessionists."

Under Captain Wilkes' direction, salvage parties boarded the scuttled ships to determine if they might be saved by some quick action. Lieutenant Henry Wise rushed down the *Merrimack*'s ladders to her berth deck. She was sinking fast and Wise knew it. The splash of the block he threw down the hatch told him the water was already over the orlop. Taking a boat to the *Pawnee,* he reported that unless a diver closed the sea cocks the ship was lost. No one had thought to include diving gear, and the *Merrimack* groaned slowly into the harbor mud.

Hiram Paulding now faced some critical choices. His primary mission, as he saw it, was to save the vessels at the navy yard. Because of McCauley's stupidity that was no longer possible. His next option was to hold the facility until reinforcements arrived. He had roughly a thousand men, half of them fully equipped infantry and marines. At their backs crouched the deadly broadsides of the *Cumberland* and *Pawnee.* The commodore's orders from the secretary of the navy clearly charged him to "repel force by force," and he could defend the place against anything the rebels dared to throw.

But as Captain Wilkes observed, "a panic" had taken hold and Paulding became swayed by peripheral considerations. The 3rd Massachusetts was only temporarily, and grudgingly at that, attached to his forces, and the *Pawnee* must quickly depart for the defense of Washington. In his report, Paulding claimed fear of being penned in by rebel block ships at Craney Island. But for whatever reason, Commodore Hiram Paulding, like McCauley, Alden, and Isherwood before him, flinched from taking the bold step and he ordered Wilkes to put the navy yard to the torch.

Lieutenant Wise got the job of burning the scuttled ships. Into a longboat, he loaded "a number of powder tanks filled with spirits of turpentine and cotton waste," and his crew pulled for the sunken *Merrimack.* In a **V** shape, its apex at the base of the mainmast, and reaching forward along the deck, Wise's men dumped piles of cordage, ladders, gratings, hawsers, and anything else that would take fire. Atop were laid ropes of cotton waste soaked in turpentine, while more tanks of the stuff were stove in and liberally doused over the *Merrimack*'s decks and beams. Lengths of match fuse were paid over the side. Wise and his crew jumped into their boat and rowed to the *Germantown* to continue their work. From the opposite shore, rebel sniper fire began pinging the water.

While the ships were readied for the bonfire, gangs of bluejackets and soldiers, armed with sledgehammers, set up a terrific din at the ordnance wharf. Paulding hadn't the means to take off the artillery, and the 300 Dahlgren guns must in no way fall intact to the rebels. But try as the wrecking crews might, the sturdy barrels didn't give a fraction. "One hundred men worked for an hour," Paulding said, "and such was the tenacity of the iron that they did not succeed in breaking a single trunnion."* Only a few obsolete guns were smashed and the men had to settle for spiking the rest and throwing them into the river.

The ship houses, shops, and the marine barracks were all packed with barrels of powder and slow match fuses laid. But more important than the guns and shops, more vital even than the *Merrimack,* was the granite dry dock. Without it, any hope the Confederacy had of major salvage, repair, and construction for their seminal navy was out of the question. The work fell to Commander John Rodgers and the army's Captain Horatio Wright, assisted by fifty soldiers and bluejackets. In pitch darkness they lowered a ton of black powder into the dock's hydraulic pumping gallery. Powder trains were snaked up the stone steps, and four slow match fuses prepared.

In the first hours of Sunday, April 21, all was ready, and Wilkes ordered the troops and marines back to the ships. At the landing, he and Lieutenant Wise stood by in the last boat to take off the demolition gangs. When all awaited the signal to set alight the fuses, old McCauley chose to play out his final, sad role in the affair.

Onto the *Pawnee*'s quarterdeck came the ex-commandant's youngest son, "tears streaming down his cheeks." He reported that his father refused to leave his post, preferring to die in the flames that would soon sweep the yard. With the tide running, Paulding had no time for histrionics and he sent an officer ashore to get McCauley out. According to Wilkes, the commodore "had retired to his house and was found lying, in a stupefied state, on a sofa.... He was induced with great reluctance, to remove to the *Cumberland* ... otherwise he would have been burned alive."

Just before dawn, the tug *Yankee* arrived with the flood tide, warped the *Cumberland* out and took her in tow. High water came within the hour, and with guns loaded, and armed marines at the rails, the *Pawnee* led the flotilla slowly down the Elizabeth into Hampton Roads. The instant the sloop's screws bit the river, Paulding ordered a signal rocket fired—its high, arching red tail calling down the cataclysm on the navy yard.

* Trunnions are the two solid cylinders projecting at right angles from the gun barrel, and bear the gun's weight when mounted on its carriage. As the barrel is cast in a single piece, the breaking of a trunnion renders the gun permanently unusable. The substitute method of "spiking," is simply to drive a railroad spike, or other device, through the gun's priming vent at the breech. This, however, is only temporary. Through a laborious procedure, the spike can be removed and the gun returned to service.

Ashore, the slow matches were lit, and the last of the sailors raced for Wilkes' boat. "At 4:20 [A.M.]," he reported, "the signal was made and the torch applied, in a few minutes the whole area of the yard was one sheet of flame—the two ship houses and the whole line of stores, as well as the *Merrimack*. . . . The conflagration was rapid, in vast sheets of flame, and dense smoke . . . The masts of the *Germantown* were on fire, and portions of her hull enveloped in the flames from the *Merrimack*."

At the dry dock the fuses smoldered toward the powder trains when Rodgers and Wright made their break. But so intense were the fires from the burning ship houses, they could not see. Trapped, the two men ran through the burning main gate, leaping into a stray boat a step ahead of the flames. Sniping rebels spotted it, and rather than die to no purpose, as Wright said, "we delivered ourselves up to the Commanding General of the Virginia forces."

On board the retreating ships, every ear pitched for the great explosion of the 2,000 pounds of powder in the dry dock. But nothing happened, and to this day, no one knows why. Some accounts treat it as ill luck or faulty materials. Others refer to the two feet of water in the dock that might have snuffed the powder trains. One questionable history puts the blame on "a considerate Union petty officer," who broke the slow match to protect the nearby homes of his friends. A Confederate naval history credits Lieutenant Charles Spotswood, lately of the United States Navy, "who promptly directed the opening of the [dock] gates, and thus saved [it] from destruction."

Steering by the light of the holocaust, the vessels steamed downriver, and with the sun, passed Craney Island. The *Cumberland* dropped anchor to await Wilkes and the boats. Across Hampton Roads, just as the *Pawnee* reached Fort Monroe, there hove into view the *Keystone State,* crammed with the marines and field artillery from Philadelphia.

The rebels swarmed into the yard, and at first sight the damage wrought by the demolition parties appeared monumental. "The most abominable vandalism," reported a Confederate officer. Both ship houses were burned to the ground. The rigging and sail lofts were gone, as were the rope walk, and gun carriage depot. General Taliaferro called Paulding's actions "one of the most cowardly and disgraceful acts which has ever disgraced the Government of a civilized people." But he had little real cause for complaint. With nary a musket shot, his militia companies had taken the United States Navy's largest shore facility, complete with intact dry dock, and 1,195 heavy guns. Added to this was the powder captured at Fort Norfolk, plus "many thousands of shells and shot . . . ready for our cause." Into his lap, too, had fallen the shops at Fort St. Helena, with 130 gun carriages and all its machinery in perfect working order.

It didn't take long for the infant Confederate Navy to begin putting the yard in order. Under its new commandant, Captain French Forrest, salvage and repair were taken in hand. The guns were fished up from the river bottom and unspiked. The older pieces provided coastal batteries along the entire Confederate coast, while most of the modern Dahlgrens eventually found their way afloat in Confederate ironclads. On May 30, a bare six weeks after its fall, Captain Forrest wrote to General Robert E. Lee, commanding Virginia's forces, "We have the *Merrimack* up and just putting her into dry dock."

Going South

"Had we been attacked I should have stood by my guns and performed my duty by the school. I was still an officer of the [U.S.] navy."

—**Captain William Harwar Parker, Confederate States Navy**

T he escalation of events beginning with the bombardment of Fort Sumter, leading to Lincoln's call for volunteers, the proclamation of the blockade, and the secession of Virginia, brought to a flood the resignation of Southern naval officers who, Gideon Welles said, "traitorously abandoned the Union."

By the late summer of 1861, in the navy's active list of 1,385 line, staff, engineering, and Marine Corps officers, plus the midshipmen at the Naval Academy (who accounted for about a third of the resignations), 375 men, several of outstanding stature and ability, had left the navy and gone South. Of the 78 captains, 33 of them Southerners, 12, with an average length of service of forty-seven years, chose service with the Confederacy.

Until Welles took over the Navy Department, Secretary Isaac Toucy customarily accepted these departures without complaint. Indeed, when Captain Josiah Tattnall, "Old Tat," a Georgian with forty-nine years' service, tendered his resignation, Toucy, according to Tattnall's biographer, "took leave of the Commodore with warm expressions of sympathy."

Alarmed at the increasing flight, a special committee of the House of Representatives roundly castigated Toucy, considering his conduct "at such a critical time ... without justification or excuse." The flow of resignations dragged the morale of the naval service to rock bottom. On taking up his duties at the department in March, Gideon Welles found "great demoralization and defection among the naval officers. It was difficult to ascertain who ... could and who could not be trusted. Some ... had already sent in their resignations. Others ... were prepared to do so as soon as a blow was struck. Some were hesitating, undecided what step to take."

The shore establishment provided several centers of disaffection. Commodore George Magruder of the Bureau of Ordnance and Hydrography went South, and his clerks, almost to a man, followed. Commander Raphael Semmes, who became the Confederate Navy's most noteworthy sea raider, resigned in mid-February. A Marylander domiciled in Alabama, the mercurial Semmes held no romantic illusions regarding his possible fate for that act. "There was some ... nerve required of an officer ... to go with his State," he wrote at war's end. "His profession was his only fortune; he depended on it for ... subsisting himself and family ... and promotion and honors probably awaited him; if he went South, a dark and uncertain future was before him ... and if the South failed, he would have thrown away the labor of a life-time."

The superintendent of the Naval Observatory in Washington, the crippled Commander Matthew Fontaine Maury, the world's leading oceanographer, who mapped the shipping lanes that are still in use to this day, placed state allegiance above the national good. "If we have a war between the sections," he wrote, "every man who continues in 'Uncle Sam's' service is, in good faith, bound to fight his own, if his own be on the other side. The line of duty, therefore, is to me clear—each one to follow his own state."

Until the very day of his resignation, Maury labored on his final works carrying the imprimatur of the United States Navy, "The Barometer at Sea" and "The Southeast Trade Winds of the Atlantic." On April 20, three days after the Virginia legislature voted to secede from the Union, Maury locked up the observatory and left the keys on Commodore Magruder's doorstep (who later handed them over to Gideon Welles along with his own resignation). Maury secretly decamped for Richmond and was immediately commissioned a commander in the Virginia state navy.

Until Gideon Welles dropped anchor in the Navy Department, there was generally no onus attached to a resigning officer. He simply wrote it out, and the letter was accepted by the secretary and President, and that was all. "The right of an officer to resign [had] never been disputed," said Captain William Harwar Parker of the Confederate Navy, "unless the officer is at the time under arrest [or] liable to charges." If the officer's conduct was in question, the Navy Department had three courses, all of which bore a stigma. They were: dismissal from the service; the far more serious, dismissal and "striking of the [officer's] name" from the navy's rolls; or most severely, dismissal and striking the name "by order of the President." The latter action was final, irrevocable, and the cashiered officer had no appeal, not even from a general court-martial.

But these were not normal times. The Union was staggering through a string of humiliating blows with hardly a counterpunch delivered in its name. Loyal officers looked with perplexed consternation as their lifelong colleagues quit the service to don the uniform and accept the pay of the Confederacy.

To sear a traitor's brand, Welles, in mid-April, refused to accept further resignations, except from student midshipmen at the Naval Academy. Instead he recommended to the President that all resigning officers be dismissed from the navy. "[The] officers," Captain Parker said, "were informed by Mr. Gideon Welles . . . that their names were 'dropped from the rolls.'" In August 1861, Welles pushed Congress to pass an act that any naval officer who tendered an unaccepted resignation, and then quit his post "with intent to remain permanently absent . . . shall be deemed and punished as a deserter"—a hanging offense. The officers of the new Confederate Navy, needless to say, considered these actions "spiteful and illegal."

By no means was the navy stripped of all its Southern-born or domiciled officers; about half the Southerners opted to remain with the Union. Halfway up the captains' list, with fifty years in the navy, Captain David Glasgow Farragut, Tennessee-born and living in Norfolk, held no truck with secessionism. During the April days when the Virginia legislature deliberated the state's future, Farragut, on leave, gathered in a local store daily with several naval officers and citizens to discuss events. He had witnessed firsthand in Latin America the horrors of civil war, but his companions ridiculed him as a "croaker."

On April 14, the Sunday following the surrender of Fort Sumter, Farragut and his wife attended church. Rumor had it that the customary prayer for the President of the United States was to be omitted from the service and, if that happened, he determined to stand up and walk out in a very public admission of his Unionist sympathies. The service, however, was read as usual, the psalter for the day beginning with, "Samaria is desolate." Farragut turned to his wife. "There's prophesy for you! God help the country."

When Virginia seceded, Farragut, though he had accurately gauged the local pulse, was caught amazed. "Virginia," he said, "had been dragooned out of the Union," and when he returned to the store, he discovered that most of the Southern officers had already written their resignations. Farragut tried to defend Lincoln's call for volunteers, but he was told very bluntly by a fellow officer that with Virginia's secession, Farragut must either resign or leave Norfolk. Fine, Farragut said, "I cannot live here and will seek some other place . . . and on two hours' notice."

Farragut did worry about his wife, Virginia, whose family lived in Norfolk. He returned home and put the situation plainly. "This act of mine," he said, "may cause years of separation from your family; so you must decide quickly whether you will go North or remain here." Fearing that real fighting over the navy yard might erupt at any hour, Farragut insisted that she make her decision immediately. Virginia Farragut chose to go with her husband. After some sad family farewells, the Farraguts, with their old black family retainer, Sinah (very possibly a slave), and carrying a few possessions boarded the Baltimore packet. From there, they journeyed by canal boat to Philadelphia, and thence to a cottage in Hastings-on-Hudson, New York.

Perhaps the most pathetic of all the resignations concerned Captain Franklin Buchanan, "Old Buck," commandant of the Washington Navy Yard, a man who entered the navy as a fourteen-year-old midshipman in the waning days of the War of 1812.

Handsome and ramrod-straight, a passionate Marylander, Old Buck was known throughout as an officer of the strictest temperance and highest moral character. A service reformer, he had worked diligently to improve a miserably inadequate system of officer education and to eradicate liquor and flogging in the navy. In September 1845, with the establishment of the Naval Academy at Fort Severn, Annapolis, Old Buck was the natural choice for its first commandant.

Buchanan showed no overweening sympathy for secession, and he condemned the ruinous conduct of the lower South. Yet officers are inherently conservative, and as such Old Buck maintained a horror of abolitionists, free soilers, and Northern "coersionists." Buchanan had held his post at the Washington Navy Yard since 1859, vigorously performing his duties all through that first dark winter and spring of national discontent. From the time of Lincoln's election there were frequent rumors of an attack on the capital and its woefully undermanned military installations. Buchanan prepared the yard to resist any assault, leaving no doubt of his determination. "This yard shall not be surrendered," he penned to his executive officer, Commander John Adolphus Dahlgren, "and in the event of an attack I shall require all officers and others under my command to defend it to the last extremity."

But Buchanan made a fatal miscalculation. On April 19, the 6th Massachusetts Infantry, en route to Washington, was set upon in Baltimore by an armed, rock-throwing rebel mob. The troops opened fire and nine rioters and four soldiers were killed. On Monday, April 22, Baltimore was still in turmoil and every portent indicated Maryland's secession. Captain Buchanan wrote out a terse, one-sentence resignation, and a letter to Maryland's Governor Thomas Hicks, offering "to assist in repelling any invasion of her soil by our Northern enemies."

Buchanan personally carried the resignation to Gideon Welles. To Welles' question of whether the commodore had spent a near half-century in the service of Maryland or of the United States, "had his honors from boyhood to age been derived from the state or the nation?" Old Buck replied that his first duty was to his "immediate government," the State of Maryland. Welles advised him to keep the letter and think the matter over for a few weeks, especially as, he correctly predicted, Maryland was not quitting the Union. Buchanan insisted on his course. Welles shrugged and laid the paper aside, Old Buck returned to the navy yard to bid farewell.

Even as Buchanan delivered his final orders, charging Dahlgren to defend the public property, a messenger arrived from the Navy Department. Welles refused to accept the resignation, stating it was "yet under consideration." Additionally, he formally relieved Buchanan of command, elevating the very junior Dahlgren to the responsible post.

In Annapolis, the Maryland legislature convened during the last days of April and voted overwhelmingly to stay in the Union. Buchanan pleaded with both Gideon Welles and his friend Hiram Paulding, now the secretary's chief of personnel. Grabbing at any straw, he reminded Paulding that his resignation had been drawn *very hastily . . . during the great excitement in Baltimore.* Had Buchanan reversed himself within a day or two, Welles might have been sympathetic, but over two weeks had passed, and positions had hardened. Who knew, Welles questioned, if another situation might arise when Buchanan would "falter, be faithless & doubt his flag?" He could never be trusted again. Now, Welles noted, was the time for "drastic . . . prominent" action. By return mail, he informed the hapless ex-commodore of his ultimate, crushing humiliation: "Sir: Your letter of 22nd [April], tendering your resignation as a captain in the United States Navy has been received. By direction of the President your name has been stricken from the rolls of the Navy from that date."

For four months Old Buck moped around his family home on Maryland's Eastern Shore, writing voluminous letters, as one naval historian put it, full of "hyperbolic protestations of his loyalty to flag and principle." But by early September 1861, with the war in full blow, he could stand the inaction no longer: Buchanan journeyed to Richmond and entered the Confederate Navy with the rank of captain.

It was a tense situation at the Naval Academy at Annapolis, for there was little doubt that slave-holding Maryland would soon join the seceding states in rebellion. Of the student body of 267 midshipmen, nearly half, 107, claimed Southern, border-state, or District of Columbia citizenship.

Midshipman Robley Evans, the "Fighting Bob" of Spanish-American War and Great White Fleet fame, was a Virginia member of the junior class. Regarding the early months of 1861, he remembered, "It was a time of great suspense for all hands; naturally the greatest strain came on those in authority, but the midshipmen had their loads to bear as well. Many of us came from the South, and as the States one after another either seceded or threatened to do so, we had to make up our minds what we were going to do."

Even before South Carolina's secession the lines were drawn. On the eve of the November 1860 presidential election, the midshipmen, less the freshman class, held a straw vote: John C. Breckinridge, 71; Abraham Lincoln, 36; Stephen Douglas, 34; John Bell, 32; and "a few not voting."

The academy's first resignation came on December 4. It was the senior class "honor man," Midshipman Robert C. Fonte of Alabama, and his classmates, singing a song of farewell, escorted him to the gate.

The superintendent, Captain George Blake, and his staff of half a dozen officers, Professors of Mathematics* and civilian instructors

---

* Professors of Mathematics were a special class of commissioned "civil officers," authorized in 1835, as an effort to modernize the system of officer education. Twelve were on duty at the Naval Academy, of whom two submitted their resignations and were dismissed from the navy.

tried to carry on normally within their little, insular world. But "drills became more spirited," said Acting Midshipman Albert Barker, a future commander-in-chief of the Atlantic Fleet, "and when it was learned that the *Star of the West* had been fired into, excitement ran high and the great guns in the battery were worked as they had never been worked before."

With the news of Fort Sumter, all pretense of routine vanished. Blake suspended the curriculum and prepared to defend the academy and its venerable school ship, the frigate *Constitution*. "This point is not defensible against a superior force . . . " he cabled Gideon Welles; "the only force at my command consists of the students . . . many of whom are little boys, and some of whom are citizens of the seceded States." Should Marylanders attack in great numbers, and given the volatility of the state, it was not an unlikely scenario, Blake proposed to embark his command in the *Constitution* and fight it out in the river.

All but two of the "great guns" in the harbor battery were brought into the ship. The trophy Mexican War cannon that adorned the academy grounds were spiked, and the civilian watchmen went about armed. The midshipmen were organized into two companies for active defense. "Drills were constant," said Robley Evans, "and every precaution taken to give the enemy a warm reception in case he came." On the far bank of the Severn he watched groups of rebel cavalry openly drilling.

The Southern officers at the academy faced a dilemma somewhat different than their colleagues afloat or at the yards and bureaus. These men were exemplar paragons to the teenage boys in their charge, and much at pains to create no show of disloyalty and oath-breaking. Indeed, to a man, the academy officers who resigned (in contrast to others who actively engaged in treasonous conduct) did their duty to the very end. As Albert Barker said, they "performed their duties strictly until their resignations were accepted [or they were dismissed]; hence they set no bad example to the midshipmen."

Lieutenant William Harwar Parker of Virginia headed the Department of Seamanship and had made up his mind to remain with the Union. However, his brother, Lieutenant Foxhall Parker, was equally determined to go South with his state. They met at the academy to argue their positions, and in one of the navy's great ironies, each managed to turn the other to an opposite course. William resigned to become a captain in the Confederate Navy and the superintendent of its naval academy, while Foxhall stayed with the Union.

William Parker considered the fears of a Maryland attack on the

academy and the *Constitution* somewhat inflated. On April 19, the day
he submitted his resignation, and the day of the Baltimore riots, he
calmly went about his work. That night the tocsin sounded to prepare
for an attack, and Parker found himself "placed in a most unpleasant
position." The drummers beat the long roll, "and all hands were sent to
their stations." Parker commanded the 2-gun howitzer battery, "and
like many of the midshipmen manning it who had resigned and were
waiting to hear from Washington, [I] had either to refuse to do duty or
fire on our friends. I do not hesitate to say," he later wrote, "that had we
been attacked I should have stood by my guns and performed my duty
by the school. I was still an officer of the navy."

Tensions remained high. On Saturday, April 20, word passed that
Baltimore rebels had organized some vessels to capture the academy
and seize the *Constitution*. Robley Evans remembered. "A bright lookout was kept for them, and . . . about two o'clock in the morning, the
lookout reported a large steamer coming in from the bay. General quarters were sounded, and in a few minutes we were ready; and there we
stood waiting for the word to fire . . . with grape and canister."

The mystery ship came slowly up, until from the deck of the *Constitution* the naked eye saw she was moving directly astern, as if to carry
the frigate by boarding. From his place on the quarterdeck, Lieutenant
George Rodgers, bellowed through a brass trumpet, "Ship ahoy! What
ship is that?"

Closer on she came, and the *Constitution*'s gun captains trained
their ancient 32-pounders on the crowding mass of men, now easily visible not more than 300 yards off. No answer came to the hail, and twice
more Rodgers called out, the last time ending with, "Keep off, or I will
sink you!"

Then from the milling group shouted a familiar voice, "For God's
sake, don't fire! We are friends!" It came from Reverend David Junkin,
the academy chaplain, reporting back from leave in the company of the
8th Massachusetts Infantry on a railroad ferry. Lucky they were, Evans
mused decades later, "because he seemed the only one on board who
knew enough to answer the hail . . . and in a few seconds more we
should have opened fire, and no one can doubt what the result would
have been."

The teenage midshipmen on board the *Constitution* came ashore,
formed with their classmates at the howitzer battery, and under arms,
marched to the wall covering the main gate leading to Annapolis town;
"and there," Evans said, "[we] deployed in line of battle to cover the
landing of the Eighth Massachusetts." The local secessionists were

content to throw stones over the wall, "which we caught and tossed back."

Hard on the heels of the infantry, came the 1st Rhode Island Artillery, and the midshipmen were forced to surrender their Spartan quarters to the ever-increasing numbers of troops. Blake bemoaned the academy's wartime fate. "The academic routine is completely broken up," he reported to the secretary. Further, his senior class had all but disappeared, ordered to active duty to fill the vacancies of the naval officer corps depleted by resignations. He recommended sending the *Constitution,* with the remaining midshipmen, to New York, then transferring the entire academy to Newport, Rhode Island.

Welles entirely agreed, especially since the school grounds had become a major army transfer point. On April 24 the midshipmen formed for their last parade. It was "a scene," Evans said, "which those who participated in it can never forget without a tendency to moist eyes." Those who opted to go South bade a tearful good-bye to their classmates.

As young Evans and the rest of the loyal students made ready to embark in the *Constitution,* the commandant of midshipmen, Commander Christopher Raymond Rodgers, yet another of the famed naval family, stepped forward to deliver some final words to his lads. "My boys," he choked after a strong effort, "stand by the old flag!" then he broke down. "We were all in tears," Evans remembered, "and only braced up when we heard the men of the Seventh New York cheering us, which we returned in a feeble sort of way."

The boys marched to the jetty, clambered into the boats, and pulled for the *Constitution.* Towed by the army gunboat *Cuyler,* and escorted by the *Harriet Lane,* the little convoy departed for Newport, where the Naval Academy abided for the remainder of the war.

Shaking Down

"There was entire unanimity . . . that vigorous steps must be at once taken, and the powers of the government exercised and enforced—that the rebellion must be stopped and suppressed without further temporizing with men, or mobs, or organized insurrection against the government."

—**Secretary of the Navy Gideon Welles**

The lurch into open conflict generated a whipsaw of executive actions between the opposing governments. After Sumter's surrender, Lincoln's call for 75,000 short-term volunteers to restore the Union was accepted by the Confederacy as nothing less than a declaration of war, or, as Jefferson Davis put it, "subjecting the free people . . . to the domination of a foreign power."

Proclaiming it his duty "to repel the threatened invasion," Davis spooked the Lincoln administration and Northern commercial interests by harking to the old, largely discredited maritime tactic of privateering. Although it brought the South some short-term booty from captured merchantmen, it also triggered the responsive Union strategy that guaranteed a strangling death for the Confederacy.

Lincoln moved swiftly. On April 19 he upped the ante by proclaiming a naval blockade over the entire rebel coast from South Carolina to the mouth of the Rio Grande. On April 27, following the secession of North Carolina and Virginia, he extended the cordon to begin literally across the Potomac River from Washington, D.C. All vessels violating the maritime rampart were subject to seizure and "condemnation" as prizes of war.

A coherent Union naval strategy would have dictated a blockade of the Confederate coast under any scenario, but considering the degraded state of the U.S. Navy, it would have come later rather than sooner. But privateering acted as a trip wire, and it forced Lincoln's government to confront some major political and diplomatic ramifications, as well as those strictly naval. By international law, the executive of a nation embroiled in civil war simply declared the ports in rebellion closed, and heavy penalties were leveled against ships attempting to enter, all quite similar to what the British did to Boston in 1774 following the "tea party."

But a formal blockade was another matter entirely, directed against a foreign enemy. To put it simply, no one blockaded their own coast. Thus by declaring a blockade, Lincoln bestowed on the Confederacy certain priceless rights of belligerency that were accorded to any legitimate nation at war.

Gideon Welles, initially, considered the blockade a grave error that unnecessarily waived American sovereign rights and enmeshed foreign powers into what he considered strictly a "domestic municipal duty." In the Senate, the radical Republican Charles Sumner noted, "By the use of this word, 'blockade,' the concession [of Southern belligerency] is vindicated. Had President Lincoln proclaimed *a closing* of the rebel ports, there could have been no such concession."

The legal aspects, however, were hardly one-sided. Unlike a statutory closing of ports, a blockade was a recognized act of war and gave the blockader several significant advantages which did not exist otherwise. The blockading navy could seize neutral vessels attempting to break the cordon, as well as ships on the high seas bound for blockaded ports. A blockade further admitted the right to search and seize neutral vessels carrying contraband cargoes. Had Lincoln merely declared the rebel ports closed, he would have deprived the United States of these internationally recognized powers garnered by a blockading, rather than, to use Welles' analogy, a policing fleet.

But whatever the method, the critical international question was: How would Great Britain react? Her economy was strongly based on the manufacture of cotton cloth, whose raw material came overwhelmingly from the Southern crop. Should Great Britain—the world's leading maritime power—officially recognize the Confederacy to ensure the uninterrupted flow of cotton, it meant disaster for the Union and likely guaranteed permanent division of the United States.

But secretive William Seward, for all his meddling faults, smoothed the watery path. Just before the announcement of the blockade, he had closeted himself with the British ambassador, Lord Richard Lyons, and presented both alternatives for Her Majesty's government's consideration.

Lyons made it very clear that if the navy's policing of closed rebel ports overstepped the mark, it might well force a diplomatic recognition of the Confederacy in order to protect British trade. A blockade, however, was an accepted mode of naval warfare. The British had employed blockades on many occasions and were familiar with all its nuances. As a result of this conversation, Lincoln and Seward concluded that a blockade was the safest means of isolating the Confederacy diplomatically, economically, and as strategic policy evolved, militarily as well. It proved a brilliant decision.

On May 13, the Union heaved a sigh of relief when Queen Victoria formally declared British neutrality in the conflict. Yet the South was elated. Coming so soon after the onset of hostilities, they considered Britain's stand as not only recognizing the Confederacy in a state of war, rather than a section in rebellion, but also signifying a first step toward diplomatic recognition. This reading was quite wide of the mark. British neutrality was as much to safeguard her millions of pounds sterling in trade goods and merchant vessels in Southern ports, than to any moral or political support for the Confederacy.

Still, Britain's economy, cut off from raw cotton, would suffer greatly. Surely, the Southerners thought, the cotton-milling barons of England could not permit that. "The first demonstration of blockade of the southern ports," wrote a Florida correspondent, "would be swept away by English fleets ... hovering on the Southern coasts ... to protect the free flow of cotton." The South continued to believe this chimera for a good part of the war.

But the days of the "paper blockade" were over. The body of international law on naval blockades was the recently published Declaration of Paris, to which the United States generally agreed, but was not a signatory.* "Blockades," it noted, "in order to be binding must be effective, that is to say, maintained by a force sufficient really to prevent access to the coast of the enemy." It no longer availed to merely declare a blockade to make it so—there had to be actual ships on station to enforce it. Considering the abysmal condition of the United States Navy, much of the blockade, for at least a year, was indeed close to the paper variety. With less than fifty ships in commission, it was ludicrous to imagine a continuous patrol along the 3,549 miles of rebel coast,

---

* Strangely enough, it had balked at the clauses that outlawed privateering.

from the Potomac to the Rio Grande, along which were dotted 189 harbors, river mouths, and landfalls for blockade runners.

When Lincoln declared that "a competent force will be posted so as to prevent entrance and exit of vessels" from the rebel ports, his words and reality sailed on widely divergent courses. "The force . . . hastily gathered and stationed along our coast," said David Dixon Porter, "would scarcely have been considered an 'efficient blockade' if a European power had thought fit to institute close inquiries into our proceedings." It was a fact made uncomfortably clear when Commodore Pendergrast declared every Virginia and North Carolina port under blockade, since in fact not one of his ships had ventured south of Chesapeake Bay.

Actually the blockade was established gradually, over many months, one harbor at a time. The announcement that a port was under blockade became the responsibility of individual squadron or ships' captains, and for the most part it was carried out quite informally.

Confronted by Herculean labors that would have easily defeated lesser men, Gideon Welles set about mobilizing the navy for war. Ships laid up in the navy yards were recommissioned with surprising speed. The overseas squadrons, spread about the globe on their traditional cruising stations, from the Mediterranean to the west African coast, from Brazil to the East Indies, were, except for three small vessels, summoned home. By the first weeks of summer, three dozen blockaders maintained a tenuously thin line off the rebel shores.

But simply using the navy's available resources amounted to almost nothing. In late April, Welles convened a meeting with Commodore Joseph Smith of the Bureau of Yards and Docks, and Cabinet secretaries Seward and Chase. At the top of the agenda came the urgent need for more ships, in effect, to improvise a navy. "Only a feeble force of men and vessels," Welles remembered, "scarcely sufficient for ordinary police operations, was at that time available on the Atlantic coast." Welles "stated the necessity of chartering or purchasing without delay vessels for the naval service . . . All concurred in my proposition." That day, emergency orders were drafted to the commandants at the Brooklyn, Boston, and Philadelphia navy yards to charter or purchase twenty merchant steamers capable of mounting a battery of naval guns.

The creaky, time-honored system of navy purchase and charter of civilian vessels groaned and nearly broke under the magnitude of the task. Traditionally, the government advertised for bids and relied on the yard commandants and naval constructors to inspect the vessels and haggle with ship brokers over the price, but while these officers were capable enough in selection and fitting out, they had virtually no experience in driving bargains with profiteering agents who had quickly grasped the enormous wealth to be made in the war.

There was also the pressing matter of time. In the somnolent days of peace, officers could leisurely inspect a vessel for defects; now they hadn't such luxury, and many an unfit bottom passed into the service. "Alas!" complained Commodore Du Pont at Philadelphia. "It is like altering a vest into a shirt to convert a trading steamer into a man of war." In one extreme case Naval Constructor Samuel Pook, an otherwise able officer, approved a ship that turned out badly. His doctor wrote to Welles saying Pook suffered from "extreme torpor of the liver, dyspepsia, and the hallucination that because of his mistake the Secretary . . . was going to have him hanged." Clearly the old system was not up to new demands. When incidents of "palpable and gross fraud" daily crossed his desk, Welles moved to crush the profiteers. In May, his brother-in-law, George Morgan, a shrewd, wealthy New York importer, offered his expertise in negotiating ship purchases and charters.

To appoint Morgan the navy's agent was fraught with danger. Charges of nepotism would doubtless be hurled at Welles, even though Morgan's mercantile experience gave him the proper credentials. Welles shoved those concerns aside, and appointed Morgan the navy's sole purchasing agent in New York. Results were gratifyingly immediate. Old Commodore Breese at Brooklyn had agreed to pay $560,000 for five screw steamers. Morgan rebargained the contracts and saved the government $73,000. During the next six months Morgan bought ninety-one vessels of every sort for $3.5 million dollars, with an estimated saving to the government of about $1 million between the asking and final costs.

Over the next four years the navy, by purchase or lease, acquired 418 civilian vessels—over 300 of them steamers—of every description, from luxuriously appointed passenger liners to Staten Island ferries, coal barges, harbor tugs, and scows. Most performed, if not excellently, at least passably, and the blockade, riverine, and inshore operations could not have been carried out without them.

"What we needed for this war, and the blockade of our extensive coast," Welles said, were "many vessels of light draft and good speed, not large, expensive ships, for we had no navy to encounter but illicit traders to capture." Notwithstanding the ingeniousness of the infant Confederate Navy in constructing some dangerous ironclads and the frightening prowess of a handful of ocean-raiding cruisers, Welles' statement was on the mark.

The navy's own program of new construction reflected a war of blockade, rather than a head-on collision between opposing battle fleets. Welles and the department professionals understood that the backbone of the fleet, the five husky *Wabash* class steam frigates, finely imposing flagships, were hardly suitable, because of their "great draft of water," for workaday blockading and operations in the shallows off the rebel coast.*

Completely new types of ships were obviously necessary, and Welles, loath to sit by and await the special congressional session scheduled for July, contracted with private shipyards for two dozen screw gunboats, the *Unadilla* class, of 691 tons and four guns. Using green, unseasoned timber, a factor that led to their scrapping at war's end, some of these ships were actually afloat, armed, and manned within four months of awarding the contract, a feat that nicknamed them "ninety-day gunboats." Referring to the *Tuscarora,* launched in late August 1861, Welles chuckled, "Her keel was growing in the forest three months ago."

Another new class of forty sidewheel gunboats were laid down in 1861–1862. These were novel "double-enders," having a rudder at both bow and stern and the ability to steam with near-equal facility in either direction. They proved invaluable assets in poking around the sandbar-strewn coastal waters and twisting bayous of Southern river estuaries.

The strength of the navy increased dramatically. Four months after the proclamation of the blockade, the number of ships in commission doubled; in ten months the navy expanded sixfold. By war's end, in the spring of 1865, the old, ninety-ship United States Navy would reach a short-lived pinnacle of 670 vessels of every type (including twenty-two surviving monitors), of which about 500 actively served on the blockade.

Getting the ships only partially solved the problem of maintaining the blockade and thrusting forward in active operations along the coasts and rivers. The exponential expansion of the fleet required the same of its personnel, and recruiting sufficient crews posed a nagging dilemma

---

* *Wabash, Minnesota, Roanoke, Colorado,* and their larger half-sister *Niagara.* The scuttled *Merrimack* formed the sixth unit of the class. The *Franklin,* laid down in 1854, was not commissioned until 1867, by which time she was as obsolete as a Carthaginian galley.

the navy never surmounted during the course of the war. One fifth of the officer corps had gone South, and the less than 1,000 who remained provided only a kernel of the nearly 7,000 who eventually filled the line and staff billets of the fleet and its shore establishment. An initial infusion of enthusiastic, partly trained teenagers, excused (to their ecstasy) from final examinations, came from the Naval Academy's senior class.

Several officers who had resigned in the peacetime doldrums, including Gustavus Fox, immediately offered their services to the department. Law forbade restoration to their former places in the Navy Register, and all were commissioned as acting lieutenants with the promise that Congress would provide a reinstatement to permanent rank.

By far, the biggest and most obvious pool of potential officers was the merchant service. By the end of 1861 nearly 1,000 merchant officers received a lieutenant's commission, or warrant as acting master, engineer, paymaster, or master's mate.* To prepare them for the rigorous and very different life of an officer in a man-o'-war, training schools were established at the navy yards, where, as Welles informed Congress, "the appointees have been drilled and disciplined for navy duty."

With any large influx, several men were found unfit. One senior officer in the Gulf bemoaned to Gideon Welles of "three master's mates, neither of whom can . . . take a meridian observation on the sun, and one of them is ignorant of the multiplication table." Of others, with problems less nautical, Welles informed Congress, "men possessing high and excellent traits in other respects have been found addicted to intemperance. This is a disqualification in any officer, and whenever this habit has been detected there has been no hesitation in revoking at once the appointment."

Considering the torpidity of the navy at the outbreak of the war, it is not surprising that, as David Porter wrote, "the navy list was encumbered with . . . worn-out men without brains." Welles stated the issue somewhat more delicately. "Some of them," he wrote, "were old and infirm; some were physically and others mentally incompetent; but none would admit infirmity, and all wanted employment." At Congress' special July 1861 session, Welles forced a mandatory retirement bill, on

---

* The commissioned "master," a rank just beneath lieutenant, replaced the archaic warrant of "sailing master" in 1837. In 1883 it was further modernized to the present lieutenant junior grade. Master's mates were noncommissioned warrant officers.

three-quarter pay, for all officers at age sixty-two, or forty-five years' service.

At the close of the war's first year, Welles really opened the sluice gates for the promotion of younger, regular naval officers. He recommended to Congress that four additional grades be added to the officer ranks: rear admiral, the actual rank (as opposed to the courtesy title) of commodore, lieutenant commander, and ensign. He also pursued a policy of promoting officers for gallantry in combat. The whole package was signed by Abraham Lincoln in July 1862. "It was the first gleam of sunshine," said David Porter, "that had illuminated the Navy for half a century."

By statute, the navy's enlisted force had been fixed at 7,500 men of all ratings, and when Lincoln took office it was slightly in excess of authorized strength. On March 4, 1861, Inauguration Day, the vast majority were at sea, in the cruising squadrons, leaving only 207 men in the navy yards and receiving ships for immediate, emergency service. This dearth of ready sailors had been a prime cause for the botched relief of Fort Sumter and the loss of the most valuable ships at Norfolk.

Lincoln waited nearly three weeks after his blockade proclamation to issue a summons for naval enlistments. But unlike his naive call of three-month volunteers to the army, the clarion for 18,000 sailors, "for not less than one nor more than three years" service, signified the reality it takes to train a lubberly landsman into something resembling a prime seaman.

By war's end 51,500 enlisted sailors manned the navy's vessels, but they were not enough. The military draft, begun in 1863, made no account for those preferring service in the navy, and the fleet suffered accordingly. Until 1864 the navy was banned from offering enlistment incentives, and the hefty bounties tendered by local authorities for service in state volunteer regiments turned many willing hands away from the sea.

Instead of a cash reward, the seaman recruit received three cents a mile travel money to the nearest navy yard or receiving ship for a physical examination. If between eighteen and thirty-three years old, at least five feet eight inches tall, and without a nautical trade, he was rated "landsman" at twelve dollars a month, or the more remunerative, but hellish rate of "coal heaver" at the princely monthly sum of eighteen dollars per month. Many black recruits served as coal heavers, drawing nearly double the pay they could get in the army. Boys, at thirteen, were permitted to enlist with the consent of parents or guardians, and were rated "boy," third class, with monthly pay of eight dollars.

Before the war closed its first year, the enlisted force of the navy reached 22,000 men, recruited from every sort and condition. Real, professional sailors quickly became a distinct minority, sprinkled as leavening throughout the fleet. Most of the men were trained into fairly proficient gunners, but only a minority achieved the rating of "ordinary seaman," to say nothing of the very few capable of advancing to "able seaman."

The creaky administrative bureaucracy of the navy, headed by generally proficient, if cautious men, was hardly fitted to carry out the mammoth tasks thrust upon the department. The five semi-independent chiefs of the bureaus of Yards and Docks; Ordnance and Hydrography; Construction, Repair, and Engineering; Provisions and Clothing; and Medicine and Surgery in no manner constituted an admiralty staff. By the very nature of the navy's organization, Gideon Welles communicated directly with his commanders afloat and ashore on every sort of tactical, logistic, and administration problem, often on matters in which he was out of his depth. Welles needed a first-rate naval officer to coordinate the department and advise on the strictly operational nature of the war, someone not yet in his dotage, of energetic vision, and with the confidence of his professional peers. He made a political choice, but the result could not have been better.

Acting Lieutenant Gustavus Vasa Fox, now skipper of the tug *Yankee* at Hampton Roads, constantly griped over the fiasco of Sumter's relief. To put a sock in Fox's mouth, and at the same time mollify his many influential partisans, Lincoln asked Gideon Welles to give the man a responsible job in the Navy Department. The secretary had been impressed by Fox's organizational abilities in the Sumter expedition, and commanding a navy tug clearly wasted his considerable talent. The secretary's order arrived on May 8 at Hampton Roads: "You are appointed Chief Clerk of the Navy Department, and I shall be glad to have you enter upon the duties as soon as you conveniently can."

"Captain Fox, *he* is the Navy Department," said Commander John Dahlgren. And while "Captain" was honorary, harking to Fox's days as a merchant skipper, the assumption of his influence at the department was not. Forty years old, with a great balding head, he was a man of zealous energy, absolutely unable to sit behind a desk for more than a few minutes. Single-handedly, he plunged into all the duties of what fifty-four years later would be designated the office of the chief of naval operations.

Fox's previous service of nearly two decades in the navy was a godsend for Welles and the department. He knew everyone, and with his aggressive, but usually tactful, nature got on well with most. During the summer of 1861, Welles expanded Fox's responsibilities and pushed legislation that created the post of assistant secretary of the navy, at a salary of $4,000 per annum, and in this office, Fox served as Welles' professional and confidential adviser.

Given remarkable latitude, Fox was instrumental in choosing officers for critical command appointments, strategic planning, and executing the department's technical business. In nearly every case where Welles received his counsel, it was largely carried out as suggested. When seeking guidance, President Lincoln spoke as freely with Fox as he did with the secretary. "He has a gigantic capacity for work," said Commander Charles Davis, a Harvard graduate and one of the navy's brainier officers.

One unforeseen benefit in having Fox in the department was getting the screeching East Coast merchants off Welles' back. They constantly harangued for protection against the rebel privateers, demanding an immediate, total, and hermetic blockade of the Southern ports. With his years in merchant shipping circles, Fox turned aside the barbs aimed at his chief. "A month has passed since the Blockade proclamation was published," roared Boston businessman Alfred Crea, "and . . . every port . . . except Pensacola is still open. . . . In the meantime, [three large warships] have been in the stream for nearly a week or more—What are they doing there? Waiting for orders, or failing to obey them? . . . The next excuse may be the want of tooth picks."

"Dear Alfred," Fox soothingly replied. "Come on and take my place for a week and you will feel better."

Meanwhile ships steamed or sailed off to play their roles in the blockade. On May 1, Welles elevated Captain Silas Stringham of the steam frigate *Minnesota* to command all blockading forces "from the capes of the Chesapeake to the southern extremity of Florida." And "as an honor to the commander of the Coast Blockading Squadron," he accorded Stringham the privilege of hoisting his flag "at the fore[mast] instead of at the mizzen." Previously, only captains with twenty years in grade were permitted this mark of admiralty respect, and at the time, Stringham fell two months short.

The *Minnesota* steamed off for Hampton Roads on May 8. As in nearly all the ships, there were gaps and deficiencies in her company. Stringham bemoaned the lack of seasoned physicians, "whom we need very much, because the fleet surgeon has always been sick at sea for the past ten years ... [and] the assistant surgeon has never been to sea before." Within a week of Stringham's arrival at Hampton Roads, eleven diverse vessels were taken as prizes. Their cargo was mostly tobacco, which brought a good price at the prize court.

Capturing prizes, though enriching all concerned, proved a drain on personnel. More midshipmen, Stringham told Welles, were needed as prize officers; he could no longer spare his few lieutenants for that duty. More importantly, the handful of blockading ships were barely enough to cover North Carolina, much less the entire Atlantic coast.

The blockade of the Gulf coast began unofficially with the aimless cruising of the Home Squadron off Pensacola. It was not until May 12 that copies of Lincoln's proclamation arrived, followed the next day by an official notice from Captain Adams of the *Sabine* to the Confederate authorities. But timid army officers still considered Fort Pickens in danger of attack from the mainland, and Adams, the senior naval officer on the station, reckoned himself bound by obsolete orders subordinating him to army command. Not until the last week of May were two ships ordered west to Mobile and New Orleans, and not until early July did a blockading vessel appear off Galveston.

At first, the Confederates hardly took the Gulf blockade seriously. According to the *Natchez Courier,* when Porter and the *Powhatan* arrived off Mobile, "Fort Morgan welcomed the blockading fleet by displaying the U.S. flag, with the Union down, from the same staff and below the Confederate flag." Welles selected William Mervine to command the Gulf Blockading Squadron. The twelfth senior captain in the list, with fifty-two years' service, he was described by Commodore Samuel Du Pont as "the thickest-headed fellow we have." With hindsight, Welles agreed: "He proved an utter failure.... He was long in getting out to his station, and accomplished nothing after he got there." It would take a while to shake things out on the Gulf Coast.

It was all very well for Lincoln to proclaim the blockade and for Welles to order warships off the rebel ports, but how was it really to be accomplished? Must the navy station vessels in sight of each other along 3,000 miles of shoreline, from the Potomac to the Rio Grande, or should it concentrate in force at harbor mouths? And what was the nature, so to speak, of the coming field of battle, or to coin a phrase, the lay of the sea?

The basis of Union strategy for the conduct of the war was conceived by Winfield Scott. Old Fuss and Feathers, for all his dithering, and in opposition to popular enthusiasms, knew the war was to be no ninety-day affair, and in all likelihood would protract for at least three blood-drenching years. As early as the first days of March 1861, Scott broached the idea of "strangling" the Confederacy by shutting it off from the world.

In May, he expanded his theory to President Lincoln. There were four main points: establish and strengthen the blockade; split the Confederacy along the line of the Mississippi River; maintain steady pressure on the rebel armies in northern Virginia; and actively use the navy to support the army's operations by amphibious assault, naval gunfire, and the transport of troops.

Scott's plan did not envision large-scale, pitched battles. In fact, it was predicated on avoiding them, and on defeating the Confederacy by economic strangulation. "We rely greatly on the sure operation of a complete blockade of the Atlantic and Gulf ports," he wrote to young General George McClellan, then commanding the Department of the Ohio. "In connection with such a blockade, we propose a powerful movement down the Mississippi to the ocean . . . so as to envelop the insurgent States and bring them to terms with less bloodshed than by any other plan." This long-range strategy, when made public, was laid open and derisively criticized as "Scott's Anaconda," after the South American reptile that slowly crushes its prey rather than going for the quick kill. And contrary to Scott's vision, there was lots of bloodshed, but the movements, in all fact, were exactly what happened.

No operational plans whatever existed for turning this blueprint and the Union's military and naval machinery against the Confederacy. The Mexican War of 1846–1848 and decades-long, antislavery patrols had given the navy a close familiarity with the waters and geography of the Mexican and African coasts. But the littoral stretching from the Potomac to the Rio Grande was little understood from the vantage of offensive operations, and each stretch of Southern coastline presented its own peculiarities.

The wide river mouths of coastal Virginia, inviting water-borne armies into the vitals of the Confederacy, gave way to the sandbar and island-strewn, "double" coasts of the Carolinas and Georgia. There was the great thumb of Florida—would all of its fever-racked, isolated shoreline have to be blockaded, or just the twenty possible places where a blockade runner might land the odd cargo? The Gulf, too, came belted with an outer bank of sandbars and islands, divided by the swampy bayous and passes of Louisiana, falling away to the desolate vastness of the Texas shore.

The answer came seemingly at dinner, on May 21, at the home of Professor Alexander Bache, superintendent of the Coast Survey,* the Treasury Department's nautical mapping agency. He had invited his navy colleague Commander Charles Davis, the compiler of the Nautical Almanac, to hear some of his broad ideas. Davis came away impressed. "I found Bache has a plan to carry out," he wrote to his wife the next day. "He wishes to establish [an] . . . advisory council, to determine military proceedings and operations along the coast. . . . Fox has already been brought into the scheme."

"The Secretary is willing," Fox said, but it took Welles a month to assemble what is variously called the Blockade Board, the Strategy Board, or its officially innocuous Commission of Conference. By whatever name, it constituted an embryonic, very temporary, naval general staff. Welles appointed the patrician Du Pont the chairman, with Bache and Major John Barnard of the Army Corps of Engineers as members, and Charles Davis as secretary.

Welles presented the board its initial charge, "to condense all the information in the archives of the Government which may be considered useful to the blockading squadrons." In the miserable Washington heat, they met almost daily throughout the summer of 1861, surveying the topography and military possibilities of the rebel coast. Over the summer and early autumn, the board issued seven reports that solidified and refined the Anaconda plan with operational precepts that were essentially followed all the way to Appomattox Court House.

The first report dealt primarily with the need to seize intermediate naval bases between Hampton Roads and Key West, Florida. Not only would these havens be of great assistance to the blockaders for coaling and repair facilities, but their occupation would amply demonstrate to the European powers the ability of the United States Navy to control its own coasts, and just as important, the impotency of the Confederacy to prevent it.

The conferees recommended that Commodore Stringham's blockading force be split into two squadrons, divided approximately at the line dividing the Carolinas. The reasons were not only to simplify commanding widespread forces, but the varied nature of the northern and southern portions of the coasts demanded "the treatment of the two should be distinct."

The upper portions of the North Carolina coast, "sterile . . . halfdrowned shores," Du Pont called them, contained large, sheltered

*Now the National Oceanic and Atmospheric Administration.

sounds guarded by a fringe of sandbars reaching seaward to form Cape Hatteras. Landlocked, save for some narrow cuts, a new navigable passage, Hatteras Inlet, had so recently been formed by the perpetual storms in the area, that it didn't appear on the charts and Du Pont had to pencil it in.

With the Confederacy shut out from commerce into Chesapeake Bay, the sounds provided a protected access into the Confederate interior. Stringham had already reported Hatteras Inlet a favorite passage for privateers and blockade runners, and he recommended it be taken. The board concurred.

Du Pont and his colleagues next turned their attention to the Gulf of Mexico. Along the whole of that coast, the Union held one base, Key West, but its distance to the major Confederate ports—600 miles from Mobile, and 800 to New Orleans, demanded operating points closer to the objectives. With an eye to the early capture of New Orleans, the board recommended occupying Ship Island, roughly halfway between the rebel port cities.

On July 21, the untrained Union and Confederate armies flung themselves together in the first great battle of the war at Bull Run, forty miles west of Washington. For the North it was a disastrous beginning. Its forces were routed and the military refugees streamed bloody and beaten through the streets of the capital. Not for the last time was it thought the city would fall.

Calls went out for naval officers to command the artillery in the army's perimeter forts. "So I got out my uniform frock coat," Du Pont explained to his wife, "a pair of stout shoes, some thick clothes, and a blanket, with my sword, and slept in my clothes all night—but nothing happened." Commander Charles Davis, the board secretary, also prepared to defend the city. "The Navy Department," he wrote to his wife, "is well prepared with rifles and revolvers. . . . Commodore [Paulding] . . . and the clerk [Fox] are loading the muskets in the room where I am now writing."

The booming tocsin of three cannon shots heralding a Confederate assault on Washington never sounded. On July 25, Du Pont briefed Welles and Fox on the board's reports. The secretary hadn't a qualm, and within hours presented the documents to Lincoln and the Cabinet. The President's military advisers were of similar mind. According to Du Pont, "General Scott . . . adopted every word of them; and General Totten [the chief of engineers] told me there was not a criticism made."

In early August, Flag Officer Silas Stringham, now an admiral in all but official rank, received his orders to take Hatteras Inlet. One month later, Welles bade Du Pont to organize an expedition to seize a port in the area of Charleston.

And the blockade? While the Northern press raked Gideon Welles for failing "to cover the ocean with vessels in pursuit of the busy privateers," the Anaconda slowly began to squeeze the life out of the Confederacy. "Already they begin to cry out for more ammunition," wrote Southern diarist Mary Boykin Chesnut, "and already the blockade is beginning to shut it all out."

Bricks Without Straw

"Our present navy consists of a little steamer of 500 tons, called the *Sumter,* under the command of Raphael Semmes."

—**Stephen R. Mallory, Secretary of the Navy, CSA**

A "stumpy, 'roly-poly' little fellow ... socially, most estimable," was how a New York newspaper described him. A Confederate naval officer put it this way, "If he had been placed at the head of the [United States] Navy, he would have been a popular and efficient administrator, but [in the Confederacy] he was like a chieftain without a clan, or an artisan without the tools of his art." The "little fellow" was Stephen Russell Mallory, the first and only secretary of the Confederate States Navy.

He was born in Trinidad, in 1811, the son of a Connecticut merchant skipper and an Irish immigrant mother, who raised her children as Roman Catholics.* When Stephen was nine years old, the family settled in the still wild and barely civilized outpost of Key West, Florida. His father and older brother died shortly after, and Mallory, with only three years' formal schooling, helped his mother run a boardinghouse. Turning eighteen, he was appointed the town's inspector of customs, a job that did not require much attending. Instead, Mallory spent his

---

* The only non-Protestants in either war cabinet were Stephen Mallory and the Jewish Judah Benjamin, who served successively as the Confederacy's attorney general, secretary of war, and secretary of state.

days studying law in the offices of a noted authority on maritime wreck and salvage.

In 1832, Stephen Mallory was elected to his first office, town marshal of Key West. He fought as a volunteer in the Seminole War (1835–1843), returned home, and began a very successful maritime law practice. Mallory stumped actively for Florida Democrats but he refused all offers to run for the state legislature. A conservative "Union man," he received support from nonradical Democrats and commercialist Whigs, coming to the U.S. Senate during the maelstrom generated by the abortive Compromise of 1850—the last, futile attempt to deal with the extension of slavery into the Western territories.

Senator Mallory believed in secession from the Union as a theoretical right of the individual states, but he considered it a very dangerous solution for the questions rending the country apart. Of secession he said, "I never could regard it as but another name for revolution."

As a citizen of sea-washed Key West, and a very knowledgeable maritime attorney, it was not surprising that Mallory's maiden speech on the Senate floor addressed naval affairs. Congress had just abolished flogging in the navy, and somewhat to the surprise of his colleagues, Mallory, hardly a martinet, ardently pushed for its reintroduction as absolutely necessary for upholding discipline. The speech brought with it his sometime nickname of "Cat-o'-Nine-Tails Mallory." The sobriquet was inaccurate. Stephen Mallory was no barnacled mossback. In 1853 he was selected by the Democratic party leadership to chair the Senate's Naval Affairs Committee.

The U.S. Navy, stagnating in its latest dark age, saw Mallory fight for some badly overdue reforms. He showed an early interest in experiments with ironclad ships; indeed, he was one of the very few congressmen who recognized the coming revolution in naval construction. Mallory's most enlightened progress (although it was eventually scuttled) was what the *New York Herald* described as "Mr. Mallory's bill providing for reforms in the personnel of the naval service." The legislation, designed to purge the navy of its ancient, disabled, and unfit, passed overwhelmingly. A retirement committee of fifteen senior officers was created, called the vaguely sinister "Board of Fifteen," or the "inquisitional tribune," by its detractors. It convened in secret, kept no records, and recommended 49 officers for outright dismissal and 152 others for placement on a reserve list.

The battle raged in the press and Congress, and Mallory caved in. More than 100 cases were reviewed, and the majority were reversed in favor of the grieving officer. When, a few years later, many of these

reinstated men resigned to go South, they brought with them a smoldering grudge against their new navy secretary, the senator they
blamed for their humiliation.

On February 14, 1861, at Montgomery, Alabama, the Provisional
Congress of the Confederate States planted the seeds of the Confederate Navy by authorizing its naval affairs committee "to procure the
attendance . . . of all such persons versed in naval affairs as they may
deem advisable to consult with." The chairman, Charles Conrad of
Louisiana, dispatched a sheaf of telegrams summoning naval officers
known to harbor Southern sympathies. The response was gratifying; of
officers, if nothing else, the Confederate Navy would always have a sur-
plus of wealth. The number of naval officers appointed by the President
of the Confederate States was, at first, commensurate with the sparse
resources at hand. The line billets were limited to a modest four captains, four commanders, and thirty lieutenants. Staff, warrant, and
lower ranks numbered ten surgeons, six paymasters, two chief engineers, and as many master's mates, midshipmen, engineers, naval constructors, petty officers, and seamen as the President considered necessary—the whole establishment not to exceed three thousand men,
plus six hundred marines and ten musicians.

A week later the rebel Congress passed an "act to establish the
Navy Department," providing for a secretary of the navy, a chief clerk,
"and other such clerks as may be authorized by law." Jefferson Davis
nominated Stephen Mallory for the Cabinet post of secretary of the
navy, and the reception was mixed. Not only was he disliked by more
than a few of the naval officers gone South, but the radical members of
the Confederate Congress blamed him for negotiating the early "truce
of Fort Pickens," which in their opinion prevented its quick seizure by
rebel forces.

Davis stood by the nomination and Mallory retained the President's approval. Throughout the conflict he managed the Navy Department and conducted the war afloat with virtual independence. Davis
went through six secretaries of war, but Mallory was his only navy
chief, and the only member of the Confederate Cabinet to serve in the
same office for the duration.

Given Jefferson Davis' military background: West Point graduate, lieutenant of dragoons, colonel in the Mexican War, secretary of war, major
general of the Mississippi state militia, it is not surprising that his
strategic thoughts were strictly continental and landlocked. He paid

scant attention to naval matters. The role a navy might play in bringing about a Southern victory—or stalemate, which politically amounted to the same thing—was lost on him.

Naval officers gone South saw dark days ahead. Lieutenant John Newland Maffitt noted in his journal, "Unfortunately . . . Mr. Davis was not impressed with the necessity of building ships." Matthew Fontaine Maury came away with even darker impressions, writing, "It is evidently no part of the plan of the Administration to have a navy at present or even to encourage one." Maury was prone to hyperbole, but he wasn't that far off the mark.

When Mallory arrived at the Confederacy's first capital, Montgomery, to take up his duties, he found a Navy Department without a ship. Properly speaking, there was not a single effective warship in the whole of the seceding states. The decommissioned sloop *Fulton* was at Pensacola, there were the burned-out hulks at Norfolk, and the individual states had captured several cutters of the U.S. Revenue Marine. That was all.

Building a navy from scratch, a regular navy with regular ships, able to match broadsides with the Union steam frigates and sloops, was impossible. The Confederacy's industrial capacity was minimal and much of its capital wealth was frozen in land and slaves. Cotton was its only real, convertible asset for raising the hard currency necessary to build, or buy, the machinery of war. And after the first year or so, the blockade put paid to that.

In 1860, the South produced barely a tenth of the manufactured goods in the United States. Of industrial works it had less than a tenth (in fact, the entire South had less manufacturing capacity than New York City). It forged no steel, nor had it the facilities to construct machine tools. Many of the South's foundries and mills were little better than village smithies, and those along the banks of the Tennessee and Ohio rivers quickly fell to Union forces. Of the eleven rolling mills of any size, only Richmond's Tredegar Iron Works was fitted for heavy production and had experience casting naval guns.

There was enough coal and timber, but transportation facilities were insufficient to bring raw materials to the manufacturing sites. Except at New Orleans, and perhaps, if given the opportunity, Memphis, there were no properly equipped civilian workshops for the construction and repair of naval vessels. The navy yards at Pensacola and Norfolk, though priceless resources to the Confederacy, never produced anything approaching their real potential during Confederate ownership.

The world's navies had entered the industrial age, and acquiring boilers and steam engines posed an enormous problem for the Confederate Navy. There were five facilities in the South that could put some form of propulsion machinery together. But only overworked and undersupplied Tredegar had the theoretical ability to manufacture large, complete systems. From the beginning, constructors had to rip the engineering plants from civilian steamers, or salvage what they could from wrecks. In several cases, patchwork Confederate warships on the building ways reached completion without any idea of what would constitute their machinery.

Throughout the war, nearly all of Stephen Mallory's efforts to build a navy were stymied by a lack of iron—either the ore itself, the foundries to turn it into guns or armor plate, or the transportation facilities to carry the finished products to the shipyards. In desperation, the Confederate Navy began ripping up track from militarily unessential railroads, including Richmond's streetcar tracks. Railroad iron, however, was also prized by every other agency of the Confederate armed forces. In 1863, the naval officer in charge of building the ironclad *Albemarle* reported to Secretary Mallory, "It is impossible to obtain any . . . iron unless it is seized. . . . These roads are considered a military necessity and the whole subject of Railroad iron [is] laid before the North Carolina Legislature and I am unable to obtain iron."

In 1862, following Mallory's decision to concentrate on building ironclads, the situation became really acute. At least ten ironclads had to be broken up, incomplete for want of plate. In late 1864, the navy's chief constructor reported a dozen vessels on the stocks awaiting their armor, "but the material is not on hand."

For the first half of the war, the principal source for the Confederate Navy's heavy guns were the captured ordnance stocks at Norfolk. By late 1861, the Tredegar Iron Works began casting excellent rifled pieces designed by the very talented Lieutenant John R. Brooke. Yet the navy's dependence on this single firm as its source of reliable ordnance proved worrisome. In early 1863, the navy bought and staffed Alabama's Selma Foundry Works, not only to cast guns, but to roll iron plate and manufacture ammunition as well. But the facility never had enough workers to turn out more than one rifled cannon each week, and it had no workers for the shell-making machinery. "We have not been able to furnish shot and shell for the guns we have made," said its frustrated superintendent. "We ought to supply the whole navy."

In one area, the nascent rebel navy achieved remarkable progress. The impossibility of building a conventional fleet to confront and cripple the blockade led the Confederacy to develop highly sophisticated methods of maritime mining and undersea warfare, an endeavor that sank or damaged more United States warships—about forty—than any other means employed by the Southern forces.

Stephen Mallory's strategy for conducting the Confederacy's naval war was based almost wholly on defeating the Union blockade. Ahead of most contemporaries, including Gideon Welles, he instinctively grasped certain elemental, strategic concepts of sea power. Alone in the rebel Cabinet, Mallory knew that with every additional ship added to the Union blockade, the Confederacy grew incrementally weaker. If the Union stayed committed to the war—and so long as Lincoln remained president, it probably would—any string of Confederate *battlefield* victories counted for virtually nothing.

The Confederate Navy could never match the Union fleet ship for ship, nor, save for the isolated incident, could it dictate the time and place of battle. Thrown on the strategic defensive, and forced into a reactive posture, Mallory adopted a dual approach that might well destroy the blockade, but in any case would weaken and dissipate its strength.

To confront the blockade directly, he planned to domestically build or buy abroad, a few immensely powerful, invulnerable ironclad steamers, against which no United States wooden warship could stand. These behemoths, he hoped, would concentrate off the Confederacy's principal ports, sink or drive off the blockaders, reopen the South to the world's commerce, and perhaps, even gain its recognition as a sovereign nation.

Simultaneously, while the United States Navy strove to meet the ironclad menace, a handful of fast, well-armed wooden cruisers would prey upon the Union's defenseless, oceangoing commerce and destroy the American carrying trade, then second only to Great Britain's. Mallory believed once the howls went up from the Northern merchant community—and already they were letting off some mighty bellows over a few privateers—Lincoln and Welles would be forced to squander their sea power by drawing off blockading warships in endless pursuit of the raiders.

In cruiser warfare the Confederate Navy was hugely successful. The ocean wolves spread enormous havoc on the seas, and permanently destroyed the predominance of the American merchant marine. But little else. Lincoln and Welles both displayed a far greater stoicism in the face of the damage than Mallory could have expected. In effect, they ignored the raiders, and the strangling blockade never loosened a notch.

The Confederate Navy's ironclads were potentially a far more serious and legitimate fear, and Mallory's prompt foresight in getting the project underway is perhaps his most praiseworthy accomplishment. In early May 1861, while Gideon Welles still poked around the subject, Mallory unequivocally told the chairman of the Confederate Senate Naval Affairs Committee, "I regard the possession of an iron-armored ship as a matter of the first necessity. Such a vessel at this time could traverse the entire coast of the United States, prevent all blockade, and encounter, with a fair prospect of success, their entire navy." Mallory was more than a little optimistic regarding an iron vessel's individual performance, especially one constructed in the South, but the millennium of the wooden wall as the arbiter of naval power was over, and he saw that clearly.

The twenty-odd ironclads built in the Confederacy, though a truly mammoth endeavor, were little better than armored, floating artillery batteries, suitable only for harbor defense. The point must always be borne in mind that the South lacked the domestic industrial capacity to produce anything beyond the simplest gun platforms. For that, Mallory had to look abroad, and when he did, he came as close as anyone to embroiling the United States in a European war.

In the spring of 1861, when the Confederate capital moved from Montgomery to Richmond, Mallory and his department took up quarters at the Mechanics Institute, formerly a library and lecture hall. According to the lobby directory, a visitor could find the navy on the "2nd story, right hand side."

As an institution the Confederate Navy was heir to the traditions of its parent organization, the United States Navy, and the overwhelming majority of its customs, rules, and regulations simply transferred title. There were, of course, some differences. First, in an eighty-year advance over U.S. Naval practice, Mallory established a specific personnel department, the Office of Orders and Detail.*

Mallory followed the United States model in forming the "offices" of Provisions and Clothing, and Medicine and Surgery. But he never

---

* Welles formed an "Office of Detail" as a secretarial adjunct in 1862. It was not, however, a congressionally authorized bureau. Its functions were transferred to the Bureau of Navigation in 1865, where it remained until the creation of the Bureau of Naval Personnel in 1942.

created specific agencies to administer the navy yards or oversee construction and repair or steam engineering. Nor was there really any centralized responsibility for those tasks until 1863 when he appointed an engineer in chief and chief constructor. Consequently, they remained weak departments, with less than the best at their heads. For the Confederate Navy, with the exception of such oddments as supplying coal, sailcloth, and cordage, which fell to the Office of Orders and Detail, most shore establishment functions became the stepchildren of the ubiquitous Office of Ordnance and Hydrography.

Confederate officers' naval uniforms were originally dark blue, but the lack of indigo dye forced the adoption of "steel gray." In accord with universal practice, officers provided their own uniforms. Enlisted men received an initial issue, often of British manufacture, and replacements when available. But cloth, as with everything else, became quite scarce, and enlisted sailors took to the time-honored nautical tradition of tailoring their own from scraps of sailcloth or other scavenged material.

Pay generally followed the tables of the U.S. Navy. Personnel serving in the home stations were paid in highly inflated Confederate greenbacks. To hold the large proportion of foreigners who enlisted overseas to serve in the raiding cruisers, their pay was not only at a higher scale, but in gold.

Initially, the Office of Provisions and Clothing adopted the ration system of the U.S. Navy, but as the war progressed, this proved impossible. The Confederacy grew more than enough food for its needs, but it lacked the means of distribution, and shortages were acute. The James River Squadron, because of its proximity to Richmond, often received fresh meat three times a week, but this was very much an exception in the service.

Many items on the ration list remained mere words on paper. Cheese, butter, tea, coffee, raisins, had to be run through the blockade at prohibitive cost. Yet, overall, the navy ate far better than the army, whose rations by 1864, often just parched corn and bacon, were about one third that of the sea service. During the last summer of the war, in the interest of interservice harmony, a naval board reviewed and reduced the ration allotment, giving the army commissariat the responsibility for furnishing provisions to all Confederate fighting forces.

Each enlisted man was allowed one gill—a half-pint—of spirits or wine per day. If he chose not to drink, he received a commutation of four cents a day. Naval surgeons consistently defended the liquor ration on medical grounds, line officers just as consistently opposed it for the disciplinary problems it created, and paymasters demanded its abolition as unnecessary expense. All exactly like the U.S. Navy.

One resource Mallory had aplenty: officers. More than 100 of those who had come South had from ten to fifty years' service and were nominally eligible for command assignments. There were outstanding men, and some hopelessly incompetent. The problem was that even for the smart and fit there were never enough billets commensurate with their rank and abilities. Confederate army officers were rapidly promoted. Lieutenants and captains found themselves colonels and generals, commanding brigades and divisions in the field, and more so than not, at war's end, mantled with a national reputation.

Not so with the Confederate Navy. Men like Tattnall and Buchanan, who had commanded squadrons at sea, now aspired to a handful of converted tugs and river steamers. In the middle scale, "commanders and lieutenants of many years' service," said William Harwar Parker, "were risking their reputations in command of canal boats." Most of the naval officers came out of the war with their original rank, or perhaps one promotion, and "nothing," as Parker said, "but their wants, infirmities and scars to reward them."

In April 1862, the Confederate Congress expanded the Register. The new list authorized four admirals, ten captains, thirty-one commanders, and presaging the U.S. Navy by two decades, divided the lieutenancy into one hundred "first" and twenty-five "second" lieutenants. It also cleared a passage for the deserving by a statutory provision that declared "all the admirals," four of the captains, and a proportional number of the lower grades "shall be appointed solely for gallant or meritorious conduct during the war."

Not satisfied with the results of meritorious promotion, Mallory initiated further efforts to place younger, active men in command of forces afloat. In April 1863, he lopped off the operational responsibilities of the naval station commanders, almost all of whom were the oldest captains in the service. Henceforth, they would concern themselves strictly with administrative and logistic matters ashore.

One month later, Mallory ingeniously and effectively created an entirely new naval service, the "Provisional Navy of the Confederate States." At a stroke, all men fit for duty, except commissioned line officers, were transferred into it. Its officers would, of course, come out of the "old" navy, but only by presidential appointment. By June 1864, the best of the regular officers, save the oldest captains and commanders, the ill and infirm, the chiefs of the various offices in Richmond, and the commandants of the navy's industrial facilities, had been assigned to the Provisional Navy and promoted one grade over their substantive rank. "The object being," said Raphael Semmes, the second-ranking captain in the new organization, "to cull out from [the] navy list, younger and more active men, and put them in the Provisional Navy, with increased rank. The Regular Navy became, thus, a kind of retired list." These radical measures served the purpose of advancing men of talent at the expense of the ineffectual.

The overpopulation of the navy's quarterdecks was reversed on the lower decks. Mallory hardly needed the great numbers of enlisted sailors required by the U.S. Navy; he hadn't the ships for them anyway. But there were never enough even to crew the tiny squadrons in home waters, and with no indigenous seafaring population, there existed no natural pool of personnel. The Confederate Navy's maximum enlisted strength counted barely 4,500 during the course of the war, at least 25 percent below requirements, and at any given time was probably fewer than 3,000 men.

Mallory generally followed United States practice and employed the traditional ways of recruiting. At New Orleans, Savannah, Mobile, Raleigh, Norfolk, Macon, and Richmond, a senior officer, often disabled, assisted by a couple of juniors and a naval surgeon established the recruiting stations, or "naval rendezvous." Boys and young men between fourteen and twenty-one years old required parental permission. Free blacks could enlist with the approval of the local squadron commander, or the Navy Department, and slaves were permitted to serve with their master's consent. It was stipulated that no draft of seamen to a newly commissioned vessel could number more than 5 percent blacks. Though figures are lacking, a fair number of blacks served as coal heavers, officers' stewards, or at the top end, as highly skilled tidewater pilots.

Enlistment bounties were not offered without Mallory's authorization. But as with the Union, too many men were being enticed into the army, and by early 1862, fifty dollars was paid to any recruit signing on for the navy for three years, or the duration of the war. In April 1862, the Confederate Congress permitted army-drafted seamen to apply for transfer into the navy. Mallory repeatedly badgered the War Department for his allotment, but he received very little cooperation. Only in the spring of 1864 did it release men to the navy, of whom fewer than 1,000 actually served.

*   *   *

In sum, the Confederate Navy, remarkable as some of its achievements were, never had a chance. From nothing, some old ships were converted, a few were built, and with scant, makeshift crews, they operated at widely scattered points with no possibility of strategic concentration. Isolated attempts, with some successes, at defending its seaports could not stand against the overwhelming might and projection of the U.S. Navy, which could and did dictate the time and place of battle.

Mallory proved a superior chief, and the Confederacy really could not have done better. Yet the secretary had the unfortunate tendency to dream, and his stabs at innovation and reform took little account of short commons and unreachable goals. Lacking an industrial base to build a navy, and the blockade preventing the exchange of cotton for hard currency to buy a fleet abroad, it is nonetheless quite remarkable what he did achieve.

The saga of the Confederate Navy can be read in one sentence of Mallory's to the commander of three Savannah gunboats on the eve of the city's military evacuation. "If fall they must, let them show neither weakness of submission nor of self-destruction, but inflict a blow that will relieve defeat from discredit." It could have stood as the motto of the service.

Half-Drowned Shores

"I know of no higher or nobler duty than the clearing out of those rebel and pirate rendezvous on the North Carolina Coast."

— Lieutenant Reigert B. Lowry, USN

Like the sharp ram of a great ironclad thrusting into the Atlantic breakers, the barren, wind-lashed sandbars of North Carolina's outer banks stretch nearly 200 miles south from Chesapeake Bay to Cape Lookout. Dotted with salt marshes and clumps of dwarf oaks, these rampart islets were home to a small population who gleaned their living oystering and salvaging the wrecks driven ashore at the ram's apex, the ever-treacherous waters off Cape Hatteras.

Behind the sandbanks, sheltered from the pounding seas, lay the wide, placid inland waterways of the Carolina sounds. On these waters, and their little ports, shallow-draft vessels carried on a lively coasting trade, well supported by railroads and riverways that reached deep into the heart of the eastern Confederacy.

Lieutenant Reigert Lowry, an officer very familiar with the region, wrote to Secretary Welles: "A simple inspection of the maps will convince [you] of the great advantages and facilities the enemy will have in possessing this vast internal water navigation unmolested." Captain Du Pont's Strategy Board paid close attention and considered these waters "vastly important to the rebels ... But for this, the sterile ... half-drowned shores of North Carolina might be neglected."

From the sea, entrance into the sounds came through a handful of ephemeral inlets, scoured by wind and wave, often appearing, as a naval officer said "after some gale of unusual severity." The sounds' new main gateway, Hatteras Inlet, had opened recently ten miles southwest of the cape.

Even before Du Pont's strategists turned to business, the Navy Department was painfully aware of active rebel military measures in the area. Immediately on North Carolina's secession, a state flotilla of armed steamers began patrolling the inlets, and "already," Lieutenant Lowry explained to the secretary, "their privateers prey upon our commerce, and from these very waters issue with impunity." In addition, the area had greatly increased its trade in timber, rice, and naval stores with the West Indies, and Confederate commerce and military supplies plied the sounds as a convenient back door to Norfolk and Richmond.

The Confederacy lost no time in throwing up defenses against a seaborne attack on the sounds through Hatteras Inlet. Using slave laborers on the southern tip of Hatteras Island, they constructed a pair of low sand and turf redoubts, forts Hatteras and Clark. Armed with a variety of captured guns brought down from Norfolk, they soon held a garrison of 580 North Carolina militiamen. The rebels felt no need to mask their presence. Several merchant masters, set free after their ships had been taken by privateers, spent some days at the inlet. Making their way north, they provided much valuable intelligence on the progress and strength of the rebel works.

At first independently of each other, the army and navy considered the threat and solutions to the Carolina coastal problem. In early June, Secretary Welles penned some general dispatches to his blockade commanders suggesting they sink blockships—stone-laden hulks—"across some of the harbors." Although the tactic was never embraced with any enthusiasm, Fox pushed hard, indeed to absurd lengths, for the scheme. In early summer 1861, he informed Flag Officer Silas Stringham that the department proposed to "sink vessels in all, or nearly all, the channels." With a good chart and a score of ballasted hulks, what, thought Gus Fox, could be easier?

Similarly, when Du Pont's Strategy Board addressed the North Carolina issue, its chief concern lay with preventing Confederate waterborne commerce and privateering. The most obvious method, it reported, "is by putting down material obstructions; and the most convenient form of obstruction . . . is that of old vessels laden with ballast . . . and sunk in the appropriate places."

The board gave only passing consideration to the possibility of

entering the sounds in force and executing an attack on the several
estuary towns. "The whole region of marshes and cedar swamps," they
informed the secretary, "is fatally unhealthy at this season of the year
... to our Northern constitutions."

At about the same time, the strictly naval solutions received an
expanded, military elaboration from the ambitious Massachusetts
lawyer, politician, and soldier, Major General Benjamin Butler. Butler
wrote to Secretary of War Simon Cameron pointing to the Confederate
privateering at Hatteras Inlet. "I suggested ... something should be
done to break it up," he later told a congressional committee, "and I
thought a small [combined] expedition might achieve that purpose."

Through midsummer, Welles and Stringham sent each other almost
daily letters of the operational possibilities along the Carolina coast.
Willing enough to carry out whatever departmental plan was decided
on, Stringham remained unconvinced that blockships alone provided
the solution. Having time to evaluate the merchant captains' reports,
his answer neatly dovetailed with Ben Butler's notion to the War
Department. "The inlets may, for the time being, be cleared," Stringham advised, "but I am satisfied that only permanent benefit can result
by the aid of a cooperating land force to occupy the forts ... at the
mouths of the harbors."

On August 3, Flag Officer Stringham received the department's
order to push ahead with "the stoppage of the ports of North Carolina."
The decision was as much political as military. Coming hard on the
catastrophe at Bull Run, and the expiration of the three-month enlistments of the army's initial volunteers, Lincoln knew the war was to be
no short summer affair. The Union desperately needed its first victory,
and the navy had to provide it.

Welles entrusted what he considered the major facet of the operation, the blockships, to "steady and experienced" Commander Henry
Stellwagen. As originally planned, Stringham's squadron was only to
convoy the stoppers to Hatteras Inlet, and, if necessary, lend the support of his guns. There was no mention of any participation by the
army.

Stellwagen journeyed to Baltimore, where the navy had bought
twenty-two Chesapeake Bay schooners, most of them derelict hulks,
loaded with stone ballast. To tow them to Hampton Roads, and their
final destination, Stellwagen chartered a pair of steamers, *Adelaide* and
George Peabody, for $600 a day.

Ben Butler's original idea for a combined operation began perco-
lating into the Navy Department. The navy hadn't yet succumbed to
"bombardment fever," the false notion that ships' guns alone could
batter land fortifications into surrender. According to the current doctrine, one gun ashore still equaled four guns afloat, and Welles paid
close attention to Stringham's warning's of the Hatteras forts. Wisely,
he sought the army's participation in the venture; the troops could
sail in Stellwagen's chartered steamers. To the surprise of all,
Winfield Scott agreed, ordering Butler to organize forces "to cooperate in carrying the batteries at the inlet." Scott thought the navy could
handle things after that, and the troops were slated back at Fort Monroe when done with the immediate business.

In the *Minnesota*'s spacious, chintz-upholstered flag cabin, Butler and Stringham discussed long-range effects of the operation.
As the flag officer saw it, if the army permanently garrisoned the
inlet, it would not only free his ships from patrolling "a very
exposed and strong point of the coast," but also provide the fleet
with a badly needed victualing depot nearer its blockade stations.
It was a plainly obvious argument, and Butler so informed his
chiefs in Washington.

On August 14, Stellwagen's steamers, towing nineteen hulks, "properly loaded with stone," anchored in Hampton Roads. Then nearly two
weeks of bad weather delayed the fleet's sailing. By Sunday, the twenty-
fifth, the weather cleared and the expedition was ready to proceed. Butler's command, 860 men, mustered the colorful 9th New York Zouaves,
the immigrant Germans of the 20th New York Volunteers, the odd-duck
Union Coast Guard, and a company of sixty regulars from the 2nd U.S.
Artillery.*

On Monday, Stringham wired the Navy Department, "I sail today
at noon for Hatteras Inlet." In stately procession, inky smoke rolling
from their stacks, the *Minnesota* and her sister ship *Wabash,* two of
the world's most powerful wooden men-o'-war, led the fleet out of
Hampton Roads. In ragged line astern followed the *Monticello,
Pawnee,* and *Harriet Lane.* Stellwagen's two steamers, each towing a
stone-ballasted blockship, and the army tug *Fanny* completed the

---

* The Union Coast Guard was one of several *army* organizations, including the New York Marine Artillery, the Mississippi Ram Fleet/Marine
Brigade, and the Confederate Mississippi River Defense Fleet, that were
organized for service afloat. All are dealt with in subsequent chapters.

parade. Stringham left the remaining blockships behind. He considered them so heavily laden, they would surely founder in any sort of bad weather.

The sailing was no secret to the rebels. Anyone standing with a long glass on Sewell's Point could pick out individual faces on any quarterdeck. Brigadier General Ben Huger cabled to Richmond, accurately reporting every ship, "and a body of troops . . . passed out of the capes, and steered south, I think to the coast of North Carolina."

Heavy swells, enough to make the troops seasick, paced the fleet on its voyage. In the little army tug *Fanny,* navy Lieutenant Peirce Crosby, who volunteered to command the craft, lashed her boiler to the deck to keep it from carrying away. Watching *Fanny's* gyrations from the comfort of the flagship, a reporter from the *Boston Herald* wrote, "she rolled about like a tub, but somehow held together. . . . Lieutenant Crosby who went as a volunteer, deserves much credit for his valor—perhaps less for his discretion."

On Tuesday morning, August 27, the speedier vessels skirted the blind, empty eye of Hatteras lighthouse (the rebels had carted away the lens) and reduced speed to allow the *Fanny* and Stellwagen's steamers to close up for the final leagues. In late afternoon Stringham let go his anchors in sight of Hatteras Inlet.

From the ships' mastheads, lookouts easily picked out the defensive works: the larger, Fort Hatteras, on the fingertip, commanded the eastern side of the inlet, while 700 yards up the sandspit beach, Fort Clark watched directly out to sea. Just inside broad Pamlico Sound a few rebel schooners huddled for protection under the battery guns. "Hoisted out surfboats and made preparations for landing in the morning," Stringham noted in his report.

From the parapet of Fort Hatteras, Colonel William Martin of the 7th North Carolina Infantry squinted through his glass. "I discovered a large fleet in sight," he reported. His little garrison numbered about 350 men, more than 200 of whom were needed to work the guns. "Knowing . . . I could not successfully resist a landing," he sent a pilot boat for reinforcements.

At dawn, Wednesday, the fleet's shrilling boatswains' pipes called the morning watch and turned up all hands. The swells had increased during the night, and in the lurching steamers the meal of fried salt pork, potatoes, and coffee could hardly have been a comfort to the retching soldiers.

Alongside the transports came the four heavy iron surfboats, one of which carried a pair of 12-pounder howitzers. From the heaving steamers, the troops climbed down into them. General Butler and the fleet's marines shifted to the *Monticello* for the run into the beach.*

"Our plan," wrote Butler to his wife, "is to land the troops under cover of the guns of the *Harriet Lane* and *Monticello,* while the *Minnesota* and *Wabash* try to shell them out of the forts." He would assault the beach above Fort Clark, wheel left, and march down, "my intention . . . to carry them with the bayonet." The general was worried about the state of the sea. "Even the *Minnesota* reels to and fro like a very drunken man. . . . I am afraid the seasickness of my men will unnerve them, but after we land I will feed them, fill their canteens with water, and try to get them on their legs."

Just before 9 A.M., a colorful hoist of signal flags soared to the *Minnesota*'s mizzentop: "disembark troops." Volcanoes of choking coal smoke belching from their stacks, the *Pawnee, Monticello, Harriet Lane,* and the transports—surfboats and blockships in tow—steamed to a point two miles east of Fort Clark. At the line of departure, the surfboats cut loose their towlines, and over a heavy, rolling surf, their sailor crews pulled mightily for the beach.

The *Wabash* led the heavy ships of the bombardment line directly at the fort. Up from the magazines ran dozens of powder monkeys— ships' boys carrying ten-pound woolen pouches of black powder charges for the guns. Down the bags went, into the iron muzzles. Exploding shells were rammed home atop. At the great guns (a 9-inch Dahlgren weighed more than five tons), a dozen seamen strained at the tackles, running them up to the firing ports. Over each barrel, firing lanyard in hand, a gun captain squinted at the target and awaited the order to fire. At ten o'clock, a thundering wall of blinding smoke heralded Silas Stringham's broadsides.

For the sloop *Cumberland* it marked the passing of an era: the last time a major American warship entered battle under sailpower alone. Aboard her, Lieutenant Tom Selfridge remembered "standing in under all sail . . . we executed a simultaneous evolution of shortening and furling sail, dropping anchor, and opening fire. . . . It was a very smart and inspiring piece of seamanship." Stringham, however, was mindful of the risk borne by a stationary target, and ordered the *Wabash* to pass a towline.

The fleet's shooting, save for a stray shell that sent a herd of cattle stampeding across the dunes, was deadly accurate. In the *Minnesota,* one of whose guns was manned by a crew of fugitive slaves, a particu-

---

* These were regular United States Marines, probably fewer than 100 men.

larly well-aimed shot brought a cheer from the ship's chaplain. Greatly embarrassed, the man remembered his calling, and grabbed an iron kettle to pour coffee for the sweated, powder-grimed gunners.

Steaming back and forth in a shallow oval, giving the Confederates no constant point of aim, the fleet poured what Confederate Colonel Martin described as "a flood of shells" into the rebel works. Inside the collapsing sand ramparts of Fort Clark, the Carolina militiamen loaded and fired, until Colonel Martin said, "every charge of powder and every primer was exhausted." Ammunition spent, he gathered his officers, who voted to spike their guns, abandon the post, and retreat down the beach to Fort Hatteras. "Having no proper spikes" to hammer into the cannon touch holes, they used bundles of nails instead. Hauling down their flag, "we fell back, under a most terrible fire of shell."

The Union landing, however, was not going as well as the bombardment. As the freshening easterly wind whipped the frothing breakers, two of the iron surfboats capsized, and two wooden flatboats were crushed in the driving water. In a desperate attempt to get ashore, ships' boats carried the seasick New York Zouaves from the transports to the ballasted blockships. Those craft, the regiment's Colonel Rush Hawkins remembered, were "slowly allowed to drift into the breakers" at the ends of their towlines.

There seemed every chance the stone-laden vessels would founder in the surf, taking down with them an entire regiment of Zouaves. Lieutenant Peirce Crosby brought the *Fanny* to their rescue. Once, twice, three times, he backed the tug into the pounding surf, only to be thrown out to sea. At last, by dogged skill, her crew managed to heave lines on board the hulks and towed them out to calmer water.

Only 318 men made it to the beach. Fortunately, they included all of the marines, the artillery regulars, and the two howitzers. Colonel Max Weber of the 20th New York assumed command ashore. "The condition of these troops," he recalled, "was of course a very bad one. All of us were wet up to the shoulders, cut off entirely from the fleet, with wet ammunition, and without any provisions; but still all had but one thought—to advance."

Weber sent forward a reconnaissance party, formed the main body of his troops in line, and seeing Fort Clark empty, marched in. Scrambling through the blasted embrasures, Weber ordered the United States flag hoisted on the staff. Out in the fleet it was mistaken for rebel colors, and "the Navy commenced firing upon us." Weber ordered a soldier to the beach, to frantically wave the national flag, "and the firing ceased."

With the striking of the rebel colors over Fort Clark, Stringham assumed the Confederates had surrendered at Fort Hatteras as well. At two o'clock he signaled his ships to cease fire and ordered the *Monticello* into Hatteras Inlet to take possession of the rebel vessels and small craft milling about inside. Commander James Gillis felt his way in with the deep-sea lead. "We grounded frequently, touching bow and stern," he reported. The water began shoaling fast, when the guns of Fort Hatteras "briskly" opened fire. Gillis returned the compliment, firing rapidly and with precision; "the Union now, the Union forever!" he shouted to his men.

Stringham, appalled at what he considered treachery by the rebels, hoisted the signal "engage batteries." Under the blanketing guns of the bombardment line, the *Montecello* retired from what had become a very hot corner. Stringham ordered the cease-fire, and the fleet, less the *Monticello, Pawnee,* and *Harriet Lane,* which he kept inshore to protect the troops on the beach, hauled off for the night. "Wind from the south, and weather looking squally," penned the officer of the watch in the flagship's log.

While the fleet traded shots with Fort Hatteras, the Confederate Navy tug *Ellis,* steaming about Pamlico Sound, unaware of the action, came upon the pilot boat that Colonel Martin had sent for Confederate reinforcements. Upon hearing "that the vandal horde of the North" (according to a Byronic officer in the *Ellis*) had landed and taken Fort Clark, the tug steered for the inlet. "With beating and anxious hearts," the officer continued, "[we] eagerly waited the time when we could cheer our noble companions by our presence."

As the tug approached the beleaguered fort, more help—the rebel steamer *Winslow,* flying the broad pennant of Commodore Samuel Barron of the Confederate Navy—anchored within long gunshot of the fort. Barron, with part of the 3rd Georgia infantry, had come down from Norfolk by way of the Dismal Swamp Canal. The rest of the regiment, creeping in a string of towed canal boats, lay a day behind.

Going ashore, Barron faced a truly desperate situation. "I found Colonel Martin," Barron said, "very much exhausted from exposure and hard fighting." "Utterly prostrated," was how a Confederate army officer put it, and they pleaded with Barron to take command. Strictly speaking, Barron could have refused the honor. But to the immense relief of the army officers, he gave it no thought and accepted.

Barron fully expected to be shelled out in the morning. Given luck, however, his own reinforcements might arrive that night, and any sort of bad weather would keep the Federal ships from interfering. With that much time, he could reorganize the defense and launch a counter-attack to retake Fort Clark. Barron set his tired men to work repairing Hatteras to receive the morning's assault.

Up the beach, Colonel Max Weber's Union troops spent an uncomfortable, but otherwise uneventful night. The two boat guns were positioned on the inner shore of the island, covering the rear approaches from Fort Hatteras. They had enough food, from stray sheep and geese, butchered on the spot and spitted on bayonets over open fires. Fresh water was their only real problem. The men dug some holes in the sand, but the pools were brackish and undrinkable.

At three bells in the morning watch, 5:30 A.M., a solitary gun boomed from the *Minnesota,* and signal 102, "prepare to engage batteries," snapped from the flagship's halyards. Two hours later, Stringham holsted the general signal "attack batteries." The rolling broadsides crashed out, and a terrible plunging fire fell on Fort Hatteras. "Our shot," he saw with grim satisfaction, "now falling in and around the battery with great effect."

The enemy colors were shot away, and for a few minutes many in the fleet thought the rebels had surrendered. But "no attention was paid to it," Stringham said, harking to the "treachery" of the day before. Three more hours of hellish bombardment continued, until a white flag appeared on the blasted ramparts. Up the *Minnesota*'s halyards climbed the signal "cease firing."

In the ships of the fleet, officers and seamen broke into cheers. Ben Butler sent Lieutenant Crosby with a formal surrender demand. In his reply, Commodore Barron offered to give up Fort Hatteras, with all its guns and munitions, if his officers and men were permitted "to retire" back across the sound.

Butler refused to consider it. "The terms offered are these," he wrote back. "Full capitulation; the officers and men to be treated as prisoners of war. No other terms admissible." If Barron agreed, they would meet on board the *Minnesota*. In less than an hour, Crosby returned with Commodore Barron and his senior officers to unconditionally surrender their swords, selves, and commands; 750 rebels became prisoners of war. Leaving the 20th New York to garrison the forts and the *Pawnee* and *Monticello* to patrol the inlet, the fleet dispersed to their blockading stations along the coast.

*   *   *

On September 3, the news of the Union's first real victory in the war hit the front pages. "The brilliant success of the Naval Expedition has been received here with that intense satisfaction which can hardly be described," gushed the *New York Times*. A White House watchman woke the President to give him the news. Still in his nightshirt, Lincoln ran into the Cabinet room, and literally danced a jig around Gus Fox, who had come from the Navy Department across the street bringing the official word.

In the Confederacy an opposite hysteria took hold. "The road open to invasion at any moment . . . and about 700 gallant men prisoners, taken by the Abolition Kangeroos," moaned the naval officer in the barely escaped *Ellis*. "Our coasts to be ravaged . . . defenseless women and children to be murdered," screamed a New Orleans editor.

But in the North's euphoria, some very important lessons went unnoticed. The battering of two small, weakly defended sand and turf redoubts had been so easy that the doctrine of one gun ashore equals four guns afloat was temporarily forgotten—the navy, it seemed, could do it all, and supporting troops were seen as largely superfluous. Bombardment fever had made its first, insidious inroad.

More important, Stringham and Butler also failed to follow their victory by not moving light-draft vessels through the inlet into Pamlico Sound. "The enemy made a great mistake," said Confederate naval lieutenant William Harwar Parker, "in not taking possession of the sounds immediately after capturing Hatteras; there was nothing to prevent it but two small gunboats." A landing force of Butler's troops might also have occupied Roanoke Island, slamming shut the back door to Norfolk and Richmond. "This at least could have been done," Parker said, "had the Federals seized their opportunity." Still, the attack on Hatteras inlet was the first significant Union victory of the war, coming when the North, "in a depressed condition," as David Dixon Porter observed, dearly needed one. "It was a death-blow to blockade running in that vicinity, and ultimately proved one of the most important events of the war."

But it was followed by a couple of sorry little epilogues.

Now that the navy controlled Hatteras Inlet, the question was again raised as to its ultimate use. To be sure, Stringham said, "as a depot for coaling and supplies for the blockading squadron it is invaluable." He urged the department to consider its permanent occupation, and that of Ocracoke Inlet, fifteen miles south, as well. The blockships, he suggested, should be used only on the less important exits from the sounds. Gus Fox agreed, and issued instructions to convert Hatteras Inlet into a small naval station. Further than that, the navy had no plans.

Yet the opportunity for a deep plunge into coastal Carolina remained. Commander Stephen Rowan and Colonel Hawkins of the 9th New York concocted several schemes for extending Federal control to the inner shores of the sounds. The capture of Hatteras Inlet, Rowan told Gideon Welles, "has produced a perfect panic." If the navy had a force of small steamers, they could sweep the inland waters clear of all rebel commerce, *and* take Roanoke Island, the choke point joining Albemarle and Pamlico sounds, which "is the key to Norfolk." As for the blockships, Rowan had no faith in them whatever. "It is a waste of money to sink vessels at the bulkhead," he informed the secretary. "The flats are quicksand, and as soon as the current is interrupted at one point it will open a channel at another."

Rowan pushed his plans on Fox and Stringham. "A glance at the map will show you," he wrote to both, that with a couple of armed tugs, some landing barges, and "a regiment or two," the entire coastal region was open to exploitation. Considering the value of the objective, these reinforcements were small potatoes. They could "dash through the sound for Beaufort," or up the Neuse River to New Berne and cut the railroad. Or they could operate to the north and take Roanoke Island, destroy the Dismal Swamp Canal, "and shut up communication with Norfolk." But it all had to be done quickly, for already Confederate troops were coming down from Virginia to strengthen the defenses.

The department agreed the plans had merit, and Welles informed his commanders that a flotilla of armed tugs and support craft would be sent to Hatteras as soon as they could be gotten together. Although Abraham Lincoln agreed with the validity of the objectives, to his thinking any vessel, no matter how seemingly insignificant, taken away from blockade duty meant a prolongation of the war. Lincoln told Welles in no uncertain terms that the blockade was the navy's primary duty, indeed, at the present, its only duty. Anything else would have to wait.

Welles and Fox gritted their teeth at having to halt some promising coastal operations, and were disgusted by a shallow press and public's constant clamoring for victories. Silas Stringham was not much help either. Age was creeping up on the flag officer, and he exhibited a pokiness that had no place in a quick-firing war. As Du Pont noted, "he has eleven ships in Hampton Roads and *three ports uncovered* . . . he . . . has evidently the sulks about something."

For several weeks Gideon Welles had searched for the opportunity to divide the Atlantic Blockading Squadron, as the Strategy Board recommended, into its natural northern and southern commands. Even if Stringham had displayed all the energy needed, it was too large a responsibility for one man. With tempers on edge, and pondering the move, Welles left for a few days to inspect the navy yards and visit his family in Connecticut.

On September 14, Fox, signing himself "Acting Secretary," sent a terse, shameless letter, bordering on insult, to the flag officer. It was bait for Stringham's resignation, and the old man, his pride intact, took it. The note was all niggling details. Why, the "Acting Secretary" wanted to know, did the flag officer send the *Jamestown* to her blockade station without proper provisions? Why was the *Flag* sent to New York for repair? Why, he demanded, were so many rebels able to run the blockade "in presence of our vessels." Couldn't the flag officer do anything about it; did he even know of these matters? Fox twisted the knife—did his officers even bother to send him reports?

Stung, Stringham tossed the letter across his chart table. Fox and the moronic editorial writers could go to hell as far as he was concerned. After fifty-one good years in the navy, he didn't deserve this sort of treatment. The "tenor" of the "Acting Secretary's" letter, he penned in his reply, could only mean an official "disapprobation" of his conduct. It would have been better had Welles said so straight to his face, but here it was, and he accepted it. The only honorable course was to request relief from duty, "and be permitted to serve my country . . . in a more humble and consequently less responsible position." With a frankness hitherto masked, Welles accepted the resignation with thanks. True, he regretted the tone of Fox's letter, but this was war, "the cause and the occasion demand this."*

To replace Silas Stringham, Welles dipped deep into the nether reaches of the captains' list and came up with Number 50, the skipper of the frigate *Congress.* He was Louis Malesherbes Goldsborough, a gargantuan, bearlike, tough-talking sea dog, who had begun his active service in 1816 at eleven years old. Full-bearded and smooth-lipped, Goldsborough looked every inch the stern Amish elder. Inwardly a

---

* Transferred to the retired list, Stringham was promoted to rear admiral in July 1862 and reentered active service as commandant of the Boston Navy Yard.

kindly soul, his habitual, roaring bombast sent young subordinates into paroxysms of terror. And he brooked no nonsense, a fact borne out during his recent tenure as superintendent of the Naval Academy. When a group of midshipmen set fire to his outdoor privy, it brought forth Goldsborough's classic threat, "I'll hang them! Yes, I'll hang them! So help me God, I will!"

Meanwhile, at Hatteras Inlet, Stephen Rowan watched the rebels with growing alarm. They blocked the Neuse and Pamlico rivers with sunken hulks and heavily fortified New Berne and several of the inner waterway towns. Again he alerted the department to the importance of Roanoke Island. "It is the key to Norfolk," he wrote, and if held by Union troops it commanded Albemarle Sound as well. With that, they could easily "dash" at the Dismal Swamp Canal, "and thereby cut off from Norfolk the supplies of a rich country."

On September 20, Colonel Hawkins learned the rebels had massed 1,500 troops on Roanoke Island for an expedition against Hatteras. As Hawkins informed his superiors, "they are to land, hang the people who have taken the oath of allegiance, blow up the light-house, and retake the forts." Hawkins moved quickly to block any rebel moves. He sent 300 men of a newly arrived Indiana regiment to Chicamicomico Island, the sandspit north of Hatteras and established a fortified camp.

Anxious to reinforce his men, Colonel Hawkins sent the *Fanny* with forty infantrymen, two light guns, food, clothing, and ammunition. After dawn, October 1, she departed Hatteras Inlet and seven hours later, anchored in shallow water in sight of the Indiana camp. "Captain" Morrison, the *Fanny*'s civilian master, sent a boat ashore to make contact with the regiment, then waited several hours until a flatboat put off from the beach to unload the supplies. In late afternoon, three Confederate Navy steamers came in from the west and steered directly for the tug. The rebels opened fire, cutting the *Fanny* off from any retreat. The *Fanny* ran aground, the crew paddling ashore in a canoe. Into the bag went one perfectly serviceable steam tug, two officers, forty-seven men, two rifled cannon, and "one negro."

The news reached Hatteras Inlet the next morning. Colonel Hawkins pleaded with Commander Rowan for vessels to support the hungry, isolated garrison. Rowan secured two tugs, and towing an armed launch with twenty-five bluejackets, the tiny relief expedition chugged north. With an active rebel naval force in the immediate area, there was nothing for them to do but evacuate the 20th Indiana from Chicamicomico and bring the troops, dragging their tails, back to the

Hatteras forts. The opportunity to seize Roanoke Island on the cheap had disappeared.

While the little tragedy of Chicamicomico played itself out, Gideon Welles, out of step with his professional advisers, save an insistent Gus Fox, took up hounding Flag Officer Goldsborough over the blocking of the inlets, "neglected since the capture of Hatteras." Goldsborough passed it down to Henry Stellwagen, ordering him to bring four schooners to plug Ocracoke Inlet.

What enthusiasm Stellwagen might have had for the project had long since evaporated. Confederate reinforcements and renewed activity in the sounds made any mission of this sort extremely dangerous. "It would not be wise or manly to risk an almost certain chance of failure," he wrote Gus Fox. "There is an evident soreness about the orders for this duty, and I only wish I were free of it," he said.

After losing one of the stone-laden vessels in passage, Stellwagen arrived at Hatteras Inlet on October 1, on the heels of the *Fanny* incident. "This is very serious," he informed Flag Officer Goldsborough. With the capture of that tug there were now at least six rebel steamers in Pamlico Sound. As for Ocracoke Inlet, he could find no pilot to guide the blockships in. "My further presence at Hatteras being useless," Stellwagen, thoroughly disgusted, returned to Hampton Roads and angrily demanded a new assignment.

Notwithstanding any of the Federal botches and hesitancies, the Hatteras Inlet operation, navy and army, was not a bad offensive beginning. A proper objective had been chosen for the means available, and intelligent senior commanders with motivated subordinates secured it without much of a real fuss. The fact that it was an opposed amphibious landing, one of the most difficult, dangerous endeavors in warfare, speaks doubly to the success of the effort.

The primary purpose had been met, Hatteras Inlet, a key element of the coast, was closed to the Confederacy, and would remain so for the remainder of the war. The secondary objective, wresting control of the sounds, would be launched in four months' time. The Union would be back, this time in overwhelming force to finish the job—almost.

Port Royal

"I do not apprehend much from the forts, for the concentrated fire of the ships will be terrific and crush them at once, I think."

—Flag Officer Samuel F. Du Pont, USN

T imely and important though it was, the Hatteras Inlet action was essentially local in scope, and held little significance in the Strategy Board's plan to seize a major foothold and operating base on the Confederacy's Atlantic coast. The Union's defeat at Bull Run made it all the more imperative to move speedily forward. "There is nothing that could be done now," Du Pont wrote to his beloved wife and confidante, Sophie, "so important and so sure to strike terror and do away with the recent reverse as this." But a final objective had not been decided upon. Fernandina, near Jacksonville, Florida, Bull's Bay, just north of Charleston, and Port Royal, ideally situated between Charleston and Savannah were all considered.

Organizational planning, at least, could begin immediately. On August 3, the day Silas Stringham received his directive to prepare the Hatteras expedition, Gideon Welles ordered Du Pont to New York to fit out and command the as yet undetermined operation. "You will lose no time," he lectured, "in getting afloat." Winfield Scott entrusted the army command for this expedition to Brigadier General Thomas Sherman, an artillery officer of the Regular Army (later known as "the other General Sherman," to distinguish him from the more famous General William Tecumseh Sherman). While the quartermaster general collected enough "good, sound, and safe steamers," to carry the troops, Brigadier General Sherman established his training camp on Long Island.

On September 18, at New York's posh Astor House, Du Pont opened a telegram from the secretary of the navy, a near copy of the one just sent to Louis M. Goldsborough. Gideon Welles had formally divided the Atlantic commands into the North and South Atlantic Blockading squadrons. To command the latter in the flagship *Wabash,* he elevated Samuel Francis Du Pont to the status of flag officer, jumping him eighteen places in the captains' list. "I felt convinced that this war would see the end of seniority [as the sole criterion of promotion]," Du Pont wrote to Sophie, "but I did not believe the knell would be sounded so soon."

Du Pont set out for Washington, and bumped into a puffing and very excited Gus Fox. There was just enough time, Fox said, to meet with President Lincoln and Secretary Seward for further discussions of the expedition. Du Pont found the President and secretary of state sitting on a couch. Lincoln, "not making me out much," wondered why Fox had brought a naval officer! Seward puffed furiously on a cigar, and Fox blew the smoke "into the President's eyes." No one seemed to have any idea of why they had gathered. More people were sent for: Simon Cameron, the secretary of war; General George McClellan, commanding the Army of the Potomac; and Brigadier General Sherman who happened to be in the city. Time passed and none arrived. "There's nobody nowhere tonight!" Seward harumphed.

Hours later, Cameron and Brigadier General Sherman, pushed along by the assistant secretary of war, stumbled into the sitting room. Until nearly dawn, Lincoln and his political advisers rambled on, tossing about subjects having nothing to do with the expedition. Finally, they ordered Sherman to sail from New York to Annapolis, and there assemble his forces. "This decided," a stunned Du Pont informed a friend, "then came the haste of ignorance as I call it—we must go in *four days!*"

That schedule was patently absurd, and neither Du Pont nor Sherman paid it any attention, fixing mid-October for a realistic departure. Still without a firm objective, the new flag officer set to planning with his chosen chief of staff, Commander Charles Davis, gentleman, nautical scholar, and lately secretary of the Strategy Board.

Brigadier General Thomas Sherman's command numbered well over 12,000 men, divided into three brigades of fourteen regiments. To his quartermaster, Sherman stressed the vital importance of loading the steamers so that what was needed first "can be got off at a moment's notice for immediate action."*

Jamming men into stuffy 'tween decks, (in conditions to which no sane farmer would subject his cattle) spread all sorts of contagion. "A sufficient quantity of disinfectants," he wisely ordered, "must be taken along to insure health on board each vessel." Special transports were needed for the horses, notoriously poor sailors, with "the greatest security afforded them by proper stalls and slings."

Daily, the sound directives left his pen. Smoking belowdecks on the transports was absolutely forbidden. The daily allowance of water was to be one gallon a day per man, "including that required for cooking purposes"; horses would receive three gallons.† Soldiers, under arms, would be posted to prevent fires and "any improper use of water." As for food during the voyage, "fancy cooking," Sherman decreed, "for instance, as frying meats and dough in fat, is prohibited," the danger of fire was just too great. "Soups, boiled meats, and hard bread," he advised "compose the true and healthy diet of the soldier on transports at sea."

By the middle of October, there was still no decision regarding the objective. Warships, troops, and transports crowded for space at New York and Annapolis. "This expedition has grown like a mushroom," Du Pont wrote to his brother, Henry. "I think of attacking Port Royal, though I hear of their having two hundred guns there." He ended by asking "Dear H." to mail a check for $393.78 to the Philadelphia wine merchant who supplied his flag mess in the *Wabash*.

Just before sailing, Sherman conferred with Du Pont and Davis in the flagship's finely appointed cabin. Sherman remembered, "We came to the conclusion that the capture of Bull's Bay was rather too insignificant . . . for a force of the dimension that we were to take with us." Port Royal, they decided, was a deepwater harbor of magnificent proportions. Though heavily defended, it was a far better objective, and "we thought we had a sufficient force to carry it." They would defer the final decision until the rendezvous at Hampton Roads.

On October 16, the *Wabash,* followed by three ninety-day gunboats and three army transports, passed out of New York's lower bay. Du Pont

* What in World War II became the science of "combat loading."

† The standard ration in sailing ships since time immemorial.

could not conceal his pleasure. "There is a great quiet in this ship," he wrote in his daily letter to Sophie. "The crew are young and better looking than the *Minnesota*'s; the engine works smoothly, which has enabled me to write this letter, and the officers are very superior."*

Du Pont's substantial private wealth enabled him to live very comfortably at sea, and his cabin was as well appointed as any Victorian gentleman's sitting room. For his personal servant, he took along William Wormley, son of the noted Washington hotelier. Du Pont's steward-chef, Joseph Pablo, aided by a specially ordered, newfangled "refrigerator," set a table equal to the best restaurants. Du Pont invited Davis and the staff to share it. "I told him," he said to Davis, "that feeling myself a *little* well off, it was the greatest pleasure to me to be able to do such things." At tea one day, Sophie was informed, "Pablo gave us an omelette *soufflé,* equal to a Parisian one."

The first night at sea, the warships practiced with the new "Coston" flare, a far cry from the methods heretofore used for centuries. Du Pont described them as "pyrotechnic lights, ruby, white, green, etc., burnt from a stick held in the hand, very superior to the use of lanterns."

Du Pont and the staff spent hours discussing and evaluating "our future operations." Whatever the objective, the exercise to capture a port had originally been intended as a combined operation with the army. But as a direct consequence of bombardment fever, in the plan Davis cast for Port Royal, Du Pont realized "the soldiers will have nothing to do." The rebels could bring "great forces" to counterattack a disorganized army landing force. But "upon us," the ships, he and Davis agreed, "only forts."

On October 18, the *Wabash* rounded Old Point Comfort and anchored in Hampton Roads. Daily, singly and by handfuls, the squadron and transports straggled in. Thomas Sherman and his regiments sailed down from Annapolis. On board the headquarters steamer *Atlantic,* a newspaper correspondent watched a bald eagle plummet out of the high sky, soar over the convoy's mastheads, and alight in the *Atlantic*'s maintop. "In an instant," scribbled the reporter, "all eyes were upon him . . . and we accepted the omen as auguring the full success of our enterprise."

By the third week of October the entire expedition, nearly seventy-five ships, crowded into the anchorage around Old Point. Then, as Du

* Du Pont had commanded the *Minnesota* on her maiden voyage to China in 1857.

Pont had predicted, the weather turned foul, and every day of waiting became a chore.

Sherman received a very unwelcome surprise when he learned that contrary to orders, the supply vessels had been loaded upside down, requiring four days to dig out the small arms ammunition from the bottom of the holds. In case the fleet sailed in that time, he was forced to beg for 350,000 rifle cartridges from Fort Monroe. Sherman wore out his welcome when he returned to the fort, hat in hand, asking for thousands of cooked rations to replace those already eaten by his troops.

Besides the weather, another factor entered into the delay, as the expedition awaited the arrival of Charles Boutelle of the Coast Survey. Having spent six years charting its waters, Boutelle knew more about the hydrography of Port Royal than any man alive. The place had a tricky bar, almost a dozen miles to sea of the harbor mouth, and the expedition's merchant masters demanded a marked channel over it, with at least six feet to spare under their bottoms. Boutelle finally arrived on Saturday, October 26 and satisfied Davis "upon the only point about which I felt anxious; the easy and certain entrance of this ship into the place." The chief of staff then set to the laborious writing of secret orders to all ship captains.

Meanwhile Confederate troops by Sewell's Point picked up a soldier's cap, lost over the side from one of the transports. Inside were two Boston newspapers, the latest not a week old. They accurately listed Sherman's entire order of battle and noted that the larger steamers carried surfboats. Charleston, the paper claimed, was the likely target.

At one bell in the morning watch, 4:30 A.M., October 29, a single gun from the *Wabash* cracked its signal across the jammed waterway, and a quartermaster bent a hoist of flags to her peak, "Underway to get." The magnificent, 40-gun steam frigate headed the parade of warships and transports out of Hampton Roads: fifty ships, the largest force yet commanded by an American naval officer.

The window of clear weather evaporated and strong head blows buffeted the fleet. Rough seas and a freshening easterly wind cast some of the vessels dangerously close to shoal water. By noon, November 1, seeing the smaller transports and auxilliaries could not keep up, Du Pont signaled for all ships to continue independently. "As darkness settled over a stormy sea," Lieutenant Daniel Ammen of the gunboat *Seneca* remembered, "the driven drops of rain struck the face roughly as pellets."

Smallpox broke out in the crowded transport *Vanderbilt*. Then the gunboat *Isaac Smith* hoisted a distress signal. "After dark," wrote her commanding officer, "the deck abaft commenced ripping up from the repeated heavy shocks of the sea. I therefore cut it away to save the hull." To keep her from sinking, he cast over the whole main battery of eight 8-inch guns.

By midafternoon, with ships dropping from sight, and the gale "very violent in its crisis," Du Pont signaled to heave-to. Everyone shortened sail and pointed their bows into the wind to ride it out. "The fine ordered fleet," he lamented to Sophie, "the result of so much thought, labor, and expense, has been scattered by the winds of heaven." The stern ports to his cabin hadn't been shut in time, and "my dressing room and bedroom were *flooded* by six inches of water. The carpets were ruined of course."

Aboard the steamer *Governor*, carrying 350 marines, a series of extraordinarily heavy rollers broke apart the port and starboard hog braces in two places.* Most of the civilian crew stood dumb. Having no idea of what measures to take, Lieutenant Colonel Reynolds sought out the only naval officer on board, twenty-year-old Acting Master John Weidman, just out of the Naval Academy. Under his orders, the marines, with "great exertions," lashed the braces, preventing the ship from buckling under the enormous stresses.

Just when the braces were gotten in hand, a sound like the cracking of a steel whip turned all eyes aloft. The funnel guys had snapped, and with it, the smokestack lurched overboard. A three-foot stump poking out of the deck provided barely enough draft to keep the fires alight. Seconds later, the main steam pipe burst. Pressure in the boiler was reduced to almost nothing, and the engine had to be stopped continually to build up enough steam just to keep the vessel's head to wind. Water began climbing in the hold. The rudder chains carried away, taking with it the ship's ability to steer.

Early Saturday morning, the packing on the engine cylinder head blew off. Water in the hold rose, the ship, "laboring violently," tore herself apart. "At every lurch," Colonel Reynolds remembered, "we apprehended the hog braces would be carried away, the effect of which would have been to tear out the entire starboard side, collapse the boiler, and carry away the [paddle] wheelhouse." The *Governor* lay entirely at the mercy of wind and wave. One hundred marines set to bailing water from the hold, while the rest held fast the posts supporting the vital hog braces.

* Cables stretched from a point above amidships to the bow and stern to prevent "hogging," the downward sag of the hull at its ends.

At dawn the weather brightened a fraction and two ships were visible from the deck. The battered *Isaac Smith* tried passing a towline. This, said Colonel Reynolds, "through the carelessness of the *Governor,* was soon cast off or unavoidably let go. The water was gaining on us . . . and it appeared that our only hope of safety was gone."

The sailing frigate *Sabine,* on her way to blockade duty, saw the distress signals, and passed a hawser and chain to the *Governor.* The *Sabine*'s sailors rigged some spars over the stern and made ready, Reynolds said, "for whipping our men on board." Thirty marines were rescued this way. But it was too slow and the incessant plunging caused the hawsers to part. The *Sabine* maneuvered alongside so the men could jump from ship to ship. "In our condition," reported Reynolds, "this appeared extremely hazardous. It seemed impossible for us to strike the frigate without instantly going to pieces." Forty men managed the leap. The forty-first was crushed between the grinding sides; twenty feet of the *Governor's* deck were ripped away.

The *Sabine* lowered her boats. The marines jumped into the sea and all but seven were hauled in. When Du Pont reported the incident to the Navy Department, he praised Colonel Reynolds, who, he pointed out, while not a sailor, maintained "the high sense of honor . . . in disputing with Mr. Weidman the privilege of being the last to leave the wreck." The *Governor* floated three hours and disappeared in the deep.

Daylight, November 2, brought little solace to Flag Officer Du Pont as he scanned the empty horizon through his long glass. "This morning," he penned to Sophie, "the fleet was *nowhere.*" His proud, formidable armada had scattered to the four winds. Only the day before "the ocean was alive with our numbers," said a rueful Charles Davis. But as the hours passed, ships came limping over the gray sea and formed about the comforting bulk of the *Wabash.*

On the morning of November 4, twenty-five ships anchored off Port Royal bar. As with every other Southern port, the rebels had removed all navigational aids, and the flat, sandy shores provided no features on which to take reliable bearings. In the Coast Survey steamer *Vixen,* Charles Davis and Charles Boutelle crossed the bar and commenced sounding the channel, planting marker buoys. By afternoon Davis signaled the flagship to send in the light-draft vessels. In preparation, Du Pont ordered four gunboats to conduct a reconnaissance of the Confederate batteries on the headlands fronting the entrance to the long, deep bay that constituted Port Royal: Fort Walker, the main bastion on Hilton Head guarding the west, and Fort Beauregard on Bay Point, the east. "I was beginning to congratulate myself upon the day's work," he told Sophie, "when 'bang, bang' came the booming of cannon." Du Pont knew the forts hadn't the range; "tugs, I suppose, of the rebels, who had run out to make a show."

Under a full head of steam, Confederate Flag Officer Josiah Tattnall and his little force of tugs and riverboats had come up the inland waterway from Savannah to fight.* "Old Tat," a great, ancient snapping turtle of a man, opened fire on the gunboats, wrote a New York reporter, "as proudly and defiantly as if [he] had a hundred line-of-battle ships under his command." Instantly the Federal vessels returned the salute and steered to cut off his retreat. Tattnall was brave but not crazy; he ordered a hasty withdrawal under the protecting guns of Fort Beauregard.

Before nightfall nearly every one of Du Pont's light-draft ships were inside the bar, anchored to good holding ground. The next morning Old Tat came out again, hoping to draw some of the Federals within range of the forts' guns. Daniel Ammen's *Seneca* was the first to engage, and he ordered his 11-inch pivot gun to aim at the waterline of the rebel flagship. "The shell skimmed along the water like a duck," he remembered. "The man aloft said he saw it strike the steamboat, and when we saw the vessel again she had a white patch of plank on her side."

High tide came at noon, and the *Wabash* led the deep-draft vessels over the bar, into the marked channel. No ship of her size had attempted it before, and during a few seconds of white-knuckled drama, the leadsman chanted a bare ten inches of water under the flagship's keel. While there was no hesitation, Davis recalled, "It cost us some anxiety." Du Pont signaled his captains and the army generals to come aboard. Any residual thought of landing the army in a truly combined operation vanished; too many of the surfboats had been damaged in the gale. Stoically, General Sherman agreed.

Du Pont outlined his simple plan to assault the stronger rebel positions at Fort Walker head-on, and contingencies were made should Tattnall's cockleshells try a run at the unarmed transports. The fleet weighed anchor and stood into the channel between the forts. Then, on

---

*The legendary "Old Tat" had served in the U.S. Navy since 1812, one of the most senior and prominent officers to go South upon secession. In June 1859, during the Second Anglo-Chinese Opium War, Tattnall, commanding the U.S. Navy's East India Squadron, covered the British naval withdrawal from their repulse at Tientsin. It was a wholly unneutral act, which he justified by declaring "blood is thicker than water."

the last tack before the fort, the *Wabash* and *Susquehanna* ran aground
on Fishing Rip Shoal.

Boutelle and Davis *had* buoyed it, but the marker came adrift. The
Susquehanna backed her paddle wheels and steamed away in a few
minutes. But the *Wabash*'s engine just didn't have the thrust, and she
stuck for two hours until the tide carried her off. It was too late in the
day to continue. A night attack, Davis said, "would have been attended
with confusion."

Wednesday, November 6, dawned fair, bright, and without a cloud;
"wholly propitious," Davis said, "in every respect but one." Heavy
winds brought contrary tides, and Du Pont, visibly frustrated, called off
the attack. This further delay, however, brought with it some very
favorable consequences. Charles Davis spent the day mulling over the
shot pattern of the forts when they had fired at the gunboats. There
was something not right. But he simply couldn't figure it out and went
to bed pondering the puzzle.

At the moment he woke on Thursday morning, "before I had fairly
got my eyes open," Davis had discovered the missing piece. No fire had
come from Fort Walker's inner, northern face, the point least likely to
receive a seaborne attack, and obviously its most vulnerable aspect.

Swiftly, he conceived a plan for the fleet to enter the bay, run the
rebel artillery gauntlet, then enfilade Fort Walker from the north while
steaming back on the opposite course. The oval-like maneuver would
be repeated until the rebels struck their colors. To engage the lesser
Fort Beauregard and counter any sortie by Josiah Tattnall, Davis had
the gunboats form a separate, parallel column to starboard, holding
their positions in the bay.

Still in his nightclothes, Davis rushed into Du Pont's cabin, and
the flag officer promptly agreed. The only question was whether to
stand off and fire the heaviest guns, or to engage at close range with
full broadsides. All concurred, Davis said, "to come simply to the
point, and to depend on the destructive agency, and the terror
inspired by it, of a shower of iron hail, or iron *hell,* dropped in the
briefest time and on one spot . . . We determined to put this ship close
to the battery."

Si Stringham's bombardment at Hatteras Inlet had given both sides
a profound lesson of the effects of exploding shell against earthworks;
this would be no different. Fort Walker mounted twenty-three guns,
mostly obsolete 32-pounders. Fort Beauregard, opposite, held eighteen
similar pieces. The Confederate garrisons, very short of trained sea-

coast gunners, numbered about 2,400 men, commanded by Brigadier General Thomas Drayton.

Beginning at six bells in the morning watch, 7 A.M., signals fluttered out from the *Wabash:* "go to breakfast," followed by "underway to get," "form line of battle," and finally, "prepare for action." The *Wabash,* nearest to Fort Walker, steamed forward at the head of the ten ships forming the bombardment line. To starboard, thrashed the flanking gunboats.

At five knots the parallel lines of the fleet steamed between the headlands, and at 9:26 A.M. the guns of Fort Walker opened the battle. At once, the thundering broadsides of the *Wabash* and *Susquehanna* answered. The shells of the heavy Dahlgren guns fell fast inside the earthworks, burying for an instant in the sand before exploding. General Drayton described it as "a terrific shower of shot and shell."

Standing on the *Wabash*'s quarterdeck with a powerful glass, Commander John Rodgers of Du Pont's staff described the maelstrom inside the fort.* "Shell fell in it . . . as fast as a horse's feet beat the ground in a gallop. . . . What could flesh and blood do against such a fire? I watched two men in red shirts; I saw them seated at the muzzle of a gun, apparently waiting . . . for more ammunition. They were so still that I doubted whether they were men. . . . I saw them move, and I knew they were men. They loaded the gun, a shell burst near them, and they disappeared—doubtless blown into atoms."

The *Wabash* with *Susquehanna* behind, reached the northern rim of the steaming oval, and a mile ahead stood Old Tat to greet them. Swinging to port, the *Wabash* opened fire with her forward 11-inch pivot gun, followed by a full broadside.

There was nothing that Tattnall could do, his toy boats would have been blown out of the water. With a glass, he picked out the tall, luxuriantly whiskered figure of Samuel Francis Du Pont, a friend and colleague of decades. He turned to a quartermaster. "Dip my broad pennant to my old messmate," he said. "Mr. Maffitt," he drawled to his flag captain, "we had best retire, and, like Mr. Micawber, wait for something to turn up."

The *Wabash* and *Susquehanna* began their downward approach on Fort Walker's northern face. At a range of 800 yards, accurate enfilading broadsides vomited from the muzzles of their guns. "From that moment," said a Confederate officer in the fort, "we were defeated, excepting perhaps by providential interference."

* Rodgers had previously fitted out and commanded the Western Gunboat Flotilla in its first actions on the Mississippi; see chapter 13.

The fine formation that began the battle dissolved, and popular maps and prints to the contrary, only the *Susquehanna* kept her assigned station astern the flagship. Constantly Du Pont signaled for his ships to keep better order and to follow his movements, but they were ignored in the fog of battle. Again the *Wabash* and *Susquehanna* steamed around the oval, and the gun sights were adjusted to 550 yards—point-blank range. "Shot after shot, shell after shell with the precision of target practice," said a Confederate artillery officer.

Sometime after 1 p.m. the *Wabash* and *Susquehanna* completed their third circuit of the deadly oval. Fort Beauregard hadn't fired in several minutes, and the ammunition in Fort Walker was nearly spent. General Drayton ordered three guns to continue slow firing and cover the garrison's "retreat by dispersion," in other words, for everyone to run.

Soon, the gunboat *Ottawa* reported the rebels racing across the cotton fields to Skull Creek and refuge in Tattnall's steamers. Unlike the formalities at Hatteras Inlet, there was no actual surrender at Port Royal. Du Pont reported, "The enemy ceased to reply [to our broadsides] and the battle was ended."

John Rodgers entered Fort Walker under a flag of truce. Except for the rebel dead and a few badly wounded men, it was deserted. Rodgers carried with him a national ensign, and he raised it over the fort. The effect was electrical—not since the capitulation of Fort Sumter had the Stars and Stripes flown over South Carolina. Brass bands in the fleet and transports struck up patriotic tunes. According to Du Pont, "more cried than cheered and General Sherman wept with emotion." Du Pont ordered the marines ashore and signaled for the army's transports to enter the bay.

Daniel Ammen and the *Seneca* took possession of Fort Beauregard. He landed with a party of armed sailors, and found "a single wounded soldier . . . in a tent. The only animate life . . . was a flock of turkeys that had the good taste to remain; they strutted around in stately pride in the belief that they were superior birds—as indeed [when we ate them] they were."

Once secured, the sleepy waterway of Port Royal was fast converted into the major logistics and repair depot for the South Atlantic Blockading Squadron, rivaling Hampton Roads as a forward operating base. Its capture virtually guaranteed a close blockade of Charleston and Savannah. Later in the war, it was the absolute control of these waters by the navy that permitted General William T. Sherman's obliterating march from Atlanta to the sea.

But like Hatteras Inlet, far more immediate work, especially by the army, could have been done.

Within a day of Port Royal's capture, Du Pont pushed up the Broad River to Beaufort, cutting the inland waterway linking Charleston and Savannah. It threw the coast into a flying panic. Steaming upriver, Daniel Ammen and the *Seneca* found the lush, green banks deserted, "except by squads of negroes, who appeared to regard us with curiosity and fear." Save for a solitary drunk wandering about, the white population had abandoned the tidal towns and their richly yielding cotton and rice plantations. The liberated slaves, as would happen time and again, refused to follow their masters.

A determined advance from Port Royal might have taken Savannah, or even Charleston, from the flank, and saved the Union three years of bloody work. At the least, Federal forces might have cut the Charleston and Savannah Railroad, forcing the rebels to detour hundreds of miles inland to move troops and goods between the two cities.

But the forces and mission given to General Thomas Sherman were adequate only for holding the immediate objective of Port Royal and its environs. Save for George McClellan's botched Peninsula campaign in Virginia, the army never seriously considered pushing inland from the Atlantic coast. It was a lapse of strategic proportions, since any advance would have forced the Confederacy to fight a three-front war: in Virginia, along the line of the Mississippi, and, if done, Charleston-Savannah. "A great pity," said Commander Percival Drayton of the *Pawnee,* brother of Confederate General Thomas Drayton, "but they seem to begrudge every man sent away from Washington . . . so far as operating against the enemy goes."

Stone Fleets

"They sunk so slow, they died so hard,
But gurgling dropped at last."

—Herman Melville, *The Stone Fleet*

While Du Pont's gunboats ranged freely along the coast, plans were already in motion for plugging Charleston and Savannah harbors with great fleets of blockships, that dwarfed the aborted try at Hatteras Inlet. Weeks before Du Pont sailed, Gideon Welles had made a secret purchase of twenty-five vessels, loaded with granite block, for sinking on the Savannah bar. All but one were laid-up New England whalers, recycled from a trade already dying. Two, *Herald* and *Fortune,* were nearly 100 years old, *Fortune* being described as "an ancient hulk that might have been engaged in the blubber business before the Revolution." The venerable *Corea* had served as a Royal Navy victualer until taken as a Continental prize during that same war. The condemned *Margaret Scott* was purchased from the U.S. marshal in New Bedford after her owners were convicted of outfitting her as a slaver. Of the *Tenedos,* in which Herman Melville had once sailed before the mast, the poet himself lamented,

> *An India ship of fame was she,*
> *Spices and shawls and fans she bore;*
> *A whaler when her wrinkles came—*

. . . till, spent and poor,
Her bones were sold . . .

The department specified "blocks of granite" for ballast, offering fifty cents a ton for anything of weight. At that lucrative price, 7,500 tons of stone walls and paving blocks disappeared from New England's farms and municipal storeyards. The ships' civilian masters, officers, and crew were offered a month's guaranteed wages for volunteering. "The only service required of you," read their orders, "is the safe delivery of your vessel."

On November 7, the day of the Port Royal attack, Gus Fox, very keen on the operation, wrote Du Pont that the stone ships were ready for Savannah, awaiting "a dispatch from you to send them forward." Twenty more were being bought for Charleston, which in Fox's opinion, if properly scuttled, "Charleston as a harbor will no longer exist."

Though everyone around the old New England whaling ports understood the ships' fate, the press, in a rare fit of common prudence, kept the stone fleet pretty much secret. Not until November 20, the day they sailed, did the New Bedford *Standard* inform its readers: "They will probably *sink.* . . . " At New Bedford, center of the old trade, thousands of cheering, handkerchief-waving spectators lined the waterfront to watch the stone fleet set out on its death ride. Gun salutes boomed from the harbor forts as the doomed ships crowded over the bar, eager as yachts at the start of an ocean race. Under full sail, and more or less in company, the whalers headed south. There was no naval escort. The only protection against rebel raiders were their broadly striped, painted sides, checkered with false "Fiji ports," giving the whalers the look of a sloop of war. Master Rodney French of the *Garland,* the fleet "commodore," also provided his ship with a huge "Quaker" gun, put together from a black-painted stump of old masting.*

French suggested the fleet hug the coast as the safest way of reaching Savannah. Several of the very independent masters rejected that, and boldly squared off on a direct course for the target, and the honor of being the first to arrive at their own wake.

---

* Whalers often were painted to resemble warships in order to scare off pirates and other undesirables in distant seas. The "Fiji ports" were simply false-painted gunports originally done to overawe the South Sea islanders. A "Quaker gun" was a variation on the theme, harmless, and was much used by the Confederate Army during the war as an effective means of disguising their weakness in artillery.

*   *   *

As the stone fleet breasted its way south, Du Pont and his squadron were hard at their own work around Savannah. The city never amounted to anything as a blockade-running port, but early on, under Du Pont's embarrassed nose, the runner *Fingal* brought in enough arms and munitions to enable the Confederates to fight the Battle of Shiloh the following spring.

Savannah's seaward gate was Fort Pulaski, like Fort Sumter, a brick and masonry work atop an islet, fifteen miles downstream, in the mouth of the Savannah River. Shipping channels lay to either side. The southern passage, with Tybee Island, a swampy piece of jigsaw puzzle, held the seaward key to the bastion and port.

On November 19, Du Pont ordered a reconnaissance of the narrow Tybee channel. Three gunboats spent three days in the river mouth, and for all they could see, the rebels had quit the place. On November 24, the *Seneca* and *Pocahontas* steamed over the bar and opened fire on Tybee's ancient "martello" tower, a round stone fort built by the Spanish 300 years before. Not a shot came in return. Armed landing parties stormed ashore against no resistance.

Fort Pulaski was now in range of the army's siege mortars. And as for blocking the river with the stone fleet, the rebels had already done the navy's work. Fearing a push by Du Pont upriver, they sank their own ballasted hulks athwart the channel; "and thus," the flag officer wrote, "by the cooperation of their own fears with our efforts, the harbor of Savannah is effectively closed." Charles Davis gaped at the easy victory. "We have now corked up Savannah like a bottle," he wrote. "It seems to me incredible the enemy . . . should have yielded up such an important position as Tybee Island without a blow. . . . The fall of Fort Pulaski is only a question of time. When Pulaski falls, Savannah is at our mercy."

With blockships no longer required at Savannah, Du Pont wondered what to do with the fleet of oncoming whalers. "We may use them for wharves or caissons or cofferdams." Or, he suggested, since the rebels were so willing to work on his behalf, "a half-dozen of them" might be turned over to allow them to complete the channel obstructions.

On December 3, the *Rebecca Sims* crossed the Savannah River bar and dropped anchor. Within the next days, all but one of the stone fleet straggled across, into the lee of Tybee Island. The senior naval officer there hadn't a clue of what to do with them. "Several of these vessels have arrived in a sinking condition," he reported to Du Pont. The

Meteor and *Lewis* parted their cables and drifted ashore. The *Phoenix* ran aground and lost her rudder. She was towed in and beached as a breakwater for landing supplies.

Charleston now loomed large as a fitting, final resting place, and Du Pont ordered a reconnaissance "to know if [I] can plant them on the . . . bar." The survey indicated so, and he assigned Charles Davis to command the operation. Undoubtedly, Davis, an authority on tides and currents, was the best officer for the job, but none was more reluctant to take it on. Davis knew Charleston intimately, having served on the department's harbor improvements commission. Now he was cast in the role of a destroyer. "I had always a special disgust for this business," he said; "the maggot, however, had got into Fox's brain."

Sinking obstructions also contradicted Davis' concepts to take Charleston from the flank and rear. The navy maintained total command of the tidal waters for several miles inland. "The army," he counseled, "by following these watercourses . . . would have the support of armed boats and vessels of light draft . . . and the easy means of transporting the munitions of war." But Sherman didn't move. Able enough in carrying out orders, he was not one to originate them. "This is not the tone of a strong man," Davis said.

Over the week of December 9, twenty additional ships of the stone fleet's "second division" set sail from New England, and Du Pont ordered up the leaky first arrivals from Savannah. Those gallant vessels were gradually being winnowed away. Three lay broken in the Savannah roadstead, and three more were scuttled for a breakwater on Tybee Island. The remainder, some dragged along by gunboats, others under their own canvas, limped into Port Royal Sound.

Du Pont was not deceived in thinking blockships were anything but a temporary solution, "for three or four months anyhow." He informed Gus Fox on December 16, "I shall have Charleston closed this week." The next morning, Charles Davis led his ships out of Port Royal to sea. To the eye, it was a very imposing force of five gunboats and three transports towing sixteen granite-laden whalers to their deaths. On board Davis' flagship, a reporter from the *New York Tribune* waxed eloquently of "the terrible stone fleet, on a mission as pitiless as the granite that freights it."

The convoy approached the Charleston bar opposite Morris Island on December 18. The rebels, thinking it an invasion fleet, promptly blew up the lighthouse. Davis wasn't bothered. He didn't need it for his operation, and the rebels, by destroying the beacon, just made blockade running that much harder on themselves.

The rebels had also removed all other navigational aids. That afternoon and part of the next day, Davis' boats worked along the bar sounding out and marking the main ship channel. Done, the whalers *Tenedos* and *Leonidas* were towed and anchored in eighteen feet of water, athwart the channel, an eighth of a mile apart, marking the limits of the barrier.

Davis gave much thought to positioning the rest of the ships. There had to be enough water flowing between them to keep a new channel from forming too quickly; yet the hulks must be close enough to confound any traffic in the harbor. Ever the thinker, he sketched a pattern of five parallel lines, "in a checkered or indented form," every vessel overlapping the space in the lines on either side.

Because of the whalers deep-laden draft, the operation could only go forward at high tide. Eight ships were towed into position during the afternoon and evening. "It had been rather melancholy," wrote the *Tribune* reporter, "to see the old craft ... towed in, one by one, to be sunk." The rest moved in the next day, December 20, the first anniversary of South Carolina's secession from the Union. When the last of the stone fleet, the *Archer,* came in position, the ships were stripped of sails, cordage, and anything else that might be of use to the rebels. The stuff was brought into the *Robin Hood* and the hulk torched.

Davis signaled to pull the plugs from the ships' bottoms, and slowly the vessels sank down to the bar, none completely disappearing from sight. Some died upright, settling so slowly it was difficult to believe they had touched bottom, and might yet sail away from their dreary fate. Others were on their beam ends, or down by the head, or stern, their masting a crazy, herky-jerky forest of sad, tangled confusion.

To leave absolutely nothing of value, Davis ordered them dismasted, and the boats that brought off the crews returned to dismember the settling hulks. Axes rose and fell, stays and shrouds fell away and the mizzen of the *Rebecca Sims* went over the side, quickly followed by her fore and main. Next came the *Richmond,* whose three masts went all together, "with three almost simultaneous reports," wrote the correspondent, "like irregular volleys of musketry. ... The stately masts, which one moment were standing in strength, the next are helplessly floating on the water, and left only a hulk behind them."

"That stone fleet ought to sink the Northern cause," screamed a leading Scottish journal, *Blackwood's Edinburgh Magazine.* The British press and merchant shipping interests became hysterical over the obstruction of Charleston harbor and the added dangers it placed on the extremely profitable business of blockade running. Conveniently overlooked were the Confederate hulks that stopped up Savannah, and the numberless occasions when England herself had employed the tactic in warfare. "Indefensibly barbaric," "monstrously unfair," and "an affront to all civilized nations," were but some of the rhetoric.

Secretary of State Seward, with masterly stroking and soothing promises, made sure the screeching from overseas remained only that. It was a mistake, he told the British Foreign Office, to even think the navy had planned to destroy the harbor permanently.

The stone fleet's second division lay idle at Port Royal. After Du Pont snatched the *India* and *Edward* for store and repair ships, he ordered fourteen of the remainder to complete the blocking business at Charleston's secondary conduit, Maffitt's Channel. The *Pocahontas* escorted the vessels up, and the force anchored off the bar on January 25. A scattering gale hindered the planting and the hulks were not as geometrically aligned as before. But Lieutenant Balch of the *Pocahontas* was confident, "that a very great obstruction has been placed . . . several of the ships having entirely disappeared."

As Du Pont and Davis knew they would, the currents formed new channels within a year, and the hulks broke up in the pounding of tide and storms. Chunks and timbers were carried away by the waves, and into Charleston's harbor bottom settled 7,500 tons of New England farm wall and paving block.

The *Trent* Affair

"One war at a time."

—Abraham Lincoln

O n November 8, 1861, a day after the victory at Port Royal, off the rocky north coast of Cuba, a lone American warship barely ruffled the narrow waters of the Old Bahama Channel. "It was a beautiful day," Captain Charles Wilkes remembered, "and the sea quite smooth." At 11:30 A.M., from the dizzying height of the mast-head came the lookout's shout "Smoke!" dead ahead. Wilkes squinted through a long glass at the first spidery wisps smudging the cloudless western horizon. He tucked the glass under his arm. "It was time," he later wrote, "to inform my officers of my intentions." And those intentions came as close as anything did to embroil the United States and Great Britain in war.

Old Charles Wilkes stood in the stern sheets of the final boat to escape the conflagration of the Norfolk Navy Yard. Following that, he received orders to bring the steam sloop *San Jacinto* home from West Africa, where she had spent her commission running down slavers. Ruggedly tall and handsome,* Wilkes, a difficult man with few friends, had spent forty-four years in the service, as Du Pont put it, not as a "Navy man,

---

* Quite like the American actor Charlton Heston.

but altogether a 'Wilkes man.'" On the lower deck, he was considered a stern, rigid "sundowner," a harsh disciplinarian not adverse to a liberal application of the cat to a seaman's back.

However, Wilkes was a worthy scientific rival to the great (and also difficult) Matthew Fontaine Maury, who thoroughly detested him as "a cunning little Jacob." A first-class oceanographer, author of *The Theory of Winds* and a fearless explorer, Wilkes shares with Christopher Columbus the honor of having discovered a continent—Antarctica, in 1840.

Performing bravely at Norfolk, Wilkes expected a bright future, and his appointment to the *San Jacinto* augured well. He took command of the sloop off the Guinea coast and in accord with his orders set course for Philadelphia. In late September, at the Cape Verde Islands, he learned from months-old newspapers that Confederate raiders were at work in the Caribbean, snapping up American prizes. Wilkes decided to shift course south and cruise those waters before heading home. On October 13, he anchored at St. Thomas, Danish Virgin Islands. In the roadstead were two Federal warships searching without luck for the Confederate raider *Sumter.* Wilkes learned she was somewhere farther south, and being the senior officer present, he ordered out the vessels. The *Iroquois* actually found her at Martinique, but the rebel slipped away.

Putting into Cienfuegos, Cuba, on October 23, Wilkes found nearly as big a catch: news that the Confederate envoys to Great Britain and France, James Mason and John Slidell, had landed on the island. They were at that moment being lavishly entertained at Havana, waiting passage to continue their journey to Europe. Philadelphia forgotten, Wilkes loaded the *San Jacinto* with sixty tons of coal and steamed to intercept.

Old, blowsy James Murray Mason—former United States senator from Virginia and grandson of George Mason, the great Continental statesman and founder of the republic—had been given a most sensitive and critical task: convincing Great Britain to officially endorse the Confederacy with diplomatic recognition.

Southern diarist Mary Chesnut, who knew everyone worth knowing, was appalled: "My wildest imagination will not picture Mr. Mason as a diplomat. He will say 'chaw' for 'chew' . . . and he will wear a dress coat to breakfast." As for Mason's way with words and other matters, she jotted, "I don't care how he pronounces the nasty thing, but he will . . .

chew tobacco. In England, a man must expectorate like a gentleman, if he expectorates at all."

John Slidell, former United States senator from Louisiana, had received the Confederacy's commission to France. Unlike Mason, Slidell had some diplomatic experience, although it brought on the Mexican-American War. He was furnished with generally the same instructions as Mason, and was accompanied by his wife, daughters, son, and a retinue of servants.

Originally, they were to sail from Charleston aboard the Confederate Navy steamer *Nashville*. But Federal warships ceaselessly patrolled off the bar, and the envoys couldn't take the chance of being run down and taken. A plan was drawn for night escape, using the *Nashville*'s superior speed to elude pursuit, but contrary tides and strong night winds prevented the departure.

By now news of the commissioners' presence in Charleston had reached the North, and the Federal offshore patrol was reinforced. The plan was changed to escape by the dangerous Maffitt's Channel, however, the arrival of more Union warships ended that hope. The frustrated envoys considered going overland to Mexico and taking ship from Matamoros, delaying their departure for months. Some Charleston merchants then suggested they take the steamer *Gordon,* a former coastal packet and sometime privateer. She was capable of speeds over twelve knots, easily outpacing any Union vessel. Better yet, her shallow draft allowed crossing the bar at any time.

At night, for several weeks, the *Gordon* scouted the bar, as Mason said, "going safely out to where [the Federals] lie, and keeping only out of reach of their guns." On October 3 and 4, to test the blockaders reactions in daylight, the ship, with Slidell and his daughters, moved to within three miles of the blockade line and was not molested. "The squadron," Mason reported, "has become so familiar with the . . . proximity of this boat . . . that her presence does not disturb them; they ceased to give her chase." Confederate naval officers concluded she'd have no trouble, day or night, in running the blockade.

The *Gordon*'s owners offered her to the government for $62,000 outright, or a chartered rate of $10,000 for a round-trip passage to Havana or Nassau. These generous "gentlemen" said Mason, with unconscious irony, were "only interested in our cause [and] . . . the privilege of bringing back some $7,000 worth of cigars and other light articles" as part of the transaction. It was an awful lot of money and the Confederate Treasury could not afford it. But there was a benefactor at hand. George Trenholm, senior partner of Fraser-Trenholm, a leading transatlantic cotton brokerage, and a major Confederate bank-roller, put up the charter money in return for half the ship's return cargo space.

At 1:00 A.M., October 12, with rain lashing the harbor, the *Gordon,* renamed *Theodora,* crossed the bar, passing within a mile and a half of the blockaders. Two days later she berthed at Nassau. The envoys were in for a big disappointment. They had missed the steamer for St. Thomas, the sailing point for British ships from the Caribbean to Europe. The *Theodora* upped anchor and steamed for Cuba to load her precious cargo of cigars.

She made a landfall near Havana and was met by a Spanish gunboat. Slidell went on board to be "received with great kindness and civility . . . the Spanish steamer kindly volunteering to attend and show us the way." The local governor dispensed with formalities, and the two men, family, retainers, and baggage landed without difficulty or inspection. The governor and the "principal gentlemen of the town proffered us every attention," Mason said, and from conversations in the street, he felt "the sympathies of the people are entirely with us." They had three weeks to wait for the next St. Thomas steamer.

In the meantime Gideon Welles, under the mistaken impression the envoys were taking the *Nashville,* ordered the gunboat *James Adger* across the Atlantic to intercept her. As it happened, the *Nashville* slipped out of Charleston to cross the ocean unmolested, becoming the first Confederate warship to fly her colors in British waters.

Such was the state of affairs when Wilkes entered Cienfuegos for coal. He set course for Havana, where he found Mason and Slidell the social lions of the city. Checking the commercial steamers, Wilkes noted the *Trent,* a British packet plying her trade between Vera Cruz and St. Thomas, scheduled to sail from Havana on November 7.

Having served for the past two years on the antislavery patrol, a mission fraught with complications in international law, the *San Jacinto* held several volumes of legal references. Wilkes examined the pertinent chapters and concluded that the dispatches, instructions, and sundry Confederate government documents carried by the commissioners rightly amounted to "contraband of war," just as if they were munitions. And just as if they had been munitions, bound to or from the blockaded Confederacy, any neutral ship carrying them was liable to seizure and condemnation by a United States prize court.

Wilkes carried it a step farther. Without any precedent, he hypothesized that the envoys and their staffs constituted a living "embodiment of dispatches," and were, arguably, also contraband of war. "I made up my mind," he said, "to leave [Havana] as soon as possible, to await a suitable position on the route of the steamer ... to intercept her and take them out." After replenishing his coal bunkers and water tanks, "I made every provision for their entertainment and particularly in the stores of eatables and drinkables, well knowing the propensities of these Commissioners to indulge in the alcoholic beverages."

The *San Jacinto* weighed anchor on November 3, with Wilkes confiding the plan to his executive officer, Lieutenant Donald Fairfax. Quite shocked, Fairfax opposed the whole scheme and stated it plainly. He considered it contrary to the American interpretation of international law, and particularly hazardous to the Union should the British take offense, which, he pointed out, they obviously would.

On November 8, within a minute of spotting the *Trent,* Wilkes assigned Lieutenant Fairfax the duty of boarding. He was to "demand" the steamer's registry papers, her customs clearance from Havana, and the passenger and crew list—all very proper in a belligerent warship's right to stop and search neutrals in wartime. If any of the rebels were aboard, Fairfax was to send them to the *San Jacinto* and take the *Trent* as a lawful prize. "I do not deem it necessary to use force," Wilkes told him. "The prisoners will have the good sense to avoid any necessity for using it, but if they should, they must be made to understand that it is their own fault. They must be brought on board." Lieutenant Fairfax and his boat's crew, he knew, would conduct themselves "with all the delicacy and kindness which becomes the character of our naval service." Yet, inexplicably, Wilkes omitted specific orders to search for the pertinent Confederate documents, the factual, unarguable contraband of war! It was a lapse of great consequence.

Steadily the *Trent* approached the unknown warship in her path and hoisted the red duster proclaiming her British registry. Wilkes waited until she was about a mile off, broke out the stars and stripes, and fired a shot across her bow.*

The *Trent* maintained course and speed, showing no inclination to obey the age-old order to stop. Wilkes ordered an exploding shell as the next warning, which as he said, "brought her to." As Lieutenant Fairfax remembered, the *Trent*'s captain "showed how provoked he

---

* As weather tore them to shreds in a matter of days, ships normally did not fly their national colors, save in port, in battle, or for identification.

was by impatiently singing out through his trumpet, 'What do you mean by heaving my vessel to in this manner?'" Wilkes shouted he was sending a boat.

At the *Trent's* side, Fairfax left his heavily armed crew in the cutter and boarded alone. "I was impressed with the gravity of my position," he said after the war, "and I made up my mind not to do anything unnecessary in the arrest . . . or anything that would irritate the captain of the *Trent* or any of his passengers." He was met by a ship's officer and escorted to the upper deck to confront the indignant captain, James Moir.

Calmly, Fairfax stated that he knew Mason and Slidell were on board. A large group of passengers had gathered on the promenade deck and one of them stepped forward. "I am Mr. Slidell," he said; "do you want to see me?" Mason, too, stepped forward and identified himself. Their Virginia families had known each other since colonial days, and Fairfax nodded a polite greeting. Where are the secretaries, he asked, and Mason pointed them out. Fairfax was distinctly relieved at not having to search the passengers, and "in the briefest time," he reported, "I had the four gentlemen before me."

It had all gone fairly smooth. But that ended quick enough when Fairfax announced their arrest and his orders to take them as prisoners of war to the *San Jacinto*. "There was an outburst of rage and indignation from the passengers . . . many of the Southerners," he recalled. Shouts of "Throw the damn fellow overboard!" came from the crowd.

Fairfax kept his composure, requesting Captain Moir to restore order among the hissing mob. For the benefit of "the excited passengers," Fairfax pointed to the *San Jacinto*, guns run out, reminding them that "any indignity to any of her officers or crew . . . might lead to dreadful consequences." The warning, together with Moir's "commanding manner," had its desired, quieting effect, for the moment.

The commotion brought the cutter's armed crew scrambling up the accommodation ladder. Captain Moir was appalled at their shoving among the hanky-sniffing civilians on the promenade deck. Fairfax agreed that the sailors' presence would "alarm the ladies present," and he ordered them back to the boat.

Mrs. Slidell asked who gave the orders for the arrest of her husband. "Your old acquaintance, Captain Wilkes," said the lieutenant, for indeed, Wilkes had been a frequent, prewar guest at her popular Washington home. "Really," she answered in a huff, "Captain Wilkes is play-

ing into our hands!" Fairfax then invited her and Mrs. Eustis, wife of
one of the secretaries, to avail themselves of the *San Jacinto*'s cabin.
Both ladies haughtily refused.

Fairfax turned to the delicate task of taking off the four men. They
declined to come peaceably, and he sent to the *San Jacinto* for reinforcements. The cutter, commanded by Lieutenant James Greer,
returned carrying twenty-five heavily armed sailors and marines. After
fruitless efforts "to induce [the gentlemen] to accompany me," Fairfax
called four United States officers into the *Trent*'s cabin. "Gentlemen,"
he said, "lay hands on him." Taking hold of each arm, they unceremoni-
ously delivered James Murray Mason into the boat. Fairfax returned to
the cabin for Slidell.

There was more trouble. Several of the passengers, including the
prisoners' families, had gathered here from the promenade deck,
Slidell retreating farther, to his stateroom. Fairfax reported the rebel
insisted "that I must apply considerable force to get him to go with me."
Lieutenant Greer formed the marines outside the stateroom. Within, he
remembered, "Mr. Fairfax appeared to be having an altercation with
someone. There was much confusion . . . [and] the passengers and
ship's officers . . . were making all kinds of disagreeable and contemp-
tuous noises and remarks." Greer heard somebody shout "Shoot him,"
and he ordered in the marines. "As they advanced," he said, "the passengers fell back."

Whatever happened has never been made entirely clear. Greer
diplomatically reported that Fairfax was "engaged in conversation."
The *Trent*'s government mail agent, a retired Royal Navy pest named
Williams, later told a cheering audience that Miss Matilda Slidell "did
strike Mr. Fairfax . . . but she did not do it with the vulgarity of ges-
ture which has been attributed to her." Fairfax glossed over the whole
incident. The ship took an unexpected lurch, the girl fell against him,
and he had merely steadied her. As for any slapping by her daughter,
Mrs. Slidell was mortified "that such a story should have been circulated."

Suddenly, the crash of breaking glass announced the ungraceful
exit of John Slidell, helplessly hanging half out of his stateroom window. "By a gentle application of force," he was marched to the gangway
and placed in the cutter. After a short protest, the secretaries, Eustis
and Macfarland, quietly followed. It was only a short pull to the *San Jacinto,* and Wilkes received the four men at the gangway "with due
politeness." Mason and Slidell bowed "& touched their hats" on reaching the quarterdeck.

It took two hours to transfer the baggage from the *Trent,* and several notes were exchanged between the families and the prisoners. All passed through Wilkes, who claimed to be "greatly entertained by the contents of abuse written by the Ladies, Mrs. Slidell in particular." Mr. Slidell, "greatly excited" by their tone, tried to apologize. "I laughed," Wilkes remembered, "and remarked . . . I was not [offended]—Ladies had privileges which could not be extended to our sex."

The large question now arose whether to seize the *Trent* as a prize, or let her go. Wilkes would have saved his government several months' worth of anxiety by bringing the steamer to a Federal prize court for adjudication. The incriminating documents would have been discovered, but by no means was it certain that the court would have condemned the vessel *per se.*

In fact, Wilkes had every right to take her. Captain Moir's refusal to produce the passenger list and other pertinent ship's papers *had* made the *Trent* liable under international law to seizure. In later years, Wilkes offered the rather lame excuse that he had not known "of the abuse the Captain of the *Trent* had used in the presence of my officers." Otherwise, "I should have pursued another course and . . . kept possession of the vessel. . . . My mind was very near a balance." At 3:30 P.M., the ships parted company—this was Wilkes' second big mistake.

Wilkes offered the prisoners the comforts of his cabin, and ordered his steward "to attend to their wants and furnish everything they might call for." He invited them to luncheon, but recalled, "they hesitated. Although they did [not] refuse exactly, there was a bottle of fine brandy . . . and this was more acceptable . . . than anything to eat." To pass time, Wilkes provided the envoys "games of cards," to be used during weekdays, "and interdicted on the Sabbath." In all, it was not a wholly disagreeable passage, "and as soon as the stiffness wore off, we were sufficiently at our ease."

Until the *San Jacinto* arrived at Hampton Roads a week later, the world remained unaware of the incident. In that time, however, there occurred some interesting developments in Great Britain. In London, at the lord mayor's annual dinner, Prime Minister Palmerston took the American ambassador, Charles Francis Adams, aside for an informal talk.

There was rancor enough on both sides of the Atlantic. For decades the British had self-righteously chided the United States over the slavery issue, all the time fueling her industrial revolution and economy by milling Southern cotton grown and picked by African slaves. In sentiment, most of the British governing class, and their newspapers, wholeheartedly supported the dismemberment of the United States as a sure way to squelch the expansive growth of the burgeoning Yankee colossus across the sea. And very much in contravention of the Queen's neutrality proclamation, British merchants were making a fortune selling the Confederacy arms, munitions, and military stores—attitudes and practices that enraged bitter Unionists.

Over the past several months, Confederate diplomats seeking British recognition had been held at arm's length by Palmerston and his ministers. But the Confederacy remained optimistic. Surely, the hardships of the cotton famine brought to England by the Federal blockade would eventually force the British to intercede on the South's behalf. Palmerston told the United States ambassador not to worry. "He touched gently on our difficulties," Adams remembered, "and at the same time gave it clearly to be understood that there is to be no [British] interference for the sake of cotton." Adams' relief was palpable.

On November 11, three days after the incident in the Bahama Channel, Palmerston met with the Lord Chancellor, the Crown's supreme legal authority. The topic was the Federal gunboat *James Adger,* hanging around the fringes of British home waters, hoping to intercept the Confederate envoys, still thought to be in passage from the West Indies.

The prime minister recorded the meeting. According to international law, as practiced in British courts, he wrote, "a belligerent has a right to stop and search any neutral . . . on the high seas . . . suspected of carrying [an] enemy's despatches." The *James Adger,* therefore, "might, by our own principles . . . stop the packet, search her, and if the Southern men and their despatches and credentials were found on board, either take [the men and papers] out, or seize the [ship] and carry her back to New York for trial."

Earl Russell, the foreign secretary, received the same counsel, but added, the American warship "would have no right to remove . . . Mason and Slidell and carry them off as prisoners, leaving the ship to pursue her voyage." Thus, according to British interpretation, it had to be all or nothing; the envoys were inviolate without the incriminating documents.

Palmerston was still uncomfortable. Even considering the *James Adger*'s belligerent rights, no practical good could come if she seized the incoming packet. It mattered not a whit if the new Confederate legate plied his questionable skills, and would "scarcely make a difference in the action of [Her Majesty's] government" to remain neutral. The prime minister would shortly be tested on his principles.

On Friday, November 15, the *San Jacinto* glided passed Fort Monroe and anchored in Hampton Roads. Taking on coal and sending his report to Washington, Wilkes continued to New York. The message reached the Navy Department the next day. Governor Andrew of Massachusetts, sitting in Welles' office was, according to the secretary, "literally swept off his feet, he . . . then sprung upon a chair . . . prominent in the tumult of cheering which followed the announcement."

Gideon Welles sat in purse-lipped silence. To him would fall the government's first, official recognition of Wilkes' action, and at once he realized the problem. Wilkes had not taken the *Trent,* nor had he recovered any compromising documents, nor any documents at all. Significant questions loomed unanswered, and it was too soon, Welles noted, "either to congratulate or censure him on his achievement." Welles put on his coat and crossed the street to the White House. Lincoln, too, held his enthusiasm in check. "His chief anxiety," Welles said, "was to the disposition of the prisoners, who, to use his own expression, would be 'elephants on our hands,' that we could not easily dispose of."

Welles' next consideration was getting the envoys out of the navy's jurisdiction as soon as possible. He went to Seward, who publicly expressed considerable joy and elation. Only to his diary did the secretary of state confide any reservation, and that only if the British launched a vigorous protest. Wilkes, after all, had acted independent of any government instructions. Whatever way it went, there would be no egg on the administration's face, "which might have resulted if the act had been specifically directed by us."

A cable to the U.S. Attorney at New York ordered Federal marshals to intercept the *San Jacinto* and deliver the prisoners to the commandant at Fort Warren in Boston harbor. Keying on the critical point, Seward ended, "Let their baggage be strictly guarded and delivered . . . for examination."

On Saturday, at New York's Narrows, the *San Jacinto* was met by a tug carrying a pair of United States marshals, handing Wilkes his new orders for Boston. Severe winds and biting weather took its toll on "the delicate health" of the four manifestly suffering prisoners. In the cabin, it was "most uncomfortably cold," and Wilkes had to send them up buckets of hot shot from the fireboxes.

On November 23, the *San Jacinto* dropped anchor at Boston, and the prisoners were interned at Fort Warren. Their luggage, searched by the marshals turned up nothing—all documents had been left in the *Trent*. Wilkes came ashore to a tumultuous welcome. Feted and banqueted as the hero of the hour, he was praised by the mayor of Boston for his "sagacity, decision, and firmness"; Governor Andrew hailed his firing a shot across the bow of "the ship that bore the English lion's head."

The North went wild. So what if Wilkes had forcibly taken the rebels from a British mail packet? Overseas British consuls were all too eager in cooperating with the Confederacy anyway. The British, went the general tone, must be made to realize the United States was determined to enforce its belligerent rights. As for Wilkes, one metropolitan daily urged the government to "consecrate another 4th of July to him." But one man in Boston, Senator Charles Sumner, chairman of the Foreign Relations Committee, saw it differently: "We shall have to give them up."

The *Trent* topped the agenda for the weekly Cabinet meeting. There *was* justification for Wilkes' actions in international law, said Attorney General Bates. But that, he cautioned, was of little matter. The British, already angered by the damage to her trade done by the blockade, might well chose this incident as sufficient cause to recognize the Confederacy. Postmaster General Blair favored releasing the prisoners immediately, denouncing their capture as "unauthorized, irregular, and illegal."

Seward, though, felt the incident would not lead to any serious complaint—how could it? Wilkes had acted entirely on his own, actually contrary to his orders to bring the *San Jacinto* to Philadelphia. President Lincoln, with the approval of the Cabinet, thought it best to defer any action or official statement until all of Wilkes' reports had been carefully examined.

Before the transoceanic cable, it took about a month for news to travel round-trip across the Atlantic. This lag time proved fortunate for the Union, since it allowed passions to subside and permitted the diplomats to wrest the issue away from the mob and the press.

Like everyone else on this side of the Atlantic, the British ambassador, Lord Richard Lyons, knew only what he read in the newspapers. Lyons rightly divined, however, that stern demands would soon thunder forth from Whitehall. He had a stone-faced meeting with Secretary of State Seward, who although still publicly euphoric, did sober up a bit.

Lyons also wisely informed his government that any demands must be couched as delicately as possible. "The American people," he wrote to Earl Russell, "would more easily tolerate a spontaneous offer of reparation made by its Government from a sense of justice than a compliance with a demand for satisfaction from a foreign minister."

On November 20, came the first public qualms over the seizure. On Wall Street shares collapsed. "War with England was the theme," noted the *New York Times,* "and stocks were thrown out with the same eagerness that they were sought only a day or two ago." Disquieting news came from a pillar of the British Empire. The *Toronto Leader* expressed "horror at Yankee audacity ... the most offensive outrage which Brother Jonathan has dared to perpetrate upon the British flag."

Gideon Welles had his own problems to deal with. The deadline for his Annual Report to the President and Congress was only days off, and he still hadn't decided whether to officially treat Wilkes as a hero or an idiot. Again and again, he considered the arguments. On its face, the Queen's neutrality proclamation had cast the *Trent* unquestionably into the prize courts. The document explicitly prohibited British vessels from "carrying officers, soldiers, despatches, arms" of either belligerent. And if they did, and were caught, they would "incur and be liable" not only to the "penalties and consequences" of British law, but "the law of nations" as well. In other words, to condemnation as a prize of war. But Wilkes had let the *Trent* go, and Welles knew the British would surely jump on that large technicality.

Having neither the ship nor the incriminating paper, Welles supported the view of Postmaster General Blair: give the rebels up and cut any diplomatic losses immediately before the Union had two wars on its hands. Yet he also had the navy to consider. No matter what the diplomatic consequences, he just could not outright censure Charles Wilkes for exhibiting energy and boldness in a dicey situation. For now only, without compromising the administration, the morale of the navy came uppermost.

On November 30, Welles crafted a careful letter of official endorsement to Wilkes, his officers, and crew. "I congratulate you on the great public service," he began. The conduct of all hands had been marked by "intelligence, ability, decision, and firmness, and has the emphatic approval of this Department."

That said, Welles turned to the question of letting the *Trent* continue on her voyage. Wilkes, he noted, however, had exhibited "a too generous forbearance" in not capturing the ship. But this, he lectured, by no means constituted a future precedent "for the treatment of any case of similar infraction of neutral obligations." By a masterly stroke of the pen, Welles had managed to simultaneously slap Wilkes' wrist and put the British on notice.

By now, the news had reached England. On November 30, the day of Welles' congratulating admonition, Palmerston and Russell dictated Her Majesty's government's position. Contrary to their views of weeks past, the *Trent* had engaged in "a lawful and innocent voyage," and the United States Navy did nothing less than perpetrate "an act of violence . . . an affront to the British flag and a violation of international law." Lord Lyons was ordered to demand the immediate release of the prisoners to his custody and a suitable apology from the Lincoln administration.

From the wording it can be inferred that neither Palmerston nor Russell desired a war with the United States. The British government were willing to believe that the naval officer "who committed this aggression" acted on his own, or he had "greatly misunderstood" his orders. If Secretary Seward needed time to consider "this grave and painful matter," Lord Lyons could give him seven days. If Seward refused to give them up, or gave an unsatisfactory reply, Lyons was to sever diplomatic relations, shut the legation, "and to repair immediately to London." That would probably mean war, and Earl Russell so informed the Lords Commissioners of the Admiralty. The North Atlantic and West Indian squadrons were put on alert, and 8,000 troops prepared to sail for Canada.

The popular outcry in Britain, in part fueled by large-scale unemployment brought on by the cotton famine, mirrored that on the other side of the ocean. Lincoln was described in the British press as "a feeble, confused and little-minded mediocrity"; Seward, "the firebrand at his elbow." How dare the Americans, "with their dwarf-fleet and shapeless mass of incoherent squads, which they call an army," screamed the *London Morning Chronicle,* fancy themselves an equal to a great power. "The navies of England will blow out of the water their blockading squadrons."

The Confederacy treated the whole affair as akin to divine providence. "Something good is obliged to come from such a stupid blunder," wrote Mary Chesnut in her diary. "The Yankees must bow the knee to the British, or fight them."

Congress convened on December 2, and without dissent, voted Wilkes its unanimous thanks. Amid loud applause, a bipartisan resolution was adopted calling on Abraham Lincoln to confine the four prisoners in the jail cells of common felons.

*   *   *

On December 19, Lord Lyons, having now heard from Palmerston and Russell, entered Seward's office. He had taken great pains to keep this meeting as nonthreatening as possible and planned to discuss the situation only in the most general terms. The written demands were purposely left behind at the legation. But, he told Seward, the only "redress" that would satisfy Her Majesty's government was an immediate release of the prisoners into his protection and "a suitable apology for the aggression which had been committed." Lyons hoped the United States would offer the reparation of its own accord, and he would gladly be guided by Seward's advice so long as the results were mutually satisfactory.

The affably serious secretary of state thanked the ambassador for his "friendly and conciliatory manner," and asked for forty-eight hours to confer with the President. Two days later—a Saturday—Lyons returned for his answer, and Seward was all smiles and apologies. He had so much else to do, what with the war and all, that he just hadn't gotten to the subject at hand. As a friend, he asked Lyons to postpone the formal demands for just a little while. "It would," said Seward, "be a great convenience . . . personally, and a great advantage in all respects."

Tomorrow was Sunday, could Lord Lyons wait until Monday? Lyons testily agreed, but it must be early in the day, he would defer no longer. True to his word, Lyons appeared at 10 A.M., Monday morning. Without any preliminaries he read Seward the official note, and the secretary of state pledged to "lay it before" the President and return a written reply "without delay."

The Cabinet session that met to pass on Seward's response was a stormy one. Attorney General Bates felt the threat of war exaggerated. As he interpreted it, Wilkes' actions were basically correct and there was case law backing him up. But this was no time to chide the British on their past behavior in stopping neutral vessels during previous wars.* The British were very touchy regarding real or imagined insults; give the rebels up, Bates recommended, they aren't worth the trouble.

Gideon Welles would have none of it. He felt the Union completely within its belligerent rights, and if any mistake had been made, it was not for stopping and searching the *Trent,* but in letting her go. So vehement were his objections, that his brother-in-law, George Morgan, felt it

---

* The odious impressment of American seamen on the high seas by the British was a prime cause of the War of 1812.

wise to counsel: "Do not let the Mason & Slidell affair place you in opposition to the President. The general feeling [in New York] is to do almost anything rather than fight England now."

The consensus answer given by Secretary Seward to Lord Lyons, a rambling, and elaborate dissertation on international law, showed (as Gideon Welles said later) "the dextrous and skillful dispatch which he prepared on his own change of [public] position." The rebel envoys, Seward argued were indeed contraband of war, liable to seizure, and Wilkes had acted correctly. It was, he said, "a simple, legal, and customary belligerent proceeding." Nonetheless, Seward continued, even though he considered the British position fallacious, the United States would now—and only for now—concede the point. Wilkes, he smoothly rationalized, had "acted upon his own suggestions of duty, without any ... instruction ... on the part of this Government." Given these facts, Great Britain could "justly infer" that the United States "had no purpose ... which could affect in any way the sensibilities of the British nation." He would give the prisoners up. Lyons considered that "apology" enough, and the crisis was over.

In secret, on New Year's Day 1862, Mason and Slidell left Fort Warren for Provincetown, where they boarded a Royal Navy sloop to complete their passage to Europe. For the duration of the war, they never accomplished a thing, and were treated with official neglect.

For the navy, the whole thing left a sour taste. Career officers were divided on the issue, based in part on their amount of dislike for Wilkes. Percival Drayton accused him of engaging "in a little cheap glory." For the Union, he wrote, "to get out of it in such a sneaking way, makes the matter ten times worse. An honest backing down would have been respectable in comparison." In contrast, David Dixon Porter harked to America's traditional policy of resisting the right of search upon the high seas; "and by way of being consistent," he noted after the war, "we had but one course to pursue, and that was to repudiate the acts of Captain Wilkes."

Samuel Du Pont placed the Union's capitulation square at the feet of braggarts and penny-pinching office holders. "I hope we will draw some lessons," he wrote in December 1861, "that there is something else required to make a nation respected than sharp politics and great boasting. . . . Thirty ships like the *Wabash* with an ironclad frigate or two . . . would have spared us this."

Up the Sounds

"I was rather surprised to find myself alive, and congratulated myself upon having one night more before me."

—Lieutenant William Harwar Parker, CSN

With crushing odds and killing broadsides, Flag Officer Silas Stringham and Brigadier General Ben Butler had muscled their way onto North Carolina's half-drowned shores at Hatteras Inlet in August 1861, giving the Union its first victory of the Civil War. Stopping up a bolt hole for rebel privateers proved a boon to the Federal naval blockade.

But it was only a partial victory. Confederate forces still held sway over the wide waters, canals, and estuaries of the Carolina sounds, easing the strain on the South's fragile railroads, and admitting free movement of men and supplies through back doors to Richmond and Norfolk. The key to it all, as Commander Stephen Rowan had pointed out, was swampy, ten-mile-long, pickle-shaped Roanoke Island, smack between Albemarle and Pamlico sounds.

After losing Hatteras, the rebels had moved almost 3,000 troops onto the island, fortifying its inward-facing shores on the shipping channel of Croatan Sound. As a further check to any Federal naval advance, gangs of slaves hammered a double line of piles into the mucky channel bottom between the island and the mainland. Yet considering the strategic importance to the Confederacy of Roanoke Island and the sounds, their defenses were very understrength.

*   *   *

Not long after the Union's seizure of Hatteras Inlet, plans were afoot to move inside and complete the work of slamming the doors. As the new commander of the North Atlantic Blockading Squadron, Flag Officer Louis M. Goldsborough's first mission was to secure the waters of Pamlico Sound. He envisioned a combined navy-army attack on Roanoke Island, followed by an advance up Albemarle Sound to the Dismal Swamp Canal system feeding Norfolk. Gideon Welles gave his "cordial approval," and the navy moved ahead, appropriating the necessary vessels.

The army's scheme originated with somewhat different strategic motives. In the fall of 1861, Brigadier General Ambrose Burnside, a genial, intelligent Rhode Island West Pointer, fond of big hats and luxuriant whiskers, suggested raising an amphibious or "coastal" division from the Northeastern states. Burnside knew that among its men, "would be found a goodly number of mechanics to fit out a fleet of light-draught steamers and barges ... to transport the division, its armament and supplies, so that it could be rapidly thrown from point to point on the coast." It was a far-reaching idea, much ahead of its time.

George McClellan, the army's new general in chief and a proponent of combined operations, admired the concept. Actively planning his own inspired campaign to capture Richmond by advancing up Virginia's York Peninsula, he saw that Burnside's capture of Roanoke Island would pose a major threat to the Confederacy's interior lines of communications. Using Roanoke Island as a base, Burnside, with the navy's assistance, could exploit the estuaries, snap up the coastal towns, and perhaps charge inland to cut the railroads. Roanoke's military value "was so evident," said Lincoln's secretary, John Nicolay, "that it needed little urging upon the attention of the Government." Thus, when Gideon Welles learned of the army's idea, he pledged the navy's fullest cooperation.

Burnside had no trouble raising his amphibious division, a big one, 15,000 men, a corps in all but name, counting attached units. While they drilled at Annapolis, Burnside collected his vessels in New York. That was a problem. The navy had already taken most of the seaworthy craft able to mount a gun. Still, from the gleanings, he gathered "a motley fleet" of Hudson River barges, ferries, and "propellers." At local yards, their hulls were braced and stiffened with oak planking, "so arranged," the general noted, "that parapets of sandbags or bales of hay could be built upon their decks."

By the new year 1862, Burnside commanded a worthy fleet of more than eighty vessels, including nine gunboats, five floating batteries, and a full train of troop and horse transports, colliers, water boats, and tugs. The army gunboats each had a naval officer in command, assisted by a couple of master's mates and a midshipman. An army regiment, the 1st New York Marine Artillery, provided most of their fighting crews. All its personnel, officers and men, wore navy uniforms with distinctive insignia. "We were like the navy in drill and discipline," recalled one of its members. "We were especially well drilled in the use of naval light artillery, either afloat or ashore."

In the first days of January 1862, the smartly marching amphibious division embarked at Annapolis for Hampton Roads. Flag Officer Goldsborough shifted his flag from the *Minnesota* to the sidewheeler *Philadelphia,* in calmer times a workaday Potomac River steamer. Command of the expedition's "naval division," a mishmash of nineteen converted steamers, every bit as diverse as the army's, went to Commander Stephen Rowan in the iron-hulled sidewheeler *Delaware.* On January 11, the combined forces sailed for Hatteras Inlet.

Hatteras in winter is one of the world's most miserable places, and moving the ships through the shallow, tortuous inlet, into Pamlico Sound, or as Burnside put it, "worried through this perplexing gut," tested seamanship to the extreme.

Almost all of the army vessels had to be lightened on the seaward side, dragged across the bar and the inlet's unique, inner bulkhead, then with back-breaking labor, reloaded once inside. Every craft touched bottom at least once. Collisions were a daily event. Three, including a horse transport, ran hard aground, knocked to bits by the seas. Everyone ran short of water. "At times," Burnside said, "it seemed as if nothing could prevent general disaster."

Goldsborough was very anxious to get going, because all the milling around at the inlet provided the Confederates with a perfect opportunity to attack. The Confederate naval forces in the area didn't amount to much. But their handful of paddle steamers and canal tugs had already proved very annoying.

The "Mosquito Fleet," as the rebels called it, sailed under Flag Officer William Lynch, an explorer of the Jordan River and Dead Sea. On January 21, as Goldsborough feared, the mosquitoes reconnoitered the Hatteras Inlet and saw just about everything. At his base on Roanoke Island's Pork Point, Lynch spoke with his captains. Should the Mosquito Fleet meet the Federals from behind the pile line, in support of the shore batteries, or below it, at the "marshes," a group of swamp

islets scattered across the channel? Some wanted a forward defense at
the marshes, others to defend at both points. But "the majority," said
Lieutenant William Harwar Parker, skipper of the armed tug *Beaufort,*
"thought it better not to divide our forces at the eleventh hour." Lynch
would make his stand at the pile line.

The morning of Wednesday, February 5, arrived clear and cool. Goldsborough signaled "Underway to get," and the combined fleet, Rowan's
naval division in the van, formed columns for the thirty-five-mile passage to Roanoke Island. The grand progress was tied to the speed of
the slowest, pig-nosed, converted ferry-gunboat. It took a good ten
hours before the island was sighted right ahead, and at Stumpy Point
they anchored for the night.

Thursday's clouds, said Surgeon Lorenzo Traver of the *Delaware,*
"were passing to and fro, as if they anticipated some commotion or
shock below." With the gunboats *Ceres* and *Putnam* scouting ahead, the
expedition steamed forward "in columns and brigades." From the
Delaware's halyards, hoists of colored bunting snapped out, "Prepare
for action."

At nine the sky, "thick and threatening," cleared just enough for
lookouts to see the Mosquito Fleet forming behind the pile line. As
Rowan threaded into the marshes the rains came. "In torrents," Dr.
Traver remembered. "How discouraging," he wrote, "when only a few
hours before, the prospect of giving the rebels a good whipping, to
have them blasted a few minutes later by the sudden change in the
weather." The ships anchored.

For the Confederate sailors in the Mosquito Fleet it was an equally
miserable time. "We remained underway all day," Parker recalled. "The
galley fires were out, and we could have no cooking done ... The
weather was cold, with a drizzling rain."

After dinner, Parker took his gig to the mosquito flagship, *Sea Bird.*
He found Flag Officer Lynch in a dressing gown, sitting quietly in his
cabin reading the pages of *Ivanhoe.* The two officers, who had spent
nearly their whole lives in the United States Navy before going South,
passed the night not in planning how to defeat their old comrades, for
"neither of us believed that we would be successful," but in a pleasant
discussion of literature; and "I never spent a more delightful evening,"
Parker remembered.

At midnight, from the 100 ships—Union and Confederate—huddled about in Croatan Sound came the brassy striking of eight bells.
Hands came up from their damp, smelly berth decks to relieve the

watch, and Parker took his leave. "Ah!" said Flag Officer Lynch at the gangway, "if we could only hope for success; but come again when you can."

"Let the men take their breakfast," was Goldsborough's signal in the morning. He and Burnside had made good use of the menacing weather to gather intelligence of the enemy, and they finalized their tactics. Rowan's naval division would lead, "dashing without delay" straight at the Mosquito Fleet. While the navies engaged, the army regiments, supported by their own gunboats and armed navy launches, would land at Ashby's Harbor, midway up the inner face of the island.

Amphibious warfare is extraordinarily difficult and dangerous. But over the weeks and months Burnside had worked out a clever method for getting his men from boat to beach. The transports each came fitted with specially designed ladders, down which the troops climbed into large surfboats. In strings of twenty they were towed inshore by a steamer, cast off and rowed the final yards over the surf. In concept and practice, it pointed a direct evolutionary line to the United States' amphibious assaults of World War II.

At midmorning, Friday, February 7, Goldsborough, borrowing from Nelson at Trafalgar, hoisted the signal, "Our country expects every man to do his duty." Watching from the turf embrasures of Fort Bartow on Pork Point, Lieutenant Benjamin Loyall of the Confederate Navy remembered, "there was a movement among the ships of the enemy, and it soon became evident that they were advancing their gunboats in full force."

The vessels scouting the landing sites at Ashby's Harbor reported no hostile batteries in range, and the transports steamed to the line of departure. The Mosquito Fleet temporarily unreachable behind the pile line, Rowan led the naval division to Pork Point and opened the attack on Fort Bartow. "The men," said Dr. Traver in the *Delaware,* "were in excellent spirits, having had an extra ration of grog. Their jokes and laughter could be distinctly heard between the discharge of the artillery."

At Fort Bartow's first return shot, Goldsborough signaled, "Close in upon the enemy," and soon every ship was engaged. The captain of the *Valley City* reported "the whole fleet pouring an incessant fire of shot and shell into the fort." Exploding shells set afire the gunners' barracks. But some of the rebel shots, "brisk exchanges," noted a Union officer, found their marks.

In the Union gunboat *Hetzel* a round shot smashed through the waterline, and a fragment of exploding shell struck a master's mate in the head, which, noted the report, "killed him instantly." One of the *Hetzel*'s own cannon burst. Every man in the gun crew was thrown to the deck, six of them bleeding from wounds. The blast blew the gun's trunnions off, and a large chunk of the breech went overboard, taking with it the portside bulwarks. Another big piece soared over the mast-head, splashing into the water just alongside. The remaining section, a half-ton of run-amok iron, drove through the deck and beam under-neath, hurling its way through the magazine, finally lodging in the bottom, against the keel. The magazine caught fire. Only by the actions of the ship's surgeon, who shouted for the engineer to get the pumps going and grabbed men to bear the hoses and flood the com-partment, were the *Hetzel* and all aboard saved from being blown to rags.

The *Delaware* had her own close call with eternity. "During the action," Surgeon Traver wrote, "one of the ... gunners, who had charge of the magazine, obtained a key which fitted the spirit room, unlocked the door and helped himself." Traver discovered him and another man, both reeling drunk, "using threatening language about blowing up the ship." The doctor hauled them on deck to the captain, who instantly clapped them in double irons.

The Mosquito Fleet was down to six fighting vessels. In the *Beaufort*, Lieutenant Parker remembered, "the first shell that exploded over us scattered the pieces over our decks. Midshipman Mallory, a youth of 14, brought some [fragments] ... to me with much glee; he looked upon the whole proceeding as great fun. Poor boy!"

Parker ordered his chief engineer to send all available men up from the fire room to the tug's single gun. Another shell burst overhead and he called to the crew to lie down, "and when it was over I ordered them to jump up and go at it again." All obeyed except a very green, very scared coal passer. "Get up!" Parker shouted from the hurricane deck. The man "turned his head like a turtle and fixed his eye on me, but oth-erwise did not move." It was time for the ultimate lesson in naval disci-pline. Parker drew his Colt revolver, cocked the hammer, and aimed. "'Get up, or I will kill you.' He hesitated a moment ... then sprang to the gun, and behaved well during the rest of the engagement." Parker holstered his pistol.

In late afternoon, a 9-inch shell shot through the deck of the rebel tug *Curlew* and dropped out her bottom. She filled so fast there was barely time to run aground. Her commanding officer, "Tornado"

Hunter, whom Parker described as "a very excitable fellow," fought the entire battle without his trousers.

After Flag Officer Lynch ordered the *Appomattox* to Elizabeth City for powder, there remained but five vessels in the Mosquito Fleet, all very cut up and nearly out of ammunition. He sent a plea to the shore batteries, but they had only ten charges to spare. With "conviction and ... hope" that Fort Bartow could hold one more day, that perhaps a night counterattack might drive Burnside off the beaches, Lynch broke off the battle. Taking the damaged store ship *Forrest* in tow, "I proceeded with my little squadron to Elizabeth City for ammunition."

Near dusk, under close cover of naval bombardment, the army landed on the drenched, uninviting beaches. By 9:30 P.M. Burnside reported 6,000 men ashore, increasing by a thousand an hour. He planned to attack at daylight. Because the troops would advance north, into the line of naval gunfire, Goldsborough ordered the ships to check fire unless requested by the army for specific targets—another arrangement well in advance of its time.

Saturday broke cold and rainy. The smoke of heavy musketry easily located the front lines, and using that reference, the gunboats returned to pound Fort Bartow. According to Goldsborough's flag secretary, the rebels "replied languidly and finally not at all." After half an hour the sailors heard gunfire in the rear of the enemy's works, and the vessels ceased firing. The army had come up behind the fort.

Goldsborough, taking for granted the army was sweeping all before it, felt the time ripe to break the pile barrier above Pork Point and charge up the sound to destroy the remnants of the Mosquito Fleet. Up the flagship's halyards flew the signal for nine gunboats, led by Lieutenant William Jeffers in the *Underwriter,* "to perform the service."

The *Ceres* had just found the channel between an unfinished row of piles and a sunken schooner when Jeffers' eye caught the Union flag "entering the battery at Pork Point." He ordered his ships forward. Closing fast on the narrow passage, the gunboat *Lockwood* discovered a chain that held a pair of hulks to the barricade. The sailors cut it, floated one of the hulks out, and *Lockwood* headed up the sound. With dark and a thick mist gathering, the gunboats passed through. Before them, all Albemarle Sound lay open and defenseless to the Union's guns.

The flag seen by Jeffers marked the storming of a silent, abandoned Fort Bartow. "At 4:30," penned the skipper of the *Valley City* in his log, "observing the American ensign flying over the enemy's battery, cheered ship." Shortly after, came Goldsborough's one-word general signal, "Victory." At a cost of less than forty killed, he and Burnside, in as neat a combined operation as happened in the war, had shattered the back door to Norfolk and Richmond, taking nearly 2,500 prisoners in the bargain.

For Flag Officer Lynch and the Mosquito Fleet, Elizabeth City, twelve miles up the Pasquotank River, was a trap. To their dismay they found the Dismal Swamp Canal's lock machinery broken, which meant any vessel trying to escape by water to Norfolk had to run the Yankee gauntlet back through the sounds. As for getting ammunition, Lynch found hardly enough for two vessels. There was a fort of sorts, at Cobb's Point, on the west bank of the river just below the town. Lieutenant Parker found it "a wretchedly constructed affair;" its designer must have felt "Elizabeth City was the last place the Federals would attack." The magazine "resembled an African ant-hill," and its front door faced the river, entirely exposed to hostile fire.

Until midday Saturday, the rumblings of battle carried over the waters from Roanoke Island. When quiet settled over the sound, Parker knew the place had fallen, and "we felt sure Elizabeth City would be the next place attacked." Ill and despondent, Lynch appointed Lieutenant Parker to organize the town's defense. Parker wanted to strip the *Forrest*'s guns, and together with some local field artillery, site them in position on both sides of the river. But there wasn't enough time. Instead, he pressed into service the civilian schooner *Black Warrior,* anchoring her on the east bank, opposite the fort, and placed the remaining vessels: *Sea Bird, Ellis, Appomattox, Beaufort, Raleigh,* and *Fanny* in a line, higher up across the channel.

On Sunday, February 9, Stephen Rowan, at the head of fourteen Union gunboats, advanced into Albemarle Sound. By the light of the moon, they steamed slowly over the bar of the Pasquotank and anchored ten miles below Fort Cobb. To economize on his own acute ammunition shortage, Rowan ordered the gunboats to revert to ancient ways, and "engage vessels hand to hand" with pistols, fixed bayonets, cutlass, and boarding pike.

The men of the doomed Mosquito Fleet spent the night dividing what powder they had. Parker, after making sure the men took breakfast before daylight, staggered exhausted to his cabin, "and threw myself on my berth 'all standing.' I really believe I did not take off my sword and pistol," he remembered years later; "I know I did not remove my cap." It had been a week since he had really slept, or changed clothes for that matter. He had fought in one desperate battle, was ready to begin another, and "I was never so tired in my life." Sleep came instantly. Yet it seemed less than a minute before the executive officer nudged him awake. "The enemy was underway and coming up."

Parker sprang to the deck. He didn't need a glass to see the massed Federal gunboats steaming up with the flood tide. A boat alongside demanded his attention. A messenger from Flag Officer Lynch ordered Parker and his crew to abandon the *Beaufort* and mount the defense of Fort Cobb. "Where the devil," Parker demanded, "are the [militia]men who were in the fort?" "All run away," replied the messenger.

"I did not fancy this taking charge at the last moment," Parker said, "but there was no help for it." Leaving four men with the *Beaufort* to escape or blow her up, Parker and his crew took to the boats. While the oarsmen pulled, officers and sailors tore bedsheets into bandages, "a cheerful occupation under the circumstances." Fort Cobb held four old 32-pounders, scavenged from the Norfolk Navy Yard, and Parker had enough men for only two of them.

Cleared for action, Rowan in the *Delaware* led six gunboats in the Union van. At long cannon shot, two miles, Parker opened the fight. Paying scarce heed to the rebel fire, the Federal gunboats steadily advanced. When three quarters of a mile from the battery, Rowan's signal floated out in the morning breeze, "Dash at the enemy." Commanding officers shouted for full speed, and their coal heavers maniacally threw shovelfuls into the glowing fireboxes. Up went another signal from the *Delaware,* "Commence firing."

The gunboats piled on the knots, "at the same time," noted Lieutenant Quackenbush of the *Delaware,* "doing terrible execution with our guns." Twelve minutes from the first gun, the *Black Warrior* was set afire by her crew. Once the fleet passed upriver, Parker in Fort Cobb had no targets and was in real danger of being surrounded. Taking his men and Flag Officer Lynch, he loaded his command into farm wagons and struck out overland for Norfolk.

The Mosquito Fleet breathed its last. "In gallant style," the *Commodore Perry* rammed the flagship *Sea Bird.* The rebel crew took to the river and were cut down with pistols and muskets as they swam to shore. The *Ceres* took on the rebel tug *Ellis.* The Confederate skipper, Lieutenant Cooke, had prepared demolition charges in the hold to blow her up and take the Yankee down with her. But this was prevented, Cooke said, "by one of my negro coal heavers." This black Confederate sailor was not a slave, nor were several others in the *Ellis* and *Sea Bird,* who Lieutenant Cooke "was sorry to say" deserted to the Union at the close of the battle.

The *Fanny* was run ashore by her crew and torched. The *Appomattox* tried to ram her way into the Dismal Swamp Canal, but jammed in the lock gates. Only the *Beaufort* and *Raleigh,* neither of which took part in the general action, survived and somehow escaped to Norfolk through the Dismal Swamp to fight another day.

For the Federal squadron there was a single moment of fright. A Confederate shell lanced the hull of the *Valley City,* passed through the magazine, and exploded on the berth deck, setting the forward end of the ship afire. The skipper dived below to direct the damage control, and found Gunner's Mate John Davis, "seated with commendable coolness on an open barrel of powder as the only means to keep the fire out ... while at the same time passing powder ... for the gun divisions on the upper deck."*

Fifteen minutes after Rowan hoisted his "Dash" signal, up fluttered "Cease firing." Parts of Elizabeth City burned to the ground, torched by her citizens fleeing inland. Gunboat landing parties reached the Confederate quartermaster's warehouse before the flames and salvaged large stores of fresh beef, bread, and flour. At the small shipyard, Rowan burned the *Forrest* and another gunboat on the stocks.

Four Federal gunboats headed west along the sound to Edenton, where another unfinished hull met the flames. Two schooners were taken and sent north, up Currituck Sound, to block the Chesapeake and Albemarle Canal. But these were penny prizes compared to the strategic consequences of the operation.

While Goldsborough guarded his water flank, Burnside jumped to the mainland, and in March 1862, combined army-navy assaults captured the major coastal towns of New Bern, Beaufort, and Morehead City. Along with the sounds, the Union now controlled eight North Carolina rivers and four canals. Seeing nothing but open country ahead, Burnside sent an urgent request to McClellan for enough cavalry to sweep inland and sever the railroads. This, however, "Little Mac" refused. He needed every horse and man; for his great hammer, the Army of the Potomac, was poised to strike up the Peninsula to Richmond and end the war.

As a Confederate naval base, Norfolk, now virtually surrounded on

---

* For this act of heroism, Davis was one of the first recipients of the newly created Congressional Medal of Honor.

all sides, was doomed. "Confederate affairs are in a blue way," wrote Mary Chesnut in her diary. "Roanoke taken, Fort Henry on the Tennessee open to them, and we fear for the Mississippi River too. . . . New armies and new fleets are swarming and threatening everywhere." But up the Elizabeth River, at the Norfolk Navy Yard, the Confederate Navy was putting the finishing touches to its own hammer that would rock the U.S. Navy off its keel blocks. The *Merrimack* was about to take her trials in Hampton Roads; nothing, by far, was over.

"our friends, the enemy"

"I am going to ram the *Cumberland*. . . . The moment we are in the Roads I'm going to make right for her and ram her."

—Flag Officer Franklin Buchanan, CSN

T he day couldn't have been better, indeed, with the warm breeze, the weather at Hampton Roads felt more like late spring than the gray, rainy, fits of a dying winter. It was Saturday, March 8, 1862, and the majestic, oaken warships of the North Atlantic Blockading Squadron bobbed quietly at anchor. The afternoon flood tide had nearly reached high water.

By Fort Monroe and Old Point Comfort, the flagship *Minnesota,* her sister *Roanoke*—with a broken propeller shaft—and the sailing frigate *St. Lawrence* swung round their hooks.

Flag Officer Goldsborough was off conducting operations in the half-drowned shores of the North Carolina sounds, and in his absence Captain John Marston of the *Roanoke* conducted the duties of senior officer afloat. On board, he had just convened a board of enquiry (to this day, no one knows why).

Seven miles west of Fort Monroe, at the upper end of Hampton Roads, in the mouth of the James River at Newport News, were a pair of sailing vessels, the *Cumberland,* last seen during the capture of Fort Hatteras and the old 50-gun frigate *Congress*. In light of recent intelligence, they had no business being in a forward area.

Secretary Welles had been receiving almost daily reports from sundry sources on the progress of the *Merrimack*'s conversion into an ironclad, and by all accounts the rebels were nearly done. Welles' own secret weapon, the bizarre little *Monitor,* had been rushed to completion, and was at that very moment sloshing her way down the coast. But if the *Merrimack** beat her to it, the sailing ships were in gravest danger. Welles had ordered tugs from Baltimore to tow them out. Gus Fox himself was coming down to make sure things went right.

Aboard the *Congress,* and all the men-o'-war in the roads, it had just struck one bell in the afternoon watch, 12:30 P.M. Hands were cleaning up from dinner, dumping buckets of galley slops over the sides. As always this brought hundreds of scavenging gulls. "Then they chatter and scream," said Surgeon Edward Shippen of the *Congress,* "and fight for the remnants as they drift astern . . . until we pipe to dinner again."

Saturday, as regulations provided, was wash day, and the clothing of the *Congress'* 400 men flapped on lines rigged between the masts; white clothes to starboard, blue to port, according to naval custom. Her crew were anticipating going to Boston for a refit, Surgeon Shippen said, "and being relieved from the monotony of a blockade at anchor."

For some minutes the quartermaster of the watch had been looking at something passing the fringe of woods over by Craney Island, south across the roads, in the Elizabeth River. He turned to the officer of the deck. "I wish you would take the glass and have a look over there, sir. I believe *that thing* is a-comin' down at last." Someone else had seen it too, the tug *Mount Vernon* flew the signal 551—"Coming enemy vessel is."

"Sure enough!" Shippen remembered. "There was a huge black roof, with a smokestack emerging from it, creeping down towards Sewell's Point." Slowly, ominously, the "thing" lurched into the main shipping channel. Two outriding tugs scouted before her across the shoals of the Middle Ground. The *Merrimack*—even the lowliest coal passer and powder monkey in the Union vessels knew that now— pointed toward the anchored ships at Newport News. Down came the *Congress's* clotheslines, and the marine drummers beat to quarters.

After something like an hour, the rebel was close enough for the men in the *Congress* to make out her iron plating. At 200 yards, Lieutenant Joseph Smith ordered a ranging shot. At this distance it was impossible to miss. But Dr. Shippen watched the 32-pound iron ball

---

* Though renamed *Virginia* for her Confederate service, virtually no one on either side called her anything but *Merrimack.*

glance off the iron casemate "like a drop of water from a duck's back. This opened our eyes!"

The *Congress* then fired a full broadside point-blank. Nine hundred pounds of hurtling metal smashed fully home. In horror the gunners saw the balls ricochet into the air like pebbles off a roof.

The monster took no notice of the hits, none at all. Shouldering the *Congress* out of the way, the *Merrimack* cracked a four-gun broadside of her own, and the old frigate's oaken walls disintegrated like papier-mâché. The carnage, Shippen remembered, was "simply terrible. Our clean and handsome gun deck was in an instant changed into a slaughter pen, with lopped-off legs and arms, and bleeding, blackened bodies." Blood and brains actually dripped from the overhead beams. John Leroy, the quartermaster who had first seen the "*thing* a-comin' down," lay smashed and broken, a gutted rag doll, both his legs blown off at the waist.

Confederate Navy Secretary Stephen Mallory's vision and a leaky, knockabout, patched-together salvage job had tossed the U.S. Navy on its beam ends. Hampton Roads, main base of the North Atlantic Blockading Squadron, lay a shambles. For one heady day, the Confederacy had broken down the wooden walls of the blockade. In England the cotton famine had reached crisis proportions. Now, with this stunning victory, could European recognition of the embattled Southern cause be far off?

Mallory's first thoughts of armored ships came in April 1861, in his initial report to Jefferson Davis on the state of the nonexistent Confederate Navy. In all probability he had ironclads on his mind when he wrote, "I propose to adopt a class of vessels hitherto unknown to naval service . . . a combination of the greatest known ocean speed with the greatest known floating battery and power of resistance."

In a few weeks, he carried the project a step further. In a letter to Representative Charles Conrad, chairman of the rebel Congress' Naval Affairs Committee, Mallory pointed to the success of French armored floating batteries in the recent Crimean War. These vessels, he pointed, admirably suited the Confederacy, whose resources could never match the U.S. Navy's fleet of conventional, wooden warships. "Inequality" of numbers could be matched by individual "invulnerability."

Given this theory, he informed the legislator that an "iron-armored ship [was] a matter of the first necessity. Such a vessel . . . could traverse the entire coast of the United States, prevent all blockades, and encounter, with a fair prospect of success, their entire Navy." He asked for $2 million to buy an ironclad in Europe, and the Congress agreed.

But in this scenario, Mallory came away empty-handed. The European naval powers were in the midst of a battleship-building race of their own and had no extras for sale.

Disappointed with his initial foreign ventures, Mallory turned domestic. In May, he asked Captain Lawrence Rousseau, commanding at New Orleans, the Confederacy's leading maritime city, to investigate whether its firms could manufacture wrought-iron plates five inches thick. No, said Rousseau, they could not. Mallory queried Captain Duncan Ingraham, chief of the Office of Ordnance and Hydrography; could the plates be rolled by ironworks in Tennessee, Kentucky, or Georgia? The answer was the same, no.

The Confederacy's few commercial iron foundries were already sagging under the burden of army contracts and were very reluctant to undertake the expensive conversion to roll heavy plate for the navy. There was one exception—the Tredegar Iron Works of Richmond, which had the facilities to roll two-inch plate.

On June 3, 1861, Mallory journeyed with the Confederate government from Montgomery to its new seat at Richmond. That night, though exhausted by the trip, he met with one of his intimate advisers, long-faced, long-bearded, Lieutenant John Mercer Brooke, lately one of the U.S. Navy's premier ordnance experts. The discussion centered on the possibility of building an ironclad within the Confederacy itself. A few days later, Brooke wrote to his wife, "Mallory wants me to make some calculations in regard to floating batteries which I shall do today."

As Brooke recalled, "the first idea presenting itself" was a simple one, in accord with the Confederacy's skimpy resources and manufacturing capability. His design showed an oblong timber casemate, or "shield," two feet thick, resembling nothing so much as a steeply pitched roof, plated with three inches of iron, atop a submerged hull of roughly similar scale. On immediate examination, however, Brooke realized that a ship of these dimensions would be so beamy as to be unnavigable, if indeed, it would even float. He extended the underwater hull portions fore and aft, and drafted a vessel of more conventional lines on its water plane.

The use of the inclined armored casemate did not originate with Brooke. The French had done it with their floating batteries in the Crimean War, and Spanish naval experiments went back 150 years. Brooke's novelty, a dangerous one, lay in the completely submerged hull, "so that nothing was seen afloat but the shield itself."

Theories of iron buoyancy were incompletely understood in 1861. The overwhelming majority of ships, merchant and naval, were built of wood, and unless there was a disastrous design flaw, wood floated. With iron ships, an entirely new science of naval construction appeared and the prototypes were very much a hit-or-miss proposition. Brooke, a superior ordnance designer but no naval constructor, received a Confederate patent for inventing a submerged hull. But his claim that this feature would actually *increase* buoyancy and speed was very much the opposite.

Brooke delivered his rough "outline drawings—body, sheer, and deck plans" to Mallory's office. When the secretary approved them, Brooke suggested he summon Constructor John L. Porter and Engineer in Chief William P. Williamson from Norfolk to execute the design.

On June 23, 1861, Porter and Williamson reported to the Navy Department. As a naval constructor, Porter's career, at best, was a checkered one. He had dabbled in ironclad design for several years, but failed his first examinations as a constructor in the U.S. Navy. Later, achieving that goal, he was tried, and acquitted, by a court-martial for gross neglect of duty in connection with building the screw sloop *Seminole*.

He brought with him to Mallory's office an ironclad model. Like Brooke's design, Porter also made use of the gabled roof casemate, but his vessel was intended strictly as a harbor defense craft. Mallory wanted a seagoing, or at least a coastal vessel. He chose Brooke's design and assigned Williamson and Porter the task of accommodating the engines and boilers. To Brooke he said, "Make a clean drawing in ink of your plan, to be filed in the department." Brooke had already picked up a drafting pen when Porter interrupted. "You had better let me to that," he said, "I am more familiar than you are with that sort of work." Brooke handed him the materials, and went off with Williamson to the Tredegar Iron Works to look for engines.

Finding nothing of worth, the officers decided to poke around in Norfolk. By all accounts, it was here that Williamson hit upon the idea. The *Merrimack,* burned nearly to her copper in the Federal rout from the navy yard, had been raised from the bottom and now rested on keel blocks in drydock. Why not examine her? Williamson asked. The lower portions of the ship were still sound, and if the engineering plant was salvageable, they had a ready-made hull on which to build their ironclad. An inspection proved him correct.

There were almost as many reasons for rejection. Of the five *Wabash* class frigates, the engines of the *Merrimack* were undoubtedly the most unreliable of the lot, and she was a coal-eater of prodigious appetite. "They were deficient in her best days," said Midshipman Virginius Newton of the Confederate Navy, "time had not improved them." Nor had being under water for a month. As for the hull itself, Brooke had his doubts. "We all thought the draught too great, but we could not do better."

Returning to Richmond, they discussed the possibilities with Porter and the three officers prepared a joint report to Secretary Mallory. In their opinion, "it would appear that this is our only chance to get a suitable vessel in a short time." Mallory concurred, and on June 28 Brooke noted in his journal, "my plan . . . will be applied to the *Merrimac*."*

For the next two weeks, Porter prepared the detailed drawings for converting the burned-out frigate into "a shot-proof steam battery," and his name, to Brooke's consternation, appeared on the final blueprints. On July 11, 1861, Mallory ordered Commodore French Forrest at Norfolk to begin work immediately.

Presenting his construction program to the Confederate Congress, Mallory informed the body he needed at least half a million dollars to rebuild the *Merrimack*'s charred hulk into her former manifestation as a 42-gun screw frigate, but only $172,523 to convert it into an ironclad. Banking on the natural parsimony of legislatures, he was not disappointed. The vote was quickly taken, and passed on the lesser amount, exactly what he wanted.

Mallory divided responsibility among the three principals. Porter and Williamson returned to their offices at the navy yard to supervise building the casemate and overhauling the machinery. Brooke remained in Richmond to prepare the armor and guns, and act as Mallory's liaison officer. Making several "visits of inspection," Brooke frequently suggested major improvements and alterations in the design. Sound as they were, they aggravated the constructor no end.

By the end of July, the *Merrimack*'s burned timbers had been cut down to the berth deck, which in conversion became the main deck. Work began on the casemate. Fore and aft, a series of live oak "knees," reaching about eight feet high, and angled inward thirty-five degrees, were bolted to the hull's original framing. On these load-bearing members were placed the backing for the iron, two layers of Georgia heart of yellow pine, twenty inches thick. Brooke considered it not enough, recommending an additional course of four-inch oak planking. When

---

* Though often, then and now, spelled without the *k*, the correct spelling of the ship is *Merrimack*.

done and ready to receive the armor, the casemate presented two feet of solid timber, open at the top, with rounded ends, the whole caulked through and waterproofed.

As designed, the rudder and screw were completely unprotected from ramming, a feature of many Confederate ironclads. In the *Merrimack*'s case, it was partially rectified by placing a heavy oaken fantail over the stern.

Tredegar received the armor contract, which specified about 1,700 tons of one-inch iron plates, eight feet long, eight inches wide. To the practical exclusion of other vital work, the *Merrimack* engaged most of the foundry's capacity. Pacifying one disgruntled railroad customer, Tredegar's managing director wrote, "It is a most fortunate thing that we could render this assistance to our little navy, it could not have been done elsewhere in the Confederacy."

But almost all the finished product was late arriving at the navy yard. The Confederacy just didn't have enough flat cars. "We have iron . . . that has been lying on the bank for four weeks," moaned a Tredegar official; "the railroad has been unable to transport it." Even with the highest government priority, shipments were lost for days, shunted to sidings to make way for the army's transport. Commodore Forrest frequently had to send officers to follow the tracks and find the missing cars.

Brooke's plan called for three layers of one-inch plate. It could be quickly rolled, and bolt holes punched with machinery previously used in the manufacture of railroad and streetcar seats. Brooke, however, doubted his original specifications and conducted a series of tests. He was correct—an 8-inch solid shot penetrated the three layers. But his new calculations, demanding a double layer of two-inch plate, were too thick for machine punching and required time-consuming drilling for the bolt holes. Design changes, and there were several, each required a shifting of the bolt holes, and a sharp rise in cost. Tredegar increased its price a penny to $7\frac{1}{2}$ cents a pound. When at last done, the armor was fastened to the timber backing with $1\frac{1}{2}$-inch-thick iron bolts, clinched inboard with quarter-pound iron nuts.

The armor plate extended two feet below the waterline, protecting the upper hull. It was intended to be three inches thick, but contained only an inch, and according to Lieutenant Catesby Jones, the ship's executive officer, "it was not well fastened." Indeed, it was her weakest point, and a well-placed shot between wind and wave would have sent the ship, and all aboard, to the bottom. Fore and aft, the deck ends were sheathed in one-inch plate, and the fantail and bow stem each received a one-inch iron border, or "shoe."

The casemate was left open to the sky, topped with a grating of two-inch iron bars. At its forward end stood a conical, twelve-inch-thick armored pilothouse.

Within the casemate were seven gunports on each broadside, and unlike a conventional warship not opposite one another. This was a necessary feature because the inward sloping sides greatly constricted the width of the gun deck, and opposite ports would have impeded loading.

In Porter's design there were only single gunports fore and aft. Brooke considered this absurd, as it left "four points of approach without fire." On his recommendation, additional embrasures were cut at the casemate's rounded corners. Hammered iron shutters, worked by chains from within, were intended for each gunport. Only those on the ends were fitted, Brooke thought them "good for nothing."

The *Merrimack* carried into battle a very powerful battery of ten guns, and here Brooke really came into his own. As an ordnance man he was among the best, and four of his newly designed pieces were mounted: a pair of 7-inch rifles fore and aft, and two 6.4-inchers at the forward corner ports. The remaining six guns on the broadside were the U.S. Navy's standard 9-inch Dahlgren smoothbores, fished up from the bottom at Norfolk.

The *Merrimack* also shipped a weapon more akin to a Grecian oared galley than any newfangled gadget of the industrial revolution—a 1,500-pound cast iron ram. Fitted as an extension of the submerged forecastle, it jutted out two feet from the stem, coming square at the business end. Ironically, it was fortunate for the crew that the navy yard blacksmiths did such a bad job of bolting it in place.

By November 1861 Secretary Mallory's patience with the ship's slow progress had reached its limits. Frustrated by the Confederacy's lack of skilled labor, proper tools, tardy iron deliveries, and the constant friction between Brooke and Porter, he sent the able Lieutenant Catesby Jones to Norfolk as the ironclad's executive officer. His orders were to expedite construction, mount the guns, assemble a crew, and get the *Merrimack* ready for sea.

In January 1862, a labor strike paralyzed the navy yard. The blacksmiths walked out over wages, all ironwork came to a halt, and it took the personal intervention of the station commander, Commodore French Forrest, to break the strike. Appealing to their Southern patriotism, he actually persuaded the smiths, and the machinists and bolt-drivers as well, to work overtime, until 8 P.M., every day without extra pay. Jones was still not satisfied. "Somebody ought to be hung," he wrote to his friend Lieutenant Brooke.

Until Jones' arrival, security at the navy yard bordered on criminal negligence—not so very different from any other military facility on both sides in the war. Visitors had a free run, and numerous, informative articles appeared in the Southern press. The *Lynchburg Virginian* printed an especially good one, giving an accurate description of the *Merrimack*'s iron casemate and battery. "Do you suppose a cannon ball can have the courage to go through all of that?" asked the helpful columnist. "She will carry ten tremendous guns."

Eventually, Commodore Forrest closed the gates, permitting no visitor unless armed with a pass from legitimate authorities. The cities of Norfolk and Portsmouth established municipal water patrols to prevent slaves, many of whom labored at the yard, from escaping to the blockade squadron or the Federal lines at Newport News. The army stationed an artillery battery near the dry dock and posted sentries on the *Merrimack*'s weather decks to shoo away loiterers. Finally, all navy yard workers had to sign in and out at the gate or lose a day's pay.

In early February, the *Merrimack* was floated in dry dock, and her many flaws became glaringly visible. The high center of gravity caused her to nearly roll over. When righted, the bottom caught on the keel blocks and required emergency patching. To lower the center of gravity, Porter increased the iron deck plating, and also loaded 200 tons of "kentledge"—pig iron ballast—in the bilges.

"This is a bad piece of work," noted the *Mobile Register.* The Norfolk *Day Book* assured its readers that if the *Merrimack* didn't work as an ironclad ship, "she will make an invaluable floating battery for the protection of Norfolk, better good for something than nothing." Supposedly these stories were placed as deliberate disinformation to lull the Federals into thinking the *Merrimack* was a flop. Yet they were all too true—she *was* a bad piece of work.

With none of the traditional ceremony, the ironclad was finally launched on February 13, 1862. Only a corporal and four marines were on board. Private William Cline remembered: "There were no invitations to governor and other distinguished men, no sponsor nor maid of honor, no bottle of wine, no brass band, no blowing of steam whistles, no great crowds to witness this memorable event. The launching was accomplished quietly, only officers and men stationed at the navy yard witnessed it." Four days later, she was commissioned a warship in the Confederate States Navy and named *Virginia.*

The crew reported on board. Living conditions, as they were in all Civil War ironclads, North and South alike, were awful. Damp and unhealthy, the ill-ventilated berthing spaces were choked with noxious boiler gas and retained the heat and cold transmitted by the tons of surrounding iron. More than one fifth of the hands were at the naval hospital at any time.

Like most everything else with the *Merrimack,* mustering the crew was a makeshift, make-do affair. The daunting responsibility for young Lieutenant John Taylor Wood, he did the best possible with poor means. A handful of actual sailors came from the wrecks of the Mosquito Fleet, and some gunners volunteered from the militia batteries of the Norfolk United Artillery. But the majority marched right from General John Magruder's army camps at Yorktown.

Wood initially chose about 200 volunteers, but when he came to collect them, he found the army had concocted a human version of three-card monte. Only two of the original men answered to their names, "the others," Wood complained to Captain Franklin Buchanan, chief of the navy's Office of Orders and Detail, "are certainly a very different class of men from those I selected." Old Buck passed it up to Mallory, who in turn had the "honor" to present the problem to his colleague, Secretary of War Judah Benjamin. When the round robin came back to General Magruder, Wood finally had his crew.

The whole complement mustered at the navy yard, and Midshipman Virginius Newton found them "as trusty a body of men as anyone would wish to command; but what a contrast they made to a crew of trained jack tars!"

The ship's executive, division, and junior officers had been appointed, and the crew formed; now what about her commanding officer? The truth is, the *Merrimack* never actually had one, and the reason lay in the ironbound traditions of the United States Navy, from which the Confederate Navy was cloned.

Commanding a major warship requires a captain's rank, usually one of some seniority. The Confederate Navy had several of these, and two, French Forrest and Victor Randolph, applied for the post. But Mallory had never liked the traditional system of selection by seniority only, and he considered both officers too old for such a critical assignment. His choice was Franklin Buchanan, Old Buck, a relative junior, having just short of forty-six years' service in the old U.S. Navy.

By an extremely adroit measure, Mallory sidestepped tradition and got what he wanted. Instead of naming Captain Buchanan the commanding officer, he bestowed on him the title of Flag Officer, James River Defenses, flagship, the *Merrimack*. Old Buck, the disgraced former commandant of the Washington Navy Yard, reported to Norfolk on February 24, 1862, and shouldered the responsibility for the her completion and fitting out.

As outlined in Mallory's orders, the *Merrimack*'s mission was quite simple: drive off the Federal blockaders at Hampton Roads, and by so doing, expose McClellan's flank and defeat his ambitious drive up the York Peninsula to Richmond.

That was the "what." As to the "how," Mallory had several ideas. The *Merrimack*'s "powers as a ram are regarded as very formidable," he wrote Buchanan, "and it is hoped that you may be able to test them." The secretary compared the ship's iron beak to the infantryman's bayonet, and the tactic of ramming to the bayonet charge. To Mallory, this method of attack had a double purpose. Not only was it the "most distinctive" in terms of shattering the enemy's resistance, he noted, but it "will commend itself to you in the present scarcity of ammunition." But whatever Old Buck decided, the secretary hammered that it must be "action—prompt and successful action."

An able administrator, Mallory was no naval tactician, and he hadn't the vaguest notion of the *Merrimack*'s capabilities. Old Buck must have choked when he read the secretary's question on whether the ship could pass Old Point Comfort "and make a dashing cruise up the Potomac as far as Washington." Not only was her draft too great to steam over the Potomac bar, but she would have eaten her coal before getting there.

Buchanan's plans were more realistic. Action the secretary wanted, and action the secretary would get, but on Old Buck's terms. He envisioned a joint army-navy operation with General Magruder striking down the York Peninsula to the Federal camp at Newport News, while Buchanan attacked the blockading ships anchored off the town.

Magruder, receptive at first, soon backed off, telling the War Department, "I am . . . satisfied that no ship can produce such an impression upon the [enemy] troops at Newport News as to cause them to evacuate." Besides, the roads were a quagmire, impassible to artillery, and Magruder advised against the joint plan.

It was not until Sunday, March 2, that Buchanan was told the combined operation had been canceled. Earlier that day, he had informed General Magruder that unless some accident prevented it, the *Merrimack* and her escorts would be off Newport News early Friday morning, the seventh. "My plan," he wrote, "is to destroy the frigates first . . . and then turn my attention to the battery on shore. . . . I sincerely hope that acting together we may be successful in destroying many of the enemy." Old Buck's reaction on learning he was to attack alone is buried with the ages—only the horrific results have come down with time.

Even this late, on the very eve of operations, there were problems with the ship. Lieutenant Jones was still not satisfied with her high-riding displacement. A full load of ammunition and 150 tons of coal brought it down another foot, and Constructor Porter added more pig iron "on her ends and in her spirit room." It was not enough. Brooke's weird design of a hull awash, and Porter's lack of waterline armor could not be reconciled with sound principles of naval architecture. "The ship will be too light," Jones wrote, "[and] we are least protected where we most need it."

To the shrill of boatswain's pipes, Flag Officer Buchanan formally took command on March 4, and ordered all the yardbirds off the ship, save those engaged in the most vital work. "This vessel," he announced, "is about to face the enemy just as soon as I can get her there." Commodore Forrest protested. She wasn't ready, there was still work to be done on the underwater plating, and only two gunport shutters had been fitted. Old Buck, high-strung and taut as an archer's bow, would have none of it: "I mean to try her against the enemy, sir! There will be time to complete the shutters and armor after we have proved her in action!"

Buchanan would not, indeed, could not wait. The targets in Hampton Roads were just too fat. More important, everyone knew the Union's first ironclad was but days away, and if Old Buck dallied—for armor, for port shutters, for more powder, for armor-piercing shot—the battle would not be against the wooden fleet, but with the "Yankee cheesebox," as the papers called it. All these reasons were valid for an immediate attack, but there was another why Buchanan strained at the bit. His personal hatred of Gideon Welles for his dismissal from the U.S. Navy was so great as to intrude on all other considerations. He fixed the *Merrimack*'s maiden voyage for the night of Thursday, March 6.

Getting down the Elizabeth River at night required lights in the channel. The Confederates had removed all navigational aids, replacing them with obstructions. Without lights, the civilian pilots refused to move the ship, so temporary lights were installed. Still, the chief pilot, William Parrish, a civilian not subject to naval discipline, a man who had trained his entire professional life never to assume the slightest risk to any vessel in his charge, outright refused to budge. He told Buchanan that lights or not, under no circumstances would he take the responsibility for bringing the *Merrimack* downriver at night. Purple with rage and frustration, Old Buck had no option. He canceled the sortie, telling Parrish to be ready at daybreak. But the pilot wouldn't do this either. The *Merrimack*'s draft of twenty-three feet could only clear the bar at high tide, about 2 P.M.

Forced to accept this further delay, Buchanan was pushed to the limits of self-control. Come dawn, Friday, March 7, the pilots found more reasons not to move, and the ship's officers began to question the civilians' courage. In fairness, the pilots had a point. The day came with heavy clouds, strong winds, and patchy rain. The converted *Merrimack,* as unwieldy a lunker as ever took the water, required over half an hour to turn a half circle. No, they wouldn't cast off, and again Buchanan could do nothing about it.

Saturday morning, March 8, saw the sun rise glorious and warm, giving the pilots no excuse. Faced with the flag officer's steel gaze, and who knows what else, they agreed to take the ship over the bar at the flood tide. Just before 11 A.M., Buchanan ordered Catesby Jones to make all preparations for getting underway. Workers were on board until literally the last moment, tightening a bolt here, burnishing a rod there. Yardbirds had already slushed the casemate with buckets of melted tallow and pork fat to help glance off cannon balls. Pacing the iron grating of the hurricane deck, Buchanan called for the chief engineer, Ashton Ramsay. The engines, he said, "were in bad shape in the old ship, I understand. Can we rely on them? Should they be tested by a trial trip?"

As the *Merrimack*'s third assistant engineer in her Federal screw frigate days, Ramsay was as familiar with the plant as anyone, but he thought for a moment before answering. The ship would have to steam ten miles downriver before entering Hampton Roads; if anything went wrong, that's when it would happen. "Sir," he addressed the flag officer, "if any trouble develops I'll report it. I think that will be [a] sufficient trial trip."

At exactly six bells in the forenoon watch, 11 A.M., a gun at the navy yard boomed the historic moment. It appeared, "to be a signal for something," wrote a Confederate soldier in a letter home. "In an instant the whole city was in an uproar, women, children, men on horseback and on foot running down toward the river from every conceivable direction, shouting 'the *Merrimac* is going down.'" The lurching, lumbering iron monarch was waited upon by a pair of handmaidens, the *Beaufort,* commanded by William Harwar Parker, and the *Raleigh,* survivors of the Mosquito Fleet, keeping apace at half-speed.

In the engine room Ashton Ramsay kept careful watch on the rods and pistons, gauges and dials, as sweaty firemen heaved shovel after shovel of coal into the insatiable fireboxes. Satisfied, he climbed to the hurricane deck and asked a pilot what speed. The man did a rapid calculation from passing objects on the riverbank. She was making close on nine knots, faster than the old frigate had ever done with a full blossom of sail. Ramsay went forward. "The machinery is all right, sir," he reported.

It had been nearly two hours since the ironclad had cast off. She came up to Sewell's Point and Hampton Roads lay open ahead. Ashton Ramsay looked across the peaceful waters to the mouth of the James River and Newport News, where, he recalled, "gleamed the batteries and white tents of the Federal camp and the vessels ... *Congress* and *Cumberland,* tall and stately, with every line and spar clearly defined against the blue March sky, their decks and ports bristling with guns, while the rigging ... was gay with the white and blue of sailors' garments hung out to dry."

Flag Officer Buchanan knew what was next. Lieutenant Jones and the midranking officers, though officially ignorant, most likely knew as well. But for the others—the midshipmen, master's mates, petty officers, and crew—any clinging thoughts that this was a trial voyage were immediately dispelled. From the lantern-lit gloom of the gun deck, Old Buck addressed the ship's company. Ashton Ramsay remembered a ringing summons, "to strike for your country and your homes." Marine William Cline recalled the words, "The eyes of the whole world are upon you this day." From his battle station at the after 7-inch rifle, John Taylor Wood watched Old Buck point through a gunport to Newport News. "Those ships must be taken," he growled, "and you shall not complain that I do not take you close enough. Go to your guns."

Ramsay, making his way along the cavelike gun deck was just about to descend the engine room hatch when the mess steward touched his elbow. "Better get your lunch now, Mr. Ramsay," he whispered, "it will be your last chance." The passage to the wardroom went by the sick bay, and Ramsay, watching the surgeon lay out the instruments of his trade, lost his appetite. Sailors should always have a full stomach before battle, but Ramsay "merely tasted some cold tongue and a cup of coffee."

As the *Merrimack* and her escorts steamed into Hampton Roads, the Confederate naval officers standing on their weather decks watched scores of small craft scurry to the far shore, as Ashton Ramsay said, "like chickens on the approach of a hovering hawk." Huge columns of black smoke suddenly poured from the stacks of the *Minnesota* and *Roanoke* at Old Point Comfort. Bright-colored signal flags ran up the masts of every ship in the Federal fleet. With long glasses to their eyes, the rebel officers saw the clotheslines drop and the *Congress* shake out her topsails.

Lieutenant John Eggleston commanded the starboard 9-inch guns. Unlike the officers on the grating topside, Eggleston's view of Hampton Roads was restricted to the three-by-four-foot picture frame of the gunports. Four bells in the afternoon watch, 2 P.M., had struck sometime back. Ahead, to the left, two points off the bow, lay "our friends, the enemy." Peering out, he could just see the *Beaufort* and *Raleigh* steaming across the shoals of the Middle Ground, waiting for the lumbering *Merrimack* to complete her progress into the main channel.

Then, like the change of picture cards in a parlor stereopticon, Eggleston's gunport framed the looming sides of a great ship, all her guns run out—the *Congress,* less than 100 yards off. Eggleston had served in her as a midshipman. But memories were abruptly kicked away, when "there leaped . . . the flash of thirty-five guns, and as many shot and shell were hurled against our armor only to be thrown from it high into the air." The *Merrimack* rocked slightly from the impact. Lieutenant Jones ordered the starboard battery to return fire and the *Congress* was transformed into a butcher shop.

The *Cumberland*'s sails lay slack, drying in the warm sunlight. Captain Radford had gone off to the *Roanoke*, and Lieutenant George U. Morris, the executive officer, was in command. He had watched the *Merrimack* come out past Craney Island and cleared the ship for action. For the men of the *Cumberland* it was poetic justice. They had been there at the very beginning, at the humiliating retreat from Norfolk, when old, drunk McCauley scuttled the ships, and old, scared Paulding burned the navy yard.

Now, said Lieutenant Thomas Selfridge, "the long-expected occasion had finally come." From his station at the forward 10-inch pivot gun, he looked over the precisely ordered deck, sanded and holystoned by decades of sailors to a smooth whiteness not seen in nature. Years later, he proudly remembered the crew, "standing at their guns for the last time; cool, grim, silent and determined Yankee seamen." They held fire and watched the *Congress'* broadside as it "merely rattled from the sloping armor like hail upon a roof," and then saw her wooden sides crushed like an egg. Now it was their turn. Let the "thing" come; nothing, they were sure, could stand up to the *Cumberland*'s twenty-two 9-inch Dahlgrens, each loaded with thirteen pounds of powder instead of the regulation ten.

But the *Cumberland*'s guns stood mute. The *Merrimack* approached from almost dead ahead, and no gun could bear on the iron target. Even the 10-inch bow pivot gun was useless, its aim fouled by the head rigging. The *Merrimack* opened fire with her forward Brooke rifle. The shell passed through the hammock nettings to explode among the marines. "Their groans," Selfridge said, "were something new to us and served as an introduction to a scene of carnage unparalleled in the war."

Unstoppable, the *Merrimack* smashed into the *Cumberland* at right angles, just aft the bow on the starboard side, the iron ram biting deep into her wooden vitals. The sloop heeled over from the impact. Her masts swept the sky like enormous pine whips, her oaken hull gored through with a hole large enough, said an amazed John Taylor Wood, "to drive in a horse and cart."

Inside the *Merrimack's* armored casemate, the men were all but blinded by the reeking smog of exploding black gunpowder, and few realized what happened. "Scarcely had the smoke cleared away," Lieutenant Eggleston recalled, "when I felt a jar as if the ship had struck ground." A few seconds later, Buchanan's flag lieutenant, Bob Minor, came running along the deck, waving his cap, and calling out, "We've sunk the *Cumberland*."

Catesby Jones ordered the engines full aback, and—nothing; she would not move! The iron ram held the ships in an embrace of death. From the *Cumberland* came a vomiting revenge of powder and smoke. Eleven 9-inch Dahlgrens, their mouths almost touching the sloping sides of the *Merrimack's* casemate, threw nearly 800 pounds of solid shot in a murderous broadside. Smashing through the ironclad's unshuttered ports, they tore off one gun at the trunnions, ripped the muzzle off another, demolished the bow rifle, swept away the anchors and boats, riddled her smokestack, and killed or wounded nineteen men.

Were it not for the slipshod work of the Norfolk blacksmiths the *Merrimack* would have gone down, underneath her victim. But in all the lurching about, the ram broke from its boltings, and she backed away free. For some minutes the ship sat dumbly immobile, refusing to answer the helm, shuddering to her oaken bones as three more of the

Cumberland's broadsides hammered the forward angles of the case-mate.

Then the rudder bit and Catesby Jones conned the ship to a position sharp on the *Cumberland's* bow, where he could rake the dying sloop without danger. Every one of the *Merrimack's* shots cut a swath of gore. "It was a situation to shake the highest courage and the best discipline," Tom Selfridge remembered, "but our splendid crew never faltered." One gun captain had both arms taken off at the shoulder. "He passed me while being carried below, but not a groan escaped from him."

The carnage defied description, but according to those who lived through it, not a man of the *Cumberland* flinched, every gunner went on, loading and firing as if at drill. Great, jagged splinters tore off the deck, bringing excruciating wounds. A gun captain with both legs shot away still managed three steps on his horrible stumps to jerk the lanyard for a last shot before falling dead. In Selfridge's division, every gun captain was killed or wounded, "and with a box of ... primers in my pocket, I went from gun to gun firing them as fast as the decimated crews could load."

She was fast making water, going down by the bow. The forward magazine flooded, and the men at the pumps could not keep up. Water reached the berth deck where the badly wounded lay, and above the battle, Selfridge heard "the heart-rending cries ... from the poor fellows as they realized their helplessness to escape slow death from drowning."

Selfridge, face blackened with powder, uniform torn, looked around him at the once well-ordered deck of a handsome sloop of war. Dead and wounded lay in piles, the ripped oak ran with blood. Some guns lay unattended, run in at their last shot, surrounded by broken rammers, sponges, and bodies.

For nearly an hour the two ships hurled at each other iron and death. On the *Merrimack's* casemate, the melted pork fat took fire, until, said Midshipman Littlepage, "it seemed that [we were] literally frying from one end to the other." One of Littlepage's gunners turned to his mate. "Jack, don't this smell like hell?" "It certainly does," Jack called back, "and I think we'll all be there in a few minutes."

Flag Lieutenant Bob Minor quit the cramped pilothouse for the open hurricane deck, and with a halling trumpet shouted across for the *Cumberland* to surrender. George Morris had fought the sloop to within an inch of her life. The water was up to the main hatch, there was no more powder, and she was going down quickly by the head. But to him, there was but one answer, "Never!" he yelled back. "I'll sink alongside first!" Morris ordered the walking wounded to the upper deck; those unable to move would die with the ship. They "were so mangled," he later told Gideon Welles, "that it was impossible to save them." He then gave his last order. "Every man to look out for himself." On board, 376 men had opened the battle, 121 of them were now dead. Slowly, the *Cumberland* settled to the bottom, until only the mastheads showed above water, her ragged, shot-torn flag still flying.

It was the turn of the *Congress*. In order to double back, the *Merrimack* had to come around a full circle in the mouth of the James River, a maneuver that took almost an hour. From the James, the rest of Buchanan's command, the armed steamers *Patrick Henry, Jamestown,* and the tug *Teaser* ran full speed past the Federal batteries at Newport News and joined the fight. Meanwhile, down at Old Point, thrashing tugs frantically hauled the *Minnesota, Roanoke,* and *St. Lawrence* up to the scene of the action. And then by the hand of a capricious fate pulling them like giant toys on a single string, the lofty frigates, one after the other, nosed aground into the soft, lumpy bottom. Less than two miles from Newport News, they waited like tethered goats, for the approach of the tiger.

While the *Merrimack* and *Cumberland* were hotly engaged, the *Congress'* Lieutenant Joe Smith set the frigate's sails, and with the assistance of the tug *Zouave* tried to get her into shoalwater where the ironclad could not follow. Instead, helpless, she grounded stern-out to the enemy. At 2:30 P.M., the *Merrimack* and her escorts took position 150 yards off and began raking the frigate.

When a shell splinter caught Joe Smith in the chest, killing him, Lieutenant Austin Pendergrast took command of the dying ship. For two hours the *Congress* absorbed the punishment, unable to fire a shot in reply. Marines and sailors grabbed muskets and tried pathetic volleys at the *Merrimack*'s gunports. John Taylor Wood could see the *Congress'* decks "reeking with slaughter," blood running out of her scuppers.

From belowdecks came reports of fire creeping toward the after magazine. Pendergrast faced the worst decision of his life, but first he turned to Commander William Smith. This officer had recently commanded the ship before turning her over to Joe Smith, and was still aboard. The old skipper agreed they could do no more, and "we deemed it proper," Pendergrast reported, "to haul down our colors without any further loss of life on our part." Up the main to half-mast, and at the spanker gaff, a pair of white flags signaled Pendergrast's surrender.

The *Beaufort* was closest, and William Harwar Parker sent a boat to take possession of the prize. As it neared the gangway, one of the *Congress*' marines leveled his musket at the teenage midshipman in command. Unfazed, the boy repeated his orders, telling the marine he was "bound to do it." The marine lowered his weapon, the rebels boarded the frigate and took down the flag. For the first time since the opening gun three hours before, quiet settled over Hampton Roads.

From the *Merrimack,* Old Buck ordered Lieutenant Parker to take off the officers and wounded, let the rest swim ashore, and burn the ship. Parker took the *Beaufort* alongside the luckless prize.

Pendergrast and William Smith boarded the *Beaufort* to formally surrender, but they hadn't brought their swords. "I thought it proper," Parker said, "to request them to return . . . and get them." Lieutenant Pendergrast could only find a ship's cutlass. Parker repeated Buchanan's instructions to get the wounded out because "I wanted to burn the ship," and he ordered the *Raleigh* to assist. No sooner had he spoken when a tremendous volley of musketry and field artillery crashed out from the Federal positions at Newport News. Every man on the *Beaufort*'s weather deck was hit. Four bullets passed through Parker's clothes, one took off his cap and glasses, another shattered his knee. The firing from shore increased as more Union regiments and field batteries galloped and wheeled into line. The ships were only 200 yards from the beach. "So near," said Virginius Newton, "that I could plainly see the faces of the men." To remain was suicide. Parker sounded his steam whistle recalling his prize crew from the *Congress* and backed out of range.

Flag Officer Buchanan took it for granted that Parker had torched the *Congress,* and he "waited some minutes to see the smoke ascending her hatches." But when the *Beaufort* and *Raleigh* sheered off, he couldn't chance allowing the Federals to retake the prize. He turned to his flag lieutenant, Bob Minor, saying, "That ship must be burned." Minor instantly volunteered to lead the party.

In a ship's launch, Minor approached to within fifty yards of his target, which still flew a white flag of surrender. Lieutenant Eggleston says there were three, Catesby Jones says two, and none dispute that there was at least one. From the shore and the *Congress* herself came another ragged volley of musketry. Minor took a slug in the stomach and several of his crew were hit. The violation of surrender by the stranded frigate drove the Confederates to unbounded fury. Catesby Jones called it an "outrage upon the usages of civilized warfare." In his official report, Buchanan called it "vile treachery." Eggleston noted it as "unparalleled treachery."

From his exposed position on the *Merrimack*'s hurricane deck, Buchanan bellowed down the hatchway, "Burn that damn ship, Mr. Jones." Old Buck grabbed a carbine from a marine and began shooting. Perhaps he got off one shot before a musket ball went through his thigh, grazing the femoral artery, and he went down in a heap. "Tell Mr. Jones to fight the ship to the last," he said as he was carried below to the sick bay.

Up from the fireboxes to Lieutenant John Eggleston's guns came the sand buckets holding the hideous, glowing, 72-pound, red-hot shot. First the woolen cartridge holding ten pounds of powder was rammed down the muzzle, after which came a dry wad and then a soaking-wet mess of wadding. With tongs the red-hot shot was transferred from the bucket to a special cradle, lifted by two men and tipped into the cannon's mouth. Another stew of wet wadding was placed atop and the whole was rammed home. Twelve men strained on the tackles and ran the gun up to the port.

"Then," said marine William Cline, "we did pour hot shot and shell into the *Congress.*" Whoever still lived and could move in the burning hulk escaped over the bow. The rest died in the flames where they lay, to the number of 120 out of 434 who began the fight, "till out of pity," remembered Lieutenant Eggleston, "we stopped [firing] without waiting for orders."

It was nearing 5 P.M. Catesby Jones would have liked to finish the day by going at the grounded *Minnesota*. But dark was settling in, and in truth, the *Merrimack* was in no condition to fight. John Taylor Wood counted ninety-eight hits in her armor. She was leaking forward where the ram had been pulled out, three guns were damaged, coal bunkers were low, and many men, including Old Buck, were badly wounded. The flagstaff had been shot away, replaced with a boarding pike, and the funnel, recalled Surgeon Phillips was so riddled, it "would have permitted a flock of crows to fly through it without inconvenience."

After running through the *St. Lawrence*'s broadsides, the last shots of the day, Jones brought the ironclad to Sewell's Point, where the dead and wounded were taken ashore. Jones made his rounds of the ship. Passing a powder-blackened John Eggleston, the younger officer said, "A pretty good day's work, sir."

"Yes," Jones answered, "but it is not over."

Near midnight, every wakened eye in Hampton Roads watched the burning *Congress,* waiting for her magazine to explode. But something else nearby caught the attention of one of the *Merrimack*'s pilots. He called over to Lieutenant Jones, who picked up a glass and squinted into the dark, where "passed a strange looking craft, brought out in bold relief by the brilliant light of the burning ship." At first light it became a little clearer. John Eggleston looked out at the *Minnesota,* still hard aground, "and near her was the strangest looking craft we had ever seen before. A cheese on a raft."

Cheese on a Raft

"My men and myself were perfectly black with smoke and powder. All my underclothes were perfectly black and my person was in the same condition."

—**Lieutenant S. Dana Greene, executive officer, USS *Monitor***

I t was Sunday morning. Across from the White House, at the Navy Department, Gideon Welles sat at his desk reading the overnight dispatches. He looked up at some commotion in the hall and saw the gasping assistant secretary of war. Without ceremony, he handed Welles a telegram. It was from General Wool at Fort Monroe, the first message sent over the new "submarine" cable, and addressed originally to Secretary of War Edwin Stanton.

Welles read the few lines: the *Merrimack* had come down from Norfolk, "sunk the *Cumberland,* and the *Congress* surrendered"; the *Minnesota* and *St. Lawrence* were aground, and "probably both will be taken." It was Wool's view that the *Merrimack* and her escorts would steam into Chesapeake Bay that very night. Welles had hardly finished when a messenger burst in "requesting my immediate attendance at the Executive mansion."

With President Lincoln stood Seward, Treasury Secretary Salmon Chase, General McClellan, and Edwin Stanton, a vitriolic, hard-line Democrat and the new secretary of war. Shock was the general impression. Lincoln's young secretary, John Nicolay, recorded the scene in his diary: Stanton paced the room "like a caged lion," Chase contributed nothing except "to utter blame." McClellan, the man who felt himself another Napoleon, sat "dumfounded and silent." Seward said nothing. Lincoln, according to Welles, was "so excited . . . he could not deliberate." Welles remembered the scene as the worst moment of the war, worse even than Bull Run.*

Edwin Stanton was "at times almost frantic," Welles said. In fact, the secretary of war seemed to have lost all control. The *Merrimack,* he railed, would sink every vessel in the navy, capture Fort Monroe, cut off Burnside in the Carolina sounds, retake Port Royal, and lay New York and Boston under "contribution." McClellan's grand Peninsula campaign would have to be canceled to protect the government from this "formidable monster."

To dramatize the danger, Stanton flung open a window that afforded a fine view down the Potomac. It was "not unlikely," he carried on, that "we shall have a . . . cannon-ball from one of her guns in the White House before we leave this room." What ship or means, he demanded of Welles, had the navy to prevent the *Merrimack* from literally destroying the Union?

Measures, actually, were going forward that very moment. Yet, because the submarine cable had parted just after General Wool sent his telegram, none in the Cabinet Room had the faintest idea of anything beyond the reported catastrophe. Welles knew the "Ericsson battery" had left New York three days back; if on schedule, it should be at Hampton Roads right now. But Wool's telegram had not mentioned that. Holding no evidence, Welles did his best to dampen the fears.

Calm down and listen to reason, he told his colleagues. The *Merrimack* was not going to pass over the Potomac's Kettle Bottom Shoals, much less go to New York. Though it was only guess and hope, Welles assured the frightened men that the U.S. Navy's own ironclad, the *Monitor* was, in fact, at Hampton Roads, "and I had confidence in her power to resist and I hoped to overcome the *Merrimack*." Seward, for one, breathed again. These remarks, he said, brought the "first moment of relief [I] had experienced" in the day. Stanton, however, continued to rave. He dashed from room to room, jumped up and down, waved his arms. Welles noted with some disgust that he constantly ran to the windows "to see if the *Merrimac* was not coming to Washington."

---

* The only national panic similar to this day occurred on December 7, 1941, following the attack on Pearl Harbor. The Japanese fleet was reported off San Francisco, Japanese airborne troops dropping on Honolulu, and other such nonsense.

Near the closing hour of that most vexing day, a telegram came from Gus Fox at Hampton Roads. Welles read it with overwhelming relief. The *Monitor* had arrived late last night. This morning she had saved the *Minnesota* and driven the *Merrimack* off, though with what damage he could not say. The *Monitor* herself, Fox assured his boss, "Is uninjured and ready at any moment to repel another attack."

Gideon Welles was always a convenient public scapegoat for any supposed faults in the navy's war effort. Certainly there were blunders—neglecting to have tugs in reach of the *Cumberland* and *Congress* certainly ranked right up there. But ignoring or dawdling on the question of building ironclads—an accusation often thrown by his contemporaries and latter-day critics—does not bear the light of truth.

Prior to the war, the tradition-bound navy hadn't shown much interest in the ironclad revolution that engaged France and Britain. True, Congress in 1854 had funded the partly armored Stevens Battery, a 6,000-ton white elephant. But the money petered out, and she sat unfinished at Hoboken, New Jersey.

By May 1861, Captain Andrew Harwood, the conservative chief of the Bureau of Ordnance, had a pile of ideas and designs on his desk. But there was no system whatever to judge and cull, nor was there anyone in the navy experienced in the new architecture and engineering of ironclad construction.

But Welles knew he had to move. The radicals, Gus Fox and Engineer in Chief Benjamin Isherwood, were badgering him to get the design process moving, and the State Department was receiving alarming reports of Confederate agents attempting to buy the latest in European ironclads. Congress would meet in special session on July 4, and Welles prepared his initial ironclad program. The date, significantly, came seven days *before* Stephen Mallory authorized work to begin on the *Merrimack*.

At Welles' arm-twisting insistence, Congress authorized "a board of three skillful naval officers" to vet the plans and proposals for "iron-clad steamships or steam batteries." Should they report favorably, the secretary could spend up to $1,500,000 on their construction.

On August 7, Welles solicited plans and bids for a ship of "iron or . . . wood and iron combined." He provided no specific dimensions, only the general and conflicting guidelines of shallow draft "for either sea or river service," the ability to carry between 80 and 120 tons of armament, provisions for up to 300 men for sixty days, and eight days' coal. "The vessel," he stipulated, was "to be rigged with two masts, with wire-rope rigging, to navigate the sea." The deadline for bids was September 9, less than a month away. The following day Welles appointed the "ironclad board." As chairman he picked Commodore Joseph Smith of the Bureau of Yards and Docks; Commodore Hiram Paulding, head of Welles' improvised "office of detail," was the second member; and the third was the ubiquitous maritime scholar Charles Davis, from the Strategy Board.

By the first week of September 1861, they received sixteen proposals of nearly every description, including one for a "rubber-clad vessel." It finally came down to two, both masted and sparred, and conventional in their outfit of broadside guns.

The smaller, eventually the unsuccessful, 950-ton *Galena,* was submitted by Cornelius Bushnell, an old Connecticut friend of Welles, and designed on the "rail and plate" principle—thin slats of iron armor affixed to the ship's frames, much like clapboard siding. The larger ship was a modest version of the latest European designs and came from Merrick and Sons of Philadelphia. The board looked upon it favorably, as "the most practicable one for heavy sheathed armor"; she became the powerful *New Ironsides,* a wood-framed, iron-cased steam frigate of 3,480 tons.

But before ruling, the board demanded that Bushnell prove his design's innate stability. Bushnell could foresee no problem, yet could not mathematically guarantee it. He put the dilemma to Cornelius Delamater, a leading New York iron-founder and proprietor of the Novelty Iron Works. Delamater had not a clue, but he certainly knew who did.

John Ericsson was a true genius of the nineteenth-century industrial revolution. Prickly, difficult, and extremely egotistical, the fifty-eight-year-old Swedish engineer was convinced there was absolutely nothing beyond his capacity to invent or improve upon. The inventor of the "spiral propeller," Ericsson had designed much of the machinery for the U.S. Navy's first screw vessel, the ill-fated *Princeton.* His patron, Captain Robert Stockton, supervised the construction, took all of the credit, and served as the ship's first commanding officer. The guns were Ericsson's brainchild. These two monsters, the "Oregon," and the "Peacemaker," were 10-ton giants, able to throw a 250-pound solid shot five miles. The Oregon was designed and manufactured to Ericsson's exacting specifications and proved a sturdy piece of ordnance. Stockton oversaw the casting of the Peacemaker, an incalculable disaster.

The *Princeton* generated great interest. On February 29, 1844,

Stockton hosted President John Tyler, the whole Cabinet, and about 200 guests for an excursion down the Potomac. At a demonstration firing, the Peacemaker burst, killing the secretaries of state and navy, the chief of the Bureau of Construction and Repair, two congressmen, and the President's black servant, and wounding about twenty others. Stockton shifted the onus for the catastrophe to Ericsson, and a navy court of inquiry agreed. The government still owed $15,000 to the Swede for his work on the ship, but they refused to pay, and indeed, he never got a dime of it.

Ericsson went off extremely bitter, so it was with some fear that Bushnell, seventeen years later, approached the house on New York's Franklin Street to seek advice. But the man received him cordially, and after examining the plans, assured Bushnell that his ship could take the weight and not capsize.

As Bushnell was ready to leave, Ericsson asked if he had some time to look at *his* plan, an ironclad, "absolutely impregnable to the heaviest shot or shell." The engineer brought out a small, dusty box and from it lifted a cardboard model of a raftlike structure, topped with a rotating, hemispheric cupola, mounting a single gun. Five years before, Ericsson had displayed it to Napoleon III, but the Crimean War ended and the French lost interest. It was nothing less than the most revolutionary warship of the nineteenth century. In the basic concept of an armored hull, carrying a revolving gun turret, it set the theory and architecture for the capital ships that dominated naval warfare for the next eighty years. Ericsson had no intention of personally involving himself with the Navy Department, but Bushnell was welcome to handle it.

Gideon Welles was in Hartford and Bushnell took the model there. Examining it, the secretary was struck with the "extraordinary and valuable features ... involving a revolution in naval warfare." Welles sent Bushnell and the model to the ironclad board. The time for submitting ideas had lapsed, and Welles, fearing a rejection, prepared to lend his personal support.

Bushnell arrived in Washington on September 13, and through Seward he obtained an interview with the President. Examining the cardboard model, Bushnell remembered Lincoln saying that "he knew little about boats, unless it was a flatboat ... of which he was master in earlier life." He was, though, impressed with the model, and while Lincoln had no direct influence with the board, he did accompany Bushnell to his presentation the next day—no small favor.

In addition to the board members, the assembly included the Presi-

dent, Gus Fox, and several interested naval officers. The very mention
of Ericsson's name soured the board; and the model was so odd, so
unlike anything they had ever seen, or even imagined. Davis, in particular, was very skeptical. The debate droned on for hours until Abraham
Lincoln ended the meeting with one of his pithy anecdotes. He picked
up the cardboard ship and squinted along its queer lines. "All I have to
say," he told the board, "is what the girl said when she put her foot into
the stocking. 'It strikes me there's something in it.'"

The ironclad board did not know what to do, and dawdled for some
days. Bushnell's pleading hit a wall. Davis handed back the model,
advising him to "take the little thing home and worship it, as it would
not be idolatry, because it was made in the image of nothing in the
heaven above or on the earth below or in the waters under the earth."
Bushnell knew that the project would die unless Ericsson himself came
to Washington. Containing his substantial pride, Ericsson convinced
the board in less than two hours. On September 16, Welles received its
formal report. "Distrustful of our own ability," wrote Commodore
Smith, the members did nothing to hide the fact they were sailing in
uncharted waters. These grizzled officers never lost their skeptism of
armored vessels as high seas warships, but so long as foreign nations
were building them, "we must not remain idle."

Commodore Smith and his colleagues recommended three experimental ships, headed by the design of "J. Ericsson, New York." They
feared her poor seagoing properties, in which they were proved right.
But they were impressed by its "novel" features, "which will render the
battery shot and shell proof." Bushnell's *Galena* and Merrick's *New
Ironsides* received the other nods.

Ericsson's contract, a joint venture financed by Bushnell and two
New York businessmen, cost the government $275,000. For their
part, Ericsson and partners were obligated to furnish their ship, an
"Iron-clad Shot-Proof Steam Battery of iron and wood combined,"
complete and ready for sea in 100 working days. As Ericsson told it,
even as the department's clerks wrote up the contract, "the iron
which now forms the keel plate of the *Monitor* was drawn through
the rolling mill."

To build the hull, Ericsson engaged the Continental Iron Works at
Greenpoint, Brooklyn, two miles by horse car from the navy yard.
Three weeks later, the keel was laid in their East River ship house. The
countless components for the ship were manufactured in dozens of
foundries and shops from Buffalo to Baltimore. Everything was done to
Ericsson's plans, and when the parts arrived at one of three New York

assembly points—Continental Iron for the hull, Novelty Iron Works for the turret, and Delamater and Co. for the engines—the pieces fit together with hardly an alteration required.

The ship measured 172 feet long, by a boxy 41 feet wide, with just over a 10-foot draft. The hull was composed of two elements: an overhanging, armored raft deck, nearly awash, and a lower, timber hull holding the machinery, magazines, and berthing spaces. Heavy oak beams formed the base of the raft deck, over which lay a strake of seven-inch oak, plated with an inch of iron. The raft's five-foot sides were composed of an inner skin of half-inch iron plate and twenty-six inches of white oak, armored with five inches of laminated, hot-riveted iron.

Just aft the raft's bow, Ericsson installed one of his most ingenious devices, an enclosed anchor well that allowed the crew to raise and lower the ground tackle totally shielded from gunfire.

Aft the anchor well was the pilothouse, a squat, rectangular structure of wrought-iron bars, rising nearly four feet above the deck. An extremely claustrophobic structure of less than twelve square feet, it housed the pilot, helmsman, and commanding officer during battle. Narrow sight holes passed around its perimeter, and access was by means of a ladder to the berth deck in the lower hull. The iron top was not bolted on, but sat in grooves, as an emergency escape hatch.

The pilothouse proved to be one of the ship's weak points. Too low for good visibility, it was high enough to interfere with the guns trained directly ahead. A speaking tube was fitted to communicate with the turret, but the device did not function unless the guns *were* trained directly ahead.

The revolving turret rose nine feet above the deck. Ericsson was the first to admit it was not an original idea. Patented designs already existed in the United States and Great Britain, but it was Ericsson who first put the theory on the anvil. It had an interior diameter of twenty feet, no timber backing, and was built of one-inch iron plate, eight layers thick, with an extra inch around the two gunports. On the roof, an iron-sheathed timber grate with a sliding hatch served as the main entry from topside to belowdecks.

In repose, the turret sat on a brass ring inset into the raft deck. Traversing was done by four huge, horizontal gear wheels, doughnutted around a vertical shaft extending into the lower hull, taking power from its own donkey engine. In battle, the turret was jacked up, the entire weight, and that of the guns, borne by the central spindle. In theory, the whole apparatus was designed to be operated by one man.

Ericsson wanted two 15-inch guns. None were yet available, and the navy settled for a pair of 11-inch Dahlgrens, powerful pieces nonetheless, that could throw a 166-pound solid shot one mile every seven minutes. During loading, the gunners were protected by an internal pair of very heavy iron pendulums. Working these shutters with an inefficient block and tackle proved so cumbersome that only one gun could be fired at a time, in effect halving the *Monitor*'s broadside.

The propulsion machinery consisted of two boilers and two engines of Ericsson's own design, generating 320 horsepower driving a single propeller shaft. Its four-bladed screw and the ship's balanced rudder were completely covered and protected by the overhanging armored raft. Designed speed was nine knots, but the *Monitor* would be lucky to steam at six.

The boilers were fed by forced air, sucked down by large, belt-driven fan-blowers from two openings in the raft deck behind the turret. Ericsson intended the blowers to ventilate the magazines and berthing spaces as well. They brought 7,000 cubic feet of fresh air per minute into the lower hull, forcing out the old, heated, foul air. Though one of Ericsson's ingenious inventions, it was a serious flaw in the design. With the ship's very low freeboard, any sort of sea would bring water down the holes, directly onto the blowers. If the belts slipped, smoke and boiler gasses having no escape through the stacks—two small, telescoping boxes on the afterdeck—would back up into the engine rooms, and eventually asphyxiate anyone below.

Living quarters were forward in the lower hull. For the enlisted men, Ericsson economically designed hammock spaces for only half, since half would be on duty at any time. Officers had their own eight-by-six-foot staterooms built around a central wardroom, the captain having a separate cabin. For the officers Ericsson spared no expense. Their decks were covered in oilcloth, tapestry rugs, and soft, goat hair mats. The woodwork was all polished black walnut, with brass railings and fixtures. Bed curtains were of lace, and the spreads of damask. The evacuation of body wastes applied the same system later used on World War II–era submarines. Waste dropped into a pipe closed at its lower end. The upper end was then shut, the lower seal opened, and a force pump drove the contents into the sea.

By January 1862, though somewhat behind the very tight, 100-day contract schedule, the vessel was nearly ready for launching,

It was time to appoint a commanding officer. On January 11, 1862, Commodore Smith wrote a private letter to Lieutenant John L. Worden, on recruiting duty in New York. After delivering secret orders to Pensacola, and nearly being lynched by the rebels as a spy, his status had been righted to prisoner of war, and in November 1861, he was exchanged for the Confederate Samuel Barron.

"I have only time," Commodore Smith wrote, "to say I have named you for the command of the battery under contract with Captain Ericsson, now nearly ready at New York. I believe you are the right sort of officer to put in command of her." Worden took the horse car to Greenpoint. "After a hasty examination," he told Smith, not neglecting to thank him first, "I am induced to believe that she may prove a success. At all events, I am quite willing to be an agent in testing her capabilities."

The vessel had yet no name. The launch date being close at hand, Fox asked Ericsson to provide one. Praising the ship's "impregnable and aggressive character" and its intended effect on the Confederacy's leadership, Ericsson stated, "The iron-clad will thus prove a severe monitor to those leaders." In addition, the British, for whom naval supremacy was paramount, could hardly view with "indifference this last 'Yankee notion,' this monitor.... On these and many similar grounds I propose to name the new battery *Monitor.*"

On Thursday, January 30, a sizable crowd gathered at Thomas Rowland's Continental Iron Works. Inside the barnlike ship house, the workers waited for high tide. Gawkers anticipated the *Monitor* sinking to the bottom, and Thomas Rowland himself had a couple of temporary airtight tanks fitted under the stern, just in case. In midmorning, near the peak of the flood tide, the shipwrights knocked away the holding wedges, and the hull slid down the ways into the East River. According to a reporter from the New York *World,* "It was evident even to the dullest observer that the battery hadn't the slightest intention of sinking."

Fox sent the inventor a congratulatory telegram, ending, "Hurry her for sea, as the *Merrimack* is nearly ready at Norfolk ... " Three more weeks were needed to finish, and in that time Worden collected his crew. Officers and enlisted men were all volunteers, and Worden had the authority to pick anyone off any ship at the Brooklyn Navy Yard.

William Frederick Keeler, a successful forty-year-old businessman from LaSalle, Illinois, could have spent the war at home. Instead, at the first call, he joined the navy and was appointed an acting assistant paymaster. Stationed at Brooklyn, he volunteered for the *Monitor* as her supply officer. Keeler's letters to his wife, Anna, provide excellent insights into the war afloat. Writing of Lieutenant Worden, one of the toughest, saltiest officers in the navy, he described a man "tall, thin . . . & quite effeminate looking, notwithstanding a long beard hanging down his breast, he is white & delicate . . . & never was a lady the possessor of a smaller or more delicate hand."

As executive officer Worden appointed twenty-two-year-old Lieutenant Samuel Dana Greene, a mustached, black-eyed 1859 graduate of the Naval Academy, a classmate of Alfred Thayer Mahan.

For the enlisted crew Worden and Greene mustered the hands of the yard receiving ships *North Carolina* and *Sabine.* Worden explained fully the dangers of a sea passage, with the absolute certainty of a battle to follow. "The sailors responded enthusiastically," Greene recalled, "many more volunteering than were required." Worden picked forty-nine men.

On February 19, the *Monitor* was turned over to the navy for trials. Fires were lit under her boilers, steam was gradually admitted into the engine cylinders, and immediately the engineers found a mistake. Someone had improperly set the cut-off valves, dropping power by nearly two thirds. Limping the few miles downriver from Greenpoint, one of the blower engines popped a valve, and it took nearly six hours before Worden brought the ship to anchor off the navy yard. Once it was towed in, an examination of Ericsson's drawings proved the design correct, although it took a week to fix the problem.

The next day, Worden received orders to take the *Monitor* to Hampton Roads. Ericsson opened a parallel communication from Gus Fox. The department had just gotten some vital intelligence indicating the *Merrimack* "will positively attack Newport News" within five days. They were cutting things awfully close, and it was "very important," the assistant secretary said, that he know "exactly" when the *Monitor* would arrive on the scene.

Loading ammunition held up her sailing date once again. But at dusk, Wednesday, Chief Engineer Alban Stimers reported "the last shell was snugly stored."* Unless the weather interfered, the *Monitor* would be off on Thursday at daylight.

A wind-driven snowstorm came howling up the coast. Nonetheless, Worden attempted putting to sea—a calamity. Ericsson's balanced rudder exerted too much leverage, and the vessel refused to

---

* Stimers' most recent job afloat had been chief engineer of the frigate *Merrimack* (and thus Ashton Ramsay's boss) during her final U.S. service as flagship of the Pacific Squadron.

answer the helm. "She steered so very badly," Worden reported. "We ran first to the New York side," wrote Keeler, "then to the Brooklyn & so back & forth across the river . . . like a drunken man on a sidewalk, till we brought up against the gas works with a shock that nearly took us from our feet."

By navy yard messenger Worden sent after Ericsson, who promised repairs in three days. Assisted by Stimers, Ericsson compensated for the overbalance by multiplying the leverage of the ship's wheel on the tiller ropes. Two turns of the wheel were now needed where one served before. It took a bit more time and a lot more muscle to steer, but a veteran quartermaster could handle it.

Final trials were held on March 4. For the first time, the ship fired her 11-inch Dahlgren guns. Following the *Princeton* explosion eighteen years before, the navy had issued categorical instructions that "until further notice, no gun will be fired aboard any ship with more than half its intended weight of powder." The causes for bursting guns had been largely rectified, but there never came any "further notice," and the decree was still technically in force. However individual captains acted as the situation warranted. If full charges were needed, full charges were used (or even excess charges, as evinced by the *Cumberland* four days hence). But Worden was a man bound by regulations. The 11-inch Dahlgren gun held a full charge of fifteen pounds of powder; he ordered test firing with seven and a half.

She was due off on Wednesday, March 5, but the coastal storm that kept the *Merrimack* in port at Norfolk served the same purpose for the *Monitor* at New York. Waiting out the weather, the officer of the watch penned in the log, "John Atkins deserted [and] took with him the ship's cat and left for parts unknown." The next morning the storm eased to a moderate wind. The quartermaster struck six bells, 11 A.M., and the *Monitor*'s deck force made fast a 400-foot towline to the tug *Seth Low.* The gunboats *Sachem* and *Currituck* escorting, the little convoy steamed down the East River into New York Bay, through the Narrows into the Atlantic.

On the stormy Wednesday of March 5, President Lincoln convened a council of war to discuss details of the coming Peninsula campaign. Because Confederate batteries still harassed Potomac River traffic, McClellan's army of 121,500 men, 14,592 horses, and 300 guns were scheduled to take ship at Annapolis. Lincoln argued against this. He had no problem with the military aspects of the movement, but politically it might appear that after a year of war, the rebels still threatened the national capital. Could not a fraction of the troops, Lincoln asked, say 10,000, embark at Washington?

McClellan opposed the diversion. The transports, he argued could not safely pass the enemy batteries. Fox replied the navy could deal with that, but unless the army landed permanent detachments, the rebels would just reoccupy the positions. McClellan refused. On purely political grounds Lincoln decided the issue. A portion of the invasion force would leave from Washington, and the navy would sweep off the rebels "if only for a temporary and moral effect." He instructed Gideon Welles to make the necessary arrangements.

Inexplicably Welles had forgotten all about the *Merrimack* and cabled Commodore Paulding at Brooklyn, "Let the *Monitor* come direct to Washington." With immense fortune for the Union, the order arrived just hours too late; she was gone, Paulding replied. Given that, Welles notified Captain Marston, the senior naval officer present at Hampton Roads, "Direct . . . the *Monitor* to proceed immediately to Washington." Marston acknowledged, he would send her back "immediately."

On Friday, March 7, Marston got another order: "Send the *St. Lawrence, Congress,* and *Cumberland* into the Potomac River." The next day, Welles changed his mind. He telegraphed Marston that Gus Fox was coming down to sort things out: "Do not move the ships until further orders." By then, however, none of it mattered.

The four little ships steamed into the gray, rolling swells of the North Atlantic. With less than two feet of freeboard, the *Monitor* took it badly. Ericsson had mistakenly placed the air blower intakes *behind* the smokestacks, sucking gas and smoke into the fire room. For the engineers, this was extraordinarily dangerous. The *Monitor* had to keep a head of steam to operate all her power-assisted machinery—pumps for instance. The towline was a means of assistance only, to take the strain off the wheel and rudder.

Keeler wrote a few lines to his wife. "The steady & monotonous clank, clank of the engines assure us that they are still at work . . . but as the day advances some anxious faces are seen." That came when the wind picked up and green seas began rolling across the deck. "It was at once evident," Lieutenant Greene recalled, "that the *Monitor* was unfit as a sea-going craft."

By late afternoon what had seemed minor mistakes in design and adjustment became life- and ship-killing nightmares. Ericsson claimed that the turret, resting on the bronze base ring, provided its own watertight seal. The navy had not been so sure; they tackled the problem by jacking up the turret to its fighting position and packed the space with oakum—unraveled hemp ropes impregnated with tar. The sea washed it away. Water came down under the turret "like a waterfall" and waves slammed into the pilothouse with such force that it knocked the helmsman off the wheel.

Keeler went below and met a choking engineer climbing up, "pale, black, wet & staggering along gasping for breath." He went to get the man some brandy and in the passageway ran into several "stifled" sailors "dragging up the fireman & other engineers apparently lifeless." The whole 'tween decks was reeking with gas, steam, and smoke. Crawling over heaps of coal, Keeler pulled a half-dead fireman up to the turret hatch.

Waves broke over the blower pipes, water cascaded onto the fan belts and they slipped their mountings. Without forced air, the fires under the boilers began to die, the engines slowed their revolutions, and the boiler exhaust gases found no escape through the smokestacks. Men fell to the deck, unconscious.

Chief Engineer Alban Stimers and Assistant Engineer Isaac Newton led a gang of men into the propulsion spaces. They "behaved like heroes," Lieutenant Greene wrote his mother, and "fought with the gas endeavoring to get the blowers to work until they dropped down as apparently dead as men ever were." The gassed hands huddled with the watch standers under a scrap of sailcloth on the turret roof. Worden turned the national flag upside down as a distress sign, but the escorts didn't see it.

"Then," Greene said, "things looked rather blue." Deprived of power, the pumps gave out. The men rigged handy-billys, but they had not the pressure to bring water up from the bilge, out the turret hatch. Bucket bailing was useless. The *Monitor* was in real danger of foundering when the wind providentially blew itself out. The blowers were repaired, the engines restarted, and the ship ventilated of gas. Around 9 P.M. the crew ate an evening meal of crackers, cheese, and water. "Of course," Keeler wrote Anna, "there was no sleep on board that night."

Worden and Greene had been awake far longer than anyone else. For the safety and sake of the ship and crew, one of them needed to sleep. They opted to begin "watch and watch"—four hours on, four hours off—until normal conditions returned. Greene volunteered for the first, and Worden went below to his stateroom. Things were looking well. A smooth sea, clear sky, a bright moon, "and the old tank," Greene remembered, "going along 5 and 6 knots very nicely. All I had to do was to keep awake." At midnight he assured the captain he needn't leave his berth. Greene lay down in his clothes, and if anything happened, "I would turn out and attend to it."

He had scarcely fallen on his bunk, when in tremendous force a wall of headwinds drove solid seas over the *Monitor*'s deck from bow to stern. Ericsson had neglected to make the anchor well watertight, and water gushed in, forcing air in and out of the hawse pipe, turning it into a giant bassoon. "The noise resembled the death groans of twenty men," Greene said, "and was certainly the most dismal awful sound I ever heard." Water came down into the berth deck, and washed over the wardroom table. Desperately the crew stuffed the pipe with sail-cloth and hemp mats. They had just about done it, when word came from the fire room of water pouring down the blower hatches.

From the turret roof Worden hailed the *Seth Low,* 400 feet ahead, but the tug heard nothing. In the haste of getting underway from New York, no one remembered to stow lights for night signaling. Lieu-tenant Greene's father had recommended fitting a steam whistle, but that hadn't been done either. Every few minutes Worden called down to the fire room to ask about the blowers. They were turning dead slow and wouldn't last much longer. "We began to think then the *Monitor* would never see daylight," Dana Greene remembered.

He was nearly right. Steep pitching in the head seas jammed the wheel ropes, and the ship became unmanageable, yawing wildly, hundreds of feet to either side of the towline. At about 3 A.M., the sailors working frantically to keep the vessel afloat, the sea calmed just enough for the blowers to keep the fires barely alight and get the pumps going. At dawn, Saturday, March 8, a soaking quartermaster could finally signal the tug, and she dragged the *Monitor* toward shore and smooth water.

The crew spent the morning making repairs and drying out. At 4 P.M. the convoy rounded Cape Henry, twenty miles from Fort Monroe. Ears distinctly heard the booming of heavy guns, which Worden correctly judged a battle between the *Merrimack* and the fleet. He ordered the *Monitor* stripped for action and cast off the towline. As darkness fell, the men saw red and orange flashes lighting up the western sky. "Oh," wrote Keeler, "how we longed to be there—but our iron hull crept slowly on & the monotonous clank, clank of the engine betokened no increase of its speed."

Passing Old Point Comfort and Fort Monroe, Greene remembered "we could see the fine old *Congress* burning brightly." Steaming into Hampton Roads, the *Monitor* came to anchor and Worden reported to Captain Marston in the *Roanoke.*

The captain had Secretary Welles' telegram giving explicit instructions to send the *Monitor* back to Washington. Not every barnacled officer—and Marston had served forty-eight years—would have had the courage, or indeed the common sense, to disobey an obviously out-of-date order. But without hesitation he ordered Worden to stand by and save the *Minnesota*.

By the fires of the dying *Congress*, the *Monitor* slowly made her way up the Roads, and at midnight dropped anchor alongside the grounded flagship. Captain Gershon Van Brunt, Worden remembered, "was very glad to make our acquaintance." The *Minnesota* was a huge, wounded thing, her oaken sides badly splintered, and there seemed to Worden a lot of confused yelling, shouting of orders, and throwing things over the side. Bone weary, wet, hungry, and knowing they would fight in the morning, the *Monitor*'s crew prepared for battle; "there was no sleep," Worden wrote.

If the *Merrimack* emerged the victor on the morrow, the blockade at Hampton Roads would be broken. Lieutenant Greene, mindful of the navy's hopelessly dated prohibition against full powder charges for the guns, put the critical question to his commanding officer, "May I have your permission to use full-weight charges tomorrow?" Worden refused to deviate. No, he said, "we will carry out all department orders precisely."

After a short while the *Congress* blew up, "not instantaneously," Greene said, "but successively." One by one, the powder casks exploded, throwing showers of fire and sparks high into the night sky, "a grand but mournful sight." Nearby, in red silhouette, he could see the *Cumberland*'s flag hanging from her mast top, just above water. For Lieutenant Greene and the rest, surrounded by wrecks, disaster, and gloom, the long, dreary night "dragged slowly on."

Not so in the *Merrimack*. Granted, officers and men had a good deal of work in taking off the wounded, cleaning up, and patching the ship and engines as best they could. But it was a work of victory, never as tiring as labor in defeat. The crew also slept, a luxury denied to the *Monitor*. Before dawn, Sunday, March 9, the marine bugler sounded reveille. Private Cline remembered, "we began the day with two jiggers of whiskey and a hearty breakfast."

At the first hints of dawn, Lieutenant Rochelle of the *Patrick Henry* swept Hampton Roads with his glass. He saw the *Minnesota* where they had left her. But there was something else, right alongside, "such a craft as the eyes of a seaman never looked upon before—an immense shingle floating on the water, with a gigantic cheese box rising from its center; no sails, no [paddle] wheels, no smokestack, no guns. What could it be?" he asked. Some guessed a floating water tank, others, a floating magazine. A few, though they were not at all sure, "feebly intimated that it might be the *Monitor* which the Northern papers had been boasting about for a long time."

Catesby Jones paced the hurricane deck. With Old Buck in the naval hospital, he would take the *Merrimack* into battle. The *Minnesota,* the blockade squadron's queenly flagship, now aground, looked like the big prize. But Jones knew the *Monitor* changed everything. The *Minnesota* could wait. He would first attack and ram the *Monitor,* and "keep vigorously at her" until one of them emerged the victor at the end of the contest.

From her night anchorage the *Merrimack* steamed along the channel to Sewell's Point and crossed the Roads, heading for the target. Then it all happened very suddenly. Ashton Ramsay saw "a black object that looked like . . . a barrel-head . . . with a cheese-box on top of it." It moved slowly out from the *Minnesota*'s shadow, "and boldly confronted us." Catesby Jones ordered the forward 7-inch Brooke rifle to open fire.

The morning was fine, just like the day before, and a little breeze from the east blew off the early fog. Around the *Minnesota* all was turmoil. The stranded flagship was surrounded by pulling and shoving tugs, and no amount of work could get her off the shoal. The crew, desperate to lighten her draft for the morning flood tide, jettisoned everything imaginable into small craft alongside. From the *Monitor,* Paymaster Keeler watched "the bags & hammocks of the men, & barrels & bags of provisions, some of which went into the boats & some into the water, which was covered with barrels of rice, whiskey, flour, beans, sugar."

The *Monitor*'s crew were just biting into a cold breakfast. The quartermaster struck four bells in the morning watch, 6 A.M., when the *Minnesota*'s drums beat to quarters. Hailing the flagship from the turret roof, Worden asked Captain Van Brunt his plans. The captain replied he would get the *Minnesota* afloat, or burn her. "I will stand by you to the last if I can help you," Worden promised. "No, Sir," said Gershon Van Brunt, forty-three years inside the wooden walls of the old navy, "you cannot help me." Worden intended to offer battle as far forward of the *Minnesota* as possible and to Van Brunt's "astonishment," he steered a course directly at the enemy.

Keeler and Surgeon Logue were on deck when the *Merrimack*'s first shell howled over their heads and crashed into the *Minnesota*'s battered side. Worden came over. "Gentlemen," he said in sterner tones than they had heard before, "that is the *Merrimack,* you had better go below." The two men, followed by their skipper, scrambled up the turret and down the hatch. Inside, the gunners manhandled a 166-pound solid shot into the muzzle of one of the Dahlgrens. Worden turned: "Send them that with our compliments, my lads."

Lieutenant Worden, Quartermaster Peter Williams, and Samuel Howard, a volunteer pilot from the *Roanoke,* were jammed into the pilothouse. Lieutenant Greene took charge of the turret. Paymaster Keeler, who had no regular battle station, found one at the base of the pilothouse ladder, and he began running back and forth transmitting orders.

Worden discarded his original notion to fight at long range and instead altered course to come alongside the enemy. Keeler remembered a palpable quiet in the ship that took almost physical form. "If there had been a coward heart there its throb would have been audible," he told his wife, "so intense was the stillness."

Except for the men in the pilothouse, and one or two peering through the turret gunports, no one in the *Monitor* could see anything. They could, however, hear the *Merrimack* and *Minnesota* exchanging shots over their heads.

Dana Greene yelled down into the passageway. "Paymaster, ask the Captain if I shall fire." Keeler ran forward to the pilothouse ladder. "Tell Mr. Greene," Worden hollered back, "not to fire until I give the word, to be cool and deliberate, to take sure aim and not waste a shot." Then it came, a bellow carried along the passage on the forty-year-old legs of a volunteer acting paymaster: "Commence firing!"

Greene sighted his eye along the 11-foot gun barrel, took steady aim at the barn roof that wrapped his whole field of vision, and pulled the lockstring. The *Merrimack* wasted no time in replying. She returned "a rattling broadside, and the battle fairly began," history's first duel between armored ships.

Shooting all the while, the ironbound combatants hovered about in gradually contracting circles, closing to point-blank range. The *Merrimack* fired exploding shells that burst on contact, striking the *Monitor* in her sides, deck, and turret but doing no damage.

Damage to humans was something else. Acting Master Louis Stodder, operating the turret-turning gear, "incautiously" leaned against the wall just as it was struck. Knocked out by a concussion, he was carried

below. Stimers came up from the engine room to take his place. No[
of this affected the crew in the least, and Lieutenant Greene watched [
"a look of confidence passed over the men's faces, and we believed t[
Merrimac would not repeat the work she had accomplished the d[
before."

Inside the *Merrimack*'s smoke-filled casemate, Lieutenant John Egg[
ston watched the circling pigmy, "receiving our fire as she went, a[
delivering her own." In the engine room, Ashton Ramsay remembere[
"the noise of the cracking, roaring fires . . . and the loud and labor[
pulsations of the engines . . . the roar of battle above, and the thud .[
of the huge masses of iron which were hurled against us"; it compar[
only "with the poet's picture" of hell.

Engulfed in his inferno Ramsay's seaman's instincts were n[
dulled; he lurched forward slightly. The *Merrimack* had stopped! Sl[
had nosed aground, a situation critical in the extreme. Ramsay thre[
off all caution. He lashed down the safety valves and ordered the fir[
men to throw kerosene-soaked cotton waste into the furnaces, buildir[
their pressure to dangerously high levels. No help. "The propell[
churned the mud and water furiously, but the ship did not stir." Spl[
ters of wood, tar-smeared oakum, casks of turpentine, anything th[
burned faster and hotter than coal was thrown into the fires, until [
seemed the boilers could stand it no more. The *Merrimack* would lur[
off, or would blow herself up, there were no other possibilities. The[
"just as we were beginning to despair there was a perceptible mov[
ment, and the [ship] slowly dragged herself off the shoal. . . . We we[
saved."

From the gun deck, Lieutenant Eggleston watched his shells bre[
into fragments against the *Monitor*'s turret. He shouted through t[
thunder to Catesby Jones topside, "It is a waste of ammunition to fire
her."

"Never mind," Jones yelled back, "we are getting ready to ram."

Worden saw the movement, and if he had any doubt of Jones' intentio[
the gathering of a large boarding party on the *Merrimack*'s hurrica[
deck erased it. He called down to Keeler, "They're going to board u[
put in a round of canister," a can of iron balls that would turn an 11-in[
Dahlgren into a man-killing shotgun of horrific proportions.

Through the running paymaster-messenger, Dana Greene answer[
back, "Can't do it—both guns have solid shot."

"Give them to her then," Worden yelled.

Greene yanked the lanyard, the shot roared off and struck the *Merrimack* blunt on the casemate, ripping away a section of armor to expose the wood. A full charge behind that 166-pound ball might well have begun the disintegration of the Confederate ship. Even with half-charges, another shot in the same place would have penetrated through, and the *Merrimack* couldn't stand much of that. "You've made a hole through her," Worden hollered, "quick, give her the other."

Greene pulled back on the lockstring, "snap" went the primer, and—nothing. In the haste of battle, the charge had not been rammed fully home. Greene tried depressing the gun to roll it out, but the ball stuck in midbore. He needed fifteen minutes to worm it through the muzzle, and the *Monitor* hauled off into shoal water where the *Merrimack* could not follow.

The *Merrimack* maneuvered to ram. But Catesby Jones had second thoughts, and they dictated prudence: she herself might not survive the collision. He rang down two bells to Ramsay at the throttle platform—reverse engines—too late.

"Look out now, they're going to run us down," Worden shouted to Keeler. "Give them both guns." Just in time the *Monitor* shied away and took a glancing, halfhearted blow. Keeler remembered "a heavy jar nearly throwing us from our feet." He looked at the bulkhead, expecting a rush of water, and was relieved to see none.

In the *Merrimack*'s engine room, Ashton Ramsay "did not feel the slightest shock." That may have been, but the crash restarted yesterday's bow leak. Brushing by, at a distance where men could have touched, Dana Greene delivered two quick shots that hit halfway up the rebel's casemate, driving in the armor by several inches. Inside, the concussion knocked the crews of the after guns to the deck, bleeding from their noses and ears. "These shots must have been effective," Worden said, "for they were followed by a shower of bars of iron." Yet, his insistence on using half-weight charges denied the final punch to penetrate through the oak backing, into the ship.

The two fighters continued to maul at close range. At one point the *Monitor* rode so close to the *Merrimack*'s submerged stern that she nearly snapped off its propeller. But there was no crippling damage. Catesby Jones came down into the gun deck and was surprised to see Lieutenant Eggleston's gunners standing at ease. "Why are you not firing, Mr. Eggleston?" he said. In the light of service courtesies and naval discipline, Eggleston's reputed answer to his senior officer is highly questionable. But John Taylor Wood recorded him saying,

"Why, our powder is very precious, and after two hours' incessant firing I find that I can do her as much damage by snapping my thumb at her every two minutes and a half."

Meanwhile, in the *Monitor* Lieutenant Greene was having his problems in the turret keeping a sense of direction. Before the action he had chalked white marks on the stationary deck beneath his feet to indicate forward, aft, port, and starboard, but the signs were obliterated early on. He constantly sent Keeler shuttling to the pilothouse ladder to ask, "How does the *Merrimac* bear?"

In addition, the steam-driven turning wheel had rusted during the storm and Alban Stimers found it impossible to stop the turret on the firing bearing. "It finally resulted," Greene wrote, "that when a gun was ready for firing, the turret would be started on its revolving journey in search of the target, and when found, it was taken 'on the fly.'"

Sometime before noon Worden hauled off into shoal water to replenish the turret with powder and shot. Taking the opportunity to check the ramming damage he crawled on deck through a gunport, "lay down upon my chest, and examined it thoroughly."

Sharpshooters topside on the *Merrimack* opened fire, and their bullets, "were falling on the iron deck all about me as thick as hail-stones in a storm." Worden found one plate torn away but no damage to the hull. He stood up, walked back to the turret, and squeezed inside. In the few minutes before steaming back to the fight he told his drooping crew "that the *Merrimac* could not sink us if we let her pound us for a month. The men cheered; the knowledge put new life into all."

Ten yards off the *Merrimack*'s quarter, Worden's eyes were jammed into the pilothouse vision slit when John Taylor Wood fired his 7-inch rifle. The shell exploded right in Worden's face, it cracked the pilothouse iron, dismantled the roof, and drove a shower of iron splinters and gunpowder into Worden's face and eyes. Staggered, he threw up his hands. "My eyes," he screamed, "I am blind."

Seriously hit, the *Monitor* had not suffered critical damage, and was still very much in fighting trim. But Worden, left eye destroyed, his face pouring blood, could not know that. "Sheer off," he gasped to the helmsman.

Keeler scrambled up and helped his captain to the berth deck. Lieutenant Greene left Alban Stimers in charge of the turret and ran forward. Worden lay at the base of the pilothouse ladder. "He was a ghastly sight," Greene recalled, "with his eyes closed and the blood . . . rushing from every pore in the upper part of his face." Taken to his cabin, Worden turned over command to his young executive officer. "I leave it with you," he said, "do what you think best. I cannot see, but do not mind me. Save the *Minnesota* if you can."*

Greene held a hurried discussion with the ship's officers, and it was their unanimous decision to continue the battle. For about fifteen minutes, however, the *Monitor*'s helmsman, receiving no orders since "Sheer off," had opened the range. Greene pointed her back toward the *Merrimack* and maneuvered to reengage. He tried aiming his shots where the rebel's armor had already been torn away. "I thought I would keep right on pounding her as long as she would stand it," he said. But that lasted only for a couple of rounds. A problem developed with one of the pendulum shutters, and he steered for the Middle Ground Shoal.

It was now 12:15 P.M., and Catesby Jones assessed the situation. The *Monitor,* clearly damaged, had retired to shoal water, and he could not follow. The *Merrimack* was leaking from the bow, the men were exhausted, and the tide had begun to ebb; she must leave now or remain in the Roads for the night.

All in all, though, it had been another good day's work. The *Minnesota* was still aground, and Jones "did not believe that she could ever move again"; they would come tomorrow and finally finish her off. He visited the ship's divisions and put the question to his lieutenants: "I propose to return to Norfolk for repairs. What is your opinion?"

Ashton Ramsay felt they must withdraw. "Our ship," he wrote, "was working worse and worse," her smokestack was shot away, and he could hardly keep steam in the boilers. All the officers except John Taylor Wood recommended breaking off the action. Lieutenant Eggleston remembered Wood champing at the bit, and wanting to go down to Fort Monroe and "clean up the Yankee ships there or run them out to sea."

Listening to the counsel, Jones considered meeting the crisis halfway, to fall back on the batteries at Sewell's Point, wait for the tide, and attack again. He ordered Ramsay to bank his fires, "but be prepared to start up again later in the afternoon." After further thought, Jones changed his mind. To say nothing of carnage of the day before, the ship had been hit about twenty times *today.* There were damaged guns, the waterline rode ever higher due to expending coal and ammunition, and to deal with the *Monitor,* he needed full lockers of solid shot.

---

* Worden's face forevermore bore a grayish cast from the tiny iron splinters and black powder grains that embedded themselves permanently in his skin.

He ordered a course back up the Elizabeth River to Norfolk.

In the engine room, Ashton Ramsay was astonished to hear the *Merrimack*'s crew cheering. He went on deck to see Craney Island to starboard, and knew it was over. "I remember feeling as though a wet blanket had been thrown over me," he recalled years later. He did not question Jones' decision. Given the circumstances, it was the only correct one, "but it ignored the moral effect of leaving the Roads without forcing the *Minnesota* to surrender."

Lieutenant Greene followed the *Merrimack* for a time, and after some parting shots, turned away. He could not hazard running too close to the rebel batteries, "so I came back to the company of our friends."

At 12:30 P.M., the *Monitor* bore up to the *Minnesota* and let go the anchor. The hatches were thrown open and the men poured on deck. A score of vessels from Fort Monroe and Newport News surrounded her. Worden was taken off. Gus Fox came on board expecting to see a big butcher's bill, but with the exception of Worden and Stodder, there were no injuries. He joined the officers for lunch in the wardroom, and Keeler remembered "enjoying some good beef steak & green peas."

"Well, gentlemen," said the assistant secretary of the navy, "you don't look as though you were just through one of the greatest naval conflicts on record." "No, Sir," Lieutenant Greene answered, "we haven't done much fighting, merely drilling the men at the guns a little."

The fight had ended in a tactical draw, not a man killed in either ship. Strategically, however, it was an enormous Union victory. The blockade stood, and with it, the Confederacy lost its last real opportunity for European intervention.

Back at Norfolk, the *Merrimack* underwent extensive repairs. Old Buck, recuperating in his hospital bed and promoted to rear admiral, was replaced by Flag Officer Josiah Tattnall, Old Tat. In the *Monitor* Tom Selfridge took over temporary command and was shortly relieved by William Jeffers. In early April, General McClellan's host landed at Old Point and began their march up the York Peninsula to Richmond. Three more times the *Merrimack* sortied down the Elizabeth River and challenged the *Monitor* to another fight. But Jeffers, heeding orders, stayed safely under the guns of the Union shore batteries.

McClellan's advance broke the Confederate lines at Yorktown, and now the Army of the Potomac stood poised to race all the way to Richmond. The movement up the peninsula made the Confederate positions around Norfolk untenable and that meant the end of the *Merrimack*.

Dawn, May 9, found her anchored at Sewell's Point, and, to the shock of her crew, no Confederate flag flew on the battlements. Old Tat sent a boat ashore and learned the position had been abandoned during the night without informing him. Infinitely worse, Norfolk had been evacuated by the Confederacy; the navy yard was deserted and on fire. The *Merrimack* was trapped.

The pilots told Old Tat that if the ship were lightened by five feet they could get her up the James River almost to Richmond. Tattnall agreed; if nothing else, he could help defend the city against McClellan's advance. The fantail iron was pried up and jettisoned, as were all spare stores—everything except ammunition. Her waterline had been raised three feet when the pilots changed their mind. Westerly winds had kept the tides down, and they would not take the responsibility of moving her into the river.

"This extraordinary conduct of the pilots," said John Taylor Wood, "rendered some other plan immediately necessary." Faced with no alternative, Tattnall ordered the *Merrimack* destroyed. The crew landed, taking their side arms and two days' provisions. With a skeleton force, lieutenants Jones and Wood ran the vessel aground and set her afire. Before dawn, May 11, her magazine blew up, leaving hardly a trace of the ship. The crew marched overland and boarded the train for Richmond.

They found the capital in a panic. With the *Merrimack* threat eliminated, there was nothing to prevent the U.S. Navy from steaming up the James. Indeed, the Federals were coming "and the result," Wood said, "was great alarm." The *Merrimack*'s crew hurried seven miles south, to Drewry's Bluff, the first high ground below the city. "Here," Wood said, "for two days, exposed to constant rain, in bottomless mud and without shelter," they constructed a battery to defend the Confederate capital. The *Jamestown* and some other vessels that escaped Norfolk were sunk as blockships.

On May 15, a force of five vessels, headed by the *Galena* and *Monitor,* steamed up to Drewry's Bluff. The attack failed, the *Galena* suffering badly, and she withdrew with thirteen men killed and eleven wounded. The *Monitor* played virtually no role in this engagement—the 11-inch guns could not elevate enough to hit the target.

The *Monitor* stayed the summer in the James. Dana Greene remembered being "suffocated with heat and bad air if we remained below, and a target for sharpshooters if we came on deck."

During November, she underwent repairs and improvements at

Washington, and became the city's foremost tourist attraction. "They rushed in by thousands," Keeler wrote, noting that whole regiments, headed by their officers, marching to the navy yard "to see the sight." The number of women that came was considered extraordinary. "We couldn't go to any part of the vessel without coming in contact with petticoats," he informed his wife. "There appeared to be a general turn out of the sex in the city . . . [and] an extensive display of lower extremities was made going up & down our steep ladders."

From Hampton Roads, on December 29, 1862, under Commander John P. Bankhead, her fifth skipper, the *Monitor* set out in tow of the storeship *Rhode Island* for blockade and bombardment duty at Charleston. For a time, all was well, until the winds blew hard and green seas again broke over the pilothouse. Off Cape Hatteras her nightmare voyage from New York was reenacted, only worse. More than once slamming down into a trough, the tremendous shock loosed the joint between the iron deck and lower hull.

The overhang at the bow gave way, and the inrush of water into her vitals could not be stemmed. Even with the pumps working and bucket details bailing like madmen, water was soon a foot deep in the engine room. The *Rhode Island* lowered boats to take off the crew, but twenty-one men, eight of them from the storeship, were lost. At 1:30 A.M., December 31, the *Monitor* disappeared into the waves.

Stinkpots and Turtles

"Let not your heart be troubled: ye believe in God, believe also in the gunboats."

—**young niece of Rear Admiral Andrew H. Foote, USN**

T he Mississippi River, the natural highway through North America, played a supreme role in the Civil War, and the naval operations on its broad, muddy waters contributed decisively to the defeat of the Confederacy. For the Union, conquest of the lower river—Cairo, Illinois, to the Gulf of Mexico—holds equal strategic rank with the coastal blockade and Sherman's march from Atlanta to the sea in winning the war.

It was a most arduous campaign, grinding down both ships and men, and not ending until the fall of Vicksburg in July 1863. With that triumph, the Union's control of the continental aorta severed off a third of the Confederacy and extended the naval blockade along the full inland seam of the military frontier.

For the Confederacy, *its* control of the Mississippi at any point was as good as holding it all. Not until every rebel battery and ram from Kentucky to the Gulf was cleared from the banks would one Northern hog, bushel of corn, or sack of flour pass down the Father of Waters. For the Lincoln administration, the opening of the Mississippi to national commerce was as vital an economic issue as its military aim of splitting the Confederacy asunder.

After first securing the line of the Ohio, the Anaconda plan of Winfield Scott envisioned a methodical advance by troops and gunboats down the river to New Orleans, there to rendezvous with the Gulf blockaders and complete the gigantic encirclement of the eastern Confederacy. Old Scott's formula was correct and would be doggedly followed until the Union capped its western victory in the summer of 1863.

The government's military departments were not the sole catalysts in devising the western strategy. Right after the surrender of Fort Sumter, James B. Eads, a wealthy St. Louis businessman and engineer, wrote to his friend, and fellow Missourian, Attorney General Bates that "vigorous action must be taken to defeat the South." What Eads had in mind was an interior blockade, halting the movement of the Confederacy's food and war material along the Mississippi. Six months, he thought, and the South would be starved into surrender.

President of the Missouri Wrecking Company and as intimate with the river as anyone, Eads suggested converting one of his steam-driven "snag boats," into a gunboat. "With $2,000 or $3,000 worth of cotton bales arranged properly upon her," he wrote, "she could be made exceedingly effective for offense or defense." Bates replied within a week. "Be not surprised if you are called here suddenly by telegram. If called, come instantly."

On April 29, Eads addressed the assembled Cabinet in the White House. The members, with the exception of Secretary of War Cameron, rallied to the idea of building an inland navy for service on the lower river. Gideon Welles invited Eads to submit his thoughts directly to the Navy Department, causing Cameron to reverse himself simply as a parochial matter of guarding the army's turf. He announced the navy had no legal authority over inland waters; that river gunboats and their operations were strictly the army's domain. The navy, however, could send competent officers to command individual vessels and advise on purchasing and conversion to arms. The Cabinet, including Welles, agreed, and Eads returned to St. Louis to await the government's pondering.

Some weeks later, Major General George McClellan then commanding the Department of the Ohio, was told that a naval officer had been assigned to his headquarters. Welles picked a good one, Commander John Rodgers, ocean surveyor and explorer, veteran of thirty-three years service with much experience in steam technology, and a member of the United States' leading naval family.

Welles drew Rodgers' attention to the anomalous nature of the assignment. Riverine operations, or "interior nonintercourse" as he put it, were the army's province. But for the gunboats' crew, armament, and stores, Rodgers would call, "by proper requisition," of course, upon the navy. It was, frankly, an inefficient way of running a war. Its consequences were felt soon enough, and the arrangement would not last.

George McClellan was well pleased that an officer of Rodgers' standing and ability had been assigned to him. Having no clear idea of the sort of naval force necessary to support an offensive, he permitted Rodgers a free hand in cobbling together the early river fleet. The first priority, he told Rodgers, were some gunboats to defend his base at Cairo, terminus of the Illinois Central Railroad and the jump-off point for the whole western offensive. The strategically placed "city of stinks" was a dismal river town. "When the world was made," said a local wag, "the refuse materials were washed up at the junction of the Ohio and Mississippi and the composite is Cairo. It is, in fact, nature's excrementitious deposit."

To help Rodgers in his quest for suitable craft, Welles ordered out Naval Constructor Samuel Pook, who once feared the secretary was going to hang him over a converted merchantman gone bad. Pook's first task involved the inspection of three new sidewheelers that Rodgers had chosen on the Ohio River: *Tyler, Lexington,* and *Conestoga.* Rodgers bought the steamers at the bargain price of $62,000, "for naval service in these waters." As an investment in the war, they would pay large dividends. Pook advised cutting their high sides down to the main deck and building a bulwark of oak planking to protect the crews against small arms fire. In addition, they would have to be considerably strengthened internally with stout timbers and beams to carry a naval battery of any weight.

The disparity between the navy's deep-hulled oceangoing steamers and these floating wooden "bandboxes" was starkly evident in their engineering plants, which were above water. Pook half solved the dangerous problem by dropping the boilers and steam pipes from the main deck into the vessels' shallow holds. As for the "black gang"—stokers, boiler tenders, and engineers—Rodgers sought the navy's permission to engage the men locally.* "The management of these engines in the

---

* All engineering personnel in the U.S. Navy, even to the present day, are called the "black gang." This has nothing to do with race, but with the arduous, dirty job of servicing a coal-fired plant. As it happened, during the Civil War, many of the black gang, especially coal heavers, were indeed black, either freed slaves or enlisted black citizens of the North.

muddy waters of the Mississippi," he said, "requires a peculiar experience." The boats would be ready, he wrote the secretary, in less than three weeks, "the united crews being 198 souls."

Gideon Welles' response was small-minded, militarily shortsighted, and out of character. He admonished Rodgers for vastly exceeding the original orders to merely submit requests for armament and crews. "The movement in that quarter pertains to the Army and not the Navy. Nor must the two branches of service become complicated and embarrassed by ... any attempt at a combined movement on the rivers." As for the three gunboats, "they are not wanted for naval purposes." Welles officially disavowed Rodgers' contracts.

Fortunately George McClellan was at the top of his administrative form. He had asked Rodgers to get him the nucleus of a fleet, and Rodgers, with hardly a bother, had done it. Without hesitation McClellan endorsed the bills for the three steamers on behalf of the War Department. The army now had a trio of perfectly serviceable vessels undergoing conversion into river gunboats that would shortly require naval officers, crews, guns, and ammunition.

However, once the ownership question had been resolved, Welles saw no reason to renege on his promise to provide their ordnance. Rodgers had his pick from the navy's depot at Erie, Pennsylvania, and he came away with ten 8-inch Dahgrens and seven 32-pounders, heavy metal for what had once been peaceful, pine-clad vessels plying the Ohio River.

In July, at Cincinnati, Rodgers chartered a small steamer for a receiving ship, tied her at the levee and started recruiting for what was officially the United States Army's Western Gunboat Flotilla. It was very discouraging, with fewer than thirty men signed the first week, but that wasn't his only problem.

Rodgers had contracted with a local firm, the Marine Railway and Drydock Company of Cincinnati, to convert the "stinkpots" as they were now called, into serviceable gunboats. The company was already a month late on the job when Rodgers' assistant, the magnificently side-whiskered navy Lieutenant Sam Phelps, inspected the progress. Phelps was appalled at the shoddy work.* There were no boat davits, nor iron over the boilers, nor hatchways to the upper deck, nor entrance to the pilothouse. "The more I examine the work on the *Conestoga*," he

---

* The word "shoddy" actually entered the language during the Civil War as a substitute material for making uniforms. It was described by *Harper's Monthly,* as "the refuse, stuff and sweepings of the shop, pounded, rolled, glued, and smoothed to the external form and gloss of cloth ... the shadow ... to the substance."

reported, "the more disgraceful patching it appears to be. The *Lexington* is best done, but none well, and the joiner-work all round is more like the work of Irish laborers than of mechanics."

Then came supply problems. The navy had no understanding with the army's quartermasters over the responsibility of supplying these ships. Perhaps aware of the futility of complaining, Rodgers, on his personal line of credit, bought quantities of dried beef, vegetables, crockery, flatware, pillow cases, mattresses, hammock canvas, chairs, skillets, and lamp wicks for the stinkpots' galleys, wardrooms, and berthing spaces.

It was now high summer and the Ohio River fell. Rodgers, alarmed that the still-unfinished gunboats might be stranded by low water at Cincinnati, managed to enlist enough men to work the boats downriver to Cairo. The boats, without their guns drew less than six feet of water, but still they grounded at the Louisville shoals. Sam Phelps hired some local dredges to scoop a channel, but the cut filled almost as fast as the buckets emptied their muck. Rodgers then hired the river correspondent of the *Cincinnati Daily Commercial* to prepare a statistical table of the Ohio River covering the past seven years. He calculated a five-to-one chance the water would rise enough in late July to get the boats over the shoals.

During the anxious wait, Phelps continued the fitting-out work nonstop. "There is no paint for the boats," he wrote. The craft were still unarmed and there were constant rumors that pro-Southern mobs planned to seize them in a raid. Phelps begged thirty muskets from the army and distributed them among his skeleton crews.

Shortages were everywhere. Phelps reported his dissatisfaction with the poor quality of enlisted personnel. "I am not pleased with the river men material. We ought to have some few old men-of-war men. . . . Clothes and hammocks would encourage enlistments." As for the handful of naval officers, some pettifogging Treasury auditor had determined they were not entitled to sea pay. As Rodgers' agent had predicted, the river rose enough to move the steamers. The *Tyler* and *Lexington* dragged the *Conestoga* over the shoals, and on August 12, they secured to the wharf at Cairo.

While Rodgers and company sweated through the summer, Constructor Samuel Pook made a quick study in shallow-draft design, and came to understand what most naval officers did not. That river craft, plying tideless, waveless natural highways, require almost none of the sleek, seakeeping features that characterize bluewater shipping.

Instead of a "conventional" design, Pook proposed a hull that resembled nothing so much as a piece of rye bread—175 feet long, a chunky 51 feet in the beam, flat-bottomed, drawing six feet of water, and having a speed of about eight knots. Atop the hull, he placed an angled, oaken casemate plated with 2½ inches of iron slabs forward and abreast the machinery. Over this, rose an octagonal, iron-sheathed pilothouse. Ports were cut for thirteen big guns. Rationalizing that in confined waters the craft would likely fight bows-on, the three heaviest pieces pointed forward. The remaining guns were placed four on either side, and two aft.

Pook dispensed entirely with exposed sidewheels, and instead designed a single, centerline wheel completely enclosed within the after portion of the casemate. Unfortunately, because of a design flaw and weight restrictions, the vessels had a couple of tender points where the iron plating did not reach. Rodgers rectified this by increasing the casemate's oak to twenty-four inches, but it proved not enough.

Yet they were very powerful vessels, squat, hunkering, and menacing in their aspect, the first purpose-built ironclads in the Western Hemisphere.* "If well handled," Rodgers said, "these boats will be most formidable adversaries." They were immediately dubbed "Pook turtles."

On August 5, 1861, army Quartermaster General Montgomery Meigs opened the construction bids and awarded the building contract to James Eads. The St. Louis engineer blithely promised to deliver seven gunboats at $89,000 each, "including engines, boilers & iron plating" by October 10, an incredibly short time, or forfeit $250 per day, per boat, for every day beyond the deadline. An editorialist for the *St. Louis Democrat,* breezily noted, "We hazard nothing in saying that the whole fleet will be ready to deal out death and terror to traitors by . . . the time set for their delivery to the government."

Within weeks Eads had 4,000 men mining, foresting, milling, blacksmithing, and fabricating parts in seven states stretching from Pennsylvania to Minnesota. He leased facilities at Carondelet, just outside St. Louis, and offered bonuses to all who labored for the entire project; work went on around the clock. As the historian Reverend Charles Boynton wrote, "Neither the sanctity of the Sabbath nor the darkness of night was permitted to interrupt it."

---

* The *St. Louis'* bottom was laid down on September 27, 1861, nearly a month before the *Monitor*'s. The first ironclad of any sort in the Western Hemisphere was the Confederate *Manassas,* converted from a wooden tug sometime during the summer of 1861.

*   *   *

In late July 1861, George McClellan went east to the Army of the Potomac and his place was taken by Major General John Frémont. Popularly known as the "Pathfinder of the West," he was, in reality, an unstable, self-promoting puffer, who had been the 1856 Republican presidential nominee. Arriving in St. Louis, he quickly demonstrated his inability to command a rapidly expanding army facing a dangerously complex military situation.

From the first, he found Commander John Rodgers an irritating presence, especially because of Rodgers' friendship with Quartermaster General Montgomery Meigs (in fact, they were brothers-in-law). The Pathfinder, however, still had some high political connections. "It would serve the public interest," he wrote Postmaster General Blair, "if Commander John Rodgers were removed. . . . Show this to the President."

By late summer, the stinkpots were ready for their first foray. On August 12, eager to make "an excursion," Rodgers distributed his personnel between the *Tyler* and *Conestoga,* obtained some ammunition from local army stores, and steamed downriver to New Madrid, Missouri. They found nothing of worth, and chuffed back to Cairo. A week later Rodgers steamed upriver from Cairo to subdue some thousand marauding rebels at Commerce, Missouri. On sighting the gunboats, the rebels broke camp, taking with them fifty wagons of looted corn and doing much property damage, according to Rodgers, "breaking furniture, carrying off and tearing up women and children's clothes."

That same day Welles uncharacteristically caved in to the political hacks. A letter went out over Gus Fox's signature ordering Captain Andrew H. Foote, commanding the Brooklyn Navy Yard, "to report in person at the Department." Rodgers' days in the West were numbered.

The ax fell on August 3, when Rodgers was, precisely, in the face of the enemy. Welles handled the matter badly, but the relief was justified on one very important point. Rodgers' relatively low rank pulled no weight with the army's bureaucrats on whom he completely depended for his beef, bread, and bullets—to say nothing of the fact that it left him open to being kicked around operationally, which any amateur colonel of volunteers might legally do. Someone of senior rank, stature, and reputation was necessary, and Andy Foote, boyhood schoolmate of Gideon Welles, was the perfect candidate.

The bearded, mastiff-jawed Foote was one of those naval officers who looked as if they had walked out of the prophetic pages of the Old

Testament. Foote was zealously religious, a naval Savonarola, albeit a humane one. Appointed acting midshipman in 1822, he saw continual service around the world, fighting pirates in Sumatra, slavers off West Africa, and in 1856, during the Anglo-Chinese Arrow War personally leading a naval landing force against the Chinese Barrier Forts at Canton. As a junior officer, Foote habitually carried a "colt," a length of knotted rope, in his cap ready for instant use against laggardly posteriors. A fanatic in the temperance movement, Foote, when executive officer of the *Cumberland,* turned her into the navy's first "dry" ship, and led the fight that saw the end of hard liquor in the navy in 1862.* Now on the train to Cairo, Foote's orders were "to take command of the naval operations upon the western waters."

The stinkpots were on the move. On September 3, substantial Confederate forces under the Episcopal bishop General Leonidas Polk marched into Columbus, Kentucky, just twenty miles below Cairo. The next day, at the request of a dumpy, unknown brigadier named Ulysses S. Grant, Rodgers took the *Tyler* and *Lexington* to reconnoiter the rebel positions. South of Columbus they spotted the armed steamer *Jackson* and gave chase.

The rebel craft ran down to Hickman, Kentucky, where Rodgers spied the enemy's tents along the riverbank. Confederate field artillery made uncomfortably close practice. The swift river current carried his boats dangerously close to the enemy's guns, "with which we were in no condition to cope, having very little powder on board and only half enough gun tackles for working the battery." Returning the fire with a few shots, Rodgers discreetly ordered the stinkpots back up the river.

On September 5, Grant kicked off the Mississippi valley campaign, which would end nearly two years later at the surrender of Vicksburg. Rodgers, taking the *Tyler* and *Conestoga,* convoyed the general and 2,000 men up the Ohio to Paducah at the mouth of the Tennessee River.

As it happened, Foote had just arrived in Cairo, and at midnight set off aboard a fast steamer. Within a few hours he overhauled the *Tyler* and presented Rodgers with the unexpected news of his relief. "He behaved well," Foote said, "officer-like and gentlemanly." Approaching Paducah, several Confederate flags were clearly seen flying over the town. As Foote reported, "we were at our guns ready to respond to

---

* The teetotaling, pacifist Secretary of the Navy Josephus Daniels banned all nonmedicinal alcohol in 1914.

masked batteries, but found none." The troops landed unopposed. With the taking of Paducah, Grant had outflanked the rebels at Columbus. Better, he now possessed an advance base for a deep strike into the enemy's middle that would save Kentucky for the Union and force the rebels to evacuate all of western Tennessee.

The next foray of the stinkpots covered a Federal advance along the west bank of the Mississippi. Below Columbus, Lieutenant Phelps discovered "the enemy in force," on the Missouri side. Exploding shells from the gunboats burst among their cavalry "with apparent great effect." Phelps turned about and headed north, when up from Columbus came the rebel steamer *Jackson*. The *Lexington*'s skipper loaded one of his 8-inch guns with a long-fused shell, and at maximum elevation let fly. "I had the satisfaction," he reported, "of seeing the shell explode in her starboard [paddle]wheel house, careening her smokestack, and otherwise crippling her."

Back to Cairo went the stinkpots, pleased with the day's work. Indeed, they had every right to be. Confederate General Leonidas Polk wrote to Stephen Mallory, "The gunboats the enemy have now in the Mississippi River are giving us most serious annoyance." Without at least one armed boat of his own, Polk told the Confederate Navy secretary, "our operations would be very seriously obstructed, if not to an extent paralyzed." The bishop-general was a prophet as well.

For paralysis, however, Polk needn't have looked farther than the turtles, whose building pace mirrored their nickname. Eads' skilled artisans, earning two dollars for a ten-hour day, plus twenty-five cents an hour overtime, threatened to strike for still higher wages. To speed things up, Eads contracted with the Mound City Marine Railway and Ship Yard to build three of the turtles nearby on the Ohio. By mid-September, Eads was nearly broke. The government owed him thousands of dollars, and he hadn't a dime to buy the engineering plants for the Mound City boats. Almost daily he pleaded with the War and Treasury departments for funds, but there wasn't enough to pay every clamoring war contractor, even honest ones like James Eads.

The turtles' heavy guns came late, a motley combination, old and new, good and bad, from the navy and army ordnance bureaus. The most notorious guns were a bunch of antiquated army 42-pounders, bored out to 8-inch rifles, whose ammunition didn't always fit. None of the naval officers trusted them to serve well in battle—and they were right.

The Eagle Iron Works of Cincinnati received the contract for the
gun carriages, and didn't have the first idea of what to do. Its chief engineer wrote to a "Mr. Chase, of the State Department," for a copy of "the
Naval Ordnance Manual." The letter was passed to Gideon Welles,
whose reply—"The Department has no such work as you describe."—
pointlessly split hairs. Even the peach-fuzziest midshipman was aware
of the tome entitled *Ordnance Instructions for the United States Navy,*
which was known throughout the service as the "Ordnance Manual."

On Saturday, October 12, forty-five days after laying her first
planks, and two days after *all* the turtles were supposed to be delivered
complete to Cairo, the first ironclad designed and built in the Western
Hemisphere, was, an observer noted, "gradually lowered into the
'father of waters' . . . and such was the noiseless, and almost impercepti-
ble manner of the operation, that we found the boat floating gracefully
upon the water, and nobody hurt, and not even a lady frightened." In
their launching sequence, the immortal seven took the names of river
cities: *Carondelet, St. Louis, Louisville, Pittsburg, Mound City, Cincinnati,* and *Cairo.*

The stinkpots ranged freely about the rivers. In October, Phelps in the
Conestoga moved up the Ohio, turned right at Paducah, and ascended
the Tennessee within sight of the rebels' Fort Henry. Along the banks
he found foundries hammering the plate for three steamers the Confederates were converting into ironclads farther upriver. A week later, he
took the *Conestoga* sixty miles up the Cumberland River to the bridge at
Eddyville, Kentucky, "a neighborhood where Union men have been
driven from their homes. . . . I found it necessary," he reported, "to use
strong language to the citizens in regard to the persecution of Union
people."

In November 1861, the army underwent a senior command shake-up.
The venerable Winfield Scott passed into retirement and was replaced
by George McClellan. In the West, Lincoln relieved the dashingly ineffective Frémont with the bumptiously ineffective Major General Henry
Halleck. Known in military circles as "Old Brains," Halleck spent most
of his energy preserving his reputation as a military intellectual, and all
of his time in preventing things from happening.

On the day Old Brains arrived in St. Louis, Foote paid a call to
inquire of some mortar scows, about which there was great delay. "May
I fit out the mortar boats?" he asked. "No," Halleck answered, "it cannot
be done." Foote wrote to Welles with his opinion of the new theater

commander. "Halleck," Foote insisted, was "a military imbecile, though he might make a good clerk."

At Cairo, on November 6, Grant loaded 3,000 men into six steamers, and with *Tyler* and *Lexington* in the van, dropped downriver to keep an eye on the rebels at Columbus, Kentucky. They came soon enough. The next morning Grant learned that a sizable rebel force had crossed over from Columbus and established a fortified camp on the Missouri side, at Belmont. He asked Commander Henry Walke in the *Tyler* to keep the enemy busy at Columbus, while he attacked the new outpost.

By midmorning, Federal troops were ashore and moving on the town. Walke, a talented pen and ink artist who often sketched the battle as he fought, maneuvered to bring the gunboats against the rebel batteries on the cliffs at Iron Bank. The rebels fired high, but in so doing, their shot landed uncomfortably near Grant's transports. Walke broke off the engagement, and with steam whistles and hails, ordered the steamers to keep out of range.

At noon, while Grant waged the battle ashore, Henry Walke renewed the contest at Iron Bank. This time, however, the plunging fire of the Confederate guns found their mark. A round shot banged into the *Tyler.* It "struck us on the starboard bulwarks," Walke remembered, "and continuing . . . through the spar deck took off the head of Michael Adams . . . and broke the arm and otherwise seriously injured James Wolfe." The stinkpots, "such frail vessels," Walke said after the action, had no business trading shot and shell with entrenched batteries, and "were only expected to protect the land forces in case of a repulse." After a parting broadside, Walke cocked an ear to the west bank. Where there had been the clash of musketry, Walke heard nothing. He thought it "an ominous circumstance."

The battle, at first, had gone well for Grant. His men drove the rebels out of Belmont to the riverbank. But instead of pushing the assault home, the green troops took to looting the enemy camp. Grant had his hands full regaining control and in the time it took to re-form, the rebels ferried over reinforcements. Grant had no choice but to fall back. Unaware of the situation, Walke brought the gunboats to the landing stage. The transports, which had retired upriver, took their leisure coming down, and until then, there was nothing, save the two stinkpots, between Grant and disaster. It wouldn't be the last time.

When the dilatory steamers arrived, the rebels, Walke remembered, came crashing "*en masse* through a cornfield, and opened a desperate fire of musketry and ... artillery upon ... our retreating soldiers." The stinkpots blasted the packed enemy with grapeshot, and the results were devastating. "The enemy's artillery," he recalled, "was seen tumbling over, and his ranks were soon broken." Grant and his little army were saved.

However gratified by the success of his gunboats, Foote was outraged that he had known nothing of the operation. Grant had simply "forgotten" to inform his naval commander, issuing the orders directly to Henry Walke. It was a situation directly traceable to Foote's inferior status. Even as a lofty captain, the navy's highest statutory rank, he was still junior to a brigadier general, and he would tolerate it no more. "I can not much longer serve effectively," he wrote Secretary Welles, "unless rank is given me corresponding to my command and its responsibilities." On November 18, Foote was elevated to flag officer, ranking him with a major general.

The Western Gunboat Flotilla, however, was still the poor cousin. "We cannot from either Army or Navy get any powder," Foote wrote to Gus Fox, and he was forced to beg the governor of Indiana for a bargeload of inferior state militia stuff. Also, "we are refused swords, pistols, rifles and muskets with cartridges by both Army and Navy. I am trying to get clothing, also, refused by both."

There were never enough men. When Foote appealed, someone at the department remembered the 500 sailors still guarding Washington from Shuter's Hill, and off they went. Yet so pressing were the needs of the whole navy for personnel, that Fox had the temerity to ask Foote if *he* had any officers to spare. "We have," the flag officer tartly replied, "barely officers enough, with all well and on duty, for *one* to each vessel."

For the burgeoning flotilla, soon to include not only the stinkpots and turtles, but two big snag boats converting into similar ironclads, *Benton* and *Essex,* Foote needed over a thousand new hands. McClellan, for one, understood, and ordered 1,100 unarmed soldiers into the turtles. Grant was also willing to transfer forty chronic drunks to the flotilla. "Things brighten a little ahead," Foote wrote.

On January 16, just over three months after their contract dates, the seven turtles were commissioned into the Western Gunboat Flotilla. Henry Walke, senior commander of the stinkpots, moved into the *Carondelet.* In his new crew, he had "more young men perhaps than on any other vessel in the fleet ... and just enough men-o'-war's men to leaven the lump with naval discipline."

*   *   *

The Confederate forward defense line extended from Columbus, east 180 miles across Kentucky to Bowling Green, a key railroad junction connecting Louisville, Nashville, and Memphis. To the Union officers, the obvious point to assault this line was in the center, up the bisecting natural highways of the Tennessee and Cumberland rivers. Control of these rivers would sever the Confederacy's northernmost lateral railroad, open a way into Alabama, outflank every rebel position on the Mississippi above Memphis, and lead straight to Nashville, a huge rebel manufacturing, military, and communications hub.

There were two obstacles to this approach: Confederate Major General Albert Sidney Johnston and Union General Henry Halleck. To defend the two rivers the Confederates had erected forts Henry and Donelson, and until they were reduced, no one was going anywhere. As for Halleck, the problem was in convincing Old Brains to take the initiative. Grant and Foote devised a basic plan to storm the forts with a combined force of turtles and troops. Halleck, Grant said, thought the operation "preposterous." He would permit nothing but a "demonstration"—a feint—to mask the main army's deliberate movements marching down the railroad line from Louisville.

Grant and Foote tried it again with Old Brains, this time almost challenging him to refuse. "With permission," Grant said, "I will take Fort Henry." When Foote kept badgering about the onset of low water, Halleck finally committed himself to the action, though not before piling on "detailed instructions" that his field commanders simply ignored.

Lieutenant Sam Phelps steamed up the Tennessee with the *Lexington* and *Conestoga* to do some advance scouting. At daylight, January 31, 1862, he came up to Panther Island just below the fort, finding the river in "good stage." In the main channel were spotted numerous buoys, which Phelps rightly suspected marked the location of "some kind of explosive machine." On February 1, Foote ordered the flotilla, four turtles and the stinkpots, to rendezvous at Paducah. The next morning Grant, with 17,000 men packed into several dozen transports, moved out from Cairo.

Waiting for the army to arrive, Foote issued the instructions for what one historian has aptly called an "experimental battle." For the first time, American sailors in American ironclads were to be tested in action. The turtles would fight in line-abreast, bows-on to the enemy. Foote granted that their first shots might be off target, but warned, "there is no excuse for a second wild fire . . . random firing is not a mere waste of ammunition, but it encourages the enemy." The first priority was to dismount the enemy guns.

The weather was unseasonably warm, and the winter ice in the Tennessee had melted away. Early rains flooded the tributary streams, and all vessels easily breasted the swift-flowing water. At 4:30 A.M., on a wet February 4, Confederate Colonel Adolphus Heiman, commander of Fort Henry, was shaken awake by his orderly. A rocket had just been fired by the pickets at Bailey's Landing, three miles off. Then three more rockets went up, signaling the gunboats' approach. Heiman ordered his drummers to beat the long roll. The sleepy garrison turned out, eleven heavy guns bearing on the river were manned and loaded, and a courier started the twelve-mile gallop to General Lloyd Tilghman, the district commander at Fort Donelson.

Until he arrived, it was Heiman's responsibility to hold the line— not a cheery thought. Whoever had chosen the Tennessee's east bank muddy bottomland for Fort Henry was no engineer. An entire company's only duty was "trying to keep the water out of the fort." The magazine already had two feet of water, and ammunition had to be moved aboveground, where it was protected only by sandbags. The defenders numbered about 3,400 men. But with the exception of two regiments (less than a quarter of the total) they were raw recruits. Heiman recalled, "They were not drilled, were badly equipped, and very indifferently armed with shotguns and [hunting] rifles." In addition, camp sanitation was awful and sickness had whittled the garrison down to 2,600 men fit for duty.

At daylight, the Confederate outposts reported the fleet coming up. Captain Jesse Taylor, a rebel artillery officer formerly of the U.S. Navy, remembered: "Far as the eye could see, the course of the river could be traced by the dense volumes of smoke issuing from the flotilla—indicating that the long-threatened attempt to break our lines was about to be made in earnest."

At noon, the turtles crept in sight. They advanced cautiously, testing the defenses. When about two miles off, the boats crabbed into line-abreast and opened fire. After a short, ineffective exchange, the flotilla withdrew.

General Tilghman arrived at the fort in late afternoon, and a council of war revealed every weakness. He ordered the garrison to escape overland, east to Fort Donelson, while he, his staff, and fifty-four gunners remained to hold the position in a desperate rear-guard fight. "To this end," he said, "I bent every effort."

.*   *   *

Grant intended landing his troops as close to the fort as possible. To reconnoiter suitable points along the riverbanks, he boarded the iron-clad *Essex,* commanded by David Porter's brother, "Dirty Bill." After they had gone some distance the guns of Fort Henry searched them out. On the second fire they hit the *Essex* on her upper deck, right where Grant and Bill Porter were standing. According to Second Master James Laning, an army volunteer officer, the solid shot penetrated into the casemate, through the officers' quarters, "visiting in its flight the ... commander's pantry and cabin, passing through the stern; doing, however, no damage except breaking some of the captain's dishes, and cutting the feet from a pair of his socks ... hanging over the back of a chair." Porter ordered the engines full aback. The troops, Grant decided, would have to march some sodden distance overland to reach the fort.

Watching from the earthen ramparts, Captain Jesse Taylor described the next day as one "of unwonted animation on the hitherto quiet waters of the Tennessee ... the flood-tide of arriving and departing transports continued ceaselessly."

That afternoon Foote visited the gunboats. James Laning remembered him admonishing the *Essex*'s crew not to throw any ammunition away. "Every charge you fire costs the government about eight dollars." At the time of sunset, the low, gray sky burst apart, sending the already flooded river to new heights of chaos. Great bulwarks of rushing flotsam, including whole trees torn out by their roots, piled up around the bows of the vessels. "The swift current," recalled Henry Walke, "brought down an immense quantity of heavy drift-wood, lumber, fences, and it required all the steam-power of the *Carondelet,* with both anchors down, and the most strenuous exertions of the officers and crew ... to prevent the boat from being dragged down-stream."

Thursday dawned in deep mist. The *Carondelet*'s lookouts spotted a number of large, white objects, "which through the fog," said Henry Walke, "looked like polar bears, coming down the stream." These were the mines that Sam Phelps had guessed lay beneath the surface of the river, torn from their hidden moorings by the swift moving current. Walke signaled the danger to the flag officer. Foote didn't immediately comprehend their considerable danger, that one bump would have sent any of his vessels to the bottom. Only when several were reported floating down on the flagship *Cincinnati* did he order the stinkpots to lower boats and begin a full day's careful work, dragging them ashore.

A breeze came up, Walke remembered, "mild and cheering," which cleared the fog and invigorated the tired crews; the warships hoisted anchor and got underway. Fighting the river, the ships took most of an hour to steam the three miles up to Panther island, where trees gave some concealment before the advance to the guns.

Thrashing in the van, line-abreast, left to right, steamed the *St. Louis,* the *Carondelet,* the flagship *Cincinnati,* and the *Essex.* Behind them, in the second line, came the stinkpots. Walke recalled the scene well: "As we slowly passed up this narrow stream, not a sound could be heard nor a moving object seen in the dense woods which overhung the dark and swollen river." Inside the iron casemates, the gun crews waited silently. Behind each piece stood its gun captain, one single, precious, saltwater sailor of the Regular Navy, firing lanyard in hand. At noon, Fort Henry and its red-barred Confederate flag came suddenly in view.

Captain Jesse Taylor of the rebel artillery watched the turtles creep inexorably forward, "until as they swung into the main channel . . . they showed one broad and leaping sheet of flame."

The *Cincinnati's* opening gun commenced the engagement. In the *Essex,* James Laning waited until he could see the effect of her shooting. As he recalled, the flagship's first three shots "fell short, so there was $24 worth of ammunition expended." He ordered a slight increase in elevation. "The No. 2 port-bow gun belched forth her fiery flame, and sent a 9-inch shell plumb into the breastworks, which exploding handsomely, caused a considerable scattering of earth, and called forth a cheer from the fleet." Slowly the turtles closed the range. Fifteen-second fuses were cut to ten, then five seconds. Gun elevations came down nearly flat, "and every shot went straight home."

Fort Henry's gunners wasted no time in replying. "At once," Henry Walke recalled, "the fort was ablaze with the flame of her heavy guns. The wild whistle of their rifle shells was heard on every side of us." And they were scoring hits. Eight heavy projectiles struck within two feet of the *Carondelet's* gunports, "and scattered our iron plating as if it had been putty." Walke remembered more than one solid shot passing completely through the casemate, "but our old men-of-war's men infused life and courage into their young comrades. When [they] saw a shot coming toward a gun port, they had the coolness and discretion to order their men to bow down, to save their heads."

Thirty minutes into the battle, someone told Dirty Bill Porter in the *Essex* that officers on the other ironclads were quitting their exposed upper decks. "Oh, yes, I see," he said, "we will go too, directly." A shot then struck the *Essex*'s pilothouse. The iron plates lay somewhere back in St. Louis, and deadly splinters of naked oak whizzed the air. Porter ordered everyone below.

Shouting above the din, he congratulated the bow gunners "for their splendid execution," ordering them relieved by the men in the stern battery who had yet to fire a shot. A few were reluctant to quit the post of the hottest action and hung back. Then, James Laning said, "in the twinkling of an eye the scene was changed from a blaze of glory to a carnival of death and destruction."

Henry Walke recorded the scene in his memoirs. "S. B. Brittan, Jr., master's mate was standing between the captain and paymaster when the top of his head was shot off, scattering the brains over their clothes." The 32-pounder ball then smashed through an interior bulkhead into one of the boilers. A hideous brew of gaseous fires, tons of boiling water, and a wall of superheated steam shot through the forward end of the *Essex*'s casemate and up the hatchway into the pilothouse.

The helmsman was killed instantly, his clothing and skin flayed away. "The scene," Laning remembered, "was almost indescribable. The dead man, transformed into a hideous apparition, was still at the wheel, standing erect, his left hand holding the spoke, and his right hand grasping the signal bell-rope.... A seaman named James Coffey ... was on his knees in the act of taking a shell from the box to be passed to the loader. The escaping steam ... had struck him square in the face, and he met death in that position."

Men hurled themselves through the gunports to avoid being scalded, some managed to grab handholds on the low hull, but others were swept away in the river. Bill Porter, badly scalded, flung himself in agony through a gunport and was saved by an alert seaman who dragged him back in. Laning, the only unwounded officer, ordered the boats lowered. Guns still firing, the badly mauled *Essex,* thirty men killed, wounded, and missing, drifted slowly downriver, out of the battle.

From inside Fort Henry, Jesse Taylor noticed "the fleet seemed to hesitate." But it was only for a moment. "His shot and shell penetrated our earth-works as readily as a ball from a navy Colt would pierce a pine board." One after another, the fort's guns were knocked out, until only four were capable of fire. The *Carondelet,* whose shells had done a good part of the damage, was struck about ten times. "She was the object of our hatred," a Confederate gunner later said, "and many a gun from the fort was leveled at her alone." The flagship *Cincinnati* came in for her share. Conspicuous by Foote's broad pennant, her entire upper works were riddled. Walke saw a heavy solid shot hit her broadside. "It had the effect, apparently, of a thunderbolt," ripping her side timbers and scattering splinters over the vessel. But she steamed on "as though nothing unexpected had happened." Her skipper reported only one man killed, "head shot away."

It was nearing 4:00 P.M. In the reeking smoke of the battle, General Lloyd Tilghman looked around at the dead, the maimed, the useless artillery with muzzles pointing at crazy angles. "It was now plain to be seen," he noted, "that the enemy were breaking the fort directly in front of our guns." He found a white rag, "which I waved from the parapet myself." But no one in the flotilla saw it, and after five more minutes of furious cannonading, which Henry Walke described as "throwing tons of earth over the prostrated gunners," Tilghman, on the advice of his officers, hauled down the stars and bars.

Continuing their approach in rigid formation, the gunboats held fire and there came a bit of comedy. The *St. Louis*'s crew, released from the agony of battle, broke into wild cheers. The turtle broke line, rushed ahead, and landed at the fort. Flag Officer Foote signaled for all vessels to stop, and at that instant the *Carondelet* ran aground. The *Cincinnati* began drifting downstream. But at first sight, it appeared that *she* was standing still, and the *Carondelet* was steaming ahead.

As Henry Walke wrote years later, Andy Foote hailed him, "with a few sharp technicalities to keep station. . . . Here was a scene! The flag officer—in the midst of the excitement came forward in haste, trumpet in hand, and called out again and again [for me] to stop . . . (unaware that his own vessel was all the time drifting down the river) until at last he gave up the undertaking in favor of a junior officer, whose lungs (poor fellow) proved quite inadequate to the task of moving the *Carondelet*."

General Tilghman and a couple of his staff officers came out in a small boat to the flagship, once again in its proper station, and surrendered. Until the army arrived, Commander Walke took temporary charge of the fort. "On every side," he remembered, "the blood of the dead and wounded was intermingled with the earth and their implements of war." The Confederates had suffered ten killed and missing, eleven wounded, and ninety-four prisoners.

Foote, giving the rebels no rest after their defeat, sent Sam Phelps and the stinkpots on a charge upriver. After destroying the vital railroad bridge connecting Bowling Green and Nashville to the

Mississippi, he pushed over 200 miles into northern Alabama, seizing several vessels crammed with military stores and iron ore. At Cerro Gordo he took a great prize, the big steamer *Eastport,* nearing her conversion into an ironclad ram, along with an "immense" quarter million board-feet of the best quality ships' timber, her "machinery, spikes, plating, nails, etc."

There was no mistaking the enthusiasm coming from Washington. Andy Foote was deluged with congratulatory letters. "We all went wild over your success," wrote Lieutenant Wise from the Navy Department. "Uncle Abe was joyful . . . and spoke of you in his plain, sensible appreciation of merit and skill." Gus Fox was ecstatic, telling the flag officer, "Another fort knocked over by the Navy is my reward."

General Albert Sidney Johnston cabled his secretary of war. Kentucky was lost and the Bowling Green line no longer tenable. The seemingly invincible gunboats prowled the rivers, and the fall of Fort Donelson was a matter only of time. Once that happened, the Federals had clear steaming up the Cumberland. Forced to avoid the "disastrous consequences" of being cut off north of the river, Johnston ordered a withdrawal to Nashville.

Had Johnston done only that, concentrated his strength at Nashville, he might have changed the course of the western campaign. But instead, he siphoned 15,000 troops, a third of his strength, and sent them into the trenches of Fort Donelson; a fatal division of forces that left him without enough to defend either.

Johnston compounded his error by giving command of Fort Donelson to the feckless Major General John B. Floyd, President Buchanan's miscreant secretary of war. His subordinates were Brigadier General Gideon Pillow, a pretentious Tennessee lawyer who should have stayed at the bar, and Simon Bolivar Buckner, an old friend and West Point classmate of U. S. Grant.

Fort Donelson, sited on a commanding bluff along the south bank of the Cumberland, was more an entrenched camp than a properly bastioned fort. On its river face, engineers had cut a series of terraces, twenty, fifty, and one hundred feet above the water, wherein loomed ten guns of questionable lineage. It gave the rebels, however, the ability to deliver a crippling plunging fire onto the river, something the flooded batteries at Fort Henry sorely lacked.

At Paducah on February 10, Henry Walke received orders to bring the *Carondelet* upriver. Not wishing to waste coal, or add extra wear to his engines, he trailed on a towline behind the steamer *Alps.* Foote, from Cairo, followed the next day. As always, the flag officer bemoaned the scarcity of crews. He was forced to shift men from vessel to vessel, with demoralizing effect, and twenty-eight hands deserted on learning they were to be transferred out of their craft.

At noon, February 12, when just out of sight of the fort, Henry Walke cast off his tow and steamed along the lead-colored river into long cannon shot range. Around him, the bleak, wintry country lay covered in a light mantle of snow. After the war, he recalled, "Not a living creature could be seen, [only] the black rows of heavy guns, pointing down on us, reminded me of the dismal-looking sepulchers cut in the rocky cliffs near Jerusalem, but far more repulsive."

Tired of waiting around without anyone seeming to take notice, he lobbed a few shells into the fort, "to announce my arrival to General Grant" whose men were to come overland from Fort Henry. Except for the crack-boom echo bouncing against the hills, not a thing stirred, and he dropped a few miles downriver to anchor in midstream for the night.

In the morning, the boatswain's pipe called the hands. At the front of sandbagged boilers, iron firebox doors clanged open, and the rasp of shovels digging into small mountains of coal spread a veil of black, choking dust inside the casemate. Walke ordered the engines slow ahead and the *Carondelet* steamed up to the fort again. Finally, a message arrived from General Grant. He was ready to open the attack. "If you will advance with your gun-boat at 10 o'clock in the morning, we will be ready to take advantage of any diversion in our favor."

Walke maneuvered into the cover of a heavily wooded point, and at a mile, opened fire. At first, the rebels replied with their only two guns that could reach, both shot high and over. Then, at maximum elevation, the rest of the batteries joined in. Most fell short, but one 128-pound solid shot came smashing through the *Carondelet*'s side, knocking down and badly wounding a dozen men. The ball struck the sandbags around the boilers, passed over the steam drum, ricocheted off the overhead beams, and carried away the engine room railing, before rolling like a demented thing around the decks. As one of the engineers said, it "seemed to bound after the men like a wild beast pursuing its prey." A cloud of iron and oak splinters filled the gun deck. "Some of them," Walke said, "fine as needles, shot through the clothes of the men like arrows." It happened so suddenly that several crewmen were unaware of their wounds, "until they felt the blood running into their shoes."

At the passing of noon, the *Carondelet* withdrew. Walke sent the wounded to the *Alps* and the rest of the crew to dinner. The army opened its attack and, hearing gunfire, Walke renewed the exchange. His gunners expended nearly all of their large-caliber shells, but in a parting shot, they struck and dismounted one of the fort's 32-pounders, killing the rebel officer commanding the batteries. Back at the anchorage, Walke received his second message from Grant: Foote and the flotilla would arrive tomorrow.

When they came, convoying the bulk of Lew Wallace's* division from Fort Henry, it was nearly midnight and snowing heavily. Preparing for battle on the morning of February 14, Lieutenant Egbert Thompson in the *Pittsburg* had 100 bread bags filled with coal piled around the boilers as some protection against solid shot. Against the bags the crew stacked their rolled hammocks. Carpenters hammered makeshift cots for the wounded. In all the gunboats, chains, lumber, and bags of coal were laid along the vulnerable upper deck in hopes of deflecting plunging fire.

Foote's plan was a simple one. He would bring the turtles right up against the lower water batteries, knock the gunners senseless from their pieces, then steam past and enfilade Fort Donelson from its open rear. But he considered the operation, "not in my opinion properly prepared." Foote would have preferred to wait a couple of weeks until he had men enough for all the gunboats, and some mortar scows as well. He could then lay off at long range and demolish Fort Donelson methodically stone by stone.

Signal flags snapped from the *St. Louis'* stumpy mast and the flotilla weighed anchor. In line-abreast the turtles (*Carondelet* on the starboard wing, nearest the fort, then *Pittsburg, St. Louis,* and *Louisville*), advanced upriver. In the rear of the ironclad line came the *Tyler* and *Conestoga*. Except for the thudding of the engines and the gurgled screech of a flight of startled geese, nothing broke the profound silence that had settled over the snowy valley.

At three o'clock, a half-mile from the target, the *St. Louis* opened the battle, immediately followed by shattering, smoke-belching volleys across the front of the iron battle line. Lew Wallace, whose division held the center of Grant's line cocked an ear to something odd in the fort's counterfire—a jarring, metallic clash. It was, he thought rightly, "the impinging of their shot on . . . iron armor and was heard distinctly . . . for a mile and a half away."

* Brigadier General Lewis Wallace, who would go on to write the novel *Ben-Hur.*

For a hellish hour the gunboats delivered a very heavy and accurate fire, blasting away the defending parapets, chasing the rebel gunners to the rear. On the turtles crept until they were only 400 yards from the mouths of the Confederate guns. With 200 more yards, the Union gunboats could slip past the rebel batteries "and we would have mowed them down."

At Albert Sidney Johnston's headquarters, the superintendent of the military telegraph handed the general a message, "Operator at Donelson says gunboats passed and are right on him." Victory for the Western Gunboat Flotilla was a hairbreadth away. But the plunging fire from the bluffs smashing into the turtles' angled sides and unarmored upper decks exacted its toll. Struck nearly sixty times, the *Louisville* took a critical hit in her steering gear. General Pillow described it: "I could see distinctly the effect of our shot . . . to one of his boats, when he . . . shrunk back and drifted below the line. Several shots struck another boat, tearing her iron case, splintering her timbers and making them crack as if by a stroke of lightning, when she, too fell back."

A repair party ran out of the *Louisville*'s casemate to hook relieving tackles to her rudders and regain control. Shells from the stinkpots falling short of the fort, exploded right over the sailors' heads, driving them away from their task. Unable to steer, the *Louisville* lurched backward out of the line.

In the flagship *St. Louis*, Foote bled from a slight wound in the arm. Needing a better vantage than the gun deck, he climbed into the pilothouse. A plunging, solid shot struck it square-on, ripped through over an inch of iron, thirteen more of solid oak, and demolished the wheel. The pilot died instantly, and Foote fell to the deck, blood pouring from his left boot. Relieving tackle held the gunboat hardly a minute when a shell from the *Tyler* exploded across her stern, ripping out the tiller ropes. Unmanageable, the flagship drifted from the fight.

The *Pittsburg* was staggered by two hits in the bow, right on the waterline. She, too, yawed out of the line, and was able to keep afloat only by running in the forward guns to raise her bow out of the water.

Of the four ironclads, only the *Carondelet* remained to slug it out in the face of the rebel guns. "We heard the deafening crack of the bursting shells," Commander Walke said, "the crash of the solid shot, and the whizzing of fragments of shell and wood as they sped through the vessel."

He took the turtle to point-blank range, perhaps as little as 200 yards, where the rebels couldn't miss. A heavy ball struck the anchor, "smashed it into flying bolts," then bounded over the upper deck, taking with it part of a stack. A shell hit the pilothouse. It knocked the plating to bits, and sent jagged, iron splinters into the pilots, killing one of them. Hits came relentlessly, "tearing off the side armor as lightning tears the bark from a tree."

Through the hellish maelstrom, the *Carondelet* kept up a constant, unwavering fire. John Hall, an experienced seaman, took command of the forward battery. Each time he saw a rebel cannonball he shouted, "Look out! Down!" and the men threw themselves to the deck. Some of the younger hands, Walke recalled, "from a spirit of bravado," ignored the veteran's cries. "The warning words 'Look out! Down!' were again heard; down went the gunner and his men, as the whizzing shot glanced on the gun, taking off the gunner's cap and the heads of two of the young men who trusted to luck." An instant later it decapitated a third man. Each head hideously exploded with a sharp "spat," sending blood and brains over Henry Walke and everyone standing nearby. "There was so much blood on the deck," he said, "that our men could not work the guns without slipping."

A shell jammed in the bore of one the old 42-pounders. Regulations specified a time-consuming removal, but the gunners fired anyway. The cannon burst, breaking into four large pieces, the barrel rolling stupidly along the deck outside the casemate. Walke, writing bitterly from hindsight, felt he could have finished the deadly run past the water batteries. Yet because of Foote's public scolding of him at Fort Henry, "having so recently received the *admonition* not to precede the flag steamer," Walke chose, instead, to follow his superior officer and retired downriver.

Whatever his motives, and uncharacteristically petty they seem, the opportunity for bold action quickly disappeared. The *Carondelet* was hit again in the pilothouse, breaking her steering wheel. Then the *Pittsburg* rammed the *Carondelet's* stern, snapping off the starboard rudder. His gunboat was now, Walke saw, "terribly cut up, with the pilot house and smoke pipes riddled; port side cut open fifteen feet, and decks ripped up." The turtle had been struck thirty-five times, four men killed, two more were in their final agony, and thirteen bled from wounds. Two shots then struck the bow "between wind and water," and only the compartmented underwater hull kept her from sinking. Leaking badly, the *Carondelet,* "last out of the enemy reach," retreated from the fight. For the navy, the heady opiate of "bombardment fever," first tasted at Hatteras Inlet, then savored at Port Royal and Fort Henry, proved a fatal draft at Fort Donelson.

On the summit battery a Confederate soldier tossed his gray cap in the air, yelling, "Come on, you cowardly scoundrels; you are not at Fort Henry." The Confederates had every reason to rejoice, albeit the celebrations were premature and temporary. Floyd, who had predicted the fort must fall in twenty minutes, now rushed off a telegram to Albert Sidney Johnston: "The gunboats have been driven back." With pardonable elaboration, Pillow claimed, "the fiercest fight on record."

In the Federal lines, the first news was that all the ironclads had been severely disabled and were limping back to Cairo. Grant "felt sad enough," but there was no sense of calamity, just a lot of headshaking. "I shall always remember the disappointment of the army," said Lew Wallace, "when Commodore Foote's attack upon the water battery failed." Grant began fortifying his positions, awaiting repairs to the turtles before renewing the attack. Fortunately, for him and the Union, the two senior Confederate generals showed themselves as true poltroons.

When their euphoria subsided, the rebels understood that they had inflicted little more than a temporary check. Grant's army still surrounded Fort Donelson on its landward sides, and the flotilla, though damaged, still controlled the river. The weather now closed in bringing a storm of driving sleet, and soldiers on both sides huddled miserably around their fires.

Very late that day generals Floyd, Pillow, and Buckner decided to boldly hit Grant's right wing and cut their way out along the road to Nashville. Before dawn, February 15, the Confederates attacked, scattering the forward Union division and occupying its lines. The escape road to Nashville lay open before them. But that was not all; the rebels found themselves in position to roll up Grant's entire right flank, pulling out a splendid battlefield triumph. But instead, the rebel commanders managed to snatch defeat from the jaws of victory. Pillow ordered Buckner to deal with an imaginary threat in the rear. He refused, and an argument ensued. Floyd rode up, took one side, then the other, and finally resolved the conflict by ordering the entire force back into the fort!

Grant immediately ordered a counterattack and the Union regiments advanced under the cover of the *St. Louis'* and *Louisville's* battering artillery. Lew Wallace recalled, "the guns of the fleet opened fire again. I recollect yet the positive pleasure the sounds gave me."

The Confederate generals now faced three choices: surrender; hope for a battlefield miracle; or try again to cut their way out to Nashville. Buckner advised giving up. The troops, he said, were in no condition to sustain another battle. Nonsense, Pillow replied, and he insisted the regiments had the stamina to break through again.

Floyd offered his advice. The rebel firebrand agreed with Buckner. Yes, he said, surrender was the only alternative, though not, however, for him. Despised in the North for his corruption and treason on the eve of the war, criminal indictments for John B. Floyd were not out of the question. "Gentlemen," he announced, "I cannot surrender; you know my position with the Federals; it wouldn't do; it wouldn't do." Then Pillow, solemnly professing "Liberty or Death," addressed his colleagues, "I will not surrender myself nor the command; I will die first." Floyd, only too eager to promote the histrionics, turned to the lawyer-general, "I turn the command over to you, sir." "I pass it," Pillow said eagerly. "I assume it," sighed Buckner, his integrity, if nothing else, intact. "Give me pen, ink, paper, and send for a bugler."

Leaving a shocked rear guard to hold the river landing, Floyd snatched two steamers and with 1,500 men escaped upriver to Nashville. Pillow, opting for liberty *over* death, managed only a skiff to row across the Cumberland. About 700 cavalry, led by the negrophobic psychopath Nathan Bedford Forrest, also made it away. Buckner, 14,000 prisoners, and forty pieces of artillery went into the bag. "The trophies of war," cabled Andy Foote to the department, "are immense."

Foote ordered the damaged vessels to Cairo for repair and refit. With two turtles and the stinkpots he steamed for Clarksville. On February 17, he wrote to Gideon Welles, "I go up with the gunboats. . . . My foot is painful, but not dangerous." Near the town, he burned the Tennessee Ironworks, a heavy blow to Confederate shipbuilding. Clarksville fell with nary a shot. But General Halleck, fearing a phantom rebel attack from Columbus, refused to let the boats go farther, missing a grand opportunity to round up 10,000 rebel troops trapped north of the river.

From all directions, Albert Sidney Johnston's forces fell back on Nashville. Then, seeing no hope of holding it, the rebels opened the storehouses and abandoned the city to the mob. Union cavalry clattered up the streets on February 23. Two days later, the *Cairo* brought the troop convoy from Fort Donelson. Albert Sidney Johnston had lost nearly a third of his army and the rest were isolated from each other. He ordered Columbus evacuated, and maneuvering south and west, concentrated his forces at Corinth, Mississippi, not far from Pittsburg Landing, near the tiny habitation of Shiloh Church.

*   *   *

From London, James Murray Mason, the Confederate envoy, wrote
his government in Richmond, "The late reverses at Fort Henry and
Fort Donelson have had an unfortunate effect upon the minds of our
friends here." And from his berth in the *Conestoga,* Andy Foote penned
to his wife the horrors of war. "I will not go so near again," he com-
forted her.

"on to Memphis"

"As the battle progressed and the Confederate fleet was destroyed, all the cheering voices on shore were silenced . . . the lamentations which went up from the spectators were like cries of anguish."

—**Commander Henry Walke, USS** *Carondelet*

Like a giant suction pump, the collapse of the Confederate center at forts Henry and Donelson drew their western army down to positions along the Memphis and Charleston Railroad. Memphis, the South's fifth city, anchored the new line on the Mississippi. At Corinth, eighty miles east, Albert Sidney Johnston mustered every available regiment until he had 40,000 men to face Grant's forces advancing up the Tennessee River.

While the gunboat flotilla refitted at Cairo, the rebels strengthened their defenses. On the Mississippi, ninety miles north of Memphis, at the bottom of a double hairpin loop in the river, just upstream from the town of New Madrid, Missouri, sat Island No. 10—the tenth island south of Cairo. At a glance it appeared that nothing could pass it.

On the island and the Tennessee side of the riverbank, the rebels had constructed a mutually supporting series of batteries and fortifications that numbered seventy-five guns and 6,000 men. Included was the Pelican dry dock, which Henry Walke called the Confederacy's "great war elephant." Towed up from New Orleans and loaded with fourteen guns, it was intended as a mobile barrier to be used up and down the river.

Surrounded by the moat of the Mississippi, whose banks at this point were nothing but sloughs and swamps, Island No. 10 was unapproachable by a marching army. If the Federal forces were to continue their drive on Memphis, there was no option but to meet the river guns head-on, or so most people thought.

Flag Officer Foote was certainly one of them, and the prospect of having to fight his turtles *down*river did nothing to cheer him. In their previous fights at Henry and Donelson, the boats had thrashed *up*, allowing their queer designs to make use of the opposing current to keep station during a bombardment. Also, when fighting upstream, a damaged vessel could drift back with the current to safety. But not so in the reverse, where a battered craft would drift helplessly forward onto the muzzles of the enemy's guns.

But in early March, Union General John Pope, with a fine show of energy and 25,000 men, invested New Madrid from the rear, and captured it. If he could cross the river quickly, the whole enemy position at Island No. 10 would be cut off, surrounded by the same moats and swamps the rebels had so counted on for its defense.

At Cairo, a lately aroused General Halleck sought the gunboats to support Pope's timely coup. Flag Officer Foote, however, insisted he needed more time to refit the flotilla after its recent bang-up. "I must be the judge of the condition of the fleet," he told Gideon Welles, "and when it is prepared for battle." Furthermore, if Halleck wanted him to confront the rebel guns head-on, the flotilla needed an army landing force to hold the captured positions, "as we cannot take prisoners with gunboats."

In addition to perpetual troubles with General Halleck, Foote's health had deteriorated, and with it he had lost his old vinegar. Still comparatively young at fifty-seven, Foote had aged ten years on the river. The painful foot wound received at Fort Donelson refused to heal, confining him to a chair and crutches. Working sixteen-hour days at his desk, suffering from headaches and loss of weight, the once robust sailor complained in cranky letters to his wife, "I would this moment give all I am worth could I be on the Atlantic . . . instead of being out here under a pressure which would crush most men." When his thirteen-year-old son died, the grief sapped him further.

Yet by March 14, Foote had everything ready. In his new flagboat, the heavily gunned ironclad *Benton,* the most powerful craft on the river, the flag officer set out from Cairo leading seven turtles, eleven mortar scows, and transports bearing an infantry brigade that he had shaken free from General Halleck. The next day, in miserable rain and dense fog, the river armada arrived in front of Island No. 10.

The river was in full spring flood. The water surged over the mud banks, ripping up great chunks of shoreline, "and carried away every movable thing," said Henry Walke. "Houses, trees, fences, and wrecks of all kinds were being swept rapidly downstream." Each vessel made fast to a stout tree to ride it out.

At Tiptonville, a few miles below Island No. 10, Confederate Flag Officer George Hollins collected his command. With only a wooden gunboat and five armed river steamers, he stood no chance of beating back a determined assault. Nor did Hollins want to be there in the first place. The Federals, he knew, were preparing to attack New Orleans from the Gulf, and from his perspective, that was the real threat.

The gunboat flotilla spent their Sunday towing the mortar scows into position and lashing the tortoiselike *Benton* between the *Cincinnati* and *St. Louis.* Monday, March 17, Foote opened the bombardment. Many of the huge, 13-inch mortar shells burst prematurely, well short of their target. They had been cast fifteen years before for the Mexican War, and should have been condemned.

Anchors down, engines aback, barely holding their way in the rushing current, the three bound-up gunboats opened fire at 2,000 yards. The rebels in the bluff batteries replied promptly and four times hit the *Benton.* One shot bounced around her upper deck, broke through the casemate, and according to an observer, "finally lodged in the flag officer's desk, depositing itself in the drawer as quietly as possible."

The flotilla managed to silence all but one of the shore batteries, but not without cost. In the *St. Louis,* one of the old army 42-pounders exploded, killing two men and wounded thirteen; "another proof," Henry Walke noted, "of the truth of the saying that the guns furnished the Western Flotilla were less destructive to the enemy that to ourselves."

Forced to send the *Louisville* and *Cincinnati* back to Cairo for engine repair, Andrew Foote settled in, as Walke said, for a "monotony of long and tedious investment." General Pope had other ideas. During the day's action, he had sent his chief engineer by a roundabout route to deliver a letter to the flag officer. If Foote could run the gauntlet to New Madrid with a couple of gunboats, the army could safely cross the river and "capture every man of the enemy at Island No. 10 and on the mainland."

Foote hedged. With only five turtles he felt he could not risk it, and neither he nor inch-along General Halleck saw any need for haste. But as day passed day with no progress, it became obvious to everyone that bombardment by the flotilla could not reduce the rebel bastion alone. Sadly, Foote turned into an object of ridicule for the army officers. One colonel, when asked of the flotilla's operations said, "Oh, it is still bombarding the State of Tennessee at long range."

On March 20, Foote held a council of war in the *Benton*. All but one of the skippers agreed that a run past the island, with fifty rebel guns bearing directly on the channel, "would result in ... almost certain destruction." Henry Walke was the exception. Given favorable circumstances and good preparation he believed an attempt could be made at night. Furthermore, there was a need for haste. The rebels were building the ironclad ram *Arkansas* at Memphis. If she sortied while the flotilla was still butting heads with Island No. 10, they might never get through. Foote and Pope both knew this, and they were getting very impatient with each other—something had to give.

Near the end of the month, one of Pope's engineers scouted a bayou that emptied near New Madrid. He thought a canal could be dug to link the meandering backwater with the Mississippi *north* of Island No. 10. The general ordered up a regiment of engineers and they commenced one of the great sapping feats of the war.

For two weeks soldiers and sailors sweated with axes and saws through six miles of swamp and a mile of solid earth. Trees were cut four feet below the water, just enough to allow a vessel that could float on a heavy dew. And if she must float through empty, Pope could arm the craft with his own howitzers. "Please communicate with me as soon as possible," he begged the flag officer. Getting no satisfaction, he complained to General Halleck. If Foote was so afraid to risk the gunboats, Pope wrote sarcastically, "I would ask, as they belong to the United States Army, that he be directed to remove his crews from two of them and turn the boats over to me. I will bring them here." With that, he began work on a coal barge to carry a piece or two of field artillery.

On March 29, Foote held a second council of war, and again Walke wanted to try running past Island No. 10 at night. The flag officer let go an audible sigh, thanking the commander for relieving him from a "heavy responsibility." What Foote had considered impossible for the whole flotilla, he now entrusted to the *Carondelet* alone.

By April 2, Pope's transports were hiding in the canal, ready to move into the river "at a moment's notice." The only thing the general waited for was finishing his coal barge floating battery. "I have no hope of Commodore Foote," he wrote General Halleck; "we must do without him."

Foote, however, did not idle away. A boat expedition landed under the rebels' noses and spiked five guns in the bluff batteries. On April 3, the ironclads and mortar scows shot up the rebels' Pelican dry dock, tearing it adrift from its moorings. These two actions subtracted fourteen guns from those that would bear on the *Carondelet* when she made her dash.

"For the ordeal," Henry Walke and his crew prepared the *Carondelet*. They collected a mountain of loose timber and piled it on deck to protect the gunboat against plunging shot. Hawsers and chain cable were wrapped around the pilothouse. To deaden the great puffing of her boilers, the engineers led pipes aft, channeling the escape gasses through the paddle wheelhouse rather than up the stacks. On her port side, outboard the powder magazine, the crew lashed a hay-laden coal barge. Looking her over, Walke thought the *Carondelet* easily "resembled a farmer's wagon prepared for market."

On April 4 she was ready. A volunteer platoon of army sharpshooters were "gratefully accepted." To repel any boarders, Walke broke out the gunboat's pistols, cutlasses, muskets, and pikes. Boxes of hand grenades were placed in easy reach, and the engineers rigged a hose to the boilers to throw scalding water. At moonset, "whatever the chances," he would make the run. "Having gone so far," he wrote after the war, "we could not abandon the project without an effect on the men almost as bad as failure."

To the joy of everyone in the flotilla, an unexpected thunderstorm "spread itself over all the heavens." At four bells in the evening watch, 10:00 P.M., the *Carondelet* drifted downstream enveloped in total blackness. When abreast of Island No. 10 Walke rang for full speed. The engines turned over, the wheel thrashed, and the *Carondelet* pushed ahead.

When the engineers had rigged the steam bypass to the wheelhouse, nobody gave it much thought. But without the steam's dampening effect in the smokestacks, the packed layers of soot had dried out. Suddenly the stacks took fire, shooting an umbrella of sparks straight up over the boat. The cat was out of the bag, and from three sides rebel guns opened up. A correspondent aboard from the *New York Herald* likened it to "a stray washtub being pelted with pebbles by a party of schoolboys." The night, the storm, and the surprise of a moving target all served to cloak the turtle from harm. The *Carondelet* clanked by unscathed—the turning point of the Memphis campaign.

Near midnight, she nosed around the hairpin turn and tied up at New Madrid. Pope's soldiers threw their caps in the air and tossed the sailors from shoulder to shoulder in wild celebration. Commander Walke, at the suggestion of his paymaster, "spliced the main brace," ordering an extra ration of spirits for the crew.

That morning Pope sent another message to Flag Officer Foote. According to his artillery officers it was "positively impossible" for the rebels to hit a moving target at night and the *Carondelet*'s dash proved it; send another gunboat! Though peevishly objecting to the general's needling tone, Foote promised every effort. On the night of April 6, the *Pittsburg* ran past the batteries and joined the *Carondelet* at New Madrid.

Pope's staff took the *Carondelet* downriver, reconnoitering the far bank as far as Tiptonville. At several points, landing parties stormed rebel batteries and spiked the guns to prepare the way for crossing. The Confederate garrison commander pleaded with Flag Officer Hollins to chase them off. Hollins, however, declined to fight a suicidal battle with the Federal ironclads and withdrew downriver.

At sunup, April 7, without delay, accident, or losing a man, Pope's transports, screened by the two turtles, steamed across the river. As soon as they saw the movement, the garrison on Island No. 10 hoisted the white flag and surrendered. Everywhere else the rebels bolted and ran. The only overland escape road led south, and Pope's troops quickly blocked it. Completely surrounded, the entire Confederate force of 5,000 men, 100 guns, several transport steamers, the gunboat *Grampus,* and huge quantities of military stores were given up to the Union. The river road—seventy-five miles to the next obstacle at Fort Pillow, forty more to Memphis—lay open to invasion.

Another action was fought these same two days of April 6 and April 7, 1862, 110 miles to the southeast, on the west bank of the Tennessee River, near tiny Shiloh Church. Gathering his forces for a mighty punch, Albert Sidney Johnston moved out of Corinth and hit Grant's surprised and unprepared lines. In a horrific battle, he nearly split the Federal army in two, driving its left onto the river, and came very close—in fact, within an eighth of a mile—to achieving a strategic victory.

But into the chaos that was Grant's collapsed left flank, came the stinkpots *Tyler* and *Lexington.* Their heavy metal provided just enough of a check to give Grant's reeling regiments time to consolidate and make a stand. "The enemy was forced to retreat in haste," Lieutenant Gwin reported to Flag Officer Foote. "Your old wooden boats rendered invaluable service." Against Grant's losses of 13,000 men, the Confederacy lost over 10,000, including the irreplaceable Albert Sidney Johnston. Following the action, Halleck, blaming Grant for the near loss of the army, temporarily took over personal command and began a plodding advance on Corinth.

On the Mississippi, there was no thought of hanging back. By April 9, Pope was ready to move south to the next rebel bastion, Fort Pillow. Though his health and stamina worsened by the day, Foote went with the momentum. The flotilla, seven turtles in the van, dropped downriver on April 12, anchoring for the night fifty miles above the fort. Pillow, a string of batteries and fortlets emplaced on the high east bank bluffs, held forty guns. As Federal long glasses picked out suitable targets, the rebels had 1,200 slaves at work strengthening the works. Foote spoke to some Union loyalists by the riverbank. "[They] express the opinion" he wrote to Gideon Welles, "that resistance will be very determined."

Cooperation between Flag Officer Foote and General Pope, strained at Island No. 10, here showed great promise. Constricted by the same terrain factors as upriver, Pope planned to cut another canal on the Arkansas side, push his transports through, and assault the position from below. Foote asked Henry Walke's opinion of the gunboats' using the detour and was assured the *Carondelet* was "ready at any time." But the scheme came to nothing since Halleck ordered all of Pope's army, less one brigade with the flotilla, to break off operations and join his forces advancing on Corinth.*

The withdrawal brought river operations to a near standstill. Only the mortar scows were active, monotonously lobbing shells into the rebel revetments. For Andrew Foote, it presented the timely opportunity for a convalescent leave. Needing a deputy commander, someone who could handle the burden while he took a well-earned rest, the flag officer recommended his old friend from midshipman days, Captain Charles Davis.

Davis arrived on May 9, aboard the mail boat from Cairo. In the *Benton* he found Foote in bed and was shocked at his condition, "fallen off in flesh, and depressed in spirits . . . he was so overpowered at the sight of me that he was unable for some moments to speak." Though Foote was supposed to be gone for only two weeks, the two friends

---

* Pope, like Ambrose Burnside, was capable enough until placed in senior command. Ordered east, his reputation and army were shattered in the coming August during the Second Battle of Bull Run.

knew intuitively this was the end. Unashamedly they held each other, Davis telling his wife, "we both shed tears."

At dawn the following morning, Acting Master Thomas Gregory of mortar scow No. 16 made fast to the bank at Plum Point Bend, ready to begin another day's bombardment of Fort Pillow, two miles away. The *Cincinnati* lay moored nearby, steam down, her crew holystoning the decks. It was a beautiful Saturday morning. Inside the casemate, Seaman Eliot Callender sat writing a letter, when the sharp bark of command broke him from his idyll. Callender gawked downstream. There, he said, "steaming rapidly around the point below us, pouring dense clouds from their funnels, came first one vessel, then two, then more, until [eight] war vessels under full head of steam came surging up the river barely a mile below us." The *Cincinnati* had barely enough steam to turn her paddlewheel, and the rest of the flotilla were at least three miles upstream.

These vessels, steaming hell for leather, as Charles Davis put it, "handsomely . . . gallantly . . . fully prepared for a regular engagement," were the cottonclad rams of the Confederate War Department's River Defense Fleet. Adamantly *not* navy, this motley collection of lightly armed river steamers with the odd 32-pounder gun was mastered and crewed by independent rivermen, and few knowledgeable military people had much confidence in the organization. General Mansfield Lovell, commanding at New Orleans, thought they contained "too much 'steamboat,' and too little of the 'man-of-war,' to be very effective."

Maybe so, but "Senior Captain" James Montgomery and his comrade, "General Jeff" Thompson, a Missouri guerrilla bushwhacker, had conceived an audacious plan to cut out the bombarding mortar scow or, better yet, its covering gunboat. General Jeff divided up his "Swamp Rats" among the eight vessels, himself commanding from the sidewheel steamer *General Bragg*. Montgomery flew his "pennant" in the *Little Rebel*.

Master Gregory and his fifteen men watched the rams rounding Plum Point. The range was less than three-quarters of a mile, ridiculously short. They pointed the monster 13-inch mortar nearly straight up, and Gregory had the satisfaction of watching his first shell explode directly over the targets. The crew set to for another shot.

The *Cincinnati* slipped her lines and slowly swung into the stream, the black gang throwing oil and all things flammable into the fireboxes to build up steam and get underway. On came the *General Bragg* pushing brown foam ten feet high around her built-up bow. The *Cincinnati* fired a broadside. Four 32-pounder shells slammed into the cotton bales, tumbling the soft bulwark, sending splinters flying through the enemy craft.

"But on she came," said Elliot Callender. When less than fifty feet off, the *Cincinnati* slew around and the two vessels came together in a fearful, crashing blow. The *Bragg* tore a twelve-foot piece out of the gunboat's hull, flooding the magazine. Like the *Merrimack* at Hampton Roads, the *Bragg*'s ram stuck in her victim. "Give her another broadside, boys!" bellowed Union Commander Roger Stembel. The *Cincinnati*'s muzzles were literally jammed against the side of the *General Bragg* when the gun captains pulled their lockstrings. Port to starboard, the 32-pounders blew an immense hole right through the wooden steamer. Stembel roared into his trumpet, "Board the enemy!"

In that instant, the rebel *General Sterling Price* rammed the *Cincinnati* in the fantail; more water rushed in and she began to sink. Then came the *General Sumter.* Someone aboard the rebel boat shouted across the water, "Haul down your flag, and we will save you." From the *Cincinnati* came the defiant answer, "Our flag will go down when we do!" The *Sumter* struck the turtle in her port quarter with such force the ironclad's bow was thrust under water. The river poured in from three gaping wounds. Her engineers stood waist deep, the fires sputtered out, and the only dry ammunition was in the guns.

Rebel sharpshooters began picking off exposed men. Stembel took a minié ball in the mouth and collapsed badly wounded. Bill Hoel, the pilot, came down into the casemate and took command. "Boys," he hollered, "give 'em the best you've got! We ain't dead yet!" The men cheered and fired their last rounds. The *Cincinnati*'s hull gave a last, convulsive shudder, and down she went. The crew scrambled atop the wheel; "and now," said Eliot Callender, "perched like so many turkeys on a corn crib," they watched the rest of the action.

The *Carondelet* and *Mound City* were quickly steaming downriver. Thrashing past the foundering *Cincinnati,* Henry Walke opened fire on the three damaged, retreating rams. With a 5-inch Dahlgren rifle at zero elevation, he put a shell into the *General Sumter*'s boilers. Steam poured from every chink and hole, and he saw "men running out . . . and falling down on her deck."

In a cut and thrust melee, the *Mound City* was badly rammed in the bow by the *General Van Dorn.* Swinging free and run onto a shoal to keep from sinking, she gave the rebel a crippling broadside, shoving her rudely in front of the Union flagship *Benton.*

In the *Benton,* skipper Sam Phelps had first fired on the *General*

Lovell with an 8-inch shell, "and I had the satisfaction," he reported, "to blow up the boilers." Phelps then took on the *Van Dorn,* hit her in the boilers and watched her drift downstream. Facing annihilation from the iron turtles, the River Defense Fleet ran for the shelter of Fort Pillow.

The Federal gunboats suffered only five men wounded in the action. But Charles Davis estimated horrendous losses for the enemy. "Their vessels," he wrote, "were literally torn to pieces, and some had holes in their sides through which a man could walk. Those that blew up—it makes me shudder to think of them." Some days later Confederate deserters said they had buried 108 men from the action.

As much as Davis' reports tried to put a gloss on the day's events, it was a Confederate victory. Two Union vessels had been sunk and Union progress halted. Flushed with overconfidence, Master Montgomery vouched to his superiors: keep the River Defense Fleet in coal and ammunition, and "of this you may rest assured . . . [the Federals] will never penetrate farther down the Mississippi."

With two boats temporarily out of the contest, Charles Davis, as Andrew Foote before him, began weeks of slow bombardment, and it seemed another stalemate. Then On May 25, there came downriver from Cairo what Henry Walke called "a useful acquisition" to the flotilla, Colonel Charles Ellet and his seven steamers of the United States Army's Mississippi Ram Fleet.

Civil Engineer Ellet, a passionate Unionist, had received a direct commission from the secretary of war to fit out and command, independent of the navy, a force of rams for duty on the western waters. With commendable energy, he purchased nine fast Ohio River steamers, bracing their hulls and bows with heavy, oaken timbers. Conceived solely as rams, they mounted no guns whatever, and no iron either; the "brown paper rams," they were called derisively.

Like the Confederate River Defense Fleet, Ellet's boats were definitely not "navy" but Ellet and his command were nonetheless a first-class fighting force. Ellet arrived full of spunk, suggesting to Captain Davis that the whole river force, rams in the van, push down to Memphis while the season still permitted it. New Orleans had fallen to Flag Officer David Farragut a month before, on May 1. He was likely advancing up the river now; and "now," Ellet said, was the time to move.

Davis put him off. The reduced flotilla could not chance a run past Fort Pillow's guns. Besides, he said, the gunboats "should take the front rank in a naval engagement with the enemy." But Davis had no authority over Ellet, and with or without the gunboats, the colonel planned to take on the defenses of Fort Pillow. Confederate movements, however, on May 30, took matters out of his hands. General Pierre G. T. Beauregard, who had taken over theater command from the late Albert Sidney Johnston, evacuated Corinth without a fight and left the disease-wracked pesthole to Henry Halleck. Fort Pillow, left dangling on the river by the retreat, was untenable. Loading the River Defense Fleet with everything they could, the garrison blew up the position before hightailing downriver to make a stand at Memphis.

Forty miles south, in the summer twilight of June 5, Memphis strollers on the river's eastern heights saw ominous clouds of brown and black smoke slowly making their way downstream. Then they heard the belching wheezing clank of engines and the thrashing churn of dozens of paddlewheels. Davis, Ellet, and their fleets had come, and according to a witness, "laid on 'Paddy's Hen and Chickens' in sight of Memphis." The city was defenseless—every gun and man had been ordered downriver to stop Farragut's advance at Vicksburg. The uncompleted ironclad *Albemarle* was evacuated south to the Yazoo River. Memphis held just 200 local troops and what remained of the River Defense Fleet.

At 4:20 A.M., June 6, just after the turn of the morning watch, the *Benton, Carondelet, Louisville, Cairo,* and *St. Louis* got under way, and sterns first* covered the mile and a half until they were off the city wharves. The eight vessels of the River Defense Fleet formed two lines abreast in midstream. The Federals, Master Hart of the *Beauregard* remembered, were "now in full view, coming down in line of battle." The *Jeff Thompson* fired the first shot. The *Benton* replied with stern guns and the ironclads hauled around and steamed forward to the attack. On the bluffs, thousands of Memphis's citizens crowded to watch the big show.

The vessels closed the range, exchanging a hot, enthusiastic fire. Presently, Ellet's "brown paper rams" overtook the slower turtles, and as Henry Walke later wrote, "the rams rushed upon each other like wild beasts in deadly conflict." Ellet's flagboat, *Queen of the West,* made a beeline for the *General Lovell.*

The *Lovell* and *Beauregard,* very close together in midstream, held firm, pointing their rams directly at the onrushing *Queen.* Ellet couldn't decide which one to hit, and the distance got "dangerously small." He had only seconds when the rebels, "apparently quailing" at the prospect of the collision, backed water—a fatal error. The *Lovell* presented her soft midships and the *Queen* crushed it in, toppling over the rebel's twin stacks.

* The author is at a loss to understand or explain why.

"The crash was terrific," Ellet wrote, "everything loose about the *Queen* ... tables, pantryware, and a half-eaten breakfast were overthrown and broken by the shock." The *Lovell* filled with water, drifted off, and sank on the Arkansas shore. Boats tried to rescue the crew, but they were picked off by the flotilla's infantry sharpshooters. Of the *Lovell*'s eighty-six men, only eighteen were saved.

The *Beauregard* turned on the *Queen of the West*. Having no time to maneuver, she took the *Beauregard*'s ram in her port wheelhouse. Out of control, Ellet somehow worked her to the Arkansas side, where he was felled by a musket ball in the leg, which proved a mortal wound.

So thick was the smoke that it was impossible to pick out individual vessels. In the *Queen of the West*'s wake came Lieutenant Colonel Alfred Ellet in the *Monarch*. From opposite sides, the *Beauregard* and *General Sterling Price* headed for her. She slipped between them, and the *Beauregard,* momentum unchecked, smacked into the *Sterling Price*'s wheelhouse, tearing it away. The *Monarch* then steamed ahead at the *Beauregard* ramming open her side.

The turtles muscled into the thick of it, and began, as Sam Phelps noted, "an execution really terrible." The *Beauregard* tried a pathetic match with the *Benton* and received a shot in the boiler that blew her up. The turtles opened on the *Jeff Thompson,* and Phelps watched her burn "in a splendid explosion." Backing downstream, pursued by the flotilla's guns and two of Ellet's rams, the surviving vessels of the River Defense Fleet kept up the hopeless fight. Only the *Van Dorn,* loaded with powder and military stores, escaped to Vicksburg.

Lieutenant Phelps went ashore with the demand for the city's surrender. He passed through "immense" crowds, and somewhat surprised, saw neither "scowling women," nor a "bitterly hateful" population. At 11:00 A.M., the flotilla's brigade of infantry marched in and took possession.

For Charles Davis and the Western Gunboat Flotilla, the prize was indeed great. The fifth city of the Confederacy, astride the junction of four railroads, Memphis yielded up mountains of cotton, a number of large steamers, some salvageable vessels of the River Defense Fleet, and the charred bones of the rebel ironclad ram *Tennessee.* There was also the Confederate navy yard, which in a few months became one of the flotilla's principal repair and victualing bases. Davis remained to coal and refit. Then, on June 28, he informed Gideon Welles of a "communication from Flag Officer Farragut, below Vicksburg, inviting my cooperation in the reduction of that city. I leave at the earliest possible moment."

New Orleans

"We drove them from their guns and passed up to the city in fine style."

—**Flag Officer David Glasgow Farragut, USN**

S even frustrating months after he had slipped off on his secret adventure to Fort Pickens and the Gulf of Mexico, Commander David Dixon Porter brought the *Powhatan* back to the Brooklyn Navy Yard. The ship badly needed repairs. Her timbers, he said, were so rotten that "only the barnacles frozen to her bottom kept the oakum from washing out." Thus far, Porter had found little success, but he had formed a plan to break the Gulf stalemate and wanted to lay it before the Navy Department. After paying off his crew, he entrained for Washington.

On November 15, 1861, the day when newspaper headlines shouted Du Pont's victory at Port Royal, David D. Porter strode into the plain, redbrick building across the street from the White House. As to his reception, it was anyone's guess. "I was out of favor since I ran off with the *Powhatan,*" he said after the war, and old Commodore Smith's greeting, "Well, you didn't run away after all!" was hardly a confidence. Gus Fox, who had arranged his promotion to commander instead of a general court-martial, studiously avoided him. Secretary Welles was too busy with the day's business to grant an interview. Crowded by people who kept avoiding his eye, "I wandered about like a cat in a strange garret."

*   *   *

Of the whole rebel coast, from Hampton Roads to the Rio Grande, the blockade was weakest at the mouth of the Mississippi. Like the spread of a four-fingered hand, the Mississippi divides south of New Orleans into four main channels, spanning thirty miles point to point at the Gulf. Fifteen miles up from the Gulf the fingers join at a strategic junction called Head of the Passes. Above this confluence hunkered the city's principal defenses, the masonry bastions of forts Jackson and St. Philip.

While still in the *Powhatan,* Porter had pleaded with the department in a stream of letters and reports for swift, light-draft gunboats that could chase runners and raiders up the passes, into the river. But in the summer of 1861 there just weren't any gunboats to spare.

Du Pont's Strategy Board had examined the problem and were frankly awed. "New Orleans has so many outlets," they told the secretary, "that the blockade of the river does not close the trade of the port."

When the late summer hurricane season came, the navy's blockaders had a choice of sheltering in the mouth of the Mississippi River, or heading out to sea. To Porter's thinking, the answer was plain. Instead of beating around *outside* the exits, why not shelter *inside,* and choke the traffic from Head of the Passes? It was also an obvious point from which to embark an advance upriver to New Orleans. "There is a field here for something to do," he wrote his chief, Flag Officer Mervine. That was the germ of Porter's ultimate plan, and it never left his thoughts.

The Strategy Board came to similar conclusions. In the fall of 1861 the blockaders crossed the bar and moved up to Head of the Passes. The force was a mixed lot: screw sloop *Richmond,* sailing sloops *Vincennes* and *Preble,* and some small gunboats. In the predawn quiet of October 12, they lay anchored, with the *Richmond,* commanded by Captain "Honest John" Pope, taking coal from a schooner alongside.*

At the time, the United States Navy had no ironclads, but the Confederate Navy did. According to intelligence reports, the tug *Enoch Train* had been radically converted into a cigar-shaped, turtle-backed, ironclad privateer, "a hellish machine" renamed *Manassas.* The ship carried a 32-pounder gun poking out the foredeck and underwater iron spikes to rip into an enemy's hull. Resolved not to let such a splendid weapon remain in civilian hands, Confederate Flag Officer George Hollins seized her at gunpoint from her startled owners and crew. With

* No relation to the general of the same name.

bold initiative, he took the ram and some armed steamers down from New Orleans to attack the Federal ships at Head of the Passes.

Captain Pope opened fire to cover the escape of his sailing vessels. The *Manassas'* deck came less than three feet out of the water, making it a very tough target. The ram bored into the *Richmond's* oaken flank and ripped out a sizable chunk of timber. Both the *Richmond* and *Vincennes* touched ground, and the *Manassas* withdrew. Aboard the *Vincennes,* Commander Robert Handy compounded the mess by misreading Pope's signal "retire from action," for "abandon ship."

The panicked Handy cast most of the *Vincennes'* guns overboard and himself lit the demolition fuse in the magazine. The ship was saved by an old quartermaster who snipped off the smoldering end. Handy wrapped himself in the flag, ordered his crew to the boats, and brought them on board the *Richmond.* Honest John Pope stood speechless in amazement.

For two hours Handy and his guilt-ridden crew fidgeted about, absolute laughingstocks. Finally convinced that the ship was not going to blow up, he returned to refloat her with the tide. Immediately after, Pope relieved him of duty. The New Orleans papers trumpeted the confusion sown by the *Manassas* as "perhaps the most brilliant and remarkable exploit on record!"

Tired of hanging around the lobby, Porter decided to enter the lion's den. At the door to Welles' office he met senators Hale and Grimes of the Naval Affairs Committee, waiting to congratulate the secretary on the victory at Port Royal. To these powerful men, Porter outlined his New Orleans plan and they ushered him inside. Welles, to Porter's surprise and relief, received him "kindly."

Porter's basic plan consisted of a dozen big ships to run past the forts and 20,000 troops to seize and hold the city. But what piqued everyone's interest was his innovative scheme to deploy a flotilla of specially converted schooners, each mounting a 13-inch mortar. Forts Jackson and St. Philip, he explained to the civilians, were not the hasty mud and turf affairs the navy had so lately vanquished. Jackson was an especially tough nut, with a tier of bombproof, casemated guns.

The forts had to be softened up, their fire unhinged, their garrisons demoralized. That, Porter perceived, was the job of the mortar flotilla—an intense, forty-eight-hour bombardment before the main fleet's dash up to the city. Porter's time frame proved optimistic, but the concept was solid.

Welles needed no further convincing. As regards New Orleans, nothing had really gone beyond some conversations. Here was something concrete, a well-thought-out operation that would wreak untold damage to the Confederacy. He called for Fox, and taking Porter in tow, walked across the street to the White House. The President, too, was impressed, and couldn't help chivvying Welles over the service's recent bungles, "Now, Mr. Secretary," Lincoln said, "the navy has been hunting pet rabbits long enough; suppose you send them after skunks." He suggested they go see General McClellan about the troops.

At McClellan's reckoning, the expedition needed at least 50,000 men to reduce the forts by a time-consuming, classic sap and siege, and he wasn't about to strip Washington's defenses for that. But when Porter explained his "bomb flotilla" Little Mac came around. The conferees imposed a clamp of "profound and impenetrable" secrecy on the operation, and for once, it held. As the first orders were written, intentional rumors spread that the expedition was being readied for the Texas coast, or maybe Mobile; "and to make matters still more indefinite," Welles said, strikes against Savannah and Charleston were given wide play.

The expedition commander, as Welles described it, required "courage, audacity, tact, and fearless energy, with great self-reliance." It was a utopian combination that few senior officers possessed and a mistake here could doom the whole enterprise. Welles considered seniority, but was not bound by it, looking for a man of unquestioned loyalty, ability, and experience who had not yet risen to a high posting—perhaps even a Southerner. Fox wanted to recommend Porter, but as a mere commander, he was really out of the question; instead, Porter received the plum assignment of the mortar flotilla. Together, Welles and Fox bent their heads over the top half of the captains' list.

Number 38 was David Glasgow Farragut of Tennessee, a man with a good, though not conspicuous record. Welles had met him once during the Mexican War and remembered him favorably. He was devoid of affect or vanity and stressed tough, thorough training. Further, when many of his Southern colleagues went South, Farragut, born in Tennessee, with a Southern wife and Virginia home, had picked up his family and decamped North. "The fact interested me," Welles jotted in his diary.

Welles had pretty much decided on his man, but he had to be sure. Given his role for the coming campaign, Porter's opinion carried a lot of weight. No officer knew Farragut better than Porter, in whose family Farragut had grown up as his adopted older brother. Indeed, Farragut's first service, as a ten-year-old midshipman, had been in old Commodore

David Porter's *Essex* during the War of 1812. Under the cover of an inspection trip to New York, Welles gave "young" Porter orders to interview Farragut, and learn his "ideas, feelings, and views."

The meeting took place in December. Porter found the captain a vigorous man of sixty, who unlike many of his rank, had not forgotten that his primary job was to fight. Porter put the questions: Did Farragut think New Orleans could be taken from the Gulf, and was he the man for it? "I answered that I thought so," Farragut said after the war, "and, if furnished with the proper means, was willing to try." This conversation sealed the careers of both men.

On December 15, 1861, Farragut was detached from dead-end duty on the retirement board and ordered to Washington, though Welles still kept him at arm's length. This appointment was his most important of the war, not only for the navy's sake, but for the Lincoln administration as well. An awful lot of political capital would be striding some flagship's quarterdeck. He called in Gus Fox.

The irreplaceable, ubiquitous assistant secretary conveniently boarded with his brother-in-law, Postmaster General Blair. Welles suggested they invite Farragut to breakfast, and "a free, social, and discretionary talk." It went well. Farragut had his doubts about the need for the mortars, but "it will succeed," he said.

From there Farragut went straight to Welles' apartment at the Willard Park Hotel for what the secretary described as "a delightful and heartwarming chat." Farragut, he said, promised to "restore New Orleans to the Government, or never return. He might not come back . . . but the city would be ours." Welles had found his man.

"Keep your lips closed, and burn my letters," an elated Farragut wrote to his wife, "I am to have a flag in the Gulf, and the rest depends upon myself. . . . I shall sail in three weeks."

On December 23, Welles published orders dividing the Gulf blockade into East and West squadrons, allowing him to appoint Farragut to the West Squadron without jeopardizing the secrecy of the planned attack on New Orleans. Farragut's command stretched from St. Andrew's Bay, Florida, to the mouth of the Rio Grande and his flagship would be the screw sloop *Hartford,* a sleek 24-gun greyhound, fitting out at Philadelphia. One veteran seaman in a Gulf blockader prophetically greeted his appointment: "If Davey Farragut came down thar, it wouldn't be long till the fur was flying."

Farragut boarded the *Hartford* in early January 1862, hoisting his flag in the ship that would be his home for the next two years. Before sailing, he incorporated some of his own ideas into her, such as mounting a couple of light howitzers in the tops, behind a shield of boiler iron. "This is a little kink of mine," he said, "but if it saves one man only, I will consider myself well repaid for the trouble." From Philadelphia it was on to Hampton Roads, where on February 2, the *Hartford* departed for the Gulf.

Almost from the day of the conference at McClellan's house, Porter had worked nonstop organizing the mortar flotilla. He placed orders with Pittsburgh foundries for twenty of the 13-inch monsters. In New York he scoured the waterfront for seaworthy schooners and small steamers and ferries for towing and escort. Porter had only the tiniest leavening of navy sailors. For the rest, including most of the officers, he culled more than 700 men from idled merchant ships. By February 1862, the schooners and all but one of the steamers had been sent on to Key West. For his "flagship," Porter received the speedy *Harriet Lane.*

On February 20, Farragut and the *Hartford* anchored at Ship Island. Named for its shape, and located between Mobile and New Orleans, it was an excellent base for operations against either city. General Ben Butler and his men were already there. Farragut intended to keep the rebels guessing the true objective of the expedition for as long as possible.

Quietly, he concentrated his forces, organizing the command. Besides the *Hartford* and her sisters *Brooklyn, Richmond,* and *Pensacola,* there were plenty of shallow-draft vessels for inshore and riverine work. He had the large steam corvettes *Iroquois* and *Oneida,* eleven of Welles' "90-day" gunboats, and the converted packet steamer *Varuna.* Against the better judgment of seagoing officers, however, the department also sent the steam frigate *Colorado* and the old, ponderous sidewheel frigate *Mississippi.*

On March 1, Farragut sent the fleet's boats to raid Biloxi and its post office. The haul brought stupendous news: forts Henry and Donelson had fallen, Andrew Foote was at Island No. 10, and the rebels were stampeded up and down the Mississippi River. Farragut decided to move into the river. Borrowing coal from Ben Butler, he ordered the *Brooklyn* to cross the bar at Pass à l'Outre and seize the telegraph station at Head of the Passes.

There were other compelling reasons to advance quickly. The latest dispatch boat brought the news of the *Merrimack-Monitor* battles at Hampton Roads. It was known the Confederates were building ironclads at New Orleans and Memphis, and one of them was rumored to be ready in a few weeks. If that happened, she could join with the *Manassas* and wreak havoc among Farragut's wooden fleet

Porter arrived at Key West at the end of February. He organized the mortar flotilla into three divisions, each under a lieutenant of the regular navy and exercised his command in what amounted to close-order drill. When several of the schooners' merchant masters chafed at being placed under naval discipline, Porter clapped them in irons and gave their vessels to more amenable types. On March 6, still short two tugs Porter ordered the schooners to follow as best they could, and he steamed off in the *Harriet Lane* to join Farragut at Ship Island.

While the Federal preliminaries went forward, the Confederate leadership spent their time fighting an internecine battle over strategy and the allocation of thin resources. Up to the day Farragut commenced the bombardment of forts Jackson and St. Philip, Navy Secretary Stephen Mallory was convinced that the primary threat to New Orleans came from the gunboat flotilla upriver—especially after the fall of Island No. 10. Indeed, until Porter changed a lot of minds at the Washington meetings, that was the Union's strategy. The turtles and stinkpots *would* have come down, eventually; Farragut just beat them to it.

The Confederate Navy's defense of New Orleans counted on the completion of two impressive ironclads, the *Louisiana* and *Mississippi*. There were, however, not enough heavy guns for their batteries, iron for their casemates, sailors for their crews, or money and workers to finish them. Luckless Commander John K. Mitchell got orders to "make all proper exertions" to install the *Louisiana*'s guns. As for the *Mississippi,* her propeller shaft was being forged at Richmond's Tredegar Iron Works. They had promised delivery in February; but here it was March, and the shaft still on the lathe.

When Farragut assembled his fleet at the river's mouth, the rebel ironclads were far from ready. Major General Mansfield Lovell, the district commander, thought the Confederate government "completely out of touch . . . with the real situation at New Orleans and with the impending disaster [here]." He appealed for reinforcements and got nothing but rebuff. The forts, he was told, could manage very well against a wooden fleet.

That might have been the case forty years ago, but no longer. Of the forts' combined 166 guns, most were short-range, obsolete 32-pounders. Star-shaped Fort Jackson on the west bank had settled into the Delta mud. The parade ground sometimes held over a foot of water, and the magazines needed pumping day and night. As a result, the

fort's principal weapons, the bombproofed, casemated guns came just
to the top of the levee and could not be depressed for critical hits at a
ship's waterline. The smaller Fort St. Philip, slightly upriver on the
east bank, was an antiquated Spanish work modernized by the U.S.
Army after the War of 1812. It had the advantage of delivering enfilading fire on the head of any fleet that came upriver, but all its guns
were in open positions, vulnerable to high-angle mortar fire. The garrisons, according to Confederate Brigadier General Johnson Duncan,
were mostly "foreign enlistments, without any great stake in the ultimate success of the revolution." They lived miserably in the damp
conditions with wet clothing and feet, resulting in high numbers on
the sick list.

Just below Fort Jackson stretched a hulk barrier common to Confederate river defenses: a line of eight dismasted schooners, chained
together, with their ground tackle and rigging dragging in the stream.
Behind this barrier ranged the Confederate forces afloat, about eighteen vessels, as heterogeneous a lot as ever cast an anchor, initially
reporting to three separate—and feuding—commands. The gunboats
McRae and *Jackson,* the ironclad *Manassas,* the unfinished *Louisiana*
and *Mississippi,* and some tugs, tenders, and armed launches were of
the regular Confederate Navy. The big steamers, cottonclad rams *Governor Moore* and *General Quitman,* owed their allegiance to the
Louisiana Provisional Navy. Six other cottonclads belonged to the
army's River Defense Fleet. General Lovell tried to place them under
naval command, but that was politically impossible. As he later ruefully
noted, the army's rivermen proved "unable to govern themselves, and
unwilling to be governed by others . . . "

In the year since normal river traffic had passed over the bars, they had
silted up. To Farragut, this meant added weeks of preparation and
plenty of anxious moments. Pass à l'Outre, the eastern finger, was
accessible only to the gunboats and the mortar flotilla. On March 18,
Porter's missing tugs, *Clifton* and *Westfield,* hove up at the pass and provided yeoman service for the entire operation. In less than a day the
whole mortar flotilla was over the bar and in the river. That done,
Porter brought the tugs to Farragut's aid at South West Pass.

This pass had two feet more water. The *Hartford, Brooklyn,* and
Richmond crossed, but not the deeper draft *Pensacola* and *Mississippi.*
As for the *Colorado,* it was impossible. Everything was taken out, but
she rose by only one inch to every twenty-four tons removed. After a
week, Farragut saw enough. He anchored the big frigate off the pass as

a floating replacement depot and shifted her best guns and seamen to other ships.

Getting the *Pensacola* and *Mississippi* across took eleven excruciating days. The *Pensacola* was careened on her side and four of Porter's tugs began dragging her over the bar. Things were going well and the tugs cast off their tow. Righting up on her keel, the *Pensacola* surged ahead at full steam and rammed squarely into a sunken hulk buried in the mud. She nosed over so far that her propeller lifted clear out of the water. Porter angrily placed the blame on "the fool of a first lieutenant and a very gassy pilot, who never cast a lead." He vowed to have nothing further to do with the ship, and indeed, relented only when Farragut ordered her skipper to personally beg for Porter's help and forgiveness.

Careening the sidewheel *Mississippi* was impossible. Instead, she was stripped of everything except each day's supply of coal. "We would run with full speed until the ship would stick firmly in the mud," remembered midshipman and future Admiral Albert Barker. "Then the other vessels would tug . . . to pull us off." Because the mud under her keel created a sucking vacuum, the tugs could bash her through only one foot at a time. At last, on April 8, Farragut lay full strength in the river.

When badly needed coal finally arrived, he moved the fleet a couple of miles up the pass to Pilot Town, a water village built on stilts. It was a hot, sweaty, and miserable place, impossible to breath the air without getting a mouthful of midges and mosquitoes. But Farragut was full of joy. He now had coal and an advanced base at the enemy's doorstep from which to launch the attack.

The fleet prepared under Farragut's detailed instructions. All nonessential gear was unloaded, and the vessels stripped their masts to the barest minimum to carry a scrap of sail. To better fire *into* the forts, boat howitzers were hoisted to the mast tops. For emergencies, commanding officers had hawsers ready to tow their next astern, and grapnels at hand to tow off fireships. Men were drilled in fire fighting. Tubs of water were placed for the men to have a drink during battle. The sides of the vessels were smeared with mud to hide them at night. For rapid identification, Farragut, well ahead of his time, ordered the gunboats to paint white, six-foot numbers on their stacks and hulls.

The flag officer received some innovative suggestions from his officers, like painting the gun decks white, to make serving the pieces that much easier at night. But probably the best idea was hanging garlands of heavy chain over the ships' sides as armored mail. "I wish you to understand," he told the captains in his fighting instructions, "that the day is at hand when you will be called upon to meet the enemy in the worst form for our profession."

On April 8, Porter brought the mortar flotilla up to Head of the Passes. The schooners were called "bummers" by the real sailors in the fleet. But the weeks of constant drill under Porter's stern eye showed, and the flotilla passed through the fleet brisk and proud, dipping their colors in turn. "They looked very pretty," said an old hand in the *Hartford,* "as they ranged along the shore in line of battle, with their flagship, the *Harriet Lane,* at their head."

Porter knew that the narrow twenty miles of constantly shifting channel between Head of the Passes and the forts needed to be mapped, and targets and anchorages plotted. This was the job of Frank Gerdes and his steamer *Sachem* of the Coast Survey. Covered by armed ships' boats, and often under heavy fire, Gerdes and his assistants surveyed the river, fixing exactly every point, including the rebel hulk line and the flagstaffs of both forts.

On the sixteenth, Porter towed three schooners to a marker 3,000 yards from Fort Jackson and lobbed a few shells to test the range. The next day, each of the twenty-one bomb vessels anchored at little white flags that Gerdes had precisely placed on both banks. As camouflage from counterbattery fire, the schooners wrapped their masts with cottonwood and willow boughs, and some crews dressed their whole sides with foliage. "The bummers think this is a holiday!" grumbled a number of salts in the fleet.

At 9 A.M., April 18, "the enemy," said General Johnson Duncan at Fort Jackson on the west bank, "opened fire with his entire mortar fleet." Each schooner, firing every ten minutes, rained down a punishing bombardment for ten straight hours, expending nearly 3,000 shells. The fort's garrison quarters burned along with the soldiers' blankets and the clothing not on their backs. Shells destroyed the hot-shot furnace, and drove the crews from the parapet guns. The citadel caught fire, and as the day wore on, Duncan said, "it became impossible to put out the flames, so that when the enemy ceased firing it was one burning mass." He reported the mortars "accurate and terrible ... the shells falling everywhere within the fort ... "

At nightfall Porter hoisted the signal lanterns to cease fire. He took an armed launch to reconnoiter upriver, rowing within spitting distance of Fort Jackson. Inside, the glowing fires silhouetted the heavy damage. He determined to reopen the bombardment in the morning and continue it around the clock. Yet ammunition was running low, and he slowed each schooner's fire to one bomb every half-hour. Despairing, he realized how badly he had miscalculated. Reducing the forts in two days was a fantasy.

Waiting for the assault, the rebels tried some harassing measures. They sent down nightly fire rafts—"one of the pleasantries of the enemy to try our nerves," wrote young Lieutenant George Dewey of the *Mississippi*. Built of logs heaped with enormous piles of pine knots soaked with resin and tar, these contraptions were very impressive in their display, with flames easily reaching 100 feet in the air. But they were ineffective. Instead of pushing the rafts as close to the Federal ships as they could get, the River Defense Fleet simply set them adrift. Farragut's small craft, vigilant for just such peril, had no trouble in grappling and hauling the pyres to the riverbanks, where they burned harmlessly away. "Every attempt seemed to prove a perfect abortion," reported rebel General Duncan.

Another rebel defensive measure that Farragut faced was the hulk line directly below the forts. "This I propose to remove," he said, "by blowing their bows out and allowing the chain to sink." On Sunday night, April 20, covered by a particularly heavy mortar fire, he sent an expedition under his chief of staff, Commander Henry Bell. The plan was quite ingenious and called for three gunboats, each carrying two 100-pound barrels of powder, holed to receive a glowing portfire. Aboard the gunboat *Pinola* was a civilian "submarine operator" and his electric "petards"—an early type of satchel charge. The petards would be placed to sever the bow chains and the powder barrels would explode the hulks, bringing everything down with them. Not trusting completely in newfangled devices, Farragut reminded the gunboats to bring "crowbars, sledges, cold chisels, hammers, and steel saws for breaking the chain." Heavy Confederate fire and a strong current defeated the electrical mining, but the tried and true methods of hack and saw did the job just well enough for ships to pass up channel along the eastern bank.

The Confederate flotilla continued to have command problems. Commander John K. Mitchell assumed charge of the Confederate Navy and the Louisiana State vessels, but Master Stevenson of the army's River Defense Fleet balked, claiming his men had entered service "with the distinct understanding" they would never be placed under naval officers. He said he would cooperate, but would not accept orders from Mitchell, and he specifically refused to station his rams at the hulk line.

"He reserved to himself," Mitchell said bitterly after the battle, "the right of obeying, or not."

Mitchell's primary task was getting the *Louisiana* out of the builder's yard and down to the forts, where she could do some damage to the Federal fleet. Even in that age of trial and experimentation, the ship was highly unusual. Externally, she was a basic, casemate-type ironclad. But internally, the vessel had four engines driving two enclosed, tandem paddle wheels. Astern, a pair of maneuvering propellers aided twin rudders in steering. Her makeshift armament was a mixed outfit of fourteen guns: Brooke rifles, 9- and 8-inch smoothbores, old 32-pounders. Her plating lay elsewhere, and she had no capstan for weighing anchor. In all respects, she was unfinished, unmanned, and unready.

The day the hulk line was broken, Commander Charles McIntosh towed the ship, with mechanics on board, down to Fort St. Philip. He tried to make a trial of her engines and found them "lamentably deficient." The rudders "seemed to be utterly powerless to control her." Bulkheads leaked, there were no hatch combings, and water came into the magazines. Under any sort of steam, the heat in the casemate was so intense the men could not serve the guns.

Mitchell and McIntosh could do nothing more. Above Fort St. Philip, just out of mortar range, they tied the *Louisiana* to the east bank for service as a floating battery. From across the river General Duncan watched her arrival with "extreme pleasure," though in his opinion the best place for the *Louisiana* was below the forts, at the remains of the hulk line, where she could engage the mortar schooners *and* provide an effective crossfire. He asked Mitchell to move her, and Mitchell, after conferring with his officers, refused. In that exposed position, he explained, it would be impossible to continue any work on the ship. Bitterly, Duncan turned away.

By April 22, the fifth day of bombardment, the mortar flotilla's ammunition dwindled down. Porter hadn't changed his uniform since opening fire, the men were exhausted, and Fort Jackson's casemate guns continued the duel.

Farragut resolved to break the deadlock. Meeting with all commanding officers, he outlined his plan of attack. He divided the fleet into three divisions. The van force, flying the Red pennant, he gave to Captain Theodorus Bailey, leading from the little "pilot fish," the ninety-day gunboat *Cayuga.* In her wake came the *Pensacola, Mississippi, Oneida, Varuna,* and three gunboats. Farragut commanded the Blue division main body, the heaviest broadsides in the fleet: *Hartford, Brooklyn,* and

Richmond. Chief of Staff Henry Bell led the rear Red and Blue division: *Iroquois* and five gunboats. The complete mission was simply to dash past the forts, sweep aside any rebel craft, then sprint upriver. Supporting the operation, the mortar flotilla moved to an exposed position by the hulk line to deliver its most furious bombardment.

Most of the officers were wary: the forts still fired back and shouldn't the bombardment continue until the enemy was smashed? Farragut agreed, in principle. But he told the assembly that mortar ammunition was running very short, "and the men [were] fagged out." The attack would go forward the next night. That, however, was immediately contradicted. Melancton Smith of the *Mississippi* would not budge until his carpenter and mates returned from some business at Pilot Town. Mortified, Farragut postponed the attack twenty-four hours.

The flag officer made good use of the extra day, visiting each ship and making certain that officers understood their orders. Because the operation would take place at night, there was a good deal of knuckle biting. "Everyone looked forward to the conflict with firmness, but with anxiety," he reported. At dusk, April 23, Farragut ordered a final reconnaissance of the hulk line. Half the hulks were piled ashore, their chains were "disarranged," and soundings found no obstructions in the channel. The entire fleet could pass through.

On the blasted parade ground of Fort Jackson, General Johnson Duncan had given up hope of any naval support, and once again turned his men to repairing damages "under a very heavy fire of the enemy." Around noon he noticed a clear slackening of effort, something he put to "an exhaustion" of the mortar flotilla. To Duncan, a professional artillerist who stood high in his old West Point class, it also signified "an attack with broadsides" by the main fleet. Vainly he urged Commander Mitchell to bring the *Louisiana* to the hulk line "to meet the emergency," and again Mitchell, sustained by his officers, refused. Mitchell's aide, Lieutenant George Shyrock, assured the general that the ironclad would be finished the next night—an absurd and deliberate falsehood. In any event, that was too late for Duncan. Time, he seethed at Shyrock, was critical, "the final battle was imminent within a few hours."

At four bells in the morning watch, 2 A.M., Thursday, April 24, a pair of dull, red lanterns ascended the mizzen peak of the *Hartford.* Pawl by pawl, two-score capstans clanked in the steamy night, dragging their anchors up from the river mud. The fleet was underway.

On board the venerable *Mississippi,* Captain Melancton Smith strode the hurricane deck between the big wheels and ordered up hot coffee and hardtack for the crew. "He refused to furnish grog," Albert Barker remembered, "as he was opposed to anything like 'Dutch courage.'" Smith called to his executive officer, whose brave, mustached lip did nothing to hide his youth. "I cannot see in the night," he told Lieutenant George Dewey. "I am going to leave that to you. You have younger eyes." For the battle, Smith would take charge of the guns and gave Dewey the ship—it was quite unheard of. "For a man of twenty-four," recalled the victor of Manila Bay, "I was having my share of responsibility."

Albert Barker took a moment from his quarterdeck guns to watch the grand parade. They were the third ship of the van, Red division, and he could hardly see the outlines of the *Cayuga* and *Pensacola* right ahead. The *Oneida* and *Varuna* were weighing anchor astern, he could hear their cables grinding in the hawse holes. "We steamed slowly up the river against the strong current in silence," he remembered, "awaiting in intense suspense the first shot of the enemy. At last, a flash—the whiz of a shell over our backs, and the battle had begun."

Above the hulk line, by Fort St. Philip, the Confederate naval forces clustered around the *Louisiana*. Commander John K. Mitchell made no attempt at concerted operations—the River Defense Fleet precluded that—and it was decided that each captain would act independently.

Mitchell, however, stationed a trip-wire, an armed launch, below Fort St. Philip, with orders to keep a bonfire going on the river and to shoot signal rockets at the first sign of Federal activity. Instead, the launch crew bolted into the swamp. Mitchell didn't get his first alarm until 3:30 A.M., when a sudden cannonade erupted from the mortar flotilla. Ten minutes later he watched helplessly as the first ship of Theodorus Bailey's Red division passed over the hulk line and opened fire on Fort St. Philip.

The fort responded immediately, striking the leading *Cayuga*, in Bailey's words, "from stem to stern." Trading shots wasn't her business and she pressed on to engage a swarm of rebel craft; "hot, but more congenial work." With point-blank fire she set one aflame, running her ashore. Two others tried to board. But the *Oneida* and *Varuna* skirted out of the line and "came dashing in" to finish the rebels off.

The *Oneida*, commanded by Sam Phillips Lee (called "Old Triplicate" for his devotion to detail), passed so close to Fort St. Philip "that the sparks from its . . . battery seemed to reach us." Just above the fort, the deadly *Manassas* appeared out of the gloom on the gunboat's port side and another rebel crossed the *Oneida's* bow. With a full head of steam, Lee crashed into it "and cut her down with a loud crash." The *Oneida* then checked speed and engaged targets at all points of the compass.

The *Varuna* entered the battle under orders from Commander Charles Boggs to load with grapeshot and "work both sides." When the range opened she switched to five-second shells, blew out the boiler of one rebel, set afire and ran ashore three others. Then came the cotton-clad steamer *Governor Moore* of the Louisiana Provisional Navy.

Lieutenant Beverly Kennon had just resigned his commission in the Confederate Navy to serve as an unpaid state volunteer. Within three minutes of the first gun, he had steam up and steered for the battle. It took effort to get past the aimlessly milling mass of "friendly" vessels. Twice the rebel army tug *Belle Algerine* fouled his way; the third time, Kennon rammed and sank her to get through. By the time he reached the scene of slaughter, he had taken the fire of every ship in the Federal Red division. Over half his gun crews were dead or wounded. The powder monkeys and shell passers had been so depleted, he recalled, that "I had to assist in their duties."

He came up to the *Varuna* from astern, and both ships fired simultaneously. Double stands of grapeshot "cut us up horribly." The two ships were so close that Kennon could not depress his bow gun to fire. His crew were mowed down in swaths, and marines in the *Varuna*'s tops picked off men at will. There were no more options. "I now pointed the [bow] gun through our own deck . . . and fired." Again, Kennon loaded and fired the 32-pounder rifle through his deck. Only ten feet separated the two ships, when Kennon put his helm over and squarely rammed the *Varuna*, crushing in her side. "In the twinkling of an eye," he wrote, "the crashing noise made by her breaking ribs told how amply we were repaid for all we had lost and suffered."

Kennon backed off and rammed again. He wanted to board and carry her off, but hadn't enough men. The *Varuna* limped toward shore, let go the anchors, and kept on firing until the river flowed over the gun trucks.

Twice wounded himself, and with sixty-four of his ninety-three men dead or wounded, Beverly Kennon drifted away in the *Governor Moore*. "Finding that no human being could possibly do anything with the vessel," he ordered the wounded taken off, lashed down the safety valves, and lit the torch. As he said from his Northern prisoner of war camp, "The pennant and the remains of the ensign were never hauled down. . . . I burned the bodies of the slain."

*   *   *

The *Pensacola,* second ship of the Red division, lost her bearings, stopped abreast of Fort St. Philip, then sheared over to the west bank of the river. Behind her thrashed the *Mississippi,* George Dewey on the hurricane deck, conning the frigate through a gauntlet of flying iron. He felt calmer now, being shot at. He directed all of his attention on keeping station astern of the lurching *Pensacola.* He was so close to Fort St. Philip that he could clearly hear rebel officers' shouting commands. The rebels shot back steadily, and men dropped mangled to the decks, heads and limbs torn off; the mortar bombardment was not having the smothering effect everyone hoped for.

Alfred Waud, artist and correspondent of *Harper's Weekly,* shouted down from the foretop where, above the battle, he had a far better view than on the deck. "Here is a queer-looking customer on our port bow," he yelled. Dewey turned. "I saw what appeared to be the back of an enormous turtle . . . which I identified as the ram *Manassas.*" Dewey instantly turned the *Mississippi* to run it down.

The rebel ram's skipper, Lieutenant Alexander Warley, had no luck this night. He missed the leading ships of the Red division and was insultingly rammed for his troubles by one of the River Defense vessels. Now even with the *Mississippi* dead ahead, the frigate's lumbering maneuvers proved "too quick" for the *Manassas,* and Warley struck only a glancing blow aft.

The *Mississippi* trembled, listed over, then righted herself on an even keel. The *Manassas* had delivered a punch that would have sunk any other other ship. Nonetheless, Dewey said, "the effect of the shock was that of running aground." Looking over the port rail Dewey saw the *Manassas* had ripped out a section of oak seven feet long and four wide, and "about fifty copper bolts had been cut as clean as if they were hair under a razor." Warley ducked under the hail of the *Mississippi's* broadside and headed the *Manassas* back into the fight. Athwart the channel he saw the *Brooklyn* tangled up in the hulk line.

Until they got abreast of the forts, the Blue division had absorbed for over an hour what Captain Thomas Craven of the *Brooklyn* described as "a raking and terribly scorching fire." In the pitch darkness and "blinding smoke," Craven had lost sight of the flagship ahead and ran into the remnants of the hulk line. Crushing a wreck under, "we steamed on," but when nearly by, the *Brooklyn* lurched over and stopped dead. Craven leaned over the quarterdeck rail and saw that one of his stern anchors had torn away, catching in the crushed hulk; "the hawser . . . which was fast to it, was as taut as a bar."

Help came from the river itself. The fast, five-knot current swept the ship over to the east bank, and gave just enough time for furiously axing seamen to sever the manila line. Again under control, the *Brooklyn* steamed past Fort St. Philip, at what Craven said "might be called double-quick time," pouring in three broadsides for good measure. That's when he spotted "this queer-looking gentleman."

In the *Manassas,* Lieutenant Warley fired his 32-pounder gun point-blank into the *Brooklyn's* side and rammed her amidships. The impact disabled the rebel's gun and knocked everyone in the ram to the deck. Warley backed clear for another go.

Thomas Craven of the *Brooklyn* was convinced his ship would sink. Yet the contact point came exactly where the hanging garlands of chain cable protected the engines. Damage was serious, but not fatal. The *Brooklyn* piled on steam, and as Lieutenant Warley remembered, "she . . . left me as if I had been at anchor."

In the *Hartford,* Farragut tried to use the enemy's lights as guides. But the smoke hung so heavily that the fleet advanced blind. There was nothing, he said, "but the flash of their guns." It was impossible to distinguish friend from foe, and he hadn't a guess as to how the battle was actually going. At 4:15 A.M., the Confederate army tug *Mosher* appeared right ahead, pushing a raging fire raft. The *Hartford,* swinging to clear, grounded on a shoal by Fort St. Philip as the tug shoved the raft hard up against the *Hartford's* port quarter. In return, the rebel took a Federal broadside that killed her and the entire crew of a dozen men. But they had done their job.

In a blink, the *Hartford's* side presented a single, blazing sheet, with fires licking her rigging halfway to the mast tops. The forts redoubled their shooting. The flagship's gunners replied in kind, not slackening a moment as fire parties were called away and deck pumps started. Backing off the shoal, the *Hartford* cleared the raft and in a few minutes her crew doused the flames and she steamed on. Passing the wrecks of the *Varuna* and her victims, Farragut sensed an easing of fire. The smoke cleared, dawn broke, "and we saw to our surprise, that we were above the forts."

Singly or in small groups, the fleet advanced to the Quarantine station. Vessels needing to mend battle damage stopped for hasty repairs. The *Brooklyn,* for example, suffered eight killed and twenty-six wounded. Water was pumped over her decks to wash away the blood and mangle, the dead were taken ashore and buried, and the carpenter's crew set to work patching the hull. Then Lieutenant Warley reappeared with the *Manassas.*

The *Mississippi* again sighted her first. Melancton Smith called his hands back to quarters and was about to attack. "[We had] an individual score to settle," George Dewey remembered, "but so deeply was [Captain Smith] imbued with the spirit of ante-bellum days, when officers might be censured for acting on their own initiative," that he felt he must first ask permission. With valuable minutes ticking away, Smith shouted across to his division leader, Captain Bailey in the *Cayuga,* "I want permission to run down the ram!" At that moment the fire-blackened smoking *Hartford* came up. Farragut, standing in the rigging, bellowed through a trumpet, "Run down the ram!"

Old Smith turned to Dewey, "Can you turn the ship?" "Yes, sir," the young exec answered, later saying, "I knew that either I was going to do so or else run aground." If Lieutenant Warley in the *Manassas* had any thoughts of ramming the charging frigate, he gave it up. With his crumpled bow and single gun damaged beyond redemption, he had done all he could to defend the river. The *Mississippi* fired two killing broadsides, and there was nothing else for Warley to do but save his crew. He cut the steam pipes, ran the vessel to the east bank, and ordered everyone out through the gunport, "the enemy," he said, "firing grape into us as we landed." Slogging breathless and bleeding through the marshes, Warley and his men joined a hopeless naval huddle aboard the stranded ironclad *Louisiana.*

The *Mississippi's* boats went after the prize. Albert Barker's reached her first. The valves were open to the sea, the machinery all broken, and too much time needed to get her afloat. Barker set the derelict afire. She slipped off the muddy bank, smoke pouring from every rent and shot hole, and floated down the river to sink.

Farragut collected his fleet. Less the sunken *Varuna,* only three gunboats from the rear division had not made it, and turned back at the hulk line. With the fleet above the forts, Farragut sent word to Porter to demand their surrender, and for Butler to bring up the army transports from Head of the Passes to assist. At 11 A.M. the fleet piled on steam and headed for New Orleans. Fifteen miles below the city, Farragut anchored for the night. "Weary as we were," George Dewey recalled, "there was very little sleep for anyone, as fire rafts and burning ships were drifting past us all night."

Reveille sounded before dawn, April 25 and in roughly the same formation of the day before, the fleet steamed upriver. Everyone was eager for the first sight of the city, "whose location we knew by the smoke," Dewey said. Standing on the hurricane deck, he thought the progress would be "in the nature of a parade." When the Chalmette batteries below the city, site of Andrew Jackson's victory in 1815, opened fire, the ship's elderly purser burst out, "Oh! that rash man Farragut! Here we are at it again." They were just earthworks cut into the levee, and the *Cayuga* and *Hartford* swatted the rebels away like chaff. "We did not mince the matter," Farragut reported, "but dashed directly ahead." Hammering broadsides of exploding shell and scything grapeshot exacted what he called "spiteful revenge . . . and those who could run were running in every direction." Dewey watched the smothering crescendo of battle. "Soon," he recalled, "we were abreast of the panic-stricken city." The battered ships anchored and trained their guns on the raging mobs in the streets. Thus far for the Union, it was the supreme moment of the war.

General Lovell had torched the levee and retreated out of the city. Everything was burning: steamers, stores, coal, cotton, molasses, frames of unfinished rams. Farragut called the fires "one common blaze." He dispatched a gunboat to seize the rebel ironclad *Mississippi,* "which was to be the terror of the seas," but she came floating by, wrapped in fire, and passed downriver.

The flag officer sent marines to take possession of the Federal mint, post office, and customs house. On all the public buildings, they hauled down the secession banners, and hoisted the "old" flag. Captain Theodorus Bailey, commander of Farragut's Red division, demanded the city's formal surrender. The mayor claimed to be under martial law and without authority. Farragut threatened a bombardment, and the mayor and Common Council, with plenty of ill grace, declared New Orleans an open city.

The forts had refused Porter's surrender demand and the nonstop mortar bombardment continued. He proffered a second offer two days later with the same result. But when rumors drifted down to Fort Jackson of New Orleans' capitulation, "a reaction," said General Duncan, began to permeate the garrison. At midnight, April 27, the troops mutinied. Half ran off; the rest, "broken detachments," demoralized to apathy, just sat down. Duncan acceded to the inevitable.

From across the river, Commander John K. Mitchell saw one of Porter's gunboats hoist a Confederate flag beneath her own colors. He knew Duncan had surrendered, but did not consider himself bound by the compact. Boiling with anger at General Duncan's action, Mitchell took a boat to Fort Jackson. The general refused to cancel the capitulation, and Mitchell returned to the far bank.

In the *Louisiana,* the mechanics had run off during the battle, and the army artillerists returned to their own units. What remained were the naval officers and crew, plus the survivors of various sunken ships.

On board the useless ironclad, Mitchell and his officers determined to blow her up.

Decks holystoned and dressed as if for a parade, the *Harriet Lane* led the procession up to Fort Jackson. In her tiny wardroom the articles of surrender were just being signed, when word came that the *Louisiana* was on fire and drifting down onto the Federal vessels. Porter was shocked. He had understood that everything was being given up. "This is sharp practice," he said. General Duncan shrugged, "We are not responsible for the acts of these naval officers." Amid the real danger of everything being blown to bits, the officers played a nineteenth-century version of "chicken," sitting calmly at the wardroom table and discussing terms, when Lieutenant Whittle of the Confederate Navy entered. On Mitchell's orders, he informed the assembly that the *Louisiana* had burned through her moorings, and as anyone could see, was now adrift. Pointedly ignoring the uncomfortable messenger, Porter asked the *army* officers if the ironclad carried any powder. They presumed so, but really had no idea. Porter turned to Lieutenant Whittle, "Say to Captain Mitchell I am much obliged."

The *Louisiana*'s overloaded guns cooked off. Porter refused to notice it, saying instead to General Duncan, "If you don't mind the effects of the explosion which is soon to come, we can stand it." Not a man moved from the table but everyone, Union and Confederate, each as vehement as the other, burst out in heated condemnation of "the ever-memorable" Commander John K. Mitchell, the "archtraitor," and his "infamous act." Soon, not far from where she had cast adrift, the *Louisiana* blew up. Her five tons of powder utterly destroyed the vessel and also killed a man in Fort St. Philip.

Mitchell and his command boarded some tugs to wait their fate. The *Harriet Lane* fired a single shot across his bow, and Mitchell lowered his flag.

On May 1, Ben Butler and the army came up from Quarantine to begin full military occupation of New Orleans.

The decision to go ahead with the capture of New Orleans ranks as one of the strategic milestones of the war. At a blow, the South's largest city, premier port of entry, and the mouth of the Mississippi, fell to the Union. But for all that, the operation fell short. Nothing was conceived beyond linking up at Vicksburg with the Western Gunboat Flotilla. But ships and gunboats cannot hold enemy real estate, the Union needed substantial accompanying troops for that, and it would pay long and dearly for the lack.

Vicksburg Rebuff

"The elements of destruction in this river are beyond anything I ever encountered, and if [it] *continues the whole*
Navy will be destroyed in twelve months."

—**Flag Officer David Glasgow Farragut**

N ew Orleans taken, Farragut faced the dilemma of what to do
next. He could either head up the Mississippi and rendezvous
with the gunboat flotilla somewhere around Vicksburg, or
take his big ships back into the Gulf and attack Mobile. Gideon Welles'
dog-eared orders of three months' back ambiguously pointed in both
directions, but Farragut lacked the resources to accomplish both aims
simultaneously.

Because his blue-water ships were far better acclimated to operations in the Gulf, Farragut leaned toward Mobile. In early May, he
detached Porter to lob a few mortar shells into the barrier forts at the
entrance to Mobile Bay, and await the flag officer's arrival with the
main squadron.

Farragut, however, could not neglect Vicksburg and the river. The
orders were very explicit on that point. Forced by circumstance to
divide his command, Farragut sent Old Triplicate, Sam Phillips Lee,
with the gunboats and 1,400 troops under Brigadier General Thomas
Williams, to destroy the railroad terminus at Vicksburg, and if possible
seize the town.

This was the moment for a grand convergence in the west, a three-
pronged general advance that could have gained complete control of

the Mississippi River in the summer of 1862. But Davis and his flotilla tarried too long at Fort Pillow, Old Brains Halleck refused to move on Corinth without fortifying his line of march, and Farragut dreaded taking his ships up 500 miles of brown water. Three precious weeks were wasted, which cost the Union a year of war.

But Porter delivered good news from the Gulf. His practice shots at Mobile Bay had spooked the Confederate commander at nearby Pensacola. Evidently prepared for this moment, he evacuated his sick, set fire to "every combustible from the navy yard to Fort McRee," and withdrew his forces. With poetic justice, Porter arrived in the *Harriet Lane* to help ferry the Union troops from Fort Pickens to the mainland. Though nearly destroyed, the navy yard was still a sheltered harbor with serviceable wharves—a great improvement over Ship Island. Porter recommended moving everything over. "We are leading rather an inactive life for us," he wrote to Farragut. "It will be gratifying when we hear that our services will be needed again." It came soon enough.

On May 2, Farragut summoned his captains. "Who is ready to go, right off?" he asked. The *Brooklyn* and four gunboats were ready, and he started them upriver to Vicksburg. A few days later, he followed on with the *Hartford* and *Richmond*.

Above Baton Rouge the navigational difficulties increased by the hour. The river, higher than anyone remembered, lapped the tops of six-foot earthen levees. Even so, as Chief of Staff Henry Bell noted in his diary, "every gunboat grounded repeatedly, some of them three times a day." Coal was another problem. To escort colliers up from New Orleans, Farragut had to detach his gunboats to sweep roving bands of rebel guerrillas or field artillery from the riverbanks.

On May 12, the squadron assembled at the state capital, Baton Rouge, grabbing the local coal yard before the rebels could fire it. From here, Lee took his gunboat division to Vicksburg. The squadron followed. At nightfall, below Natchez, the *Hartford*'s make-do pilot mistook some bushes on a mudflat for the encroaching forest and grounded the ship. Running the crew from side to side accomplished nothing, and there would be no tide to lift her off. Towlines to the gunboats snapped like kite string. They tried kedging-off with a three-ton stream anchor shackled to an eleven-inch hawser. "No go," said Henry Bell. Coal and three 9-inch guns were taken out, but she didn't move.

The next evening she was still stuck fast in the mud. A Gulf steamer came up, made fast a heavy towline, and thrashed downriver at full throttle, ripping the hawse chock out of her deck without starting the *Hartford* in the slightest. Farragut knew real fear. The river had crested, and the only thing it could do was fall; if that happened, the *Hartford* would stay grounded for weeks, maybe the whole summer. After more unloading of coal and stores, she was finally dislodged from the mud by the *Itasca*. "[We] got her off in two days," Farragut informed Gideon Welles, "but my health suffered from anxiety and loss of sleep."

On May 18, Lee, shepherding Brigadier Williams' transports, arrived before Vicksburg. The town rose up a series of terraces, 300 feet high along the eastern bluffs of a steep horseshoe bend. Had Farragut and Butler sent a force immediately after the fall of New Orleans, they just might have taken it, but not now. The Confederates had been given three precious weeks to build their first batteries, and several regiments, perhaps 2,000 men, were already at work digging the soon famous trenches.

Under a flag of truce, Sam Phillips Lee demanded the town's surrender "to the lawful authority of the United States." The Confederate military governor threw back an insulting reply, which the Federals never forgot. "Mississippians," he said, "don't know and refuse to learn how to surrender to an enemy. If Commodore Farragut and . . . General Butler can teach them, let them come and try." Lee gave the rebels twenty-four hours to evacuate their women and children before he opened fire.

Farragut anchored the squadron sixty-miles south at Natchez. Unaware of the real situation, he fretted at the delay and Lee's "dilatory movements" in capturing the town. With uncharacteristic naivete, he assured Henry Bell that the rebels would abandon the place if presented with an "imposing" show of force.

At Vicksburg, Brigadier Williams discovered that nature had already done the work assigned to his men. The western railroad he was supposed to destroy—the Vicksburg, Shreveport & Texas—terminated across the river at De Soto, on Young's Point, the sodden tongue of land that formed the west inner horseshoe bend. The track bed was flooded for twenty miles back. The only other military objective for Williams and the army was storming and occupying Vicksburg itself, and he had neither the numbers nor stamina for that. His troops were in miserable shape. Racked with malaria and dysentery, begging food from the navy, they lived crammed in their fetid vessels, as Williams said, "more like livestock than men."

When informed of these seemingly insurmountable difficulties,

Farragut headed up in the gunboat *Kennebec*. On May 22, two miles from Vicksburg's water batteries, he saw a pair of Confederate River Defense rams tied to the wharves. His blood up over the rebel insults, he ordered the gunboats to take them in a surprise cutting-out attack that night. Two skippers were willing to give it a try, but most considered it "impracticable madness." Lee, according to Henry Bell, "carried his objection so far as to say anyone who would undertake it might have his vessel." Farragut took Old Triplicate at his word, replacing him in command of the gunboat division with James Palmer of the *Iroquois*.

Against the advice of his captains, who feared for their ships' safety in the unpredictable river, Farragut ordered the heavy ships to continue up to Vicksburg, leaving the rebel rams unharmed. On May 25, ill with dysentery, he dragged himself to a council of war. Once and for all, Farragut wanted to know, do we attack the town? Brigadier Williams feared landing his transports at the waterfront until the fleet had silenced the hilltop batteries. Even if that happened, there were barely enough troops to mount the cliffs and spike the rebel guns. He pointed out that it was impossible to hold Vicksburg with 1,400 sick men.

Most of the senior officers agreed that the ships' flat trajectory guns couldn't reach the highest batteries. Henry Bell recalled Commander Palmer and some of the gunboat skippers wanting to "go into it and smash them up," to avenge the insulting remarks to the flag officer. Neither for the first nor the last time, Commander James Alden of the *Richmond* wavered. "Alden thought we should attack, and should not attack, and hid his face in his hands."

Farragut was beaten and he knew it. Without a strong, cooperating military force, the town stood inviolate. The first attempt at Vicksburg had failed. Later, Farragut said, "I was very sick at the time and yielded to advice, which I think was good; but I doubt if I would have taken it had I been well." Leaving Palmer and the gunboats to blockade the town and throw an occasional shell into the batteries, the ships and transports dropped down to New Orleans. At Baton Rouge, Williams landed his brigade to chase some guerrillas up the main street. The action presented a good excuse to occupy the state capital, and the soldiers were finally given the chance to take a bath.

Back at New Orleans Farragut received a rude shock when he opened his official mail. Of the navy's squadron commanders, he was the farthest from Washington, which greatly confounded timely communications. In contrast to Davis' telegraph at Cairo, a day's turnaround, Farragut's link was a fast steamer to Hampton Roads, taking about twenty days round trip. When a Memphis newspaper on May 11 claimed that Farragut's squadron had turned back at Natchez, not even reaching Vicksburg, it created a panic within the Lincoln administration. Fox called in Captain Theodorus Bailey, who had brought Farragut's New Orleans victory dispatches of six weeks ago. There was nobody in Washington with more recent official information. How many ships, Fox wanted to know, did Farragut send upriver? As of the end of April, Bailey answered, "None."

"Impossible," Fox exploded, "the instructions were positive." Bailey volunteered that the flag officer might have forgotten his original orders. Lincoln ordered Gideon Welles to send new orders in triplicate by three steamers.

Farragut nearly choked at the words: "Carry out your instructions of January 20 about ascending the Mississippi River, as it is of the utmost importance." In a private letter, Fox implored the flag officer, "Everything sinks into insignificance compared with this." Farragut took up his pen. The passage to Vicksburg, he informed the secretary, had been his farthest from seawater since childhood days, and a journey "of greater anxiety I never had." There was never enough coal, no regular pilots, constant grounding of ships, chronic disease for everyone, no rations for the army, and because of that, half rations for the fleet.

All that aside, he wrote, "the elements of destruction in this river are beyond anything I ever encountered." He had lost more anchors and seen more vessels damaged than in a lifetime on the ocean. Not a third of his ships were fit for duty, "their sides are smashed in, their cutwaters entirely broomed up and removed. . . . They all require docking—ribs broken, plank-sheer gone, stems torn off to the wood ends." He had also been lucky the ironclad ram *Arkansas* hadn't made an appearance. She was up the Yazoo, a tributary north of Vicksburg, and everyone, North and South, waited for her daily. Had she come, it would have been a Hampton Roads slaughter all over again. "Why can not the Department spare us a monitor?" he pleaded, it would be "worth all the gunboats in the river."

His missive sent off, Farragut spent a hectic week at New Orleans repairing his vessels, making arrangements for towing coal barges, and tripling the number of transports and store ships. He asked Porter to send six mortar boats from Mobile Bay, and Ben Butler doubled the army contingent to 3,200 men, all he could spare, "to take the town or have it burned." But he knew they were not enough. Porter, too, was apprehensive. It was late in the season, and the Mississippi River must soon fall. "We are not prepared for it and [the expedition] will fail," he forthrightly told the flag officer. Chief of staff Henry Bell, confiding to his diary, felt the same way. "Our force for ascending the river is neither adequate nor of proper organization. Coal and ammunition cannot be brought up for want of river steamers; troops are too few; river falling. . . . Weather very sultry and hot."

Nobody wanted to go, but the situation at Vicksburg was dire. Besides being nearly out of coal, Commander Palmer wrote, "the gunboats are all . . . in a most crippled condition," and the crews sick with scurvy. "Unless supplies come up, we cannot stay here a week longer." At dawn, June 8, the *Hartford* weighed anchor and led the squadron back upriver to Vicksburg.

The next day, Porter arrived at New Orleans. In place of the penny packet of mortars Farragut had asked for, Porter brought the whole flotilla. "I never like to send a boy on a man's errand," he told Ben Butler, "so instead of six . . . I bring nineteen." He headed up immediately, steamers towing the schooners, passing Farragut along the way. On June 20, Porter dropped anchor just below Vicksburg. Other than the *Brooklyn* and the gunboats firing a shot into the high terrace batteries, everyone and everything dragged in the miserable humid torpor of a Mississippi bottomland summer.

Porter was appalled at what he found. The men simply could not stand the heat. Under ravening clouds of mosquitoes, ships' crews tried to snatch what sleep they could in the day, doing their heavy work at night. When a supply vessel came up, Captain Thomas Craven, very jealous of Porter's elevated stature, refused to honor the flotilla's victualling requests, sending the forms downriver to higher authority. "We of the mortar fleet," Porter wrote to his friend and patron, Gus Fox, "are living on *half rations,* no flour, no bread, no butter, no sugar, no molasses, and a store ship . . . laying close alongside of us—but we are outsiders and not expected to eat."

On June 25, the *Hartford* came to rest below Vicksburg. That night, the first thread of the naval noose that eventually strangled the Confederacy at its watery margins was woven along the river. Medical Cadet Charles Rivers Ellet, rowing in a small skiff, bumped the flagship's side and climbed aboard to deliver dispatches from his uncle, Colonel Alfred Ellet, who now commanded the brown-paper rams. The Ellets offered to undertake anything Farragut suggested, and to pass his communications up to Flag Officer Davis at Memphis. Farragut was profoundly grateful. He asked Alfred Ellet to assume control over the twelve miles of river between the mouth of the Yazoo and Vicksburg, and to inform Davis the Gulf squadron would run the by Vicksburg batteries within forty-eight hours.

Farragut's plan had much in common with the dash below New Orleans. He would steam upriver, past the town and batteries, in two parallel columns, *Richmond, Hartford,* and *Brooklyn* on the starboard hand, nearest the enemy, and eight gunboats, led by the *Iroquois,* on the port, Young's Point side of the river. Farragut recommended "the free use of shrapnel" as a good man-killer for the rebel gun crews. For the water batteries lower down by the wharves, "give them grape." The mortar flotilla dropped anchor where their high trajectories lent the best support with smothering shellfire. The flag officer stressed this would not be the undisciplined mad rush of New Orleans. Rather, the big ships of the starboard column would take their time to destroy the fortifications. He also ordered ample gaps between the heavy ships for the gunboats to shoot between, and not over them.

Something, however, was not clear, and a good amount of trouble and disunity it caused. Twice Thomas Craven of the *Brooklyn* asked, "Is it your desire for me to leave any batteries behind me that have not been silenced?" And twice Farragut answered, "No, sir; not on any account."

There was another flaw in the whole operation and clarity had nothing to do with it; there were not enough troops to occupy the city. Brigadier Williams had no qualm about charging up the hill with fixed bayonets to spike the guns, but not with 3,200 men against a garrison of like number and 12,000 reinforcements within a day's march. Instead he landed his artillery on Young's Point, across the river, and engaged the uppermost guns on the terraced heights.

As four bells, 2 A.M., struck in the middle watch of June 28, two red lanterns rose up the *Hartford's* mizzenmast, and the squadron weighed anchor. From both sides of the river, the mortar flotilla commenced the bombardment, shells tumbling over and over, the burning fuses leaving tails of crisscrossing fire through the night sky. From Young's Point, Williams' artillery joined in. Under the canopy of fire, the squadron steamed upriver in stately array.

Until they came abreast of the town, broadsides were useless, and the ships took the enemy's metal without reply. At 4:15, the *Hartford* opened fire. The elevation was far too great, and only a fraction of shells actually exploded among the batteries 190 feet atop a ridge.

Farragut, as was his custom, climbed up the mizzen rigging, "my

favorite stand. . . . The scene," he remembered, "soon became ani-
mated, both parties doing their best to destroy each other."

As usual, the rebels shot high, canceling their advantage of plunging fire, but playing havoc with masts and upperworks. The gun captain
on the *Hartford*'s poop yelled up that the flag officer blocked his aim,
"and requested me to get down." Farragut did, and a moment later, the
whole mizzen rigging was swept away. The damage snared his flag to
half-mast. No one in the *Hartford* noticed it, but "this circumstance,
caused the other vessels to think that I was dead."

At sunrise, *Hartford* came abreast the town, and the *Richmond* and
two gunboats passed out of sight around the horseshoe bend. *Hartford*
followed on, raked in the stern, "cutting our lower rigging severely,"
wrote Henry Bell. Behind the flagship, the *Brooklyn, Katahdin,* and *Kennebec* were still at the batteries, taking fire. Not yet beyond the town, both
Thomas Craven in the *Brooklyn* and the skipper of the *Kennebec* had
interpreted Farragut's verbal orders to mean keeping below the town,
trading blows until the rebel guns were knocked out. When they did not
appear around the horseshoe bend, Farragut worried over their fate.
"What is the difficulty?" he asked Craven in a solicitous letter.

Uncharacteristically, Farragut refused to accept Craven's answer
and issued a damning, official censure. "It was your duty," he wrote, "to
have followed your flag-officer until his situation justified you in abandoning him as hopeless." For Captain Craven, the humiliation was too
much. To remain in the squadron, he felt, degraded him "to the level of
a serf." Craven requested his own immediate relief and was replaced in
command of the *Brooklyn* by Henry Bell.

Costing fifteen dead and more than thirty wounded, the squadron,
most of it, had passed above Vicksburg, "but," Farragut told Gideon
Welles, "to no purpose." Without at least 12,000 troops, nothing further
could be done. To General Halleck he wrote, "My orders are to clear
the river. This I find impossible without your assistance." In a letter to
his family he expressed hope: "As soon as General Halleck sends the
soldiers to occupy it by land, we will drive them out of the forts."

Farragut's situation was actually quite precarious. All of his supplies were below Vicksburg, he was above it, and the river began to fall.
"My orders are so peremptory," he wrote Charles Davis, that no option
remained than to attack the batteries again. Cadet Ellet carried the dispatch up to Memphis. Davis opened the seal, read the communication,
and penned a letter to the Navy Department: "I leave [for Vicksburg] at
the earliest possible moment."

On July 1, under their usual heralding mass of black smoke, the

Western Gunboat Flotilla rounded the point and appeared above Vicksburg. "Every vessel cheered us," Davis wrote. Led by the *Benton,* the ironclads steamed along the line of Farragut's saltwater ships, the crews of both yelling themselves hoarse. For the officers, old friends met again, and for many an amazed enlisted man in the flotilla, it was their first sight of a regular man-o'-war. Davis, the junior flag officer, boarded the *Hartford,* and he and Farragut took each other by both hands. "A memorable day," wrote Henry Bell, "it rejoiced all hearts. Davis looking well; brought no troops. Bah!"

To keep the rebels from constantly fortifying their defensive positions, the mortar flotilla kept up a slow fire throughout the daylight hours, "we drive them off," Porter said, "as often as they attempt to work." Already the mortars had dismounted two of the enemy's guns on the heights. To blunt an expected counterattack on the boats, Porter built a line of earthworks, studded with fourteen boat howitzers, along the riverbank south of the city. In front, nearly up to the rebel trenches, his pickets placed a large ship's bell to herald the foe's approach.

On the nights of June 30 and July 2 they came, three regiments strong charging the anchored schooner line. The bell clanged, and all vessels opened gun and mortar fire for a mile along the riverbank. "The result," Porter said, "was a perfect stampede on the part of the rebels." Badly led, they got literally stuck in the mud and many were captured with all their weapons and equipment. Porter claimed that with 100 men on the riverbank, he could have put the whole lot in the bag. "I hope that the army will soon come along," he told Farragut, "for we won't do much without them. Ships can not crawl up these hills. If they could, we could soon settle the business."

On Independence Day, the vessels flew more than their usual number of flags, and all fired a twenty-one-gun national salute at noon. In marked frustration, Farragut waited news of reinforcement by the army. A few days later, he read a message from General Halleck. Complaining of the "scattered and weakened condition" of his army, Old Brains could do nothing for Vicksburg now. "This may delay the clearing of the river," he blathered, "but its accomplishment will be certain in a few weeks." The letter was dated July 4, 1862—he was off by exactly a year.

"We are still at this place," Farragut wrote to Gideon Welles, "bombarding it by the mortars from both sides of the peninsula." Every night, Porter had to beat off attacks of rebel infantry, and every morning he hauled in his booty of prisoners, shoes, packs, and muskets from the swamps around his flagship. Farragut joined Davis for a reconnaissance in the *Benton,* his first experience in an ironclad. A heavy shot crashed through the casemate, killing a man. Farragut looked at the gory mess. "Everybody to his taste," he said to Davis; "I am going on deck; I feel safer outside."

For the vessels above Vicksburg the torpid summer weeks brought a time, Henry Walke said, "of comparative rest." But it was also, as Farragut reported, the "sickly season." The *Brooklyn* had sixty-eight men down with malaria and dysentery, and there wasn't enough quinine for one ship, let alone all. The river had dropped sixteen feet from high water, and inside of two weeks, Farragut's big ships would be trapped. Barely masking his frustration, he asked Secretary Welles, "Shall they go down[river], or remain up the rest of the year?"

The Gulf coast, he wrote, was where the squadron belonged. Up here his seagoing ships were absolutely wasted and rotting away. Give Davis enough troops and the turtles and stinkpots could handle Vicksburg and the river. The sole Confederate naval threat, the ironclad *Arkansas,* still lay far up the Yazoo, "from whence I do not think she will ever come forth." Welles had already come to many of these conclusions, and Farragut's reports crossed several departmental orders and announcements.

While Farragut had been laboring up the Mississippi, Welles had pushed through the most sweeping naval reforms in a generation. He got Congress to open up the ladder of naval promotion, creating the ranks of rear admiral, commodore, lieutenant commander, and ensign. Four rear admirals were created immediately: Farragut, Goldsborough, Du Pont, and Foote; Stringham, Paulding, and six others were promoted to rear admiral on the retired list. Charles Davis was promoted to commodore.

Admitting the deleterious effects of daily alcohol, Congress ruled "the spirit ration of the United States Navy shall forever cease." All enlisted personnel would receive five cents a day in lieu. Porter, and other officers who enjoyed a drink, took to imbibing "vinegar bitters," "Mrs. Winslow's Soothing Syrup," and other "medicinal" concoctions that were permitted on board. Finally, though the actual switch would not take place for three months, Congress approved the long-needed bill transferring the Western Gunboat Flotilla from the army to the navy.

Meanwhile General Halleck decided against sending any troops to Vicksburg. Instead, Old Brains divided his army to cover western Tennessee and Kentucky, and then he went east to become general in chief of the United States Army.

The breakup of Halleck's army decided Farragut's future at

Vicksburg. On July 14, the orders went out from the department: return to the Gulf. Commodore Davis, the turtles, and the stinkpots would take over the job on the river. Porter, very ill with malaria, "intermittent fever" he called it, got welcome orders to bring the gunboat *Octorara* and a dozen mortar schooners all the way back to Hampton Roads.

However, before learning any of this, the commanders at Vicksburg had planned a reconnaissance foray up the Yazoo. The *Carondelet, Tyler,* and *Queen of the West* would head up the next morning, July 15.

In the last days of May, Lieutenant Isaac Newton Brown, described by his old messmate Henry Walke as "one of the best of the Confederate officers," arrived at Greenwood, Mississippi, 100 miles up the Yazoo. He found his new command, the ironclad *Arkansas,* in complete disarray: hull unplated, engine in pieces, guns without carriages, and hardly any crew. Regarding his predecessor who had overseen the work, Isaac Brown said, "I came near to shooting him."

The ironclad began at Memphis, of scrap and railroad iron gathered from all over western Tennessee, and her reputation was bad from the first. The executive officer, Henry Kennedy Stevens, told his wife, "She is such a humbug, and badly constructed." In appearance, the *Arkansas* was a basic Confederate casemate ironclad, having sloped front and rear faces, oddly perpendicular sides, a squat pilothouse forward, and a hugely prominent funnel rising amidships. In the nick of time, the Confederates had snatched her from the cataclysm at Memphis, and brought the ship up the Yazoo for completion.

Isaac Brown found the barge carrying the armor plate "carelessly sunken" on the river bottom, and he conducted a major salvage operation with professional divers to retrieve it. Brown towed the *Arkansas* downriver to better facilities at Yazoo City, and he pressed into Confederate service every blacksmith and mechanic for 100 miles around, jailing those who refused the work. Fourteen forges were hauled from nearby plantations, and a foundry and floating workshop were set up in the steamer *Capitol;* 200 soldiers came as laborers. But still, the armoring was never completed, and the *Arkansas* could have presented bare timber on her quarters, stern, and pilothouse except, "we tacked boilerplate over it for appearance sake."

The armament of ten guns, was as usual, a very mixed lot: 9-inch Dahlgrens, Brooke rifles, ancient army 42-pounders, and navy 32-pounders. Brown recruited more than 160 men from the crews of sunken Confederate naval vessels, and General Jeff Thompson's Missouri bushwhackers. Some artillerymen were even pried from the army. Passable gun carriages were manufactured locally.

Brown, however, never solved the problem with the engines. Twin-screwed, "they were built (or botched, rather)," said Lieutenant George Gift, "at a foundry on Adams Street," Memphis. They had the maddening tendency of suddenly stopping, but never together, slewing the ship around in a circle despite any action of the rudder. Yet, within five weeks of his arrival, Brown had the *Arkansas* ready—or at least as ready as possible—for action.

Isaac Brown understood the unanimous wish of his officers and crew to attack the enemy at Vicksburg. But he was not certain that was the best approach. The *Arkansas,* he thought, should remain in the Yazoo and operate defensively. There were still a number of good steamers on the river, and the Yazoo valley was capable of furnishing large quantities of food and other agricultural products to the Confederate armies. With batteries along the riverbanks, Brown and the *Arkansas* could ensure uninterrupted production and delivery within the theater of operations. If, on the other hand, she sortied to attack the Federals off Vicksburg, she might damage some targets of opportunity, but not accomplish anything of lasting value.

General Earl Van Dorn, the Confederate commander at Vicksburg, had other ideas. He wanted the *Arkansas* to exit the Yazoo, run past the combined fleets, and attack the *Brooklyn,* mortar boats, and supply vessels below the town. That presented a measure of tactical logic, and perhaps success. But Van Dorn, a capable, experienced officer, might have had a touch of fever when he suggested that Brown steam down the entire Mississippi, destroy everything in his way, exit at New Orleans, and head for Mobile! "It is better to die game and do some execution," he said, "than to lie by and be burned up in the Yazoo."

Isaac Newton Brown never needed anyone to tell him his duty, and he required none now. Van Dorn and other critics he called "impatient spectators. . . . If the army will attack against the same odds as that which awaits me, the war will soon be over."

On July 13, Brown took the *Arkansas* down the Yazoo to Sartatia. The next morning, leaking steam seeped into the magazine, wetting the gunpowder. Brown pulled up at an abandoned sawmill and spread tarpaulins over the sawdust. In the clear and very hot day, by constant shaking and turning, the crew had their powder dried before sunset.

Well before dawn, July 15, the *Arkansas* stripped for battle and steamed down through the heavily wooded countryside. When about ten miles from the Mississippi, the sun rose over the stern on a perfectly warm and calm day. Lieutenant Charles Read remembered the quiet, "save the dull thump, thump, thump of the propellers." The crew were at quarters, guns loaded. "Pretty soon we discovered smoke above the trees, winding along the course of the crooked Yazoo: we saw . . . ahead, under full steam, three Federal vessels in line approaching," *Tyler, Carondelet,* and *Queen of the West.*

Lieutenant William Gwin in the *Tyler* opened fire, and backed downriver, stern first, keeping up a fire from his bow guns. Seeing he would be overtaken before reaching the relative safety of the *Carondelet,* he rounded and loosed a broadside at 300 yards, "which apparently had no effect, although the shot struck her." Stinkpot against ironclad ram was suicide, but Gwin held his position to give what support he could to Henry Walke's lone turtle and the Ellet steamer.

"All was calm, bright and beautiful," Walke remembered, when he saw the *Arkansas,* "coming down boldly." He had never fought an ironclad before, and his crew was so reduced by sickness that only one division of guns could be served at a time. He ordered Gwin to put on all speed and sound the alarm at Vicksburg, but got no response. The *Queen of the West* hugged close to the *Tyler* apparently waiting for orders.

It was madness to continue steaming bows on against the ram. Walke turned the *Carondelet* downriver to the Mississippi, and at 500 yards, fired his stern guns into the enemy. He was later faulted for "running away," as some ignorantly thought. "I was not such a simpleton as to 'take the bull by the horns,'" he wrote after the war, "to be fatally rammed, and sacrifice my command through fear of the criticisms of any man. . . . A collision, which the enemy desired, would have been inevitable, and would have sunk the *Carondelet* in a few minutes."

But it was not all one-sided by any means. Accurate shooting took its toll on Confederate personnel and the ram's soft points. Rebel Lieutenant George Gift recalled how "an Irishman, with more curiosity than prudence, stuck his head out a broadside port, and was killed by a heavy rifle bolt which had missed the ship." Headless, the corpse fell back, pouring blood all over the sanded deck. Lieutenant Stevens, the *Arkansas'* executive officer, feared the sight would demoralize the gun crews and called to a nearby man to help throw it over the side. "Oh! I can't do it, sir," he pleaded, "it's my brother"; but into the river the body went.

A company of the 4th Wisconsin formed in ranks on the *Tyler's* deck, and fired by volleys at the only visible target aboard the rebel:

Isaac Brown atop the casemate. He took a glancing minié ball in the head and fell. "But this gave me no concern," he remembered, "after I failed to find any brains mixed with the handful of clotted blood which I drew from the wound and examined."

A moment later, a shot from the *Tyler* struck at his feet, penetrated the unarmored pilothouse—taking off a section of the wheel—killed the chief pilot, and disabled another. One of the Missouri bushwhackers took the helm. "Keep the ironclad ahead," Brown ordered, before falling down the hatch to the gun deck. After some minutes, he recalled, "I awoke as if from sleep, to find kind hands helping me to a place among the killed and wounded."

Patched and bandaged, Brown climbed topside. The *Carondelet* was still ahead, but much closer, perhaps 100 yards off, and the helmsman, having gotten no orders since Brown's wounding, shadowed the prey into a willow marsh. The turtle was badly damaged. Brown could see the white wooden backing where raking fire had gone through her stern and smoke poured from every gunport. The distance came down to twenty feet, and the *Carondelet,* her steering ropes shot away, scraped into the bank. The *Arkansas,* with her thirteen-foot draft, could not follow or she would ground.

Henry Walke brought his men up the hurricane deck to repel boarders. When the *Arkansas* sheared off slightly the two ironclads came parallel, and he ordered the crew back to their guns. Lieutenant Charles Read of the *Arkansas* remembered the cannon muzzles touching, and "we poured in a broadside of solid shot when his colors came down." The *Carondelet* lurched over from the impact and took a flood of brown water over her foredeck. To the crew of the *Arkansas* she appeared sinking and they cheered the victory. Steam from burst pipes filled the turtle's gun deck, six men were dead, and the wounded were carried topside.

Isaac Brown conned the *Arkansas* back to the main channel, where the *Tyler* and *Queen of the West* waited, watching the battle of the ironclads. The *Queen's* skipper, an army lieutenant, let slip a golden opportunity for ramming, and made off at top speed for the Mississippi. He was "followed," said a seaman in the *Tyler,* "by a storm of what the darkey called the 'wustest kind of language' from [Commander] Gwin."

Gwin, seeing the *Arkansas* emerge from the willows, could not remain and live. Keeping 200 feet ahead, "I stood down the river with all speed." The stinkpot was hit eleven times and counted eight dead and eighteen wounded. But in the uneven stern chase, she exacted a remarkably heavier toll on the rebel.

Banging away through his stern ports, Gwin smacked the *Arkansas* repeatedly at the base of her stack, shooting away the boiler uptakes and destroying the furnace draft. The rebel's speed dropped to a crawl, barely enough for steerage way, and she glided on with the current. Flame and gasses from the machinery spaces filled the gun deck, and the temperature rose to 120 degrees. Brown went below to inspect the engines and found the black gang working in 130 degrees of hell. Lieutenant Stevens had been relieving the stokers and engineers every fifteen minutes.

Then suddenly, she was out of the Yazoo and in the Mississippi. Brown saw nothing ahead, save "the two chases driven before us." He shouted an order into the wrecked pilothouse, and the *Arkansas* started the final crawl to Vicksburg, with nothing in the way except most of the U.S. forces afloat on the Mississippi. Pushed by the current, Brown rounded the horseshoe point, and saw just ahead, "a forest of masts and smokestacks—ships, rams, ironclads, and other gunboats ... the genius of havoc could not have offered a finer view."

The combined Union squadrons had heard the shooting for over an hour, had seen the *Queen of the West* and *Tyler* running out the Yazoo for their lives, and were still caught asleep, steam down, boilers cold. For both Farragut and Davis, it was an inexcusable lapse.

Through his glass, Brown could actually pick out certain officers, old "valued friends," on the Federal quarterdecks. Brown had a ram under his feet, but no speed to use it—the *Tyler* had seen to that—else it might have been a Hampton Roads slaughter all over again. He ordered a course to Vicksburg, shaving Farragut's line as close as possible, and opened fire on the *Hartford.*

Awakened from their torpor, 100 Federal guns blasted out, their smoke mingling with the blanketing heat of the river, turning the air black. "As we advanced," Brown remembered, "the line of fire seemed to grow into a circle constantly closing." Shot after shot smashed into the *Arkansas'* hull and casemate, shaking loose whole patches of armor, knocking over her stack.

For twenty minutes it went on, and only the continual roar of guns showed the *Arkansas* still lived. Then, out of the maelstrom, said a reporter from the *Cincinnati Times,* "the big smoke" made for the town. With ten dead and sixteen badly wounded, Isaac Brown, blood streaming down his face, brought the crippled, victorious *Arkansas* to rest at Vicksburg. The whole military command, Van Dorn at their head, the population behind, rushed cheering down to the waterfront. Brown took off his cap, showing a hole in his head, and turned to the

crew. "Boys," he choked, "I never was under fire before, but I am not so
scared as I expected to be."

Farragut never experienced greater humiliation in his whole career
than on that day. Sam Phelps blamed the admiral's "inattention" for the
whole debacle. When Farragut conferred with Davis aboard the *Benton,* Phelps described him "full of going down immediately to destroy
the rebel with his fleet—going off at once; couldn't wait a moment."
Davis urged waiting until dusk when the sun would be in rebel eyes,
not their own. "But it was hard to dissuade him," Phelps said, "from his
. . . desperation in destroying the *Arkansas.*"

The plan was for Davis and the mortar scows to engage the Vicksburg batteries from upriver and Young's Point, while Farragut's
squadron, with the captured cottonclad *General Sumter,* ran past, guns
pouring fire into the ironclad. On the chance of a closer engagement,
anchors and grappling hooks were hung from yardarms, ready to drop
on the *Arkansas'* deck.

At 6 P.M., Davis opened his bombardment of the town. But by the
time all were underway, dark had fallen, and the *Arkansas* lay hidden in
the gloom. Farragut, leading in the *Hartford,* steamed past Vicksburg.
"As we turned the point," wrote the commanding officer of the gunboat
Sciota, "the bullets began to fly over us very thickly." He returned the
fire with muskets in the hands of sick officers and men, "too feeble to
work the heavy gun." The *Sumter* was holed twice below the waterline,
five more Union sailors were killed, and the gunboat *Winona,* badly hit,
ran aground to keep from sinking. "The thing was a failure," wrote Sam
Phelps.

The following day, July 16, Farragut suggested a combined daylight
assault on the Vicksburg waterfront to engage the water batteries,
while the turtles and Ellet's rams dealt with the *Arkansas.* Davis
refused. He could not chance being cut off, stranded below the town
with his bases above it.

On July 22, they made a last attempt. Just after daylight, three turtles opened fire on the batteries at the apex of the horseshoe. Under
the umbrella of shells, Dirty Bill Porter in the *Essex* and Alfred Ellet in
the *Queen of the West* advanced on the Vicksburg waterfront. From
below, Farragut opened a bombardment of the lower batteries. The
General Sumter moved up, converging on the target.

With forty-one men fit for duty, the *Arkansas* cleared for action.
"The cannonading was tremendous," Lieutenant Read recalled, "and
fairly shook the earth." After half an hour, the *Essex* emerged from the
smoke, steamed directly for the rebel, and hurled a 10-inch solid shot

into a forward gunport; twenty men were swept away. The *Essex* came on at ramming speed. A rebel sailor let go the bowline, the *Arkansas* drifted just enough, the *Essex* delivered a grazing blow and "ran," Dirty Bill said, "with great force high on the bank."

The two ironclads traded broadsides with cannon depressed to their lowest limits, before the *Essex,* the target of 100 Confederate guns, backed off the bank and dropped downriver. The *Arkansas* had not yet reloaded, when the *General Sumter* was spotted heading right for her. The vessels collided broadside, swung free, and the *Sumter* ran aground, her bow completely out of the water. Now came the *Queen of the West.* But she lost precious headway in maneuvering, and failed, Alfred Ellet said, to crash "a full blow." Every rebel artilleryman shifted fire, and the *Queen,* "completely riddled with balls and very much damaged," withdrew from the fight.

Farragut and Davis hadn't received it yet, but over the telegraph wires, and down by steamer from Cairo, came Gideon Welles' response to the whole fiasco. "I need not say to you," he chastised both commanders, "that the escape [of the *Arkansas*] and its attending circumstances have been the cause of serious mortification to the Department and the country."

But the strategists in Washington had no idea of what the sailors and soldiers faced on the river at Vicksburg. Brigadier General Williams had just a quarter of his men fit for duty. Farragut was reduced to bribing rivermen to drift a coal barge past the Vicksburg gauntlet: "I will pay them liberally," he promised. "Sickness and death," Charles Davis told the secretary, had ravaged his command. The turtle crews were reduced by half. "The department," Davis said, "would be surprised to see how the most healthy men wilt and break under the ceaseless and exhausting heat of this pernicious climate."

For Farragut, the time was either now, or wait until the fall, rotting for months in front of Vicksburg. On July 24, the orders came, "Go down river at discretion." Davis could not remain alone in close blockade. He established a fortified outpost upriver at Helena, Arkansas, and withdrew his main force all the way back to Memphis.

The second attempt at Vicksburg had ended in failure.

From Jackson and Mobile, mechanics arrived to repair the *Arkansas.* Isaac Brown left for a short convalescent leave, and the executive officer, Lieutenant Henry Stevens, assumed temporary command. In early August, taking advantage of the Federal retreat, Earl Van Dorn pro-

posed an expedition to retake Baton Rouge using Major General John
C. Breckinridge's 6,000 men. Intelligence reported the Union forces at
Baton Rouge consisted only of the *Essex,* a couple of gunboats, and
Brigadier Williams' 2,500 soldiers convalescing from their ordeal at
Vicksburg.

Breckinridge outlined a combined assault, his force attacking by
land while the *Arkansas* hit the town on the river. Stevens didn't like it.
Indeed, Brown had left him clear instructions not to sortie until his
return. The army, however, was eager to get going. On August 4, with a
new crew, the *Arkansas* headed downriver to Baton Rouge.

With the current helping her along to a truly phenomenal speed of
twelve knots, the ship passed what Lieutenant Read called "many signs
of the wanton and barbarous destruction of property by the enemy."
Friendly crowds waved from the banks, "and hailed with exclamations
of delight" the sight of the Confederate flag waving over the fast-
moving ironclad.

After midnight, on the fifth, less than two hours from their objective, the *Arkansas'* engines stopped. The chief engineer had been left
behind with malaria, and each of his assistants had a different idea of
the problem. They finally got her underway at daylight, just as the
sound of Breckinridge's artillery came rumbling over the river.

In a dense fog, the rebels attacked, overran the Union camp, and
forced them nearly to the riverbank. Williams was killed and losses
mounted. But as the stinkpots had done at Shiloh, the navy at Baton
Rouge staved off catastrophe. Firing salvos of grape and canister, the
Essex and gunboats *Kineo* and *Katahdin* stopped Breckinridge in his
tracks. The battle stalemated.

The *Arkansas* could have tipped the balance. But just above the
town the starboard engine stopped. Skidding over to the west bank of
the river, the current shoved her aground, stern firmly wedged in a
grove of cypress trees. By sunset the engines were working then
stopped again and were repaired again. Before sunrise August 6, she
raised steam and lurched over with only one engine turning. For Lieutenant Stevens, that was all. He tied up to the bank; his sole thought
now was getting the *Arkansas* into a defensive position until "permanent" repairs could be made.

Within hours, under black smoke moving upriver, came the *Essex,*
Kineo, Katahdin, and *Sumter.* As luck would have it, the engines suddenly answered to orders. The crew cheered and the *Arkansas* steamed
to intercept. At pistol-shot range, Stevens rang for full speed, and the
starboard engine stopped dead. Again, she was shoved to the west

bank, but this time she smashed onto tree stumps, her thin, boiler-plated stern facing the enemy. Stevens ordered the *Arkansas* abandoned, distributed small arms to the crew, and blew her up. Down in Baton Rouge, Breckinridge retreated out of town, leaving a good number of his men dead.

Shortly after, the Union withdrew from Baton Rouge as well. It was too far up from New Orleans, and the army had not enough troops to defend it. The retreat of Farragut and Davis from Vicksburg and the army from Baton Rouge ceded 300 miles of the lower river back to the Confederacy. The falling water level at Young's Point brought the western railroad to Vicksburg back into operation, and with it, began a resupply of the rebel armies with Texas beef, grain, and horses, and blockade-run goods from the Gulf. In leaden summer heat, the war on the western waters exhausted itself. The Confederacy still held the key to the great river.

Vicksburg Return

"Admiral Porter, meet General Grant."

—Captain McAllister, U.S. Army

O n July 26, 1862, David Dixon Porter's mortar flotilla, returned east from the Mississippi quagmire, sailed into Hampton Roads. After reading in the newspapers of the *Arkansas* episode at Vicksburg, Porter sent a personal letter to Gus Fox at the department. What was really needed on the upper river, he unsubtly hinted, was a "more energetic" flag officer than the gentleman scholar, Commodore Charles Davis.

When Porter reported to the Navy Department on the twenty-eighth, Washington lay prostrate in a blanketing heat wave. Secretary Welles greeted him genially, sat him down, offered a cold glass of lemonade, and was appalled at Porter's physical condition. He ordered the exhausted naval officer to take two weeks' leave with his family at Newport, Rhode Island. Truly, the whole war stagnated on every front. On the Mississippi, Union forces had drawn back from Vicksburg. Grant straddled the railroad west of Corinth, and William Tecumseh Sherman idled at Memphis. In the east, McClellan stalled before Richmond.

At the fashionable Newport Club amid a noisy argument over war strategy, Porter was asked his views. "McClellan's troops," he sneered, "have not been taught what discipline is.... They ought to shoot a thousand soldiers and hang a dozen or so officers. After that they would have an army that could fight!" Not only was the outburst inappropriate, it was also patent nonsense. The reason the Army of the Potomac didn't fight was that McClellan acted like a hypnotized rabbit in the face of Robert E. Lee's rattlesnake. Porter's remarks reached some important ears, and he was ordered back to Washington.

Welles refused to see him, and Fox handed over the new orders. He was being sent to Cincinnati as aide to Commodore Joseph Hull, an elderly relic on the retired list, inspecting gunboats on the Ohio River! Porter was struck dumb and demanded to see the secretary. Sorry, Fox said, the secretary was "engaged." Porter was desperate. If he wanted to save his career, there was only one man left to whom he could appeal. With a rapid step, he walked across the street to the White House.

The long, gangly form rose from the chair and held out his hand. "Well, what can I do for you?" asked Abraham Lincoln. Porter launched into a narrative of the Mississippi campaign. When he recounted the wild battle below New Orleans, Lincoln nodded. "It reminds me," the President said, "of a fight in a barroom at Natchez." But when Porter described the Confederate fortifications at Vicksburg, Lincoln had nothing to say—the news came as a revelation. He rang for a messenger to bring Gus Fox. Porter prudently hurried out.

The Cincinnati orders never went beyond "pending," and Porter remained in Newport through September. Exhibiting confidence in a destiny that was by no means assured, he also refused command of the Potomac River flotilla as too confining for his energies and too close to McClellan. At the end of the month he was summoned to the department for what was nebulously described as "duty west." Entering the inner sanctum, the chief clerk smiled and Gus Fox was full of cheer. Gideon Welles, as usual, remained quiet and deliberate; "[he] gave me his two fingers to squeeze, and asked me to be seated." Porter sat, like a stone, hardly believing.

Welles had put a lot of thought into this conversation. In his diary, he had written of Porter's "stirring and positive qualities . . . fertile in resources, great energy." But there was the other side to the ledger. Twice he had been elevated above his rank, first to the *Powhatan,* then to the mortar flotilla. Also, Porter was still but a commander, who exhibited "excessive and sometimes not over-scrupulous ambition," and lacked "high moral qualities." But Welles knew talent when he saw it. The "field of operations is peculiar," he penned, "and a young and active officer is required."

The secretary explained to Porter that he was investing him with the temporary rank of "acting rear admiral" to command the new Mississippi Squadron. Commodore Davis would come back to Washington to head the Bureau of Navigation. Porter tried very hard to deal stoically with this. He had already made up his mind to show no emotion if Welles cast him on the beach for insubordination. But he could not hold it back. If the secretary ordered him "over Niagara Falls in an iron pot," he would do it!

The army also went through command changes. Following the breakup of Halleck's immense host at Corinth, Grant was elevated to command the Army of the Tennessee, currently deployed in northern Mississippi. For the march on Vicksburg, Lincoln appointed a fellow Springfield, Illinois politician, General John A. McClernand, to recruit a new army. It was a bad choice. McClernand was regarded as an officer of small merit, prone to puffery, very out of his league in senior command.

In Maryland, on September 16–17, 1862, Robert E. Lee's first invasion of the North ended in the hugely inconclusive Battle of Antietam. George McClellan and the Army of the Potomac caught the wily Confederate at a total disadvantage. But Little Mac's hesitations fudged the engagement that might have ended the war with a crushing Union triumph. The battle, however, *was* touted by the administration as a strategic victory, which in a narrow sense it was. Thus Lincoln, on September 23, issued his Emancipation Proclamation from a position of arguable military superiority. In November he appointed General Ambrose Burnside to command the Army of the Potomac.

At New Orleans, Ben Butler managed to put the entire city in an uproar. He hanged a professional gambler for pulling down the national flag at the U.S. Mint. Responding to provocation, Butler published his infamous "Woman Order," whereby any female who exhibited disrespect or contempt to Federal personnel would be treated as a common prostitute. Giving too much grief to the administration, Butler was replaced by Major General Nathaniel P. Banks, formerly the governor of Massachusetts and speaker of the U.S. House of Representatives.*

---

* Banks was also a former president of the Illinois Central Railroad, in whose boardroom once sat Vice President George McClellan, Treasurer Ambrose Burnside, and General Counsel Abraham Lincoln.

In October, Porter headed west, stopping at the industrial centers along the Ohio and upper Mississippi to inspect a new generation of ironclads soon to augment his command. Both the *Indianola* and *Chillicothe* had shocking design flaws. The first had no berthing space for the crew. The second's steering wheel was jammed between the forward guns, making it impossible for the helmsman and gunners to function simultaneously. Porter, however, was very pleased with the conversion of a score of commercial river steamers into lightly armored, shallow-draft "tin clads," which "could float wherever the ground was a little damp."

When Porter arrived at Cairo, he found most of the squadron collected under the temporary command of Captain Henry Walke. The welcome from officers and enlisted men was genuine and enthusiastic. The vessels fired a rear admiral's thirteen-gun salute, and the flag of Acting Rear Admiral David Dixon Porter flew from the *Benton*. At once, Porter sent Walke downriver to Helena, Arkansas, to take charge of the naval forces above Vicksburg.

But before Porter could consider aggressive action, he needed to rearm, refit, and reorient his command. The U.S. Navy's new Mississippi Squadron included every type of river vessel imaginable, and some that were not. There were turtles and stinkpots and specially designed rams like Ellet's timber-butters. There were catamarans like the *Benton,* propeller and paddle-wheel combinations like the *Indianola.* There were tugs, snag boats, supply steamers, coal and fodder barges, mortar scows, floating forges and machine shops, as well as a floating shack town that housed former slaves and the USS *Red Rover,* the navy's first hospital ship. The naval station commandant, Captain Alex Pennock, operated from a rented riverfront building in Cairo. The navy yard lay a few miles up the Ohio at Mound City, where for the most part, the storehouses, shops, smithies, and quarters stood on barges in the river. Since October 1861, Pennock had managed the squadron's complete logistical needs, and Porter considered him a "trump."

The real work of transferring the organization from the army to the navy was accomplished not by the act of Congress, but by the hard labor of men on the scene. Pay scales had to be regularized according to the navy's rates, and many an army-enlisted landsman was reduced to the level of his navy mates, who filled the squadron in ever-increasing numbers. Army hands refusing to serve under these conditions were discharged. In most situations, their berths filled with former slaves enlisted into the navy.

The Ellet ram fleet, after much acrimony that reached to the White House and Cabinet, was re-formed into the Mississippi Marine

Brigade,* temporarily attached to Porter's Mississippi Squadron.

Four hundred sick were discharged immediately. Porter rented a hotel at Mound City to take patients from *Red Rover* and circulated a general order of squadron hygiene. Hereafter, crews were to be inspected for fitness at morning and evening quarters. Officers were to see their men were properly and "comfortably" dressed, "and have their under flannels on."

In the ironclads, where little sun penetrated below, drying stoves were installed for wet clothing. Echoing a common fear, when the cause of malaria was yet unknown, Porter forbade men to sleep in the open air, where "night dews can affect them." He ordered breakfast served as soon as the crew were turned from their hammocks, "before washing the decks." Fresh meat and vegetables he ordered served three times a week. "The comfort and health of the men," the acting rear admiral announced to his officers, "must be the first thing to be looked after."

Working up to eighteen hours a day, Porter supervised rearming the turtles, replacing their dangerously obsolete guns with modern, 6-inch Parrott rifles. All the army's powder, having no protection against damp, was exchanged for the navy's stuff. Uniform regulations were strictly enforced. From the flagstaff of his new flagship, the palatial steamer *Black Hawk,* came daily instructions: a white flag meant white uniforms, a blue flag signified blue uniforms.

On November 12, Porter received a letter from General William T. Sherman at Memphis. Grant with 40,000 men had marched into Mississippi, establishing his base on the railroad at Holly Springs. Facing him were General John Pemberton and 6,000 Confederates. Sherman suggested that a naval thrust up the Yazoo to the railroad junction at Grenada would trap Pemberton between Grant to his front and the gunboats in his rear. Grant could then advance to Jackson, which lay astride the railroad linking Vicksburg to the east. Porter was all for it, declaring himself "ready to be of any service to the army."

On November 28, Henry Walke arrived with the *Carondelet, Mound City,* and tinclads *Signal* and *Marmora* at Milliken's Bend, by the mouth of the Yazoo. At first light, the tinclads leading, the vessels headed up for a reconnaissance in force. After a few miles the turtles could go no further. The tinclads continued, marking on charts the rebel positions

* A name only, having no association with the U.S. Marine Corps.

along the Chickasaw Bluffs, the defensive ridge line overlooking the Yazoo just north of Vicksburg.

December 1 found Porter at Cairo, having dinner on a ramshackle riverboat with Captain McAllister of the army Quartermaster's Department. During the courses, McAllister was called out and returned with a stumpy, bearded man, wearing a civilian brown coat and wrinkled gray trousers. He was dusty, seedy, very travel-worn, and next to the tall, stately McAllister, looked like a dwarf. "Admiral Porter," McAllister said respectfully, "meet General Grant."

They shook hands warmly, and sat apart at a small table with a bottle of champagne. "While I was looking earnestly at Grant," Porter wrote in his journal, "trying to make out how much there was under the plain exterior, the General was regarding me to see what amount of work there was under all the gilt buttons and gold lace with which the Department had bedizened my coat."

Embellishments to the original plan that Sherman had outlined in his letter to Porter were discussed. While the navy launched a diversionary attack and landed an army division at the foot of the Chickasaw Bluffs, Grant and Sherman would advance south together from Holly Springs to Jackson. Besides keeping the Confederates guessing as to where the main blow would fall, it trapped them in a giant nutcracker, with Vicksburg as the nut. Porter ordered a concentration of fighting vessels to assemble under Henry Walke for the feint up the Yazoo.

But a week later things changed. On December 8, it was learned that McClernand's commission, commanding the new "Army of the Mississippi," elevated the politician-general to seniority above General Sherman, nominally a corps commander in Grant's Army of the Tennessee. Neither Sherman nor Grant would tolerate that. To get a jump on operations, they pushed forward the date of attack and heavily altered the distribution of forces. Instead of a divisional jab at the bluffs, Sherman would assault the heights with nearly his entire corps, 25,000 men.

A thorough reconnaissance of the ground from the Yazoo riverbank to Chickasaw Bluffs, a bare two miles, would have revealed a very disturbing picture. The land formed a natural moat of marsh and drowned forest, crossed and split by creeks and bayous. Its half-dozen farms, including the homestead of the late Albert Sidney Johnston, were hemmed by high dikes honeycombed with Confederate outposts and dugouts. What were termed "roads" on the maps were actually the flattened tops of these dikes. Every path inland from the landing sites was presighted and ranged by rebel artillery along the crest. The river also presented problems. There was a hulk line by Drumgould's Bluff and, most dangerously, the lower Yazoo had lately been sown with hundreds of electric-fused mines, detonated by operators concealed in camouflaged pits along the riverbank.

Warned of the mines by a runaway slave on December 11, Henry Walke sent the tinclads *Marmora* and *Signal* to reconnoiter. On the water, beneath Drumgould's Bluff, the crews saw "an unaccountable number of small scows and stationary floats." A sailor fired his musket at one of the objects, and the explosion rocked the vessel. Another exploded close aboard. Snipers opened fire from the levees. The tinclad skippers reported they could destroy the mines if they had a turtle to cover the sweep. Walke, already familiar with the deadly things from his experiences at Fort Henry, sent the *Cairo, Pittsburg,* and *Queen of the West* as escorts, cautioning their officers "to be very careful not to run their vessels in among the torpedoes." Commander Thomas Selfridge, last seen on the burning foredeck of the *Cumberland,* now skipper of the *Cairo,* directed the operation.

On the morning of December 12, the sweepers steamed up the Yazoo, beating the woods with shellfire and canister. Cautiously, they nosed ahead until the *Marmora* opened with a rattle of musketry at a wooden float. A naval shore party cut the mooring lines, and the mines, five-gallon, glass demijohns, filled with gunpowder, popped to the surface.

Neither Selfridge nor his helmsman had been attending to the *Cairo*'s position. She drifted close on the bank, and the rebels on Drumgould's Bluff opened fire. Selfridge tried backing clear when two explosions, port and starboard, violently shook the vessel, crushing her bottom. The river poured in, said one of her boys, "like the roar of Niagara." Water swamped the foredeck, and Selfridge ran the boat aground. Steam pumps and handy-billys were useless. The *Cairo* slipped off the bank and disappeared into the Yazoo with only the tops of her twin stacks and the jackstaff poking through the surface.* Though his career did not suffer for it, Selfridge received a mountain of criticism. One officer stated that Selfridge "found two torpedoes and removed them by placing his vessel over them."

On December 13, 1862, in Fredericksburg, Virginia, General Ambrose Burnside threw the Army of the Potomac in suicidal frontal assaults

* The wreck was rediscovered in 1956, and with much difficulty raised and restored. The *Cairo* now resides as a central exhibit of the Vicksburg National Military Park.

against Lee's entrenchments on the heights above the town. Union losses amounted to 12,700 men killed and wounded. Lee, criticized for not pursuing a beaten foe, lost 5,300 men. Burnside publicly admitted his failure and was replaced in command by General Joseph "Fighting Joe" Hooker.

On December 14, Porter and the squadron arrived at Memphis, where Sherman's reinforced corps were loading their transports. The two commanders had not yet met, and Porter, thinking the general to be "in full feather," put on his gold-laced uniform coat. Sherman, in the mistaken belief that Porter scorned formality, wore a suit of ordinary blue flannel. Each was comically surprised at the other's appearance. "Hello, Porter," said Sherman, "glad to meet you. Do you suppose we can get all this crowd down to Vicksburg by Christmas?" The two men hit it off like a couple of swells.

Singing "Yankee Doodle" and "John Brown's Body," Sherman's 40,000 men embarked in seventy steamers, and convoyed by the squadron, churned downriver. But a menacing situation in Grant's rear derailed the operation and with it, the eventual direction of the whole campaign. On December 20, Earl Van Dorn raided Grant's base at Holly Springs, capturing 1,500 prisoners and a million dollars' worth of military stores. Simultaneously, Nathan Bedford Forrest's rebel cavalry destroyed seventy miles of track from Jackson, Tennessee, nearly to the Mississippi River at Columbus. Grant's logistics were cut and with his arm of the nutcracker attack neutralized, there was no way he could cooperate with Sherman's amphibious attack on Vicksburg.

Knowing nothing of this calamity, the fleet arrived at Milliken's Bend on Christmas Eve. A division of minesweeping tinclads, guarded by the *Benton,* entered the Yazoo and moved up to the landing sites. When ambushing rebels opened fire from Albert Sidney Johnston's plantation, U.S. Marines put it to the torch. The big house, sugar refinery, sawmill, the cotton gin, and quarters for 300 slaves went up in smoke.

On Christmas Day, Porter and Sherman reconnoitered the area, their horses sinking to their bellies in mud. All day, Confederate infantry on the bluffs harassed the minesweepers. The night, clear and frosty, heard no bells or whistles in the fleet. Sailors hung sheets of wet canvas around the fireboxes to hide the glare from rebel snipers, and no one lit a Christmas cigar on deck.

On December 26, two days behind schedule, Sherman's men

landed. The fleet's guns hadn't the range to silence the hilltop batteries to the army's front, so Porter headed a few miles farther up the Yazoo to Drumgould's Bluff. After thoroughly sweeping the channel, the warships anchored behind a tree-covered point and opened fire.

Commander William Gwin of the *Benton* was hampered by the forests. Rather than approximate the range by indirect fire, he moved beyond the point, permitting both his forward and starboard guns to bear. But it placed the *Benton* in full view of the rebels on the bluffs, and they directed all their fire into her.

The funnels were knocked away, roundshot came in the gunports and through the hurricane deck. In the casemate, one man was killed and eight wounded. Gwin, a very promising officer, who had served on the river from almost the beginning, refused to fight from the safety of the armored pilothouse. "A captain's place is on the deck," he said. In a few minutes he was struck by a roundshot, horribly mutilating his right breast and arm, wounding him mortally. After more than an hour, the gunboats retired. The *Benton,* funnels gone, limped between two supporting tinclads.

On December 28, the army, ears pitched for the sound of Grant's artillery, pushed its patrols to the base of the Chickasaw Bluffs. But instead of Union guns, the bluecoats heard the clank and whistles of packed troop trains, and saw signal rockets arching in the eastern sky. It heralded the arrival of 6,000 rebel reinforcements. The Vicksburg garrison had been effectively doubled on the eve of battle.

In the morning, in terrible rain, Sherman threw four divisional columns in a frontal assault against the ridge line. It was a Fredericksburg slaughter in miniature. Concentrated Confederate fire dropped the Federal infantry in its tracks, and the few who actually reached the summit were hurled back. The gunboats in the Yazoo pounded both ends of the enemy line, but at maximum range, they were ineffective. The Union lost 2,000 men for not an inch of gain.

Withdrawing his advanced brigades, Sherman, exhausted, drenched, and covered with mud, boarded the *Black Hawk.* In Porter's cabin, a steward mixed a hot whiskey punch, and the two commanders spoke in whispers so as not to disturb Lieutenant Gwin, who lay dying in the admiral's bed. The report had just come of Nathan Bedford Forrest's cavalry raid on the railroad and telegraph, without, however, mentioning the catastrophe at Holly Springs. Still expecting Grant to arrive on the field from the east, Porter and Sherman planned a second attack a few miles farther up the Yazoo, at Haynes's Bluff. It was the very end of the Confederate right flank, upriver from the hulk line, where the enemy would least expect it. It came to nothing when a careless, floating smithy rammed a laden coal barge, sinking Porter's fuel reserve.

Looking to salvage a scrap of victory and divert public attention from the mess at Vicksburg, Sherman suggested a quick operation to seize a large Confederate cavalry camp on the Arkansas River, known as Arkansas Post, and its companion, Fort Hindman. The mouth of the Arkansas empties into the Mississippi roughly between Helena and Vicksburg and plugging it would stop another source of supplies to Vicksburg and also eliminate a major annoyance to river communications.

On December 31, a young colonel in a spanking new uniform entered Porter's cabin to announce General McClernand's arrival at Milliken's Bend with his new bride, several maids, a deckload of baggage, and an entourage of reporters. Waving his presidential commission and very put out over Sherman's independent actions, McClernand relegated "the crazy West Pointer" to a subordinate command in the Army of the Mississippi.

At midnight, January 4, the two generals came to the *Black Hawk* for an unannounced conference. Porter, who had already gone to bed, received them in his nightshirt. The admiral agreed to supply two ironclads for the attack on Arkansas Post, but bristled at McClernand's insolent attitude. "If General Sherman goes in command of the Army," said Porter, nose in the air, "I will go along with my whole force and make a sure thing of it. Otherwise, I will have nothing to do with the affair." Sherman beckoned him to a corner. "My God, Porter!" he whispered. "You will ruin yourself if you talk that way to McClernand. He is very intimate with the President and has powerful influence."

"I don't care who or what he is," replied the acting rear admiral, who had some influence himself. "I'll be damned if he shall be rude to you in my cabin!"

When the three senior officers had calmed down, they set to working out the details. Sherman would lead the attack, starting at daybreak, before the reporters in McClernand's entourage could "let the cat out of the bag," Sherman joked.

"I suppose," said McClernand, "there's no objection to my going along?" If Sherman had no objections, Porter said, neither did he; he glanced at his colleague. "None in the world," Sherman answered with a straight face.

On January 5, nearly 30,000 men, fifty transports, and thirteen warships plowed upriver. Two days later the force reached the town of

Napoleon at the mouth of the Arkansas and White rivers. The tinclads, each with two seamen casting a lead, and boats at the ready for sweeping mines, formed the van. Behind came the *Louisville, Baron De Kalb* (the former *St. Louis*), *Cincinnati*, and Porter in the *Black Hawk*. Next came the army transports, escorted by Ellet's rams. *Lexington* and *Conestoga* brought up the rear. In all the warships, guns were loaded with shrapnel, and fuses cut to one second. No one was to wait for orders before opening fire, and any vessel could let fly as soon as the enemy were observed.

It was as bleak a country as anyone had seen. There was hardly a village along the banks of the Arkansas, just some wretched farms, burning corncribs, and the odd plantation sinking into decay. Sixty miles upriver, at a farm landing just below the objective, the troops went ashore on both sides of the river. In the distance could be heard the sound of axes felling trees across the single access road. Arkansas Post and Fort Hindman sat on a strip of bottomland, barely above the water, defended by General Tom Churchill and 5,000 men. The fort proper, mounting eleven guns, was commanded by Lieutenant John Dunnington of the Confederate Navy.

On January 11, the Union troops deployed along their line of departure to attack Fort Hindman head-on, advancing across a cotton field. The turtles moved up to calibrate ranges and the tinclad *Rattler* swept the enemy's rifle pits. All day, General Churchill rode along the Confederate earthworks; there would be no retreat, he commanded, the men must die where they stood.

It was nearly dark when Porter received word from McClernand that the assault was ready. The turtles advanced to within 400 yards of Fort Hindman and opened fire. The bombardment was very destructive, with shrapnel and exploding shell killing most of the fort's artillery horses. But it was too late in the day to attack across the cotton field, and the fleet dropped down to await the sunrise.

At dawn, the warships commenced firing. The tinclads *Rattler, Glide,* and Ellet's *Monarch* ran past the fort, cutting off any Confederate retreat. The guns of Fort Hindman grew silent, and presently a white flag appeared on the ramparts. Lieutenant Dunnington, "late of the U.S. Navy," as the report noted, would surrender only to his erstwhile comrades, and Admiral Porter received his sword. One rebel officer told him, "You can't expect men to stand up against the fire of those gunboats."

Tom Churchill reluctantly handed his blade to General McClernand, who according to witnesses gloated and behaved badly. Sherman, in disgust, turned away. Into the bag went nearly 5,000 Confederate prisoners. McClernand's report, borne by a fast tug to the telegraph at Memphis, claimed the entire laurels for himself. Porter's report, sent from Cairo, was slower to arrive at Washington. Still, Gideon Welles was pleased. The little victory erased some of the funk caused by the retreat from Chickasaw Bluffs, but he couldn't help needling Porter to speed up the process of naval communications. The admiral wired back, "You will receive the first account of the next battle we have."

No matter the outcome, the expedition to Arkansas Post raised some hackles. Grant considered it, perhaps too strongly, "a wild goose chase" that diverted resources. Conveniently forgetting that the attack had been Sherman's idea, he warned McClernand not to engage in any effort unconnected with "the one great result, the capture of Vicksburg." In mid-January, with a nod from the White House, Grant disbanded the Army of the Mississippi, absorbing it into his own Army of the Tennessee, and took personal command of the Vicksburg campaign.

Although Grant condemned the operation at Arkansas Post as irrelevant, it served to erase from the public's mind another minor disaster, which Gus Fox called "the disgraceful affair at Galveston."

Late in 1862, Farragut, corking the leaky blockade along the Texas coast, ordered several of the steamers of the old mortar flotilla to Galveston. Under Commander William Renshaw, the *Westfield, Clifton, Harriet Lane,* and *Owasco* occupied the coastal city without opposition. Three companies of Colonel Isaac Burrell's 42nd Massachusetts Infantry fortified the immediate area around the waterfront docks. A wagon bridge, over which any counterattack had to cross, was left intact and unguarded. Army transports with field artillery arrived, but the guns were not landed. The naval vessels disposed themselves around the harbor and bay, and for the next two months, neither side did anything else.

On December 31, 1862, "Prince John" Magruder, commanding the Confederate forces in Texas, emplaced several guns just outside the town, near the *Harriet Lane.* Before dawn, January 1, 1863, he attacked. The concentrated fire of the Federal infantry, ably supported by the guns afloat, stopped the rebels short. As the sun rose Magruder was about to order a retreat, when his cottonclads, *Bayou City* and *Neptune,* carrying three guns between them and 400 troops, snatched success from a sure defeat.

Running alongside the *Harriet Lane,* the *Bayou City* opened a withering volley of musketry. Despite the surprise, Commander Jonathan Wainwright put up a gallant defense.* He rammed his antagonist, and was rammed in turn by the *Neptune*. Severely damaged by the collision, the *Neptune* sank in the shallows. The *Bayou City* then rammed the *Harriet Lane* with such force that the two ships could not separate. With a curdling rebel yell, the enemy infantry boarded and took the gunboat at the point of the bayonet. Wainwright and his executive officer were killed in the hand-to-hand fighting.

The shooting stopped to allow Commander Renshaw to consider a demand to surrender all the vessels in the bay. He refused, and in the confusion, the flagboat *Westfield* ran aground. Set afire to prevent capture, she blew up, killing Renshaw and several seamen. The *Clifton* and *Owasco* escaped with what remained. Ashore, the three companies of the 42nd Massachusetts, their support disappearing over the horizon, surrendered the town.

For the Confederacy, it was a surprising little victory, and the blockade, since there were no longer any Federal vessels off the port, was legally raised until the *Brooklyn* and several gunboats arrived to reestablish it on January 8. But for the Union, as Gus Fox wrote to Porter, "It is too cowardly to place on paper. Poor Wainwright did well. Renshaw—bah! he is dead. The others ran."

On January 29, when Grant arrived at Milliken's Bend, he found the fleet at the mouth of the Yazoo ready for action. In Porter's clubby cabin, the admiral, Grant, and Sherman hatched a scheme to envelop Vicksburg by an expedition around the top, through an abandoned barge canal called Yazoo Pass. The choked way wound up the tributary Coldwater and Tallahatchie rivers to Yazoo City. Porter suggested cutting the levee fronting the pass and raising its trickling levels enough to float in the gunboats. By this route, Union forces could flank the defenses at Chickasaw and Haynes's bluffs, and turning the rebels' right flank, sever Vicksburg from its provisioning larder. It was an all-around good plan, depending on surprise and especially speed for its success.

Unfortunately, newspaper correspondents tipped off Confederate spies. Taking the threat seriously, General Pemberton had gangs of slaves felling trees across the streams, and built an earth and cotton-clad fort deep inside the Yazoo valley.

---

* Commander Wainwright was the grandfather of General Jonathan Wainwright of Bataan.

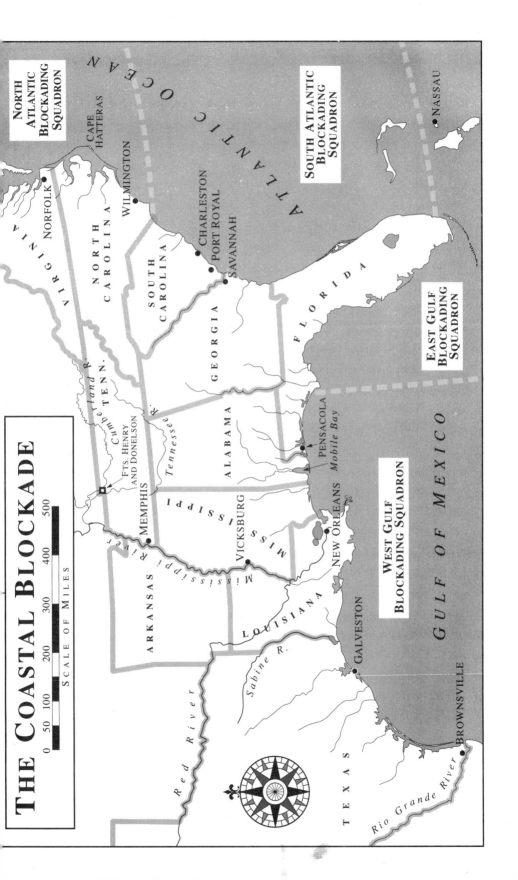

THE COASTAL BLOCKADE

SCALE OF MILES

0 50 100   200   300   400   500

NORTH ATLANTIC BLOCKADING SQUADRON

SOUTH ATLANTIC BLOCKADING SQUADRON

EAST GULF BLOCKADING SQUADRON

WEST GULF BLOCKADING SQUADRON

ATLANTIC OCEAN

GULF OF MEXICO

NASSAU

CAPE HATTERAS

NORFOLK

WILMINGTON

CHARLESTON

PORT ROYAL

SAVANNAH

VIRGINIA

NORTH CAROLINA

SOUTH CAROLINA

GEORGIA

FLORIDA

TENN.

ALABAMA

MISSISSIPPI

ARKANSAS

LOUISIANA

TEXAS

Cumberland R.

FTS. HENRY AND DONELSON

MEMPHIS

Tennessee R.

VICKSBURG

Mississippi River

Red River

Sabine R.

NEW ORLEANS

PENSACOLA

Mobile Bay

GALVESTON

BROWNSVILLE

Rio Grande River

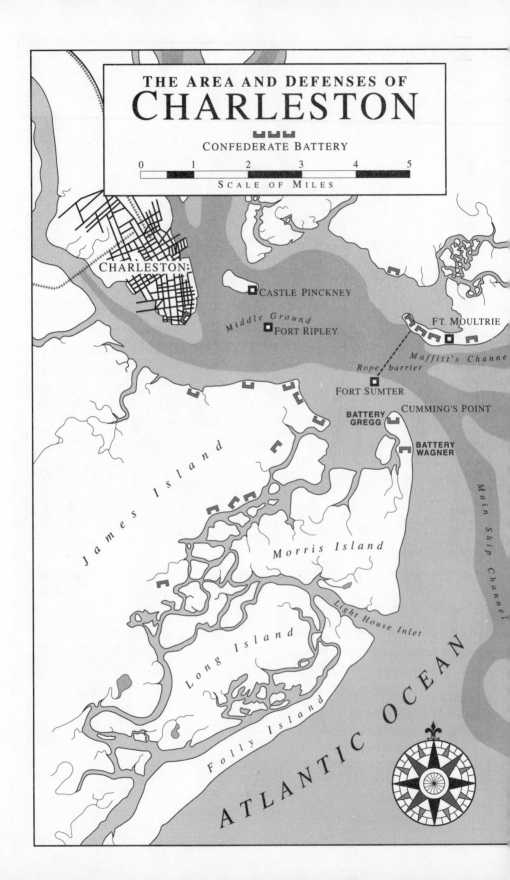

THE AREA AND DEFENSES OF
CHARLESTON

CONFEDERATE BATTERY

0 1 2 3 4 5

SCALE OF MILES

CHARLESTON

CASTLE PINCKNEY

Middle Ground
FORT RIPLEY

FT. MOULTRIE

Maffitt's Channe

Rope barrier
FORT SUMTER

CUMMING'S POINT

BATTERY
GREGG

BATTERY
WAGNER

James Island

Morris Island

Main Ship Channel

Light House Inlet

Long Island

Folly Island

ATLANTIC OCEAN

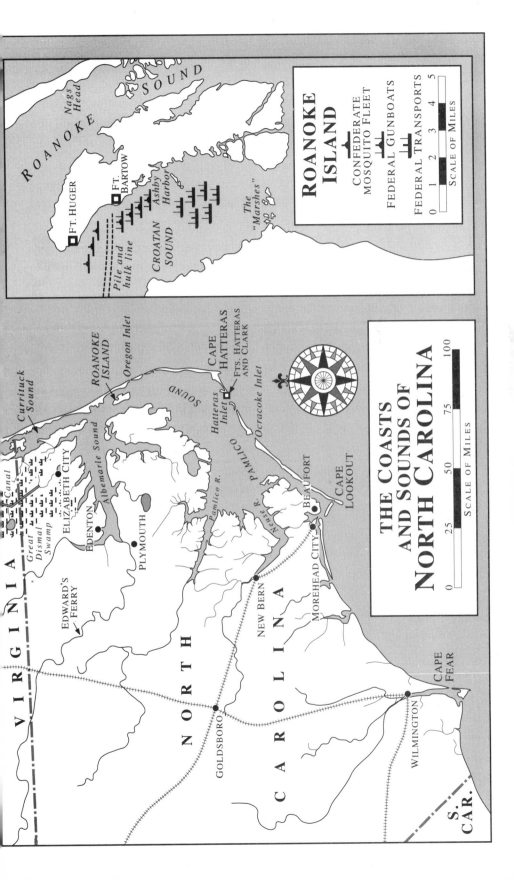

ROANOKE ISLAND

CONFEDERATE MOSQUITO FLEET
FEDERAL GUNBOATS
FEDERAL TRANSPORTS

SCALE OF MILES
0 1 2 3 4 5

Nags Head

ROANOKE SOUND

ROANOKE

FT. HUGER

FT. BARTOW

Ashby Harbor

Pile and hulk line

CROATAN SOUND

The "Marshes"

THE COASTS AND SOUNDS OF NORTH CAROLINA

SCALE OF MILES
0 25 50 75 100

VIRGINIA

NORTH CAROLINA

S. CAR.

Currituck Sound

Great Dismal Swamp

Canal

EDWARD'S FERRY

ELIZABETH CITY

EDENTON

PLYMOUTH

Albemarle Sound

ROANOKE ISLAND

Oregon Inlet

PAMLICO SOUND

Pamlico R.

Neuse R.

CAPE HATTERAS

FTS. HATTERAS AND CLARK

Hatteras Inlet

Ocracoke Inlet

GOLDSBORO

NEW BERN

MOREHEAD CITY

BEAUFORT

CAPE LOOKOUT

WILMINGTON

CAPE FEAR

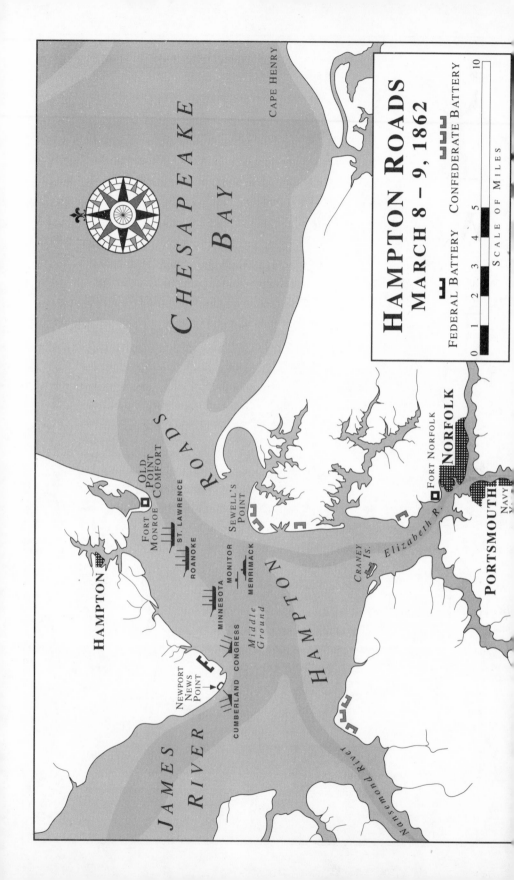

HAMPTON ROADS
MARCH 8 – 9, 1862

FEDERAL BATTERY   CONFEDERATE BATTERY

0   1   2   3   4   5   10
SCALE OF MILES

CAPE HENRY

CHESAPEAKE BAY

HAMPTON

JAMES RIVER

FORT MONROE
OLD POINT COMFORT

ST. LAWRENCE

ROANOKE

MINNESOTA

MONITOR

MERRIMACK

CUMBERLAND

CONGRESS

NEWPORT NEWS POINT

Middle Ground

HAMPTON ROADS

SEWELL'S POINT

CRANEY Is.

Elizabeth R.

FORT NORFOLK

NORFOLK

PORTSMOUTH
NAVY

Nansemond River

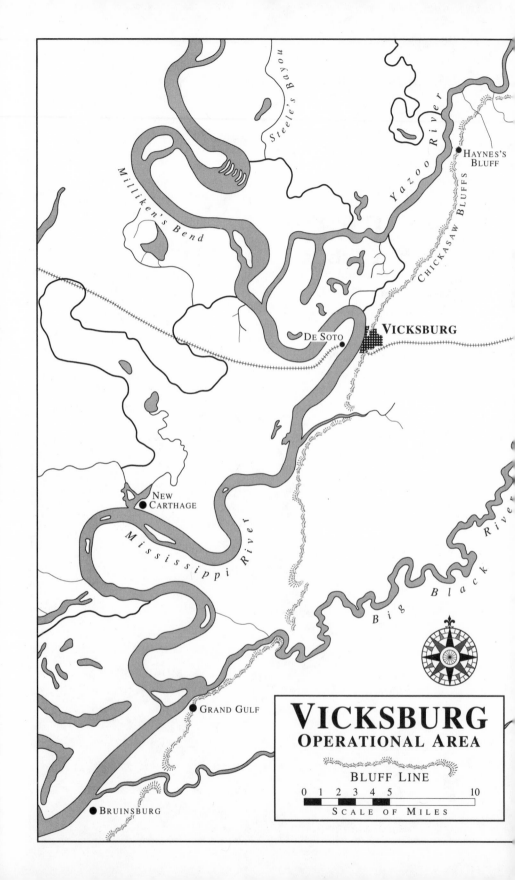

Steele's Bayou

Yazoo River

HAYNES'S
BLUFF

Milliken's Bend

CHICKASAW BLUFFS

DE SOTO

VICKSBURG

NEW
CARTHAGE

Mississippi River

Big Black River

GRAND GULF

VICKSBURG
OPERATIONAL AREA

BLUFF LINE

0 1 2 3 4 5   10
SCALE OF MILES

BRUINSBURG

Gideon Welles, Union secretary of the navy. A great spotter of bold talent, he promoted the brave and sacked the incompetent.
(Used by permission, Book Sales)

Gustavus Vasa Fox, the navy's first assistant secretary, the department's "Mr. Outside" to Welles' "Mr. Inside." *(Courtesy National Archives)*

Stephen Mallory, former U.S. Senator from Florida, the Confederacy's first and only secretary of the navy.
(Courtesy National Archives)

Admiral Franklin Buchanan, "Old Buck," and Flag Officer Josiah Tattnall, "Old Tat," Confederate States Navy. *(Used by permission, Book Sales)*

Vice Admiral David Glasgow Farragut, the U.S. Navy's first rear admiral and its only vice admiral in the Civil War. Gideon Welles thought him the finest officer in the Navy. *(Courtesy National Archives)*

Rear Admiral David Dixon Porter. Never wholly trusted by Gideon Welles, the secretary knew a winner and by successive steps, elevated Porter from disgruntled lieutenant to rear admiral in command of the North Atlantic Blockading Squadron. *(Courtesy National Archives)*

Rear Admiral Louis Malesherbes Goldsborough. In command of the North Atlantic Blockading Squadron, he opened North Carolina's tidal sounds for the Union. But it was his bad luck to be away from Hampton Roads when the *Merrimack* came out for her day of slaughter. *(Used by permission, Book Sales)*

Rear Admiral Samuel Francis Du Pont, chairman of the navy's Strategy Board, victor at Port Royal, and commander of the South Atlantic Blockading Squadron. His career was undone in April 1863 in the failed attack of the monitors at Charleston. *(Courtesy National Archives)*

Commander John Lorimer Worden, skipper of the *Monitor* in her famous fight with the *Merrimack* on March 9, 1862. *(Courtesy National Archives)*

Rear Admiral Andrew Hull Foote symbolized God, gunboats, and temperance. A fiery abolition moralist commanding the Western Gunboat Flotilla, he led it through actions at forts Henry and Donelson and at Island No. 10. *(Courtesy National Archives)*

Rear Admiral Charles Henry Davis, scientist, scholar, and Harvard graduate. Davis relieved Foote on the Mississippi but was not sufficiently aggressive to the task. *(Courtesy National Archives)*

Captain Raphael Semmes, CSN. As commander of the Confederate Navy's ocean raiders *Sumter* and *Alabama,* he in large part drove the American merchant marine from the sea lanes. Always quick to take offense, Semmes eventually met his match and defeat in the war's only significant battle on the high seas. *(Courtesy National Archives)*

The result of drunk, incompetent senior command, the Norfolk Navy Yard and its shipping went up in flames on April 20, 1861. The screw frigate *Merrimack* is seen here burning to the waterline. *(Used by permission, Book Sales)*

The steamer *Governor,* carrying a battalion of marines in Du Pont's Port Royal expedition, breaking up at sea. *(Used by permission, University Press of Mississippi)*

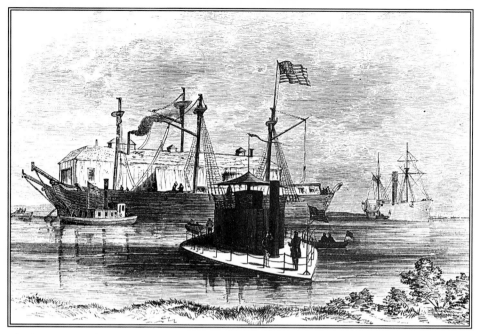

The hulked New England whalers *India* and *Edward,* converted into a floating repair shop, Port Royal, South Carolina. *(Used by permission, University Press of Mississippi)*

In December 1862 and January 1863 thirty old New England whaling ships were scuttled on Charleston bar in a failed effort to block the harbor. *(Used by permission, U.S. Naval Historical Center)*

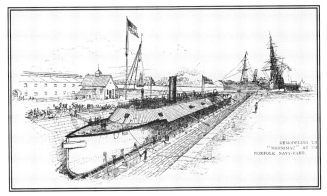

February 1862: the CSS *Virginia* completes her conversion from the wooden screw frigate *Merrimack* in Norfolk's Dry Dock Number 1, a facility still in use. Note the cast iron ram bolted to her bow. No photographs of this historic ship are known to exist.
(Used by permission, Book Sales)

March 8, 1862: *Merrimack* rams and sinks the Union sloop *Cumberland* at Hampton Roads.
(Used by permission, Book Sales)

An accurate rendering of the world's first battle between iron ships, *Monitor* and *Merrimack*, March 9, 1862. *(Used by permission, Book Sales)*

A group of the *Monitor's* sailors loaf on deck. Dents in the turret iron from the fight with the *Merrimack* can be seen to the left of the gunport. The man-high box at left, one of two, was fitted after the battle as protection for the smokestacks.
(Courtesy Mariners Museum, Newport News, Virginia)

USS *Tyler* with a mortar scow in the foreground. Together with *Lexington* and *Conestoga*, she was one of the original three "stinkpots" that formed the Western Gunboat Flotilla.
(Used by permission, U.S. Naval Historical Center)

An excellent rendering of the "Pook turtle" *St. Louis*. Note the conical pilothouse immediately forward of the stacks, the enclosed paddle wheel aft, and the strakes of armor on front and sides. The seven "city" class ironclad gunboats bore the brunt of the river war on the Mississippi. *(Courtesy National Archives)*

February 6, 1862: Flag Officer Andrew Foote leads the Western Gunboat Flotilla in the attack on Fort Henry on the Tennessee River.
(Used by permission, University Press of Mississippi)

June 6, 1862: the naval Battle of Memphis, seen from the Arkansas side of the river. Flag Officer Charles Davis led the Western Gunboat Flotilla, supported by Colonel Charles Ellet's Mississippi Ram Fleet, in the capture of the Confederacy's fifth largest city. *(Used by permission, University Press of Mississippi)*

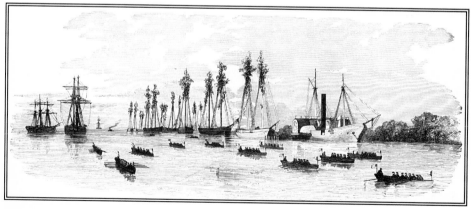

Below New Orleans, the vessels of Commander David Dixon Porter's Mortar Flotilla, masts camouflaged with tree branches, are towed into position for the bombardment of Fort Jackson. *(Used by permission, University Press of Mississippi)*

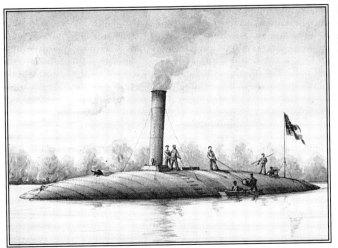

CSS *Manassas,* the "hellish machine," first ironclad warship in the Western Hemisphere. Formerly the tug *Enoch Train,* she was radically converted into an ironclad ram and met her death in the battle for New Orleans.
(Used by permission, U.S. Naval Historical Center)

July 15, 1862: a fanciful interpretation of the Confederate ironclad ram *Arkansas'* debauch from the mouth of the Yazoo River, north of Vicksburg, catching the Federal fleets completely by surprise.
(Used by permission, University Press of Mississippi)

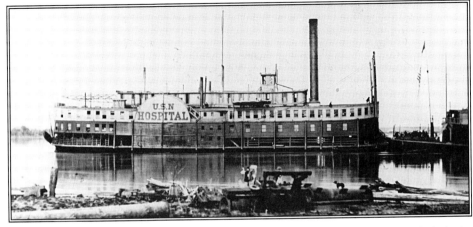

The U.S. Navy's first specifically commissioned hospital ship, *Red Rover,* on the Mississippi. Formerly a rebel floating barracks, she was captured at Island No. 10 and thoroughly converted with such features as steam-powered elevators, ice machines, a laundry, operating room, and separate galley for patients. *(Used by permission, U.S. Naval Historical Center)*

The vessels of Colonel Charles Ellet, Jr.'s Mississippi Ram Fleet, the "brown-paper rams." A very odd duck of an organization, it was one of several of the U.S. Army's forces afloat, and served on the Mississippi and its tributaries. *(Courtesy National Archives)*

The sternwheel river monitor *Osage,* which served as rear guard in the retreat down the Red River. The turret held two 11-inch guns that blew rebel cavalry away like dust. *(Used by permission, U.S. Naval Historical Center)*

The log dam that saved the Mississippi Squadron from stranding and certain destruction above the falls at Alexandria, Louisiana, May 11, 1864. The *Carondelet, Pittsburg, Ozark,* and *Mound City* prepare to shoot the gap. *(Used by permission, University Press of Mississippi)*

Admiral Farragut's flagship *Hartford* engages the Confederate ironclad ram *Tennessee* at point-blank range during the Battle of Mobile Bay, August 5, 1864.
(Used by permission, University Press of Mississippi)

CSS *Alabama*, the most successful of the Confederacy's high seas raiders. Her fine hull lines and full spread of canvas provided the ship remarkable powers of speed and endurance. *(Used by permission, University Press of Mississippi)*

In a legitimate, if unsavory ruse of war, Raphael Semmes and the *Alabama* set fire to a captured prize as a lure for others. *(Used by permission, University Press of Mississippi)*

The Confederate States ram *Stonewall* in the Washington Navy Yard after the war. Built at Bordeaux, France, she eventually found her way to the infant Imperial Japanese Navy as *Azuma*. *(Courtesy National Archives)*

January 31, 1863: rebel ironclads *Chicora* and *Palmetto State* sortie from Charleston to attack the Federal blockade. *(Used by permission, University Press of Mississippi)*

The monitor *Weehawken* engages Fort Sumter during Du Pont's abortive attack on Charleston harbor, April 7, 1863. *(Used by permission, University Press of Mississippi)*

A Confederate *David* torpedo boat, possibly the original, aground at low tide in Charleston harbor, 1865. *(Used by permission, U.S. Naval Historical Center)*

CSS *Hunley,* the only true submarine in the Civil War, her after hatch open, on a Charleston wharf. Note the diving planes forward. *(Used by permission, U.S. Naval Historical Center)*

The massed bombardment of Fort Fisher by the North Atlantic Squadron, January 15, 1865. The monitors are closest to the beach, upper right. The Mound battery is clearly visible on the far left. *(Used by permission, Book Sales)*

Typical of the several types of mines used by the Confederates. The explosives are held in the lower tanks, kept afloat by watertight casks.
(Used by permission, University Press of Mississippi)

On February 3, the Federal tinclad *Forest Rose* blasted the levee, and the Mississippi River, eight feet higher than the canal bed, roared in, a muddy, smashing flood that tore away huge masses of earth, sweeping whole forests before it. In a few hours the cut widened to fifty yards; the next morning it was near eighty. It took more than a week for the water levels to even out, and nearly another to clear the debris from Yazoo Pass. Not until February 20 did the Union vessels enter the old canal.

Lieutenant Commander Watson Smith, one of Porter's original division commanders in the mortar flotilla, led the naval element. It was a formidable force: the ironclads *Chillicothe* and *De Kalb,* five tinclads, two Ellet rams, and the tug *S. Bayard* towing three barges of coal. Thirteen transports carrying Brigadier General Leonard Ross' 4,500 men formed the army's contingent. Grant had allocated an entire corps, 12,000 soldiers, but lack of transport prevented anything beyond Ross' brigade.

Traveling approximately three miles a day, progress was excruciatingly slow. Some of the felled timber was nosed aside by the ironclads, but the rest needed to be dragged away, log by log. Watson Smith had to send to Memphis for six-inch hemp cable that could handle the strain. Pioneer companies from the embarked troops hacked at the debris, foot by miserable foot, wrapping chains around the tree trunks and hauling them to the banks Over the disused waterway, low branches overlapped the column to form a dank, vaulted forest tunnel. For the squat ironclads, this wasn't much of a problem. For the tinclads and transports, with their high deck houses and funnels, it was a nightmare. Stacks toppled and boats and cabins were stove in.

To make it all worse, a group of Confederate mounted guerrillas, the "Partisan Rangers," hovered ahead and on the flanks, bushwhacking the pioneers, clogging the pass with ever more obstacles. Whenever a warship needed to coal, or a transport lost her funnels, or fouled a paddle wheel, the entire line halted front to back. Fortunately, the tinclads didn't need to bother with coal. Instead, the crews stripped every passing farm and habitation of its fence rails.

Watson Smith, good enough under orders, was out of his depth in independent command. Army and navy officers alike crabbed at his caution, faulting him for not plunging ahead with the fastest warships, a company of troops in each, leaving the transports and the rest to catch up. "So much for speed," wrote the sarcastically blunt-spoken Lieutenant Colonel James Harrison Wilson. "I have no hope of anything great, considering the course followed by the naval forces under the direction of their able and efficient Acting Rear Admiral, Commodore, Captain, Lieutenant-Commander Smith." Wilson elaborated: "Smith . . . I don't regard as the equal of Lord Nelson. Walker and Foster [skippers of the ironclads] . . . are good men, and will cheerfully do what they are ordered, but both think of Commodore [sic] Smith just as I do." None realized that Watson Smith was very ill physically and close to nervous collapse. He would not long survive past the ordeal.

On February 28, the force squeezed out of Yazoo Pass and entered the broad, serpentine Coldwater River. On farms lining both banks, raging cotton fires pointed the way ominously forward. In the high water, the expedition made better time, reaching the Tallahatchie in little more than a week. On Tuesday, March 10, after what a contemporary historian gently called "rather dilatory navigation," they came to the end of the line.

In the time taken by the Union forces to bump and heave 200 miles, the Confederates had thrown up a cottonclad earthwork at Greenwood, where the Tallahatchie joins the Yalobusha to form the Yazoo. Fort Pemberton was armed with a British Whitworth rifle and some old 32-pounders. A log raft lay across its narrow front, impeded further by a sunken hulk.* The rebels had barely finished when the moving cloud of black and brown smoke appeared over the trees.

On the morning of March 11, Watson Smith and General Ross took the *Chillicothe* to within half a mile of the fort. The rebels hit the "Chilly Coffee" twice, cracking the iron plate and smashing through the pine backing. Porter had considered her a bad piece of work, and he was right. In late afternoon *Chillicothe* advanced to attack, and it lasted all of seven minutes. She was hit four times. Lieutenant James Foster, her commanding officer wrote, "One gun crew rendered perfectly useless . . . 3 men being killed outright, 1 mortally wounded, and 10 others seriously wounded . . . the other 5 of the gun's crew had their eyes filled with powder." Angrily, he pointed to "the ease with which the enemy's shell . . . penetrates the armor of the *Chillicothe* . . . she is almost a failure."

The navy spent the next day repairing damage. Cotton bales, scavenged from slim gleanings along the river, were piled on the decks of

---

* Formerly the steamer *Star of the West,* which had attempted the first relief of Fort Sumter. Captured in late 1861, she was renamed *St. Philip* by the rebels.

the two ironclads. Light guns were landed in the woods to occupy the enemy from another angle, and a mortar scow readied for high-angle fire. The narrowness of the channel meant the ironclads could fire their bow guns only, and both vessels were securely tethered to trees, hauling on the lines to shift fire.

Again the *Chillicothe* was severely knocked about. Struck repeatedly, on fire, and ammunition exhausted, Foster withdrew for hasty repairs. "She . . . does not withstand the enemy's shot and shell near as well as expected," he reported. The *De Kalb,* a stout turtle, fared better, firing deliberately at the fort for the remainder of the day, making good practice. But it was impossible for the infantry to attack the Confederate position, because, as General Ross said, "the rebels' works were so surrounded by swamps, bayous, and overflowed country . . . inaccessible for land forces."

About that, there was some question, especially in the minds of naval officers, as each service sought a scapegoat for the failure. After the *Chillicothe* withdrew, rebel prisoners and deserters reported Fort Pemberton had fired its last ammunition and *De Kalb*'s fire had passed through seven banks of cotton bales, which, as Porter later noted, "must have made the place untenable." Mending and replenishment occupied the navy all the next day. On Sunday, Colonel Wilson wrote, perhaps sarcastically, "[Attack] put off today out of respect for the Sabbath."

On Monday, March 16, Ross put his three best regiments aboard three tinclads, ready to throw them at Fort Pemberton the instant its fire slackened. At noon, the brigade's field guns opened fire from the woods and the Confederates replied. As Wilson watched through his field glasses, the ironclads, *Chillicothe* leading, advanced "with the intention of 'going in' upon the well-established principle of gunboat warfare, 'close quarters and quick work.'" After the "Chilly Coffee" fired her opening salvo, and the guns run-in for reloading, she was struck by four simultaneous shells on her closed gunports. The armored bolts were driven out, making it impossible to open the shutters to fire. Unable to engage his forward guns, and the channel too narrow to fight anything but bows-on, Foster pulled back. In the three days of fighting, the ship had lost twenty-two men, killed, wounded, and drowned.

Watson Smith, faced with bloody failure, reported himself "no longer fit for duty." He asked Admiral Porter for his relief and turned over command to James Foster. Reading the original orders, Foster was much taken by their emphasis on speed, and Smith's neglect of it. "Had these instructions been carried out," he wrote to Admiral Porter,

"I have no doubt that the expedition would have been successful."

Foster held a council of war. The officers of both services agreed it was impossible for naval forces "alone" to "conquer" the fort; or for the army "to combine in the attack, in consequence of water, etc." The *Chillicothe* needed an overhaul, and both ironclads were short of ammunition. There was also the danger of the entire force being cut off by the enemy coming behind. "It has been deemed advisable to retreat," he dispatched to Admiral Porter.

On March 17, the very next day, the retiring river column literally bumped into General Isaac Quinby and 10,000 men sent by Grant as reinforcements. Returning to their old positions facing Fort Pemberton, the ironclads fired three shots to draw the rebels out. Receiving no reply, they backed off. "We remained twelve days awaiting for the army to do something," Foster reported. On April 5, everyone retreated back to the Mississippi, a miserable failure, with blame enough spread around for all.

At the time Admiral Porter sent forward the Yazoo Pass expedition, he also attempted to disrupt Confederate shipping between Vicksburg and the Red River. On February 1, the steamer *City of Vicksburg* was seen unloading cargo at the city. Porter ordered nineteen-year-old ex-Medical Cadet Charles Rivers Ellet, son of the late Charles Ellet, and now a lieutenant colonel in the Mississippi Marine Brigade, to run the batteries before daybreak and ram the vessel at her moorings.* Porter made it clear to Ellet that humanity was not a priority. "It will not be part of your duty to save the lives of those on board," he said. In a final bit of advice, the admiral suggested Ellet fire turpentine balls from his howitzers, "it will make a fine finish to the sinking part."

On February 2, at 4:30 A.M., the *Queen of the West,* double-banked in a breastwork of cotton bales, glided past the upper batteries. By rotten luck her steering gear malfunctioned, and after an hour's emergency repair, dawn peeked over the bluffs. The rebels opened fire. Alone, in daylight, and, as a contemporary historian termed it, "in true Ellet fashion," the teenager in his brown paper ram raced past the booming Confederate guns.

Ellet rounded, lost way, and rammed the *City of Vicksburg* a glancing blow. At the instant of the grinding crash, the *Queen* took a 68-pounder shell through her cotton. Then Ellet fired a treble-shotted

---

* The only known photograph of Charles Rivers Ellet depicts a man having an uncanny resemblance to the actor Sean Penn.

load of turpentine incendiaries which "set the rebel steamer in flames"—and himself as well.

With the *Queen's* own cotton cladding on fire, the smoke pouring into the engine room suffocated the black gang. Ellet wanted to ram the target again, but to remain meant certain destruction. He ordered course downriver, cut loose the burning cotton, and out of enemy range repaired the damage.

Along the forty-mile stretch of the Mississippi between Red River and the Confederate forts at Port Hudson, Ellet started gobbling up prizes. Having no telegraph south of Vicksburg, the rebels were taken unawares. "Not a word of our coming had reached [this] place," Ellet said, "and the people scarcely knew who we were."

The first catch, the *A. W. Baker*, had on board several Confederate officers and women passengers. It was hardly secured when another steamer, the *Moro*, came down. A shot brought her to. This was a fat prize: 55 tons of pork, 500 hogs on the hoof, "and a large quantity of salt." Ellet burned 25,000 pounds of sacked cornmeal at a boat landing, and at the mouth of Red River, he put the women ashore, "who did not wish to go any farther." The *Berwick Bay* came into view, carrying 200 barrels of molasses, 10 hogsheads of sugar, 30,000 pounds of flour, and 40 bales of cotton. There was no escape for her either.

The three steamers in his wake, Ellet headed up the Red River. The captured vessels couldn't keep up, and the *Queen's* emptying coal bunkers "would not permit us to wait." Ellet ordered them burned, and the *Queen's* crew watched as perhaps $200,000 in prize money went up in smoke. No mention was made of the fate of the live hogs.

On February 5, three days after setting out, Ellet returned to Vicksburg. The mission had been a resounding success. Admiral Porter sneaked the little army tug *De Soto* and a full coal barge past the batteries at night, and on February 10, he sent Ellet back to Red River. "Hoping to hear a good account of you," he ended his orders, then added a postscript, "Don't be surprised to see the *Indianola* below." On the night of February 13, the ironclad *Indianola,* towing a pair of coal barges, ran past the Vicksburg batteries to "burn, sink, and destroy" rebel commerce in the Red River.

The *Queen of the West* and *De Soto,* towing her coal barge, ascended the Red River on February 12, going several miles to the junction of the tributary Atchafalaya, capturing and destroying a dozen army wagons laden with general military stores and barrels of salt beef. Ellet exchanged some musket shots with "a party of overseers and other civilians," and suffered one casualty, First Master

James Thompson, shot through the knee. For civilians to fire at uniformed troops was a serious violation of the rules of war, and the next morning, Ellet burned three large plantations for sheltering the bushwhackers.

On the fourteenth, they captured the steamer *Era No. 5,* with 4,500 bushels of corn. Leaving the prize under guard, the *Queen* and *De Soto* steamed farther upriver, reaching the bend near Fort DeRussy. As Ellet said, "The dense smoke of several boats, rapidly firing up, could be seen over the tops of the trees as we approached." He ordered the pilot to proceed dead slow, and just poke the *Queen*'s bow around the point. The rebels spotted her and opened fire. Ellet ordered the pilot to back the *Queen* out. Instead, the man ran her aground. Throwing the engine aback did nothing but drive the hull deeper into the mud. "The position at once became a very hot one," Ellet wrote in his report. In the fast-closing night, her cabin lights were a beacon to rebel balls, and nearly every shot hit. A rush of steam around the boat told Ellet the main steam pipe had been cut in two, and all power went dead. "Nothing further, of course, could be done." He ordered a boat lowered to carry First Master Thompson and discovered that someone had already made off with it. Cutting loose the cotton bales, most of the crew used them as rafts to the *De Soto*.

It would have been the easiest thing to burn the *Queen* if they could just have evacuated the wounded Thompson to the tug. It was, however, impossible to get at him. "All the passages," said Ellet, "had been blocked up with cotton, the interior . . . was intensely dark, full of steam, and strewed with shattered furniture." To bring the *De Soto* alongside would have ensured her destruction also. Ellet had no option than to retreat, leaving the *Queen of the West* to fall intact to the enemy.

The *De Soto* had hardly started downriver when a dense fog enveloped the whole area, and she pushed into the mud, losing her rudder. Poling off the banks, Ellet drifted the tug fifteen miles down to where he had left the *Era No. 5.* Moving everyone into that prize, he burned the *De Soto* and the coal barge. With the enemy right on their heels, Ellet pushed at full speed all night in the endless, wrapping fog, "throwing off the corn to lighten her."

At dawn the *Era* reached the relative safety of the Mississippi, when the pilot ran the vessel hard aground, in Ellet's words, "actually permitting her wheels to make several revolutions after she had struck." Ellet was now convinced that this accident and the *Queen* also running aground had been intentionally done—"deliberate treachery"—and he placed the pilot under arrest. With difficulty, they got the *Era* off and headed upriver.

The following afternoon, Ellet met the *Indianola* near Natchez. The ironclad's skipper, Lieutenant Commander George Brown, turned both vessels back to the Red River to recapture the *Queen of the West*. They had not gone three miles, when a break in the fog showed a steamer a mile off, coming right up at them. Ellet shrieked his steam whistle in alarm. She was the Confederate timberclad ram *Webb,* lead vessel of Ellet's baying pursuers.

Indianola opened fire, and it was now the hunters' turn to run. The fog socked in again, so dense that lookouts on the *Indianola* could not even make out the enemy's smoke. The following morning the ironclad continued down, anchoring at Red River. Brown sent Ellet and the *Era* back to Vicksburg. Then, for four days he blockaded the mouth of the Red River, unable to enter for want of a pilot. From local gossip he learned the rebels had repaired the *Queen,* and together with the *Webb* and some cottonclads were preparing an attack on the ironclad.

Thinking Admiral Porter would send another vessel to assist in operations, Brown, coal barges lashed alongside, headed back toward Vicksburg. At 9:30 P.M., February 24, "the night being very dark, four boats were discovered in chase of us." Brown cleared for action, went about, "and stood downriver to meet them." The Confederate vessels, *Dr. Beatty, Queen of the West, Webb,* and *Grand Era,* were commanded by Major Joseph Brent. At 150 yards he gave the order to fire and simultaneously surged ahead in the *Dr. Beatty* to ram. "Our bow went crashing clear through the [coal] barge," he reported, shattering the *Indianola* amidships. For almost five minutes, the two vessels were stuck fast. Rebel marksmen fired at every chink of light. Brent reported "no living men were to be seen on the enemy's decks."

The *Indianola* and *Dr. Beatty* were locked in a deadly embrace, and the *Webb* dashed up and rammed *Indianola* with "terrific force" near the bow. Iron plates were jarred loose and the starboard engine stopped, but the *Webb* paid for it, cleaving her own bow down to the keelson.

It was now the turn of the *Queen of the West*. At full speed, she struck the *Indianola* right aft, crushing the hull framing. The *Queen* herself became almost unmanageable, listing so far out of the water that a paddle wheel thrashed the air. Then the *Webb* careered on with a full head of steam, ramming the *Indianola* in exactly the place just evacuated by the *Queen*. "She struck us fair in the stern," Brown said, "and

... water poured in in large volumes." The wounds were critical and the *Indianola* could not be saved.

With damaged rudders, Brown conned her to midchannel, "and the leaks were increasing rapidly." The enemy rams gathered for another charge, and if they hit, the *Indianola* would go down with little hope of saving the crew. Stern underwater, Brown grounded on the west bank and surrendered.

For the Confederates it was a tremendous coup. Even considering the Galveston affair and the capture of the *Queen of the West,* the rebels hadn't such a victory afloat since Hampton Roads. The nearest salvage equipment was at Vicksburg, and the *Queen of the West* was sent to bring down some pumps.

On February 21, three days *before* the *Indianola* battle, Ellet arrived at Young's Point and reported his losses to Admiral Porter. With the powerful *Queen of the West* in Confederate service, the admiral rightly considered the *Indianola* to be in danger. He had no ironclads, however, to send in her support, except the turtles, and they could not return upriver without a tow.

Before this crisis, a weird idea had been thought up in the flagship's drawing room. When the *Queen* and the *Indianola* first ran the Vicksburg gauntlet, several rebel guns had burst in their preventive fire. Hoping to take advantage of this self-destruction, Porter sent a mortar scow to bombard the town from a safe distance, but the rebels refused the bait. As Porter wrote, "Finding that they could not be provoked to fire without an object, I thought of getting up an imitation Monitor." The admiral produced a sketch of the hokum, which his officers pronounced "very formidable."

Around Wednesday, February 24, Porter took a rotting coal barge in hand. Pine boards simulated paddleboxes and a boxy turret, armed with Quaker guns. Empty pork barrels served as funnels, old canoes for her boats. The boilers were of riverbank clay, in which were placed smudge pots filled with damp oakum and pitchpine knots. The whole thing, taking half a day to build and $8.63 of taxpayer money, was finished with a coat of black tar. At her launching, a pirate's skull and bones flag was tacked to a mast, and across the paddleboxes, some wag painted "Deluded People Cave In." The navy christened her the "Black Terror."

At midnight, February 25, her smudge pots were lit, smoke poured from the pork barrel funnels, and the Black Terror was cast adrift to run past Vicksburg. Ensign Cort Williams wrote, "With all the speed that her mud furnaces and a five knot current could give, she moved proudly on with majestic dignity." The Confederate gunners on the heights opened a terrific fire. "The earth fairly trembled," Williams recalled, "and the shot flew thick around the devoted craft." The *Queen of the West,* loading salvage gear, turned and ran for it. The panic spread before her. From the capital at Jackson, General Pemberton telegraphed the rebels on the river, "You must, if possible, blow up the *Indianola.*"

The Black Terror touched land at the base of Young's Point, "as naturally," Ensign Williams wrote, "as if guided by the hand of a skilled pilot." Some Union infantrymen shoved her back into the stream and she drifted slowly down toward the grounded *Indianola.* The *Queen of the West* came tearing by, in the bitter words of a Confederate cavalry officer, "in great haste, reporting a gunboat of the enemy approaching." The Confederate flotilla at once got underway, abandoning the wreck. Seeing the Black Terror two miles off, the lieutenant commanding the deserted salvage party burst the *Indianola*'s guns and blew her up. Totally unintended, the mock warship destroyed what might have been a very serious Confederate obstacle on the river. The loss of the *Queen of the West* and *Indianola* deterred Admiral Porter from ever attempting to interdict the Red River while the main squadron remained above Vicksburg. It did not, however, hinder another attempt to encircle Vicksburg from the north. During the waning days of the Yazoo Pass expedition, Porter, acting on information gotten from runaway slaves, informed the department "that by cutting our way through the woods, which are all under water," a way could be found into the Yazoo, "and thus get into the rear of Vicksburg without loss of life or vessels." If successfully completed, Grant could push through the new route to high, dry land behind the city. In early March, Porter took the *Carondelet* on a reconnaissance thirty miles up Steele's Bayou, "which at low stages of water," he noted, "is nothing but a ditch."

The route went up Steele's and Muddy bayous to Black Bayou, east to Deer Creek, up the Rolling Fork, then down the Big Sunflower to the Yazoo at Haynes's Bluff, passing through some of the most picturesque willow and moss-draped plantation country in the Old South. In fact, the expedition would pass right by the semifictional "Shelby" place, Harriet Beecher Stowe's setting for *Uncle Tom's Cabin.*

On March 14, Porter started with five turtles, four mortar scows, and their tugs. Grant accompanied the column for a day to work out the fine points of the army's cooperating effort. Everyone was in good spirits. Porter obliterated the cypress trees growing in the channel by ramming them. Each turtle took a turn, butting its 800 tons against the trunk, backing off and doing it again. The branches rained an angry fall of lizards, snakes, weasels, opossum, and other arboreal life on the decks.

On the sixteenth, they entered Black Bayou, the first of the lateral passes. They "found the water very black," wrote an officer in the *Cincinnati*, "the trees meet over our heads, and there is great danger of knocking down the chimneys." They were in the heart of lazy, magnolia plantation country, and to the residents along the banks, especially the slaves, the incredible vision of the snorting iron turtles, creeping along under their moving cloud of smoke, seemed a vision from another world.

"The inhabitants," wrote Admiral Porter, "looked on in wonder and astonishment, and the negroes flocked in hundreds . . . to see the novel sight." The white inhabitants also ran, the other way, leaving their valuables and slaves behind. Foraging parties spread over the fat land, bringing back boatloads of chickens, hams, eggs, butter, "bed quilts, etc." The grand progress did not last. They were finally spotted by a Confederate government agent, and, as if by a single hand the riverbanks became consumed in an endless pyre of cotton fires. "All along," said Admiral Porter, "as far as the eye could see, there was nothing but cotton fires burning up, and many dwellings consuming with it."

The expedition, with gunports closed and decks wetted, forced its way through twisting waters, lined with miles of flame on either side. Porter, on the upper deck of the *Cincinnati,* stood with Lieutenant George Bache and the helmsman. A hose pointing up a deck hatch at their feet kept all completely drenched. The heat was insufferable, and the officers retreated into the pilothouse. The helmsman stayed at his post, swathed in a water-soaked flag.

General Sherman came up the eighteenth, looked at the creeks, and refused to believe a channel for his transports could be hacked out. "Before you fellows get through," he told the admiral, "you won't have a smokestack or a boat among you." Porter laughed at that. "So much the better," he said, "it will look like business. All I need is an engine, guns, and a hull to float them." Sherman ordered the transports up.

The next day, with only seven miles left until they reached "plain sailing" at the Rolling Fork, an escaped slave reported the rebels felling trees ahead. Porter rushed the armed tug *Thistle* to the site. Too late. "The enemy," he wrote, "succeeded . . . in getting a large tree down, which stopped . . . progress, and then the negroes, with muskets [aimed] at their breasts, were made to ply their axes until the creek was . . . sealed against our further advance."

Porter landed 300 men to cover the flotilla from an Indian mound on the riverbank and all that night, with neither food nor sleep, the sailors worked in brutal, mosquito- and snake-infested swamp water to clear out the felled timber. By morning the turtles were within half a mile "of the end of this troublesome creek."

Forward appeared a stretch of water covered with what seemed a layer of green scum. Taking the lead, the *Thistle* stuck fast, snared helpless in a tangling web of willow switches. The *Carondelet* tried to ram her way through and got stuck in the mess. The crew poured out with knives, cutlasses, and saws. As soon as one switch was cut, another popped up from below. The *Carondelet* lurched ahead three feet.

The landing parties holding the riverbank were driven back to the vessels by ever-increasing numbers of enemy troops with artillery. More slaves came to tell Porter the rebels were now cutting timber behind him. There was real danger of the entire force being cut off. "I hesitated no longer what to do," the admiral said. He ordered everyone on half-rations and dictated specific instructions for blowing up the flotilla should it come to that.

On a piece of tissue paper, Porter scribbled a hasty note to Sherman, wrapped it in a tobacco leaf, and dispatched it with a black crewman. At night, snipers opened fire. To lessen the chance of boarding, the casemates were smeared with thick coats of bottom slime. The turtles buttoned up their hatches, the men stifled below. Placing his best shots in the pilothouses, and loading the big guns with grape, Porter ordered all rudders unshipped, and sterns first, the flotilla dropped downstream, "the vessels rebounding from tree to tree." The scary night passed, and on Saturday, March 21, they bumped into the army's advancing transports. "We were quite pleased," Porter wrote, "as I never knew before how much the comfort and safety of ironclads, situated as we were, depended on the soldiers."

At midday the sounds of skirmishing came upriver, and with it, covered with mud, astride an old horse with a rope bridle, rode General William Tecumseh Sherman. A great roar of cheers greeted him. All along Deer Creek, the sailors looked at the welcome sight of Sherman's men slaughtering cattle and spit-roasting sides of beef. The soldiers raised a cheer when Porter's tug chugged by, and the admiral hooted his steam whistle back. Behind the turtles tramped an exodus of contraband slaves, whole families and plantations of them. The *Cincinnati* diarist wrote, "the lame, the halt, the blind, as well as the stalwart and active . . . on horses, mules, and afoot, in high glee—'going to freedom, sure,' they say."

The Steele's Bayou expedition failed in its primary mission of encircling Vicksburg. It did, however, capture or destroy huge stocks of cattle, horses, mules, food, and provisions sorely needed by the Confederates at Vicksburg—indeed, all of its commissary reserve. At the same time, it forced General Pemberton to extend his lines ever farther to the north, away from what would become Grant's eventual line of advance.

Near the mouth of the Yazoo, Admiral Porter was handed a message just come from the *Black Hawk*: Farragut had run the batteries at Port Hudson!

In the summer of 1862, after the initial failures to capture Vicksburg, Farragut had written to his chief of staff, "I will not take another place without troops to hold it." In December, the arrival of General Nathaniel Banks and 20,000 men at New Orleans led Farragut to plan a push against the other remaining Confederate bastion on the river. "I hear that Porter is knocking at the upper door at Vicksburg," he wrote at year's end, "and we must go to work at the lower door, Port Hudson."

But Banks shied away. A reconnaissance convinced him that Port Hudson was too tough a proposition, and his soldiers were still green as peas. Disingenuously, he wired General Halleck, "the naval force here is insufficient." Farragut learned of this backbiting from the columns of the commercial press. To his wife, Virginia, he wrote, "You will no doubt hear more of 'Why don't Farragut's fleet move up the river?' Tell them, because the army is not ready."

Angered by the innuendo, which he blamed on the War Department, Farragut pondered an advance upriver by the fleet alone. Trusty Captain Thornton Jenkins had reported as his new chief of staff, and this experienced officer listened with interest. A broad thinker, Farragut knew the object was not only to reopen the river to Federal commerce, but to strategically divide the Confederacy, crippling the Southern armies, he told Jenkins, "by cutting off their supplies from Texas . . . their main dependence for beef cattle, sheep, and Indian corn." With ships alone, it would be extraordinarily dangerous, and both men knew it. "If we can get a few vessels above Port Hudson," Farragut hoped, "the thing will not be an entire failure, and I am pretty confident it can be done."

Port Hudson stood, in almost the exact configuration of Vicksburg, on 100-foot heights along an eastern elbow of river bluff, twenty miles above Baton Rouge. Along the ridges, the Confederates had built a series of fortified batteries that both covered the river approach from below the town, and enfiladed the sharp, shoaling, left turn immediately above. The positions were held by about 16,000 entrenched troops.

However much Farragut wanted to make the attempt sooner rather than later, he was hampered by the siphoning of vessels taking care of business in the Gulf, especially after the miserable events at Galveston. Chafing at the enforced idleness, he "amused" himself in the New Orleans social season. At a young ladies' concert for the city's poor, the admiral purchased a box for his staff. "I could not but feel," he wrote Virginia, "that I was giving my money to those who would not give me a Christian burial if they could help it."

In late February 1863, the inactivity suddenly ended with news of the loss of *Indianola* and *Queen of the West.* "The time has come," he announced to Captain Jenkins, "there can be no more delay. I must go—army or no army." Convincing a reluctant General Banks to lead a diversion on Port Hudson by land, Farragut set his mind to run the batteries, "or be sunk in the attempt."

On March 11, the fleet assembled at Baton Rouge: *Hartford, Richmond, Monongahela, Mississippi,* the ironclad *Essex,* five gunboats, and a division of mortar schooners. Preparations for battle began. Running rigging and topmasts were taken down, splinter nettings placed on the starboard—engaged—side, sandbag bulwarks piled about engines and boilers, chain cables garlanded over the side, and boat howitzers hoisted in the mast tops for short-range work.

Another bit of innovation came from Farragut's active brain. As each ship passed the batteries, it would have to execute a sharp turn to port, against a strong current, at the same time exposing their sterns to raking fire. To aid this movement he ordered a gunboat lashed to the disengaged side of each of the big ships: *Albatross* to the *Hartford, Genessee* to the *Richmond, Kineo* to the *Monongahela.* It jury-rigged the ships with the maneuvering capacity of a twin-screw steamer and at the same time protected the gunboats with the thicker sides of their brethren. The arrangement could not, however, be done with the *Mississippi,* whose massive paddleboxes would not allow it.

On the morning of the fourteenth, the fleet came in sight of Port Hudson. For the preliminary bombardment, Farragut stationed the mortar schooners, the weak-engined *Essex,* and two gunboats along the forested east bank, below the batteries. That done, he summoned his commanding officers for a council of war. Remembering the misunderstanding with the *Brooklyn* at Vicksburg, Farragut said, "I expect all to go by who are able, and I think the best protection against the enemy's fire is a well directed fire from our own guns." Aboard the flagship, a sailor remembered the tense wait "as quiet as death."

Each big ship carried an experienced pilot, or so the admiral thought. In the *Hartford,* the man was stationed in the mizzentop, communicating to the quarterdeck by means of a speaking tube. In the *Mississippi,* the pilot stood in one of her boats, lashed outboard, below the guns on the disengaged port side.

When it was true and fully dark, an army tug—lights flaring, steam whistle screaming, wigwagging away with a signal torch—came alongside the *Hartford.* Captain Jenkins remembered Farragut as "calm . . . but he saw at once that the enemy's attention had been specially called to him." And what was the momentous message? Only that General Banks was "five miles in rear of the Port Hudson works," nothing else. Would Banks attack the town? Farragut thought not. Turning to Jenkins, he muttered, "He had as well be in New Orleans . . . for all the good he is doing us."

At that moment, a rocket split the air over the first enemy battery. Lieutenant George Dewey in the *Mississippi* remembered, "the whole crest of the bluff broke into flashes." The rebels, learning from their mistakes at the New Orleans forts, had set huge bonfires of pitch pine to illuminate the river and the passing targets. At two bells in the evening watch, 9 P.M., Farragut signaled the fleet to get underway.

The Confederates held their fire until the fleet came within 800 yards, then, accompanied by a screeching rebel yell, they loosed a rain of iron on the river. The heavy, misty air hadn't a whisper of breeze, and the smoke from engines and guns hung over the ships in a choking blanket, "thickening," Dewey said, "with the progress of the cannonading." The *Hartford* was able to run beyond her own smoke, but the *Mississippi,* last in line, breathed it from every vessel.

At the bend just above the town, the current swung the flagship's bow toward the east bank, and for a few harrowing minutes she touched bottom, head to the enemy. This was exactly the sort of situation perceived by Farragut when he ordered the gunboats lashed to the disengaged side. He lifted a hailing trumpet. "Back! Back [the engine] on the *Albatross!*" The "little chicken," as she was affectionately called, threw her screw in reverse and got the *Hartford* off.

A report came of a ram bearing down on the port bow. Farragut, sixty-two years old, hefted a cutlass. "I am going to have a hand in this myself," he said. But it was a false alarm. In a couple of minutes, just past midnight, the flagship and her little chicken were in the bend, above the Confederate guns, crews cheering like maniacs, and they came to anchor.

They were the lucky ones. The *Richmond* took a shot in the engine room that knocked off the steam safety valves. The propulsion spaces and berth deck filled with escaping steam and pressure dropped. Against the current, her lashed gunboat hadn't the strength for both of them. The *Richmond*'s executive officer, Lieutenant Commander Cummings saw his leg blown off. "Quick, boys," he said to those helping him, "pick me up, put a tourniquet on, send my letters to my wife, tell them I fell in doing my duty." When the dying officer learned the ship had gone about he was stunned. "I would rather lose the other leg than go back," he groaned. "Can nothing be done? There is a south wind. Where are the sails?"

Next in line, the *Monongahela* and gunboat *Kineo* received volleys of musketry from the opposite bank. The *Kineo* silenced it, but took an unlucky shot that disabled her rudder post. The *Monongahela,* having to steer for both vessels, lurched aground. The *Kineo,* swept by the momentum, tore free from her lashings. For a desperate half-hour, she stood by the stranded sloop, then drifted, rudderless, downstream, out of the fight. Then the *Monongahela*'s bridge collapsed, knocking out her commanding officer, and the "exec" took over. Freed from the bottom, he tried to follow Farragut around the turn, but the engines froze, and she drifted down. Confederate grapeshot swept across her decks, killing six men and wounding twenty-one.

In the *Mississippi,* last in line, Captain Melancton Smith and Lieutenant George Dewey knew the "destiny" of their stout, old ship rested in the hands of the pilot. "There was nothing to do," Dewey said, "but to fire back at the flashes on the bluffs and trust to his expert knowledge." The enemy shells were coming so close together, that it appeared the rebels were firing chain shot.*

The ship steamed ahead very slowly, feeling her way forward with the lead, approaching the shoal that jutted from the inner elbow of the turn. When the pilot thought the hazard past, he called out, "Starboard the helm! Full speed ahead!" The order was carried out smartly, and the *Mississippi* ran hard aground straight on to the shelving bottom and listed over. The paddle wheels were backed immediately at full power and the portside battery run in to get her on an even keel; nothing. As Dewey recalled it, there was remarkably little confusion. They had

* Two cannon balls secured to a length of chain, used to demolish rigging at long ranges.

been under severe fire at the New Orleans forts, "but," Dewey said, "no amount of training could altogether prepare men for such a situation."

Half an hour's thrashing did not budge the ship an inch, yet Dewey wrote, "steadfastly and even unconcernedly the engine-room force stuck to their duties." The hits mounted, and so did the toll of dead and wounded. The flash of bursting shells took over from the night, and the brief intervals of darkness were "baffling to the eyes." Dewey found old Captain Melancton Smith on deck, casually lighting a cigar. "Well," Smith commented coolly, "it doesn't look as if we can get her off."

"No, sir," replied the young exec, "it does not!"

The ship was now on fire forward, in the paint locker, from red-hot shot. In a desperate attempt to lighten her, Smith ordered the port battery thrown overboard, but it was too late. He turned to Dewey, "Can we save the crew?" "Yes, sir!" he replied. There was, literally, not a minute to lose, not with the wounded piling up and the paint fire creeping toward the magazine. The guns must continue shooting until the last possible instant. The gunners never flinched, working their pieces as if sure of victory.

Dewey moved about the deck, giving orders to abandon ship. Half the boats were smashed, and the wounded were lifted into what remained. Some of the uninjured crew began crowding in. "For the moment," Dewey noticed, "the bonds of discipline had been broken. The men were just human beings obeying the law of self-preservation." He gave orders for the boats to return immediately after making the west bank, but none had. To swim in the swift current was impossible, "it would be a choice of drowning or of burning." Determined to get the boats back, he jumped into the last one as it pulled for the shore. Only then did he realize what he had done. To any man not there, it seemed as if he had deserted his ship. "All the world would say that I had been guilty of about as craven an act as can be placed at the door of any officer." It was the most agonizing moment of his sixty-year naval career.

Under fire all the way, the boat reached the bank and Dewey ordered everyone to take shelter behind the levee. Four men he detailed to return with him to the ship. Only the *Mississippi*'s black cook came to his side. "I am ready to go with you, sir!" said the man. Dewey called out to the rest, "shaming them, in the name of their race, for allowing a negro to be the only one who was willing to . . . save his shipmates, [then] I did not lack for volunteers." Seeing the other boats having the same problem, he ordered their fuzz-cheeked midshipmen to shoot anyone who did not obey.

Back aboard the burning ship, Dewey and Melancton Smith went up and down the decks. "We must make sure that none is left aboard alive," said the captain. They turned over every dead man, and found one alive, a small lad, "little more than a boy, who was so faint that he could scarcely speak." The two men pulled him from under a pile of the dead, all killed by a single, bursting shell.

Their next duty was making certain the rebels did not take the *Mississippi* intact. Dewey and Ensign Oliver Batcheller began in the wardroom. Dewey grabbed his mattress, ripped it open, dumped the horsehair under the dining table, piled the furniture around it, and threw an oil lamp. In the engine room, Smith cut the delivery pipes and the ship filled with water astern.

The last boat returned alongside. Captain Smith, Dewey, Ensign Batcheller, and four enlisted men, including the wounded boy, were the only living left. Dewey stood back, waiting for his juniors to precede. And "then the captain waited for me, so that he was the last man ever to press his foot on the *Mississippi*'s deck." The order of their departure was in strict accord with naval custom, "as if it had been some formal occasion in a peaceful port."

Filling aft brought the ship's bow out of the water and she slid free of the shoal. The current took her, swung her head around, and the *Mississippi* drifted, all aflame, downriver. The heat reached the guns, and they cooked off, as Dewey watched, "a dying ship manned by dead men, firing on the enemy." Most of the crew were picked up by the *Richmond,* and from her deck, they witnessed the frigate's death throes. In the words of a *Richmond* sailor, "their emotions almost too great for words." At 4:30 A.M., the *Mississippi* blew up. Of her crew of nearly 300 men, 64 were killed or missing.

After the *Hartford* anchored above Port Hudson, Farragut sent up rockets in a vain endeavor to communicate with the rest of the fleet. In the runs past New Orleans and Vicksburg, only one or two vessels had failed to make it, now all but two had been turned back or destroyed. For the admiral, there was nothing to do but bury the flagship's dead, holystone the blood off her decks, and head upriver.

On March 25, the *Hartford* and *Albatross* arrived below Vicksburg. Porter was off with the Steele's Bayou expedition, and Alfred Ellet, in direct contravention of orders, sent two of his rams in broad daylight past the batteries to open communications. The *Lancaster* was sunk and the *Switzerland* badly damaged with many men killed. Porter banished Ellet to the guerrilla-infested creeks of Tennessee.

On the twenty-sixth, Porter drifted a barge of coal and provisions past the city down to Farragut. "It will be an object for you to remain at

Red River as long as possible, and I hope you will do so," read the accompanying, coded letter. "It is death to these people; they get all their grub from there." The next day, Farragut headed south to block-ade the mouth of Red River.

The lengthy and so far unsuccessful maneuvering of Grant, Porter & Co. in the morasses around Vicksburg manifestly perplexed Abraham Lincoln. True, Porter had put to him the correct picture of the diffi-culties during their last meeting. But Lincoln was confounded that the town, the war's primary strategic objective, continued to hold in spite of all that was hurled against it. By springtime, 1863, he was all for sending thousands of men vainly besieging Charleston and all the available monitors to the west. Halleck relayed the President's anxi-eties to General Grant, and Gideon Welles sent Admiral Porter a direct order to run the fleet past Vicksburg. By the time Porter received it, the combined great movement at crushing the Confeder-ate bastion was underway.

In early April, Grant gave up the idea of enveloping Vicksburg from the north, and instead, started his army south along the west bank levee to New Carthage, twenty-five miles below the city, across the river.

Porter needed no shove from the Navy Department, and in the days leading up to April 16, he took the squadron in hand. All the iron-clads needed repairs after their banging up in the expeditions along the Yazoo. The vessels were given new coats of paint—black hulls and casemates and buff cabins with painted gunports. For the run, he had seven ironclads: *Benton,* four turtles, and the new monsters, *Lafayette* and *Tuscumbia.* Each had shields of logs and piles of wet hay abreast their engines, with either a tug or coal barges lashed alongside.

The admiral found time to pen a letter to Gus Fox. The rebels at Vicksburg, he wrote, "are like a man inside of a house, windows barri-caded, muskets out of a thousand loop holes, a 'cheval de frise' [wooden barricades of pointed spikes] all around, and a wide ditch out-side of that—*we* are in the position of boys throwing grass at him and expecting him to cave in—yet we win after all—we don't go backwards. . . . I hope to see us yet with Uncle Abe's foot on Jeff Davis's neck!"

Benton, with Admiral Porter and the staff on board, would lead, fol-lowed by *Lafayette,* Henry Walke's new command, the four turtles, three army transports crammed with stores and fodder, and *Tuscumbia* bringing up the rear.

Near 10 P.M., on April 16, the *Benton* flashed two white lights, and the squadron, hugging the far bank, drifted without steam down to Vicksburg with the current. At the apex of the horseshoe turn, when Porter could make out the lights of the city, he ordered the flagboat to cut in her engines. The rebels spotted them and set an abandoned house afire to spread the alarm. Tar barrels at the water batteries were also lit. From the heights above Vicksburg, a calcium flare burst forth, sending shafts of blinding light onto the river, illuminating every vessel as if on a stage. Ensign Elias Smith of the *Lafayette* said, "New York conflagrations and Fourth of July pyrotechnics—they were nothing to it!"

The current grabbed the *Benton,* never the handiest of craft, and swung her completely around in a circle. Steadying up, she steamed to within a few yards of the wharf batteries, vomiting broadsides as fast as her gunners could fire. Porter, topside, could actually see the crashing bricks of collapsing buildings. The flagboat took one hit, a solid shot that went right through her iron and forty inches of oak, taking off the leg of one man and mangling another.

Most of the coal barges were cast off, to give the ironclads better purchase in the current. Behind them, the army transports, crewed by green volunteers, spun in the eddies and tried in their fear to steam back upstream. But Commander Jim Shirk of the *Tuscumbia,* an old hand from the stinkpot days, brusquely turned them back into line. The transport *Henry Clay,* her decks piled with bales of cotton and forage, was hit and abandoned to the flames. The rebel gunners, thinking they had gotten an ironclad, set up a tremendous cheer, "a fiendish yell of triumph," said Ensign Smith. Porter heard it, and for some minutes he, too, thought *Tuscumbia* had gone.

By 1:30 A.M., the squadron had passed to safety. Below the town, at the base of Young's Point, a rowboat pulled for the flagboat. "*Benton,* Ahoy!" came the hail. "Halloo!" Porter answered. It was General Sherman. He shook Porter's hand in admiration. "You are more at home here," he said, "than you were in the ditches grounding on willow trees. Stick to this, Porter. It suits you Navy people better."

With remarkably little damage to either men or vessels, the squadron had run the Vicksburg batteries. On the eighteenth, Porter anchored off New Carthage. Four days later, Grant was marching down the levee road with the main body of the army. It was Grant's plan to ferry his men across the river to Grand Gulf, in operational terms, the southern extremity of the Vicksburg defense line. At the same time, Sherman's corps, supported by what was left of the squadron above

Vicksburg, would occupy the rebels with another play at Haynes's Bluff.

On April 29, Porter led the ironclads head-on against the Grand Gulf batteries. For nearly five hours, the massive artillery duel rocked the river, and the Confederates gave better than they received. The *Tuscumbia, Pittsburg,* and *Benton* were hit repeatedly. Porter was wounded by a shell splinter, and the *Benton* took a damaging shot in her paddle wheel and drifted a mile downriver, spinning like a top, completely out of control. The defenses were too strong, and Grant wisely marched a few miles further south, opposite the undefended town of Bruinsburg.

The fight at Grand Gulf had been witnessed by a party of special military and civilian commissioners sent by President Lincoln to report on Grant's fitness for high command. The night after the bombardment, Porter gave his berth to the army's elderly adjutant general, Charles Thomas. The admiral helped unpack his bags, and as Thomas got into a nightshirt, mixed him a hot whiskey toddy. In confidence, General Thomas told the admiral that complaints had come to the President regarding Grant's management of the Vicksburg campaign. Thomas swore Porter to secrecy. If necessary, he said, he carried the order to sack U. S. Grant and appoint a successor. "General," said Porter, handing over a brimming crystal cup, "don't let your plans get out, for if the army and navy found out what you . . . gentlemen came for, they would tar and feather you."

Up the lower Yazoo at Haynes's Bluff, Lieutenant Commander K. R. Breese gathered his forces: ironclads, tinclads, transports, store boats, and a floating forge. With a great show of blowing boiler tubes and hooting steam whistles, he landed 10,000 of Sherman's men. Before reembarking, the soldiers tramped around in the woods, making as much noise and spectacle as they could. It was so realistic that the Confederates were completely taken in and they ignored the real threat at Bruinsburg. By May 1, when General Pemberton realized he had been fooled, Grant was ashore with 30,000 troops on the hard, east bank of the Mississippi, advancing north to the state capital at Jackson. On May 2, the outflanked rebels abandoned Grand Gulf. The noose around Vicksburg wound one notch tighter.

In the east, during the first week of May, near an isolated Virginia manse called Chancellorsville, Robert E. Lee fought his greatest battle, pitting 60,000 men against Fighting Joe Hooker's 133,000. Half the Union Army of the Potomac disintegrated, with losses of nearly 17,000 men. Lee's casualties numbered over 12,500, including the death of Stonewall Jackson. Hooker was relieved of command, replaced by Major General George Gordon Meade. Lee made plans to invade the North again, this time through Pennsylvania.

It would be at least two weeks before Grant advanced to the Vicksburg fortifications, and Porter left for a quick foray into the Red River. On May 5, he exchanged salutes with Farragut in the *Hartford* and pushed into the heart of Louisiana. The ironclads could go no farther than Alexandria, over sixty miles upriver, and the rebels, barely a step ahead, retreated to Shreveport. Porter turned the tinclads loose up the shallows, where they destroyed $300,000 worth of salt, sugar, rum, molasses, and bacon. Porter returned to Vicksburg, crossed over at Young's Point, and resumed command from above the town. On May 7, Grant had 44,000 men marching north. By midmonth Federal troops occupied Jackson, severing the Confederates at Vicksburg from any reinforcement.

In the Yazoo on the morning of May 18, Porter, ears straining for the sound of Grant's artillery, his eye anxiously scanning the heights through a glass, heard the distinctive pop-pop-pop of skirmishing behind Chickasaw Bluffs. By noon, they could see blue-coated cavalry galloping along the crest, sabers out, driving the rebels from the guns.

Foraging for two weeks on "hog and hominy," Sherman's corps had broken through to the Yazoo, and the fleet sent up a great cheer. The *De Kalb* steamed to Haynes's Bluff to shell out the remaining enemy, and found them already in full retreat. Within two days, the rebels abandoned every position between Vicksburg and the Yazoo. The Mississippi at their backs, and Grant to their front and flanks, General Pemberton's 20,000 men were trapped inside a meat-cleaver-shaped position four miles long and two miles wide at the blade.

The battle for Vicksburg settled into a regular siege. The navy's 13-inch mortars rained destruction on the trenches and town around the clock. On May 22, Grant ordered a general attack. The din from the covering naval bombardment was so great that those on the river could not hear the firing inland. McClernand's corps on the left captured an outpost, which he reported to Grant as a lodgement in the main Confederate works. Taking McClernand at his word, Grant ordered a second assault, which was thrown back with heavy losses. When McClernand trumpeted his "victory" to the press, Grant finally had enough and sacked him.

Inside Vicksburg, cattle on the hoof suffered terribly from the mortar fire. When the rebels moved the herds to a secluded valley south of town, the animals were literally ripped apart by fire from the turtles coming up from below. By May 25, the stench of death and corruption on the battlefield became unbearable, and Grant and Pemberton agreed to a two-hour truce to bury the dead.

On May 27, General Nathaniel Banks with 12,000 men launched an unsuccessful attack on Port Hudson, and was thrown back with 1,000 killed and wounded. For the rebel garrison, the deprivation there was as bad as Vicksburg. One Confederate soldier said he and his comrades eventually ate "all the beef—all the mules—all the Dogs—and all the Rats."

By the end of June, Confederate deserters from Vicksburg swam out to the squadron in increasing numbers. The garrison, they said, subsisted on cornmeal "bread" and mule meat, "Confederate beef." As for the civilian population, they lived in holes dug into the cliffs. The deserters told Admiral Porter that the besieged army were tearing down damaged houses to fashion rafts and paddles for a mass escape across the river. Porter ordered everyone to be ready to repel boarders.

On July 3, while directing the round-the-clock bombardment, Admiral Porter received a message from General Grant. The rebels had asked for an armistice to arrange terms of capitulation. "Will you please cease firing until notified, or hear our batteries open? I shall fire a national salute into the city at daylight if they do not surrender."

Half a continent away, on July 3, at Gettysburg, Pennsylvania, the war's greatest battle climaxed when Robert E. Lee's assault across a wheat field lapped to the edge of the Federal batteries, and staggered back, bloody and beaten.

The next day, July 4, at Vicksburg, General Pemberton surrendered the town and garrison to General Ulysses Grant. At 11:30 A.M., the Confederate flag was lowered from the courthouse, and up the staff went the stars and stripes. From above and below, the warships converged on the waterfront. Grant and his staff boarded the *Black Hawk,* and Porter accommodated them by emptying out his wine locker.

The admiral, remembering the petty humiliation of having the army's report of Arkansas Post reach Washington before his own, this time made certain the navy came first. His terse message to Gideon Welles, "I have the honor to inform you that Vicksburg has surrendered to the U.S. forces on this 4th of July," reached the national capital ahead of Grant's, and was carried across the street to the White House by the secretary of the navy himself.

Gideon Welles found President Lincoln looking at a Vicksburg map "when I gave the glad tidings." Lincoln stood up. "I myself will telegraph this news to General Meade" at Gettysburg, he said. Lincoln picked up his hat and suddenly stopped, "his countenance beaming with joy." He took Welles' hand, and threw an arm around the secretary's shoulder. "I cannot, in words, tell you my joy over this result. It is great, Mr. Welles, it is great!"

On the New York Stock Exchange, gold dropped fifteen points, a sure indicator of confidence in ultimate Union victory. Some weeks later, the President personally signed David D. Porter's commission to permanent rear admiral on the active list, retroactive to July 4. From Cairo, Captain Pennock read it in the papers, and wrote, "I have ripped all the gold lace off my pants, and will send it down to you with pleasure."

On July 9, Port Hudson surrendered to Nathaniel Banks. Farragut, as ordered by the Navy Department, turned over all duties on the river to Admiral Porter, and the "Father of Waters," in the words of Abraham Lincoln, once more "flowed unvexed to the sea." The Confederacy had been cut in two. It was the beginning of the end.

Red River

"There is a faint attempt to make a victory out of this, but two or three such victories would cost us our existence."

—**Rear Admiral David D. Porter, USN**

f ever a military expedition began with the seeds of disaster already planted, this was it. Since the fall of Vicksburg and Port Hudson in the summer of 1863, the military value of the western Confederacy—Texas, Arkansas, and Louisiana west of the Mississippi—had declined to almost nothing. When the flow of cattle, horses, grain, foodstuffs, and recruits ceased to supply the eastern Confederacy, the isolated western region should have been allowed to simply wither away.

But in the summer of 1863, certain political and economic considerations took precedence over strictly military judgment. The establishment of the puppet French empire in Mexico, plus the fact that in all of Texas, the U.S. flag flew over not an inch of territory, sounded alarm bells in the State Department. At a July Cabinet meeting, Secretary of State Seward stated his fears of French designs on Texas. The immediate retaking of Galveston was suggested.

A month passed, and General Halleck, prodded by Seward, dropped the decision on General Nathaniel Banks, commanding the Department of the Gulf in New Orleans. "There are important reasons," Halleck wrote, "why our flag should be restored in some point of Texas with the least possible delay." He gave Banks the choice of marching overland to "any ... point you deem preferable," or, if he wished, moving by sea, where "Admiral Farragut will cooperate." But before Banks received the message, Halleck wrote a second. While not changing the gist of his original suggestions, he pointed Banks to Louisiana's Red River as a means for occupying northern Texas. In addition, an advance up the Red River had other advantages, specifically to uncork a flood of Louisiana cotton.

Following the second letter, Banks dispatched a staff officer to confer with Grant, Sherman, and Admiral Porter. Banks wanted nothing of the Red. It was barely a trickle this time of year, something Halleck seems not to have known. Instead, he proposed an amphibious assault on Sabine Pass in the Gulf, on the very southeastern tip of Texas. The mouth of the Sabine was a persistent irritant to the blockaders. If the object were to plant the flag somewhere in Texas, this was as good a place as any. The three senior commanders believed it more important for Banks to move in the opposite direction and cooperate with Farragut at Mobile, but they promised to lend what support they could.

Banks' attack turned into one of those small disasters that peppered four years of war. On September 8, 1863, army transports, convoyed by a detachment of the West Gulf Blockading Squadron, brought 4,000 troops to the muddy mouth of Sabine Pass. Against a small fort and a cottonclad tug, the navy lost two gunboats, ten men killed, and the crews taken prisoner. The expedition withdrew in abject defeat.

In November Banks and the navy redeemed themselves, achieving all goals, diplomatic and military, in a neat series of virtually bloodless conquests. Federal troops landed on Brazos Island at the mouth of the Rio Grande. Crossing to the mainland and driving off the rebels, Banks marched into Brownsville. Not only had a major Texas town been taken, but it cut Confederate communications with Mexico, eliminating one more of the South's ever-dwindling blockade-running ports. For Secretary of State Seward, the operation served notice on the French that their aggrandizing adventures ended at the Rio Grande.

With this foothold, Banks planned to leapfrog back along the Texas coast, taking the island passes all the way east to the Sabine, and he nearly succeeded. Corpus Christi fell late in the month, and by the end of the year, the American flag flew over Matagorda Bay, over halfway to Galveston. These advances across the western rim of the Gulf, the highlight of Banks' brief military career, should have ended all talk of large-scale operations west of the Mississippi. But that was not to be, and the Red River beckoned anew.

Halleck, for domestic political reasons, had never taken his eye off it. Eastern Louisiana, that part of the state occupied by Federal forces, was undergoing the process of "reconstruction." A new state government of Unionists, under Banks' guidance, convinced many erstwhile rebels to take the oath of allegiance to the United States. The rebels moved the secessionist capital of Louisiana to Shreveport, which also happened to be their chief military depot west of the Mississippi. Halleck and Lincoln feared that Confederate armies could march north into Arkansas and stymie that state's efforts at reconstruction.

A Federal seizure of Shreveport, they reasoned, would provide an excellent base for an overland invasion of Texas. True, but militarily speaking, the whole Confederacy west of the Mississippi had been strategically isolated since the fall of Vicksburg and Port Hudson, and was hardly worth a major campaign into its railroadless void.

During the last weeks of 1863 the plan congealed in Halleck's brain, although he issued no operations order, merely some general correspondence for the army's senior commanders to consult with one another. In what Banks considered "the government's instructions," he had 17,000 men, reinforced by 10,000 detached from Sherman's command, to bring up the line of the Red River to Shreveport. This marching column would be joined by another 10,000 advancing south from Arkansas. Admiral Porter provided the heavy naval support.

There was also an economic reason for the move up the Red River. Since the opening of the Mississippi, the pressures for the resumption of the cotton trade were enormous. The Red River country was prime cotton land, and rumors of 300,000 bales lining the riverbanks whetted everyone's appetite. Even Lincoln was not immune to granting favors to relentless commodity speculators, and he signed safe-conduct warrants for several political favorites who would accompany the expedition.

Seized cotton, that part of the crop bought and paid for by the Confederate government, was treated as a prize of war, and the profits of sale at the prize court went into the U.S. Treasury. Less, of course, the commission paid to the soldiers and sailors who took it. Cotton had an export value of $400 a bale, and the system, ripe for corruption, brought out the worst in everyone.

On Christmas Day, 1863, Porter and Sherman met at Cairo. The admiral very much wanted Sherman to take charge of the expedition, but the general brushed this aside. Preparations for his thrust at Atlanta were moving forward and he refused to jeopardize the main objective. The loan of 10,000 men to Banks had been made reluctantly, and only with the proviso they return after thirty days on the river. Porter, bitten by the Red River before, mentioned his concern over the depth of water. Sherman, familiar with the river from his years as super-intendent of a military academy at Alexandria,* assured the admiral of plenty of water during the spring floods.

In early March 1864, Porter collected the cream of the Mississippi Squadron: thirteen ironclads, four tinclads, plus the *Lexington* and *Black Hawk* at the mouth of Red River. At the bar, he saw the water "was just sufficient to allow the larger boats to pass," not an encourag-ing sign. Shortly, there came the transports carrying Sherman's bor-rowed men, the veteran Brigadier General A. J. Smith's division. While the troops deployed ashore, Porter sent Sam Phelps with a powerful advance guard to reconnoiter the obstructions at Fort De Russy, where the *Queen of the West* had been lost the year before.

The rebels had been at work here for months. Laboring slaves had driven a double pile line into the bottom mud, chain-braced in all direc-tions and clamped together with heavy iron plates. Below the line lay a timber raft of sodden, sunken logs, secured to both sides of the river. "When I first saw these ... obstructions," Admiral Porter wrote after the war, "I began to think that the enemy had blocked the game on us ... but after looking carefully for a few minutes, I said 'Bosh!'. . . . Why, this is simply silly. . . . What a waste of money and horse-power! Blessed is the power of steam, by which we can undue, in a few hours, the labor of years." The rebels had reinforced the fort proper with an iron-sheathed casemate mounting ten guns, including two 9-inchers lifted from the *Harriet Lane* and *Indianola*. Around 5,000 troops gar-risoned the place and its environs, and they considered the position impregnable.

Early on March 14, Phelps' advance force came up to the obstruc-tions. The tinclad *Fort Hindman* dealt with the sunken raft, and Phelps employed the big ironclad *Eastport* as a pile-puller and ram.† The work took all day. Near sunset the vessels burst through, steaming eight miles to the fort, where the sounds of a heavy exchange of musketry drifted over the river. A. J. Smith's troops, marching parallel to the stream, had come in behind and attacked the bastion at its weakest face. Most of the rebels escaped to Alexandria. But 300 went into the bag, along with all the fort's artillery and large quantities of ammunition.

---

* Now Louisiana State University.

† The same vessel captured unfinished by the stinkpots after the victory at Fort Henry.

Writing to Gideon Welles, Porter couldn't help shoveling up the scorn. "The efforts of these people," the rebels, "to keep up this war remind one very much of the antics of Chinamen, who build canvas forts, paint hideous dragons on their shields, turn somersets [sic], yell in the faces of their enemies to frighten them, and then turn away at the first sign of an engagement. It puts the sailors and soldiers out of all patience with them after the trouble they have had in getting here."

Porter hurried Phelps to Alexandria, seventy-five miles upriver. Leaving the *Benton* and *Essex* to destroy the fort and hold the rear, the admiral, with Smith's embarked troops, pushed up with the main body. Phelps reached Alexandria, a cotton port of 1,500 people, half an hour too late. The smoke of the last Confederate steamer disappeared in the western sky, and the flames consuming another, blazed along its grounded hull. Because of a double barrier of rock-strewn rapids, or "falls," above the town, pursuit with ironclads was impossible. The tinclads might have followed, but the rebels had an ironclad ram at Shreveport and Phelps could not hazard the tinclads against her.* He secured the town and waited for the fleet to come up.

The fleet came the next day; then, everyone waited for General Banks. His cavalry arrived on the nineteenth, but the infantry and train of 1,000 wagons, coming overland from New Orleans, bogged down in the muddy, rained-out roads.

Porter put the time to profitable use. He ordered Thomas Selfridge, now commanding the river monitor *Osage,* "to pick up some cotton," and only an officer of the rectitude of Andrew Foote would not have been tainted by the experience. This was prize money without risk, and there for the taking. Selfridge took the *Osage,* a tinclad, and an empty transport to scour every plantation between Alexandria and Fort De Russy. *Benton* and *Essex* did the same down to the Mississippi bar. Among the white population, Selfridge later wrote, "genuine sympathy and loyalty to the Union cause was almost nonexistent." Given that, neither he nor any other officer closely questioned if the cotton was privately or rebel-government owned. Selfridge's foraging party cut their own stencils, "C.S.A."—Confederate States of America, and stamped every one of 800 cotton bales accordingly, instantly creating a prize of war. "While I did not authorize this procedure," he said, "I knew of and winked at it."

---

* This was the *Missouri,* armed with one of the *Indianola*'s 11-inchers. Though complete and ready for active service, she spent her entire career in mining and transport work on the upper Red River.

Up the Oauchita River, into northern Louisiana, the admiral sent another division of harvesting tinclads. At Alexandria, he landed horses from the *Black Hawk* and went scouting inland. Every cotton bale was stamped "U.S.N. Prize" in big letters at each end, rolled down to the river, and into the coal barges. Porter watched a large wagon hauled by four big mules with "U.S.N." painted in red letters on the animals' flanks. Cotton bales in the wagon were painted "C.S.A." in the same size and color. "What do they mean?" asked someone. "They mean," answered the admiral, "the United States Naval Cotton-Stealing Association." By the time Nathaniel Banks arrived on March 25, Porter reported to the department that 2,129 bales of contraband cotton were on their way to Cairo.

The moment Banks' headquarters steamer, also named *Black Hawk,* tied up at the Alexandria wharf, a crowd of civilian cotton speculators ran ashore. Rumors spread that Banks' political supporters were using the commodity profits to finance the general's bid for the Republican presidential nomination. When Banks prohibited private speculation, the civilians attempted to bribe the naval officers to "seize" their cotton, offering one twentieth of the value just for removing it from Banks' control.

During the week of foraging, the river rose one inch every twenty-four hours, just high enough to try climbing over the falls. The *Eastport,* heaviest of the ironclads, went first, and under a full head of steam grounded on the rocks. It took three days, Porter said, "hauling her over by main force," to get above the falls. The hospital boat *Woodford* of Ellet's Marine Brigade was wrecked in the attempt. Nor could many of Banks' heavily laden supply boats get over. It forced the general to establish a logistics depot at Alexandria, and the slicing of 4,000 soldiers to guard it.

At the end of the month, Banks received a figurative kick in the pants from the new general in chief of the armies of the United States, Ulysses S. Grant. Sherman was ready to move on Atlanta, and the Red River sideshow could not be permitted to siphon any forces away. Of A. J. Smith's division, Grant said, "Should you find that the taking of Shreveport will occupy ten or fifteen days more [than the month's detached service allowed] ... you will send them back ... even if it leads to the abandonment of ... your expedition."

By April Fool's Day, the last of the thirteen gunboats and thirty transports that would advance to Shreveport were above the falls. The remainder of the warships—*Eastport,* four turtles, and some tinclads—remained below to protect the thin line of communications. Banks' army advanced parallel to the south bank of the river, and the Confederates fell back before his advancing host, burning everything of value.

Admiral Porter shifted his flag to the tinclad *Cricket,* and leading eight of his fastest vessels, spearheaded the twisting, riverine thrust to its next stop, Grand Ecore, a tiny, unpainted hamlet, fifty miles farther up. The biggest problem now was lack of coal. Foraging parties stripped the surrounding countryside of fence rails. "If the rebels had been clever enough to burn rails, instead of cotton," wrote Tom Selfridge, the fleet should have "been greatly hindered" at all points above the Alexandria falls.

Porter steamed into Grand Ecore on April 3 and was handed a letter from Sherman, carried up by a following transport. "We are getting ready for big licks," he wrote, reminding Porter that A. J. Smith's division must be out of the Red River in a week. Porter expected Banks to be ready for an immediate advance, but the general spent a couple of precious days supervising elections before at last stepping out along the south bank road for Shreveport.

On April 7, Admiral Porter started off with *Cricket, Fort Hindman, Lexington, Chillicothe,* river monitors *Osage* and *Neosho,* and twenty transports carrying T. Kilby Smith's brigade. The heavier vessels were left behind at Grand Ecore. It was no different from the old hells upon the Yazoo. The river became an endless hairpin of curves winding back and forth on itself, and even the little tinclads had trouble making the bends without touching ground. Along the slippery clay banks, cotton fires gave evidence of the Confederate retreat. Springfield Landing was next, the midway point from Grand Ecore to Shreveport. Here, Porter planned to rendezvous with Banks' advance guard, then continue the parallel advance.

The river column reached the appointed place at the appointed time and found not a soldier in sight. Refusing to get alarmed, Porter pushed on. But a few miles up, at Loggy Bayou, the rebels had scuttled a big steamer right athwart the channel. Her back was broken and a sandbar was already making up under the bottom. In big letters on its side, the rebels invited the "Yankees" to a ball at Shreveport. Porter and Brigadier T. Kilby Smith spent the day preparing to blow the vessel up. In late afternoon, a breathless courier galloped in. Banks had been whipped in battle at Sabine Cross Roads, sixty miles to the southwest, in Porter's *rear,* and was now in full retreat. The admiral received the information as if he had been struck a blow. If the gunboats were not to be trapped in the river, they must get back to Grand Ecore ahead of Banks' army.

*　　*　　*

Advancing through the pine barrens on the south bank of the river, Banks had dictated an order of march not taught in any military school. Between the cavalry of the van and the supporting columns of infantry, he inserted an eight-mile train of 1,000 wagons with their civilian teamsters. On April 8, at Sabine Cross Roads, only forty miles from Shreveport, Confederate General Dick Taylor wheeled about and struck Banks' cavalry head-on. The confused fight turned into a rout as the horsemen were thrown back onto the mob of wagons, teamsters, and camp followers. Were it not for a stand made by Banks' divisional commanders, the entire van would have been wiped out. At the end of the day the rebels had captured 250 wagons, 400 mules, and 18 field guns. Losses in Union personnel were very high, with 2,235 killed, wounded, and missing out of 12,000 men engaged.

The army withdrew several miles to Pleasant Hill, and the next day the rebels attacked again. This time they were thrown back, driven into the forests by a vicious bayonet charge. The army camped on the field of battle, hoping to renew the fight the next day. But before sunrise, April 10, Banks ordered a retreat back to Grand Ecore. The stink of mutiny began to pollute the air, and discipline was significantly tightened. It was reported that A. J. Smith had asked General William Franklin, the deputy commander, to join him in arresting Banks for incompetence and continue the march to Shreveport. Franklin declined.

Upriver Porter ordered an about face for Grand Ecore. The army's retreat had left the riverbanks free to harassing rebels, whose numbers increased by the mile. "We had every reason to suppose that our return would be interrupted in every way and at every point," Porter later wrote to Gideon Welles, "and we were not disappointed." The place of greatest danger in any retreat is the rearguard, and for this critical task, the admiral chose Tom Selfridge with his river monitor *Osage* and the trusty stinkpot *Lexington*.

Maddeningly, the river began dropping by fractions of an inch, making the *Osage* unmanageable in the shallow currents and innumerable bends. Selfridge was forced to lash an army transport to his starboard quarter. Jury-rigged, he moved downriver until grounding opposite a place called Blair's Landing. The *Lexington* doubled back to aid the monitor in freeing herself from the bottom. The south riverbank—a mud dike—was twenty feet high, and everything behind it was invisible, except from the tethered transport's upper-deck pilothouse.

Amid the work of getting afloat, came a yell from the pilot: a large force of men was pouring out of the woods. Selfridge climbed up to look, "and from their being dressed in Federal overcoats, thought they were our troops." The coats, however, were booty from Sabine Cross Roads, as Selfridge soon realized. The rebels, two brigades of dismounted cavalry, numbered not less than 2,500 men, many of them drunk. They were commanded by Brigadier General Tom Green, a leader much loved by his men.

Selfridge cleared the grounded *Osage* for battle and ordered Lieutenant Bache and the *Lexington* to a position for enfilade firing. The rebels came with "unusual pertinacity," across the fields in column of regiments, a formation no sane officer would order in the situation, and no sober man would obey. Using an ingenious, mirrored periscope mounted behind the turret, Selfridge directed the fire of his twin 11-inch guns. He ordered them loaded with canister and grapeshot, elevated the barrels to clear the top of the mud bank, "and as the heads of the first line became visible, fired." The result "was something indescribable." The transport's civilian crew bolted below, while her embarked troops, a company of the 95th Illinois, settled behind a rampart of oat sacks and opened volleys of musketry at the rebels surging up the dike.

The *Lexington* commenced firing on the rebel field guns, disabling one, driving the rest away. The charging troopers, however, came right up to the bank, so close that part of it caved in at the *Lexington*'s bow. The enemy officers, said Lieutenant Bache, were "yelling and waving their side arms." He estimated killing at least 150 men at a range of twenty feet. General Tom Green galloped up and his head was taken off, atomized by an exploding shell. His horse dashed madly on, its headless rider in the saddle.

In the hour-long action, Selfridge fired all his cannister and grape, and in the last salvos, used only shrapnel with fuses cut to one second. Suddenly, the rebels broke in great confusion, leaving the ground covered with perhaps 700 dead and wounded, muskets, knapsacks, and canteens stinking of Louisiana rum. Talking to some of his prisoners, Selfridge learned they were recently recruited Texans, "who had been told by their officers that the gunboats would surrender, if attacked in a determined way."

The incident at Blair's Landing was the most serious Confederate attempt to block the navy's withdrawal to Grand Ecore, but it was not the last. Small groups of snipers continually shot from the woods. But the greatest impediment was the constant groundings of the transports.

At the hamlet of Campti, a dozen miles above Grand Ecore, virtually the entire column touched bottom during a hailstorm of sniper fire. Porter took the *Cricket* downstream and fortunately found A. J. Smith, who promptly sent up 2,000 men to clear the banks of tormentors. By April 15, the last of the vessels chugged into Grand Ecore to rendezvous with Banks and the army.

During the advance upriver, the admiral had left Sam Phelps and the deep-draft *Eastport* to guard the line of communications at Grand Ecore. When the army fell back on the town, Phelps moved the ironclad above its small rapids to cover the retreat.

When the river dropped, she was stranded. Phelps unshipped the guns and dragged her over the rocky rapids to the town. A mile farther downriver, she grounded again. Tugs, working all night, got her off. On the fifteenth, eight miles below Grand Ecore, she came afoul of a small mine. Most on board hardly felt the shock of the explosion, and damage, by all accounts, was slight. A leak, however, started forward, and after all their searching, the ship's carpenters could not find it. To contain the water, they hastily erected internal bulkheads. Pumps were rigged, keeping the leak in check, and the vessel steamed on, grounding eight times in the ever-shallowing stream. Twenty miles farther down, she ran onto a bed of sunken logs. Wedged hard into the timber, she leaned over at a crazy angle until the water lapped over her deck. Phelps sent to Alexandria for a pump boat. Admiral Porter ordered two and himself went up in the *Cricket*. On April 21, at Grand Ecore, General Banks ordered the army to continue the retreat to Alexandria. Brigadier T. Kilby Smith wrote to the admiral, "General A. J. Smith and I both protest at being hurried away. I feel as if we [are] shamefully deserting you."

The rebels now controlled both sides of the river, surrounding the stranded *Eastport,* along with three tinclads, and two pump boats in attendance. After heroic efforts, all the while being shot at by rebel snipers, Admiral Porter ordered the ironclad destroyed. On April 26, an army engineer failed to blow her with a galvanic battery wired to a ton of gunpowder. Several hundred guerrillas opened fire from the banks and attempted to board the *Cricket,* but the tinclads *Juliet* and *Fort Hindman* drove the rebels off in a crossfire of grapeshot. Using tried and true methods, Commander Phelps stove kegs of gunpowder all around the machinery spaces, ran fire trains of turpentine-soaked cotton and tar into the magazine, and lit the match. He barely made it to the *Fort Hindman* when eight separate explosions rocked the river.

"The vessel was completely destroyed," reported Admiral Porter, "as perfect a wreck as ever was made by powder." The *Cricket* led the tinclads and pump boats, the latter crowded with families of escaping slaves from Grand Ecore, downriver to Alexandria.

Porter kept the little flotilla in close order, no stragglers, cleared for action. On the south bank, rounding a bend near the top of the Cane River, they came upon 1,200 rebels, with eighteen field guns, engaged in harassing Banks' rearguard. Instead of firing on the run, the *Cricket*'s skipper stopped engines and opened with his 24-pounder howitzers. The rebel artillery shifted target and delivered a terrible salvo with all their guns, and every shot hit home.

Porter ordered the tinclad full ahead, "but not soon enough," he said, "to avoid the pelting shower . . . which the enemy poured into us—every shot going through and through, clearing all our decks in a moment." Hearing the howitzers slacken fire, he ran down to the gun deck. Two gun crews were dead or wounded, blasted apart by exploding shells. In the fire room, every stoker but one lay with wounds, "leaving only one man to fire up." The chief engineer was killed. The little tinclad had suffered twenty-five killed and wounded, half her company. Forming a gun crew from the contraband slaves, "who fought the gun to the last moment," the admiral climbed to the pilothouse. He found the pilot mortally wounded, the vessel drifting and afire. Porter took the wheel and steamed past the rebel artillery, "under the heaviest fire I ever witnessed." In sight of the enemy, but mercifully out of range, she ran aground.

Sam Phelps in the *Fort Hindman* took command of the scattered brood, barely rescuing them from complete slaughter. The pump boat *Champion No. 3* took a shot in the boiler that killed the master, 3 engineers, and scalded to death over 150 crew and contrabands. The boat drifted onto the far bank and was later taken by the rebels. The *Juliet*, her machinery damaged, was lashed to the *Champion No. 5*, which received a hit in her own boiler, killing another eighty fugitive slaves on board.

The night was spent making feverish repairs. In the morning, the horror continued. The *Juliet*, again under her own power, though very cut up, got through, as did the *Fort Hindman* with only a damaged rudder. The rebels reserved their fire for the sinking *Champion No. 5*, packed with screaming, doomed, contraband slaves. Only minutes too late to prevent the butchery, the monitor *Neosho* arrived to cover the escape of the remnants to Alexandria. All these atrocious losses were utterly unnecessary, entirely caused by Nathaniel Banks' untimely and inexcusable retreat from Grand Ecore.

Admiral Porter limped into Alexandria on April 28 and found another catastrophe in the making. The river continued to drop, and the depth at the falls measured less than three-and-a-half feet; seven feet was the minimum for getting the ironclads over. Trapped above were *Carondelet, Mound City, Baron de Kalb, Pittsburg, Chillicothe, Osage, Neosho, Ozark, Lexington,* and two tinclads—$2 million worth of Federal warships.

Porter had lost all confidence in General Banks and daily expected him to cut and run as he did at Grand Ecore, which would literally leave the squadron high and dry. Army provisions were short, and the horses nearly out of forage. At most, Banks had a ten-day supply.

For a solution, General Franklin turned Porter's attention to a certain lieutenant colonel of the 4th Wisconsin Cavalry. Joseph Bailey, a lumberman and civil engineer, wanted to build a dam below the lower falls, at a point where the river stretched 738 feet bank to bank. No civilian contractor would have estimated less than six months for the job. Bailey, if he had enough men and horses, thought he could get it done in ten days. The plan, as Porter remembered, "looked like madness, and the best engineers ridiculed it." Banks, however, proved surprisingly willing to try it, and turned over to Colonel Bailey 3,000 men and 400 wagons and teams.

Most of these soldiers, from Maine regiments, were experienced lumberjacks. By May 2, the work was feverishly underway, "with a vigor," said Admiral Porter, "I have seldom seen equalled." Trees, plentiful along the north bank, were cut and dragged to the river's edge. Wagons fanned out bringing in bricks, rubble, and iron scrap from demolished cotton gins. Quarries were opened along the river above the town, and flatboats were built to haul the stone to the building site.

On the north bank, the dam stretched 300 feet into the river, and consisted of thousands of cottonwood trees, weighted down with stone and brick, cross-tied and strengthened with heavy timbers. Soldiers worked up to their waists and necks in the dangerous nine-knot current placing every trunk in its precise location. From the south, town side of the river, where the forests had been long since cleared for farms, sailors built wooden cofferdams that they floated 300 feet out and loaded with stone and rubble until they hit bottom. This left a sluice gap of 100 feet in midchannel. Backed up, the water over the upper falls rose substantially, but not enough. Three coal barges were weighted with broken machinery and sunk in the gap.

Most ammunition and guns were taken out of the ironclads and carted downstream. Iron plating was unbolted and hauled below the falls. What could not be saved or carried was thrown into quicksand to prevent salvage.

By Monday, May 9, after eight days of heroic work, the water over the upper falls had risen enough for the *Lexington, Osage, Neosho,* and *Fort Hindman* to pass over into the deep channel between the rapids and the dam. Porter and Colonel Bailey planned to get all the vessels into the channel and then blow up the sunken barges in the sluice gap.

But the river beat them to it. Early on May 9, with only the light-draft vessels in the channel, the barges gave way. Admiral Porter saw it, mounted a horse, and galloped to the upper falls. Breathless, he ordered Lieutenant Bache to take the *Lexington* over. Bache steered directly for the gap in the dam, "through which," Porter said, "the water was rushing so furiously that it seemed as if nothing but destruction awaited her." Wheels thrashing under a full head of steam, the old stinkpot shot through, pitched down into the rolling current, lurched stupidly two or three times, bumped onto the broken coal barges, and careened away into the river. "Thirty thousand voices rose in one deafening cheer," said the admiral, "and universal joy seemed to pervade the face of every man present."

The *Neosho,* hatches battened down, followed. But as she closed on the gap, her pilot panicked and stopped the engines. For a minute the monitor's hull literally disappeared under the rush, and every watcher thought her lost. Then she rose, swept along the rocks by the current, over the dam with only one hole in her bottom. The *Osage* and *Fort Hindman* had no trouble at all. There were still the four turtles, *Chillicothe, Ozark,* and two tugs above the falls, and Bailey had to do something to get them over. Admiral Porter collapsed with sickness and fatigue. He retired to his berth in the *Cricket* and turned over the navy's end of the rescue to Tom Selfridge.

The force of the current made it impossible to build a continuous dam, 600 feet across, in the short time available. Bailey solved the problem with "wing dams," a series of lighter structures across the upper falls. These raised the level another foot over the rocks, and were completed in three days. On May 11, to the cheering of the troops, the *Carondelet, Mound City,* and *Pittsburg,* with scarce enough room on either side, hurtled through the upper falls, steadied in the deep channel, then crashed over the lower dam. "The passage of these vessels," wrote Porter from his sickbed, "was a most beautiful sight, only to be realized when seen."

The next day, *Chillicothe* and *Ozark* went over, leaving only the *Baron De Kalb*, heaviest of the turtles, with six inches too much draft. Colonel Bailey impressed a full brigade of 2,000 men and a band. The men took up a series of four-inch hawsers run out from the turtle and the band struck up a march. As Tom Selfridge watched in amazement, the soldiers, "stamping their feet in unison with the inspiring music," hauled her over the upper falls. As soon as the last vessel went over, the army evacuated Alexandria.

After much "embittered testimony," by partisans and participants, the meddlesome Joint Congressional Committee on the Conduct of the War decreed the Red River campaign a total fiasco, and so it was. Banks received the bulk of censure, but Admiral Porter did not come out unscathed, and was officially criticized for paying too much attention to grabbing cotton and not enough to the falling state of the river.

The real blame, however, rested with the Lincoln administration. If Secretary Seward's desire for a foothold in Texas was the paramount objective, it had been accomplished with Banks' occupation of Brownsville and Corpus Christi. If Lincoln, Stanton, and Halleck were persuaded of the military necessity of the Red River operation, they should have appointed someone other than Banks to command it. Recuperating at Cairo, and sitting as a self-appointed judge and jury of Nathaniel Banks, Admiral Porter emptied himself of venom in a letter to Gus Fox. "If the Court knows herself, it is the last one of the kind I will get mixed up in. I shall be sure of my man before I cooperate with any soldier."

Mobile Bay

"Damn the Torpedoes! Full speed ahead!. . . "

—**Rear Admiral David G. Farragut, USN**

"Well, Johnston, fight to the last! Then to save these brave men, when there is no longer any hope, surrender."

—**Admiral Franklin Buchanan, CSN**

O ver three years had passed since the spring of 1861, when David Dixon Porter and the runaway *Powhatan* proclaimed the blockade of Mobile. The city still held out, now the sole Confederate Gulf port. That, however, was due less to rebel tenacity than to the Union's attention toward other objectives.

After his capture of New Orleans, Rear Admiral Farragut had wished to move on Mobile immediately, before the rebels recovered from the shock and before they could reinforce Mobile's seaward defenses. Accordingly, he had dispatched Porter and the mortar flotilla to take up position outside Mobile Bay's barrier islands. "Mobile is so ripe now," Porter wrote, "that it would fall to us like a mellow pear." Rebel deserters brought him information that Fort Morgan, the principal work guarding the bay, held only "two fire companies."

President Lincoln opted instead for sending Farragut 500 miles up the Mississippi to Vicksburg. The decision was strategically sound, and, had Vicksburg fallen in 1862, it might have shortened the war by as much as a year. But Farragut's blue-water ships were completely unsuited for brown-water work, and there were not enough supporting troops to seize the moment.

By summer 1862, the first opportunity to successfully advance into Mobile Bay had evaporated. By the time Farragut's splintered fleet limped down in retreat from Vicksburg, Fort Morgan's casemated, brick pentagon boasted a garrison of 700 men and seventy-nine guns.

The next chance, or so Farragut thought, came shortly after, in the autumn of 1862. Patched, resupplied, and hoping for reinforcements, the admiral logically wished to take his fleet to Mobile and run the gap of the outer defenses into the bay. But the cockpit of the war had shifted east, and Farragut's needs were considered less vital than operations along the Atlantic coast. There was an acute shortage of warships, a situation not to be alleviated for at least another year. As for the new monitors, they were slated instead for Du Pont at Charleston. As soon as that place fell, Farragut was promised, the ironclads would be sent to the Gulf.

Over the next year, as operations moved up and down along the line of the Mississippi, the blockade of Mobile lapsed into a desultory affair. The only excitement came when the Confederate raider *Florida* dashed through the cordon to reach safety at Fort Morgan.

After the surrender of Port Hudson, Farragut turned the squadron over to Commodore Henry Bell and took the *Hartford* to New York for an extended period of leave. "I am growing old fast, and need rest," he noted in a letter. The latest opportunity for the Gulf had come in November 1863, when at the conclusion of the Chattanooga campaign and before the march on Atlanta, Grant suggested an attack on Mobile. A success, linking up with Sherman somewhere between Atlanta and Montgomery, would have sliced all of Mississippi and most of Alabama from the active theaters of the war. But it was shunted aside in favor of Banks' operations along the Texas coast.

About 130 miles north of Mobile, at Bassett's yard, Selma, the hulls of three great ironclads were taking shape along the Alabama River. In all, eight Confederate ironclads were under construction on the Alabama and Tombigbee rivers. Only one would be complete in time for service. She was launched in February 1863 and named *Tennessee*. From cast-iron ram to sternpost, the ship measured 209 feet and displaced 1,273 tons. The casemate, crowned forward with an armored pilothouse, was of twenty-three-inch yellow pine and oak, sheathed in six inches of iron forward and four inches aft. Unlike most Confederate ironclads, she had complete armor protection below the waterline.

All of the *Tennessee*'s timber was cut in the immediate neighborhood, but nearly everything else had to be brought over unconnected railroads between the Yazoo and Atlanta. There were delays in getting her iron at every step, from the mines, to the punch press, to the lack of rolling stock to haul it. As late as September 1863, Admiral Franklin Buchanan, Old Buck of Hampton Roads, now the station commander at Mobile, complained to Secretary Mallory "for want of plate and bolt iron."

The armament she carried into battle was cast under Catesby Jones' eye at the Confederate Navy's gun foundry at Selma: two 7-inch Brooke rifles on revolving pivots fore and aft, and four 6.4-inchers on the broadside. The engine, twin-screwed, was taken out of a Yazoo steamer and could drive the ironclad at six knots.

There was an obvious fatal flaw. The rudder chains, like the *Merrimack*'s, lay exposed in open grooves along the quarterdeck. They were plated over with sheets of boiler iron, but not enough to compensate for the structural error. "We were compelled to take the consequences of the defect," said Commander James Johnston, her captain, "which proved to be disastrous."

The Confederate Navy always had problems getting enough enlisted bodies on board its ships, never mind their quality. "The crews of the vessels under my command," Old Buck complained to Richmond, "are of all nations, and many of very bad character." To a colleague, he wrote, "One or two such hung during this time would have a wonderful effect." The personnel situation was somewhat improved when he received a draft of Tennessee soldiers who provided an amount of disciplined leavening.

On February 16, 1864, the *Tennessee* was placed in commission and brought downriver to complete at Mobile. Once that was done, Buchanan and Johnston had to move the ship over Dog River Bar into the lower bay. Even riding light, the *Tennessee* drew thirteen feet, and the bar held only nine feet of water at high tide. Discouraged, Buchanan wrote, "What folly to build vessels up our rivers which cannot cross the bars at the mouths."

The difficulty was solved with specially built caissons, "camels," as they are nautically called. Designed to fit exactly against the ram's hull, they were filled with water, lashed to her sides with heavy chains and pumped out. Alas, it raised the *Tennessee* only two feet. Six larger camels were built. They were nearly ready when a careless workman dropped a candle into a pile of tarred cotton, and up in flames they went.

By mid-May a new set was ready. The *Tennessee* was taken in tow by a steamer, and with barely enough water under her bottom, safely crossed the bar into the lower bay. On May 22, crewed, ammunitioned, coaled, and provisioned, Old Buck hoisted his flag in her and took command of the squadron. It was virtually the same sort he had led at Hampton Roads: the ironclad and wooden gunboats *Gaines, Morgan,* and *Selma.*

The public, North and South, held an exaggerated view of the new ship, an opinion shared by Jefferson Davis, who put significant pressure on Buchanan "to strike the enemy" offensively. Old Buck, a four-star admiral, senior officer of the Confederate Navy, was not amused. Unhappily, he wrote to a friend, "Everybody has taken it into their heads that *one* ship can whip a dozen and if the trial is *not made,* we who are in her are damned for life, consequently the *trial* must be made. So goes the world."

Buchanan's only chance lay in surprise, to attack the blockaders before they knew the *Tennessee* was in the lower bay. On May 23, all hands mustered on the afterdeck to receive the admiral's fighting orders with three cheers. Rough weather delayed the sortie until the next night, when the *Tennessee* grounded by Fort Morgan. She floated free with the tide, but by then any element of surprise had been lost.

After spending a very pleasant four-month leave in New York, Rear Admiral David G. Farragut itched to get back into the war. Fueling his restlessness were urgent rumors from Gideon Welles reporting the *Tennessee* complete and ready to break the blockade in a month's time. The only thing that prevented Farragut's immediate departure was a shortage of 140 men for the *Hartford.* He would have the old flagship again, but with a new captain and chief of staff, Percival Drayton, who had seen hard service in the Charleston blockade.

On January 3, 1864, Welles authorized the flagship to complete her crew from the *Niagara.* When Farragut received a note from Gus Fox asking how many monitors he needed to blast his way into Mobile Bay, he answered, "Just as many as you can spare; two would answer me well, more would do better." To his son, Loyall Farragut, a cadet at West Point, the admiral wrote, "Buchanan has a vessel which he says is superior to the *Merrimac* with which he intends to attack us. . . . So we are to have no child's play."

Off the Mobile barrier forts in late January, Farragut shifted his flag into the double-ender *Octorara* to conduct a personal reconnaissance. Fort Morgan on the east, the primary work, sat at the tip of a long, narrow, sand-duned peninsula known as Mobile Point. West, three miles opposite, the smaller Fort Gaines covered the entrance from Dauphin Island. Fort Powell, on the mainland, guarded the intercoastal passage from Mississippi Sound. Farragut took his gunboat in close, where "I could count the guns and the men who stood by them."

The main shipping channel was quite narrow, about a quarter mile, hugging right up against Fort Morgan. Across the shallows from Fort Gaines to the main channel, the rebels, as usual, had sunk a triple pile line, whose eastern corner was anchored by a minefield marked with a conspicuous red buoy, "the object of which," said Farragut, "is to force [our] ships to keep as close as possible" to Fort Morgan.

Formidable it all looked, but he was not impressed. "I am satisfied," he wrote to Gideon Welles, "that if I had one ironclad at this time I could destroy their whole force in the bay," and with 5,000 cooperating soldiers from the army, "reduce the forts at my leisure." What Farragut really wanted was to smash into Mobile Bay and catch the *Tennessee* while she was still fitting out above Dog River Bar.

A bold strike of this kind, akin to an old-fashioned cutting-out expedition with cutlass and pistols, required a special, light-draft monitor, something the navy had foreseen months earlier. The keels for twenty turtle-backed vessels, the *Casco* class, had already been laid down. Drawing but nine feet, a foot-and-a-half less than the original *Monitor,* and theoretically able to carry a similar battery, they were meant for precisely the job Farragut required. But when the *Casco* was launched at Boston in May 1864, the overweight vessel nearly went to the bottom. The navy declared her unseaworthy, as indeed were the whole class. Most were only completed after the war's end, failures in every respect.

However, before this fiasco, Gideon Welles had paid close heed to Farragut's reports, and earmarked four new monitors for operations in the Gulf. Two, *Manhattan* and *Tecumseh,* were large, improved vessels, mounting a pair of 15-inch Dahigren guns behind eleven inches of turret armor. They were the most powerful warships in the world. The other two, completing at St. Louis, *Chickasaw* and *Winnebago,* were twin-turret, quadruple-screwed river monitors, having a battery of four 11-inch guns. Together, these four monitors constituted an armored naval squadron unmatched on the waters of the globe.

But these ships required at least four months more of work, and several weeks of postcommission tuning and towing before they could join Farragut for active service. Until then, the admiral contented himself by harassing Fort Powell with his mortar schooners and maintaining a tight blockade of the port.

In the spring of 1864, Abraham Lincoln finally sacked Old Brains Halleck, and promoted U. S. Grant to commanding general of the army. Excess troops from the Gulf Coast were transferred east, and Grant replaced Nathaniel Banks with Major General Edward Canby, a career infantry officer of the Regular Army, a man Farragut found to be a willing, businesslike colleague.

Farragut and Canby planned a joint venture against Mobile for July, to coincide with the arrival of the monitors. But heavy losses in the Army of the Potomac forced Grant to shift most of Canby's forces east as well. It canceled any full-scale campaign against the city, and limited the eventual operation to its naval aspects and reduction of the barrier forts.

In the second week of May, the Southern press trumpeted a proposed sortie by Admiral Buchanan to drive off the blockaders, perhaps even to recapture Pensacola. "No doubt is felt of his success," wrote Farragut to Secretary Welles. Coming on the heels of the rebel successes in the Red River, "the public mind in the rebel states is in such a state of excitement." Old Buck and his little squadron, however, remained safely behind the guns of the barrier forts, never really contemplating anything beyond defending Mobile Bay against Farragut's inevitable attack.

By July, the monitors were on the way. On the twelfth, Farragut issued General Order No. 10 to his captains: "Strip your vessels and prepare for the conflict." He intended on closing Mobile Bay to the outside world, destroy the *Tennessee,* and isolate the barrier forts from the city, very much as he had done at New Orleans. The lower bay would then serve as a sheltered anchorage for the squadron. Taking the city of Mobile was impossible, since the big ships drew too much water to pass over Dog River Bar.

Borrowing a leaf from Port Hudson, the squadron advanced in tight line-ahead, gunboats lashed to the port, disengaged sides of the heavy ships. Farragut stationed the four monitors in the van, echeloned slightly right, toward Fort Morgan, to draw enemy fire away from the wooden ships.

Once inside the bay, the monitors would engage the *Tennessee,* the gunboats pursue their rebel opposites, and the big ships add their broadsides to the army's operations against the forts. To fight as rams against the ironclad, *Hartford* and her consorts had inch-thick boiler-plate bolted to their bows.

Farragut wanted to get as close to Fort Morgan as possible before opening fire. "The flagship will lead," he told his captains. They would not have it. A cost of their true devotion for him, the senior officers refused the admiral the point of greatest danger. To Gideon Welles, Farragut wrote: "It was only at the urgent request of the commanding officers" that he yielded. Much like the initial, futile attempt at Vicksburg, Farragut ever after thought his caving in was a mistake.

The *Brooklyn,* however, for which he stepped aside, was well suited for the task, with four bow chasers to return end-on fire, and what Farragut called "an ingenious arrangement" of minesweeping gear. Her skipper was Captain James Alden, the officer who fretted at spiriting the old *Merrimack* out of Norfolk and who hedged his bets during the first go-up at Vicksburg.

As Farragut had done before previous battles, upper spars and rigging came down, and splinter nets and chain garlands were draped over the starboard sides. "Barricade the wheel and steersman with sails and hammocks," ordered the admiral. Sandbags, according to one officer were piled "from stem to stern, and from the berth to the spar deck."

In the days that followed, Farragut honed his attack plan to a fine edge. The *Hartford's* carpenter fashioned several wood blocks into toy boats, and with them the admiral experimented on a chart table. His aide, Lieutenant John C. Watson, remembered, "I used to help him maneuver the little blocks ... to concentrate and maintain as heavy a fire as possible upon Fort Morgan when we should be going in." On July 29 came General Order No. 11, elaborating on the previous fighting instructions. Once past the forts, the gunboats could cast off from their big-ship partner at the discretion of the senior officer of each pair. Special note was made of the pile line and the red buoy marking the eastern edge of the minefield. The whole line must pass to the east of it, at most, a bare quarter-mile from the guns at Fort Morgan.

Three monitors arrived by August 1. The *Tecumseh,* however, was still undergoing final patching at Pensacola. The delay put Farragut and Drayton very out of sorts. Every day gave the rebels that much more time to prepare. On the third, Farragut sent a gunboat to bring the *Tecumseh* over—"otherwise she will be of no use to me in my operation."

That day, a mixed Union army brigade of 1,500 troops, consisting of infantry, dismounted cavalry, and "Cobb's Colored Regiment of Engineers," all commanded by Brigadier General Gordon Granger, landed at the west end of Dauphin Island, in the rear of Fort Gaines. Farragut had wanted to open the naval battle simultaneously, forcing the enemy to divide its strength and attention. But for the missing *Tecumseh* and her captain, an old friend, T. Augustus Craven (brother of Thomas Craven), he decided to wait forty-eight hours.

To better communicate between forces, Farragut and Granger stationed army signal officers and their flagmen aboard the larger vessels. Into the *Hartford* came Captain Marston, Lieutenant John Coddington Kinney, and five flagmen. Farragut ordered they remain belowdecks during the fight and help with the wounded. They were, after all, on board to open communication with the army after the battle. At sunset, the *Richmond* and *Tecumseh* arrived and anchored in the lee of Sand Island.

Farragut retired to his cabin, and in a grip of fatalism penned a letter to Virginia. "I am going into Mobile in the morning if God is my leader, as I hope He is, and in Him I place my trust." No one had successfully done this before: run past a fort, over a minefield, beyond which loomed an enemy ironclad squadron pouring in a raking fire. "If He thinks it is the place for me to die, I am ready to submit to His will." Farragut sealed the letter and turned in for a restless sleep in the muggy Gulf summer night.

Aboard the *Tennessee,* conditions were horrendous. The officers and crew had lived atrociously since crossing Dog River Bar. Rains came nearly every day, and with them, said Confederate Navy Surgeon Daniel B. Conrad, "the terrible moist, hot atmosphere, simulating that oppressiveness which precedes a tornado." It was impossible, because of the heat, to sleep inside the ship. "From the want of properly cooked food, and the continuous wetting of the decks at night, the officers and the men were rendered desperate." All hands, from Old Buck, to the meanest coal heaver looked forward to the impending battle, whatever its outcome, "with a positive feeling of relief."

For weeks Conrad had watched the Federal ships multiply outside the bay. Stripped for action, they "appeared like prize fighters ready for the ring, we knew that trouble was ahead." He feared even more when he saw "strange-looking, long black monsters—the new ironclads."

At daybreak, Friday, August 5, the doctor and his admiral were roused by the quartermaster. "Admiral," the old sailor announced from the companionway, "the officer of the deck bids me report that the enemy's fleet is under way." They climbed to the hurricane deck, Old Buck painfully limping on his wounds from Hampton Roads; "and sure enough," said Conrad, "there was the enemy heading for the passage past the fort." Clench-mouthed, Old Buck nodded and turned to the skipper. "Get under way, Captain Johnston; head for the leading vessel of the enemy, and fight each one as they pass us."

At 5 A.M., the Federal fleet heaved thick, hempen fenders over their inboard sides, and maneuvered parallel for lashing. The operation took about an hour. Farragut, having finished his breakfast, ordered Captain Drayton to signal the fleet into line of battle. To starboard, slightly ahead of the van, lumbered the monitors—the 15-inch-gunned *Tecumseh* and *Manhattan* leading the twin-turreted *Winnebago* and *Chickasaw.* The wooden ships and their lashed gunboats followed: *Brooklyn* with *Octorara, Hartford* with *Metacomet, Richmond* with *Port Royal, Lackawanna* with *Seminole, Monongahela* with *Kennebec, Ossipee* with *Itasca,* and last, *Oneida* with *Galena.**

The ships hoisted their battle flags, an oversized stars and stripes to each masthead and gaff, except for the *Hartford,* which flew Farragut's two-starred blue flag at the mizzen. In the maintop, the *Hartford*'s longtime pilot, the Gulf fisherman Martin Freeman, communicated to the quarterdeck through a speaking tube. Farragut climbed a half-dozen rungs up the port main rigging. Lieutenant Kinney and Captain Marston, thinking their presence would go unnoticed in the confusion of battle, ignored Farragut's order to keep safely below and remained on deck. Their game lasted about one minute, as long as it took the *Hartford*'s executive officer, "who never allowed anything to escape his attention," to firmly instruct them the admiral's order must be obeyed. Down the signal officers went, into the "stifling hold." Here sat the surgeon, his assistant, and their helpers, "with their paraphernalia spread out ready for use. Nearly every man had his watch in his hand awaiting the first shot."

A little after 6:30 the *Tecumseh,* leading the monitor line, opened the battle, firing a ranging shot from each of her 15-inch guns. Farragut signaled "Closer order," and the column of wooden ships compressed, each pair of vessels only a few yards from the next ahead, echeloned a bit to starboard. Helped by the morning tide, the fleet swept majestically on. At 7:10, range half a mile, Fort Morgan opened fire, replied to immediately by the *Brooklyn* with her forward Parrot rifles. "Soon after this," Farragut said, "the action became lively."

In the confusion of the smoke the admiral climbed higher in the rigging, until he found himself in the iron futtock shrouds, just below

* The failed, third ironclad of the original trio: *Monitor, New Ironsides, Galena.*

the maintop. Farragut could now reach through a hole above his head, and communicate with pilot Freeman by grabbing his ankle. Captain Drayton, who remembered the admiral suffered mildly from vertigo, sent a quartermaster to secure him about the waist with a piece of lead-line.

In the bowels of the *Hartford,* army Lieutenant Kinney and those around him felt a great relief at the rumble and jolts of the flagship's opening guns. "Soon the cannon balls began to crash through the deck above us," he remembered, "and then the thunder of our whole broadside . . . kept the vessel in a quiver." Firing a broadside meant the *Hartford* was nearly abreast the fort. No wounded had come down yet. Kinney estimated they had been in action for about twenty minutes when an officer shouted down the hatch, "Send up an army signal officer immediately; the *Brooklyn* is signaling."

So far, Captain Alden in the *Brooklyn* has done his job well, leading the battle line and engaging Fort Morgan with volleys of grapeshot. "Several of their batteries were almost entirely silenced," he reported. Ahead, the *Tennessee* and her little ducks crept out from behind Mobile Point and took position across the near side of the bay, just behind the minefield. Old Buck had executed the classic naval maneuver of crossing Farragut's T. In minutes, raking fire from the Confederate naval guns shot down the long axis of the Federal line.

The *Brooklyn,* with her superior speed, had drawn level with the rear monitors. If Alden continued on course, it meant the wooden ships, not the monitors, would be the first to engage. At this point, one of the *Brooklyn*'s lookouts reported shoal water to port, in the direction of the minefield, a stretch of water that in any case was out of bounds. Then Alden, or someone else, saw "a row of suspicious looking buoys . . . directly under our bows"—empty shell boxes from Fort Morgan. Unsure of whether to stop or press on, Alden backed engines to clear the hazard. Wigwag signaling being faster than a flag hoist, he ordered his army signaler to inform the flagship.

That's when Kinney got the word. He rushed to the *Hartford*'s forecastle and copied the message, "The monitors are right ahead; we cannot go on without passing them." The situation threatened to bring the whole fleet crashing into the sterns of the next ahead.

Forty feet above the deck, Farragut grabbed the pilot's ankle through the hole in the maintop. "What is the matter with the *Brooklyn?* Freeman, she must have plenty of water there!" The pilot thought so too. "Plenty of water and to spare, Admiral, but her screw is moving; I think she is going ahead again, Sir."

But no, Alden was backing, compressing the van of the battle line hindmost onto the center. The rebel gunners in Fort Morgan, just driven to shelter by the fleet's broadsides, returned to their pieces, hurling a murderous counterfire. From ahead, came the raking fire of the enemy squadron, against which Farragut could not reply.

Ominously, the guns of the battle line fell silent. Because of the smoke, Lieutenant Kinney climbed to the foretop. He remembered the *Hartford*'s men "being cut down by scores . . . The sight was sickening beyond the power of words to portray. Shot after shot came through the side, mowing down the men, deluging the decks with blood, and scattering mangled fragments of humanity." Hypnotized, he watched a shell flying through the air from the rebel gunboat *Selma*. Tumbling butt-end first, fuse sputtering, it struck the foremast right over his head. On deck, the dead were collected in a row on the port side and the wounded sent below.

Farragut hailed the *Brooklyn*. "Go on!" he bellowed through his brass trumpet. Alden did not obey, in all likelihood, he did not hear. Lieutenant Watson, the admiral's flag lieutenant, recalled the *Brooklyn*'s reply was something about "torpedoes." The battle turned on the edge of a razor.

The *Tecumseh*, leading the monitor line, her twin 15-inch guns loaded with 350-pound solid shot, reached the point of greatest peril, between Fort Morgan and the minefield. Behind her the *Brooklyn* had just stopped; T. A. Craven in the *Tecumseh* probably had no idea why. Ahead, across the near corner of the minefield, beyond the red marker buoy, loomed the *Tennessee*. Craven ordered his helmsman to steer straight for the Confederate ram.

In the rebel ironclad, gunners loaded the bow 7-inch Brooke rifle with a steel-cored, armor-piercing bolt. Lieutenant Arthur Wharton squinted over the iron sight. Ram and monitor converged, and his fingers tightened around the lockstring. Commander Johnston called down from the pilothouse, "Do not fire, Mr. Wharton, until [we] are in actual contact."

Anticipating "a deadly fight at close quarters," Wharton didn't move his eye. Not an instant passed when he saw ahead a huge fountain of water explode up from the *Tecumseh*'s bow. The monitor heeled to port, "as from an earthquake shock." A few of her crew leaped wildly from the turret, the screws turned once in the air, and she was gone, plunging headfirst to the bottom.

"Immediately," said Surgeon Conrad of the *Tennessee*, "immense bubbles of steam, as large as cauldrons, rose to the surface of the water

. . . only eight human beings could be seen in the turmoil."

John Collins, the *Tecumseh*'s pilot, was one of them. He and Commander Craven had stood at the ladder to the turret roof. Ahead lay safety, to stay meant death. "After you, pilot," said T. Augustus Craven. "There was nothing after me," Collins said later. "When I reached the utmost round of the ladder, the vessel seemed to drop from under me." Ninety-three men went down to their deaths.

The *Hartford*'s crew, thinking the *Tecumseh* had sunk the *Tennessee,* leaped to the hammock rail, giving three defiant cheers, taken up by the squadron down the line. The surge of elation was met by the paralyzing shock of reality. "At this critical moment," a naval officer recalled, "the batteries of our ships were almost silent, while the whole of Mobile Point was a living line of flame."

The slightest flinching by Farragut meant losing the battle. A great commander by nature, every bit as bold and intelligent as the transcendent Nelson, Farragut's outstanding qualities of leadership carried the day; it was the supreme moment of his life. "O God . . . Shall I go on," he said to himself. "And it seemed as if in answer a voice commanded, 'Go on!'"

First, he shouted to Commander Jouett of the *Metacomet* to lower a boat and rescue the *Tecumseh*'s survivors. He reached up through the hole in the maintop and grabbed pilot Freeman's ankle. "I shall lead," he said. Then, to the *Brooklyn* and history, he bellowed out, "Damn the torpedoes! Full speed ahead! Drayton! Hard-a-starboard! Ring four bells! Eight bells! Sixteen bells!"*

To Jouett again, he yelled to reverse the *Metacomet*'s engine, giving the pair of ships the ability to turn on their keels. "By this movement," Lieutenant Watson knew that Farragut was going to cross the minefield, something he had expressly forbidden, and a caution the *Tecumseh*'s sinking had certainly justified. "Some of us," Watson said, "expected every moment to feel the shock of an explosion . . . and to find ourselves in the water." Several officers distinctly heard the popping of percussion caps under the hull. As Farragut said later, he believed the mines had been in the water long enough to make them "probably innocuous, I determined to take the chance of their explosion."

---

* There are other versions, more or less similar. This is Lieutenant Watson's. The reader must also take into account the opposite gearing between the ship's wheel and her rudder, exactly the same action as a hand-held tiller in a small sailboat. Farragut's order, "Hard-a-starboard!" is for the quartermaster to turn the wheel to starboard, thus steering the ship to port.

The battle now witnessed the remarkable sight of the *Hartford* and *Metacomet* lashed together, hawsers straining, sides grinding against their hemp fenders, turning sharply to port, past the *Brooklyn-Octorara,* directly across the minefield into Mobile Bay.

Ahead the rebel squadron continued to deliver a raking fire. The *Hartford,* in the van, took the brunt of it. One shell from the *Selma* killed ten men and wounded five at the forward guns. According to Captain Drayton, not a man faltered. "There might perhaps have been a little excuse," he said, "when it is considered that a great part of four guns' crews were at different times swept away. . . . In every case, the killed and wounded were quietly removed, the injuries at the guns made good, and in a few moments except from traces of blood nothing could lead one to suppose that anything out of the ordinary routine had happened."

From the moment of the *Hartford*'s turn, her starboard battery, followed by the *Brooklyn* and the ships behind, opened fire at Fort·Morgan in full fury, driving the rebel gunners to shelter. A race began between the *Brooklyn* and *Richmond* pairs as to who would follow in the flagship's wake. Lieutenant Watson watched with a professional eye, "and probably no straighter course was ever kept than by these ships in passing over that torpedo field."

While the fleet sorted itself out in the bay, the *Tennessee* turned to the main body of the Federal squadron, now steaming by the fort in their tandem pairs. "The ram received from us three full broadsides of 9-inch solid shot, each broadside being eleven guns," said Captain Thornton Jenkins of the *Richmond,* still awed by it years later. "They were well aimed and all struck." When he examined the rebel ironclad, next day, all he found were some scratches.

If Farragut erred in placing the *Brooklyn* at the head of the line, he also miscalculated in assigning the weakest vessels to the rear. By the time the last two pairs were up to Fort Morgan, its gunners had nothing to fear keeping them hunkered down. The last tandem, *Oneida-Galena,* suffered badly for it. A shell smashed through the *Oneida*'s chain garlands and exploded in the starboard boiler, killing or fearfully scalding the entire watch: eight men dead and close to thirty wounded. A second shell exploded aft, cutting the wheel ropes; a third set fire to the deck above the forward magazine. Commander Mullany, her skipper, was wounded in two places. Mullany, his executive officer, and the chief engineer rallied the crew, rigged relieving tackles for the wheel, and closed off the starboard fire room from the rest of the ship. The *Oneida,* assisted by the *Galena,* limped on.

The rebel gunboats retreated, leaving the *Tennessee,* advancing at a two-knot crawl, to hammer at the Federal ships sweeping into the lower bay. Surgeon Conrad recalled, "Their fire was so destructive, continuous and severe that after we emerged from it [we had] nothing left standing as large as your little finger." Undaunted, Old Buck turned to the *Tennessee's* skipper, "Follow them up, Johnston; we can't let them off that way."

Commander James Jouett, skipper of the *Metacomet,* asked repeatedly to cast off from the *Hartford.* Finally, a little past eight, a mile into the lower bay, Farragut ordered her cut loose, hoisting the signal, "Gunboats chase enemy gunboats." The *Metacomet,* a handy double-ender, intended for coastal shallows, was soon, nonetheless "dragging her bottom." If the *Metacomet* grounded, the whole game with the rebel gunboats would be turned around. Jouett, considered a "strict constructionist" by his peers, gave a wholly unexpected order, "Call the leadsman in from the chains, Mr. Sleeper!" Amazed, the lieutenant thought he had misunderstood. "I tell you," Jouett said in a tone that brooked no dallying, "the admiral has directed me to follow those gunboats, and I am going to do it. Call the men in from the chains at once, sir; they are demoralizing me!" The *Metacomet* shot through the shallows in pursuit of the three rebels.

Crippled, the rebel gunboat *Gaines* retreated to Fort Morgan. The *Morgan,* the only Confederate to survive under her own flag that day, escaped in the direction of Mobile. The *Selma* fought it out in a stern chase. It was a hopeless duel. Outclassed in every respect, eight men dead, the injured strewn about the deck, her bleeding commanding officer, Lieutenant Murphey, called the scene "a perfect slaughter pen." When he saw the *Metacomet* take position to rake with grape and shrapnel, "I did not believe that I was justified in sacrificing more of my men . . . [and] gave the order to haul down the colors."

In the quiet interlude the ships regrouped. "Go to breakfast!" ordered Commander Johnston in the *Tennessee.* It was unthinkable to eat below. Surgeon Conrad remembered "intense thirst universally prevailed," and men rushed to the scuttlebutts to drink long swallows of warm water. Hardtack and coffee were served out, "the men all eating standing, creeping out of the ports on the after deck" to get fresh air. Officers climbed to the upper deck. Conrad described Old Buck as "grim, silent and rigid."

After some fifteen minutes, the crew of the *Tennessee* noticed that instead of making for a safe lee at Fort Morgan, "our iron prow," Conrad said, "was pointed for the enemy's fleet." As the fact penetrated, and the surgeon heard muttered comments from every rank, he ventured to ask the question himself. "Are you going into that fleet, admiral?"

"I am, Sir!" Old Buck answered. Conrad, not intending the admiral to hear, whispered to an officer, "Well, we'll never come out of there whole." Old Buck turned around, and in the sharpest tone, put everyone back in their place. "That's my lookout, Sir!" Conrad, afterward, learned the reason for this apparently suicidal decision. The *Tennessee* had only six hours of coal, and Buchanan wanted to burn it fighting to the end. "He did not mean to be trapped like a rat in a hold, and made to surrender without a struggle." An escape up the bay to Mobile was impossible, there was no way to get across Dog River Bar.

Four miles beyond Fort Morgan, the Federal fleet lay anchored in the lower bay, the crews at breakfast. For a few minutes a heavy rain squall passed over, and when pushed away by the wind, a call came down from aloft, Ensign Joseph Marthon at the main topsail yard: "The ram is coming for us." Farragut refused to believe it. "I did not think Old Buck was such a fool." He descended to the deck and gave orders to the fleet, wigwagged by the army signal officers: "Destroy the enemy's principal ship by ramming her." Drayton ordered the anchor hoisted in. A jammed shackle pin left it hanging from the hawsepipe, and in that state, the *Hartford* steamed directly at the ironclad foe.

In the *Tennessee*, Surgeon Conrad watched "one after another of the big wooden frigates sweep out in a wide circle." The *Brooklyn* lunged first, firing steel-cored shot from her bow chasers. At the very last moment the *Tennessee* sheared off, as Alden noted, "giving us some heavy shots in passing." For the *Brooklyn* that ended the day, eleven dead, forty-three wounded.

Monongahela, with the *Kennebec* still lashed on her port side, separated from the circle of ships, and with a tower of white foam creaming up her boilerplated bow, steered for the target, "which we on board of the *Tennessee*," said Surgeon Conrad, "fully realized as the supreme moment of the test of our strength." Commander Johnston passed the word: "Steady yourselves when she strikes. Stand by and be ready!" In the casemate total silence prevailed, men standing rigid by their guns, awaiting their fate.

The *Monongahela* struck the ironclad's armored knuckle with tremendous, but glancing impact, tearing away her own boilerplate bow, shattering the butt ends of her planking. The shock threw most of the men in both ships to the deck. Confederate Lieutenant Wharton remembered, "The *Tennessee* ... spun around as upon a top. I felt as though I were going through the air."

At the moment of impact, the *Tennessee* fired two shots that completely penetrated her wooden antagonist, passing out the opposite side. The *Monongahela* loosed a full broadside that did no more damage to the ram than scrape the paint.

So close were the two ships during the exchange, that several of the *Tennessee*'s crew were injured by the blasts of the guns. The wounded started coming down to Surgeon Conrad's cockpit. He saw curious dark blue "elevations and hard spots" on their skin. "Cutting down to these, I found that unburnt cubes of cannon powder, that had poured into the ports, had perforated the flesh and made these great blue ridges under the skin. Their sufferings were very severe, for it was as if they had been shot with red-hot bullets."

The *Monongahela* was hardly away, said the *Tennessee*'s Lieutenant Wharton, "when a hideous-looking monster came creeping up on our port side," the *Manhattan*. Wharton shouted for everyone to stand clear when a 15-inch solid shot, 350 pounds of iron, "admitted daylight through our side, where before ... there had been over two feet of solid wood, covered with five inches of solid iron."

The *Tennessee,* with hardly time to recover, now found herself the target of the *Lackawanna.* Under the fullest head of steam the engineers could coax out of her, the wooden ship smashed at right angles into the after end of the rebel's casemate. The *Lackawanna,* too, had her stem crushed by the impact, bringing a considerable leak into the bargain. The two ships swung parallel, head to stern. Several of the Confederate crewmen poked their heads out, and according to the *Lackawanna*'s skipper, used "most opprobrious language." Marines drove them inside with a volley of musket fire, spittoons, and holystones.

The *Lackawanna* followed with a shot that jammed the *Tennessee*'s thinly protected rudder chains, lurching her steering gear in a lazy left turn; another hit jammed the after port shutter. Old Buck sent for a repair party of firemen to clear it with sledgehammers. Two braced their backs against the casemate, holding the shutter bolt steady, while their mates slammed away.

"Suddenly," said Surgeon Conrad, "there was a dull sounding impact, and at the same instant the men whose backs were against the shield were split in pieces. I saw their limbs and chests, severed and mangled, scattered about the deck, their hearts lying near their bodies." Everyone in the area, including the admiral, "were covered from head to foot with blood, flesh, and viscera." Commander Johnston said they were turned "into sausage." The gore was shoveled into buckets and hammocks and struck below. Lost in the horror was Old Buck, cut down by a splinter, alone in his agony.

Conrad, called to the gun deck, recalled, "lying curled up under the sharp angle of the roof, I discovered the old, white-haired man." Silent, in awful pain, he uttered no sound. "Admiral," Conrad asked, "are you badly hurt?"

"Don't know," the old sailor groaned. Conrad saw that one of Buchanan's legs was twisted and crushed under his body. He could get no one to help; every able-bodied man served the guns. Lifting the old man with "great caution," he carried him on his back down the ladder, "his broken leg slapping against me as I moved slowly along." The surgeon diagnosed the wound as a compound fracture, and from every indication it appeared the leg would have to come off. Old Buck sent for the captain. "Well, Johnston," he gasped in frightful pain, "they've got me. You'll have to look out for her now. This is your fight, you know." "All right, sir," he replied in the only admissible answer, "I'll do the best I know how."

The *Hartford* was the third vessel to make a try at ramming, and she steamed at full speed toward the enemy. Farragut jumped from the deck into the port mizzen shrouds, just above the poop. "He laughed at my remonstrances," Lieutenant Watson recalled years later, "as I seized the tails of his frock coat and tried to prevent him from getting up there." After tying Farragut to the rigging, "I stood near him . . . with a drawn revolver, ready to get the drop on anybody aboard the ram who might try to pick him off."

At the very last second, the *Tennessee*'s momentum caused the ships to pass at a range of eight feet. The *Hartford* fired a full broadside, 980 pounds of smashing iron; every shot bounced off. The *Tennessee* loosed two shots in reply, ripping through the flagship's berth deck, into the sick bay, among the wounded.

The *Hartford* had just steadied from the blow, when the *Lackawanna,* misjudging the swiftly changing positions of a dozen vessels all converging upon a single point, rammed the flagship starboard, aft, "cutting us completely down to within two feet of the water," according to Captain Drayton. Lieutenant Kinney thought she was sliced through, and she might have been, had the *Lackawanna* still carried her boiler-iron prow.

It did, however, for five minutes, create "general consternation" on board. The cry went up, "Save the admiral! Save the admiral." Farragut, truly remarkable for a man who had just passed his sixty-third birthday, unbound himself and scampered down to the deck. Looking over the side, he saw a few inches of plank above water and ordered Drayton to advance at full speed toward the enemy.

The *Hartford* was right on course to ram, and truthfully no one aboard was paying attention to anything else. All eyes were riveted ahead, when the *Lackawanna* again loomed up to starboard. Farragut, whom Kinney described at that moment as "excited," yelled to the army signal officer, "Can you say 'For God's sake' by signal?"

"Yes, sir."

"Then say to the *Lackawanna*, 'For God's sake get out of our way and anchor!'"

As Kinney remembered it, "In my haste to send the message, I brought the end of my signal flag-staff down with considerable violence upon the head of the admiral who was standing nearer than I thought, causing him to wince perceptibly." The *Hartford* steamed ahead.

The *Tennessee* was in her death throes. The twin-turreted *Chickasaw* took position to rake her by the stern. The stack went over, riddled by a hundred holes. The gunport shutters were all jammed, and for half an hour, she fired not a round. Solid shot were battering in the casemate, and from sheer inactivity, the crew became demoralized and sought shelter, which Commander Johnston said without rancor, "showed their condition mentally." He went below to inform Admiral Buchanan. "Well, Johnston," said Old Buck, with what must have tasted like the bitterest gall, "if you cannot do any further damage you had better surrender."

Johnston returned to the gun deck and saw the *Ossipee* bearing down to ram. "Realizing our helpless condition. . . " convinced that the ship "was now nothing more than a target," he climbed to the hurricane deck and and lowered the Confederate colors, "which had been [fastened] onto the handle of a gun scraper and stuck up through the grating. I then decided . . . with an almost bursting heart, to hoist the white flag."

The *Ossipee* could not check her way and caromed into the stricken ironclad. Her skipper, Commander William Le Roy, a comrade from the old navy, hailed, "Hello Johnston, how are you? Le Roy—don't you know me?" He sent a boat and Johnston came aboard. "I'm glad to see you, Johnston," he said. "Here's some ice-water for you."

Farragut sent orders for Buchanan's sword, and Old Buck surrendered it to a volunteer lieutenant of the *Ossipee*, who delivered it to the flagship. Within the hour, Commander Johnston stood before Admiral Farragut on the deck of the *Hartford*. Courteously, Farragut expressed his regret at the circumstances of the meeting, "to which I replied," Johnston said, "that he was not half as sorry to see me as I was to see him."

Farragut always considered the battle "one of the hardest-earned victories of my life." His casualties were far heavier than in previous engagements. Federal losses amounted to 150 dead (ninety-three of whom went down in the *Tecumseh*) and 170 wounded; the rebel ships had twelve killed, nineteen wounded. The wounded, Union and Confederate, including Admiral Buchanan, needed more care than ships' surgeons could provide. Farragut sent a flag of truce to Fort Morgan, where the rebels agreed to the safe passage of one vessel to carry all wounded to the naval hospital at Pensacola.

The rebels evacuated Fort Powell that night, blowing it up. Fort Gaines surrendered two days later, and Fort Morgan in a fortnight. The *Tennessee* and the gunboat *Selma* passed into Federal service.

On August 6, Gus Fox telegraphed General Ben Butler, now on the James River, "Please try and get a Richmond paper to see how Farragut is getting on at Mobile." Butler got several copies of the *Richmond Examiner* that detailed the entire operation, ending with an article headed, "The enemy's fleet has approached the city." Alone in his tent, Butler gave three cheers for Rear Admiral Farragut and cabled the news clippings direct to the President.

When Gideon Welles brought the official dispatches, he came away somewhat disappointed at Lincoln's apparent lack of enthusiasm. After three years and four months of war, the Gulf had been eliminated as a Confederate military frontier, and all its blockade running had virtually stopped. "It is not appreciated as it should be," he wrote in his diary.

Mobile itself was of no importance without egress to the sea. Isolated from the main theaters of war, the city held out until after Lee surrendered at Appomattox.

On the High Seas

"She certainly kicked up a fuss, but we doubt very much whether she weakened the military resources of the Yankee Government to any appreciable extent."

—*Wilmington Daily Journal,* September 20, 1864

O verwhelmingly, the naval campaigns of the Civil War occurred in the rivers, estuaries, and coasts of the southern Confederacy. In none of those places, from Hampton Roads to Galveston, did the Confederate Navy achieve anything but incidental, temporary success. Not so on the high seas, where a dozen ocean raiders, indifferently armed and manned, drove U.S. merchant shipping from the world's sea lanes, for all intents permanently crippling American seaborne commerce. In no phase of the war did the Confederate Navy exhibit more skill and dash in its mission, or the U.S. Navy more frustration in countering it.

The strategic aim of Confederate naval commerce raiding was to disrupt the American carrying trade to a point where Abraham Lincoln would have to negotiate an end to the war to prevent economic disaster. Given the President's invincible determination for unquestioned military victory, this was a naive assumption. The raiding, however, did achieve the goal of ridding the seas of Yankee-flagged trading vessels, which in 1860 were a close second to that of Great Britain, the world's leading maritime power.

These incidents are romantic and full of derring-do, and the considerable success of the Confederate Navy in this sphere should not be discounted. But for all of the long-range economic damage visited upon the United States, it is doubtful whether the commerce-raiding campaign effected the outcome of the Civil War by as much as a single day.

It began very early, before Abraham Lincoln proclaimed the blockade, when the Confederate government issued letters of marque to several privateers. As the first coastal prizes were grabbed up by small, weakly armed vessels, panic gripped the Northern merchant community. Insurance rates rocketed skyward, and the flood of ship registries and freight goods to neutral flags began. The strictures of international law and the Federal blockade squadrons soon put paid to the privateers, and they did not last beyond the first year of the war.

But from late 1862 to *past* the war's end, Confederate ocean depredations wrought truly significant economic and political damage. The pressure from Northern governors, chambers of commerce, insurance companies, and President Lincoln and the Cabinet eventually forced Gideon Welles to permanently detail a force of fast, powerful warships to hunt the rebel cruisers down.

The first commerce destroyer of the Confederate Navy was also its first regularly commissioned ship, the 437-ton steamer *Sumter.* A handsome little vessel, formerly the *Habana,* she was purchased at New Orleans and armed with an 8-inch pivot gun and four 32-pounders. The machinery was not much; she was slow, with ten knots her maximum speed. Equally deficient were the coal bunkers, a paltry eight days' supply. It was not the best combination for an ocean raider, whose very concept dictates an ability to outrun anything it cannot outfight.

The *Sumter* was fitted out and commissioned under Commander Raphael Semmes, "Old Beeswax," the most successful raider of the war and the second of the Confederate Navy's two admirals.* A difficult man, a trained lawyer, annoying in his self-righteousness, he affected the imperial mustaches and goatee then popular in France and a patent aping of European manners and surface culture. Semmes, who had served thirty-five years, was not highly regarded by his officer colleagues of the prewar navy. David Dixon Porter thought him "indolent and fond of his comfort . . . his associates in the Navy gave him credit for very little energy."

His energy level, though nothing else, changed the moment South Carolina seceded from the Union. When Stephen Mallory was appointed Confederate Secretary of the Navy, Semmes introduced him

---

* Franklin Buchanan was the other.

to the strategy of commerce warfare and specifically requested that duty, considered by many officers a coward's path. Mallory gave him command of the *Sumter.*

In June 1861, Semmes had a full company of ninety-three officers and men, plus twelve marines. He picked the lower-deck hands from the large number of unemployed merchant seamen hanging around New Orleans. All were inexperienced in naval work and discipline, but willing enough to ship out with the prospect of prize money ahead. In the *Sumter's* flag locker was a complete outfit of the world's national flags and naval ensigns, legitimate ruses in commerce warfare. Expecting to live off his prizes, Semmes carried but a small sum of gold and U.S. greenbacks for wages and expenses.

The *Sumter* dropped down to Head of the Passes and waited for the opportunity to slip through the blockade. On June 30, 1861, the *Brooklyn* left her station to chase a strange sail and Semmes, the strong river current at his back, dashed out. Under Mallory's orders "to do the greatest injury in the shortest time," Semmes shaped course for Cape São Roque, the northeast corner of Brazil, the most trafficked headland in the Western Hemisphere.

On July 3, the *Sumter* took her first prize off the south coast of Cuba, the bark *Golden Rocket,* sailing in ballast to Cienfuegos for a cargo of sugar. Semmes, as he did with every prize, first removed the vessel's chronometer (for which he had a fetish), then put her to the torch, waiting until night to do so. The method of burning was to chop up the cabin and forecastle bunks, empty their straw mattresses over the pile, dump any galley lard and grease on top, and apply the match. Night burning was a legal practice followed throughout the war by raiders to lure other potential prizes to the scene of the conflagration. Nevertheless, the Northern press went hysterical over the tactic.

The following day Semmes took a pair of sugar-laden Maine brigs. Putting a prize crew of a midshipman and four hands in each, he headed for Cienfuegos,* where two more New England sugar vessels fell into his bag. Approaching the harbor entrance on the morning of July 5, a tug was spotted towing three vessels to sea. As soon as they cast loose, Semmes grabbed them and shepherded the prizes into port. With a straight face, he blandly asked the governor of Cienfuegos for permission to park his captures until he could bring them into a Confederate harbor for adjudication. Though Semmes would not learn the

---

* Unknown to Semmes, the crew of one of them, the *Cuba,* retook their ship, made prisoners of the prize crew, and sailed her into New York.

decision for many weeks, the Spanish authorities refused. To do otherwise violated neutrality, making them accessories to the seizure. Semmes, as usual, saw himself as the aggrieved party and found no merit in the argument. He was convinced the Spanish had been turned by Yankee bribes. Compounding his fragile sense of injustice, the captain-general of Cuba "deliberately handed back all my prizes to their original owners."

After filling with coal, *Sumter* headed south. Off the Venezuelan port of La Güiria she took the schooner *Abby Bradford*. Needing a ship to carry dispatches home, Semmes sent the prize to New Orleans, where she was recaptured by the blockaders and restored to her owners. When the *Sumter* captured the bark *Joseph Maxwell,* the Venezuelans were ready to investigate whether she had been taken in their territorial waters. Getting the prize out of reach, Semmes, still misreading the Spanish attitude, sent her to Cienfuegos, where she was duly repatriated.

At Paramaribo, Dutch Guiana, Semmes spent almost two weeks enlarging his coal bunkers to give an extra four days' steaming. On September 4, the *Sumter* crossed the equator to anchor in the Brazilian port of São Luís. Another political storm erupted. The nations of the *Sumter*'s previous ports of call had already recognized the Confederacy as a belligerent, though not a sovereign power. Brazil had not yet done so, and its government could legally brand Semmes, the *Sumter,* and her crew as pirates subject to hanging.

The local governor was in a dilemma as to what to do with Semmes' request to buy coal and provisions. The U.S. consul set up a vigorous protest, but permission was eventually granted. Semmes, however, was nearly broke and was forced to borrow $2,000 from a local Texas businessman.

Despite Semmes' humiliation and paltry haul of prizes, this solitary and not very successful raider was having an influence far beyond her actual conquests. The U.S. consul wrote to Secretary of State Seward, "Your excellency cannot imagine the effect which the presence of the *Sumter* on this coast has had on American trade. It is quite possible that it will be entirely suspended."

Refitted, repainted, and coaled, Semmes put to sea and headed north to the "calm belt," the area just above 5 degrees north latitude. For ten days he saw nothing. Then came the brigantine *Joseph Parke,* sailing from Pernambuco, Brazil, to Boston in ballast. Echoing the U.S. consul's note, her master explained his empty hold was the result of fear. No one wanted to trust their goods to American vessels when rebel raiders were in the neighborhood. Semmes used the craft for target practice and then burned her.

Semmes headed northwest for the Lesser Antilles. He sighted no enemy sail for a month, and the crew began showing signs of scurvy. On October 27 their luck, and health, changed. They captured the schooner *Daniel Trowbridge,* out of New Haven with a full cargo of provisions, including beef, pork, hams, live sheep, geese, chickens, "fancy crackers," cheese, and flour, enough to last the *Sumter* five months.

On November 9, short of coal and fresh water, and needing to rid himself of his latest prisoners, Semmes entered Fort-de-France, Martinique. While the *Sumter* was coaling in nearby St. Pierre,* the USS *Iroquois,* a fast steam sloop with the ability to blow the *Sumter* out of the water, stood into the harbor. So as not to come under the "twenty-four-hour rule" of international law, whereby the vessel of one belligerent may not leave a neutral port within twenty-four hours of an enemy, Commander James Palmer took the *Iroquois* out, far enough to keep from being charged with "hovering," and waited.

Palmer arranged with the master of an American merchantman in the harbor to signal the *Sumter*'s movements. But to Gideon Welles, he displayed deep and hardly reassuring doubts. "I feel more and more convinced," he wrote, "that the *Sumter* will yet escape. . . . Even now, moonlight though it be, she may yet creep out under the shadow of the land and no one be able to perceive her . . . if she escapes me we must submit to the distress and mortification."

It was exactly that. Semmes waited five nights for the moon to wane and began his dash to sea. The American schooner in port burned a light, giving Commander Palmer the direction of steaming. Heeding the signal, the *Iroquois* raced south.

In total darkness, Semmes ran to the southern headland of the harbor mouth, until he came under the shadow of the mountains, and stopped. There came a providential rainstorm, and at that moment he reversed course and sped north. It was a teeth-gritting time, as Semmes said of the lookout, "If he saw one *Iroquois* that night he must have seen fifty," and had to be relieved. "Groping like a blind man," the *Sumter* nearly ran into the breakers. But she was at large again. Palmer emerged with nothing more lethal than a board of enquiry and a reduction in standing on the commander's list; others would not be so fortunate.

By now, the *Sumter,* bottom foul and leaky, requiring a thorough

* Temporarily obliterated by a volcanic eruption in 1902.

overhaul, crossed the Atlantic, taking three prizes, and on January 4, 1862, entered the harbor of Cadiz.

Her arrival came at a critical period of British and Confederate pressure for Spanish support during the *Trent* affair. Not surprisingly, the American chargé d'affaires at Madrid, Horatio G. Perry, did his utmost to persuade the Spanish government to act otherwise. He secured the opposition party's allegiance in the Spanish parliament and brought effective propaganda to bear in the local press.

In the interests of European solidarity, Spain agreed to Britain's proposals of support, but only on condition of restoring Spanish rule in Santo Domingo (the modern Dominican Republic), and receiving a share of France's imperial adventure in Mexico. Until then, Spain would observe strict neutrality on the question of the American Civil War.

Into this diplomatic hot pot sailed Raphael Semmes and the *Sumter.* Perry cabled every American legation and consulate in coastal Europe to dispatch U.S. warships to Cadiz. The American diplomatic pressure paid off, and Semmes was allowed to make only minimal repairs and take enough coal to ensure the *Sumter's* immediate seaworthiness and nothing more. With further efforts by the U.S. consul at Cadiz, the local tavern keepers and prostitutes suborned several of the *Sumter's* "misguided men" to desert their ship.

Semmes was also financially broke and cabled the Confederate mission in London for funds. When these were not immediately forthcoming, he asked for local credit and was denied. Eventually, he was able to convince the Spanish authorities that two days in a government dock was absolutely necessary for the safety of the ship, and he was granted $7.00 worth of essential repairs.

Following that, he received a peremptory order from the port admiral to sail or risk internment. In virtually the same condition as she arrived, the *Sumter* put to sea, hoping for a better reception at nearby Gibraltar. Rounding the Trafalgar corner, she took the bark *Neapolitan,* bound from Messina to Boston with a hold full of brimstone and fruit. To make a point, Semmes burned her in the straits, well within sight of the British and Spanish forts on either side.

Shortly after, on January 18, came the eighteenth and last prize, the *Investigator* of Searsport, Maine, carrying a neutral cargo of iron ore. In lieu of immediate seizure, her master signed a surety bond for $11, 250, the cost of the vessel, payable to the President of the Confederate States of America within thirty days of the conclusion of the war. Of course, if the Confederacy lost, the bond was just so much paper. The next day, Semmes dropped anchor in the shadow of the Rock of Gibraltar.

Alerted by Chargé Perry, the U.S. consul at Gibraltar persuaded local coal merchants not to sell or provide credit to the *Sumter* unless they wished to lose substantial American business. Semmes tried to get some Royal Navy coal on credit, but this was refused on orders from London.

When two Federal steam sloops began a close blockade of the harbor, Semmes knew the raiding life of the *Sumter* had come to an end. The ship began to rot at her moorings, and the crew, singly and in small groups, deserted. On April 11, 1862, Semmes discharged the remainder, about fifty men, and decommissioned the ship. She was sold to a subsidiary of the Anglo-Confederate cotton brokers Fraser, Trenholm and Company, spent a short time as a blockade runner, and then disappeared, literally, from the seas.

As a commerce raider the *Sumter* was not a great success, being too small, slow, and short-legged for effective cruising. Her real value to the Confederacy lay in the fear and upheaval she inspired throughout the Northern merchant community and the lessons gained by Semmes and his officers. These men journeyed to London, then to Nassau, where orders dictated their return to Liverpool for a new ship, known thus far only as "Hull No. 290."

The U.S. warships that came to Gibraltar had originally engaged in the pursuit of the *Nashville,* a fast, lightly armed, 1,200-ton sidewheeler commanded by Lieutenant Robert Pegram. In a short career paralleling the *Sumter,* she took her first of only two prizes off the Irish coast, the *Harvey Birch* of New York. Thirty-one crew and passengers were taken off and the vessel, its value estimated at $65,000 (and ironically owned by a Southern sympathizer), was burned.

On November 22, 1861, *Nashville* anchored in Southampton. Expressing its sympathy for the cause, the *Times* of London noted that "great excitement has been created . . . by the arrival in our waters . . . of a steamer of war bearing the flag of the Confederate States of America." Less than a week later, came news of the *Trent* affair and the brief flurry of war fever. Taking advantage of anti-Union sentiment over the incident, the *Nashville* spent more than a month refitting in a Southampton dry dock, a clear violation of British neutrality.

On January 8, 1862, she was ready for sea, when T. Augustus Craven* and the Union steam sloop *Tuscarora* came into port. Twice the superintendent of the dockyard had to chase off night prowlers

---

* The same officer who met his death in the *Tecumseh* at Mobile Bay.

sent by Craven to spy, and possibly burn, the raider at dockside. On January 11, with the *Nashville* obviously preparing to sail, both captains were officially warned of the twenty-four-hour rule. Craven, to avoid it and turn the tables, took the *Tuscarora* out beyond the "marine league"—three miles—and waited for the *Nashville* to sail.

On January 27, the port captain notified Lieutenant Pegram that he must depart in twenty-four hours or suffer internment. Shocked, Pegram complained to the First Lord of the Admiralty, the Duke of Somerset. As the *Nashville,* hardly "a war vessel," had no chance whatever against the U.S. sloop, "your grace can not fail to observe," he wrote, "I am thus . . . to be placed at the mercy of a powerful man of war which it would be madness to attempt to cope." Pegram ended the self-serving whine with "a solemn protest . . . in the name of common humanity."

The duke bent, and word was sent to Craven, then coaling at Cowes on the Isle of Wight, that even though in another port, he must wait twenty-four hours before chasing the rebel. To complete the insulting charade, the steam frigate HMS *Shannon* escorted the raider to sea. Having no wish to precipitate a major diplomatic row, Craven was powerless.

The *Nashville* crossed the Atlantic, burning the schooner *Robert Gilfillan.* Flying U.S. colors, she ran through the blockade into Morehead City, North Carolina. It was a great embarrassment, and petitions circulated throughout the North demanding Gideon Welles' dismissal. The *Nashville* was then sold to Fraser, Trenholm for service as a blockade runner. Before her conversion, however, Burnside and Goldsborough had burst into the sounds and she was forced to escape again. She ended up at tiny Georgetown, South Carolina. After a few runs to Nassau, the ship was bottled up near Savannah, in the Great Ogeechee River, where her fate will be described later.

The *Sumter* and *Nashville* were both of home origin, and beyond these the Confederacy had to seek their ocean cruisers abroad. From beginning to end, the Confederate Navy maintained a large establishment in Europe. Personnel and operations were directed by Flag Officer Samuel Barron in Paris; procurement and purchasing, in the main, by Commander James Bulloch, in London.

Bulloch, a maternal uncle of Theodore Roosevelt, was an officer much like Gus Fox, in that he had left the prewar, dead-end service to command government mail steamers. In May 1861, he reported to Secretary Mallory, was commissioned a lieutenant in the Confederate

Navy, and received orders to buy or build six "steam propellers" for commerce raiding. By rail he traveled to Canada and took ship for Liverpool. On arrival Bulloch learned quickly enough that Confederate treasury notes were so much wallpaper "that no contracts or purchases could be made without cash actually in hand." Only when Fraser, Trenholm agreed to honor his drafts with gold run through the blockade did construction begin. Bulloch arranged with two British builders on plans for one "gun vessel" each, the work to begin when the entire costs were safely deposited to their account.

Money was not Bulloch's only problem. There was also the Queen's proclamation of British neutrality and, even more important, a criminal statute known as the Foreign Enlistment Act. It had been passed in 1812 for the express purpose of preventing private British expeditions in aid of rebellious Spanish colonies in South America. The act deemed it a misdemeanor for anyone without a special license to equip, furnish, fit out, or arm vessels for a belligerent, or to knowingly assist in doing so. Conviction meant fines, imprisonment, and forfeiture of the ship. It became Bulloch's delicate task to skate as close to the edge as the statute allowed. To assist in that regard, he engaged a firm of Liverpool solicitors who claimed the ability to "sail a fleet of ships through the Foreign Enlistment Act," and they well-nigh did.

Bulloch maintained the fiction that no builder or vendor was ever informed of the final purpose of the ship they built, supplied, or fitted out. Bulloch's vessels were constructed as nominal merchantmen for a shadow client, with little vestige of naval purpose. Armament was contracted from one manufacturer, gun carriages and their gear from another; small arms and ammunition from yet a third and fourth. Bids for the large quantities of stores, clothing, hammocks, and other necessities were spread as wide as possible. So long as the ship, armament, and naval crew did not come together in Great Britain, all this activity did not literally constitute an "armed expedition" under the Foreign Enlistment Act.

When complete, the ship, under a British master, and flying British merchant colors, sailed for a remote rendezvous with another merchant ship. That vessel carried the armament, naval stores, and a group of passengers who just happened to be Confederate naval officers. Transfer of title was made at sea, and the erstwhile merchantman was commissioned a warship in the Confederate Navy. All of this, naturally, was known to anyone who cared to know. The U.S. ambassador to Great Britain, Charles Francis Adams, laid thirty-four protests against violations of the Foreign Enlistment Act, but in nearly every instance, the British courts found no criminal behavior.

Bulloch's first success followed the pattern exactly. He began with an engine and building contract with the Liverpool firm of Fawcett, Preston & Co. The hull, masts, and rigging were given to Wm. C. Miller & Sons, and conformed to the general specifications of a British gunboat. The ship, 700 tons, bark-rigged, with twin, folding stacks, was ostensibly intended for a merchant firm in Palermo, Sicily, and was registered as the *Oreto*.

On March 22, 1862, she sailed from the Mersey River under command of Master John Low, with a British crew of fifty-two men, theoretically bound for her fictional home port. In fact, the ship set course for Nassau, consigned to Adderly & Co., local agents for Fraser, Trenholm. At the same time, the steamer *Bahama* departed the North Sea port of Hartlepool, loaded with guns and ammunition. On May 4, there arrived at Nassau the blockade runner *Gordon,* bearing Lieutenant John Newland Maffitt, CSN, an Irish-born Georgian with twenty-eight years in the old navy. He found the *Oreto* already there, "her position daily becoming perilous and precarious," under a great cloud of suspicion and a flurry of diplomatic huffing. She had already taken on board certain arms from the *Bahama*.

The U.S. consul had forced the British authorities to detain her for violating the Foreign Enlistment Act, and when Maffitt stepped ashore, the *Oreto* was under the jurisdiction of the Nassau admiralty court. During the *pro forma* trial, she was inspected by an officer of the Royal Navy, who reported the ship, "in every respect fitted as a man-of-war, on the principle of the despatch gun-vessels in Her Majesty's service."

For the defense, a sympathetic Nassau merchant testified he had been aboard her, and the ship, to his eyes, seemed to be strictly a commercial undertaking. To the disgust of the U.S. consul, the *Oreto* was released to Adderly & Co. For legal fees, "boat hire, bribes to police, and runners," Maffitt billed the Confederate Navy $248.

Under her British master, the *Oreto* steamed sixty miles to uninhabited Green Key, with Maffitt and eight officers going as passengers. Only thirteen men of the original crew, much less than Maffitt expected, volunteered to remain as Confederate sailors, and to fill out, he needed about 120 more. On August 10, the schooner *Prince Albert* stood in from Nassau bearing the *Oreto*'s armament of two 7-inch and six 6-inch rifles, a 12-pounder howitzer, ammunition, and stores. Maffitt's orders from Secretary Mallory were to commission the ship and "cruise at discretion." Of that large and complicated business, Maffitt wrote, "The complacent order to equip, fit out, and proceed on a cruise of aggression, as though a navy yard and enlisting rendezvous were at my disposal, clearly indicated that the Navy Department had failed to . . . consider the very many obstacles and difficulties. . . ."

He began a week of "a task more difficult and painfully laborious" than anything yet experienced. Guns, shot, shells, powder, and stores were shifted into the ship. When all was nearly ready for Maffitt's inspection, someone discovered that forgotten at Nassau were the rammers, sponges, sights, and firing locks for the broadside 6-inch rifles. "Deplorable," wrote Maffitt in his journal. Worse, one man died, and "the yellow appearance of the corpse excited in my mind grave misgivings." On the morning of August 17, Maffitt read aloud his orders of command and commissioned the ship CSS *Florida*. "The English colors hauled down" he wrote, "and with loyal cheers . . . we flung the Confederate banner to the breeze."

Maffitt's fears regarding the dead man came true. The crew had brought yellow fever on board. Several were taken ill and the wardroom steward died. Having no surgeon, Maffitt was pressed into the duty. Within days, "the yellow fever . . . had gained complete ascendency." Inside a week, Maffitt was himself infected. He determined to run the blockade into a Confederate port before all on board were dead. Men continued to fall. On September 3, when in sight of Mobile, only the officers and four seamen were available to work the ship. Having no pilot for a night dash, Maffitt had to try it in daylight. Rising from his sick berth, unable to stand unaided, without enough able bodies to man a single gun, he hoisted British colors and brassed it out.

The blockaders off Mobile this day consisted of the sloop *Oneida* and gunboat *Winona*—the former repairing her boilers, the latter off chasing a suspected runner. At fourteen knots, the *Florida* stood in. The *Oneida*'s Commander George Preble spotted the red ensign soon enough, the ship "having every appearance of an English man-of-war." He signaled the *Winona,* and the two Federal ships closed the stranger. When 100 yards abeam Preble hailed, got no answer, and fired a shot across her bow. Maffitt hauled down his false colors and continued on. The Federals continued firing, hitting the *Florida* several times, but doing no significant damage. Passing under the guns of Fort Morgan, Maffitt outpaced his pursuers by an eyelash and dropped anchor in Mobile Bay.

The hail of invective against Gideon Welles, not for the first or last time, reached thunderous heights. New York Republican Thurlow Weed said that Lincoln might as well have a wooden figurehead for a navy secretary. Press cartoons portrayed Welles, "in a nebule of whiskers, smoke, cobwebs and musty newspapers," as the rebels played havoc with American shipping. The pro-South British humor magazine *Punch* published a special poem for the occasion:

> *There was an old fogy named Welles,*
> *Quite worthy of cap and bells,*
> * For he tho't that a pirate,*
> * Who steamed at a great rate,*
> *Would wait to be riddled with shells.*

For President Lincoln and his secretary of the navy, none of it mattered. Welles refused categorically to materially weaken the blockade for the sake of commerce protection, and Lincoln wavered not an inch in his support.

Someone's head, however, had to be placed on the block, and it was the unfortunate Commander George Preble's. "Preble, by sheer pusillanimous neglect, feebleness, and indecision, let the pirate run the blockade," Welles angrily wrote in his diary. "The time has arrived when these derelictions must not go unpunished." A board of inquiry or a general court-martial would "likely excuse him," and Welles refused to countenance that. Instead, he chose the ultimate professional disgrace by submitting the case to the President. "Dismiss him," answered Abraham Lincoln. "If that is your opinion, it is mine."

Welles showed no pity, sending Preble the perfunctory letter: by order of the President, "You will from this date cease to be regarded as an officer of the Navy of the United States." By custom, it was read to the assembled crews of every ship in the navy, and was entered verbatim into the deck logs.*

The *Florida* remained in Mobile four months, where Maffitt received a nearly full crew for his coming voyage of destruction. On the night of January 16, 1863, camouflaged with a coat of whitewash, and burning coke to avoid telltale smoke, Maffitt ran past Fort Morgan. The blockaders were caught, literally asleep. The fast gunboat *R. R. Cuyler,* stationed specifically to catch her, wasted at least five minutes in slipping her cable—the time for the skipper to awake, come on deck, and give the order. All night and all the next day the *Cuyler* pursued, but at last, the *Florida* dropped beneath the horizon.

---

* In February 1863, responding to a request by Farragut and pressure from the U.S. Senate, Welles restored Preble to duty. He retired from the navy in 1878 with the rank of rear admiral.

The next morning, off the north coast of Cuba, Maffitt burned the brig *Estella* and headed for Nassau, torching two more prizes on the way. The *Florida* was greeted with a rousing reception by the British colonials, who permitted her to remain thirty-six hours and to take a three-month supply of coal. The raider headed south to the Atlantic narrows between the bulges of Africa and Brazil, through which passed the ocean traffic of four continents.

On February 12, east of the Lesser Antilles, the *Florida* took the clipper ship *Jacob Bell,* sailing from Foochow to New York, loaded with $2 million in tea, cinnamon bark, camphor, and firecrackers. She was a singular example of the pinnacle of American nineteenth-century ship-work, and one of the greatest captures by any Confederate raider in the war. As Midshipman Terry Sinclair later wrote, "As she lay thus, with black hull, gilt strake, scraped and varnished masts, and snow-white sails, there was a general exclamation of admiration, coupled with regret that such a thing of beauty must be destroyed." Not mentioned was the loss of a fortune in prize money. Forty-seven passengers and crew were taken off, including the captain's very pregnant wife, for whom Maffitt surrendered his cabin.

Off Barbados came the *Star of Peace,* sailing from Calcutta to Boston with 840 tons of saltpeter for the E. I. du Pont gunpowder works. After using her for target practice, Maffitt set the prize alight, and the night sea glowed for thirty miles around. Next was the schooner *Aldebaran,* en route from New York to São Luís, Brazil, with flour, provisions, and clocks. Paying no mind to the master's protestations of Southern sympathies, Maffitt took what he needed to replenish his larder, burned her, and transferred his prisoners into a British vessel.

On March 28, in midocean they overhauled the bark *Lapwing* sailing from Boston to Batavia with, Sinclair recalled, "a fine assorted cargo of Yankee notions, canned meats, fruits, vegetables," lumber, furniture, a horse carriage, and most important, several hundred tons of coal. Maffitt wished to use the prize as a tender and put on board Master's Mate Richard Floyd, Midshipman Sinclair, fifteen men, and two 12-pounder guns.

The *Lapwing* soon took a prize of her own, the 1,278-ton *Kate Dyer,* bound for Antwerp with a full cargo of guano. The prize being twice the size of the *Lapwing* the rebels took her by trick. Cutting and painting a spar to mimic a naval gun, they mounted it upon the wheels of the "family carriage found on board. With this trained on the enemy," Sinclair said, "we hove him to with a shot from our 12-pounder." The guano being neutral cargo, the *Kate Dyer* was bonded and allowed to go her way.

Off the Brazilian penal island of Fernando de Noronha, at the very tip of the bulge, the *Lapwing* and *Florida* rendezvoused for coaling. On parting, Maffitt set coordinates for future meetings. The *Lapwing,* however, proved unseaworthy. On May 30, in sight of Barbados, Floyd set her afire and rowed ashore with his crew. Floyd and Sinclair took passage in a British merchantman to eventually rejoin the *Florida* at Brest, while the enlisted sailors were released of their obligation.

After parting from the *Lapwing,* Maffitt took four prizes, landing his prisoners at Fernando de Noronha. As bad luck would have it, the raider *Alabama* had touched here a week before, and the welcome reception she received from local officials had not gone down well with the Brazilian government. Consequently, Maffitt was given only twenty-four hours in port. On May 6, he captured the large brig *Clarence,* bound from Rio de Janeiro to Baltimore with a cargo of coffee.

One of Maffitt's officers, Lieutenant Charles Read, put forward the bold suggestion "to take the brig . . . and with a crew of twenty men, to proceed to Hampton Roads and cut out a gunboat or steamer of the enemy." If that failed, it might be possible "to fire the shipping at Baltimore." Maffitt gave the scheme his full, unqualified approval, adding, "I . . . will not hamper you with instructions." It began as wild an adventure as any in the naval war.

On June 6, Read and the *Clarence* passed Cape Hatteras. First they captured the bark *Whistling Wind,* bound from Philadelphia to New Orleans with government coal; she was burned. The next day witnessed the capture of the schooner *Albert H. Partridge,* sailing from New York to Matamoros with small arms, clothing, and a special license to trade with, as Read put it, "our citizens in Texas." Read, not having the corruption of the Federal official who granted the permit, demanded a written guarantee from the master to complete the voyage and deliver the cargo as consigned. Two days after, he burned the *Mary Alvina,* en route from Boston to New Orleans with army stores.

From prisoners and newspapers in the prizes, Read knew his original plan to penetrate Hampton Roads was no longer possible. Even had the *Clarence* sailed in good faith, she would not have been permitted to pass Fort Monroe. Nothing was allowed in except government cargoes under naval escort. Undaunted, Read continued on, hoping to capture an army transport.

They were off Cape Henry on June 16, and before daylight took three vessels. The bark *Tacony* was first. In empty passage from Port

Royal to Philadelphia, Read lured her in by flying his colors upside down, the clear signal of distress. The *Tacony* closed on her mission of mercy, and Read boarded her from an armed boat, forcing the crew's surrender at pistol point. She looked a much better craft than the *Clarence,* and he decided to transfer his little command into her.

Almost immediately the schooners *A. M. Schindler* and *Kate Stewart* came near and were taken. Thus, before breakfast, Read had four prizes to dispose of. Putting the *Kate Stewart* under bond, he loaded her with nearly fifty prisoners, setting the other craft afire. The rebels sailed off in the *Tacony.* When the *Kate Stewart* landed on the New Jersey shore, the *Tacony's* master immediately telegraphed the Navy Department. Gideon Welles ordered the Atlantic navy yards to commandeer any suitable vessels and give chase. Within two days more than thirty took to the sea, a very mixed lot.

Unmolested for nearly two weeks, the *Tacony* sailed up the Atlantic coast, taking fifteen prizes ranging from fishing schooners to the big liner *Isaac Webb,* en route from Liverpool to New York with 750 passengers. Read sent her off in bond of $40,000. Most of the rest were burned.

On June 24, Read took the fish schooner *Archer,* transferred into her, and burned the *Tacony.* Out of ammunition, he boldly planned to enter an exposed New England port, destroy everything possible, then escape by cutting out a steamer. "No Yankee gunboat would even dream of suspecting us," he wrote in his journal. The *Archer's* career lasted two days. On June 26, Read sighted Maine's Portland light. "I picked up two fishermen," he reported, "who, taking us for a pleasure party, willingly consented to pilot us into [the harbor]." They were a talkative pair, and the rebels learned the revenue cutter *Caleb Cushing* and the New York packet, "a stanch, swift propeller," were both in port for the night. Read determined to take one or both.

They entered port at sunset and anchored "in full view of the shipping." The cutter *Caleb Cushing,* a topsail schooner with one 32-pounder gun, sat pierside. Her skipper was ill ashore, and half the crew and all but the second officer were in town. Shortly after midnight, leaving three men in the *Archer,* Read boarded her without resistance, and locked the crew in irons below. By daybreak they were out of the harbor.

When first seen missing, it was thought the *Cushing's* Georgia-born second officer had run off with her; the next guess was she had been taken by pirates. The Treasury Department's collector of customs armed two steamers and a tug with a few light guns, some local infantry, and a posse of armed citizens and set off in chase. Twenty miles to sea they caught the cutter.

Read offered no resistance. He torched the vessel, took to his boats, and surrendered. The *Archer* meekly gave up later in the day. Much to the anger of the Portland police and civilians, the Confederate prisoners were taken to Fort Warren in Boston, the *Portland Transcript* noting, "Our citizens could scarcely reconcile themselves to the idea of not hanging somebody."

Having no clue of Read's adventures, Maffitt and the *Florida,* over the strenuous objections of American consuls, coaled and repaired at Brazilian ports, then headed north to meet the *Lapwing* and ravage the New England traffic.

On June 16, the raider captured the big ship *B. F. Hoxie,* sailing from the west coast of Mexico to Falmouth, England, with logwood and $105,000 in silver bars. Examining her manifest, Maffitt did not believe it a neutral cargo. He removed the silver and burned the ship. Had he been able to bring it to a prize court, the *Florida*'s crew would have been rich men. Instead, Maffitt used the silver for mundane expenses.

Burning two vessels en route, Maffitt arrived at Bermuda on July 16, exchanging a twenty-one-gun national salute with the harbor batteries. While extending this courtesy to the Confederacy, the island's governor took the precaution of sending Maffitt a copy of the British neutrality laws. They required belligerents, as Maffitt well knew, to leave port within twenty-four hours. Maffitt, with the benign neglect of the Empire, departed when he was ready, eleven days later.

Since leaving Mobile, the *Florida* had been at sea continually for five months, and was in dire need of an overhaul and replacements. Maffitt steamed for Brest, where he arrived on August 23, and found the French very accommodating. The protests of U.S. Ambassador William Dayton were of no avail. He declared the *Florida* capable of proceeding under sail, and thus repairs to her machinery were not necessary to her basic seaworthiness. But Emperor Napoleon III replied, "Because a duck can swim is no reason for clipping her wings."

Maffitt gave his officers shore leave in Paris and two-thirds of the enlisted crew deserted the ship. When Ambassador Dayton objected to the local recruitment of men to replace them, a clear violation of international law, Commander Bulloch rounded up sixty adventurous souls in London and shipped them off to Brest. Maffitt, seriously debilitated by his bout with yellow fever, was relieved of command. For her final cruise, the raider was skippered by Lieutenant Charles Manigault Morris.

On February 10, 1864, nearly six months after her arrival, the *Florida,* in thick and rainy weather, slipped away for the familiar hunting grounds in the South Atlantic narrows. There were many sail, but none of them American. Not until March 29, did they spot the *Avon* of Boston, bound from Howland Island to Cork with guano. The likeliest seamen were forcibly pressed into the *Florida*'s crew, and the *Avon* burned.

Finding poor hunting around the equator, Morris brought the *Florida* to Bermuda, where the usual courtesies were rendered on both sides. British warships dipped their colors, and officers doffed their hats in salute. In mid-May she took the schooner *George Latimer* with a welcome cargo of bread, flour, and lard. The ship was burned. Only two more prizes came the *Florida*'s way until July 1, when she took the *Harriet Stevens,* carrying lumber and 312 pounds of opium. The drugs were transferred to a runner at Bermuda, and run through the blockade as a priceless commodity for Confederate military hospitals.

At Bermuda, Morris received a communication from Secretary Mallory suggesting another "dash at New England commerce and fisheries." Risks were great, but so were the rewards. On July 8, heading north, he burned the whaler *Golconda,* home from the Pacific with 1,240 barrels of sperm and 600 of oil. Two more prizes, one of them carrying coal for the Gulf squadrons, were burned next day off the Virginia capes.

Off Hampton Roads prizes abounded. July 10 proved the most profitable day of her career. First came the *General Berry* with army hay. Two others quickly followed, Morris putting the last under bond for sixty-eight prisoners. The fourth prize was a fine catch, the steamer *Electric Spark,* bound from New York to New Orleans with general cargo, forty-two passengers, a crew of thirty-nine, and $12,000 in U.S. postage stamps. Morris stopped a British vessel carrying a load of fresh fruit. He bought the cargo for $750 to make room for his prisoners; the *Electric Spark* he torched that night.

Word of the *Florida* loose off the coast brought ghost sightings of her at every point from the Grand Banks of Newfoundland to Cherbourg. In fact, Morris headed south, planning a foray into the Pacific to attack the American whaling fleet. On September 26, 1864, in her old cruising ground between the continental bulges, the *Florida* took her last prize, a thin little victory, the bark *Mondamin,* sailing from Rio to Baltimore in empty passage.

Before proceeding further, Morris turned the ship to Bahia, Brazil, for a final refit and shore leave. The *Florida* entered port at 9 P.M., October 4, noting nothing amiss in the night. Daylight, however, disclosed the powerful steam sloop USS *Wachusett*. Commanding the Federal warship was Napoleon Collins, a heavy-browed plodder formerly of the South Atlantic Blockading Squadron, a man Du Pont described as "sensible in some things and very stupid in others." Employing both traits, Commander Collins brought the *Florida*'s career to an ignominious end.

Local officials exacted promises from Lieutenant Morris and U.S. Consul Thomas Wilson to respect the port's neutrality. Significantly, Commander Collins took no part in the arrangement, not that it excused him from subsequent actions, but it preserved his honor in technically not breaking an oath. Through Consul Wilson, Collins sent Lieutenant Morris a challenge to steam into international waters and fight. Morris responded to the challenge, telling Collins that when he was done refitting, he would steam out of port and take what followed. However, Collins had other plans. Mindful that he shared the harbor with an enemy directly responsible for the capture of thirty-three defenseless merchantmen—and doubtless preparing to ravage again—he prepared the *Wachusett* for a major violation of international law. In a private letter to that other creator of diplomatic incidents, Captain Charles Wilkes, Collins indicated his intent to ram the *Florida* "full speed amidships," without firing a shot of any kind, "or a loud word being spoken." If successful in sinking her, he would back off and head quietly to sea; if still afloat, "to go on board with revolvers," drive the crew below, and tow the rebel out.

The second option happened exactly as Collins described. At six bells in the middle watch, 3 A.M., October 7, the *Wachusett* got quietly underway. Under a full head of steam she struck the *Florida* abaft the mizzen mast on her starboard side, according to Collins' log, "crushing it in, carrying away mizzen-mast and doing other serious damage." The *Wachusett* backed clear, and receiving some pistol shots, returned fire with a volley of marine musketry. Then contrary to orders, the executive officer boomed off two broadside guns.

Morris and about half his officers and crew were ashore. The *Wachusett*'s boarding party forced the remainder—twelve officers, fifty-eight men—to surrender at gunpoint. In the harbor, the commanding officer of a Brazilian corvette would have been completely within his rights to open fire on the *Wachusett* for violating a neutral port. Instead, he sent an officer who protested to the Federals in Portuguese and was answered in English. From the harbor fort came a shot in the *Wachusett's* general direction. According to international law, Brazil had upheld her honor in the face of wanton aggression.

At dawn, Collins towed the *Florida* out, set a full spread of sails on both ships, and headed home. In Hampton Roads, on November 28, 1864, very probably in response to Brazil's demand for her return, which the United States could not legally refuse, the *Florida* was "accidentally" rammed and sunk by the army transport *Alliance.**

The most famous of the Confederate sea raiders was also the best of the "six propellers" that Commander Bulloch's money and orders could buy. Her keel was laid on June 27, 1862, at Laird's yard, Liverpool. On the building slip stood a sign, "No. 290"—the two hundred and ninetieth hull laid down by the firm. She was a matter of common talk around the dockyard. Everyone knew the ship was being built for a Confederate cruiser, and was thus a finesse of the Foreign Enlistment Act. The ship "was built for speed rather than battle," said her stoic executive officer, Lieutenant John McIntosh Kell. "Her lines were symmetrical and fine; her material of the best." A relative match to several classes of United States steam sloops, the vessel displaced 1,050 tons, was 220 feet long, and thirty-one feet, nine inches in the beam. Her armament, impressive for a raider, consisted of a forward 7-inch pivot rifle, one 64-pounder smoothbore aft, and six 32-pounders on the broadside.

"She was a perfect steamer," Kell said, and under normal conditions could sustain ten to twelve knots, reaching fifteen with special measures. The novel propeller was housed in a "banjo" frame and could be hoisted free of the water in fifteen minutes. The rig was barkentine, with long lower masts, giving an immense spread of canvas. On her varnished, inlaid wheel was inscribed the motto *Aide toi et Dieu t'aidera*—"God helps those who help themselves." A full crew numbered twenty-four officers, several of whom, including Kell, had served in the *Sumter*, and approximately 120 men on the lower deck. Her captain was Raphael Semmes.

---

* In March 1865, Collins was tried before a general court-martial with Rear Admiral Louis M. Goldsborough presiding. He stoically offered no defense and pleaded guilty to the charge and specification of "violating the territorial jurisdiction of a neutral government," in which he "did unlawfully attack and capture the steamer *Florida*." Save for objecting to the word "unlawfully," Collins remained silent. He was sentenced to dismissal from the service, but Gideon Welles rejected the punishment, and he retired from the navy a rear admiral in 1874.

In London, U.S. Ambassador Charles Francis Adams dunned Earl Russell with a pile of documents proving beyond doubt what everyone knew, that No. 290, under the current name of *Enrica,* was a warship being constructed for the rebels. On July 26, 1862, these papers arrived on the desk of Sir John Harding, Queen's Counsel, Russell's expert on the Foreign Enlistment Act. Harding chose the moment to suffer a nervous breakdown and became insane, a condition hidden by his wife for three days.

By now the *Enrica* had nearly completed fitting out and undergone a successful builder's trial; her bunkers and holds were full. On the day of Harding's collapse, Commander Bulloch "received information from a private but most reliable source that it would not be safe to leave the ship at Liverpool another forty-eight hours." Taking advantage of a contract clause permitting a second trial, Bulloch ordered her out, literally hours before detention bills arrived at the dockyard. The ship's master was Captain M. J. Butcher, late of the Cunard steamship line. Carrying a party of civillians as a further disguise, the *Enrica* glided down the Mersey. Once out of harbor, the guests returned to Liverpool by tug, and the *Enrica* shaped course seaward for the Azores.

At the island of Terceira she met the bark *Agrippina,* carrying the armament and ammunition. Shortly after, there arrived the *Bahama* with Raphael Semmes and his officers. In the lee of the island, but carefully outside the marine league, the ships were lashed together for the transfer of guns and stores.

On August 24, George Townley Fullam, a young British subject and the *Enrica's* second officer, wrote in his diary, "Captain Semmes read his commission, and formally took command of the Confederate States Steamer *Alabama* . . . hoisting the Confederate ensign at the peak, the English St. George at the fore." Giving an impassioned speech to the foreign crews of the three vessels to enlist in the Confederate Navy, Semmes received eighty-three volunteers, including Fullam as acting master's mate, which formed the nucleus of the *Alabama's* company throughout her life.

On September 5, 1862, the *Alabama* took and burned her first prize, the whaler *Ocmulgee* of Martha's Vineyard, its dead prey alongside. Nine more whalers in the seas around the Azores fell to the raider in the next month. Semmes steered west into the North Atlantic shipping lanes, and during October captured ten large vessels with valuable cargoes of grain and flour. One of the ships, the *Brilliant,* was nearly as large as the *Alabama.* Her master tried to convince Semmes that a portion of the cargo was British-owned. There was some evidence of this, but not the legal proof of a consular seal, and Semmes the lawyer knew it. "Do you take me for a damned fool?" he raged at the master. "Where are the proofs that . . . your cargo is on English account?"

The *Brilliant,* which Semmes estimated with her cargo at $164,000, was fired. Thinking of his destitute countrymen in the English Midlands, Fullam wrote, "It seemed a fearful thing to burn such a cargo . . . when I thought how the [workers] of the cotton [milling] districts would have danced with joy had they shared it among themselves. I never saw a vessel burn with such brilliancy, the flames completely enveloping the hull and rigging in a few minutes, making a sight as grand as it was appalling." Two more were taken and burned in the next week.

Then came the *Tonawanda,* en route from Philadelphia to Liverpool with seventy passengers, half of them women. It was a fine ship, but Semmes reluctantly bonded her a few days later to carry the load of civilians from the recent captures. Two crew members remained aboard the *Alabama.* One, a deserter from the *Sumter* whom Semmes could have hanged for desertion, proved so worthless that he was later set ashore on a barren Caribbean island. The other was a seventeen-year-old black slave, David White, in the charge of his master, a citizen of loyal Delaware. As such, under the laws of war as interpreted by Semmes (and the Dred Scott Decision of the Supreme Court), David White was contraband cargo just as Union wheat.

Assigned as the personal servant of the *Alabama*'s surgeon, Dr. Galt, "there at once arose," Semmes wrote, "between the Virginia gentleman and the slave boy, that sympathy of master and servant, which our ruder people of the North find so impossible to comprehend." Semmes entered David White's name in the ship's books as one of the crew, and allowed him the pay of his grade, second-class boy. "In short," Semmes noted, "no difference was made between him and the white waiters of the [officers'] mess." In several ports, White was offered his freedom by American consuls. He always refused.

Five more prizes were taken by the end of October, one yielding a cargo of live pigs. The last vessel of the month, an old lumber brig was caught 300 miles east of Atlantic City, New Jersey. Semmes bonded her to carry prisoners, telling its master to advise the New York Chamber of Commerce the *Alabama* would be off that port by the time they heard the news.

Semmes did intend to raid New York, a feat scotched by a shortage of coal. "To astonish the enemy in New York harbor, to destroy their vessels in their own water," Fullam noted, "had been the darling wish of all on board." Semmes turned the ship south to Martinique and a coaling rendezvous with the *Bahama*. On the way he burned two prizes, taking a store of cabbages and turnips from one, and turning out some *Alabama* officers from their cabins to accommodate two women and three little girls from the other. He also got nine recruits, which, added to the eleven enlisted from other prizes, nearly filled out the crew.

At Martinique, Semmes gave the slip to a Federal warship, and coaled from the *Bahama* off the Venezuelan coast. Taking two small prizes, he turned back to the Caribbean, hoping to catch one of the Vanderbilt liners inbound from Panama with California treasure. Off the coast of Cuba, Semmes captured the steamer *Ariel,* outbound from New York to Panama with $8,000 in Treasury notes, $1,500 in silver coin, 532 civilian passengers, and 140 U.S. Marines for the Pacific Station. It was a good catch, but hardly the treasure ship she would have become had he grabbed her on the return leg. Semmes paroled the marines until properly exchanged and bonded the ship and cargo for $261,000. Following this incident, the California steamers, inbound and out, were considered strategic assets and provided with naval escorts.

On January 11, 1863, the *Alabama* arrived off Galveston, temporarily in Confederate hands, and Semmes was astonished to find five U.S. warships in the process of bombarding the town. Under sail, flying the white ensign of the Royal Navy, the raider approached carefully. The first vessel to spot her, the converted gunboat *Hatteras,* a three-masted schooner with an auxiliary engine, stood out to investigate. Slowly the *Alabama* drew away, taking the *Hatteras* farther and farther from the Federal ships. Her skipper, Lieutenant Commander Homer Blake, cleared for action and narrowed the distance to 400 yards. On hailing the mysterious sail, "What steamer is that?" Semmes replied, "Her Britannic Majesty's ship *Vixen.*"

Night fell, becoming quite dark. Blake, certain of deception, lowered a boat to investigate. It was hardly in the water when the *Alabama* struck her false colors, and in its place flew the stars and bars of the Confederate Navy. Simultaneously a broadside crashed out.

It was no contest. In minutes the *Hatteras'* walking-beam engine was shattered and the ship ablaze in two places. Blake continued to fire, hoping to attract the blockaders off Galveston. The fires crept to the magazines. There was nothing Blake could do but shoot a gun to leeward in token of surrender. Semmes picked the *Hatteras'* crew from the sea and headed for Jamaica, where they were landed under parole.

Against his better judgment, Gideon Welles was forced by this incident, together with the escape of the *Florida* from Mobile five days later, to detach several vessels of the North Atlantic Blockading Squadron to the West Indies. None, however, had any success in bringing either raider to book. Semmes turned south to the Atlantic narrows, and together with the *Florida* and the soon-commissioned *Georgia*, he veritably swept American commerce from the ocean highways. By the time the *Alabama* crossed the equator on March 29, thirteen more prizes had fallen into her bag. The *Louisa Hatch* yielded an especially valuable cargo of coal, and Semmes brought her to Fernando de Noronha to await the arrival of the *Agrippina*. Not only did the Brazilian governor permit the *Alabama* to loot her prize in a neutral port, but he also turned a blind eye when the *Alabama* darted out to capture a pair of whalers.

Semmes waited eleven days for the *Agrippina*, then sailed away on April 21 for Bahia. Four prizes were taken and burned, packing the *Alabama* with more than 100 prisoners, including several women. As usual, officers were turned out of their cabins to accommodate them. "The ladies, bless their sweet hearts," wrote Lieutenant Arthur Sinclair, "are desirable company at all times and places with but few exceptions. One of the exceptions is the crowded wardroom of a man-of-war. . . . What would become of these women if we should get alongside of an enemy's cruiser?" He needn't have worried, at least not for another fourteen months.

She entered Bahia on May 11. Cruising off the Brazilian bulge after a ten-day stay, the *Alabama* captured eight ships, burning five and bonding two. About the eighth vessel, the bark *Conrad,* sailing from Buenos Aires to New York with a cargo of wool and goat hides, Sinclair said, "A more beautiful specimen of American clipper could not be produced, new, well-found, and fast." Semmes armed her with two 12-pounders, ordered a lieutenant and fifteen men aboard, and commissioned the vessel CSS *Tuscaloosa.*

Semmes decided to try the Cape of Good Hope to grab what he could of the traffic returning from the East Indies. The *Tuscaloosa* would join after cruising independently. For sixteen days the *Alabama* saw nothing and then only neutral vessels. Her effectiveness was nearly done. She had taken fifty-four prizes, and would seize but ten more in the time remaining of her life. On July 29, she anchored in a small harbor north of Cape Town.

The crew, a volatile mix of foreigners, with a scattering of ex-Royal Navy sailors, were never a trustworthy lot and they became a serious problem. "I have a precious set of rascals on board," Semmes wrote at the Cape, "faithless in the matter of abiding by their contracts, liars, thieves, and drunkards." To deny them liberty ashore after two months at sea risked a mutiny. He had to permit it, and lost twenty-eight men through the hospitality and shelter of the American consul. Semmes, with his warped sense of injustice, appealed to the local police for a roundup of the deserters. But the chief constable saw no reason to arrest British subjects to compel them to serve in a foreign warship. Semmes was forced to pay a crew broker—a "crimp"—to supply him with a dozen "passengers"—drunken merchant sailors looking for a berth—and enlisted them outside the three-mile limit.

The *Tuscaloosa* came in mid-August. The American consul demanded that as a legally uncondemned prize, she must be detained by the port authorities and restored to her owner. The consul was upheld by the senior Royal Navy officer on the station, Rear Admiral Sir Baldwin Walker. But the Cape attorney general overruled, and she was permitted to go to sea. Eventually, however, the London courts found for the admiral, but by that time the issue was moot.

On September 24, the *Alabama* entered the Indian Ocean and for a month sighted not one U.S. flag. Her arrival in the Dutch East Indies was completely unexpected, but pickings were very slim; most American vessels remaining safely, and uselessly, in port. In the first two weeks of November three prizes were burned in the Sunda Strait. There was more trouble with the crew. The first officer of the clipper *Contest,* aboard as a prisoner, wrote, "Crew much dissatisfied, no prize money, no [shore] liberty, and see no prospect of getting any. Discipline very slack; steamer dirty, rigging slovenly. Semmes sometimes punishes but is afraid to push too hard; men excited; officers do not report to captain; crew do things for which they would be shot on board American man-of-war."

Semmes' journal confirms this. Tired, homesick, discouraged by war news (which he read in Singapore newspapers), disgusted with the crew, and taking only three more prizes by Christmas, he was forced into an inevitable decision. Not that he had much of a choice. A dockyard refit and complete change of crew could be done only in Europe. France was a better bet than England, where questions of the Foreign Enlistment Act were sure to compound his problems, and France had the advantage of housing the European headquarters of the Confederate Navy.

On December 31, 1863, the *Alabama* headed west into the Indian Ocean. In March she rounded the Cape, spent a month in the South Atlantic, and took her sixty-fourth and last prize, the clipper *Tycoon,* outbound from New York to San Francisco with general cargo. On June 11, 1864, the *Alabama,* foul-bottomed, filthy, and demoralized, steamed into Cherbourg.

Almost immediately Semmes realized his mistake. Mid-1864 was rather late in the game to play on European sympathies for the Confederate cause. The only dry docks at Cherbourg were those of the French Navy, and to use them, permission was needed from the Emperor, who as it happened, was on vacation. No decision could be gotten for several days. Le Havre, with private docks, would have been a better port. Furthermore, the U.S. ambassador in Paris sent telegrams announcing the *Alabama*'s presence to every U.S. warship in northern Europe.

On Sunday, June 12, the steam sloop *Kearsarge* rode to her anchor in the Scheldt, off Flushing. Her surgeon, John M. Brown, recalled, "The cornet suddenly appeared at the fore, and a gun was fired." Signals soared aloft calling officers and men back to the ship. The moment there was enough steam in the boilers, she hoisted in her anchor and passed down the English Channel. Underway, Captain John Winslow called all hands aft to tell them the "welcome news." Surgeon Brown remembered that "the crew responded with cheers." Two days later the *Kearsarge* arrived off Cherbourg. Inside the breakwater the Confederate flag was easily seen, and the crew crowded the rail and rigging to get a look at the most notorious of the rebel sea raiders.

For Gideon Welles, hunting needle-in-a-haystack enemy raiders on the high seas had one interesting advantage: it provided a convenient place to stash Federal officers who had incurred his displeasure, or were otherwise found wanting. John Winslow was one of them. As commanding officer of the *Benton* and the *St. Louis* on the Mississippi, he had publicly stated his opposition to David Porter's promotion to acting rear admiral. Worse, in August 1864, after the Union defeat at the Second Battle of Bull Run, he had uttered a wish the rebels "would bag old Abe." For these indiscretions he was banished from the scene of active operations. But bad politics and *lèse-majesté* aside, Winslow was neither stupid nor a coward.

The *Kearsarge* entered the harbor intending to bring out the *Alabama*'s merchant seamen prisoners, who had just been put ashore. Semmes objected that such "reinforcements" materially increased the enemy's crew, and the port admiral agreed. Without anchoring, the *Kearsarge* steamed out, taking up station just outside the marine league.

With a glass to his eye, Semmes kept her under very close scrutiny, carefully weighing the odds. He turned to his trusted executive officer, John McIntosh Kell. "I am going out to fight the *Kearsarge*," he said, "what do you think of it?"

On paper the two antagonists seemed fairly evenly matched, but this was deceptive. At 1,550 tons, the *Kearsarge* outweighed her opponent by a third. The rebel ship carried one more gun, and her 7-inch Blakeley rifle gave an advantage at long range. But the *Kearsarge's* two 11-inch and four 9-inch Dahlgrens provided a smashing capability at close quarters the *Alabama* could not match. In weight of metal, the Federal ship threw 430 pounds of iron, the rebel, 360. And critically, the *Alabama's* powder had deteriorated badly during the long voyage. Theoretically faster, the *Alabama's* designed speed of thirteen knots was now, due to her foul bottom, significantly reduced to perhaps ten, a knot slower than her foe. Her crew, 149 officers and men, was fourteen less than the Federal sloop's, and far less trained and disciplined.

Winslow had garlanded the *Kearsarge's* sides with hanging loops of chain cable. For sea-keeping and aesthetic reasons, they were sheathed in light planking, painted the same black as the ship's hull. Even from close aboard it was almost impossible to spot the extemporaneous armor, and Semmes did not see it either. Finally, the *Kearsarge* had been built as a regular warship, with timbers and scantlings to match, and she could absorb considerable punishment, which the *Alabama* could not.

In typical fashion, Semmes, through the Confederate agent in the port, issued a challenge to combat. "I desire to say to the U.S. consul," he wrote, "that my intention is to fight the *Kearsarge* as soon as I can make the necessary arrangements." Coaling and the removal of personal effects, including Semmes' large collection of chronometers taken from the prizes, would take no more than two days "at furthest. I beg she will not depart before I am ready to go out." He need not have worried.

For his part, Captain Winslow informed the U.S. consul that he, too, had come to Cherbourg "to fight, and had no intention of leaving." Winslow summoned his officers for a council of war. In all probability the ships would engage on parallel courses and the *Alabama,* if defeated, was likely to seek safety in neutral waters. Thus, Winslow sought to begin the action several miles from the harbor breakwater. "It was determined," Surgeon Brown said, "not to surrender, but to fight until the last, and, if need be to go down with colors flying." Bulwarks down, guns trained to starboard, "the whole battery loaded," shell, grape, and canister ready at hand, the *Kearsarge* waited her moment.

On Sunday, June 19, at two bells in the forenoon watch, 9 A.M., the *Alabama* weighed anchor and steamed to battle. Escorting her out were the French ironclad frigate *Couronne* and the steam yacht *Deerhound*, owned by a wealthy English "gentleman of leisure." The day was bright and beautiful, with a light breeze. The Confederate officers donned full uniforms, and the crew were neatly dressed in clean clothing. Cherbourg civilians in the thousands lined the shoreline, and an excursion train from Paris deposited hundreds more.

The *Alabama* rounded the breakwater and the *Kearsarge* was spotted about seven miles to the northeast. "We immediately shaped our course for her," said Jonathan Kell, "called all hands to quarters, and cast loose the starboard battery." He reported the ship ready, and Semmes called all hands aft, where, mounting a gun carriage, he addressed the crew. This, he told them, was their first opportunity of meeting an armed foe since sinking the *Hatteras*. They had driven American commerce from the seas, and the *Alabama* had become a household word in the civilized world. "Shall that name be tarnished by defeat?" Semmes roared. "The thing is impossible! . . . Go to your quarters."

Aboard the *Kearsarge,* the decks were holystoned white, brightwork gleamed in the morning sun, the guns reflected a dull black polish, and the crew, Surgeon Brown recalled, "were dressed in Sunday suits." After inspection at quarters, they were dismissed to attend services. "Seemingly no one thought of the enemy."

They had waited for days and "speculation as to her coming had nearly ceased." At 10:20 A.M., the officer of the deck reported a steamer standing out of harbor, a common enough occurrence, and hardly a man gave it attention. "The bell was tolling for [divine] service when some one shouted, 'She's coming, and heading straight for us!'" The officer of the deck whipped the glass to his eye: "The *Alabama!*" Down the wardroom hatch he repeated the yell, "The *Alabama!*" Marine drummers beat to quarters, Winslow put down his prayer book, took up a brass hailing trumpet, and went on deck. He ordered the ship about and headed seaward, ensuring the battle would take place outside of territorial waters.

After forty-five minutes, at a range little over one mile, the *Kearsarge* spun around on her keel, presented the starboard battery, and made straight for the *Alabama,* as Surgeon Brown said, "with the design of running her down." The *Alabama* sheared off, presenting *her* starboard broadside. Winslow rang for more speed. When the range came down to 1,800 yards, the *Alabama* belched a dirty cloud of smoke and the dull boom of a heavy gun rippled over the water. The *Alabama* followed with a broadside, then another. In the *Kearsarge* some rigging was cut, but most of the shot passed over or fell short. "It was apparent," said Surgeon Brown, "that Captain Semmes intended to fight at long range."

In minutes, after a third and fourth Confederate broadside were fired, the range fell to 500 yards. To prevent raking fires, each ship kept its rudder hard to starboard, and the battle formed around a common center, drawing into connected circles that turned seven times before the final curtain. Semmes stood on the quarterdeck, a glass to his eye. "Mr. Kell," he barked, "use solid shot; our shell strike the enemy's side and fall into the water"—a clear result of the *Kearsarge*'s chain armor and the *Alabama*'s deteriorated powder.

The *Kearsarge*'s 11-inch guns began their fearful work. Three shells swept away numbers of the rebel gun crews, the spanker gaff carried away, and the stars and bars fell by the run. The *Kearsarge* kept it up, pouring a deliberate, accurate fire into the *Alabama*. "Our decks," said Kell, "were now covered with the dead and the wounded, and the ship was careening heavily to starboard from the effects of the shot-holes on her waterline."

Semmes ordered all sail set to bring the *Alabama* on the port tack and continue the action on her disengaged side, at the same time attempting an escape back into French waters. According to Kell, "The evolution was performed beautifully . . . the action continuing almost without cessation." The damage, however, was becoming critical. "The port side of the quarterdeck," Kell went on, "was so encumbered with the mangled trunks of the dead that I had to have them thrown overboard in order to fight the after pivot gun."

The *Kearsarge* took thirteen hits, the most serious a 7-inch shell that struck the sternpost and did not explode. Had it done so, it might well have shattered the rudder, rendering the ship helpless. Nonetheless, it was felt. "The blow," said Surgeon Brown, "shook the ship from stem to stern."

The battle had just completed the seventh circle. To watchers in the *Kearsarge* she "showed gaping sides, through which the water washed." Winslow ordered the helmsman to steer between the enemy and the shore. "Then," said Surgeon Brown, "the *Alabama* was at our mercy."

Semmes' chief engineer reported his fires out and the engine no longer working. A further examination indicated the ship could not float another ten minutes. "Then, sir," Semmes said to Lieutenant Kell, "cease firing, shorten sail, and haul down the colors; it will never do in this nineteenth century for us to go down, and the decks covered with our gallant wounded."

Following the surrender, shots were fired by both ships, each captain blaming the other for violating a white flag. Semmes said it was done "deliberately." Winslow called it "a trick . . . extraordinary conduct" on the part of the rebels, and laid the *Kearsarge* across the *Alabama*'s bow to rake her with grapeshot. The *Alabama* lowered a boat officered by George Townley Fullam and carrying some wounded men. It came alongside the *Kearsarge* and Fullam hailed the deck, reporting the *Alabama* disabled, sinking, and asking for help. "Does Captain Semmes surrender his ship?" Winslow asked. "Yes," Fullam answered. A second boat came with Dr. Galt and more wounded. On Fullam's promise to return and surrender, Winslow granted him permission to rescue men from the water. Fullam shoved off—and that was the last Winslow saw of him.

The *Alabama* went down stern first; her bow lunged high in the air, and then she was gone. Semmes, Kell, and several others were picked up by Fullam's boat and brought to the *Deerhound,* which meant freedom from capture. Two French pilot boats also rescued many, and the *Kearsarge* picked up 70. In all, out of a crew of 150 men, the *Alabama* lost 9 killed in battle (including the slave David White), 10 dead by drowning, and 21 wounded.

Shortly after 3 P.M., the *Kearsarge* entered port, where ambulances ordered by the French admiral relieved Winslow of the Confederate wounded. Among the *Kearsarge*'s crew of approximately 160 men, she suffered no fatalities and only 3 seriously wounded. The formerly blacklisted Captain Winslow received a congressional "vote of thanks" and was immediately promoted to commodore.

The Lincoln administration and the Union considered the *Kearsarge*'s triumph a sweet moral and political victory over Great Britain as well as the Confederacy. The British had built the *Alabama,* armed and manned her, and provided every assistance in the way of material support. Admiral Porter wrote, "When it came to fighting, the *Kearsarge* did her work so quickly and effectively that the blindest could . . . detect the difference between the true and the false coin."

*   *   *

The third foreign-bought cruiser, after the *Florida* and *Alabama,* was acquired by Commander Matthew Fontaine Maury. In late 1862, armed with his reputation as the world's leading oceanographer, he landed in England partly to influence public opinion on behalf of the Confederacy and partly to obtain and fit out ships of war. In March 1863, he purchased at Dumbarton on the Clyde the new iron-hulled screw steamer *Japan.* The building contract was drawn from the personal account of a member of Fraser, Trenholm as a regular merchant ship. At her launching, the name was changed to *Virginia.*

She was an excellent vessel of 600 tons, capable of fourteen knots, but a poor choice for a sea raider. Bulloch, for one, would never have bought her, and for the very reason of her modern features. An iron hull required a shipyard for even minor repairs, and the lack of full sail severely restricted her cruising range to the amount of coal in her bunkers.

On April 1, 1863, under marked suspicion of her true vocation, the *Virginia* departed from Greenock with a civilian crew ostensibly bound for Singapore. Off the Breton coast, she rendezvoused with the tug *Alar,* which carried the armament, war stores, and the remainder of the crew. When these new men in the *Alar* understood the charade, they refused to transfer over. As a sop to Ambassador Adams, the recruiters were later tried and convicted of violating of the Foreign Enlistment Act and fined £50 each.

On April 9, armed with a pair of 7-inch rifles and three smaller guns, the *Virginia* was commissioned by Commander William L. Maury (a distant relative of Matthew Maury), and renamed CSS *Georgia.* Shorthanded, Maury steered south. By the Canary Islands, off the bulge of Africa, he captured and burned the New York–registered *Dictator,* sailing to Hong Kong with coal. Maury induced a good number of this vessel's crew to enlist in the Confederate Navy, and he now had a workable number of hands.

By the end of October 1863, the *Georgia* had snapped up nine prizes, mostly in the Atlantic narrows hunting grounds. One was the bark *Good Hope,* bound from Boston to Cape Town with general cargo. Her master was dead, and his eighteen-year-old son had preserved the corpse in brine. Maury burned the prize, but brought the body on board, wrapped it in an American flag, and conducted the regular service for burial at sea. While the service was being read, a lookout hailed from the mast top of an approaching sail. Maury concluded with, "We commit his body to the deep. Beat to quarters." She was the bark *W. F. Seaver,* en route from Boston to the Amur River with machinery. Her master, not recognizing the *Georgia* for a raider, but full of concern for the burning prize, came aboard. "Can I be of any assistance?" he asked. "How did she catch fire?" According to Midshipman James Morgan, Maury said he "would stand court-martial before he would burn the ship of a man who had come on an errand of mercy to help fellow seamen in distress." Instead he bonded the *Seaver* and sent her off with his prisoners.

By July, the *Georgia*'s hull had become so foul that she dragged a lawn of sea grass six inches deep, and there was no way of scraping it without a dry dock. In late October, she entered Cherbourg and waited four months before being permitted to dock. In January 1864, she was declared unfit for service and moved to an anchorage near Bordeaux. There were plans to rendezvous with the raider *Rappahannock* and transfer the battery into her, but that came to nothing. In May, Commodore Barron ordered the ship to Liverpool for sale to a local merchant. At this Ambassador Adams raised strong objections and the deal collapsed.

On August 11, the *Georgia* put to sea under charter of the Portuguese government, bound for Lisbon. Four days later, unarmed and under English merchant colors, she was captured by Commodore Thomas Craven and the *Niagara,* "as a pirate, formerly cruising under the rebel flag." Taken to Boston, she was judged a lawful prize of war by the district court.

Matthew Maury's second purchase began life as the Royal Navy dispatch vessel *Victor,* condemned and bought at auction in November 1863, under very suspicious circumstances. Even the British authorities could not overlook the sale, and she was ordered held in the Thames for investigation. On November 24, with workmen still aboard and only a skeleton crew, she escaped under the pretext of sea trials. Once clear of the estuary, she dropped all pretense and commissioned as CSS *Rappahannock.* Her career was ludicrously short. With the engines failing in the English Channel, she drifted aground off Calais.

On orders from Flag Officer Barron, Lieutenant Charles Fauntleroy, who considered the *Rappahannock* a "white elephant," was placed in command. At Calais, the master of the French steamer *Nil* tried literally to bump the *Rappahannock* from her berth, "a reckless passionate attempt to compel this vessel to make way for his," said the rebel's executive officer, Lieutenant George Shyrock. The *Nil*'s owners sued for damages, and the court awarded a judgment of 200 francs. Shyrock called it "the most wanton insult that I had ever known to be offered to a vessel of war by the people of any nation, barbarous or civilized." The court sent a bailiff to nail the judgment to the *Rappahannock*'s mainmast, "in the presence of the flag." Even more insultingly, they placarded the city with bills advertising the ship's sale if Fauntleroy failed to pay.

This comedy of errors came at the height of a war scare involving the United States and Britain and France over the building of European ironclads for the Confederacy. France was not about to let the situation in Calais get out of hand. A French gunboat anchored near to keep watch, and the rebel raider remained interned for the duration of the war.

The career of the raider *Tallahassee* lasted forty days, when the lights were going out all over the Confederacy and the Cause declining to its certain end. She was built on the Thames as the *Atalanta,* a 546-ton, twin-screwed, high-speed channel ferry, a veritable flyer at fourteen knots and the very latest thing in naval architecture. During her early life as a blockade runner she was spotted by John Taylor Wood, late of the *Merrimack,* at Wilmington, where he recommended converting her into a commerce destroyer.

She commissioned on July 20, 1864, with Wood in command. The crew were handpicked veterans of the James River Squadron, making the vessel unique in having an all-naval crew and operating throughout her raider career from a Confederate home port. On the night of August 5, she ran the Wilmington blockade, as Wood said, "so close under the stern of one [Federal ship] that a biscuit could have been tossed on board," and headed for New York.

Flying U.S. colors Wood took his first prize off the New Jersey shore, the schooner *Sarah A. Boyce.* Seven sail were in sight off Fire Island light, one of which, the *James Funk No. 22,* sent a boat. In a few minutes, said Wood, "a large well-dressed man in black with a high hat, heavy gold watch, a small valise and a bundle of papers under his arm, stepped over the side"—a New York harbor pilot, seeking engagement! Up the *Tallahassee*'s mast soared the Confederate ensign. "My God," he choked, "what ship is this?" As Wood remembered it, "A more astonished man never stood on deck of any vessel. He turned deadly pale, and drops of perspiration broke from every pore."

Wood took the schooner's fresh beef and vegetables and placed on board two officers and twenty men to herd the coastwise shipping to the raider. In a short while, three vessels bobbed alongside and forty prisoners sat in irons on deck. Late in the afternoon he bonded the *Carroll*

Wood for $10,000 to take them ashore. The last prize of the day was another pilot boat, *William Bell,* which offered a $30,000 bond. Instead, Wood ordered the boarding party to "turpentine her and set her on fire." The next day, August 12, he took six prizes, of which the packet *Adriatic,* in passage from London to New York, with terror-stricken German immigrants, was the largest of the raider's entire bag. "It was some time," Wood noted, "before they could comprehend that we did not intend to burn them also." They were loaded into a bonded vessel and the liner was torched. Wood steamed for the New England coast as the fires of the *Adriatic* "illuminated the water for miles, making a picture of rare beauty."

Near Boston he took the bark *Glenarvon,* en route from Glasgow to New York with pig iron. Wood wrote of one of her passengers, the wife of a retired merchant captain, who "came on board scolding and left scolding. Her tongue was slung amidships, and never tired." Wood provided the elderly couple with his cabin. A Russian steamer was hailed to take them off, and "as a final effort to show how she would serve us, she snatched her bonnet from her head, tore it in pieces, and threw it into the sea."

In the fog of the Maine coast, Wood captured the *James Littlefield* with a cargo of smokeless anthracite coal, a very valuable prize. High seas prevented its transfer, and to take the vessel into a Nova Scotia fishing cove to loot her (as the *Alabama* had done at Bahia with the *Rachel Hatch*) would have violated neutrality too close to home. Very reluctantly, Wood ordered her scuttled, "to be a home for the cod and lobster."

Other than fishing boats, American seaborne commerce was now very scarce, the inevitable and direct result of Wood's raiding predecessors on the shipping lanes. Forced inshore to ravage the coasting trade, Wood found slim pickings. On August 18, with only forty tons of coal, he entered Halifax. The *Tallahassee* was welcomed by thousands of people at dockside, and her officers were feted by the local British regiment. It being a week after Farragut's victory at Mobile Bay, the official reception, however, was decidedly cool. Admiral Sir James Hope, commanding the North American Station, was outright rude. The lieutenant governor read aloud to Wood an order requiring his departure in twenty-four hours, and stipulated only enough coal for the ship to reach her nearest home port, Wilmington.

To determine that amount, U.S. Consul Mortimer Jackson persuaded the admiral personally to investigate her bunkerage, and Wood was restricted from buying more than 100 tons. On the second day in port, Wood requested an extension to fish a new mainmast. This was hardly necessary for the *Tallahassee*—her sails being nothing but vestigial—but the request was granted as coming within the Neutrality Act. Wood, though, changed his mind. He knew Federal warships were coming, and he contracted with a local pilot to get him out of Halifax by the least conspicuous route.

At 1 A.M., August 20, the *Tallahassee* sneaked through a narrow, unlighted, little used passage to the sea, missing the USS *Pontoosuc* by four hours. Reluctantly, Wood shaped course for North Carolina, burning one prize on the way. Six nights later, he ran the cordons of the outer and inner blockades and anchored under the sheltering guns of Wilmington's Fort Fisher. Wood's raid along the Atlantic coast vindicated to some extent the recent losses of the *Alabama* and *Florida,* and brought some small solace to the defeat at Mobile Bay. But it also brought a tightening of the Wilmington blockade, and seven of the best runners were caught as a result. "She certainly kicked up a fuss," noted the *Wilmington Daily Journal,* "but we doubt very much whether she weakened the military resources of the Yankee Government to any appreciable extent." It was an epithet that could have applied to the entire campaign of Confederate commerce raiding.

The *Tallahassee* was recommissioned as the *Olustee* and made another cruise, destroying six vessels. In December 1864, she was converted into the Confederate Navy blockade runner *Chameleon,* making a single passage to Bermuda for desperately needed food. Returning, she found it impossible to enter either Wilmington or Charleston and turned away. The ship reached Liverpool on April 9, 1865, the day Lee surrendered to Grant at Appomattox. Seized by the British, she was turned over to the United States and sold to Japan as a merchantman.

Wooden cruisers, with a wink and a nod, could be built as disguised merchantmen abroad, but that charade was impossible with ironclads. No one could mistake an ironclad ram for anything else. Turrets and rams could not be provided at sea, but were part and parcel of the ship herself. With ironclads, the only thing for the Confederate agents was to conduct the business as secretly as possible, and if not, to brazen it out and trust to sympathetic British officials. This brought the United States and Great Britain as close to war as the *Trent* affair, but this time, it was Britain—and France—that blinked.

From the beginning, Stephen Mallory had been interested in European ironclads. In May 1861, studying the French armored frigate

Gloire, he penned a note to navy Lieutenant James North: "The Confederate States require a few ships of this description, ships that can receive without material injury the fire of the heaviest [warships] ...and whose guns ... with shell or hot shot, will enable them to destroy the wooden navy of our enemy." He ordered North to try to buy an existing French ironclad, or if they would not sell, to place an order for one each in France and Britain.* "Such construction," he warned, "would have to be done in such a manner as to leave us unidentified publicly with it."

In March 1862, Bulloch in Liverpool turned to the local firm of Laird & Co., an excellent facility, nearly done with his previous order for Hull No. 290. For the sum of £187,500, exclusive of guns and ammunition, he contracted for two, small seagoing rams, twin-turreted, mounting four 9-inch guns apiece. With their 10.5-knot speed they would have been formidable adversaries for the U.S. Navy.

Bulloch made the deal in his own name, so there was no secret regarding their true destination. Ambassador Charles Francis Adams protested the ships as the grossest violation of British neutrality and the Foreign Enlistment Act. For his troubles he received only adverse rulings and shifting nuances from the British government and courts.

When Adams, continuing his protests against the Laird rams, was told by Earl Russell that insufficient evidence existed for detaining them, he decided to brook it no longer. Politically, he stood on firm ground. At the time of the *Trent* incident, the Union had not much to show militarily, and Wilkes had clearly muffed the seizure. But a lot had changed since then. The Union victories at forts Henry and Donelson counted for much, the rebels had been whipped (if barely) at Shiloh; New Orleans and Memphis had fallen, and the episode of the *Monitor* at Hampton Roads opened a lot of eyes. On September 5, 1862, after pondering Russell's thin excuses for the rams, the patrician ambassador, son and grandson of two presidents of the United States, dipped his pen and replied, "It would be superfluous in me to point out to your lordship that this is war."

Britain was in no position for it. Canada lay open to attack. Russia, thirsting to avenge the Crimean War was actively seeking a diplomatic and naval agreement with the United States. British ocean commerce (her very lifeline, as two world wars later showed) was ripe for assault from American cruisers, even now being specially built for the purpose,

---

* The French had one ironclad in service, three in the latter stages of completion, and ten just begun.

and the U.S. Navy itself was expanding beyond imagination. Three days later Her Majesty's government ordered Laird to cease work on the rams.

Yet Bulloch was not through. The Khedive of Egypt was known to be in the market for a couple of ironclads, and Bulloch arranged for a consortium of French banks, acting as the Khedive's agent, to buy and complete the half-finished ships. Once at sea, the vessels, named *El Toussan* and *El Mounassir,* would transfer title and flag to the Confederate Navy.

Ambassador Adams got word of the deal and officially informed the British government, which ordered the vessels seized by Liverpool customs officers. There is no doubt that force would have been used to keep them from putting to sea—the victories at Gettysburg and Vicksburg saw to that. In 1864 the British settled with the French banks, acquired the rams at a bargain £30,000, and they were commissioned into the Royal Navy as *Scorpion* and *Wivern.* To compensate the Confederacy for the building contracts, the chancellor of the exchequer transferred a like amount into rebel accounts. These funds were turned around to purchase the vessel that became known as the *Shenandoah.*

In December 1863, following the Laird rams' detention, Stephen Mallory wrote to Commander Bulloch: "From France, we think from the lights before us, we may fairly expect a different course." The secretary had excellent reasons for this optimism, for it was the Emperor Napoleon III himself who suggested it. "My sympathies are entirely with the South," he told Commissioner Slidell. "My only desire is to know how to give them effect."

Eight months earlier, contracts for four corvettes had been signed with L. Arman of Bordeaux and J. Voruz of Nantes, "subject to the Emperor's approval." Under the fiction the vessels were being built as Asia packets and required protection from Chinese pirates, the minister of marine permitted Arman to install the ships' guns. In mid-June, Bulloch and Arman signed contracts for two ironclad rams.

In September, with news of Gettysburg and Vicksburg still fresh, and the fortunes of the Confederacy in undeniable decline, the U.S. consul general in Paris bribed a Voruz clerk for the original documents showing the actual employer of these ships as none other than the Confederate Navy. Solemnly outraged, Ambassador William Dayton laid them upon the desk of the foreign minister. Confronted with the irrefutable evidence of his double-dealing, Napoleon III exploded "with horrified amazement," ordering all activity to cease unless the parties could prove without doubt the ships were not intended for the Confederacy.

There were six Confederate vessels in France: the four wooden corvettes, Arman's two ironclad rams, and the hapless *Rappahannock*. After several tries at fake sales, Napoleon III came around to appeasing the United States, which was now undeniably winning the war. In the spring of 1864 he met with Arman and ordered him to sell all Confederate ships to *bona fide* customers, or face forfeit and seizure by the French Navy. It was now Bulloch's turn for theatrical outrage. Writing to Secretary Mallory, "I certainly thought this kind of crooked diplomacy had died out since the last century."

Arman sold two corvettes and one of the rams to Prussia. The second ram, a ten-knot, 1,390-ton vessel named *Staerkodder,* mounting a giant 300-pounder rifle in her bow, was sent off to Denmark. But that country had just lost the Schleswig-Holstein War to Prussia and no longer needed it. After unsuccessful attempts to sell the ship to any bidder, Arman and Bulloch reached a secret agreement on behalf of the Confederacy. Under its terms, the *Staerkodder* would leave Copenhagen, apparently for Bordeaux, with title transferring to the Confederate Navy at sea.

Frantic activity occupied the Confederate naval establishment in Europe. To command the ship, Flag Officer Barron chose Captain Thomas Jefferson Page, grandson of two Virginia governors, who had spent most of the war in Europe. On December 17, 1864, he left for Copenhagen. The crew came from the interned *Rappahannock* at Calais. For their rendezvous at sea, Bulloch arranged for the blockade runner *City of Richmond* to take them out.

The *Staerkodder,* renamed *Olinde,* left Copenhagen on January 7, 1865, with a Danish captain and crew, and Captain Page as a passenger. Three days later, the *City of Richmond* weighed anchor from Dover and steamed down the English Channel to the Brittany coast. Reaching the rendezvous she found nothing, and her master entered the Breton port of Houat.

The ironclad had her troubles. Hit by a snowstorm, she corkscrewed through the seas, as Page said, "diving and coming up after the fashion of a porpoise." On January 24, she, too, entered Houat. Her officers and crew exchanged places with the Danes, Page hoisted Confederate colors and commissioned the ship *Stonewall.* On the twenty-eighth, she steamed into the Atlantic and headed south.

She was a terrible seaboat. Taking green seas over her maindeck, leaking badly aft, and very short of coal, she limped into the Spanish

Biscay port of La Coruña on February 3. The Spanish were cordial in their greeting, and apologizing for their inadequate repair facilities, suggested Page take the *Stonewall* to neighboring Ferrol, a major naval and commercial dockyard. He did so and work began, but within two days the Spanish yardbirds walked off the ship and all work stopped.

On spotting the ironclad, the U.S. consular agent wired the legation in Madrid. The chargé, Horatio Perry, bombarded the Spanish government with reams of objections, demanding the *Stonewall* be seized as a pirate. But all the Spanish wanted to do was get her out of their waters before any serious diplomatic damage resulted, and they wanted to do it politely. Orders went to the dockyard to resume repairs. The *Stonewall,* the embarrassed foreign minister told Chargé Perry, could "knock the Arsenal of Ferrol about the ears of its defenders and burn the town and go out to sea whenever she pleased."

From the American legation at Madrid, news of the *Stonewall* telegraphed its way across Western Europe. Anchored at Dover was the screw frigate USS *Niagara,* commanded by Commodore Thomas Craven. Formerly skipper of the *Brooklyn* under Farragut and disgraced at Vicksburg, Craven had been shunted off by the department to the very periphery of the war.

The *Niagara,* at 5,540 tons, with twelve 8-inch rifles and twenty 11-inch Dahlgren guns, was the largest and most heavily armed warship in the U.S. Navy, alas, she was of wood, as was her consort, the screw sloop *Sacramento.* Nonetheless, Craven arrived at Ferrol on February 14, the *Sacramento* coming a week later.

Except for rising anxiety among Spanish port officials, nothing happened for weeks. Repairs continued on the *Stonewall,* and Craven, to avoid the twenty-four-hour rule, took his ships across the bay to La Coruña. Thomas Jefferson Page had no great concerns. Once the repairs were done, he would simply take the *Stonewall* out and do battle. He even took a short trip to Paris to confer with Commodore Barron. They agreed on a strike at Port Royal, and a possible foray into the Mississippi. But in the dying winter of 1865, these grand schemes indicated a departure from reality.

On March 21, the *Stonewall* sailed from Ferrol and the Federal vessels immediately stood out to meet her. Nothing happened. Page judged the seas too rough and returned to port. It was the same on the twenty-third. Tired of the game, Spanish authorities informed the Confederate skipper that when he departed the next day, he could not return.

In these anticlimactic hours, Commodore Craven took counsel of his fears. Rumors of the *Stonewall* doubled the length of her ram to forty feet and her armor to eight inches. Wanting to neither impale his own ships, nor allow the rebel to escape, he considered running her down as she lay in port, much as the *Florida* had been taken at Bahia. "I feel sorely tempted to try it," he informed Chargé Perry. "My impression is that you had better not," replied the diplomat.

On the morning of March 24, escorted by a Spanish frigate, the *Stonewall* steamed out of harbor into calm seas. As with the battle off Cherbourg, thousands of civilians lined the shoreline to watch the impending contest. But the Federal ships, with steam up, remained at anchor. Thomas Craven refused the risk. All day long, the *Stonewall* maddeningly steamed back and forth, taunting the Federals to come out and fight. At nightfall, the ironclad turned south and disappeared into the Atlantic.

Coaling at the Canary Islands, she arrived at Nassau on May 6, nearly a month after Lee's surrender. The *Stonewall* was now a ship without a country. A cold shoulder and limited coal from the British brought the ram to Havana. Gideon Welles had stationed monitors from Boston to the mouth of the Mississippi, and ordered an ironclad squadron to the West Indies to search for the "pirate." At Havana they found her, and having no further right to fight, Page, for $16,000, transferred the ship to the captain-general of Cuba, using the funds to pay off his crew. In turn, Spain handed the *Stonewall* over to the United States, which sold her to Japan, where she served her long life as the *Azuma,* the first armored warship of the new Imperial Navy.

As for luckless Commodore Thomas Craven, he was tried by a general court-martial for "falling to do his utmost to overtake and capture or destroy a vessel which it was his duty to encounter." The court, whose members numbered the elite of the navy: Farragut, Paulding, Davis, Dahlgren, plus three commodores and three captains, found Craven guilty and sentenced him to two years' suspension on half-pay. Welles disapproved of the verdict as too lenient; "ridiculous," he called it. A second court-martial reached the same conclusion ("a shocking jumble," Welles noted in his diary). He again refused to sanction the sentence, and disgustedly restored Craven to duty*

When Raphael Semmes, on the last day of the *Alabama*'s life, told his crew they had destroyed or driven to neutral flags half of the enemy's ocean commerce, he might have added that a large part of the remainder consisted only of the whaling industry. Indeed, the *Alabama* began

---

* In December 1866, Craven retired from the navy as a rear admiral.

her career destroying a dozen whalers in the mid-Atlantic. The Pacific whaling fleet lay yet undisturbed.

In the decade preceding the war, the industry had peaked, counting 595 vessels aggregating 176,848 tons. Their products were chiefly whale oil, rendered from blubber and used for soap, lubricants, varnishes, and lamp oil. "Sperm" oil, an expensive and desirable commodity recovered from the head and body cavities of sperm whales, was used as a high-quality illuminate for candles. Whale "bone," from the mouths of baleen whales, served for corset and dress stays, upholstery, fishing rods, umbrella stays, and carriage whips. Ambergris, lardlike lumps in the stomachs of sick whales, a rare and highly sought product, was used to intensify the aroma of perfumes. At its zenith, an annual whale harvest brought home 328,000 barrels of whale oil and 103,000 barrels of sperm oil.

The habits and feeding grounds of whales had been known for centuries, but not until 1852 were they codified by Matthew Fontaine Maury's *Whaling Charts of the World.* The volume eased immeasurably the task not only of the whaler, but also of anyone seeking the whereabouts of the whaling fleet.

The campaign against the Pacific whaling fleet was hatched in the minds of Commander John M. Brooke and Lieutenant Robert Carter, both of whom had participated in the U.S. Navy's North Pacific Exploring and Surveying Expedition of the early 1850s. Carter presented a plan to Bulloch in London which with Maury's charts formed the basis of the campaign. Two cruisers were assigned to the duty: the *Florida,* taken at Bahia before she could enter the Pacific, and the *Shenandoah,* which began her career on October 8, 1864, the day after the *Florida* ended hers.

Bulloch had seen the *Shenandoah* at Glasgow in the summer of 1863, a "handsome and handy ship." She was the *Sea King,* built as a Bombay trooper, and had already made one voyage east bearing British soldiers to the far reaches of empire. Iron-framed, teak-planked, and full-rigged, the vessel displaced 1,160 tons, which made her slightly larger than the *Alabama,* and she came equipped with an auxillary engine capable of ten knots. In September 1864, using funds from the disposal of the Laird rams, she was purchased by Richard Wright, a Liverpool merchant whose South Carolina son-in-law happened to be the managing partner of Fraser, Trenholm. Confederate officers secretly assembled in Liverpool awaiting orders.

On October 8, the *Sea King,* with a cargo of coal, a British master and crew, cleared the Thames for Bombay. The same day, the steamer

Laurel departed Liverpool carrying armament, ammunition, and stores in crates marked "general merchandise." On board were Commander James Iredell Waddell, CSN, his officers, and several ex-sailors of the *Alabama.* The transfer was performed at a desolate rock near Madeira, where Waddell commissioned the vessel *Shenandoah.*

Waddell offered the usual blandishments to the civilian crew to enlist in the Confederate Navy, wages four times the standard amount, plus a bounty of £15 in gold. But the fate of the *Alabama* was too recent—only nineteen signed up and they were not the cream of the service. According to one of the Confederate officers, "I never saw such a set of curs in all my experience at sea." Counting his officers, Waddell had forty-three men to handle a ship that required a full crew of eighty-five. Standing southward, Waddell and his short crew converted the transport into a warship, mounting four 8-inch smoothbores, two 32-pounder rifles, plus a pair of 12-pounder signal guns from her original outfit.

The first prize was taken off the Cape Verde Islands, the bark *Aline* with railroad iron for Buenos Aires. Seven members of the crew were pressed. All American seamen were threatened they would be "made sorry," and "it would be worse for them," if they did not enlist. No attempt was made to coerce foreigners. Even after signing on, many of the new men were kept in irons at night.

Five prizes were taken in early November, one of which, the schooner *Charter Oak* of Boston, yielded a ton of canned tomatoes and a large quantity of preserved fruit. Six more hands joined the ship's company. On December 4, in the center of the South Atlantic void, Waddell sighted the island of Tristan da Cunha, and his first whaler, the decrepit, fifty-year-old *Edward.* Most of her crew were native Hawaiians, some of whom enlisted into the Confederate Navy. Waddell also landed twenty-six prisoners and nearly doubled the island's population.

Christmas was spent in a full gale passing the Cape of Good Hope. On December 29, came the only prize in the Indian Ocean, the bark *Delphine* of Bangor, in ballast. Before the prize was burned, the master's books were returned to him—except for a copy of *Uncle Tom's Cabin,* which was thrown over the side.

The *Shenandoah* entered Melbourne on January 25, 1865. Waddell requested permission to dock for repairs. The American consul declared that the ship was a pirate and must be denied all use of the harbor, all shelter, all facilities. The locals were of many minds on this, first agreeing with Waddell, then with the consul. Complaints that Waddell was engaged in enlisting were ignored, acted upon, and ignored again. As the consul reported of the Australian officials, "They have eyes that see not; ears that do not hear." The total effect of the dumb show led to the arrest of one man for cooking and selling meals to the crew at dockside, thus aiding the vessel and violating the Foreign Enlistment Act.

After three weeks, repaired, provisioned, coaled, and with forty new men in the crew that were not aboard on arrival, the *Shenandoah* sailed. On April 1, she approached the Caroline Islands. In the harbor of Ponape four whalers were taken and burned. Waddell found himself with 130 prisoners; eight were enlisted and the rest sent ashore. The next day, on the other side of the world, Jefferson Davis and the Confederate government abandoned Richmond.

Waddell remained for nearly two weeks, during which time, Lee surrendered the Army of Northern Virginia at Appomattox, which for all intents ended the Civil War. On April 15, two days after sailing and 120 degrees of longitude away, Abraham Lincoln was shot while attending *Our American Cousin* at Ford's Theater. Steering ever northward, the *Shenandoah* passed the barren Kurile Islands and entered the Sea of Okhotsk. They found the ancient whaler *Abigail*, two years out of New Bedford, and burned her. Thirty-five prisoners were taken, of whom about half signed on.

For the next three weeks the *Shenandoah* saw only ice and fog. Twice the ship was held fast in the frozen wastes. On June 14, Waddell headed east into the Bering Sea. It was now apparent that he badly needed an Arctic pilot. The second mate of the *Abigail,* described by one of the rebel officers as "a Baltimorean by birth, anything by profession, and a reprobate by nature," volunteered his services. He proved thoroughly competent.

Two prizes later, the *Shenandoah* took the supply vessel *Susan Abigail,* which had newspapers from San Francisco that were barely eight weeks old. There was news of Lee's surrender, but also of Jefferson Davis' last gasp proclamation that the war nonetheless would continue. This presented Waddell with a very serious situation. If the war had indeed ended, any subsequent actions by the *Shenandoah* were outright acts of piracy, for which he and the crew might be hanged. But he refused to believe the Cause was lost.

Instead, he burned the *Susan Abigail* and twenty more whalers in the next five days. On June 18, *Shenandoah* took eleven ships in seven hours, sending the prisoners back in four bonded vessels to San Francisco. Heading as far north as fifteen miles below the Arctic Circle, Waddell found too much ice and turned south, hoping to grab some of the San Francisco–Panama traffic.

On August 2, he came up with a British merchantman with news of the surrender of all Southern forces and the political collapse of the Confederacy. Bereft of excuses, Waddell dismounted his guns, stowed all warlike material in the hold, and so far as possible transformed the *Shenandoah* into a merchant ship. Having no coal, moving under sail only, and touching no port, he rounded Cape Horn and finally entered Liverpool on November 5, 1865.

Waddell surrendered to the Royal Navy, and the *Shenandoah,* on the demand of Ambassador Adams, was turned over to the United States. In her career, the vessel took thirty-eight prizes, of which thirty were whalers, two-thirds of them after the cessation of the war. She was sold to the Sultan of Zanzibar as the *El Majidi,* and ended her life foundering in the Indian Ocean in 1872.

The collapse of the Confederacy placed Great Britain in a serious dilemma. As Lord Salisbury said, England "had backed the wrong horse." Throughout the war, Charles Francis Adams had been laying the basis for a mountain of financial claims against the Crown for damages wrought by British vessels under Confederate colors, and the United States now demanded restitution. Collectively these were known as the *"Alabama* claims," after the most infamous of the raiders. An international arbitration tribunal was established at Geneva, sitting from the summer of 1871 to September 1872.

The United States demanded a gross sum covering direct losses for the destruction of merchant vessels, about 244 ships, and their cargoes; the expenses accrued in pursuit of the raiders; losses due to transfer of U.S. registries to neutral flags; enhanced insurance premiums; and prolongation of the war after the Battle of Gettysburg. The figure was computed at anywhere between $2.5 and $9.95 billion.* On fact and law, the British contested all points.

The tribunal, however, found for the United States, but hardly in the amount presented. They held Great Britain in fault for the *Alabama* and *Tuscaloosa,* for the *Florida* and her three offspring, and for the *Shenandoah* following her departure from Melbourne. A flat fee of $15.5 million was adjudged as equitable for direct damages, and payment was duly made. These were paltry damages indeed to make restitution for the destruction of the American merchant marine, whose demise has continued to the present day.

* About $32.5 to $129.3 billion in 1990 dollars.

"On to Charleston!"

"On the 5th [of April] the ironclad fleet of the abolitionists, seven monitors and one double-turreted vessel, hove
in sight from Fort Sumter."

—**Brigadier General R. S. Ripley, CSA**

n the fall of 1862, Commander John Downes of the Federal
gunboat *Huron* wrote of the goings-on at the Charleston
blockade. "I would be glad," he penned to a colleague, "if I
could only impress upon you some faint notion of how disgusting it is to
us, after going through the anxieties of riding out a black, rainy, windy
night in 3 fathoms of water, with our senses all on the alert for sound of
paddles or sight of [a] miscreant violator of our blockade ... when
morning comes to behold him lying there placidly inside of Fort
Sumter, as if his getting there was the most natural thing in the world
and the easiest."

Each of the naval commands afloat had their own particular problems, and Downes' letter hit the mark regarding the frustration experienced by Charleston's blockaders through most of the war. Like Vicksburg in the west, the city's defenders were resolute and gave not an
inch in hasty retreat, delivering just enough jabs and cuts to bleed the
South Atlantic Blockading Squadron almost to the end.

Until its evacuation in February 1865, Charleston, behind only New
Orleans as a prewar Southern port, served as the principal terminal for
the Atlantic blockade runners—the sleek, misty phantoms who nightly
played deadly hide-and-seek with the likes of John Downes and the

squint-eyed lookouts of the U.S. Navy. Through the blockade came 60 percent of the Confederacy's arms, a third of its bullet lead, ingredients for three-quarters of its gunpowder, and most of the army's leather and uniform cloth.

The docks fronting Charleston's Cooper River were crowded with runners unloading military cargoes, expensively delicate luxuries, or loading bales of King Cotton for the outbound passage. "They are seldom captured and charge an enormous price for passengers and freight," wrote a British military observer on the scene. While Southern currency was worthless and Southern armies often marched barefoot on a diet of fatback and parched corn, the fortunes in gold, pounds-sterling, or U.S. greenbacks for a successful voyage were staggering. The profits of two round-trips could pay the entire cost of the ship itself. Individuals and syndicates bought shares in the runners that returned a 15 percent dividend in two months, and doubled the venture capital in four. A $3,200 investment in one share of a fast blockade runner could be sold for $6,000 after a single round-trip. An ordinary seaman might make $100 in gold in a single voyage, and a $50 bonus at its successful conclusion, easily a year's good wages in peacetime. A captain or pilot could receive $5,000 a trip.*

The blockade-running vessels were specially designed and built for the swift, final rush from Nassau, Bermuda, or Havana into a Confederate Atlantic port. They often approached fourteen knots and could outrun nearly anything a blockade squadron could muster. Hardly the traditional, round merchantman, a purpose-built runner was described by a Charleston woman as looking "like a veritable phantom-ship . . . as she glided past. No ghost could have moved more silently, or looked more mysterious." Painted smoky blue-gray, the best color to hide and blend with the sea, sky, and mist, their collapsible, sharply raked funnels and pole masts exuded a true aura of speed.

For Confederate citizens with comfortable means, the Federal blockade was a great annoyance, nothing more. Into the narrow holds of the runners were packed discriminating goods of every sort: china, liquor, carpets, cigars, silks, and Charleston's favorite wine, Madeira. All flowed into the city almost as before the war. These goods and the fabulous fortunes they made for investors and runners, however, masked the dark side of the dangerous romance of blockade running. Often as not, the delicacies in the holds of the runners came at the expense of vital military supplies and mundane cargoes of salt, brooms,

* An 1860 U.S. dollar would be worth approximately $13.15 in 1990.

matches, soap, candles, kegs, and sewing needles—the stuff of life itself.

As the war entered its third year and prices rocketed upward, mercantile competition was stifled by the monopolistic gathering of huge wealth. The less affluent middle, farming, and laboring classes of the South suffered. Their Confederate money bought little and that only at ballooning inflationary rates. Those who were able had already fled inland, where food staples were more plentiful. Those left behind, often families headed by widows or women whose men served far away in the Confederate armies, became destitute. Unable to cope with the ever-spiraling costs of living, they were forced on inadequate charity, thievery, or prostitution.

Finally, in February 1864, the Confederate government confronted the scandal and prohibited the importation of luxury goods—what it termed, "articles not necessaries or of common use." Henceforth, all merchant vessels entering or leaving its ports were required to allocate fully half their carrying tonnage to military cargoes.

Exact numbers are difficult to gauge, but figures indicate that in the four years of the war, 1,300 attempts were made by steam runners to enter Southern ports, an average of less than two per day (a tiny fraction of prewar figures). Of these a little over 1,000 were successful. Charleston, for all its importance as a port of entry, counted only 115 successful round-trip passages through the blockade.

Though howls of frustration over the leaky nature of the blockade never ceased, the average runner managed but two turnarounds before being captured or run aground by the U.S. Navy. A total of 687 runners of all types were eventually captured, aggregating over $10 million in prize money. In 1861, one runner in ten was captured; in 1862, one in eight; in 1863–1864, one in three; and in 1865, one in two. Such figures indicate that the Confederacy had reached the point of strangulation.

Of King Cotton, the South's leading source of exported wealth, over 3 million bales had been shipped out in the last year of peace, as compared to 400,000 bales during the entire course of the war. With cotton selling at eight cents a pound in the Confederacy, and sixty cents in England, fortunes were made by only a few while the rest of the South starved.

In hindsight, Charleston, the soul and cradle of the Confederacy, might have been captured in the fall of 1861, right after Du Pont's victory at Port Royal. At the time, Charleston's seaward defenses were not much stronger than Port Royal's and far slimmer than at New Orleans, where the resolute Farragut pushed through. A bold dash past Fort Sumter by the South Atlantic Blockading Squadron at the end of 1861 could have carried the day. The army, however, provided just enough troops for the local operation at Port Royal, and the slim opportunity—even if Du Pont had been up to it—vanished. The futile endeavors at sinking the stone fleets to block Charleston's harbor channels had been a complete waste of effort and resources.

But by 1862, spurred by the navy's triumph at New Orleans and the unprecedented building program of ironclad monitors armed with monster 15-inch guns, a recurrence of "bombardment fever" struck the North. The cry "On to Charleston!" became all the rage. Gus Fox also unwisely told a congressional committee the "navy would have no hesitation in taking the *Monitor* right into Charleston."

In September 1862, General Pierre G. T. Beauregard arrived at Charleston to take command of the southeast theater of operations. "I found," he wrote some years later, "an exceedingly bad defensive condition against a determined attack." The energetic general got immediately to work. He obtained a number of old army siege cannon, converted the pieces to rifles, and mounted them in vital positions on Morris Island, guarding the southern neck of the harbor, and in Fort Sumter, in the center of the main ship channel. All the forts were reinforced and additional earthworks built to afford covering fire to blockade runners.

A defensive timber boom extended across the main channel from Sumter to Fort Moultrie, but it was a flimsy thing, hardly able to withstand the tides, much less a good ramming from an ironclad steamer. Beauregard's engineers advised replacing it with a barrier of twin, heavy, hempen cables, five feet apart, one beneath the other, connected by a thin web of rope netting. To hold it in place, anchors were fastened to the lower cable, and buoys to the upper. The top cable carried a "fringe" of manila lines, fifty feet long, that lay on the water's surface like "streamers," to foul the screws of any hostile warship. To seaward of the barrier, the engineers suggested two lines of tethered mines that would float just beneath the surface at low tide, each loaded with up to 100 pounds of powder. Beauregard ordered the whole system installed as soon as it could be got together. It was no secret to the blockaders, who watched the work through their long glasses.

At the U.S. Navy Department, Gideon Welles informed his supervisor of monitor construction, Commodore Francis Gregory, that the half dozen new *Passaic* class ships had to be finished by November 1862. "A demonstration is to be made on Charleston," he wrote, and he ordered Admiral Du Pont to Washington to discuss the operation.

Like every other senior naval officer appointed, Rear Admiral Samuel Francis Du Pont had been the secretary's personal choice to command the South Atlantic Blockading Squadron. He had done a very creditable job, shutting down the rebel coast from South Carolina to Cape Canaveral, Florida, until only Charleston remained as a haven for runners on his station.

But as with David Porter, though for very different reasons, Welles never completely trusted the patrician admiral: "a courtier with perhaps too much finesse," he confided to his diary. There was also the matter of age and temperament. Du Pont, coming on sixty years old, in the navy since he was twelve, was a very mature product of wood and sail. Welles questioned whether the admiral really had the fire to press forward in the new dimension of iron and steam. For the moment, Welles gave him the benefit of doubt. "Certainly," he wrote, "while he continues to do his duty so well, I shall pass minor errors and sustain [him]."

Since Farragut's sweep past the forts at New Orleans, the normally methodical secretary had also been gripped by a severe bout of bombardment fever. If Farragut and the wooden navy could do it there, why not Du Pont and the iron navy at Charleston? With that sentiment in mind, he placed before Du Pont a plan of attack to push a force of monitors into Charleston harbor, pass the forts without engaging, and once inside, demand a surrender under threat of bombarding the city.

According to Welles, the admiral readily agreed. According to Du Pont and his defenders, the admiral had voiced significant reservations. Captain Christopher Raymond Rodgers, former commandant of midshipmen at the naval Academy, now du Pont's chief of staff, maintained the admiral was convinced that naval forces alone could not accomplish the task, and that 25,000 troops were necessary for a combined attack.

Du Pont hinted as much in a letter to Charles Davis, "The Department thinks it can be done with a few monitors, and talks of four." Unlike New Orleans, he continued, the geography of Charleston, "is 'no running by,' the harbor is a . . . *cul de sac,* to say nothing of obstructions." Unlike wooden warships with their boats, booms, and tackle, the bare-decked monitors could not readily deal with these traps. "I hope and believe we can do the job," he ended. "I shall certainly try. All this between ourselves."

*   *   *

In Washington, Captain John Augustus Dahlgren, chief of the Bureau of Ordnance, and President Lincoln's unofficial adviser and confidant, felt the war passing him by. While his brother officers steamed along the rebel coasts and rivers, he, the navy's premier gunnery expert, was bound to his drawing board at the Washington Navy Yard overseeing production of his latest masterpiece, the gigantic, 15-inch smoothbore cannon for the new monitors. If things continued as they had, he would never rise to admiral's rank. Gideon Welles' firm policy precluded that; only officers tested in battle received promotion to that exalted height. For months he had badgered the secretary for a command at sea, and each time the answer was no, his duties and talents were more important at the bureau.

Welles had other reasons that he kept to himself. Dahlgren's reputation was that of a scholar-engineer, and for the past seventeen years he had ridden a desk at the navy yard. In that time, he wrote extensively and performed brilliantly, completely reorganizing and upgrading the navy's ordnance with his famed "soda bottle" guns. However, Welles wrote, "he has yet rendered no service afloat during the war, has not been under fire," and he doubted the fleet would accept such a man as a fighting commander. Several times Abraham Lincoln hinted that a recommendation from the secretary would be very favorably received, but Welles remained diplomatically deaf, confiding to his diary: "The army practice of favoritism and political partyism cannot be permitted in the Navy. . . . I am compelled, therefore, to stand between the President and Dahlgren's promotion."

Welles did, however, sympathize with Dahlgren's keening desire to hear the thunder of the guns and recommended a compromise. He would authorize a temporary leave of absence for Dahlgren to command a monitor in action. Dahlgren flatly rejected it. A single ship for a bureau chief he considered "derogatory," especially with people like Porter, "a mere commander," given an entire squadron *and* flag rank. Ill-adept at departmental politics, he tried turning the tables by threatening to resign his fiefdom before accepting the monitor command. Welles flat-out rejected it, "This," he wrote, "I can't countenance or permit."

But now, perhaps, came Dahlgren's chance. The proposed attack on Charleston would be spearheaded by the monitors, and Dahlgren was in the very forefront of the new technology, an ardent champion of the iron revolution in naval warfare. Badly misreading Du Pont's reservations as a refusal, he penned a formal application for "command of the forces that are to attack Charleston." Through private channels, he asked Rear Admiral Andrew Foote, Welles' boyhood friend, to intercede where even the President had failed. Du Pont was thunderstruck. To Gus Fox he wrote, "Foote made a most extraordinary appeal to me to give up my command to Dahlgren." Needlessly hurtful to a brother officer, Du Pont descended into dishonest hyperbole. "As I told Foote, he [Dahlgren] chose one line in the walks of his profession while Foote and I chose another; he was licking cream while we were eating dirt and living on the *pay* of our *rank*." Coming from one of the wealthiest officers in the navy, this was an absurd, demeaning remark—in fact, a lie. Du Pont, however, had no quarrel with Dahlgren commanding one of the monitors. "I shall be glad to have him as one of my captains." But nothing was done, yet.

The ten new vessels of the *Passaic* class were a distinct improvement on Ericsson's original *Monitor:* 200 feet long, 1,875 tons, almost double the displacement. The vulnerable pilothouse was built logically atop the turret, and engineering was aided greatly by an eighteen-foot, part-armored smokestack.

The ships had been designed to take a pair of the latest 15-inch Dahlgren cannon. Not enough were ready, and they were armed with one new piece and one 11-incher. To the horror of the department, it was discovered the *Passaic's* gunports were too small to permit firing the big gun; either a mathematical error or, as the naval constructors thought, John Ericsson's stubbornness. For whatever reason, it was a monumental mistake. The gunports would have to be enlarged to twenty-seven inches, a cut Ericsson claimed would weaken the turret wall. Hiram Paulding, commandant at New York, wired the secretary, "We are helpless in the hands of the iron men."

Welles sent his troubleshooters, Fox and Dahlgren, to straighten it out. They approved an Ericsson design for a muzzle collar, or "smoke box," that permitted the gun to fire inside the turret without gassing the crew. But another month had been lost.

The *Passaic's* acceptance trials were avidly reported by the press, and she and her iron maiden sisters were pronounced invulnerable. "A fleet of monsters has been created," noted the *New York Times,* "Volcanoes in a nutshell, breathing under water, steered with mirrors, driven by vapor, running anywhere, retreating from nothing."

With the department going full-bore on its monitor program, and public support a vital element in getting congressional appropriations, several uncomfortable facts were withheld. Much of the iron, both plate and bolts, was of brittle, inferior quality, prone to cracking. The ships were very difficult to maneuver, their sea-keeping qualities questionable—Du Pont compared their stability to that of "Susquehanna rafts"—and their ability to absorb punishment from seacoast forts remained totally unknown.

On December 22, 1862, the *Passaic,* with Charleston native Captain Percival Drayton in command, in company with the original *Monitor,* left New York in tow of their respective steamers for Port Royal. When the *Monitor* sank off Cape Hatteras, the *Passaic* suffered a machinery breakdown and was towed to Washington. With no facilities for the repair of iron warships at the navy yard, Ericsson sent a work gang from New York to fix, as Drayton said, "their Little Castle Garden on a raft."*

The *Passaic* became an instant attraction. Drayton described it in letters: "We are overrun with senators and members [of Congress] who won't be kept out. The latter I think as a rule about the seediest set of individuals in appearance one often sees, they all think all is up with the South now." With Treasury Secretary Chase "and some other important people," Abraham Lincoln visited the wondrous ship. Drayton told a friend that the President "went everywhere, crawled into places that [children] would scarcely have ventured into. . . . He looks more like a gentleman than I expected."

One by one, as they were completed, the monitors, captained by the cream of the navy, were sent south for the coming attack. Du Pont diverted the *Passaic* to tidewaters around Savannah to guard against a threat by a new Confederate ironclad, the *Atlanta.* The *Montauk,* skippered by Captain John L. Worden, who had recovered from his ghastly wounds, arrived in mid-January. To test the capabilities of the monitors against fortifications, Du Pont sent the *Montauk* to rebel Fort McAllister, an earthwork of eight guns, up the Great Ogeechee River, by Savannah. The fort itself, Du Pont said, was "of no special practical importance," but served as a good rehearsal for the big attack. Behind the fort sheltered the ex-raider *Nashville,* now a cotton-packed blockade runner, "which has been rather a thorn in my flesh." She would be a fine trophy to present to Gideon Welles after all the grief the secretary had received because of her nettlesome adventures.

Escorted by four gunboats, the *Montauk* arrived amid the creeks

---

* A reference to the round, brick fort at the southern tip of Manhattan. Formerly part of New York City's harbor defenses, it had been converted into Castle Garden music hall and later served as the city's immigration processing station.

and swamp islands of Ossabaw Sound at the mouth of the Great
Ogeechee. The afternoon of January 26, 1863, she led the force upriver,
anchoring just out of enemy range. By midnight, a reconnaissance
party removed the fort's presighted range stakes. They also discovered
a pile line and a string of tethered mines, marking it with a flag.

In the morning, the *Montauk* advanced to the marker and commenced fire with both guns. The Confederate garrison replied at once.
"Their practice was very fine," Worden said, "striking us a number of
times, doing us no damage." After four hours, he had expended all his
exploding shells and retired downriver. Everything in the ship operated
well, and the chief engineer reported that during the action the temperature in the machinery spaces had not risen above 104 degrees.

The action betokened success "for the *impenetrability* of these vessels," Du Pont happily noted, but he was very concerned at the *Montauk's* slow firing and very poor accuracy. Six hits out of sixty rounds
fired "give no corresponding powers of . . . destruction. Well," he jotted
to a friend, "I asked *myself* . . . if one ironclad cannot take eight guns,
how are five to take 147 guns in Charleston harbor?"

Not all of Du Pont's ironclads were monitors; he also had the *New
Ironsides* and *Keokuk*. The first was part of the U.S. Navy's original
three experiments in the iron revolution of naval warfare. Mounting
two 8-inch Parrot rifles and fourteen 11-inch Dahlgren guns on the
broadside, she was one of the most powerful ships in the entire navy,
and matched only by two or three in the world. Consistent with British
and French practice, she was also the most conservatively designed,
flat-bottomed, with a full top hamper of rigging and spars. Du Pont
chose her for his battle flagship and ordered her dismasted to bare signal poles.

Her designers, in a strangely innovative moment, bolted the armored
pilothouse directly behind the smokestack, completely obscuring any
view to the front. The only thing for it, save for a major yard overhaul,
was to cut the stack down to within four feet of the deck. This cleared
the sight lines but brought other problems with it.

In a test run at Port Royal, her skipper, Captain Thomas Turner,
conned the ship directly into a fresh wind. Without the natural draft of a
tall pipe, sailors on the spar and gun decks could barely cope with the
furnace gasses. In the pilothouse it was worse. "I found the atmosphere
so saturated with gas as to occasion even more inconvenience and
oppression than I had felt on deck." The chief engineer reported his
firemen suffering tremendously, "as to make it almost impossible to
keep the furnace doors open." Given these additional troubles, Turner

had the stack restored to normal height. Better to be half-blind than half-dead from suffocation.

The ironclad *Keokuk,* often mistaken for a twin-turreted monitor, was an experimental failure. Small, only 677 tons, the vessel presented a steeply arched turtle back, a high midship's funnel, and a fixed, armored gun house at either end. Inside, an 11-inch Dahlgren gun rotated on a pivot mount through one of three ports. She would serve the Confederates better as a wreck than the Union in commission.

In the cold, early gloom of January 29, the Federal blockaders executed one of their most spectacular catches of the war, a fabulous capture of nearly strategic proportions.

By 1863, there were certain consignments of specially manufactured goods the Confederate government considered too valuable for the regular system of blockade running. In shipping from Great Britain and transferring the cargo to fast runners at Nassau or Bermuda, many things could go wrong: there were too many prying eyes on the wharves and too many alert U.S. consuls.

For this particular voyage, Fraser, Trenholm, agents of the rebel government, loaded the cargo into the specially chartered *Princess Royal,* an iron screw steamer, capable of eleven knots. The shipment consisted of four complete marine engineering plants—engines, boilers, propellers, and shafts; 600 barrels of gunpowder; six 6-inch Whitworth rifles; 930 steel-headed shells; 35 tons of projectile steel; a complete outfit of machine tools for manufacturing large-caliber naval ammunition, along with mechanics to erect it; 1,500 ounces of quinine; plus quantities of leather, shoes, wire, steel files, pig iron, coffee, tea, clothing, and paper. This invaluable wartime cargo was worth nearly $360,000.*

The *Princess Royal* quietly approached the channel bar and was spotted by the weakest vessel of the blockading force, the armed schooner *G. W. Blunt.* The *Blunt* ignited two signal rockets, seen by a gunboat that forced the runner aground. The entire cargo was taken intact, one of the biggest prize hauls of the war.

The next day it was the turn of the rebels to take a ship. At the back side of Morris and Folly islands, southwest of Charleston, flows the Stono River, up whose lower reaches the Union gunboats made periodic forays of reconnaissance. On January 30, it was the *Isaac Smith*

---

* About $4.7 million in 1990 currency.

and the rebels were ready. Several batteries of field artillery were hidden under thick tree cover. When the *Isaac Smith* passed above the position, the gunners opened fire, piercing the steam drum and disabling the ship. The *Isaac Smith* was trapped without wind or tide to carry her out. With eight men dead and seventeen wounded, unwilling to set the ship afire because of the casualties, the commanding officer surrendered. She was renamed *Stono* and entered the list of the Confederate Navy.

But the day was not over, not by a long, long way. Close to midnight, the Confederate ironclad rams *Chicora* and *Palmetto State* cast off from their dock and passed Fort Sumter in complete silence. Pointing their bows to sea, they slipped like wolves into the fold of the inshore blockade. Both ships were improved *Merrimack* types, the *Chicora* being funded by a popular subscription of South Carolina citizens. The *Palmetto State* was a government-built ship that, like the *New Ironsides,* carried the pilothouse abaft the stack. Each carried a 7-inch Brooke rifle at the casemate end, with the *Chicora* having two rifled 32-pounders in broadside and the *Palmetto State* a pair of 9-inch Dahlgren smoothbores. The engines were minimally adequate, and under favorable circumstances the vessels could steam at seven knots.

Finished with leaky cockleshells and little canal tugs, deserving to serve in the best the Confederate Navy had to offer, Lieutenant William Harwar Parker had reported aboard the *Palmetto State*, flagship of the station commander, Duncan Ingraham, as executive officer. Unusual among ships of the Confederate home squadrons, large numbers of the crews, including some "regularly enlisted" free blacks, were, Parker said, real "sailor-men."

Shortly after the ships were completed, Flag Officer Ingraham and his senior officers got to planning. According to Lieutenant Parker, "we commenced to think of making some demonstration, and it was decided to attack the fleet off Charleston on the night of the 30th." In marked contrast to the *Merrimack*'s sortie, there were no crowds along the shoreline, and Parker was quite sure that very few people actually knew of the attack. "Charleston was full of spies," he said, "and everything was carried to the enemy."

But not this night. Save for the steam sloop *Housatonic,* the inshore blockaders were all converted merchantmen. They were good and fast enough to catch a runner, but breakfast for the iron wolves. In calm waters, under a bright winter moon, the rams headed dead slow into the main ship channel, calculating to reach the bar at 4 A.M., high water.

Parker expected to see a couple of small steamers behind, carrying armed troops to board and bring back any prizes. But for some reason, they had not come as planned.

At midnight, knowing there were still hours ahead until battle, Parker ordered "hammocks piped down." The crew were too excited for sleep, "and I found they had gotten up an impromptu Ethiopian entertainment."* Inside an hour, passing between forts Moultrie and Sumter, "the men began to drop off by twos and threes, and in a short time the silence of death prevailed."

As the time approached, the ships moved up to the bar and lookouts spotted the blockader *Mercedita* lying at anchor just to seaward. The Confederates burned soft coal, and in the clear night, with a full moon, Parker remembered "it did seem to me that our smoke, which trailed after us like a huge black serpent, *must* be visible several miles off." If the Federals saw they were dealing with ironclads, they could pile on the steam and leave the rebels in their wakes.

Forward, Parker's friend, Lieutenant Phil Porcher, tugged on a pair of white kid gloves, and stood with an unlit cigar next to the forward rifle. Not a whisper passed between men. Parker scanned the gun deck. "Just at my side I noticed the little powder boy of the broadside guns sitting on a match tub, with his powder pouch slung over his shoulder, fast asleep." Parker, who had threatened to shoot one of his crew for funking at Roanoke Island, let the boy slumber "and he was in this condition when we rammed the *Mercedita*."

The *Palmetto State* quickened the pace and steered directly for its prey. Out of the night came a sharp, high-pitched hail, "Steamer ahoy! Stand clear of us and heave-to! What steamer is that?" "Halloo," came the answer from the ram; then something unintelligible; then, "This is the Confederate States steam ram—" The sentence hung unfinished, when from the quarterdeck of the *Mercedita* came the bellowed order, "Fire! Fire!" Steaming straight-on, the *Palmetto State* smashed into the *Mercedita*'s starboard quarter, dropped the forward gunport shutter, and opened fire with her 7-inch Brooke rifle.

The ram bit into the *Mercedita*'s soft hindquarters. The Brooke rifle shell lanced diagonally through her hull, demolishing the condenser and steam drum of the portside boiler, instantly filling the ship with scalding steam. Blasting out, the shell exploded against the ship's inner hull, tearing a hole nearly five feet across.

Henry Stellwagen, he of the blockships at Hatteras inlet, com-

---

* Blackface minstrelsy, very popular in the navies of both sides.

manded the doomed gunboat. Asleep in his cabin, he tumbled awake at
the commotion of calling the watch. Precious minutes had disappeared
in the rituals of hailing, and by the time Stellwagen gave the order to
"Fire! Fire!," the *Palmetto State* had passed inside their range.

Panicked reports came up to the quarterdeck. "Shot through both
boilers"; "Fires out by steam and water"; "Water over the fire-room
floor"; "Vessel sinking fast." From alongside came a hail from the *Palmetto State:* "Surrender, or I'll sink you!" Stellwagen, relying on the
doomsday reports, which—given what he could see—he had no reason to doubt, gritted his teeth and called back. "I can make no resistance."

"Then do you surrender?" the voice demanded.

"Yes."

Alongside the ram came a white-flagged boat with the *Mercedita*'s
executive officer, Lieutenant Abbott, reporting the name of his ship and
captain, 128 "souls on board," and sinking fast. Now, however, it was
the turn of the rams to slip the time away.

This splendid Confederate opportunity heavily depended on the
darkness cloaking their true nature from the blockaders. The moment
they were recognized as ironclad rams, every Federal vessel would
race for the horizon, "and we," Parker said, "with our inferior speed
could not force it." The dawn was fast breaking, and Flag Officer Ingraham was in a quandary. There were no seamen to spare for a prize
crew. Had the missing troop steamers come up, that would have solved
the problem.

After what Parker thought "much valuable time lost," Ingraham
required the Federal officer to "give his word of honor, for his captain,
officers and crew," that they would not serve against the Confederacy
"until regularly exchanged" for rebel prisoners of war. Abbot gave his
verbal parole and returned to the *Mercedita*. By then, Stellwagen had
already set everyone to work, caring for the wounded, pumping ship,
stopping leaks. After about two hours, the engineers raised steam, and
the ship limped off to Port Royal, its officers and crew out of the war
until a proportional number of Confederate prisoners returned South
two months later.

The *Palmetto State* pointed her bow seaward to engage the outer
cordon. Some shots were exchanged with the gunboat *Quaker City,* the
Housatonic, and several other vessels heading for the sound of the
guns. Without exception they all sheared off when, as Parker said,
"they felt the weight of our metal."

Meanwhile, the *Chicora* crept up to the *Keystone State* in much the same style as her consort had on the *Mercedita.* The *Keystone State*'s skipper, Commander William Le Roy,* watched the suspicious vessel approach, slipped his cable, and hailed the *Chicora* to stop. From the ram came an answering "Halloa!" At this, the *Keystone State* opened fire. "I fired into him seven guns," Le Roy wrote after the affair, "one after the other, hitting him at . . . 50 yards, without hurting him."

The *Chicora* let fly her own, and in no time had the *Keystone State* in flames. Le Roy put his ship before the wind and called for the fire parties. "After our fire was subdued," he said, "we got ready, manned both sides, and ran for him to run him down or [he to] sink us." The ships exchanged rapid fire when, a little after six o'clock, a shell smashed into the *Keystone State*'s port paddlebox, shooting through the base of the funnel and into the portside boiler. "Then," said Le Roy, "we were done": twenty-three men lay dead, at least another twenty wounded—in all, about a quarter of the ship's company.

Struck again and again, with four large holes in her bottom, the vessel heeled over nearly to her beam ends. The boiler emptied, the fore part of the ship filled with steam, and two feet of water sloshed through the hold. Le Roy ordered the boats ready for lowering and threw the signal book over the side. "The ram being so near," he reported, "and the ship so helpless and the men being slaughtered by almost every discharge of the enemy, I ordered the colors to be hauled down."

In the *Chicora,* Commander John Tucker, "Handsome Jack" to the navies of both sides, saw the gunboat "completely at my mercy." He ordered his executive officer, Lieutenant Bier, to take charge of the prize, "if possible, to save her; if that were not possible, to rescue her crew." As the *Chicora* lowered her boat, Bier noticed the steamer, "by working her off [paddle] wheel," was edging away. He called Tucker's attention to it, and asked permission to reopen fire. Tucker hadn't expected "any deception or treachery" and hesitated "to fire on a ship with her colors down."

What followed is controversial. Tucker claimed, impossibly, that the *Keystone State,* "owing to her superior steaming qualities," widened the distance between the ships to 200 yards, rehoisted the flag, and opened fire. "Her commander," said "Handsome Jack," "by this faithless act, placing himself beyond the pale of civilized and honorable warfare." In his report, Commander Le Roy stated the Confederates contin-

---

* Who later in the war took the surrender of the *Tennessee* at Mobile Bay.

ued to fire after the flag had been lowered. Defining an opposite breach
of the laws of war, he ordered the colors hoisted, "and resumed fire
from the after battery."

Other ships of the squadron were now engaged, and the screw sloop
Housatonic, a true warship, albeit of oak, gave chase. Unaccountably, the
Chicora and *Palmetto State* reversed course back to Charleston. After a
running fight they came to anchor under the guns of Fort Moultrie.
Given this respite, the *Keystone State* got her pumps going, bent on sails,
and limped out of danger.

That ended the naval action of the day, and it was a disappointing
one for the Confederacy, no Federal ships sunk and only two damaged,
a meager tally for what should have been a string of captures and a
sack of prize gold. The two Charleston rams, for their high proportion
of sailors, and good qualities all around, could not even bring into port
a pair of converted merchantmen, both of whom had struck their colors in surrender.

Late in the afternoon, to salutes from the harbor forts, and cheers
from crowds of citizens, the rams got underway for the city. "But I can-
didly confess," Lieutenant Parker said after the war, "I did not participate in the general joy. I thought we had not accomplished as much as
we had a right to expect. As we entered the harbor, the Federal vessels
closed in towards their old stations and resumed the blockade."

Or did they?—not according to General Beauregard, Flag Officer
Ingraham, elements of the Royal Navy, and the press as represented
by the *Charleston Mercury.* When the U.S. Navy retreated to the horizon, several foreign consuls were brought to the outer harbor to witness what Beauregard and Ingraham considered the actual raising of
the blockade. As the *Mercury* claimed, "The British consul with the
commander of the British war steamer *Petrel* had . . . gone five miles
beyond the usual anchorage of the blockaders and could see nothing
of them with their glasses." In contrast, Parker could not even recall
the *Petrel* being there and considered the public statements "foolish."

Letting their euphoria take hold, Beauregard and Ingraham issued
what Parker called an "ill-advised" proclamation. They claimed that
Confederate naval forces had "attacked the United States blockading
fleet off the harbor of the city of Charleston and sunk, dispersed, or
drove off and out of sight for the time the entire hostile fleet." Thus, the
two senior Confederate officers "formally" declared the blockade of
Charleston "to be raised by a superior force."

"Of course," said one of the Federal captains to Admiral Du Pont,
"the idea is simply ridiculous," and so it was. No honest Confederate

naval officer thought for a moment they had actually done it. Granted, the blockaders withdrew from the bar, not returning until late in the day. But all were visible on the horizon, and at no time did any Confederate or neutral ship attempt to enter or leave the harbor.

In Washington, Secretary of State Seward burst into Welles' office, "in great hullabaloo . . . over a report that the whole blockading fleet ran away." Not for the first time, Father Neptune calmed his Cabinet colleague's frenzy, "Told him most of the stuff was unworthy of a moment's consideration." The majority of Confederate naval officers felt exactly the same. James Tomb, one of the *Chicora's* engineers, wrote, "They say we raised the blockade, but we all felt we would have rather raised hell and sunk the ships." The following day, a British officer informed the *Palmetto State* of the safe arrival of the *Mercedita* at Port Royal. As Parker remembered, "Our fellows said nothing, but like the Irishman's parrot, 'they kept up a devil of a thinking.'"

Yet the foray of the rams did sharply increase anxieties in Washington. Even Gideon Welles, generally solid as New England granite, stepped back. After carefully examining the resources, he told Admiral Du Pont that the five monitors available for the big attack on Charleston, were, perhaps, "inadequate." If the admiral judged his strength not enough to ensure reasonable success, the operation "must be abandoned." However, like the razor-sharp politician he was, Welles deftly wielded a doubled–edged sword. "The Department," he assured Du Pont, "will share the responsibility imposed upon the commanders who make the attempt."

Abraham Lincoln thought about Charleston constantly. Twice on February 14, he called Captain Dahlgren to the White House. The second time, Dahlgren walked in while the President was being shaved and General Halleck and Gus Fox were relaxing on couches nearby. "He let off a joke," Dahlgren penned in his diary, "the first I have heard for a long while. Abe is restless about Charleston."

The day following, Major General John Foster, the army corps commander at Port Royal, having recently spoken of the matter with Du Pont, proposed a combined arms attack on Fort Sumter. Halleck and Secretary of War Stanton introduced him to the President, Fox was called in, and the whole matter of the Charleston campaign was laid on the table. The President wanted to send Fox to Charleston as a sort of grand operational coordinator. Welles said no, he was needed in Washington to deal with Congress at the end of the session. The navy had too many bills that required ramming through, and Fox could not be spared from that chore.

Only if the President considered his presence on the scene "indispensable" would Welles permit him to go. Chastened, Lincoln yielded. That solved, Welles, furious with Du Pont for even mentioning the navy's future plans, briefed General Foster on the department's policy, "that the Navy could move independent of the army, and pass Sumter, not stop to batter it."

That night, Welles uncomfortably confided to his diary: "This indicates what I have lately feared, that Du Pont shrinks, dreads, the conflict he has sought. . . . It is not what we have talked of, not what we expected of him; is not like the firm and impetuous but sagacious and resolute Farragut." One week later, Welles could no longer stem the political pressure for Dahlgren's promotion, and he was recommended and confirmed in the rank of rear admiral, the sixth senior officer in the U.S. Navy, behind Farragut, Goldsborough, Du Pont, Foote, and Davis.

In his first bombardment of Fort McAllister, Captain John L. Worden had seen nothing of the *Nashville,* the blockade runner that constituted "a thorn" in Du Pont's "flesh." But on the night of February 27, she was reported aground, above the fort, in a part of the river called Seven-Mile Reach. Unwilling for such an opportunity to slip away, Worden advanced with the *Montauk* and her escorting gunboats. At dawn he opened fire at long range, and the *Nashville* was swept with flames. The magazine erupted, as Worden said, "with terrific violence, shattering her in smoking ruins. Nothing remains of her." A fortune in cotton had literally gone up in smoke.

Exiting the river, the *Montauk* ran upon a mine. Engineer Tom Stephens recalled "a violent, sudden, and seemingly double explosion." When the shaking stopped, there was lots of smoke, dust, and debris, but that was all. Stephens breathed an audible sigh, it was only the condenser emptying into the bilges. Beached for emergency repairs, the water was pumped out the engine room hatches, and in less than an hour, "all those having wet clothing were relieved and ordered to dress in dry clothing and take dinner."

That, however, was not the end of it as far as Worden and Stephens were concerned. The accident exposed what the Navy Department had tried to hide, the dangerous interior design and shoddy construction of the navy's revolutionary new iron ships. "I feel bound to complain in the name of . . . all engaged in the engine departments," Stephens formally reported, of "the indifference, the negligence" by the builders "to the lives and well-being of those . . . engaged below hatches. . . . No excuse for it, but unreasoning avarice, if that can be an excuse." Worden endorsed the letter to the department without reservation.

On the other side of the line, Confederate Navy Secretary Stephen Mallory convened a board of officers to study various plans to destroy the growing fleet of monitors congregating at Port Royal and Charleston. The result was the Confederate Navy's Special Service Detachment, commanded by Lieutenant William A. Webb.

In detail, his assignment envisioned boarding the monitors from a flotilla of boats and barges, fitted with special scaffolds to bring the men atop a monitor's turret. Each storming party was divided into target teams: one equipped with iron wedges to drive under the turret; another to smother the pilothouse with wet blankets; another to toss powder down the stack; another "provided with turpentine or camphine in glass vessels, to smash over the turret, and with an inextinguishable liquid fire to follow it"; and a final group equipped with "sulpheretted cartridges . . . to smoke the enemy out."

Sometime in February or March, Webb and thirty men arrived at Charleston and outfitted ten small boats with a spar torpedo. The *Stono,* late the USS *Isaac Smith,* was selected as a tender, and her crew distributed among the assault craft. Spar torpedoes were the latest thing, and Lieutenant William Glassell of the *Chicora* became a true believer. "I was now convinced," he wrote later, "that powerful engines of war could be brought into play against iron-clad ships." This was so obvious a tactic for the Confederate Navy that Glassell confronted Flag Officer Ingraham with a daring proposal. At half the cost "of a clumsy iron-clad," he suggested that forty, small-engined boats, partly sheathed in boiler iron, be secretly built to carry a spar torpedo, "and make simultaneous attacks . . . before the enemy should know what we were about." Ingraham would have none of it. "The Commodore," said Glassell, "did not believe in what he called, 'new-fangled notions.'"

Around April 1863 (the date is very unclear), Glassell armed a number of oared boats "for a practical experiment against the blockading vessels at anchor off the bar." Ingraham interceded, refusing to permit volunteers to participate, "saying that my [Glassell's] rank and age did not entitle me to command more than one boat." In time, Ingraham relented somewhat, allowing the lieutenant to make the attempt with one boat and six men against the *Powhatan.*

Near 1 A.M. on the given night, Glassell crossed the bar on the ebbtide, approached the target, and was hailed by the watch when still 300 yards off: "What boat is that?" To the question, "I gave evasive and stupid answers," and was ordered to stop immediately and come no nearer. To repeated orders and threats of fire, Glassell answered that he was coming on board "as fast as I could," and whispered to his crew to pull with "all their might. I trusted [the Federals] would be too merciful to fire on such a stupid set of idiots as they must have taken us to be."

Inside forty feet of the *Powhatan's* side, one of the boat's crew, "from terror or treason," suddenly backed his oar and stopped the headway. The rest of the crew lay on their oars in despair. The boat drifted, until the man who faltered threw his revolver over the side. By then, the muzzles of several muskets pointed over *Powhatan's* rail, and Glassell ordered the torpedo cut loose. Resolving not to surrender, or be taken alive, "till somebody at least should be hurt," Glassell cocked his pistol and ordered the crew to pull for the harbor. Shoulders hunched, waiting the volley of musketry that never came, the boat made good its escape. The man who ruined the operation later deserted to a Federal warship.

On the third of March, Du Pont ordered a second bombardment of Fort McAllister. Because the monitors *Passaic, Patapsco,* and *Nahant* could fire only one round per gun every seven minutes, the rebels in the fort easily avoided exposing themselves, shooting, according to Captain Drayton, "either while we were loading or just as our ports came in line."

For eight hours the monitors blasted away, withdrawing when all long-range fuses had been expended, "and the crew[s]," Drayton said, "were almost beyond further work, having been occupied at the guns . . . without even an intermission to eat." The *Passaic* was hit thirty-four times, with damage from a 10-inch shell that fell "over the bread room." Fortunately, the projectile was filled with sand, "or it might have set the vessel on fire." Yet, she suffered more damage than the *Montauk* had on the first go-up, which Drayton attributed "to a worse class of iron."

The exercises at Fort McAllister demonstrated to Admiral Du Pont that monitors were indeed equipped with superior qualities of resistance, but it also revealed their inherent weaknesses: too few guns, very slow fire, poor maneuverability. Convinced their offensive power had been overrated by the department, he decided that he needed more than four of them if he was to batter his way into Charleston harbor. On March 29, Dahlgren found President Lincoln sitting in the department chief clerk's office talking with Welles and Fox. "He looks thin and badly," Dahlgren wrote, "and is very nervous. Complained of everything. They were doing nothing at Vicksburg or Charleston. Du

Pont was asking for one ironclad after another, as fast as they were built."

By the first week of April 1863, Admiral Du Pont had assembled the most powerful fleet in the world to date: seven monitors, *New Ironsides,* and the *Keokuk,* for a total of thirty-four heavy guns. Every vessel was commanded by a picked, senior officer of long service and battle experience. If the attack did not succeed, it would not be for want of leadership. "Certainly no commander," said their foe, William Harwar Parker, "not even Nelson, was ever better supported by his captains than was Admiral Du Pont."

Du Pont planned to enter the harbor in single line-ahead, and "when within easy range" of Fort Sumter, 600 to 800 yards, open fire on its weaker, northwest walls, then steam upchannel to the city.

Captain John Rodgers' monitor *Weehawken* led the battle line. For the task, she had chained to her a novel, Ericsson-contrapted, minesweeping "raft." In shape, the sixty-foot oak structure resembled a bootjack, the notch fitting against the monitor's bow, and was so nicknamed by the fleet. To explode enemy mines, Ericsson designed a 700-pound electric torpedo attached to its front. Rodgers outright refused to carry the torpedo into battle, "since we might come into contact with some of our own vessels and thus blow them up." Instead, he knotted to the bootjack a number of dangling grapnels to snare the mines' mooring lines.

Following *Weehawken* in the battle line came Drayton's *Passaic,* Worden's *Montauk,* and Daniel Ammen's *Patapsco.* In the center, Admiral Du Pont flew his flag in the *New Ironsides,* commanded by Captain Thomas Turner. In the second division, astern the flagship, were George Rodgers in the *Catskill,* Donald Fairfax with the *Nantucket,* John Downes' in the *Nahant,* and the *Keokuk,* last ship in the formation, skippered by Commander Alexander Rhind.

On Saturday, April 4, the *Keokuk,* after planting marker buoys along the bar, crossed over with *Catskill* and *Patapsco* to anchor in the main ship channel.

The next day the fleet assembled. In the *Nahant,* sixteen-year-old First Class Boy Alvah Hunter could see the harbor fortifications with his naked eye. Nearby, some officers were examining the enemy through long glasses. "This," one of them said, "isn't going to be any such picnic as we had at Fort McAllister."

On the morning of April 6, the waters were dead calm, with a light blanket of haze touching the glassy surface. Du Pont wanted to advance at the height of flood tide, a tactic that allowed any injured ship to drift out with the ebb. At his signal, the squadron formed line of battle. Then another hoist from the halyards of the *New Ironsides,* "anchor." Alvah Hunter was stumped. "Everyone expected we would be under the guns of Fort Sumter within an hour, and the signal from the flagship came as a surprise ... why should we come to anchor and wait?"

The pilots, Du Pont reported, could not see over the haze, and he called all captains to the flagship. Observing the group, the admiral found them generally "firm and calm." The attack, he told them, would go forward exactly as planned the next day.

At ten past noon, April 7, the fleet got underway. The *Weehawken,* her bottom foul, and pushing the bootjack against the ebb, led at three knots. The channel's fast-flowing, shallow water, averaging about thirty feet deep, added to the difficulty, and the formation bunched up. Alvah Hunter in the *Nahant* remembered, "The clumsy vessels were here pretty nearly unmanageable." Aboard the flat-bottomed *New Ironsides,* her deck protected by 6,000 sandbags, over which were spread a layer of reeking, "green" hides, Captain Turner found his ship "could not be depended upon in a tideway." Inside half an hour, a disturbing signal fluttered from the *Weehawken's* pilothouse, "Foul anchor." She had tangled on one of her own mine grapnels.

The fleet stopped. It took the *Weehawken's* crew over an hour to free the maddening knot of chain and cable before she signaled "All clear," and the battle line steamed to the attack. From Fort Sumter's parapet, the Confederates hoisted the stars and bars and *Palmetto* flags while a regimental band played patriotic songs.

Near 3 P.M., as the *Weehawken* passed the final marker buoy, seventy-six, presighted guns of Charleston's outer defenses crashed out. Their accuracy was superb, and they struck the *Weehawken* with everything in their arsenal: armor-piercing rifle "bolts," exploding shells, solid and steel-capped shot. Fifty-three times she was hit. Inside the turret and pilothouse, three dozen iron bolts broke free. The maddening bootjack proved perfectly worthless, loosening the bow armor with hinging motions that were the opposite of the ship's. As Rodgers recalled, "when she rose to the sea, the raft fell, and the reverse."

The *Weehawken* now approached the double rope line of obstructions, whose mines were marked by several rows of beer casks. "To the eye," said Rodgers, "they appeared almost to touch one another." One of the mines exploded very near, lifting the monitor slightly, causing no apparent damage. But it caused Rodgers to turn away, short of the point where the fleet was to take position to bombard Sumter's northwest face. *Passaic, Montauk,* and *Patapsco* followed. All vessels behind were thrown into confusion, the *New Ironsides* lost steerage way, and the battle was already lost.

Admiral Du Pont was unwilling to concede. The monitors could take punishment, that alone was true, and he ordered them to anchor 600 yards from Sumter's east face and begin smashing away with their monster Dahlgren guns.

The bunching monitors prevented the flagship *New Ironsides* from getting closer than half a mile. Badly positioned, often within a foot of the bottom, Captain Turner had to anchor to avoid grounding, "which would have involved loss of the ship." Unknown to all aboard, she came to rest directly over an electrically fused mine, operated by a magneto at Battery Wagner, on Morris Island's Cummings Point. Nothing happened. Try as they might, the rebel engineers could not detonate it. Had they been able, the flagship would have gone down like a rock.

Near 3:30 P.M., with all formation lost, Du Pont signaled the fleet to disregard his movements and act independently in action. The *New Ironsides* was hit at least fifty times. Chief of Staff Christopher Rodgers recalled, "The fires of hell were turned upon the Union fleet. The air seemed full of heavy shot, and as they flew they could be seen as plainly as a base-ball in one of our games."

The erratic maneuvering of the *New Ironsides* threw the ships astern into confusion. The *Catskill* and *Nahant,* unable to check way, collided into the flagship's stern, slew around, then charged into the melee in front of Fort Sumter.

In the *Montauk,* Worden could not hold his position in the flood tide without risking collision. To equalize the incoming current with their engines, most of the monitors checked fire, turned their heads to sea, and reopened, "as opportunity occurred." For Worden, even with his pilothouse atop, rather than before the turret, as in the original *Monitor,* maneuvers were "a serious embarrassment." Under rapid, concentrated fire, with friendly vessels "close around me, and neither compass nor buoys to guide me," with mines to his front, and shoal water on his flanks, he knew "Charleston [could] not be taken by the naval force now present."

The *Nahant,* last but one in the line, entered late in the game. Alvah Hunter remembered, "Those of us who were stationed on the berth deck, where we could hear little and see nothing, found the long wait very trying to our nerves. . . . The relief we all felt when at last our guns spoke out was very great, and we gladly hastened to such duties as came to us."

But as his captain, John Downes wrote, "We soon began to suffer from the effects of the terrible and I believe almost unprecedented fire to which we were exposed." At 550 yards, a heavy hit jammed the turret while in its traverse, arresting further movement. Two hits on the pilothouse broke off a seventy-eight-pound chunk of iron that smashed into the steering wheel. Flying bolt heads mortally wounded the helmsman, struck the pilot at the base of his neck, paralyzing him, and opened up Downes' foot. Soaked in everyone's blood, and alone able to stand in the pilothouse, with a clumsy ship under him edging closer to the mine barricade, Downes snapped orders to steer the *Nahant* from the huge, manual wheel directly above the rudder.

Alvah Hunter saw his first wounded man when the stretcher party carried the helmsman from the turret. "I heard a gasping moan, turned around and looked directly down upon the gaping wound on the side of Cobb's head. Then for a few seconds, I wished I was back in Boston."

Last to engage was the *Keokuk*. Forced in the melee to pass ahead of the *Weehawken,* the *Keokuk* drew the concentrated fire of every gun from forts Moultrie and Sumter. In half an hour she was struck ninety times by every sort of projectile, including red-hot shot; jagged holes gaped at her waterline. The gun carriage of the forward 11-incher was knocked out of action, and most of the after gun crew wounded. "In short," said Commander Rhind, "the vessel was completely riddled." The *Keokuk* began to sink, and Rhind withdrew to shallow water and anchored.

After about three hours, Du Pont asked Christopher Rodgers the time. Told it was nearly 5 P.M., the admiral ordered, "Make signal to the ships to drop out of the fire; it is too late to fight this battle tonight; we will renew it early in the morning." As Rodgers recalled, Du Pont and the staff "had not the slightest thought" of abandoning the attack and hoped to reopen the battle at the first opportunity the next day.

Around the *New Ironsides* clustered the wounded ironclads. *Keokuk* was "riddled like a colander," remarked Christopher Rodgers, "the most severely mauled ship one ever saw." Rhind limped along her deck shouting that he didn't know if he could keep her afloat.

The captains came aboard to report. Sitting exhausted around the polished table in the flag cabin, they were unanimous. "I must say," spoke Donald Fairfax, whose *Nantucket* had been hit fifty-one times, "that I am disappointed beyond measure at this experiment of monitors overcoming strong forts. It was a fair trial." John Downes reported the *Nahant's* turret and pilothouse so weakened by the hits that the structure was in danger of collapsing "for want of bolts to hold them together"; fully sixty had sprung into the turret on impact from rebel shot. John Worden was convinced that had the attack continued, "it could not have failed to result in disaster." Each presented the same litany, "and when they had done," said Rodgers, "Admiral Du Pont went to his state-room and . . . he was seen no more that night."

Alexander Rhind spent those hours trying to save the *Keokuk,* "though the water was pouring into her in many places." The wind and sea freshened, the leaks got worse, and so large and torn were the rents in her side, "that it was impossible to keep anything . . . in the holes." Rhind signaled for help, and the flagship sent the tug *Dandelion.* At daylight, he said, "I saw the vessel must soon go down." They tried a tow, and failed. At 7:30 A.M., April 8, the *Keokuk* sank in shallow water to the top of her smokestack.

When Christopher Rodgers came on deck in the morning, he found Du Pont already there. The admiral had spent the night in deep contemplation over the previous day's events, and the choices for the new day. One ironclad was already lost, two or three were damaged enough to bar their effectiveness for immediate service. The fleet had engaged only the outer line of the harbor defenses, and even if they forced their way through, there were no troops to occupy anything beyond the lower end of Morris Island. "I ask no one's opinion," he told Rodgers, "for it could not change mine. I have decided not to renew the attack. . . . We have met with a sad repulse; I shall not turn it into a great disaster." The signal for damaged vessels to retire from the bar fluttered out from the flagship's halyards.

"A feeling of disappointment and chagrin at our failure settled down upon us," wrote Alvah Hunter. "We had failed." What of the damage inflicted on the enemy? According to the Confederate officer in charge, Sumter's east wall had been "badly bruised," the "crushing effect" of the 11-inch and 15-inch guns was "very great." But there was no material injury to the fort.

On April 9, General Pierre G. T. Beauregard convened a council of war to decide how best to take advantage of the shaken Federal squadron licking its wounds off Morris Island. The meeting held only a select few: the general, "Handsome Jack" Tucker (who had relieved Flag Officer Ingraham in Mallory's bilging of the ancients in the Confederate Navy), and Lieutenant William Webb of the navy's Special Service Detachment. Beauregard thought their plans would "shake Abolitiondom to [its] foundation." It was nothing less than the first, massed torpedo boat attack in naval history.

The next day, William Harwar Parker reported to the *Chicora* and joined "Handsome Jack" in pacing the fantail. "What is your opinion to making an attack on the three upper monitors tonight with six torpedo boats?" Tucker asked.

"I think well of it," Parker answered.

"Will you take the command of them?"

"Yes, sir."

"Now I never had any fancy for this kind of service," Parker said after the war, "in fact, it was repugnant to me; but this was a case of *noblesse oblige.*"

In the *Chicora*'s cabin, Parker spent the day honing the fine details. He expanded the operation's initially limited scope, and instead planned to attack every Federal ship inside the bar, explaining to Captain Tucker, "I believe it to be as easy to surprise . . . all the iron-clads as a part of them." The boats hiding behind Battery Wagner on Cummings Point would dart out and strike in pairs. If hailed, they were to reply "Boats on secret expedition," or "Contraband," just confusing enough to permit them to get in close. It was audaciously brilliant, and the genesis of surface warfare torpedo tactics for the next eighty years.

But the means were wanting. On Sunday, April 12, Parker transferred to the tender *Stono*. "We had about fifteen boats in all," he later wrote, "and as I looked at them lying alongside . . . some of them half full of water, and with inexperienced crews, my heart sank." He called the boat officers aboard to explain his orders. They would drop down with the tide, reaching the Federal ships by midnight, an hour before moonrise. Every boat must explode its torpedo against an ironclad, then race for the beach at Morris Island, where the crews would try a desperate escape run over the dunes.

Parker, in his private thoughts, saw no possibility of success. Neither did his old friend and academy classmate Lieutenant John Johnson. "It seems to me, captain," he said, "that when I explode the torpedo, the reaction will knock the bow of my boat in." Parker knew this likely to be, "but of course I could not express it."

When everything was ready, and the boats ready to shove off, the squeal of a boatswain's pipe announced the arrival of Captain "Handsome Jack" Tucker. Parker thought he had come to wish the men "Godspeed," but no. "Parker," he said, "you have lost your chance—the monitors are leaving—they can be seen crossing the bar." Parker thought for a moment: "I am glad of it." Tucker was surprised, "Why?" Parker took his superior out of earshot and pointed over the side, to the flotilla of half-swamped boats. "Handsome Jack" nodded. The whole thing would have been suicide.

On April 12, a melancholy Commander Alexander Rhind reported to the department with Du Pont's dispatches of the battle lost. Welles at once took him across the street to the White House. Reading through the discouraging reports, Lincoln and his secretary of the navy nerved themselves to hope the action had been only a poorly done preparation for the main attack. On questioning Rhind, they were dismayed to learn that Admiral Du Pont considered the battle final, not merely a check, and a defeat.

Rhind's personal report fell on very unsympathetic ears. "Rhind, an impulsive but brave and rash man, has lost all confidence in armored vessels," Welles wrote that day, his pen spiteful in the extreme. "Why Du Pont should have sent him home to howl . . . I do not exactly understand. If it was to strengthen faith in himself and impair faith in the monitors the selection was well made." From that moment, Samuel Francis Du Pont could measure his future career in weeks. The stench that had permeated the department at the back-stabbing of Silas Stringham over his failure to exploit the victory at Hatteras Inlet over two years back wafted anew.

Chief Engineer Alban Stimers, a leading monitor proponent, who had fought in the original *Monitor* at Hampton Roads, observed the Sumter bombardment from the Coast Survey vessel *Bibb*. He inspected the monitors on the morning after, and expecting massive damage, "was agreeably disappointed" to find their injuries not so much the result of enemy fire, but of design flaws that could be rectified in the new ships currently on the building ways. That was largely true, but, of course, was small comfort to the monitor captains on the scene.

Badly stung by press criticism and Stimers' remark, Du Pont did not exhibit his stoic, patrician best. He defended his conduct in volumes of self-serving correspondence and demanded that Secretary Welles publish all official reports of the battle. He also demanded the arrest of Alban Stimers and his trial by court-martial on charges of "Falsehood" and "Conduct unbecoming an officer of the Navy." Welles, to the admiral's chagrin, refused to publicize the reports on grounds they would destroy the public's faith in the monitors. As for Chief Engineer Stimers, a general court-martial issued no verdict and dismissed the charges as without foundation.

On April 24, the monitor captains, to a man, rallied to Du Pont's defense. Considering the press accounts "perverted and falsified," they composed a long memorandum to the secretary, "in the interest of truth and of our reputations." All of the reasons for not renewing the attack were laid out for Gideon Welles to see: shoals, tides, the "imperfect" steering qualities of the monitors, the inability to damage Fort Sumter "sufficient to slacken its fire," the obstruction line, the mines. To reopen the battle under those handicaps was to them "unwise in the extreme."

In a private letter, Captain John Rodgers chided the secretary, "Where things cannot be denied, admit them. . . . If public opinion backed by all the ironclad captains, in a solid body, would sustain the admiral, for Heaven's sake, let the Department shake hands with him rather than quarrel." So involved had Du Pont become over the issue of his public flagellation that he had ignored the Confederate salvage work on the *Keokuk,* allowing them to remove, under his incensed nose, the 11-inch guns, the flags and pennants, and quite likely her signal book as well.

On May 13, John Dahlgren plopped into a chair in Gideon Welles' office. "Well," said the secretary, expecting a confirmation of his views, "what do you think of Charleston?" When Dahlgren gave an unexpectedly optimistic answer, Welles, nonplussed, wondered why Dahlgren wished to go. The chief of the Bureau of Ordnance thought hard before giving the politic answer. "Not to displace Admiral Du Pont," he said, "or to promise to take the [city], but to do the best if ordered." Du Pont, he told Welles, had been right, there were not enough ironclads "to do the work with certainty." If the secretary wanted the offensive renewed, then "I would try," and suggested preparations go forward "quietly."

"Quietly" was the key word. Dahlgren felt there was far too little discretion. "Much chat in the Department . . . about Charleston," he noted in his journal. "Too many seem to know of the project." Everyone also knew Du Pont's relief was a matter of the smallest time. It would be a plum assignment, one for which Welles, Fox, and Abraham Lincoln each had his own candidate.

The Welles-Fox solution was a brilliant political stroke, though not a smart naval one. "An idea of two commanders surfaces," Dahlgren wrote, "one for the general fleet command, and one for the intended attack." The two men under discussion were Andrew Foote and himself. "Objectionable," wrote Dahlgren to the secretary, "on the whole it does not look like unity of action."

Fox suggested another way: Would Dahlgren "volunteer" to go as Foote's second in command? No, "chiefly because two admirals would only produce difficulty, and . . . the seeds of dissension would be sown from the first." Dahlgren had his own methods of conducting business "and would not yield them to any one." Nor would he expect Andrew Foote to subordinate himself "to his second [in command], and he would not do so."

On June 2, Welles put yet a finer line to the situation. He would order the next attack on Charleston as an independent operational command, distinctly separate from the blockade and the South Atlantic Blockading Squadron. Hearing this, Dahlgren relented. Fox, enthusiasm personified, jumped from his chair. Dahlgren must immediately go to New York and talk to Foote about the new arrangement.

The next day, the two admirals met in Van Nostrand's bookstore. Dahlgren noticed Foote "in bad plight with a sick headache." By chance or design, Major General Quincy Gillmore walked in, newly appointed to the X Corps, the army's Southern theater command. Gillmore, a skilled military engineer, was confident that given naval support, he could occupy all of Morris Island, plant siege batteries, and batter Fort Sumter into capitulation. Foote made no objection to the plan, or the divided naval command, and Dahlgren so informed the department.

But Dahlgren put little faith in the design of attack. Gillmore wanted to push 10,000 men along Morris Island's narrow beach for three miles, one step at a time, a maneuver that would negate his strength and expose the head of the advancing column to the guns of Battery Wagner. Furthermore, the ironclads could get no closer to Morris Island than 1,200 yards and their supporting fire was masked from the sea by high sand hills. "This," Dahlgren said, "seemed to me a small base for hope."

Dahlgren, like Gideon Welles, considered a naval assault alone as the "feasible" method, but only "if enough guns were taken in on the iron-clads." Three new monitors had just been commissioned and four or five others might be ready in October. Fox, however, refused to commit the entire allocation. Three was all the navy could spare; the rest had to go west, to Farragut at Mobile. "The attack," noted Dahlgren sourly, "will not be what it should be." On June 4, Andrew Foote was detached as chief of the Bureau of Equipment and Recruiting and ordered to Port Royal to command the South Atlantic Blockading Squadron.

Before any changes in flag officers took place, Admiral Du Pont capped his forty-eight years in the navy with a final, and well-executed, little victory. In November 1861, the steamer *Fingal* had successfully run the cordon into Savannah with the military stores that enabled the Confederates to fight the Battle of Shiloh. Trapped by the blockade, unable to exit, she was purchased by the Confederate government and converted into a 1,006-ton, triple-screwed, casemate ironclad and renamed *Atlanta*. Her armament consisted of two 7-inch Brooke rifles fore and aft, two 6.4-inchers on the broadside, and a spar torpedo in her bow. For a time she served as Old Tat's flagship and made numerous appearances in Savannah's tidewater rivers. In the spring of 1863, she was commanded by Lieutenant William Webb, late of the Special Service Detachment.

In early June, Du Pont had good reason to believe the ironclad was ready to come down the Wilmington River into Wassaw Sound and attack the inshore blockaders. To prevent another wolf-in-the-fold episode, he ordered the *Weehawken* and *Nahant* to reinforce the wooden ships on station.

Before dawn, Wednesday, June 17, the *Atlanta* and the small gunboat *Isondiga* were underway at flood tide. Webb hoped to surprise the Union ships, intending to ram the lead monitor with the spar torpedo, then turn his guns on the other. His officers and crew believed they possessed "the strongest ironclad in the Confederacy."

John Rodgers commanded the Union vessels from the *Weehawken*. He doubted the rebels reckless enough to engage two monitors, but he planned a careful reception nonetheless, stationing picket boats in the channel to act as a trip wire and ordering the gunboat *Cimmaron* to deal with any of the ironclad's escorts. A little after 4 A.M., the *Weehawken's* officer of the watch spotted the rebels coming downriver. Rodgers took a long glass and saw "a vessel built like the *Merrimac*." The morning calm shattered as the monitors beat to quarters and cleared for action. Rodgers slipped his cable and dropped downstream to build up a good head of steam. Then at four knots, the flood tide at their backs, the monitors turned bows-on to the enemy. The *Atlanta*, apparently stopped, lay broadside, a mile and a half ahead.

Lieutenant Webb had mistaken Rodgers' initial movement as flight. He rang for full steam and the *Atlanta* touched bottom. Throwing her three screws in reverse, and with the tide quickly rising, he got the ironclad afloat in fifteen minutes. The monitors were now less than a mile off and coming fast. He ordered the *Atlanta* full-ahead, but the rudder would not answer. The combination of the tide on the starboard bow, and the nearness of her keel to the bottom brought the ship back on the sand. Webb opened fire. Perhaps the *Weehawken* would stop, and he could engage her at long range. No luck. "On she came," said Webb, unheeding my fire."

The shots passed over the *Weehawken* and splashed near the *Nahant.* At a range of 350 yards, Rodgers opened with his 15-inch Dahlgren. The 400-pound, steel-cored shot struck the *Atlanta*'s casemate abreast the pilothouse, driving in the armor and ripping away a swath of woodwork three feet wide along its full length. According to Webb's report, this hit caused "the solid shot in the racks and everything movable in the vicinity to be hurled across the deck with such force as to knock down, wound, and disable the entire [portside] gun's crew" and half the crew of the bow gun, "some thirty men being injured more or less."

The *Weehawken's* turret revolved 180 degrees, and the ship slowed as steam was diverted from propulsion to training the turret on target. Rodgers had gotten the time down from seven minutes to four, and fired both guns together. The 11-inch shot struck the *Atlanta* just above the waterline, ricocheting off and doing little damage. The 15-incher slammed into the pilothouse roof, Webb said, "cutting the top off and starting the entire frame to its foundation." Everyone inside suffered bleeding concussions and splinter wounds. The next two shots from the 15-inch gun struck the starboard gunport shutter, "ripping up the armor and throwing the fragments inside."

The two monitors took position on the *Atlanta's* quarters, where the grounded vessel could bring no gun to bear. Webb would have to wait another hour for the tide to lift the vessel off, and he had no option but surrender. Rodgers spotted her flag down, replaced by another, but he couldn't see whether it was white or blue. After just six shots he refused to believe the rebel had struck her colors. The pilot reported the flag blue, and the *Weehawken* fired another salvo, smashing another gunport shutter. At that, a breeze stiffened the *Atlanta's* flag of surrender and Rodgers ceased firing.

Webb boarded and delivered up his sword. He and Rodgers were old friends from the old navy, and to spare his late comrade, Rodgers ordered the crew not to cheer. "Poor devils, they feel badly enough without our cheering."

The prize court at Boston adjudged her value at over $350,000. Because a 1798 law dictated that prizes of equal or greater strength belonged solely to the victors, the crews of the two monitors and the *Cimmaron* became relatively rich men. As a first class boy in the *Nahant,* Alvah Hunter received $176.16, the equivalent of fourteen months' pay.

*   *   *

A day after the capture of the *Atlanta,* Admiral Dahlgren got his orders to command the ironclads "with a special view to Charleston." In New York to choose an administrative flagship, he read in the morning paper that Andrew Foote lay "dangerously" ill at the Astor House. He went at once, "and soon learned that his illness was considered fatal." Foote was glad to see him, but in too much chest pain to permit any conversation. On June 20, Dahlgren met with his friend, "Alas! he was unconscious, and had in reality taken leave of earth."

In Washington on June 21, Dahlgren sat in church. He remembered "the service had not proceeded far, when a messenger from the Secretary summoned me." Welles offered Dahlgren command of the South Atlantic Blockading Squadron, "remarking that it seemed destined that no one else should do so."

Dahlgren returned to New York. Foote, he found "very low, and seemingly unconscious to all objects." When the doctor whispered that Dahlgren had come, Foote flickered his eyes for a second. "Dahlgren? . . . Dahlgren?" he repeated. "Who will fight for Dahlgren? Dahlgren's boys." He fell back and closed his eyes. The next day Andrew Hull Foote peacefully died and Dahlgren penned in his journal, "The grave never closed on a better man."

On July 4, a day after Gettysburg, and the day of Vicksburg's surrender, the *Augusta Dinsmore* bore Rear Admiral Dahlgren into Port Royal Sound. Christopher Rodgers came aboard at "early light" to announce Du Pont not yet awake, and Dahlgren deferred his call. Rodgers quickly got to business, briefing Dahlgren on the overall situation. Gillmore was ready to attack Morris Island, but required naval assistance. Du Pont had agreed to provide it, but preferred waiting until his relief. "A very loose state of things," Dahlgren wrote, "no shape or connection."

John Dahlgren was received in the *Wabash* with a rear admiral's thirteen-gun salute, and all honors due his rank. Du Pont stepped forward on the quarterdeck to shake hands, and displayed no rancor to his successor. In the afternoon, Dahlgren went ashore to confer with Quincy Gillmore. The attack, said the general, must go forward now— delay only served to strengthen the Confederate defenses. "So I had no alternative," noted Dahlgren that night, "but to grant the aid asked." On Monday, July 6, John Dahlgren read aloud his orders to the assembled crew of the *Wabash,* "and received the command from Admiral Du Pont. . . . So," he penned that day, "ends the first act of the new play."

That Friday, the day of battle, dawned "warm and oppressive." At the first peep of light, Dahlgren broke his flag in the *Catskill* and led four monitors across the bar to bombard Morris Island. An hour later, the Federal siege batteries on adjoining Folly Island thundered out. Dahlgren recorded the army's shooting as "incessant . . . the shells cracking in quantities in the air, heavy banks of smoke encircling the view." Beyond the half-seas wreck of the *Keokuk,* the monitors opened fire at the rebel field guns and infantry on the sand dunes.

At eight o'clock Gillmore's batteries checked fire, replaced by the sharp rattle-crack of musketry. In lines of assault boats, the Federal infantry stormed across Light House Inlet to a footing on the southern tip of Morris Island. The Confederates retreated down the beach toward Battery Wagner, harried all the way by naval gunfire. As Confederate Colonel Robert Graham reported, "the iron monitors followed us along the channel, pouring into us a fire of shell and grape." By nine o'clock, General Quincy Gillmore had thrown two regiments across. The sand dunes were overrun and a halt called at the flat beach that formed the sea face of Morris Island. At the far end stood the guns of Battery Wagner.

The monitors closed to 1,200 yards. Dahlgren would have preferred a shorter range, but for the shoals, and they began exchanging fire with the rebel artillery. The first three Confederate shots struck the *Catskill,* "and it was soon apparent," Dahlgren wrote, "that my flag was to have most attention." Indeed, it did, the rebels hit the ship sixty times that day.

The Federal ground assault stopped half a mile from Battery Wagner and could advance no farther. At 6 P.M., Dahlgren signaled for the ships to cease fire, "for the men were now weary and well nigh exhausted. No one can form an idea of the atmosphere of these vessels. I was a weary man that night, after my first battle."

Though not a great operational success, the day's action signaled the opening guns of a continual, eighteen-month bombardment of Charleston's defenses, and from the U.S. Navy's standpoint, a clear downturn in Charleston as blockade-running port. For the next nine weeks only four inbound ships made successful round-trip passages; a figure that dropped to zero from mid-September 1863 to March 1864.

On July 18, Gillmore launched his second assault at Battery Wagner. It went forward without naval support and resulted in the slaughter of nearly 800 Union soldiers, 272 of whom belonged to the 54th Massachusetts Colored Infantry.*

* About whom the film *Glory* was made.

*   *   *

August 17 brought the first of three devastating cannonades of Fort
Sumter, reducing the universal symbol of the war to a shapeless heap of
bouncing rubble. At that time, Sumter mounted thirty-eight guns of
varying types, including an 11-incher salvaged from the *Keokuk*. Anticipating the onset of a formal siege, General Beauregard ordered the
stone casemates filled with tons of wet sand and compressed cotton
bales soaked in salt water. The original sally port opposite Morris
Island, the obvious direction of attack, was sealed and a new one built
opposite, facing the city. Without these preparations, it is doubtful the
rebels could have held beyond the day.

At midmorning, Admiral Dahlgren, leading in the *Weehawken,*
brought the *Catskill, Montauk,* and *Nahant* to fire upon Battery Wagner. In the main ship channel, the *Passaic* and *Patapsco,* rearmed with
8-inch rifles, took position 2,000 yards from Fort Sumter. *New Ironsides'*
broadsides would provide smashing support where needed. On the bar,
seven gunboats added their metal at long range.

Earlier, Dahlgren's new chief of staff, Captain George Rodgers,
nominally of the *Catskill,* asked whether he should resume command of
his ship for the operation, or remain at the admiral's side. "Do as you
choose," answered Dahlgren. "Well," said Rodgers, "I will go in the
Catskill, and the next time with you." After eight o'clock, the rising tide
enabled the *Weehawken* and *Catskill* to move within 1,000 yards of Battery Wagner, and for George Rodgers it was fatal. A shot striking the
top of the pilothouse fractured the outer plate, ripping away the bolts
and a foot-square piece of the interior iron. The jagged debris knifed
into Rodgers and Paymaster Woodbury, killing both, and wounding the
pilot and a master's mate.

By noon the guns of Battery Wagner lay silent, though only for
want of ammunition. As for Sumter, the admiral reported the fort
"scarcely replied ... it appeared damaged a good deal." Indeed, the
gorge wall and northwest face were crushed, and a 10-inch Columbiad
knocked out of the fight. Only one man, however, was killed, and ten
wounded. That night the rebels began removing large quantities of
ammunition and stores from Sumter, transferring them to Fort Moultrie and other points in the harbor defenses. Within a month, most of
Sumter's guns were remounted on the city's inner defense ring,
replaced in the fort with wooden Quakers.

On August 17, General Gillmore began a weeklong concentrated
bombardment against Fort Sumter. On the first day, his siege guns,
joined by the 15-inchers of two monitors, fired nearly 1,000 rounds, dis-

abling seven enemy guns and heavily damaging the fort. The west barracks were destroyed, the casemates on the east, city, side received extensive damage, and a large crack opened in the main curtain wall.

On the morning of the twenty-third, five monitors, their turrets well sandbagged, took positions and opened a merciless bombardment on the fort. Six shots only came in reply, the last being from the *Keokuk*'s gun, the last cannon shot fired by Fort Sumter in the war. In the week, the army and navy had expended nearly 6,000 projectiles, with a combined weight of metal of more than half a million pounds. "Sumter pretty well used up," Admiral Dahlgren reported, but the Union was not through.

At 9:30 P.M., September 1, the admiral led six monitors and the *New Ironsides* to a punishing night bombardment of the fort. When only 500 yards from its walls, the Confederate guns across the harbor at Fort Moultrie hit the *Weehawken* at the turret base, driving a large iron splinter into Captain Oscar Badger's leg—the third chief of staff killed or wounded in two months. Sumter remained silent, all her guns were now of the Quaker variety. The monitors edged closer to deliver a merciless pounding. The city's population escaped the deadening late summer heat by watching the nighttime show from the waterfront. When the *New Ironsides* fired her full broadside, a reporter from the *Charleston Courier* wrote, "The whole horizon at times seemed to be on fire." The east wall crumbled, shells going completely through to explode on the inner side of the west wall opposite.

On September 6, General Beauregard knew an all-out attack on the fort was only a matter of days. The fort was nothing but a pile of bricks. But if the Federals had it, they would mount some heavy guns and pound Charleston around the clock, at will. Also, in Federal hands, the U.S. Navy could sweep the minefield and remove the barrier obstructions, enabling the monitors to steam up to the city's docks inside a week. In short, Fort Sumter, a ragged silhouette of blasted masonry, remained the key to the city and soul of the rebellion.

Beauregard confronted Major Stephen Elliott, his choice as Sumter's new commander. "You are to be sent to a fort deprived of all offensive capacity, and having but one gun—a 32-pounder—with which to salute the flag. . . . It must be held to the bitter end . . . and there can be no hope of reinforcements."

"Issue the order, General," answered Elliott, "I will obey it." Under a flag of truce, Admiral Dahlgren sent a surrender demand to Fort Sumter. "Come and take it," replied Major Elliott.

Also September 6, Quincy Gillmore's engineers, under the close cover of the monitors' guns, worked their way to the ditch fronting Battery Wagner. It was the first time these sappers had been able to work in daylight. Before then, Dahlgren said, "a man could not show a finger." The following morning the rebels had gone and all of Morris Island fell to the Union. The news spread to the fleet. According to Commander Thomas Stevens, new skipper of the *Patapsco,* "speculation was rife as to what the next move would be. . . . 'On to Charleston!' was the prevailing sentiment."

The unexpected evacuation of Morris Island caught the Federals by surprise and there was no swift follow-up. Instead, Dahlgren and Gillmore set to bickering. The Confederates, in possession of the *Keokuk*'s signal book, read every visual message passing between the two men.

On September 7, Commander Stevens brought the *Patapsco, Weehawken,* and *Lehigh* up to the barricade line, within 150 yards of Sumter. "We did not see a man on Sumter," he reported, "nor any sign of a gun on the channel face." Shortly after, Stevens had dinner aboard the *New Ironsides.* "We had just lighted our pipes," he recalled, when Sam Preston, Dahlgren's young flag lieutenant entered the wardroom. He told Stevens the admiral intended to attack Fort Sumter that night, in a flotilla of ships' boats, and "You are selected to command."

Stevens wanted no part of the harebrained scheme and he let Admiral Dahlgren know it. For one thing, there was no accurate intelligence regarding the fort's garrison. Nor were means being provided for scaling walls, nor time given to prepare "for the proper organization of a force for service of so desperate a character." Stevens also felt the rebels "fully notified" by the congestion of so many boats around the flagship.

In an act of marked courage, Stevens formally declined the command, an action that might have ended any advancement in his naval career. The admiral remained silent for a moment. "You have only to go and take possession," he said softly. "You will find nothing but a corporal's guard to oppose you." Stevens saluted and wordlessly nodded his assent.

As Stevens and several officers conferred on the assault, word came that General Gillmore planned his own boat attack on Fort Sumter, a much bigger one, with two regiments under the command of a brigadier general. "To insure success," Gillmore suggested he and Dahlgren combine forces "under the command of the senior [army] officer." Stevens remembered, "the admiral would not consent to this, on the ground that it was a boat expedition and purely naval in character."

Dahlgren's refusal to cooperate with the army caused Stevens to rethink his own grudging participation. But his colleagues would not let him withdraw. "If you do not go," said Sam Preston, the flag lieutenant, "the naval demonstration will fall through and the army will reap all the glory." Stevens remained unconvinced but "I reluctantly consented to go."

Several messages now passed between the senior officers. Gillmore was appalled at Dahlgren's stiff-necked attitude. The general greatly feared "some accident" taking place between the lines of boats bumping around in the night, and were it not too late, he would have recalled his own attack.

For the next hour or so, Dahlgren fuddled around, sending insulting queries to General Gillmore. "I am waiting an answer," said his last message. As it happened, there would be no army operation that night against Fort Sumter. Gillmore's boats, hidden in the creeks around Morris Island, were held back by low tides, and it would be purely the navy's show.

On board the *Wabash,* the quartermaster struck five bells in the evening watch, 10:30 P.M., and Stevens made ready to leave. Just then, the ship's commanding officer, Alexander Rhind, suggested that one division of boats be sent around Sumter as a feint to reconnoiter rebel strength. The main body of the 400-man combined sailor and marine force was to wait in easy pulling distance for a blind-side assault. Stevens considered the merits and agreed. He shoved off in the admiral's barge, twenty ships' boats, in five divisions, behind him.

Under bright stars, the tug *Daffodil* brought them to the line of departure, marked by the comforting presence of the *Montauk* and *Lehigh.* "We moved slowly on our way," Stevens said, "and nothing was seen ahead but the grim, half-defined outline of the fort." When the tug could go no farther, Stevens cast off, and the feint division disappeared into the night. Now came the first calamity. Thinking it was a general movement, "most of the division commanders dashed off also." Stevens vainly tried to recall them. There was nothing left for him to do but order the remaining boats "to make the best of their way to the fort."

In a few minutes, they were spotted and hailed from the fort. Major Elliott had been waiting, a third of the garrison was posted on the parapet, and the rest were ready to reinforce any point "with promptness." A little to the north, the rebel ironclad *Chicora* took position against any flanking naval movement. The Confederates shot a rocket from the walls. When it exploded, Stevens recalled, "the air was filled with shrieking missiles from the [harbor] batteries, which seemed alive with

fire, while an ironclad was pouring grape and canister into the boats."
The tops of the blasted walls suddenly filled with men, "pouring a murderous fire," throwing down grenades and blocks of masonry. "The
'corporal's guard,' that we were to have encountered," Stevens wrote
after the war, "proved to exceed our own numbers." He grabbed his
hailing trumpet: "Retreat! Retreat!" he shouted.

Lieutenant Francis Higgenson,* leading the feint division, reached
Sumter's northeast face without being seen. He attempted a landing,
but it was the wrong place. "I found myself," he reported, "upon a narrow ledge of sharp rocks, in which no foothold could be obtained."
After several tries, his boats in danger of being stove on the rocks,
Higgenson withdrew. Off the southeast wall he found the unbelievable
confusion of Stevens' retreat, and he followed on. Empty boats, their
crews taken prisoner, bobbed around him. The whole thing was an
unmitigated disaster. Out of 400 bluejackets and marines, the navy had
lost 4 men killed, 19 wounded, and 102, including 10 officers, captured.

Relations between the services became very strained. In October,
two senior army officers called on Gideon Welles at the department.
"They come from Gillmore," he wrote, denouncing "Dahlgren as
incompetent, imbecile, and insane . . . totally unfit for his position." The
charges were, of course, overblown. "He is neither a fool nor insane,"
said Welles. But there came no praise either. The appointment was
wrong. "Both Dahlgren and Gillmore are out of place," he penned in his
diary, "they are both intelligent, but they can better acquit themselves
as ordnance officers than in active command."

Despite reverses, Confederate efforts at building torpedo vessels continued through the summer and autumn of 1863. The latest venture was
the product of locomotive designer Ross Winan of Baltimore. The pro-
totype was privately financed and constructed at Stony Landing, thirty
miles from Charleston. The laborers were nearly all plantation slaves
supervised by a prominent physician, Dr. St. Julian Ravenel. The cigar-
shaped craft measured about fifty-four feet by six, heavily ballasted to
ride low in the water, and held a four-man crew in an open cockpit
amidships. An old locomotive engine, ending in a tall, thin funnel forward, pushed her at six knots. A 100-pound spar torpedo extended over
the bow. At the suggestion of Ravenel's wife, the craft was named
David, a name later attached to all Confederate vessels of the type.

* Higgenson commanded the battleship *Massachusetts* at the Battle of
Santiago during the Spanish-American War.

In late summer the *David* moved by rail to Charleston and was turned over to Lieutenant Glassell for trials. They were successful, and on their completion he received permission to take her out and attack the *New Ironsides*. On October 5, a little after dark, Glassell and a volunteer crew left their wharf and slipped down harbor with the ebb tide. He knew from recent prisoners of war that the Federal fleet was expecting a torpedo attack, "and were prepared for it." Glassell concluded that if the *New Ironsides'* officer of the watch were disabled quickly, the resulting confusion would greatly aid in the operation and the escape. The *David* carried four double-barreled shotguns, and "I determined that if the occasion offered, I would commence by firing the first shot."

Glassell ordered a full head of steam, and took over the helm, "it being so arranged that I could sit on deck and work the wheel with my feet." When 300 yards from the target, they were hailed from the deck, "Boat ahoy! Boat ahoy!" rapidly repeated several times. Steaming straight on, Glassell cocked both barrels of his shotgun and made no answer. In seconds, *New Ironsides'* officer of the watch appeared at the rail, bellowing "What boat is that?" The distance was now forty yards and Glassell fired. Acting Master Howard fell back, mortally wounded.

The spar torpedo struck the *New Ironsides* under her starboard quarter, throwing up a high column of water that plunged down on the *David,* quenching her fires. The engine dead, the craft bumped along the frigate's side, potted by intense musket fire. Glassell ordered his men to grab some cork floats and swim for it. The pilot could not, and stayed with the boat. A short time later, he was joined by the returning engineer who restarted the fires, and together they brought the *David* safely back to Charleston.

Lieutenant Glassell and Seaman Sullivan were not so fortunate. After an hour in the water, Glassell was picked up and taken to the gunboat *Ottawa*. When Dahlgren learned of the capture, he ordered Glassell placed in irons, and if uncooperative, in double irons. The *Ottawa's* skipper was a friend of Glassell from prewar days. He intervened with the admiral and obtained open arrest in the ship for the prisoner. Sullivan was found clinging to the *New Ironsides'* rudder, hauled aboard, and thrown in the brig in irons.

The Northern press screamed for their heads, in fact, the New York papers demanded they be hanged for "using an engine of war not recognized by civilized nations." Taken as prisoners of war to Fort Warren, Massachusetts, both men were eventually exchanged for the commanding officer and a seaman of the ex-*Isaac Smith*.

The Confederacy also constructed the only true submarine of the Civil War, the *H. L. Hunley.* Named for one of its designer-financiers, it was built at Mobile from iron boilers and completed in the spring of 1863. The craft measured forty feet in length and carried nine men (eight cranking the propeller and a commander/helmsman). Diving and surfacing were accomplished by hand-pumped ballast tanks. Underwater navigation was by means of a compass lit by a single candle. In August 1863, following successful trials, General Beauregard ordered the boat to Charleston.

She arrived on flatcars in midmonth, and by December, had killed at least twelve men in diving accidents—five from the *Chicora* and seven civilians, "found in a bunch near the manhole." Some accounts state as many as forty men were killed in her during her career. Beauregard seriously contemplated withdrawing the craft from service. His mind was changed only when Lieutenant George Dixon, a badly wounded infantry officer who once commanded the boat, volunteered again. For a crew, Beauregard permitted him to recruit volunteers from the receiving ship *Indian Chief,* along whose side the submarine last plunged to the bottom with all on board. Not surprisingly, none stepped forward.

But a full, eight-man crew was raised somewhere, and through January 1864, the *Hunley* was more than once towed by the *David* to the harbor entrance in hopes of catching a blockader. The *David's* skipper, James Tomb, a first assistant engineer of the Confederate Navy, made it quite clear the submarine was "not under the orders of the Navy." He considered Dixon "a very brave and cool-headed man," but no seaman, and certainly no authority on naval ordnance. The *Hunley's* original weapon was a towed mine, delivered by the submarine diving beneath the target, detonating the weapon when reaching the opposite side. Tomb considered this suicidally dangerous and suggested to Dixon "The only way to use a torpedo was on the same plan as the *David*—a spar torpedo—and to strike with his boat on the surface." Dixon demurred, and adapted to reason only when the navy refused further cooperation if he did not.

Admiral Dahlgren held a fair inkling what was afoot. Since the *David's* attack on the *New Ironsides,* he had ordered all ironclads to have picket boats rowing guard, and antitorpedo nets weighted with shot, rigged outboard the hulls. Howitzers were to be kept loaded, and calcium flares ready to light. "It is also advisable," he wrote in general orders, "not to anchor in the deepest part of the channel." Shallow water impeded the submarine's diving potential, and made salvage easier should disaster strike. He also knew from deserters that "the *Diver*," as the *Hunley* was sometimes called, "is also ready."

On February 17, 1864, Lieutenant Dixon got a break in the weather, and slipped from a pier at Breach Inlet, near Fort Mouitrie. Aided by the ebb tide, his eight men at the hand-cranked propeller shaft moved the craft at something like three knots. Attached to her bow, a barbed spike held a 90-pound spar torpedo. Two miles away, anchored in twenty-seven feet of water, lay the steam sloop *Housatonic*.

The *Hunley* approached partially submerged, only her two, squat, glass-windowed conning towers showing above the surface. At 8:45 P.M., when about 100 yards off, the *Housatonic*'s officer of the watch discovered an object that "had the appearance of a plank moving in the water." He sounded the alarm immediately, but too late for guns to bear. Frantically, the crew opened small arms fire and tried to slip the cable. But in less than two minutes from the sighting, just as the ship gathered sternway, the *Hunley*'s torpedo struck starboard by the mizzenmast, in line with the magazine, blowing off the whole after end of the ship. She went down very fast, masts above the water. Somehow, two boats were launched and picked up a number of the crew, the rest climbed into the rigging to await rescue. Only 5 men out of approximately 150 were killed. She was the first ship sunk by a submarine in the history of naval warfare.

The *Hunley*, the world's first "successful" submarine, disappeared. Either she blew up with her own torpedo, was crushed by the sinking *Housatonic,* or simply washed out to sea, lost forever. That day, Admiral Dahlgren wrote in his diary, "Torpedoes have been laughed at; but this disaster ends that."

The blockade of Charleston settled into stalemate, neither side able to budge the other from its final positions. The rubble at Fort Sumter received two more major and eight minor bombardments. In all, from Du Pont's abortive attack of April 1863 until the end, the fort was subjected to 280 days of fire and 28,000 projectiles, a fantastic amount of wasted ammunition that netted a mere fifty-six dead rebels—and still it held. But in December 1864, came the strategic break.

In May that year, General William Tecumseh Sherman's group of three armies, nearly 100,000 strong, advanced along the railroad from eastern Tennessee into Georgia. Outflanking the Confederates in a series of battles astride the tracks, Sherman arrived before Atlanta on July 9. On August 31, the city fell, and he began his famous march to the sea.

On the coast, Major General John Foster pushed inland, up the Broad River from Port Royal, and by December had the Charleston & Savannah Railroad under artillery fire. On December 11, at Ossabaw Sound, contraband slaves reported Sherman's cavalry less than a day's march from the Great Ogeechee River. The next day, three Illinois cavalrymen, the tip of the Federal host, rode into Port Royal with a message for Admiral Dahlgren. He at once wrote to the President "of the arrival of General Sherman near Savannah, with his army in fine spirits."

Dahlgren described it as "a memorable event," and so it was. Equal in every way to the capture of Vicksburg, which sundered the rebellion along the Mississippi, the arrival of the three horsemen at Port Royal split the eastern Confederacy into two dying halves. On December 13, Fort McAllister fell, and the following day General Sherman took dinner with the admiral aboard the flagship in Wassaw Sound. A week later the rebels evacuated Savannah.

Sherman, using Savannah as his base, planned to move his army across South Carolina into North Carolina, crushing the rebels in a giant vise between himself and U. S. Grant in Virginia. The march bypassed Charleston, but pressure would be maintained on the city by a combined army-navy landing just up the coast. On February 12, 1865, Dahlgren and Gillmore put their men ashore at Bull's Bay.

In the harbor of Charleston, there occurred one final naval tragedy. The monitor *Patapsco,* covering the picket boats at the entrance, ran on a mine and sank in less than a minute, taking 62 of her 105 men down with her. On the night of February 17–18, the Confederates blew up their ironclads and abandoned Charleston to its fate. During those hours, the blockade runner *Chicora* (not to be confused with the ironclad ram), unaware of the situation, slipped inside the celebrating cordon of U.S. vessels and approached the bar. When realization dawned, the ship "turned away from the land," wrote her captain, John Wilkinson, of the Confederate Navy, and "our hearts sank with us . . . that the cause for which so much blood had been shed, so many miseries bravely endured, and so many sacrifices cheerfully made, was about to perish at last."

On the morning of February 18, Admiral Dahlgren cabled Gideon Welles, "Charleston was abandoned this morning by the rebels. I am now on my way to the city."

Wilmington, to the End

"The importance of closing Wilmington is paramount to all other questions, more important, practically, than the capture of Richmond."

—Gideon Welles

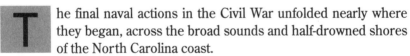he final naval actions in the Civil War unfolded nearly where they began, across the broad sounds and half-drowned shores of the North Carolina coast.

Since summer of 1862, Rear Admiral Louis M. Goldsborough was gone, his substantial pride wounded over the establishment of an independent James River Flotilla. To next lead the North Atlantic Blockading Squadron, the navy's largest and *de facto* premium command, Welles had made a surprising choice, far down the captains' list, Samuel Phillips Lee, "Old Triplicate," from the West Gulf, barely fifty years old. The promotion to acting rear admiral satisfied Lee's powerful Blair family in-laws and served as an inspiration to all young officers throughout the fleet.

Lee was not called "Old Triplicate" for nothing. Taking pride in what a historian has called, "the prompt attention he gave to routine details," Lee could never quite get beyond mountainous paper shuffling for the squadron's bread, beef, shot, and shell. For a fleet that numbered more than 100 vessels, the correspondence alone was a crushing task.

For two years, Federal forces held tightly to the North Carolina sounds and the large towns at the mouths of their tidal rivers, most

importantly Plymouth on the Roanoke at Albemarle Sound and New
Bern, on the Neuse, at Pamlico Sound. Up those rivers, beyond the
Federal reach, the rebels built a pair of primitive ironclads in an
attempt to regain control.

On the Roanoke River at Edward's Ferry, in what John Newland
Maffitt described as "an open cornfield," the ironclad ram *Albemarle*
took the familiar Confederate shape.* Gilbert Elliott, her civillian
builder, had previously done nothing more complicated than flatboats,
and his task was supervised by Commander James W. Cooke, "a quaint
little North Carolinian," and veteran of the annihilated Mosquito Fleet.
The ship's frames were of green, unseasoned timber. Her twin-screwed
engine, when it worked, was capable of four knots, and the battery
numbered two Brooke 6.4-inch rifles on pivot mounts fore and aft. "A
simple blacksmith shop," Maffitt said, "aided the mechanical part of
her construction."

Commander Cooke's first, all-consuming task was procuring enough
iron to sheath the casemate. According to Maffitt, he "ransacked the
country, gathering bolts and bars and the precious metal in any shape
that admitted . . . to his needs by the manipulation of the blacksmith. . . .
His greed for iron became amusingly notorious." In no time, Cooke was
known as the "Ironmonger Captain."

The ship was no secret. As early as June 1863, Admiral Lee warned
the department, "we must have ironclad defense on the sound." The
regular monitors' draft was too deep for the inlet bars. Lee wanted to
steam up the river and destroy the ram on her building ways, but the
low state of the river ended those thoughts. In both regards, the situation was perfect for the *Casco* shallow-draft monitors, but they were
utter failures in design. Instead, the senior Federal naval officer in Albemarle Sound, Lieutenant Commander Charles W. Flusser, reported to
the admiral, "We are driving piles in the river and preparing to receive
them [the rebel ironclads]. I do not doubt we shall whip them if they
venture down."

The *Albemarle* was launched in July 1863, and Welles gave warning
of the threat, urging a joint, navy-army operation to destroy her while
she was still fitting out at Edward's Ferry. According to Admiral Lee,
the local army corps commander "never attached any importance to it."

In the winter of 1863–1864 it was perceived in high Confederate circles that a short period of opportunity presented itself for a combined

* Maffitt commanded the ram during her inactive period in the summer
of 1864.

attack to recapture the tidewater towns and their lush agricultural hinterlands, even possibly to regain control of the sounds. It had to be done quickly, because once the snows melted and the Virginia roads dried out, Grant would begin his spring campaign, and every rebel soldier would be needed to stop him.

The original plan intended a coordinated movement against both Plymouth and New Bern using the troops of General Robert Hoke, with the *Albemarle* moving on the former, and General George Pickett, supported by the ram *Neuse,* against the latter. But as spring came, and the roads to Richmond dried out, the Confederate ironclads were still unfinished. Time was running out, and Robert E. Lee, holding the line in Virginia, wanted to call the whole operation off. Instead the New Bern effort was canceled and resources concentrated on Plymouth. On April 16, General Hoke visited Edward's Ferry and received assurances the *Albemarle* would be ready in time for the battle. Twenty-four hours later, Hoke launched his attack.

The *Albemarle,* far from done, was commissioned the same day, and Commander Cooke started her downriver. His "salty crew," he recalled, were mostly soldiers of Hoke's division, "long, lank, Tar Heels ... from the piney woods." At the last moment they were reinforced with twenty seamen sent from Charleston, "and without them I should have been almost powerless."

Towing a portable forge, Cooke literally finished the vessel on her maiden voyage. Standing atop the pilothouse, bellowing through a trumpet, he simultaneously drilled the crew at the guns while giving orders for bolting the final plates to the casemate: "Drive in spike No. 10! On nut below and screw up! In vent and sponge! Load with cartridge!" A farmer standing on the riverbank watched her pass down, and later wrote, "I never conceived of anything more perfectly ridiculous than the appearance of the critter as she slowly passed by my landing."

As could be expected, the *Albemarle's* engineering plant broke down. Repairs took six hours, and before they had gone any distance, the rudder head snapped. In all, nearly half a day was wasted in fixing what should not have broken. Late on April 18, Cooke anchored the ram three miles above Plymouth with the sounds of desperate battle clearly heard.

After a reconnaissance reported high water over the Federal pile line, Cooke weighed anchor and continued down. Before dawn, half a mile below the town, Gilbert Elliott saw ahead, coming out of the dark, two vessels, "lashed together with long spars, and with chains festooned between them."

Lieutenant Commander Charles Flusser, skipper of the Federal double-ender *Miami,* had planned this moment for months. The *Miami* was a fine new ship mounting six 9-inch Dahlgrens and a 6.4-inch Parrot rifle. She, perhaps, stood a ghost of a chance against a mediocre Confederate ironclad. But that was not the case with the converted ferries and coasters that formed the bulk of the U.S. Navy's presence in these waters. The lack of light-draft monitors would now be keenly felt. Flusser had devised a desperate tactic of lashing two ships together, heading straight for the rebel. He hoped to wedge the ironclad between his broadsides, then pummel her into submission.

Flusser's vessels had been in the thick of it, directly supporting the army's defense of Plymouth, and he had already lost the army gunboat *Bombshell* to rebel field artillery. "We have been fighting here all day," he reported to Admiral Lee. The army, for now, were holding, but he doubted they could for long without reinforcements. "The ram will be down here tonight or tomorrow," Flusser noted in his last report. He could either defend Plymouth or, "lashed to the *Southfield,*" fight the *Albemarle.* He could not do both.

After turning back the latest rebel assault on Plymouth with his ships' guns, Flusser withdrew to rest and feed the crews. He knew the morning would see the Confederate ram, and he ordered the *Miami* and the former Staten Island ferry *Southfield* lashed together. In the predawn, the *Whitehead,* picket gunboat at the pile line, came tearing downriver with her steam whistle blasting and rebel shells falling in her wake. The *Albemarle,* yelled her skipper, was right behind! Flusser came on deck. As William Welles, the executive officer, wrote, he "ordered both vessels to steam ahead as fast as possible and run the ram down."

Less than two minutes after the *Whitehead*'s alarm, Commander James Cooke piloted the rebel into the *Miami*'s bow, glanced off, and rammed the *Southfield,* shoving ten feet into the gunboat's innards. On the Federal side, Flusser, personally directing the fire, opened with every gun, pouring broadsides of solid shot at spitting range. They bounced straight up from the inclined iron casemate, and Flusser dropped, mortally wounded by flying ricochets.

Like the *Cumberland* at Hampton Roads, the *Southfield* nearly dragged her killer under. Cooke backed engines but could not extricate the ram, and down the *Albemarle* went. "Her bow," said Gilbert Elliott, "was carried . . . to such a depth that water poured into her port-holes in great volume, and she would have soon shared the fate of the *Southfield,* had not the latter vessel reached the bottom." Returning to an even keel, Cooke opened his Brooke rifles on the *Miami,* scoring several hits.

Acting Volunteer Lieutenant Charles French, skipper of the *Southfield,* along with about half his crew of eighty officers and men, jumped to the *Miami,* where he took over command from the dying Flusser. There was nothing left but to order all ships to retreat. Plymouth surrendered at noon the next day, the rebels bagging 1,600 men and twenty-five guns. Washington, on the *Pamlico,* fell on March 30.

The victory presented a clear, if fleeting opportunity for the Confederacy to regain complete control of the sounds. But even given their sole possession of ironclads on these waters, it came to nothing but a good scare. By late April, the rebels finally completed the ironclad *Neuse.* The vessel steamed down her namesake river for a rendezvous with the *Albemarle* to attack New Bern. One of the *Neuse's* crew wrote of their confidence to "take the city and sink the gunboats without much trouble . . . and have a fine time afterwards." On the twenty-seventh, she got underway, and half a mile later ran hard aground, stuck, as it happened, for a month. It was decided to continue the operation with the *Albemarle* alone. "With its assistance," wrote the new department commander, General Beauregard, "I consider capture of New Bern easy."

The *Neuse* had only to head downstream to reach New Bern; not so the *Albemarle.* For that, she had to leave the safety of the Roanoke, cross Albemarle, Croatan, and Pamlico sounds, then steam up the blocked Neuse River. She would face every Federal gunboat in the sounds. Commander Cooke, however, seemed unconcerned. He had already dealt handily with the double-enders and converted ferries, and there were still no monitors in his way.

At noon, May 5, accompanied by the salvaged gunboat *Bombshell* and the transport *Cotton Plant,* the *Albemarle* proceeded down the Roanoke, into the sound. Reaching the flat waters, Cooke spotted the Federal flotilla about ten miles off. So far, they were just the usual collection of converted whatevers. But then, four vessels "of a much more formidable class," double-enders, swung out from the dots on the horizon and headed to intercept. Cooke saw the coming battle as an "unequal contest" completely in his favor, and cleared for action.

Old Captain Melancton Smith, last seen at Port Hudson calmly smoking a cigar while the *Mississippi* burned away under him commanded the Union naval forces. His double-enders were the *Mattabesett, Sassacus, Wyalusing,* and *Miami.* Smith's plan for defeating the rebel ironclad was a simple one, albeit with a wrinkle or two. Delivering continual broadsides, the double-enders would pass as close to the ram as possible. Once by, they would round her stern, firing all the time, until each, in turn, passed her again. The *Sassacus'* bow had been reinforced with a three-ton bronze beak, and if opportunity presented, she would attempt to ram. The *Miami* came fitted with a spar torpedo over her bow, as well as a seine net, which Smith hoped to throw over the *Albemarle's* stern to foul her screws.

As the distance closed, Surgeon Edgar Holden of the *Sassacus* remembered, "all eyes were fixed on this second *Merrimack,* as like a floating fortress, she came down the bay. A puff of smoke from her port bow opened the ball." The first shells struck the flagship *Mattabesett,* cutting away some spars, damaging her boats, and wounding several men. Followed by the *Sassacus,* 9-inch solid shot from both ships slamming into the rebel's casemate, she rounded the enemy in a half circle. Other than a volcano of blinding smoke, the cannonade had no apparent effect. "The guns might as well have fired blank cartridges," Surgeon Holden said. The gunners shifted their aim to the ram's weak points and then scored hits on the stack and gunports.

The Confederate's *Bombshell* was quickly out of it, lurching astern. A gun captain in the *Sassacus,* naked to the waist, stood upon the rail. Holden recalled, "He brandished a huge boarding pistol and shouted, 'Haul down your flag and surrender, or we'll blow you out of the water!'" The *Bombshell* struck her flag, and limped in wake of the advancing Federal ships.

It was the decisive point of the battle. The *Albemarle* maneuvered to ram the *Sassacus'* stern, narrowly missed, and lay broadside to the Federal, capping the T. Lieutenant Commander Francis Roe, the gunboat's skipper, shouted for his engineer to "Crowd waste and oil in the fires! Give her all the steam she can carry." Backing to gain more headway, Roe manuevered the *Sassacus* to strike between the rebel's casemate and stern.

"Then came four [engine] bells," Surgeon Holden recalled, "and with full steam and open throttle the ship sprang forward like a living thing." For an instant, the guns ceased firing and the smoke of battle lifted over the sound. It was a moment of the most intense strain. "Straight as an arrow we shot forward to the designated spot." Francis Roe bellowed the order, "All hands, lie down!"

At a speed approaching twelve knots, the wooden *Sassacus* struck the iron *Albemarle* full and square at the junction of the casemate and hull, "careering it over," Holden said, "and tearing away our own bows, ripping and straining our timbers at the waterline."

The rebel ram twisted over to a point where she nearly could not right herself—"so much," Roe said, "that the water flowed freely over her decks and gave so great a list that . . . I hoped I should sink her." Riding a tiger, Roe knew that to back away risked his own certain destruction. Instead, "I kept the engine going, pushing, as I hoped, deeper and deeper into her."

The *Sassacus* held fast for ten minutes. The crew hurled grenades onto the ironclad's deck hatch, and tried throwing bags of gunpowder into her smokestack, all the time exchanging point-blank musketry with the rebels. The enemy immobilized, Roe desperately looked for another Federal ship alongside the ram, "opposite to me, as she was unable to harm them."

But there was nothing but wild confusion. With the two ships locked together, Federal vessels dared not fire in fear of striking their own. Surgeon Holden watched shot from his own guns, depressed virtually to right angles, "bounce from the [casemate] into the air like marbles." The *Miami* missed the *Albemarle* with her spar torpedo, the *Mattabesett* cast her seine net at the ram's propellers and accomplished nothing, the *Wyalusing* incorrectly hoisted a signal she was sinking.

Roe couldn't hold any longer. The *Albemarle* slew around, and Roe sent a parting broadside into her after gunport, which broke off twenty inches of rebel rifle barrel. In return the *Sassacus* took a shot in her starboard boiler. It burst, scalding the entire fire room crew. "The steam was terrible," Roe wrote in his report, and blinded everyone in the ship. Amid the suffocation, Roe said, "my men and officers jumped to the guns and continued pouring solid shot into the enemy."

The antagonists drifted apart. The *Albemarle,* bereft of rudder and her stack holed through, could neither steer a straight course nor raise a head of steam. For a short while, Commander Cooke actually thought of trying to reach New Bern, but there was no chance of that. Instead, he crawled back up the Roanoke. As a rebel seaman noted, "Nearly all the bacon, lard, and butter was burned, the bulkhead also, to raise steam to get back with." Tactically the battle was a draw, but strategically it was a clear Union victory. The *Albemarle* never again constituted a real threat, and Hoke's land attack on New Bern was abruptly canceled. He and his division were recalled by Lee to Virginia, where Grant had just begun the slogging campaign of the Wilderness.

*   *   *

For all its "ram fever," drama and deeds of individual bravery, affairs in the sounds constituted a distinct sideshow to the main events at Wilmington, North Carolina, whose closing Gideon Welles considered "paramount to all other questions, more important practically, than the capture of Richmond." For the U.S. Navy, Wilmington was the most difficult place of all to blockade. The city stands on the Cape Fear River, twenty-eight miles inland from two principal ocean entrances, New Inlet to the northeast and the Western Bar Channel to the southwest. Between them is the inverted triangle of wooded Smith's Island, whose bottom tip is Cape Fear. Frying Pan Shoals, one of the major hazards to shipping along the entire Atlantic coast extends from the cape a full twelve miles out to sea. A straight line between the river entrances is seven miles, but the natural obstructions draw the distance to fifty, requiring not one blockading force but two, out of sight of each other and beyond direct communications.

Because of Federal dominance at Hampton Roads, Wilmington became the port of entry for Richmond, and thus for the Confederate armies in Virginia and North Carolina. Of all Confederate ports, it was closest to the runner bases of Nassau and Bermuda. Once Charleston had been effectively sealed in September 1863, Wilmington remained the sole port through which the rebel war effort was supplied from overseas.* Indeed, in its final months of greatly intensified activity, from October 26, 1864, through January 13, 1865, thirty-one runners brought the Confederacy over 4,000 tons of meat, 750 tons of lead, 950 tons of saltpeter, 546,000 pairs of shoes, 700,000 blankets, half a million pounds of coffee, 69,000 Enfield rifles, forty-three pieces of artillery, and enough cotton to pay for all was shipped out through the blockade. On so regular a schedule did the runners penetrate, British newspapers speculated whether U.S. naval officers were conniving to prolong the war for greater shares of prize money. Nearly 300 inbound runners accomplished the journey in the course of the war.

The Confederate defenses of Cape Fear River consisted primarily of Fort Caswell on the mainland, opposite Smith's Island, covering the Western Bar Channel, and the main work, Fort Fisher, on the north side of the more frequently used and accessible entrance at New Inlet. Fort Fisher, the most intensively fortified piece of coastline in the Confederacy, was sited at the tip of the long peninsula, Confederate Point,

---

* Although Mobile was active until September 1864, it was never anything but a minor port of entry, principally from Havana.

that formed the east bank of the Cape Fear River. In shape the fort resembled the numeral 7, its elbow to the northeast. The short bar, defending against a land attack, faced north, up the peninsula, and contained nineteen heavy guns behind log and sand breastworks. Directly to its front, a nine-foot wooden stockade offered protection for sharpshooters and overlooked a minefield detonated by galvanic batteries within the fort. The elbow of the 7, known as the "center traverse," or "northeast bastion," rose forty-three feet from the beach and commanded sea and land approaches with an 8-inch Blakely rifle and a 68-pounder Armstrong cannon—British ordnance run through the blockade.

The long arm of the 7 faced the sea. It was a series of packed sand, turf, and log batteries, mounting fifteen guns, connected by covered ways, affording excellent protection for the gunners in "bombproof" traverses. At the very bottom tip of the 7, right on New Inlet, the mound battery held an 8-inch Armstrong rifle, a 10-inch Columbiad, and towered nearly sixty feet above the sands. The garrison of Fort Fisher numbered anywhere from 800 to 1,500 men, with a few thousand more available from Wilmington.

Reducing Fort Fisher required a joint navy-army operation. But in May 1863, Gideon Welles, after months of trying to persuade General Halleck to provide a landing force or sufficient reinforcements for an overland attack on Wilmington from New Bern, authorized Admiral Lee to launch a purely naval attack. The admiral ordered several night reconnaissances up the mined, heavily defended river to within a few miles of the city, but nothing came of it. No wooden ship could survive the daylight gauntlet. It was yet another instance where the failed, shallow-draft *Casco* monitors would have served their purpose.

More than a year later, on the heels of Farragut's victory at Mobile Bay, Gus Fox made a personal appeal to the new general in chief, U. S. Grant, for military cooperation against Wilmington. In principle, Grant agreed, but only if the navy replaced "Old Triplicate" Lee with someone more innovative and energetic. Welles shared the opinion that Lee was not the man for bold action. "He is true and loyal," Welles noted in his diary, "prudent and cautious. Farragut would take the place three times while Lee was preparing, and hesitating, and looking behind for more aid." Now that the Gulf was secure, Farragut was the secretary's first choice, and to make the decision more palatable, and not appear a demotion to Lee and his Blair connections, Welles simply ordered the two admirals to exchange places. But no sooner had the order gone out than Farragut requested a long overdue sick leave.

Welles read through the short admirals' list. "Neither Goldsborough nor Du Pont are men for such service," he confided to his diary
on September 15, 1864. "Nor is Davis. Dahlgren has some good qualities, but lacks great essentials." Try as he might, Welles could not avoid
the obvious: "I see no alternative but Porter, and unprejudiced and
unembarrassed, I should select him."

Porter was already in Washington, summoned for conferences following the Red River fiasco, out of which he had come with reputation
intact. As Fox had written, "After you get your feathers smoothed and
oiled, I don't see why you should not come East." On August 8, 1864, he
accompanied Fox to Grant's headquarters at City Point on the James
River. Grant's chief concerns were defeating the rebels in front of Richmond and Atlanta. Wilmington, so far as the commitment of troops, was
a secondary objective. He agreed to detach only Godfrey Weitzel's division, 6,500 men, as soon as the naval force was ready for its end of the
operation.

It was understood the objective remain secret. Weitzel would sail
under sealed orders, and a diversion launched to give the impression of
a strike at Charleston. But sometime in late September, the news
leaked to the press, and Grant, to the anger of the navy, canceled the
army's participation.

On September 22, Secretary Welles effected the command switch
of Porter to the North Atlantic Blockading Squadron, and Lee to the
Mississippi. The man who began the war number six in the lieutenants'
list, on the brink of resigning his commission for a Pacific mail steamer,
had ascended to the pinnacle of the U.S. Navy's premier command.

But before Admiral Porter could manage the great issue of Wilmington, there was still the irritant of the *Albemarle*. "As there is a ram in
your neighborhood," he wrote to the new senior officer in the sound,
Commander William Macomb, "you will be ready to attack her at all
times." Melancton Smith's death or glory tactics had met with
Porter's strong approval; he elaborated upon them. "You will make a
dash at her with every vessel you have, and 'lay her on board,' using
canister to fire into her ports." Every ship was to be equipped with
grapnels "and boarding parties appointed to lash the vessels
together." Losses were not to be considered. "Even if half your vessels are sunk you must pursue this course." At the very end of the
exhortation, Porter entered an afterthought, telling Macomb he had
ordered Lieutenant William Cushing to the sounds in a steam launch,

"if possible [to] destroy this ram with torpedoes. I have no great confidence in his success."

William Barker Cushing, just shy of twenty-two years old, four times commended by the department, recipient of the "Thanks of Congress" and the President, was one of the bravest men in the history of the U.S. Navy. William Harwar Parker, one of his academy instructors, described him as "rather a delicate-looking youth; fair, with regular, clear-cut features, and a clear, greyish-blue eye. He stood low in his classes." In fact, he was the "anchor man," bottom of his class. In March 1861, on account of poor grades, Cushing resigned from the navy, only to be appointed master's mate almost at the start of the war. He showed his audacity early on in North Carolina waters by refusing to surrender the steamer *Ellis* against large odds. Instead, he defended her with five men, and finally blew up the craft in the face of the enemy. And it was he who conducted Admiral Lee's reconnaissances up the Cape Fear River to within sight of Wilmington itself.

In the summer of 1864, Cushing had proposed to "Old Triplicate" some highly original plans to eliminate the *Albemarle*. The first called for "India-rubber boats, to be inflated and carried upon men's backs, [to] . . . transport a boarding party of a hundred men." Another entailed two steam launches, fitted with spar torpedoes and light howitzers; the lead boat dashing in to plant her torpedo under the ram's hull, while the second covered the operation from yards off. Cushing favored the latter, as did Lee and the always eager Gus Fox. Cushing was ordered to New York to purchase and fit out "suitable vessels."

He found two fine boats, forty-five-foot steam launches, and equipped each with a spar torpedo boom and 12-pounder howitzer in the bows. In early October Cushing started south, making his way through the web of intercoastal canals to Chesapeake Bay. One of the boats foundered near Norfolk. The other, with seven remaining men, passed right through rebel-held territory into the sounds. On the twenty-sixth, Cushing joined the Federal squadron at the mouth of the Roanoke River. Here Cushing disclosed his mission and asked for volunteers; each of his seven men stepped forward, as did thirteen others.

They needed to travel eight miles upriver to Plymouth, which had a rebel garrison of several thousand. Hostile pickets guarded both banks, and in midstream the grounded wreck of the *Southfield* was known to house a large guard, and possibly a gun. Once beyond all this, the volunteers must rush the target with hardly a guarantee of anything but death. As Cushing told it, "It seemed impossible to surprise them [the enemy], or to attack with hope of success." But "Impossibilities are for the timid," he went on; "we determined to overcome all obstacles."

In the first hours of October 27, Cushing's launch, towing an armed cutter with a dozen men, entered the river. They chuffed by the first enemy patrols, coming within twenty yards of the *Southfield*. The cutter cast off, boarded the wreck, and silently took prisoner the rebel guard. Cushing and the launch "made for our enemy under a full head of steam."

Cushing steered for a light which he thought must come from the *Albemarle,* and too late, coming parallel to the ram, realized he had overshot his target. Coming around, they were hailed from the ram. "We made no answer," said Acting Ensign Thomas Gay. Hailed again, the sailors remained silent while Cushing moved into position. "The next call," said Ensign Gay, "was not so pleasant, for we were discovered, and the grape and canister began to play on our small craft in rapid succession." Cushing returned fire from his 12-pounder, yelling to the rebels, "Leave the ram, or I'll blow you to pieces!"

The launch passed close and made a complete circle "so as to strike fairly, and went into her bows on." Then Cushing saw it. The *Albemarle* was shielded by a raft of logs several yards wide, far too great to reach over with his fourteen-foot spar. Undaunted, he decided to go "at the booms squarely, at right angles, trusting to their having been long enough in the water to have become slimy." With full headway, the launch, he hoped, "would bump up against them and slip over into the pen with the ram. This was my only chance of success." He also knew that once over the logs, he could never get out.

From the banks and the ram, musketry and grapeshot hammered into them as the launch surged ahead. "The whole back of my coat was torn out by buckshot," Cushing reported, "and the sole of my shoe was carried away. The fire was very severe." Again, there came a hail from the rebels. "All my men gave comical answers," said Cushing, who himself fired a shot from the 12-pounder.

The launch struck the boom and carried over. "Everything," recalled Ensign Gay, "now was in the greatest of excitement." Cushing stood up in the bow and ordered the spar lowered until the forward motion of the launch carried the torpedo under the ironclad's armored knuckle. He pulled the detaching line, waited a few seconds for the torpedo to rise under the hull, was shot in the left hand, "and by a vigorous pull," exploded 100 pounds of gunpowder, rending the *Albemarle*'s hull apart. The same instant the *Albemarle* fired her after rifle, crashing through the launch, Gay said, "filling . . . and completely disabling [us]."

Twice Cushing refused demands to surrender, but to stay was to die. Shouting "Men, save yourselves," he jumped into the river. "It was cold," he remembered, "and the water chilled the blood . . . the whole surface of the stream was plowed up with grape and musketry." He had twelve miles of enemy-infested territory to get through, "but anything was better than to fall into rebel hands." Only Cushing and Ordinary Seaman Edward J. Horton escaped. Two were killed or drowned in the fighting. Seven, Acting Ensign Gay included, were taken prisoner at the log boom. Cushing hid in the swamp for the better part of the next day, stole a skiff from some rebel pickets, and by midnight was aboard the *Valley City.*

The *Albemarle* was a total loss, and with it Plymouth lay open to naval attack. Commander Macomb opened a three-day battle on October 29, blasting his way upriver against the rebel batteries. After a huge explosion of a powder magazine, Plymouth fell on November 1. Federal control of the sounds was never threatened again. Cushing was the new man of the hour, receiving the thanks of the President and Congress, as well as promotion to lieutenant commander. Admiral Porter published a general order read aboard every ship: "The spirit evinced by this officer is what I wish to see pervading this squadron."

As for Fort Fisher, the navy was keen to get on with it, but weeks passed and Grant had not assigned a cooperating force. Welles, on October 28, complained to the President, "Every other squadron has been depleted and vessels detached from other duty to strengthen this expedition." The fine autumn weather was fast evaporating, and "to procrastinate much longer will be to peril its success." But Lincoln declined to prod his general in chief, to whom the last, slogging, trench warfare battles for Richmond and Petersburg were the key to winning the war.

Enter Major General Ben Butler, from whose command the troops for the Wilmington operation were to be drawn. At the beginning of October some powder barges had exploded with awesome noise and window-breaking on the Thames River near London. Butler suggested to Gus Fox that a similar shipload of powder detonated near forts Caswell or Fisher might stun the garrison long enough for an assault force to gain a foothold on the beach. Most ordnance authorities opposed the idea. Brigadier General Richard Delafield, the army's elderly chief engineer, considered the scheme completely impractical "toward the reduction of those works."

Fox, however, would not let go. Considering the alluring promises and low cost of the operation, he convened a Washington meeting of army and navy ordnance experts in late November 1864. The conferees' report was precisely the opposite of General Delafield's. They predicted an exploding powder ship would damage the earthworks "to a very great extent," render enough of the enemy's guns unserviceable, and stun the garrison to a degree permitting "the carrying of these works by immediate assault."

Admiral Porter was all for it. "The army and navy had plenty of bad powder and worthless vessels," he wrote some years later. "In war it is worth while to try everything." K. R. Breese, his chief of staff, thought otherwise. "Admiral," he countered, "it has about as much chance of blowing up the fort as I have of flying!" Porter ordered the *Louisiana*, a tired, iron-hulled, 145-foot gunboat to Hampton Roads for conversion into a floating bomb. She was stripped bare except for the engine, and a wooden deckhouse was built over half her length. The initial loading, 185 tons of powder, was done at Craney Island under the supervision of navy and army ordnance officers. Two original methods of explosion were planned: clockworks and match fuse, including the new Gomez quick match, calculated to ignite at the rate of one mile in five seconds. To produce the greatest possible lateral blast, most of the powder was stowed above the waterline. The berth deck was filled with fifty-pound bags, and the after hold with two tiers of full barrels, their heads knocked out, and powder bags laid on top. The remainder of the powder was stowed within the deckhouse.

On adopting the project, Porter circulated a private summons requesting volunteers, "for a most hazardous enterprise which offers the alternatives of death, capture, glory, and promotion." From the list of respondents, he chose Commander Alexander Rhind, late of the ill-fated *Keokuk,* to command the vessel. Porter's young aide, Lieutenant Samuel Preston, and twelve men from Rhind's ship, the gunboat *Agawam,* made the rest of the crew. On December 13, towed by the *Sassacus,* the powder ship departed Hampton Roads for Beaufort 100 miles up the coast from Fort Fisher.

The Fort Fisher invasion force was ready to sail on December 8, 1864. Weitzel's troops, with three days' cooked meat, and five of total rations, sat aboard their transports at Hampton Roads waiting for the weather to clear. Ben Butler, for reasons that had nothing to do with sound military judgment, decided to sail in company. Admiral Porter cursed at the news, writing to Gus Fox, "Butler is going himself to look on or direct—he had better leave it to Weitzel." Fox leaked the letter around Washington. One never knew where blame would fall, and it bode well to cover the navy's rear, just in case.

During the wait at Hampton Roads, Porter and Butler spoke but once on the coming operation. On that occasion, Butler, Weitzel, and their engineer, Colonel Comstock, came to the fleet flagship. Porter later told a congressional committee that they "asked me if I had a map of Cape Fear River. . . . They asked my opinion . . . of what I thought was the best way to go to work. They made no remarks whatever, but went into a far part of the cabin and there consulted together. . . . They got up, bade me 'good evening,' and went off." The personal animus among the senior commanders brought the departure of the fleet and invasion forces in reverse of the order intended, each unbelievably ignorant of the other's movements.

Porter planned to start with his slow monitors a day ahead of the army's transports. When Butler sailed off on windy, rainy, December 12, his troops already down to one day's food, Porter assumed they were heading directly for Beaufort. Instead, Butler, to deceive the rebels, headed north, into Chesapeake Bay. Porter and the bombardment ships left for Beaufort the next day, arriving on the sixteenth. Commander Rhind, he found, had loaded another 30 tons of powder, making 215, and completed his preparations on the powder vessel. The army, was not to be seen. Porter continued on in the flagship *Malvern* and joined the blockading squadron off Cape Fear. The ships lay over the horizon, unseen to the rebels in Fort Fisher.

Butler entered Beaufort later in the day, and not finding Admiral Porter, continued down the coast to Cape Fear. The fleet, of course, being invisibly over the horizon, Butler didn't locate the admiral there either. He did, however, steam close enough to Fort Fisher to alert the rebels to something impending. That done, he returned to Beaufort.

By December 18, the army and navy were aware of their respective positions, and the powder ship joined the fleet off Cape Fear. K. R. Breese went to Beaufort, notifying Butler the explosion would take place that night. For the army, though, it was bad timing. The troops had eaten their five days' rations, and several of the transports needed to fill up with drinking water as well. Porter consented to a short delay, with the understanding the *Louisiana* would be exploded at the first favorable opportunity thereafter.

For the next five days it blew a gale. The transports stayed in the shelter of Beaufort, while the fleet, monitors included, rode it out with sea anchors down. On the twenty-third the breakers calmed and the sun appeared. By fast dispatch vessel, Porter informed Butler the powder ship would blow before 2 A.M. the following morning. In his calculations, Porter allowed for sixteen hours until the army began landing up the beach from Fort Fisher.

The general plan called for blowing the powder vessel as near the fort as possible, "even to running her on the beach," the navy opening a bombardment from fifty ships, and the army assaulting a thoroughly stunned garrison with Weitzel's 6,500 men. If this assault succeeded, a forced march up Confederate Point might even take the city of Wilmington by surprise.

On the night of December 24, the powder vessel was towed by the tug *Wilderness* to about 250 yards from the beach, a little over half a mile north of the 7 angle of the fort. The night was perfectly clear, else Rhind would have anchored the ship half again as near. The crew took to their boat. Rhind and Lieutenant Preston remained to set the clocks and Second Assistant Engineer Anthony Mullin lit the fire in the cabin. All were off and aboard the *Wilderness* at midnight, steaming at high speed out to the fleet, twelve miles at sea, for no one could predict the effects of the blast.

At 1:40 A.M., Christmas Day, the *Louisiana* exploded. Major Thomas Lincoln Casey of the engineers watched it from the fleet. "The first thing observed was a bright flame," he reported, "which suddenly leaped into the air. ... Some ten seconds after ... two sharp and ringing reports, about as loud as those from a 6-pounder brass gun were heard." He felt his ship "sensibly jarred and shaken." Over the water came a low rumbling, like "distant thunder ... and all was then quiet."

On the beach, inside Fort Fisher, the rebels thought a gunboat might have suffered a boiler accident. The noise was heard in Wilmington, and a query was telegraphed to the fort. "Enemy's gunboat blown up," wired back Colonel Lamb, the garrison commander, and that was all. The grand scheme had accomplished exactly nothing.

At daylight, through still settling powder dust, Porter signaled the fleet to assume its bombardment stations. Five commodores led the divisions, and each commanding officer had his own copy of the position and target charts, printed on the *Malvern's* lithographic press. In a great crescent, no more than a mile to sea, overlapping Fort Fisher from the northeast bastion to the mound battery, more than fifty ships, mounting 580 guns, moved with the precision of a ponderous ballet.

The *New Ironsides* led the northernmost division of four monitors and seven gunboats against the land face, the short bar of the upside-down 7, preparing it for the assault of Weitzel's infantry. In the center, the second division, seventeen wooden walls of the old navy, including the *Minnesota, Wabash, Powhatan, Colorado,* and *Brooklyn,* ranged opposite the northeast bastion at the elbow. The long bar of the 7, the sea face and mound battery, fell to a division of eight large gunboats, mostly double-enders. Outside the bombardment line, a reserve division of seventeen gun and dispatch vessels would be used as opportunity presented.

By Admiral Porter's reckoning, Butler should have arrived at the landing beaches by 8 A.M. But when the ships' bells simultaneously struck the hour, there was nothing in sight. At 11:30 Porter declined to wait longer and hoisted the signal to engage the enemy. It continued for five hours. Porter in the *Malvern,* a lavishly converted ex-runner, hastened from point to point and in and out of the lines of thundering ships. When the admiral noticed a vessel falling out of the line, a *New York Times* reporter in the flagship recorded the exchange:

"What's the trouble," hailed Porter.

"My 100-pounder has exploded."

"Then why in hell don't you go back and use your other guns?"

To the skipper of a double-ender, he inquired, "Where are you going now?"

"To repair a damage in my side," replied the officer.

"Go back to your place, or I'll send you and your boat to the bottom."

Fort Fisher made no serious reply. Without wind, there was too much smoke around the fleet to guarantee any accuracy, and Colonel Lamb, to conserve ammunition, limited his response to one round per gun every half-hour.

For all the fire and brimstone, casualties were surprisingly light. The Confederates suffered three gun carriages disabled, half their quarters burned, one soldier dead, and twenty-two wounded. The fleet's casualties were negligible as well. The *Mackinac* of the center division was towed out with a shot-through boiler, and several sailors were killed when some faultily cast Parrott rifles burst on firing.

Porter assigned Captain James Alden of the *Brooklyn* the duty of getting the troops ashore, a task he admirably accomplished with the gunboats of the reserve division and 100 ships' boats. Covered by gunfire, 2,500 men, a third of Weitzel's force, landed five miles up the beach from the northern land face, the short arm of the 7. A skirmish line quickly formed, and it advanced toward the wooden stockade. More than 200 rebels surrendered, including two field batteries served by old men and young teenagers. A rebel flag was pulled from the parapet, and one soldier actually walked into the fort proper, killed a dispatch rider, and took his horse.

In the afternoon, storm clouds lowered the sky, bringing with it a rising surf. On the beach, Weitzel, accompanied by Colonel Comstock of the engineers, surveyed the parapets from close range, and determined the fort was largely undamaged. He reported to Butler "and told him I considered it would be murder to order an attack on that work" with the forces at hand—meaning one third the troops, or less; the rest of the division was still embarked.

Butler sent the two officers to Admiral Porter. Could not the navy alone charge into New Inlet and take Fort Fisher from the rear? Porter knew that was out of the question. The wrecks of blockade runners and sunken hulks on the unmarked bar had altered its whole formation, obliterating the original channel.

Porter ordered William Cushing to sound and buoy a channel if he could find one. A gunboat division covered the operation and swept for mines. All of this, of course, was done under fire. Cushing actually marked a narrow, crooked path into the Cape Fear River, before enemy gunfire drove him back. His knowledge confirmed, Porter told the army officers it could not be done. Butler either ignored or failed to consult his orders from General Grant, that he entrench after landing. Rather, he ordered the troops back to the transports and then sailed off to Hampton Roads. Worst of all, he left more than 600 men on the beach, claiming that he couldn't get them off because of the rising surf.

Porter's reactions went from amazement to disgust to violent anger. Yet before he could give them full vent, there was the matter of the stranded troops. "We must get those poor devils of soldiers off today, or we will lose them," he wrote in orders to Captain Alden, "and won't I be glad to get rid of them! Ain't a soldier troublesome?" Alden got them off the beach two days later.

Militarily, Butler was finished, and he was banished by the President to Lowell, Massachusetts. To commemorate Butler's escapade, the crew of the *Malvern* fashioned a tooled leather medal, the obverse depicting a pair of running legs surmounted by a major general's shoulder straps, the reverse bore the inscription "In commemoration of his heroic conduct before Fort Fisher, Dec. 1864." Porter wrote to Secretary Welles: "If this temporary failure succeeds in sending General Butler into private life, it is not to be regretted."

For Porter, the initial failure served as a stimulant for even greater energy in the next attempt. To lull the rebels into overconfidence, he ostentatiously retreated the bulk of the fleet, except for the regular blockaders. The *Richmond Whig* took the bait. "Where is it now?" it crowed. "Beaten, scattered, sunk, dispersed over all the ocean." On December 30, Porter received from General Grant the most welcome news: "Please hold on where you are for a few days, and I will endeavor to be back again with an increased force and without the former commander." Admiral Porter responded on New Year's Day 1865, "I shall be ready. . . . Thank you. . . . I knew you would do it." Grant had collected the transports, reinforced the troops with an additional brigade, and appointed Major General Alfred Terry to command.

Grant's actions showed the new importance of maintaining pressure on Wilmington as a strategic objective. The rebels could not simultaneously defend it *and* counter Sherman's march to the sea. One Confederate front or the other would have to be stripped of forces. As it happened, the rebels could halt neither.

On January 8, Major General Alfred Terry and 8,000 men arrived at Beaufort. He boarded the *Malvern* instantly, and by direction of General Grant laid his sealed orders before Admiral Porter. "The siege of Fort Fisher," they read, "will not be abandoned until its reduction is accomplished." Winter gales kept the vessels in port until the twelfth, when the combined armada steamed to Fort Fisher.

The fighting fleet took its positions for bombardment. They deployed in three lines, similar to the first action, but closer in, with the ironclads on the angle of the northeast bastion giving enfilade fire along both axes of the 7. To occupy the rebel gunners with smothering, rapid fire, Porter added the *Brooklyn* to the ironclad division.

Commanding officers were cautioned to cut their fuses and shoot carefully, there had been an element of wildness in the first action. "The object," Porter noted, "is to lodge the shell in the parapets and tear away the traverses" over the bombproof shelters. No vessel was to retire from her place in the line "unless in a sinking condition." When the troops were ready to assault, he would hoist signal "2211"— "Change direction of fire"—accompanied by a steam whistle to be repeated by every ship. Fire would shift to the sea face, the mound battery, and the interior approaches of the fort on the far, river side.

At first light, January 13, the fleet opened a deliberate, concentrated, all-day barrage. At 8:30 A.M., the first wave of Terry's troops pulled for the beach well north of the land face. Young Robley Evans, nineteen, had charge of a string of boats from the *Powhatan.** "We

---

* Evans commanded the battleship *Iowa* during the Spanish-American War, and later the Atlantic Fleet during the first leg of its famous round-the-world cruise in 1908.

made the first landing with over two hundred boats," he wrote nearly four decades later, "and the sight was a notable one as we pulled in, an occasional shell splashing among us, and the bullets spluttering on the surface of the water. As soon as the order was given to land we went for the beach at full speed."

The soldiers had difficulty in getting out with dry feet, and many rolled in the surf. "But once on shore it was glorious to see how they knew their business," Evans recalled. "As soon as they got their feet they spread out into a skirmish line, and the rifles began to crack." By midafternoon, Terry's entire force was ashore with entrenching gear and twelve days' supplies.

Through the night and the next day the fleet kept up their fire. At 11 A.M. on the fifteenth, the bombardment concentrated on the short, land face of the fort, and it dismounted every gun but one. The parapets and traverses were torn, the wooden stockade breached or knocked down in places, and the wires to the minefield obliterated. Never before had a fleet accomplished so much destruction of a fortified position, nor would it again until the amphibious invasions of World War II.

By gradual approaches the army worked down the far, river side of Confederate Point, against the open, short tip of the 7. At each forward movement, the leading brigade entrenched, while the rear brigades occupied the former positions. By this leapfrogging, they advanced to within range for the final rush.

"That we may have a share in the assault when it takes place," Admiral Porter mustered a naval brigade of 1,600 sailors and 400 marines, under Chief of Staff K. R. Breese. "The sailors," he noted in his orders, "will be armed with cutlasses, well sharpened, and with revolvers." They were supposed to land just below the elbow, against the sea face, "and board the fort on the run in a seaman-like way. . . . Two thousand active men from the fleet will carry the day."

The naval brigade, Robley Evans among them, landed at 1 P.M. in the wrong place, a mile and a half up the beach from the northeast bastion. In three "divisions," the marines leading, the force advanced half the distance to the fort. At 3 P.M. came the steam whistles from the fleet, the signal for the general assault on Fort Fisher, "and we started," Evans said, "our long run of twelve-hundred yards over the loose sand." It came a near disaster. Breese, instead of keeping his marines to cover the charge of the sailors, brought them forward. The advance became immediately confused, had no close fire support, and the column spread out dangerously. By the time the van arrived at the stockade and halted for the center and rear to come up, those divisions had stalled as well. With less than a third of his men, Breese faced an aroused Confederate defense that mistakenly considered the naval brigade the main assault.

"So the whole garrison," Evans recalled, "concentrated its fire on us . . . and as if by magic, the whole mass of men went down like a row of falling bricks." Evans got close enough to see the garrison commander, Colonel Lamb, standing atop the parapet, "calling on his men to get up and shoot the Yankees." Evans aimed his revolver, and was himself shot in the chest. "I felt a burning . . . like a hot iron, over my heart, and saw something red coming out of the hole in my coat, which I took to be blood." Staggering on at the head of his men, Evans was hit again. There were so many officers in front that there was no one to steady the rest of the column, and it broke. "Two minutes more and we should have been on the parapet."

The brigade was slaughtered. Porter's absurd wish to have a share in the assault brought the navy more than 300 killed or wounded. Disorganized, routed, they retreated up the beach. But the sacrifice of the naval brigade had a result not intended. Colonel Lamb, congratulating himself on repulsing the assault, was jerked away from the little triumph. On his left, on the river flank of the parapet, there suddenly flew three U.S. flags, with columns of blue-coated troops pouring through the gap.

The battle degenerated into a hand-to-hand, bayonet and grenade alley fight—battery to battery, traverse to traverse, trench to trench. The *New Ironsides,* whose shooting was particularly accurate, dropped shells into individual rebel positions, blasting the defenders into the open killing ground. At 9 P.M., January 15, 1865, General Terry sent up a rocket announcing victory. Fort Fisher collapsed in surrender; 1,900 prisoners and forty-four heavy guns fell to the Union.

From the flagship *Malvern* a blast of her steam whistle and rocket after rocket answered the signal from the beach. It was taken up by the whole cheering fleet. The sky became kaleidoscopic with colored pyrotechnics. Officers and sailors alike took turns pulling whistle ropes. At the fort, soldiers, sailors, and marines spent the night removing the wounded and getting drunk on captured stores. In the morning, a group of drunken soldiers entered the main magazine with uncovered torches and blew it up, killing 200 of their comrades.

The mop-up continued through the seventeenth. Admiral Porter ordered the signs of battle and capitulation removed, and the signal lights at the mound battery relit. The ruse snared the runners *Stag* and

Charlotte, inbound from Bermuda with small arms, blankets, shoes, liquor, lace, silks, and the latest ladies' hats from Paris. The blockade of the Confederate coast—all 3,549 miles of it, from the Rio Grande to the Potomac—was complete. Not an Enfield rifle, nor grain of powder, nor ounce of opium, nor bolt of uniform cloth would get through again. The Civil War, from the navy's strategic standpoint was won, if not yet over. There was still, among other matters, Wilmington itself.

The Cape Fear River, strewn with mines and obstructions, with batteries on either side, made hard going for the fleet and the army. Porter, having sent all his monitors but the *Montauk* to pound the rubble of Charleston, fashioned a dummy ironclad, as he had done at Vicksburg. She was named "Old Bogey," and Cushing piloted her upstream on the flood tide to draw the enemy's fire. On February 21, according to one gunboat skipper, "Johnny Reb let off his torpedoes without effect on it, and the old thing sailed across the river and grounded in flank and rear of the enemy's lines . . . whereupon they fell back in the night." The next day, on George Washington's birthday, Federal forces by river and road entered Wilmington.

A month earlier, on the James River below Drewry's Bluff, the largest Confederate ironclad force ever assembled in one place: *Virginia II, Fredericksburg,* and *Richmond,* escorted by a gunboat and torpedo flotilla, sortied in hopes of raiding Grant's supply base at City Point. The ironclads ran aground under the fire of Federal batteries at Trent's Reach. The U.S. naval forces, which included the double-turret monitor *Onandaga* and ten gunboats, inflicted some damage on the rebels, then hastily withdrew on orders from the monitor's commanding officer.

A short panic gripped the Federal high command. The *Onandaga's* skipper was sacked. Grant issued orders directly to naval officers on the scene, and there was talk of sending Farragut to clean up the mess before any real damage occurred. An overwhelming force was rushed from Hampton Roads, and Porter came up to take personal command before the rebels retreated, never to come down again.

On March 28, Abraham Lincoln arrived at Hampton Roads in the steamer *River Queen* to confer with Grant, Sherman, and Porter. He wanted to end the war quickly, to force the Confederate armies to surrender without further loss of life. Porter remembered the President saying to the generals, "Let them all go, officers and all, let them have their horses to plow with, and, if you like, their guns to shoot crows with." The meeting ended at noon. The following day, Grant opened the final advance on Lee's ragged army in front of Petersburg.

Lincoln and Porter spent several days together, the President very much enjoying "knocking around" in the admiral's barge. The relaxation was a sore-needed tonic for the war-weary President, and leaving Mrs. Lincoln pouting, he moved into the *Malvern*. Porter wrote to Gus Fox, "Uncle Abe is having a good time down here. . . . We pulled him through the Navy and did all we could to make him forget the cares of office, for which he seems grateful."

On the morning of April 3, came reports of the evacuation of Richmond, and two hours later, powerful explosions heralded the blowing up of the Confederate ironclads at Drewry's Bluff. The Confederate gold reserves were packed aboard the last train out of the city. Its armed escort was composed of the midshipmen of the Confederate Naval Academy, under its superintendent, Captain William Harwar Parker, who followed Jeff Davis and his government out of Richmond.

The next day, Admiral Porter and Abraham Lincoln headed up the James in the *Malvern*. At Drewry's Bluff, past the junk and debris of the Confederate Navy, they shifted with three aides to Porter's barge for the final pull to the city. Ahead they could see the fires in the rebel capital. The barge tied to the pier by the tobacco warehouse that had been the infamous Libby Prison.

Admiral Porter formed ten of his carbine carrying barge's crew into a guard around the President, six in front, four in the rear. Lincoln, with his tall hat, towered above the little procession, and they walked through the streets.

Crowds of blacks and poor whites gathered to him, the former singing hallelujahs and greeting the President as the messiah. Lincoln did not bask in the adulation, instead, he lectured the crowd on good citizenship. "I have not a particle of the bump of veneration on my head," Porter wrote some years later, "but I saw more to admire in this man, more to reverence, than I had believed possible. . . . How could one avoid liking such a man?"

Lincoln spent the night aboard the *Malvern* and told Porter he had not enjoyed himself so much in years. On April 10 came word of Lee's surrender at Appomattox, and the fleet at Hampton Roads fired a national salute of thirty-five guns. Five days later, Admiral Porter received the news of Lincoln's assassination, "the hard little man," his biographer wrote, "whose trade had taught him to jest in the heat of battle bowed his head and wept."

* * *

The war was at last over. In four horrific years, the U.S. Navy had transformed itself from a drowsy, moth-eaten organization on the fringes of the technological revolution to a maritime ironclad power briefly unmatched by any navy in the world (before it again reverted to a new dark age of twenty years of somnolent inactivity). It was the unflinching naval blockade that slowly strangled the Confederacy, denying the South the war materials and foreign intercourse without which it could not—and indeed, did not—survive the contest.

In August 1863, Abraham Lincoln addressed a meeting of "unconditional Union men" at Springfield, Illinois. After speaking of the army's great victories at Gettysburg and Vicksburg, Lincoln turned to the navy: "At all the watery margins they have been present. Not only on the deep sea, the broad bay, and the rapid river, but also up the narrow, muddy bayou, and wherever the ground was a little damp, they have been and made their tracks. Thanks to all."

SOURCES

Chapter 1: Fort Sumter

Daniel Ammen, *The Old Navy and the New;* Howard K. Beale, ed., *Diary of Gideon Welles* [hereinafter cited as Welles, *Diary*], vol. 1; George E. Belknap, "The Home Squadron in the Winter of 1860–61," *Naval Actions and History— 1799–1898;* James Buchanan, *The Administration on the Eve of the Rebellion;* French Ensor Chadwick, *Causes of the Civil War 1859–1861;* Samuel Wylie Crawford, *The Genesis of the Civil War;* Abner Doubleday, "From Moultrie to Sumter," in Robert U. Johnson and C. C. Buel, eds., *Battles and Leaders of the Civil War* [hereinafter cited as *Battles and Leaders*], vol. 1; Jeremiah H. Gilman, "With Slemmer in Pensacola Harbor," *Battles and Leaders,* vol. 1; Clarence Edward Macartney, *Mr. Lincoln's Admirals;* Allan Nevins, *The Emergence of Lincoln,* vol. 2; John G. Nicolay and John Hay, *Abraham Lincoln,* vol. 3; *Official Records of the Union and Confederate Navies in the War of the Rebellion* [hereinafter cited as *O.R.N.*], Series 1 [unless otherwise indicated], vol. 4; David D. Porter, *Incidents and Anecdotes of the Civil War* [hereinafter cited as *Incidents and Anecdotes*]; David D. Porter, *The Naval History of the Civil War;* James Russell Soley, *Admiral Porter;* W. R. Swanberg, *First Blood;* Henry Walke, *Naval Scenes and Reminiscences of the Civil War in the United States on the Southern and Western Waters During the Years 1861, 1862 and 1863* [hereinafter cited as *Naval Scenes*]; *The War of the Rebellion: A Compilation of the Official Records of the Union and Confederate Armies* [hereinafter cited as *W.R.*] Series 1, vol. 1; Richard S. West, Jr., *Mr. Lincoln's Navy;* Richard S. West, Jr., *The Second Admiral.*

Chapter 2: The Fires of Norfolk

37th Congress, 2nd Session, Senate Report No. 37, *Surrender and Destruction of Navy Yards;* Frank M. Bennett, *The Steam Navy of the United States;* Robert W. Daly, *How the "Merrimac" Won;* Clement A. Evans, ed. *Confederate Military History* [hereinafter cited as *C.M.H.*], vol. 3; William James Morgan et al., ed. *Autobiography of Rear Admiral Charles Wilkes, U.S. Navy, 1798–1877* [hereinafter cited as Wilkes, *Autobiography*]; *O.R.N.,* vol. 4; J. Thomas Scharf, *History of the Confederate States Navy* [hereinafter cited as *CSN*]; Thomas O.

Selfridge, Jr., *Memoirs of Thomas O. Selfridge, Jr.* [hereinafter cited as *Memoirs*]; Harrison A. Trexler, *The Confederate Ironclad "Virginia"*; Welles, *Diary*, vol. 1; West, *Mr. Lincoln's Navy.*

Chapter 3: Going South

Albert S. Barker, *Everyday Life in the Navy;* Edward L. Beach, *The United States Navy;* Park Benjamin, *The United States Naval Academy;* William S. Dudley, *Going South;* Robley D. Evans, *A Sailor's Log;* John D. Hayes, ed., *Samuel Francis Du Pont: A Selection from His Civil War Letters* [hereinafter cited as Du Pont, *Letters*]; Charles C. Jones, Jr., *The Life and Services of Commodore Josiah Tattnall;* Charles Lee Lewis, *Admiral Franklin Buchanan;* Charles Lee Lewis, *David Glasgow Farragut: Admiral in the Making;* Charles Lee Lewis, *Matthew Fontaine Maury;* Navy Department, *Annual Report of the Secretary of the Navy, 1861;* Navy Department, *Register of the Commissioned and Warrant Officers of the Navy of the United States . . . 1861;* Nicolay and Hay, *Abraham Lincoln*, vol. 4; *O.R.N.*, vol. 4; William Harwar Parker, "Confederate States Navy," *C.M.H.*, vol. 12; William Harwar Parker, *Recollections of a Naval Officer 1841–1865* [hereinafter cited as *Recollections*]; Scharf, *CSN;* Raphael Semmes, *Memoirs of Service Afloat During the War Between the States* [hereinafter cited as *Memoirs*]; Royce Gordon Shingleton, *John Taylor Wood;* James Russell Soley, *The Sailor Boys of '61;* Oretha D. Swartz, "Franklin Buchanan: A Study in Divided Loyalties," *Proceedings* of the United States Naval Institute [hereinafter cited as *USNIP*], December 1962; Jack Sweetman, *The U.S. Naval Academy;* Welles, *Diary*, vol. 1; West, *Mr. Lincoln's Navy.*

Chapter 4: Shaking Down

Daniel Ammen, "Du Pont and the Port Royal Expedition," *Battles and Leaders*, vol. 1; Robert W. Daly, "Pay and Prize Money in the Old Navy, 1776–1899," *USNIP*, August 1948; Charles H. Davis, *Life of Charles Henry Davis;* Jefferson Davis, *The Rise and Fall of the Confederate Government*, vol. 2; Du Pont, *Letters*, vol. 1; Gustavus Vasa Fox. *Confidential Correspondence of Gustavus Vasa Fox* [hereinafter cited as *Confidential Correspondence*], vol. 1; James M. Merrill, *The Rebel Shore;* Frank Moore, ed., *The Rebellion Record*, vol. 1, "Diary"; Navy Department, *Annual Report, 1861;* Navy Department, *Civil War Chronology*, part 1; Nevins, *The War for the Union*, vol. 1; *New York Times*, July 25, 1861; Nicolay and Hay, *Abraham Lincoln*, vol. 4; *O.R.N.*, vols. 4–5, 12, 17; Charles Oscar Paullin, *Paullin's History of Naval Administration 1775–1911;* Porter, *The Naval History of the Civil War;* Roweena Reed, *Combined Operations in the Civil War;* James D. Richardson, ed., *The Messages and Papers of Jefferson Davis and the Confederacy Including Diplomatic Correspondence 1861–1865;* Carl Sandburg, *Abraham Lincoln*, vol. 2; Scharf, *CSN;* Winfield Scott Schley, *Forty-Five Years Under the Flag;* Harold and Margaret Sprout, *The Rise of American Naval Power 1776–1918;* Craig L. Symonds, ed., *Charleston Blockade;* Welles, *Diary*, vol. 1; Welles "Admiral Farragut and New Orleans,"

Galaxy, November-December 1871; Richard S. West, Jr. *Gideon Welles;* Richard S. West, Jr., "The Morgan Purchases," *USNIP,* January 1940.

Chapter 5: Bricks Without Straw

James D. Bulloch, *The Secret Service of the Confederate States in Europe* [hereinafter cited as *Secret Service*], vol. 1; Joseph T. Durkin, *Confederate Navy Chief: Stephen R. Mallory;* Burton J. Hendrick, *Statesmen of the Lost Cause;* Jones, *The Life and Services of Commodore Josiah Tattnall;* John B. Jones, *A Rebel War Clerk's Diary at the Confederate States Capital;* Lewis, *Admiral Franklin Buchanan;* Emma Martin Maffitt, *The Life and Services of John Newland Maffitt;* Navy Department, *Dictionary of American Naval Fighting Ships* [hereinafter cited as *DANFS*], vol. 2; *O.R.N.,* vol. 16 and Series 2, vols. 1–2; Parker, "Confederate Navy," *C.M.H.,* vol. 12; Milton Perry, *Infernal Machines;* Richardson, ed. *Messages and Papers of Jefferson Davis,* vol. 1; Scharf, *CSN;* Semmes, *Memoirs;* William N. Still, Jr., *Confederate Shipbuilding;* W.R., vol. 33; Tom Henderson Wells, *The Confederate Navy.*

Chapter 6: Half-Drowned Shores

37th Congress, 3rd Session, Senate Report No. 108, *Report of the Joint Committee on the Conduct of the War* [hereinafter cited as *JCCW*], part 3; Daniel Ammen, *The Atlantic Coast;* Benjamin F. Butler, *Private and Official Correspondence . . .* [hereinafter cited as *Correspondence*], vol. 1; Du Pont, *Letters,* vol. 1; Fox, *Confidential Correspondence,* vol. 1; Arthur Gordon, "Union Stone Fleets of the Civil War," *DANFS,* vol. 5; Rush Hawkins, "Early Coast Operations in North Carolina," *Battles and Leaders,* vol. 1; Merrill, *The Rebel Shore; New York Times,* September 3, 1861; *O.R.N.,* vols. 5–6, 12; Parker, *Recollections;* Porter, *The Naval History of the Civil War; Rebellion Record,* vol. 3, "Documents"; Reed, *Combined Operations in the Civil War;* Scharf, *CSN;* Selfridge, *Memoirs; W.R.,* vol. 4; West, *Mr. Lincoln's Navy.*

Chapter 7: Port Royal

Ammen, *The Atlantic Coast;* Ammen, *The Old Navy and the New;* Roy P. Basler, ed., *Collected Works of Abraham Lincoln,* vol. 4; Edward Boykin, *Sea Devil of the Confederacy;* Charles H. Davis, *Life of Charles Henry Davis;* Du Pont, *Letters,* vol. 1; *JCCW,* vol. 3; Macartney, *Mr. Lincoln's Admirals;* Nicolay and Hay, *Abraham Lincoln,* vol. 5; *O.R.N.,* vol. 12; *Rebellion Record,* vol. 3, "Documents," "Rumors and incidents"; Scharf, *CSN; W.R.,* vol. 6; West, *Mr. Lincoln's Navy.*

Chapter 8: Stone Fleets

Davis, *Life of Charles Henry Davis;* "Naval Letters from Captain Percival Drayton, 1861–1865" [hereinafter cited as Drayton, *Letters*], *Bulletin of the New York Public Library,* November 1906; Du Pont, *Letters,* vol. 1; Fox, *Confidential*

Correspondence, vol. 1; Arthur Gordon, "The Great Stone Fleet," *USNIP,* December 1968; Arthur Gordon, "Union Stone Fleets of the Civil War," *DANFS,* vol. 5; Herman Melville, *The Stone Fleet (An Old Sailor's Lament); O.R.N.,* vol. 12; *Rebellion Record,* vol. 3, "Documents"; John E. Woodman, Jr., "The Stone Fleet," *American Neptune,* October 1961.

Chapter 9: The *Trent* Affair

Charles Francis Adams [Jr.], *Charles Francis Adams;* Charles Francis Adams [Jr.], "The *Trent* Affair," *American Historical Review,* July 1912; Du Pont, *Letters,* vol. 1; Mary Boykin Chesnut, *a Diary from Dixie;* D. Macneill Fairfax, "Captain Wilkes's Seizure of Mason and Slidell," *Battles and Leaders,* vol. 2; Norman B. Ferris, *The "Trent" Affair;* James D. Hill, "Charles Wilkes— Turbulent Scholar of the Old Navy," *USNIP,* July 1931; Drayton, *Letters;* Navy Department, *Annual Report, 1861; New York Times,* November 20–21, 1861; *O.R.N.,* vol. 1 and Series 2, vol. 3; Edward L. Peirce, *Memoir and Letters of Charles Sumner;* Porter, *The Naval History of the Civil War; Rebellion Record,* vol. 3, "Documents"; Belle Becker Sideman and Lillian Friedman, eds., *Europe Looks at the Civil War;* Geoffrey S. Smith, "Charles Wilkes: The Naval Officer as Explorer and Diplomat," in James C. Bradford, ed., *Captains of the Old Steam Navy;* Welles, "The Capture and Release of Mason and Slidell," *Galaxy,* May 1873; Welles, *Lincoln and Seward;* West, *Gideon Welles;* West, *Mr. Lincoln's Navy;* Wilkes, *Autobiography.*

Chapter 10: Up the Sounds

William B. Avery, "The Marine Artillery with the Burnside Expedition," *Personal Narratives of Events in the War of the Rebellion . . .* [hereinafter cited as *Personal Narratives*], no. 4, Series 2; Ambrose E. Burnside, "The Burnside Expedition," *Personal Narratives,* no. 6; Chesnut, *A Diary from Dixie;* Nicolay and Hay, *Abraham Lincoln,* vol. 5; *O.R.N.,* vol. 6; Parker, *Recollections; Rebellion Record,* vol. 4, "Documents"; Lorenzo Traver, "Burnside Expedition in North Carolina— Battles of Roanoke Island and Elizabeth City," *Personal Narratives,* no. 5.

Chapter 11: "our friends, the enemy"

Beach, *The United States Navy;* Sumner B. Besse, *C.S. Ironclad "Virginia" and U.S. Ironclad "Monitor". . . ;* John M. Brooke, "The *Virginia* or *Merrimac:* Her Real Projector," *Southern Historical Society Papers* [hereinafter cited as *SHSP*], 1891; "Captain Eggleston's Narrative . . . ," *SHSP,* September 1916; William R. Cline, "The Ironclad Ram *Virginia,*" *SHSP,* 1904; Daly, *How the "Merrimac" Won;* William C. Davis, *Duel Between the First Ironclads;* Charles B. Dew, *Ironmaker to the Confederacy;* Flanders, *The "Merrimac";* Catesby Jones, "Services of the *Virginia (Merrimac),*" *SHSP,* 1883; Lewis, *Admiral Franklin Buchanan;* Virginius Newton, "The Ram *Merrimac* . . . ," *SHSP,* 1892; *O.R.N.,* vols. 6–7 and Series 2, vols. 1–2; Parker, *Recollections;* Scharf, *CSN;* Selfridge,

Memoirs; Shingleton, *John Taylor Wood;* Edward Shippen, *Thirty Years at Sea;* William N. Still, *Iron Afloat; W.R.,* vol. 51, part 2; H. W. Wilson, *Ironclads in Action,* vol. 1; John L. Worden, et al., *The "Monitor" and the "Merrimac."*

Chapter 12: Cheese on a Raft

James Phinney Baxter III, *The Introduction of the Ironclad Warship;* Beach, *United States Navy;* Cornelius Bushnell, "Negotiations for the Building of the *Monitor,*" *Battles and Leaders,* vol. 1; "Captain Eggleston's Narrative"; William Conant Church, *The Life of John Ericsson;* Cline, "The Ironclad Ram *Virginia*"; Robert W. Daly, ed., *Aboard the USS "Monitor";* Davis, *Duel Between the First Ironclads;* John Ericsson, The Building of the *"Monitor," Battles and Leaders,* vol. 1; S. Dana Green, "In the *Monitor* Turret," *Battles and Leaders,* vol. 1; S. Dana Green, "*Monitor* at Sea and in Battle," *USNIP,* November 1923; G. Totten McMaster, "A Little Unwritten History of the Original USS *Monitor, USNIP,* December 1901; Navy Department, *Annual Report, 1861;* Nicolay and Hay, *Abraham Lincoln,* vol. 5; *O.R.N.,* vols. 6–7; Shingleton, *John Taylor Wood;* Welles, *Diary,* vol. 1; Welles, "The First Iron-Clad Monitor," in *The Annals of the War;* John Taylor Wood, "The First Fight of Iron-Clads," *Battles and Leaders,* vol. 1; Worden, et al., *The "Monitor" and the "Merrimac."*

Chapter 13: Stinkpots and Turtles

Edwin C. Bearss, *Hardluck Ironclad;* Charles B. Boynton, *The History of the Navy During the Rebellion,* vol. 1; *DANFS,* vol. 2; R. Ernest and Trevor N. Dupuy, *Military Heritage of America;* James B. Eads, "Recollections of Foote and the Gun-Boats," *Battles and Leaders,* vol. 1; Fox, *Confidential Correspondence,* vol. 2; Ulysses S. Grant, *Personal Memoirs of U. S. Grant* [hereinafter cited as *Memoirs*], vol. 1; Jim Dan Hill, *Sea Dogs of the Sixties;* James Mason Hoppin, *The Life of Andrew Hull Foote, Rear Admiral, USN;* Robert Erwin Johnson, *Rear Admiral John Rodgers; 1812–1882;* Macartney, *Mr. Lincoln's Admirals;* James M. Merrill, *Battle Flags South;* John D. Milligan, "From Theory to Application: The Emergence of the American Ironclad War Vessel," *Military Affairs,* July 1984; *O.R.N.,* vol. 22; Porter, *The Naval History of the Civil War;* Jesse Taylor, "The Defense of Fort Henry," *Battles and Leaders,* vol. 1; *W.R.,* vol. 7; Walke, *Naval Scenes;* Walke, "The Gun-Boats at Belmont and Fort Henry," *Battles and Leaders,* vol. 1; Walke, "The Western Flotilla at Fort Donelson, Island Number Ten, Fort Pillow and Memphis" [hereinafter cited as "Western Flotilla"], *Battles and Leaders,* vol. 1; Lew Wallace, "The Capture of Fort Donelson," *Battles and Leaders,* vol. 1; Welles, *Diary,* vol. 1; West, *Mr. Lincoln's Navy.*

Chapter 14: "on to Memphis"

Davis, *Life of Charles Henry Davis;* H. Allen Gosnell, *Guns on the Western Waters;* Hoppin, *The Life of Andrew Hull Foote; O.R.N.,* vols. 18, 22–23; Scharf, *CSN;* Walke, *Naval Scenes;* Walke, "Western Flotilla"; West, *Mr. Lincoln's Navy.*

Chapter 15: New Orleans

Barker, *Everyday Life in the Navy; DANFS,* vol. 2; George Dewey, *Autobiography of George Dewey;* Durkin, *Confederate Navy Chief;* Loyall Farragut, *The Life and Letters of David Glasgow Farragut* [hereinafter cited as *Life and Letters*]; Fox, *Confidential Correspondence,* vol. 2; Beverly Kennon, "Fighting Farragut Below New Orleans," *Battles and Leaders,* vol. 2; Lewis, *David Glasgow Farragut: Our First Admiral; O.R.N.,* vols. 16, 18, and Series 2, vol. 1; Porter, *Incidents and Anecdotes;* Porter, *The Naval History of the Civil War;* Schley, *Forty-Five Years Under the Flag;* Soley, *Admiral Porter;* Welles, "Admiral Farragut and New Orleans"; Welles, *Diary,* vol. 2; West, *Mr. Lincoln's Navy;* West, *The Second Admiral.*

Chapter 16: Vicksburg Rebuff

Isaac N. Brown, "The Confederate Gun-Boat *Arkansas,*" *Battles and Leaders,* vol. 3; Butler, *Correspondence,* vol. 1; *DANFS,* vol. 2; Davis, *Life of Charles Henry Davis;* Farragut, *Life and Letters;* Fox, *Confidential Correspondence,* vol. 2; George W. Gift, "The Story of the *Arkansas,*" *SHSP,* 1884; Gosnell, *Guns on the Western Waters;* Navy Department, *Civil War Naval Chronology,* part 2, 1862; *O.R.N.,* vols. 18–19; Charles W. Read, "Reminiscences of the Confederate States Navy," *SHSP,* May 1876; Soley, *Admiral Porter;* James Russell Soley, "Naval Operations in the Vicksburg Campaign," *Battles and Leaders,* vol. 3; Still, *Iron Afloat; W.R.,* vol. 15; Walke, *Naval Scenes;* West, *Mr. Lincoln's Navy;* West, "Relations Between Farragut and Porter," *USNIP,* July 1935.

Chapter 17: Vicksburg Return

Bearss, *Hardluck Ironclad;* Mark Mayo Boatner III, *The Civil War Dictionary; DANFS,* vol. 3; Dewey, *Autobiography;* Durkin, *Confederate Navy Chief;* Farragut, *Life and Letters;* Fox, *Confidential Correspondence,* vol. 2; Gosnell, *Guns on the Western Waters;* Lawrence Lee Hewitt, *Port Hudson . . . ;* Lewis, *Farragut: Admiral in the Making;* Alfred Thayer Mahan, *Admiral Farragut; O.R.N.,* vols. 19, 23–25; Porter, *Incidents and Anecdotes;* Soley, "Naval Operations in the Vicksburg Campaign," *Battles and Leaders,* vol. 3; *W.R.,* vol. 17, part 2, vol. 24, part 1; Walke, *Naval Scenes;* Welles, *Diary,* vol. 1; West, *Mr. Lincoln's Navy;* West, *The Second Admiral;* E. Cort Williams, "The Cruise of 'The Black Terror'. . . ," in Robert Hunter, ed., *Sketches of War History: 1861–1865,* vol. 3.

Chapter 18: Red River

Richard B. Irwin, "The Red River Campaign," *Battles and Leaders,* vol. 4; *JCCW,* vol. 2 "Red River Expedition"; *O.R.N.,* vol. 26; Porter, *Incidents and Anecdotes;* Selfridge, *Memoirs;* Thomas O. Selfridge, "The Navy in the Red River," *Battles and Leaders,* vol. 4; E. Kirby Smith, "Defense of the Red River," *Battles and Leaders,* vol. 4; Welles, *Diary,* vol. 1; West, *Mr. Lincoln's Navy;* West, *The Second Admiral.*

Chapter 19: Mobile Bay

Daniel B. Conrad, "Capture of the C.S. Ram *Tennessee* in Mobile Bay, August, 1864," *SHSP*, 1891; Fox, *Confidential Correspondence*, vol. 1; James D. Johnston, "The Ram *Tennessee* at Mobile Bay," *Battles and Leaders*, vol. 4; John C. Kinney, "Farragut at Mobile Bay," *Battles and Leaders*, vol. 4; Lewis, *Admiral Franklin Buchanan;* Lewis, *Farragut: Our First Admiral;* Mahan, *Admiral Farragut;* *O.R.N.*, vols. 18–19, 21; Foxhall Parker, *The Battle of Mobile Bay;* Still, *Iron Afloat;* J. Crittenden Watson and Joseph Marthon, "The Lashing of Admiral Farragut in the Rigging," *Battles and Leaders*, vol. 4; John C. Watson, "Farragut and Mobile Bay—Personal Reminiscences," *USNIP*, May 1927; Welles, *Diary*, vol. 2; Wilson, *Ironclads in Action*, vol. 1.

Chapter 20: On the High Seas

Adams, *Charles Francis Adams;* John M. Browne, "The Duel Between the *Alabama* and the *Kearsarge*," *Battles and Leaders*, vol. 4; Bulloch, *The Secret Service of the Confederate States in Europe*, vols. 1–2; George W. Dalzell, *The Flight from the Flag;* Du Pont, *Letters*, vol. 2; Hendrick, *Statesmen of the Lost Cause;* Kell, "Cruise and Combats of the *Alabama*," *Battles and Leaders*, vol. 4; Lee Kennett, "The Strange Career of the *Stonewall*," *USNIP*, February 1968; Maffitt, *John Newland Maffitt;* James M. Morgan, *Recollections of a Rebel Reefer; O.R.N.*, vols. 1–3; Porter, *The Naval History of the Civil War;* Scharf, *CSN;* Semmes, *Memoirs;* Shingleton, *John Taylor Wood;* Arthur Sinclair, *Two Years on the "Alabama";* G. Terry Sinclair, "The Eventful Cruise of the *Florida*," *Century Magazine*, July 1898; James Russell Soley, *The Blockade and the Cruisers;* Charles G. Summersell, ed., *The Journal of George Townley Fullam;* Welles, *Diary*, vol. 1; West, *Gideon Welles;* Wilson, *Ironclads in Action*, vol. 1.

Chapter 21: "On to Charleston!"

JCCW, part 3; Pierre G. T. Beauregard, "Torpedo Service in the Harbor and Water Defenses of Charleston," *SHSP*, April 1878; E. Milby Burton, *The Siege of Charleston, 1861–1865;* Madeleine Vinton Dahlgren, *Memoir of John A. Dahlgren . . . ;* Daly, "Pay and Prize Money in the Old Navy," *USNIP*, August 1948; Drayton, *Letters;* Du Pont, *Letters*, vol. 2; William T. Glassell, "Reminiscences of Torpedo Service in Charleston Harbor," *SHSP*, July–December 1877; Alvah F. Hunter, *A Year on a Monitor . . . ;* Johnson, *Rear Admiral John Rodgers;* Navy Department, *Annual Report, 1864–1865;* Navy Department, *Civil War Chronology*, part 3, 1863; *O.R.N.*, vols. 13–14; Parker, *Recollections;* Perry, *Infernal Machines;* Christopher R. P. Rodgers, "Du Pont's Attack at Charleston," *Battles and Leaders*, vol. 4; Scharf, *CSN;* Thomas H. Stevens, "The Boat Attack on Sumter," *Battles and Leaders*, vol. 4; *W.R.*, vol. 28, part 1; Still, *Iron Afloat;* Welles, *Diary*, vol. 1; West, *Gideon Welles;* Stephen R. Wise, *Lifeline of the Confederacy.*

Chapter 22: Wilmington, to the End

Ammen, *The Old Navy and the New;* William E. Beard, "The Fort Fisher 'Volcano,'" *USNIP,* August 1932; William B. Cushing, "The Destruction of the *Albemarle," Battles and Leaders,* vol. 4; Gilbert Elliott, "The First Battle of the Confederate Ram *Albemarle," Battles and Leaders,* vol. 4; Evans, *A Sailor's Log;* Edgar Holden, "The *Albemarle* and the *Sassacus," Battles and Leaders,* vol. 4; *JCCW,* part 2, "Fort Fisher Expedition"; *New York Times,* December 31, 1864; *O.R.N.,* vols. 8–12, 26; Parker, *Recollections;* Charles Oscar Paullin, "President Lincoln and the Navy," *American Historical Review,* January 1909; Porter, *Incidents and Anecdotes;* Porter, *The Naval History of the Civil War;* Scharf, *CSN;* Soley, *Admiral Porter;* Still, *Iron Afloat; W.R.,* vol. 42; Welles, *Diary,* vol. 2; West, *Gideon Welles;* West, *Mr. Lincoln's Navy;* West, *The Second Admiral.*

BIBLIOGRAPHY

Government Publications

37th Congress, 2nd Session, Senate Report No. 37. *Surrender and Destruction of Navy Yards.* Washington, D.C.: 1862.

———. 3rd Session, Senate Report No. 108. *Report of the Joint Committee on the Conduct of the War,* parts 2 and 3. Washington, D.C.: 1863.

Canfield, Eugene B. *Civil War Naval Ordnance.* Washington, D.C.: Naval History Division, Navy Department, 1969.

Morgan, William James, et. al., eds. *Autobiography of Rear Admiral Charles Wilkes, U.S. Navy, 1798–1877.* Washington, D.C.: Naval History Division, Navy Department, 1979.

Navy Department. *Annual Reports of the Secretary of the Navy,* 1860–1866. Washington, D.C.: 1860–1866.

———. *Civil War Chronology,* 5 vols. [plus summary]. Washington, D.C.: nd.

———. *Dictionary of American Naval Fighting Ships,* 8 vols. Washington, D.C.: Naval History Division, Navy Department, 1963–1981.

———. *Register of the Commissioned and Warrant Officers of the Navy of the United States, Including Officers of the Marine Corps and Others, for the Year 1860, 1861.* Washington, D.C.: 1860, 1861.

Official Records of the Union and Confederate Navies in the War of the Rebellion, Series1, 27 vols.; SeriesII, 3 vols. Washington, D.C.: 1894–1922.

The War of the Rebellion: A Compilation of the Official Records of the Union and Confederate Armies, SeriesI, various vols. Washington, D.C.: 1880–1902.

Books

Abbot, Willis J. *The Naval History of the United States,* vol. 2. New York: Collier, 1890.

Adams, Charles Francis [Jr.]. *Charles Francis Adams.* Boston: Houghton, Mifflin, 1900.

Ammen, Daniel. *The Atlantic Coast.* New York: Scribner's, 1883.

———. *The Old Navy and the New.* Philadelphia: Lippincott, 1891.

Barker, Albert S. *Everyday Life in the Navy: Autobiography of Rear Admiral Albert S. Barker, USN*. Boston: Badger, 1928.

Baysier, Roy P., ed. *Collected Works of Abraham Lincoln,* 9 vols. New Brunswick: Rutgers University Press, 1990.

Baxter, James Phinney III. *The Introduction of the Ironclad Warship.* Cambridge, Mass.: Harvard University Press, 1933.

Beach, Edward L. *The United States Navy—200 Years.* New York: Henry Holt, 1986.

Beale, Howard K., ed. *Diary of Gideon Welles,* 3 vols. New York: Norton, 1960.

Bearss, Edwin C. *Hardluck Ironclad: The Sinking and Salvage of the "Cairo."* Baton Rouge: Louisiana State University Press, 1980.

Belknap, George E. "The Home Squadron in the Winter of 1860–61," *Papers of the Military Society of Massachusetts,* vol. 12, *Naval Actions and History— 1799–1898.* Boston: Griffith, 1902.

Benjamin, Park. *The United States Naval Academy.* New York: Putnam, 1900.

Bennett, Frank M. *The "Monitor" and the Navy Under Steam.* Boston: Houghton, Mifflin, 1900.

———. *The Steam Navy of the United States: A History of the Growth of the Steam Vessel of War in the United States Navy, and of the Naval Engineer Corps.* Pittsburgh: Nicholson, 1896.

Besse, Sumner B. *C.S. Ironclad "Virginia" and U.S. Ironclad "Monitor"—With Data and References for Scale Models.* Newport News, Va.: Mariners Museum, 1978.

Bigelow, John. *France and the Confederate Navy 1862–1868.* New York: Harper, 1888.

Boatner, Mark Mayo III. *The Civil War Dictionary.* New York: McKay, 1959.

Boykin, Edward. *Sea Devil of the Confederacy: The Story of the "Florida" and Her Captain, John Newland Maffitt.* New York: Funk and Wagnalls, 1959.

Boynton, Charles B. *The History of the Navy During the Rebellion,* 2 vols. New York: Appleton, 1867.

Bradford, James C., ed. *Captains of the Old Steam Navy: Makers of the American Naval Tradition 1840–1880.* Annapolis: Naval Institute Press, 1986.

Buchanan, James. *The Administration on the Eve of the Rebellion: A History of Four Years Before the War.* London: Sampson Low, 1865.

Bulloch, James D. *The Secret Service of the Confederate States in Europe: Or, How the Confederate Cruisers Were Equipped,* 2 vols. London: Richard Bentley, 1883.

Burton, E. Milby. *The Siege of Charleston, 1861–1865.* Columbia, S.C.: University of South Carolina Press, 1970.

Butler, Benjamin F. *Private and Official Correspondence of Gen. Benjamin F. Butler During the Period of the Civil War,* 5 vols. Norwood, Mass.: Privately published, 1917.

Carrison, Daniel J. *The Navy from Wood to Steel: 1860–1890.* New York: Franklin Watts, 1965.

Chadwick, French Ensor. *Causes of the Civil War 1859–1861.* New York: Harper & Bros., 1906.

Chesnut, Mary Boykin. *A Diary from Dixie.* Boston: Appleton, 1905.

Church, William Conant. *The Life of John Ericsson.* New York: Scribner's, 1911.

Clark, Charles E. *My Fifty Years in the Navy.* Boston: Little, Brown, 1917.

Coletta, Paolo E., ed. *American Secretaries of the Navy,* vol. 1, *1775–1913.* Annapolis: Naval Institute Press, 1980.

Crandell, Warren D. *History of the Ram Fleet and the Mississippi Marine Brigade . . . The Story of the Ellets and Their Men.* St. Louis: Privately published, 1907.

Crawford, Samuel Wylie. *The Genesis of the Civil War: The Story of Sumter 1860–1861.* New York: Webster, 1887.

Dahlgren, Madeleine Vinton. *Memoir of John A. Dahlgren—Rear Admiral United States Navy.* New York: Webster, 1891.

Daly, Robert W., ed. *Aboard the USS "Monitor": 1862—The Letters of Acting Paymaster William Frederick Keeler, U.S. Navy.* Annapolis: Naval Institute Press, 1964.

———. *How the "Merrimac" Won: The Strategic Story of the CSS "Virginia."* New York: Crowell, 1957.

Dalzell, George W. *The Flight from the Flag: The Continuing Effect of the Civil War upon the American Carrying Trade.* Chapel Hill, N.C.: University of North Carolina Press, 1940.

Davis, Charles H. *Life of Charles Henry Davis—Rear Admiral 1807–1877.* Boston: Houghton, Mifflin, 1899.

Davis, Jefferson. *The Rise and Fall of the Confederate Government,* 2 vols. Richmond: Garrett and Massie, 1881.

Davis, William C. *Duel Between the First Ironclads.* Baton Rouge: University of Louisiana Press, 1975.

———. *The Image of War 1861–1865,* 6 vols. Garden City, N.Y.: Doubleday, 1983.

Dew, Charles B. *Ironmaker to the Confederacy: Joseph R. Anderson and the Tredegar Iron Works.* New Haven: Yale University Press, 1966.

Dewey, George. *Autobiography of George Dewey: Admiral of the Navy.* New York: Scribner's, 1913.

Dudley, William S. *Going South: U.S. Navy Officer Resignations and Dismissals on the Eve of the Civil War.* Washington, D.C.: Naval Historical Foundation, 1981.

Du Pont, H. A. *Rear Admiral Samuel Francis Du Pont.* New York: National Americana Society, 1926.

Dupuy, R. Ernest, and Trevor N. Dupuy. *Military Heritage of America.* New York: McGraw-Hill, 1956.

Durkin, Joseph T. *Confederate Navy Chief: Stephen R. Mallory.* Columbia, S.C.: University of South Carolina Press, 1987.

Evans, Clement A., ed. *Confederate Military History,* vol. 12. Atlanta: Confederate Publishing Co., 1899.

Evans, Robley D. *A Sailor's Log: Recollections of Forty Years of Naval Life.* New York: Appleton, 1901.

Farragut, Loyall. *The Life and Letters of David Glasgow Farragut: First Admiral of the United States Navy.* New York: Appleton, 1891.

Ferris, Norman B. *The "Trent" Affair: A Diplomatic Crisis.* Knoxville, Tenn.: University of Tennessee Press, 1977.

Flanders, Alan B. *The "Merrimac": The Story of the Conversion of the U.S.S. "Merrimac" into the Confederate Ironclad Warship C.S.S. "Virginia".* Norfolk, Va.: Privately published, 1982.

Fox, Gustavus Vasa. *Confidential Correspondence of Gustavus Vasa Fox Assistant Secretary of the Navy 1861–1865,* 2 vols. New York: Naval Historical Society, 1918.

Gosnell, H. Allen. *Guns on the Western Waters: The Story of River Gunboats in the Civil War.* Baton Rouge: Louisiana State University Press, 1949.

Grant, Ulysses S. *Personal Memoirs of U. S. Grant,* 2 vols. New York: Webster, 1885.

Hamersly, Lewis R. *The Records of Living Officers of the U.S. Navy and Marine Corps.* Philadelphia: Lippincott, 1870.

Hayes, John D. *Samuel Francis Du Pont: A Selection from His Civil War Letters,* 3 vols. Ithaca, N.Y.: Cornell University Press, 1969.

Hendrick, Burton J. *Statesmen of the Lost Cause: Jefferson Davis and His Cabinet.* Boston: Little, Brown, 1939.

Hewitt, Lawrence Lee. *Port Hudson: Confederate Bastion on the Mississippi.* Baton Rouge: Louisiana State University Press, 1987.

Hill, Jim Dan. *Sea Dogs of the Sixties: Farragut and Seven Contemporaries.* Minneapolis: University of Minnesota Press, 1935.

Hoppin, James Mason. *The Life of Andrew Hull Foote, Rear Admiral, USN.* New York: Harper, 1874.

Hunt, O. E., ed. *The Photographic History of the Civil War,* vol. 6, *The Navies.* New York: Review of Reviews, 1912.

Hunter, Alvah F. *A Year on a Monitor and the Destruction of Fort Sumter.* Columbia, S.C.: University of South Carolina Press, 1987.

Johnson, Robert Erwin. *Rear Admiral John Rodgers 1812–1882.* Annapolis: Naval Institute Press, 1967.

Johnson, Robert U., and C. C. Buel, eds. *Battles and Leaders of the Civil War,* 4 vols. New York: Century, 1887–1888. Includes:

Ammen, Daniel, "Du Pont and the Port Royal Expedition," vol. 1.

Bartlett, John Russell, "The *Brooklyn* at the Passage of the Forts," vol. 2.

Beauregard, Pierre G. T., "The Defense of Charleston," vol. 4.

Brown, Isaac N., "The Confederate Gun-Boat *Arkansas,*" vol. 3.

Browne, John M., "The Duel Between the *Alabama* and the *Kearsarge,*" vol. 4.

Bushnell, Cornelius, "Negotiations for the Building of the *Monitor,*" vol. 1.

Butts, Francis B., "The Loss of the *Monitor,*" vol. 1.

Chester, James, "Inside Sumter in '61," vol. 1.

Cushing, William B., "The Destruction of the *Albemarle,*" vol. 4.

Doubleday, Abner, "From Moultrie to Sumter," vol. 1.

Eads, James B., "Recollections of Foote and the Gun-Boats," vol. 1.

Ellet, Alfred W., "Ellet and his Steam-Rams at Memphis," vol. 1.

Elliott, Gilbert. "The First Battle of the Confederate Ram *Albemarle,*" vol. 4.

Ericsson, John, "The Building of the *Monitor,*" vol. 1.

Fairfax, D. Macneill, "Captain Wilkes's Seizure of Mason and Slidell," vol. 2.

Gilman, Jeremiah H., "With Slemmer in Pensacola Harbor," vol. 1.

Green, S. Dana, "In the *Monitor* Turret," vol. 1.

Hawkins, Rush, "Early Coast Operations in North Carolina," vol. 1.
Holden, Edgar, "The *Albemarle* and the *Sassacus*," vol. 4.
Irwin, Richard B., "The Red River Campaign," vol. 4.
Johnston, James D., "The Ram *Tennessee* at Mobile Bay," vol. 4.
Kell, John McIntosh, "Cruise and Combats of the *Alabama*, vol. 4.
Kennon, Beverly, "Fighting Farragut Below New Orleans," vol. 2.
Kinney, John C., "Farragut at Mobile Bay," vol. 4.
Meredith, William T., "Farragut's Capture of New Orleans," vol. 2.
"Opposing Forces in the Operations at New Orleans," vol. 2.
Page, Richard L., "The Defense of Fort Morgan," vol. 4.
Porter, David D., "The Opening of the Lower Mississippi," vol. 2.
Rodgers, Christopher R. P., "Du Pont's Attack at Charleston," vol. 4.
Selfridge, Thomas O. "The Navy in the Red River," vol. 4.
Smith, E. Kirby. "Defense of the Red River," vol. 4.
Soley, James Russell, "The Confederate Cruisers," vol. 4.
———, "Early Operations in the Gulf," vol. 2.
———, "Gulf Operations in 1862 and 1863," vol. 3.
———, "Minor Operations of the South Atlantic Squadron Under Du Pont," vol. 4.
———, "Naval Operations in the Vicksburg Campaign," vol. 3.
Stevens, Thomas H., "The Boat Attack on Sumter," vol. 4.
Taylor, Jesse, "The Defense of Fort Henry," vol. 1.
Walke, Henry, "The Gun-Boats at Belmont and Fort Henry," vol. 1.
———, "The Western Flotilla at Fort Donelson, Island Number Ten, Fort Pillow and Memphis," vol. 1.
Wallace, Lew, "The Capture of Fort Donelson," vol. 1.
Warley, A. F., "The Ram *Manassas* at the Passage of the New Orleans Forts," vol. 2.
Watson, J. Crittenden, and Joseph Marthon, "The Lashing of Admiral Farragut in the Rigging," vol. 4.
Wood, John Taylor, "The First Fight of Iron-Clads," vol. 1.
Jones, Charles C., Jr. *The Life and Services of Commodore Josiah Tattnall.* Savannah: Privately published, 1878.
Jones, John B. *A Rebel War Clerk's Diary at the Confederate States Capital,* 2 vols. New York: Old Hickory, 1935.
Knox, Dudley W. *A History of the United States Navy.* New York: Putnam, 1936.
Lewis, Charles Lee, *Admiral Franklin Buchanan.* Baltimore: Norman, Remington, 1929.
———. *David Glasgow Farragut: Admiral in the Making.* Annapolis: United States Naval Institute, 1941.
———. *David Glasgow Farragut: Our First Admiral.* Annapolis: United States
———. *Matthew Fontaine Maury: The Pathfinder of the Seas.* Annapolis: United States Naval Institute, 1927.
Macartney, Clarence Edward. *Mr. Lincoln's Admirals.* New York: Funk & Wagnalls, 1956.
Maclay, Edgar Stanton. *Reminiscences of the Old Navy.* New York: Putnam, 1898.

Maffitt, Emma Martin. *The Life and Services of John Newland Maffitt.* New York: Neale, 1906.

Mahan, Alfred Thayer. *Admiral Farragut.* New York: Appleton, 1892.

———. *From Sail to Steam: Recollections of Naval Life.* New York: Harper, 1907.

———.*The Gulf and Inland Waters.* New York: Scribner's, 1883.

Merrill, James M. *Battle Flags South: The Story of the Civil War Navies on Western Waters.* Rutherford, N. J.: Fairleigh Dickinson University Press, 1970.

———. *The Rebel Shore: The Story of Union Sea Power in the Civil War.* Boston: Little, Brown, 1957.

Millett, Allan R. *Semper Fidelis: The History of the United States Marine Corps.* New York: Macmillan, 1980.

Milligan, John D. "Andrew Foote: Zealous Reformer, Administrator, Warrior," in Bradford, *Captains of the Old Steam Navy,* op. cit.

———. *Gunboats Down the Mississippi.* Annapolis: Naval Institute Press, 1965.

Moore, Frank, ed. *The Rebellion Record: A Diary of American Events,* 12 vols. New York: Putnam, 1862–1871.

Mordell, Albert, comp. *Selected Essays by Gideon Welles: Civil War and Reconstruction,* 2 vols. New York: Twayne, 1959.

Morgan, James M. *Recollections of a Rebel Reefer.* Boston: Houghton, Mifflin, 1917.

Myer, Albert J. *A Manual of Signals: For the Use of Signal Officers in the Field, and for Military and Naval Students . . .* New York: Van Nostrand, 1872.

Nash, Howard P. *Stormy Petrel: The Life and Times of General Benjamin F. Butler, 1818–1893.* Rutherford, N. J.: Fairleigh Dickinson University Press, 1969.

Nevins, Allan. *The Emergence of Lincoln,* 2 vols. New York: Scribner's, 1950.

———. *The War for the Union,* 4 vols. New York: Scribner's, 1959–1971.

Nicolay, John G., and John Hay. *Abraham Lincoln: A History,* 8 vols. New York: Century, 1909.

Niven, John. *Gideon Welles: Lincoln's Secretary of the Navy.* New York: Oxford University Press, 1973.

Owsley, Frank Lawrence. *King Cotton Diplomacy: Foreign Relations of the Confederate States of America.* Chicago: University of Chicago Press, 1959.

Parker, Foxhall A. *The Battle of Mobile Bay . . .* Boston: Williams, 1878.

Parker, William Harwar. *Recollections of a Naval Officer 1841–1865.* Annapolis: Naval Institute Press, 1985.

Paullin, Charles Oscar. *Paullin's History of Naval Administration 1775–1911.* Annapolis: Naval Institute Press, 1968.

Peirce, Edward L. *Memoir and Letters of Charles Sumner,* 4 vols. Boston: Roberts, 1877–1894.

Perry, Milton F. *Infernal Machines: The Story of Confederate Submarine and Mine Warfare.* Baton Rouge.: Louisiana State University Press, 1965.

Personal Narratives of Events in the War of the Rebellion, Being Papers Read Before the Rhode Island Soldiers and Sailors Historical Society. Providence: Bangs Williams, 1880–1882. Includes:

Avery, William B., "The Marine Artillery with the Burnside Expedition," no. 4, Series 2, 1880.

Burnside, Ambrose E., "The Burnside Expedition," no. 6, 1882.

Butts, Francis B., "A Cruise Along the Blockade," no. 12, Series 2, 1881.

Traver, Lorenzo, "Burnside Expedition in North Carolina—Battles of Roanoke Island and Elizabeth City," no. 5.

Pollard, Edward A. *Southern History of the War,* 2 vols. New York: C. B. Richardson, 1866.

Porter, David D. *Incidents and Anecdotes of the Civil War.* New York: Appleton, 1885.

————. *The Naval History of the Civil War.* New York: Sherman, 1886.

Reed, Roweena. *Combined Operations in the Civil War.* Annapolis: Naval Institute Press, 1978.

Reynolds, Clark G. *Famous American Admirals.* New York: Van Nostrand, 1978.

Richardson, James D., ed. *The Messages and Papers of Jefferson Davis and the Confederacy Including Diplomatic Correspondence 1861–1865,* 2 vols. New York: Chelsea, 1966.

Sandburg, Carl. *Abraham Lincoln: The War Years,* 4 vols. New York: Harcourt, Brace, 1939.

Scharf, J. Thomas. *History of the Confederate States Navy: From Its Organization to the Surrender of Its Last Vessel.* Albany, N.Y.: McDonough, 1894.

Schley, Winfield Scott. *Forty-Five Years Under The Flag.* New York: Appleton, 1904.

Schwab, John C. *The Confederate States of America 1861–1865: A Financial and Industrial History of the South During the Civil War.* New York: Scribner's, 1901.

Selfridge, Thomas O., Jr. *Memoirs of Thomas O. Selfridge, Jr., Rear Admiral, U.S.N.* New York: Putnam, 1924.

Semmes, Raphael. *Memoirs of Service Afloat During the War Between the States.* Baltimore: Kelly, Piet, 1869.

Shingleton, Royce Gordon. *John Taylor Wood: Sea Ghost of the Confederacy.* Athens, Ga.: University of Georgia Press, 1979.

Shippen, Edward. *Thirty Years at Sea.* New York, Arno Press, 1979.

Sideman, Belle Becker, and Lillian Friedman, eds. *Europe Looks at the Civil War.* New York: Orion, 1960.

Silverstone, Paul H. *Warships of the Civil War Navies.* Annapolis: Naval Institute Press, 1989.

Sinclair, Arthur. *Two Years on the "Alabama."* Annapolis: Naval Institute Press, 1989.

Solely, James Russell. *Admiral Porter.* New York: D. Appleton, 1903.

————. *The Blockade and the Cruisers.* New York: Scribner's, 1883.

————. *The Sailor Boys of '61.* Boston: Estes and Lauriat, 1888.

Sprout, Harold, and Margaret Sprout. *The Rise of American Naval Power 1776–1918.* Annapolis: Naval Institute Press, 1967.

Stern, Philip Van Doren. *The Confederate Navy: A Pictorial History.* Garden City, N.Y.: Doubleday, 1962.

Still, William N., Jr. *Confederate Shipbuilding.* Athens, Ga.: University of Georgia Press, 1969.

————. *Iron Afloat: The Story of the Confederate Armorclads.* Columbia, S.C.: University of South Carolina Press, 1985.

Summersell, Charles G., ed. *The Journal of George Townley Fullam: Boarding Officer of the Confederate Sea Raider "Alabama."* Huntsville, Ala.: University of Alabama Press, 1973.

Swanberg, W. A. *First Blood: The Story of Fort Sumter.* New York: Scribner's, 1957.

Sweetman, Jack. *The U.S. Naval Academy.* Annapolis: Naval Institute Press, 1979.

Symonds, Craig L., ed. *Charleston Blockade: The Journals of John B. Marchand, U.S. Navy 1861–1862.* Newport, R. I.: U.S. Naval War College, 1976.

Taylor, Thomas E. *Running the Blockade.* London.: John Murray, 1896.

Tily, James C. *The Uniforms of the United States Navy.* New York: Yoseloff, 1964.

Trexler, Harrison A. *The Confederate Ironclad "Virginia."* Chicago: University of Chicago Press, 1938.

Valle, James E. *Rocks and Shoals: Order and Discipline in the Old Navy 1800–1861.* Annapolis: Naval Institute Press, 1980.

Walke, Henry. *Naval Scenes and Reminiscences of the Civil War in the United States on the Southern and Western Waters During the Years 1861, 1862 and 1863.* New York: Reed, 1877.

Weigley, Russell F. *History of the United States Army.* Bloomington, Ind.: Indiana University Press, 1984.

Welles, Gideon. *Lincoln and Seward: Remarks upon the Memorial Address of Chas. Francis Adams, on the Late Wm. H. Seward.* New York: Sheldon, 1874.

————. "The First Iron-Clad Monitor," in *The Annals of the War.* Philadelphia: Times Publishing, 1879.

Wells, Tom Henderson. *The Confederate Navy: A Study in Organization.* Huntsville, Ala.: University of Alabama Press, 1971.

West, Richard S., Jr. *Admirals of American Empire: The Combined Story of George Dewey, Alfred Thayer Mahan, Winfield Scott Schley and William Thomas Sampson.* Indianapolis and New York: Bobbs-Merrill, 1948.

————. *Gideon Welles: Lincoln's Navy Department.* Indianapolis and New York: Bobbs-Merrill, 1943.

————. *Mr. Lincoln's Navy.* New York: Longmans, Green, 1957.

————. *The Second Admiral: A Life of David Dixon Porter, 1813–1891.* New York: Coward-McCann, 1937.

Williams, E. Cort. "The Cruise of 'The Black Terror' (Porter's Dummy at Vicksburg)," in Robert Hunter, ed. *Sketches of War History: 1861–1865: Papers Prepared for the Ohio Commandery of the Military Order of the Loyal Legion of the United States, 1888–1890,* vol. 3. Cincinnati: Ohio Commandery, 1890.

Wilson, H. W. *Ironclads in Action,* vol. 1. London: Sampson Low, Marston, 1896.

Wilson, James Grant, and Titus Munson Coans, eds. *Personal Recollections of the War of the Rebellion: Addresses Delivered Before the New York Com-*

mandery of the Loyal Legion of the United States, 1883–1891. New York: New York Commandery, 1891. Includes:

Brown, George W., "The Mortar Flotilla and Its Connection with the Bombardment and Capture of Forts Jackson and St. Philip."

Brown, George W., "Service in the Mississippi Squadron, and Its Connection with the Siege and Capture of Vicksburg."

Farragut, Loyall, "Passing the Port Hudson Batteries."

Wise, Stephen R. *Lifeline of the Confederacy: Blockade Running During the Civil War.* Columbia, S.C.: University of South Carolina Press, 1988.

Woodward, C. Vann. *Mary Chesnut's Civil War.* New Haven: Yale University Press, 1981.

Worden, John L., Dana Green, and H. Ashton Ramsay. *The "Monitor" and the "Merrimac": Both Sides of the Story.* New York: Harper & Brothers, 1912.

Periodicals

Adams, Charles Francis [Jr.] "The *Trent* Affair." *American Historical Review,* July 1912.

Anderson, Bern. "The Naval Strategy of the Civil War." *Military Affairs,* Spring 1962.

Anderson, Stuart. "1861: Blockade vs. Closing the Confederate Ports." *Military Affairs,* December 1977.

Anonymous. "Life on a Blockader." *Continental Monthly,* July 1864.

Aptheker, Herbert. "The Negro in the Union Navy." *Journal of Negro History,* April 1947.

Banks, Carlos. "Blockaders off the American Coast." *Proceedings* of the United States Naval Institute, February 1941.

Beard, William E. "The Fort Fisher 'Volcano.'" *Proceedings* of the United States Naval Institute, August 1932.

Beauregard, Pierre G. T. "Torpedo Service in the Harbor and Water Defenses of Charleston." *Southern Historical Society Papers,* vol. 5, April 1878.

Blair, Carvel Hall. "Submarines of the Confederate Navy." *Proceedings* of the United States Naval Institute, October 1952.

Brooke, John M. "The *Virginia* or *Merrimac:* Her Real Projector." *Southern Historical Society Papers,* 1891.

Buell, Thomas B. "Saga of Drydock One." *Proceedings* of the United States Naval Institute, July 1970.

Cline, William R. "The Ironclad Ram *Virginia. . .*" *Southern Historical Society Papers,* 1904.

Conrad, Daniel B. "Capture of the C.S. Ram *Tennessee* in Mobile Bay, August, 1864." *Southern Historical Society Papers,* 1891.

[Cushing, William B.] "Outline Story of the War Experiences of William B. Cushing as Told by Himself." *Proceedings* of the United States Naval Institute, September 1912.

Daly, Robert W. "Pay and Prize Money in the Old Navy, 1776–1899." *Proceedings* of the United States Naval Institute, August 1948.

Demaree, Albert L. "The *Merrimack*—Our Navy's Worst Headache." *Proceedings* of the United States Naval Institute, March 1962.

Dillon, John F. "The Role of Riverine Warfare in the Civil War." *Naval War College Review,* March–April 1973.

Dohrman, H. G. "Old Man River, 1863." *Proceedings* of the United States Naval Institute, June 1934.

[Drayton, Percival.] "Naval Letters from Captain Percival Drayton, 1861–1865." *Bulletin of the New York Public Library,* November 1906.

[Eggleston, John R.] "Captain Eggleston's Narrative of the Battle of the *Merrimac." Southern Historical Society Papers,* September 1916.

Fornell, Earl W. "Confederate Seaport Strategy." *Civil War History,* December 1956.

Gift, George W. "The Story of the *Arkansas." Southern Historical Society Papers,* 1884.

Glassel, William T. "Reminiscences of Torpedo Service in Charleston Harbor." *Southern Historical Society Papers,* July–December 1877.

[Goldsborough, Louis M.] "Narrative of Rear Admiral Goldsborough, U.S. Navy." *Proceedings* of the United States Naval Institute, July 1933.

Gordon, Arthur. "The Great Stone Fleet." *Proceedings* of the United States Naval Institute, December 1968.

Green, S. Dana. "The *Monitor* at Sea and in Battle," *Proceedings* of the United States Naval Institute, November 1923.

Hanks, Carlos C. "The Last Confederate Raider." *Proceedings* of the United States Naval Institute, January 1941.

Hayes, John D. "Captain Fox—*He* Is the Navy Department." *Proceedings* of the United States Naval Institute, September 1965.

Heitzman, William Ray. "The Ironclad *Weehawken* in the Civil War." *American Neptune,* July 1892.

Hendren, Paul. "The Confederate Blockade Runners." *Proceedings* of the United States Naval Institute, April 1933.

Hill, James D. "Charles Wilkes—Turbulent Scholar of the Old Navy." *Proceedings* of the United States Naval Institute, July 1931.

Jones, Catesby. "Services of the *Virginia (Merrimac)." Southern Historical Society Papers,* 1883.

Kennett, Lee. "The Strange Career of the *Stonewall." Proceedings* of the United States Naval Institute, February 1968.

Martin, Harrison P. "When the *Monitor* Went Down." *Proceedings* of the United States Naval Institute, July 1941.

McMaster, G. Totten. "A Little Unwritten History of the Original USS *Monitor." Proceedings* of the United States Naval Institute, December 1901.

Merrill, James M. "Men, Monotony, and Mouldy Beans—Life on Board Civil War Blockaders." *American Neptune,* January 1956.

———. "Strategy Makers in the Union Navy Department, 1861–1865." *Mid-America,* January 1962.

Milligan, John D. "From Theory to Application: The Emergence of the American Ironclad War Vessel." *Military Affairs,* July 1984.

Neeser, Robert W. "Historic Ships of the Navy." *Proceedings* of the United States Naval Institute, December 1926.

Newton, Virginius. "The Ram *Merrimac* . . ." *Southern Historical Society Papers,* 1892.

New York Times, 1861–1865, various editions.

Paullin, Charles Oscar. "President Lincoln and the Navy." *American Historical Review,* January 1909.

Post, Charles A. "A Diary of the Blockade in 1863." *Proceedings* of the United States Naval Institute, October, November 1918.

Preston, Anthony. "The Raider That Never Made It." *Proceedings* of the United States Naval Institute, March 1968.

Price, Marcus W. "Ships That Tested the Blockade of the Carolina Ports, 1861–1865." *American Neptune,* July 1948.

Pullar, Walter S. "Abe Lincoln's Brown Water Navy." *Naval War College Review,* April 1969.

Read, Charles W. "Reminiscences of the Confederate States Navy." *Southern Historical Society Papers,* May 1876.

Roberts, John C., and Richard H. Webber. "Gunboats in the River War, 1861–1865. *Proceedings* of the United States Naval Institute, March 1965.

Rodgers, W. L. "A Study of Attacks upon Fortified Harbors—The Capture of Port Royal, S. C., in 1861." *Proceedings* of the United States Naval Institute, December 1904.

Ropp, Theodore. "Anacondas Anyone?" *Military Affairs,* Summer 1963.

Sinclair, G. Terry. "The Eventful Cruise of the *Florida,*" *Century Magazine,* July 1898.

Smith, Alan Cornwall. "The *Monitor-Merrimac* Legend." *Proceedings* of the United States Naval Institute, March 1940.

Swartz, Oretha D. "Franklin Buchanan: A Study in Divided Loyalties." *Proceedings* of the United States Naval Institute, December 1962.

Thomson, David Whittet. "Three Confederate Submarines—Operations at New Orleans, Mobile, and Charleston 1862–64." *Proceedings* of the United States Naval Institute, January 1941.

Wardle, Arthur C. "Some Blockade-Runners of the Civil War." *American Neptune,* April 1943.

Watson, John C. "Farragut and Mobile Bay—Personal Reminiscences." *Proceedings* of the United States Naval Institute, May 1927.

Welles, Gideon. "Admiral Farragut and New Orleans." *Galaxy,* November–December 1871.

———. "The Capture and Release of Mason and Slidell." *Galaxy,* May 1873.

West, Richard. "(Private and Confidential) My Dear Fox—." *Proceedings* of the United States Naval Institute, May 1937.

———. "The Morgan Purchases." *Proceedings* of the United States Naval Institute, January 1940.

Woodman, John E., Jr. "The Stone Fleet." *American Neptune,* October 1961.

INDEX

Abbott, Lieutenant, 380
Abby Bradford, 328
Abigail, 366
Adams, Captain, 60
Adams, Charles Francis, 115–16, 333, 344, 354, 355, 359, 367
Adams, Michael, 189
Adderly & Company, 334
Adelaide, 78
Adriatic, 357
Agrippina, 344, 347
Alabama, 197, 306–24. *See also* Mobile, Alabama; Mobile Bay
secession of, 12, 26
Alabama, 338, 344–54, 357, 358, 363–65, 367
Alabama River, 307
Alar, 354
Albatross, 281, 282, 285
Albemarle, 69, 215, 410–15, 418–21
Albemarle Sound, 86, 88, 123, 124, 129–32, 413–15
Albert H. Partridge, 338
Aldebaran, 337
Alden, James, 30–34, 37, 240, 425, 426
in Mobile Bay, 312, 315–16, 320
Alexandria, Louisiana, 295–98, 301–3, 305
Aline, 365
Allegheny, 34
Alps, 197, 199
Ammen, Daniel, 94, 97, 100, 101, 387
A. M. Schindler, 339
Anaconda plan, 61, 62, 64, 179–80
Anderson, Robert, at Fort Sumter, 6–14, 22–23, 25

Andrew, Governor, 117, 118
Anglo-Chinese Arrow War, 186
Antietam, battle of (1862), 258
Appomattox, Lee's surrender at, 324, 358, 363, 366, 431
Appomattox, 129, 130, 132
Appomattox Court House, 62
Archer, 106, 339–40
Ariel, 346
Arkansas, 292, 294
Arkansas, 208
in Vicksburg campaign, 241, 246–56
Arkansas Post, Mississippi, 265–67
Arkansas River, 265–67
Arman, L., 360–61
Army, Confederate, 74. *See also specific people*
at Antietam, 258
at Chancellorsville, 288–89
at Corinth, 203, 205, 210–11, 215
at first battle of Bull Run, 63
in Fort Donelson attack, 197, 200–203
in Fort Henry attack, 191–96
at Gettysburg, 290
in Hatteras Inlet action, 80–83
at Island No. 10, 205, 210
Norfolk Navy Yard and, 34–35, 39–40
promotions in, 73
Quaker guns of, 103*n*
rations of, 72
Army, U.S. *See also* Army of the Potomac; Army of the Tennessee; *and specific regiments and people*
Chicamicomico Island, 88–89
at first battle of Bull Run, 63
in Hatteras Inlet action, 78, 79, 82–84

Army, U.S. (cont.)
  in Mobile Bay, 311–13
  political appointments made by,
    90–94, 97, 100
  Wilmington and, 417, 418, 421–29
Army of Northern Virginia, 366
Army of the Mississippi, in Vicksburg
    campaign, 258, 261, 265–67
Army of the Potomac, 185, 256–58, 311
  at Antietam, 258
  Burnside and, 258, 262–63
  at Chancellorsville, 288–89
  in Peninsula campaign, 132, 165–66,
    176–77
Army of the Tennessee, 258
  in Vicksburg campaign, 260, 261, 263,
    265, 267–69, 272, 280, 286–91
Ashby's Harbor, Roanoke Island, 127
Atchafalaya River, 273
Atkins, John, 165
Atlanta, 356, 375, 396–98. See also *Talla-
    hassee*
Atlanta, Georgia, 297, 407, 418
Atlantic, 18, 26, 93
Atlantic Blocking Squadron, 87, 91
Atlantic Fleet, 427*n*
Augusta Dinsmore, 398
Australia, 365–67
Avon, 341
A. W. Baker, 273
Azores, 344
Azuma, 363

Bache, George, 278, 300, 304
Badger, Oscar, 401
Bahama, 334, 344, 346
Bailey, Theodorus, 228, 230, 234, 235, 241
Balch, Lieutenant, 107
Baltic, 18, 23–25
Baltimore, Maryland
  riots in, 45, 48
  secessionists in, 35, 45
Bankhead, John P., 178
Banks, Nathaniel, 311
  Port Hudson and, 280–82, 290, 291
  in Red River campaign, 293–99, 301–3,
    305
  in Texas, 292–93, 307
Barker, Albert, 47
  in New Orleans campaign, 225, 230,
    234
Barnard, John, 62
Baron de Kalb, in Red River campaign,
    303, 305
  in Vicksburg campaign, 266, 269, 271,
    289

Barron, Samuel, 83–84, 163, 332, 355,
    361, 362
Batcheller, Oliver, 285
Bates, Edward, 14, 180
  Trent affair and, 118, 121
Baton Rouge, Louisiana, 238, 240,
    253–55, 281
Battery, Stevens, 157
Battery Wagner (Morris Island), 389,
    395, 399, 400, 402
Bayou City, 267
Beaufort, North Carolina, 422–23, 427
Beaufort, South Carolina, 86, 101, 132
Beaufort, 126, 128, 130–32
  as *Merrimack* escort, 147, 148, 152
Beauregard, 215–16
Beauregard, Pierre G. T., 215
  in Charleston, 371
  in Charleston attack, 382, 391,
    400–401, 406
  Fort Sumter relief and, 21–23, 25, 26
Bell, Henry, 227, 229, 307
  in Vicksburg campaign, 238–40, 242,
    244, 245
Bell, John, 46
Belle Algerine, 231
Belmont, Missouri, 189
Benjamin, Judah, 65*n*, 143
Benton, 190, 206–8, 211, 213–16, 296
  in Vicksburg campaign, 244–46, 252,
    259, 263, 264, 286–88
Bermuda, 416
  sea raiders and, 340, 341
Berwick Bay, 273
B. F. Hoxie, 340
Bibb, 393
Bier, Lieutenant, 381
Biloxi raid, 222
Black, Jeremiah, 9, 10, 12–13
Black Bayou, 277, 278
Black gang, 181
Black Hawk, 297
  in Red River campaign, 295
  in Vicksburg campaign, 260, 264–66,
    280, 290
Blacks, 181*n. See also* Slavery (slaves)
  in Confederate Navy, 74, 131–32
  in U.S. Navy, 57
Black Terror, 276–77
Black Warrior, 130, 131
Blackwood's Edinburgh Magazine, 106
Blair, Montgomery, 4, 14, 185, 221
  Trent affair and, 118, 119
Blair's Landing, Louisiana, 299–300
Blake, George, 46–47, 49
Blake, Homer, 346

Blockade, Union, 26, 34, 41, 50–55, 59–64, 84, 86, 179. *See also specific cities*
  in Galveston, 267–68
  Great Britain and, 51–52
  of Gulf coast, 60, 63
  legal aspects of, 51
  Mallory's strategy *vs.,* 70–71
  in New Orleans, 218–19
  privateering as stimulus to, 50–51
  stone ships and, 102–7
  weakness of, 218
Blockade Board. *See* Commission of Conference
Blockade runners, 61, 63, 332, 334–36, 346–47
  in Charleston, 368–70
  in Wilmington, 356, 358, 416
Blockships tactic, 77
Board of Fifteen ("inquisitional tribune"), 66
Boggs, Charles, 231
Bombshell, 412, 413, 414
Boston, Massachusetts, 117–18
Boston Herald, 80
Boston Navy Yard. *See* Charlestown Navy Yard
Boutelle, Charles, 94, 96, 98
Bowling Green, Kentucky, 191, 196–97
Boynton, Charles, 184
Brazil, sea raiders and, 327, 328, 338, 342–43, 347, 357
Brazos Island, 293
Breach Inlet, 407
Breckinridge, John C., 46, 253–55
Breese, K. R., 54, 288
  Wilmington and, 422, 423, 428–29
Brent, Joseph, 275
Brilliant, 344–45
Brittan, S. B., Jr., 195
Broad River, 101
Brooke, John Mercer, 364
  ironclad ships and, 137–42
Brooke, John R., 69
Brooklyn, 9–11, 16, 27, 327
  in Mobile Bay, 312, 314–18
  in New Orleans campaign, 222, 224, 228, 232–33
  in Vicksburg campaign, 238, 242, 243, 244, 246, 248, 268, 281
  Wilmington and, 425, 427
Brooklyn Navy Yard, 15, 19–21, 30, 34, 53, 54, 217
Brown, George, 275–76
Brown, Harvey, 18
Brown, Isaac, 26

Brown, Isaac Newton, 247–51, 253, 254
Brown, John M., 349–52
Brownsville, Texas, 293, 305
Bruinsburg, Mississippi, 288
Buchanan, James, 7–10, 14
Buchanan, Franklin (Old Buck), 73
  ironclad ships and, 134, 143–47, 152–53
  in Mobile Bay, 308–9, 311, 313–15, 319–24
  resignation of, 44–46
  wounding of, 153, 170, 176
Buckner, Simon Bolivar, 197, 202–3
Buell, Don Carlos, 6
Bulloch, James, sea raiders and, 332–33, 334, 340, 343, 344, 354, 359–61, 364
Bull Run
  first battle of, 63, 78, 90
  second battle of, 211*n,* 349
Bull's Bay, South Carolina, 90, 92
Burnside, Ambrose, 132, 156, 258*n,* 332
  Army of the Potomac and, 258, 262–63
  Roanoke Island, 124–25, 127, 129, 130
Burrell, Isaac, 267
Bushnell, Cornelius, ironclad ships and, 158–60
Butcher, M. J., 344
Butler, Benjamin, 258, 324
  Hatteras Inlet action and, 78, 79, 81, 84, 85, 123
  in New Orleans campaign, 222, 234, 236
  in Vicksburg campaign, 239, 241, 242
  Wilmington and, 421–26

Cabinet, Confederate, meetings of, 21
Cabinet, U.S., meetings of, 155–56, 292
  Fort Sumter relief, 9, 10, 14, 15
  Trent affair, 118, 121–22
  western strategy, 180
Cadiz, 330
Cairo, Illinois, 179, 181, 183, 185, 187, 188, 189, 203, 205, 206, 259, 261, 294–95
Cairo, 188, 203, 215, 262
Caleb Cushing, 339
Callender, Eliot, 212, 213
Cameron, Simon, 78, 180
  Fort Sumter relief and, 14, 15
  political appointments made by, 91
Campti, Louisiana, 301
Canby, Edward, 311
Cape Fear River, 416–19, 423, 426, 430
Capitol, 247
Caroline Islands, 366

Carondelet, 188, 190, 193–201, 211, 213, 215
  in Fort Henry attack, 193–96
  at Island No. 10, 208–10
  in Red River campaign, 303, 304
  in Vicksburg campaign, 247, 249–50, 260, 277, 279
Carroll Wood, 356–57
Carter, Robert, 364
Casco, 410, 417
Casco class, 310
Casey, Thomas Lincoln, 424
Catskill, 387, 389, 400
Cayuga, 228, 230, 234, 235
Ceres, 126, 129, 131
Cerro Gordo, Alabama, 197
Chameleon, 358
Champion No. 3, 302
Champion No. 5, 302
Chancellorsville, battle of (1863), 288–89
Charleston and Savannah Railroad, 101, 408
Charleston Courier, 401
Charleston Mercury, 8, 11, 12, 382
Charleston, South Carolina, 6–7, 94, 286, 307, 368–408. *See also* Fort Moultrie, South Carolina; Fort Sumter, South Carolina
  blockade of, 102, 103, 105–7, 368–69, 377–83, 385–86, 395, 396, 399, 416
  blockade runners in, 368–70
  Confederate possession of Federal facilities in, 8
  criticism of Du Pont's atack on, 393–94
Charlestown Navy Yard, 28–29, 53
Charlotte, 430
Charter Oak, 365
Chase, Salmon, 4, 53, 155, 188, 375
Chesapeake and Albemarle Canal, 132
Chesapeake Bay, 28, 35, 63, 419, 423
Chesnut, Mary Boykin, 64, 109–10, 120, 133
Chicamicomico Island, 88–89
Chickasaw, in Mobile Bay, 310, 314, 323
Chickasaw Bluffs, Mississippi, 261, 264, 267, 268, 289
Chicora, in Charleston attack, 378, 380–83, 385, 392, 403, 406, 408
Chillicothe
  in Red River campaign, 298, 303, 305
  in Vicksburg campaign, 259, 269–72
Churchill, Tom, 266
Cienfuegos, 327–28
Cimmaron, 396, 397
Cincinnati, Ohio, 182, 183, 188

Cincinnati, 188, 207
  in Fort Henry attack, 193–96
  in Fort Pillow attack, 212–13
  in Vicksburg campaign, 266, 278–80
Cincinnati Times, 251
City of Richmond, 361
City of Vicksburg, 272
City Point, 430
Civil War, U.S., start of, 8, 23
Clarence, 338–39
Clarksville, 203
Clifton, 224, 267, 268
Cline, William, 142, 147, 153, 169
Coal, 68, 238, 269, 357
  Merrimack's use of, 138–39
Coast Blocking Squadron, 59–60, 62–63
Coast Guard, U.S., 13, 78
Coast Survey, 15, 62, 94, 96
Cobb's Point, 130
Coffey, James, 195
Coldwater River, 268, 270
Collins, John, 317
Collins, Napoleon, 342–43
Colorado, 55n, 222, 224–25, 425
Columbus, Kentucky, 186, 187, 189, 191, 203
Commerce, Missouri, 185
Commission of Conference (Blockade Board; Strategy Board), 62–64, 76–78, 87, 90, 218
Commodore Perry, 131
Compromise of 1850, 66
Comstock, Colonel, 423, 426
Conestoga, 181–83, 185–91, 199, 204, 266
Confederate Mississippi River Defense Fleet, 79
Confederate Navy. *See* Navy, Confederate
Confederate Point, North Carolina, 416, 424, 429
Confederate States of America
  British sales to, 116
  capture of envoys of. See *Trent* affair
  Fort Sumter relief and, 21–23
  industrial capacity of, 68–69
  "King Cotton diplomacy" of, 22
  Provisional Congress of, 13, 67, 73, 74
  ironclad ships, 136, 139
  splitting of, 291, 292
  Union blockade of, 50–55. *See* Blockade, Union
Congress, 134–36, 157, 166, 168, 169
  blowing up of, 169
  Merrimack vs., 135–36, 147–49, 151–55
  surrender of, 151–53, 155

Congress, U.S., 2n, 43, 56–57, 66, 259, 304. *See also* House of Representatives, U.S.
 ironclad ships and, 157
 naval reforms in, 246
 Trent affair and, 120
Connecticut, election of 1860 and, 4
Conrad, 347
Conrad, Charles, 67, 136
Conrady, Daniel B., 313, 316–17, 319–22
Constitution, 47–49
Constitution, U.S., 26
Contest, 348
Continental Iron Works, 160–61, 163
Cooke, James W., 410–13, 415
Cooke, Lieutenant, 131–32
Cooper River, 369
Corea, 102
Corinth, Mississippi, 203, 205, 210–11, 215, 238, 256, 258
Corpus Christi, Texas, 293, 305
"Coston" flare, 93
Cotton, 22, 51, 52, 116, 136, 216, 296, 384
 in Charleston, 369, 370
 Red River campaign and, 293, 294
Cotton Plant, 413
Couronne, 351
Craney Island, 32, 36, 37, 39, 135, 148, 176, 422
Craven, T. Augustus, 313, 316, 317, 331–32
Craven, Thomas, 232–33, 355, 362–63
 in Vicksburg campaign, 242–44
Crea, Alfred, 59
Cricket, 298, 301, 302, 304
Crimean War, 136, 137, 159, 359
Croatan Sound, 123, 126–27, 413
Crosby, Peirce, 80, 82, 84
Cuba, 108, 109, 111–16, 363
 Semmes in, 327–28
Cuba, 327
Cumberland, 29, 32–39, 81, 134, 157, 165, 166, 169, 186
 Merrimack vs., 147–51
 sinking of, 150–51, 155
Cumberland River, 188, 191, 197–203
Cummings, Lieutenant Commander, 283
Cummings Point, South Carolina, 12, 25, 389, 392
Curlew, 128–29
Currituck, 165
Currituck Sound, 132
Cushing, William Barker, 426, 430
 Albemarle and, 418–21
Cuyler, 49

Daffodil, 403
Dahlgren, John Adolphus, 45, 58
Dahlgren, John Augustus, 363, 418
 in Charleston attack, 373–74, 383–84, 386–87, 394–95, 406–8
Dahlgren guns, 1, 28, 37–38, 40, 81, 99, 149, 182, 376
 of *Monitor,* 162, 165, 171
Danby, Robert, 30–33
Dandelion, 391
Daniels, Josephus, 186
Daniel Trowbridge, 329
Dauphin Island, 310
David, 404–5
Davis, Charles, 59, 62, 63, 105–7, 258, 363, 372
 blockade and, 104–7
 in Fort Pillow attack, 211–12, 214, 215, 237
 Fort Pulaski and, 104
 ironclad ships and, 158, 160
 political appointments made by, 91–93, 96–98
 in Vicksburg campaign, 242–46, 251–53, 255
Davis, Mrs. Charles, 212
Davis, Jefferson, 50, 136, 366, 431
 elected president of Confederacy, 13
 Fort Sumter and, 8–9
 Fort Sumter relief and, 21–23
 military background of, 67–68
Davis, John, 132
Dayton, William, 340, 360
Declaration of Paris, 52
Deer Creek, 277, 279
Deerhound, 351, 353
Delafield, Ronald, 421–22
Delamater, Cornelius, 158
Delamater and Co., 161
Delaware, 29, 125–28, 131
Delphine, 365
Democrats (Democratic Party), 2–4
 Mallory and, 66
 Norfolk Navy Yard and, 29–30
 Welles' break with, 4
Department of the Ohio, naval operations and, 180–86
De Soto, 273–74
Dewey, George, 227, 230, 232, 234, 235
 in Vicksburg campaign, 282–85
Dictator, 354
Dismal Swamp Canal, 83, 86, 124, 130
Dixon, George, 406, 407
Dr. Beatty, 275
Dog River Bar, 308, 310, 311, 313, 320
Dolphin, 29, 36

Doubleday, Abner, 8, 12
Double-enders, 55
Douglas, Stephen, 46
Downes, John, 368, 387, 390–91, 400
Drayton, Percival, 101, 122
    in Charleston attack, 375, 386
    in Mobile Bay, 309, 312, 314, 315, 317,
        318, 322–23
Drayton, Thomas, 99–101
Dred Scott decision, 5n, 345
Drewry's Bluff, Virginia, 177, 430
Drumgould's Bluff, Mississippi, 262, 264
Duke of Somerset, 332
Duncan, Johnson, in New Orleans cam-
        paign, 224, 226–29, 235, 236
Dunnington, John, 266
Du Pont, Henry, 92
Du Pont, Samuel, 35, 54, 60, 62–64,
        90–105, 246, 342, 407, 418
    blockade and, 102–5
    in Charleston, 307
    in Charleston attack, 371–76, 382–84,
        386–91, 393–96, 398
    Commission of Conference and,
        62–63, 76–78, 90, 218
    political appointments made by,
        90–101, 370–71
    Stringham as viewed by, 86–87
    Trent affair and, 122
Du Pont, Sophie, husband's correspon-
        dence with, 90, 91, 93, 95–97

Eads, James B., 180, 184, 187
Eagle Iron Works, 188
East Gulf Blockading Squadron, 221
Eastport, 197, 295, 297, 301
Eddyville, Kentucky, 188
Edward, 107, 365
Edward's Ferry, North Carolina, 410
Eggleston, John, on Merrimack, 148,
        149, 152–54, 172, 173, 175
Egypt, Khedive of, 360
8th Massachusetts Infantry, 48
Election of 1860, 4, 6, 17, 46
Electric Spark, 341
Elizabeth City, North Carolina, 129, 130,
        132
Elizabeth River, 28, 36, 133, 145–46, 176
Ellet, Alfred, 216, 285
    in Vicksburg campaign, 242–43, 249,
        252, 259
Ellet, Charles, 214–16, 272
Ellet, Charles River, 272–76
    in Vicksburg campaign, 242, 244
Elliott, Gilbert, 410–12
Elliott, Stephen, 401, 403

Ellis, 83, 85, 130–32, 419
El Majidi, 367
El Mounassir, 360
El Toussan, 360
Emancipation Proclamation, 258
Enlistment bounties, 74
Enoch Train, 218. See also Manassas
Enrica, 344. See also Alabama
Era No. 5, 274–75
Ericsson, John, 374, 387
    ironclad ships and, 156, 158–66, 168
Essex, 190, 193–95, 252–53, 254, 281, 296
Estella, 337
Eustis, Mr. and Mrs., 114
Evans, Robley (Fighting Bob), 46–49,
        427–29

Fairfax, Donald, 387, 390
    Trent affair and, 112–14
Fanny, 88–89, 130, 132
    in Hatteras Inlet action, 79–80, 82
Farragut, David Glasgow, 4, 291, 363,
        430
    blockade and, 267
    communications problems of, 240–41
    decision to stay with Union of, 43–44
    in Mobile Bay, 306–7, 309–18, 320,
        322–24, 357
    in New Orleans campaign, 214,
        220–25, 227, 228, 233–35, 371, 372
    in Red River campaign, 286
    in Vicksburg campaign, 215–17,
        237–46, 251–53, 255, 280–82,
        285–86, 306, 307
    Wilmington and, 417–18
Farragut, Loyall, 309
Farragut, Virginia, 43, 44, 220, 221
    husband's correspondence with, 280,
        281, 313
Fauntleroy, Charles, 355–56
Fawcett, Preston & Company, 334
Fear, Cape, 416, 423
Fernandina, Florida, 90
54th Massachusetts Colored Infantry, 399
Fiji ports, 103
Fingal, 104, 396. See also Atlanta
1st New York Marine Artillery, 125
1st Rhode Island Artillery, 49
1st U.S. Artillery, 6
Flag, 87
Flogging, 66
Florida, 61
Florida, 307
Florida. See also Fort Pickens, Florida;
        Pensacola Navy Yard
    secession of, 12, 26

Florida, as sea raider, 335–38, 340–43, 347, 358, 367

Floyd, John B., 6–9, 197, 202–3

Floyd, Richard, 337–38

Flusser, Charles W., 410, 412

Folly Island, 377

Foote, Andrew H., 15, 19–21, 185–91, 196–204, 211–12, 246, 373–74
   Charleston attack and, 394–95
   death of, 398
   in Fort Donelson attack, 199–201
   Fort Henry attack, 191–93, 196
   Island No. 10 and, 206–11, 222
   as Rodgers' replacement, 185

Foote, Mrs. Andrew H., 204, 206

Foreign Enlistment Act, 333–34, 343, 344, 348, 354, 359

Foreign Office, British, 107

Forest Rose, 269

Forrest, 129, 132

Forrest, French, 40
   ironclad ships and, 139–43, 145

Forrest, Nathan Bedford, 203
   in Vicksburg campaign, 263, 264

Fort Bartow, North Carolina, 127–30

Fort Beauregard, South Carolina, 96–100

Fort Caswell, North Carolina, 416, 421

Fort Clark, North Carolina, 77, 79–83, 84

Fort Cobb, 131

Fort De Russy, Louisiana, 295–96

Fort Donelson, Kentucky, 191–92, 197–206, 222, 359

Fort Fisher, North Carolina, 416–17, 421–29

Fort Fisher (Wilmington), 358

Fort Gaines (Mobile Bay), 310, 312

Fort Hatteras, North Carolina, 79, 80, 83–84
   construction of, 77

Fort Henry, Kentucky, 133, 188, 191–96, 204–6, 222, 359

Fort Hindman, 295, 298, 301–2, 304

Fort Hindman, Mississippi, 265, 266

Fort Jackson (New Orleans), 218, 219, 223–24, 226–29, 235–36

Fort McAllister (Savannah), 375–76, 384–86, 408

Fort Monroe, Virginia, 10, 11, 36, 39, 156, 168, 176
   attempt to move *Merrimack* to, 32–33

Fort Morgan (Mobile, Alabama), 60, 306, 307, 309–12, 314–20, 324, 335

Fort Moultrie, South Carolina, 6–9, 12, 371, 379, 382, 390, 400, 401, 407

Fort Norfolk, Virginia, 29, 35, 39

Fort Pemberton, 268, 270–72

Fort Pickens, Florida, 16–21, 26–27, 60, 238
   truce of, 67

Fort Pillow, Tennessee, 210–15, 237

Fort Powell (Mobile Bay), 310, 324

Fort Pulaski, 104

Fort St. Helena, Virginia, 29, 40

Fort St. Philip (New Orleans), 218, 219, 224, 228–30, 232–34, 236

Fort Sumter, South Carolina, 6–27, 57, 371, 379, 387–91, 393, 394, 395, 400–404, 407
   Confederate firing on, 23, 30
   defenselessness of, 6, 7
   first relief of, 9–12
   Fort Pickens relief and, 18, 19
   Foster's plan for, 383–84
   Fox plan for, 13–15, 18, 22–26
   Seward's negotiating of evacuation of, 17
   surrender of, 25, 43, 50
   transfer of U.S. troops to, 6–7

Fortune, 102

Fort Walker, South Carolina, 96–100

Fort Warren (Boston), 117–18, 122, 340

42nd Massachusetts Infantry, 267, 268

Foster, James, 270–72

Foster, John, 383, 408

4th Wisconsin, 249

Fox, Gustavus Vasa, 56, 63, 77, 85–87, 217, 305, 419, 431
   appointed Chief Clerk, 58–59
   blockade and, 103, 105
   Charleston and, 371, 374, 383, 394–95
   Fanny incident and, 89
   Fort Sumter relief and, 13–15, 18, 22–26, 58
   Hatteras Inlet and, 85, 86
   ironclad ships and, 157, 160, 176
   Mobile Bay and, 309, 324
   New Orleans campaign and, 220, 221
   Peninsula campaign and, 166
   political appointments made by, 91
   Stringham's resignation and, 87
   western strategy and, 185, 190, 197, 241, 242, 286
      Galveston, 267, 268
      Vicksburg campaign, 256, 257
   Wilmington and, 417, 421–22, 422–23

France
   cotton and, 22
   ironclad ships and, 136, 137, 157, 159, 356, 358–61

France (cont.)
  in Mexico, 292, 293, 330
  sea raiders and, 340, 348–51, 355–56
Franklin, William, 299, 303
Fraser, Trenholm and Company, 110–11,
  331–34, 354, 364, 377
Fredericksburg, 430
Fredericksburg, battle of (1862), 262–63
Freeman, Martin, 314, 315
Frémont, John (Pathfinder of the West),
  185, 188
French, Charles, 413
French, Rodney, 103
Frying Pan Shoals, 416
Fugitive Slave Law, 3
Fullam, George Townley, 344–46, 353
Fulton, 68

Gaines, 309, 319
Galena, 177, 314, 318
Galt, Doctor, 345, 353
Galveston, Texas, 267–68, 281, 292
  blockade of, 60, 63, 346
Garland, 103
Gay, Thomas, 420–21
General Berry, 341
General Bragg, 212–13
General Lovell, 213–15
General Qutiman, 224
General Sterling Price, 213, 216
General Sumter, 213, 252–53, 254
General Van Dorn, 213–14, 216
George Latimer, 341
George Peabody, 78
Georgia, 61. *See also* Savannah, Georgia
  secession of, 12, 26
Georgia, 347, 354–55
Gerdes, Frank, 226
Germantown, 29, 33, 36, 37, 39
Gettysburg, battle of, 290, 291, 360, 367
Gibraltar, 330–31
Gift, George, 248, 249
Gillis, James, 83
Gillis, John, 22, 24–25
Gillmore, Quincy, 395, 398–404, 408
Glassell, William, 385–86, 405
Glenarvon, 357
Glide, 266
Gloire, 359
Golconda, 341
Golden Rocket, 327
Goldsborough, Louis Malesherbes,
  87–89, 91, 246, 332, 343*n,* 409,
  418
  North Carolina operations of, 124,
  125, 130, 132, 134

Good Hope, 354
Gordon, 110–11, 334
Governor, 95–96
Governor Moore, 224, 231
Governor's Island, 15, 18, 22
Grampus, 210
Grand Ecore, Louisiana, 298–303
Grand Era, 275
Grand Gulf, Mississippi, 287–88
Granger, Gordon, 312–13
Grant, Ulysses S., 293, 297, 307, 311,
  358, 408, 411, 430
  Army of the Tennessee command
    given to, 258
  Mississippi Valley campaign of,
    186–87, 189–91, 193, 198, 199, 202
  Corinth, 210–11
  in Vicksburg campaign, 260, 261, 263,
    264, 267–69, 272, 277–78, 280,
    286–91
  Wilderness campaign of, 415
  Wilmington and, 417, 418, 421, 426,
    427
Great Britain, 70, 325
  arms sales of, 116
  blockade and, 51–52
  collapse of the Confederacy and, 367
  cotton and, 22, 51, 52, 116, 136, 370
  ironclad ships and, 356, 358–60
  ironclad ships in, 157
  neutrality of, 52, 116, 117, 119, 333,
    340, 359
  sea raiders and, 331–34, 343–44, 348,
    353, 367
  Alabama claims, 367
  Trent affair and, 108, 111–22, 330, 331
Great Ogeechee River, 332, 375–76, 408
Green, Samuel Dana, on *Monitor,* 155,
  164, 166–69, 171–77
Green, Tom, 300
Greer, James, 114
Gregory, Francis, 371–72
Gregory, Thomas, 212
Grenada, Mississippi, 260
Grimes, Senator, 219
Gulf Blockading Squadron, 60, 180
  division of. *See* East Gulf Blockading
    Squadron; West Gulf Blockading
    Squadron
Guns, 158–59, 295, 308, 350, 352, 397
  Confederate sources of, 68, 69
  Dahlgrens, 1, 28, 37–38, 40, 81, 99,
    149, 182, 376
  Monitor, 162, 165, 171
  Quaker, 103
  soda bottle, 373

of turtles, 187–88
G. W. Blunt, 377
Gwin, William, 210, 249–51, 264

Habana, 326. *See also Sumter*
Hale, Nathan, 3, 219
Halifax, 357–58
Hall, John, 201
Halleck, Henry (Old Brains), 188–89,
      191, 203, 206–8, 211, 215, 237–38,
      258, 286, 311, 383
  Banks and, 280, 292–93
  Red River campaign and, 292–94, 305
  in Vicksburg campaign, 244–46
  Wilmington and, 417
Hampton Roads, 28, 38, 39, 58, 62, 134,
      338, 343, 416, 422–23, 426, 430–31
  arrival of *San Jacinto* in, 115, 117
  attempt to take *Merrimack* across, 30,
      32, 33
  Du Pont-Sherman rendezvous at,
      92–93
  Merrimack trials at, 133, 135–36,
      144–55, 164, 168–76
  Monitor at, 154, 156, 164, 168–76, 359
  Port Royal compared with, 100
  Stellwagen's steamers in, 78–80
  Stringham at, 59–60
Handy, Robert, 219
Harding, John, 344
Harper's Monthly, 182n
Harriet Lane, 13, 15, 23, 24, 49, 238, 295
  in Hatteras Inlet action, 79–81, 83
  in New Orleans campaign, 222, 223,
      226, 236
Harriet Stevens, 341
Hartford, 289, 307
  in Mobile Bay, 309, 311–20, 322–23
  in New Orleans campaign, 221–22,
      224, 226, 228, 229, 233, 234, 235
  in Vicksburg campaign, 238–39,
      242–45, 251, 252, 281, 282, 285
Harvey Birch, 331
Harwood, Andrew, 157
Hatteras, 346, 351
Hatteras, Cape, 63, 76, 178
Hatteras Inlet, 77–82, 125
  use of, 85–86
Hatteras Inlet action, 62–64, 98, 123
  failure of follow-up in, 85–89, 393
  Fort Clark captured in, 81–83
  press reaction to, 85
Hatteras Island, 77
Hawkins, Rush, 82, 86, 88
Haynes's Bluff, Mississippi, 264–65, 268,
      288, 289

Head of the Passes, 218–19, 222, 226, 327
Heiman, Adolphus, 192
Henry Clay, 287
Herald, 102
Heth, Henry, 35, 36
Hetzel, 127–28
Hickman, Kentucky, 186
Hicks, Thomas, 45
Higgenson, Francis, 404
H. L. Huntley, 406, 407
Hoel, Bill, 213
Hoke, Robert, 411, 415
Holden, Edgar, 414–15
Hollins, George, 207, 210, 218–19
Holly Springs, Mississippi, 260, 263,
     264
Holt, Joseph, 12–13
Home Squadron, 29, 60
Hooker, Joseph, 263, 288–89
Hope, James, 357
Horton, Edward J., 421
Housatonic, 378, 380, 382, 407
House of Representatives, U.S., Toucy
     castigated by, 41–42
Howard, Acting Master, 405
Howard, Samuel, 171
Huger, Ben, 80
Hull, Joseph, 257
Hunley, 407
Hunter, Alvah, 387–91, 397
Hunter, "Tornado," 128–29

Illinois Central Railroad, 181
India, 107
Indian Chief, 406
Indianola, 295, 296n
  in Vicksburg campaign, 259, 273,
     275–77, 281
Industry, Confederate, 68–69, 71, 137
Ingraham, Duncan, 137, 378, 380, 382,
     385, 391
Investigator, 330
Iowa, 427n
Iron, 68, 69, 137, 308
Iron Bank, Kentucky, 189
Ironclad ships, 66, 134–78, 356. See also
     Merrimack; Monitor; turtles
  Brooke's work on, 137–42
  Confederate, 358–63
Iroquois, 109, 222, 229, 240, 243, 329
Isaac Smith, 94–96, 377–78, 385. *See also*
     Stono
Isaac Webb, 339
Isherwood, Benjamin Franklin
  ironclad ships and, 157
  Norfolk Navy Yard and, 28, 30–34, 37

Island No. 10, 205–11, 222, 223
Isondiga, 396
Itasca, 239, 314

Jackson, 186, 187, 224
Jackson, Andrew, 14
Jackson, Mortimer, 357
Jackson, Stonewall, 289
Jackson, Mississippi, 260, 288
Jacob Bell, 337
James Adger, 111, 116
James Funk No. 22, 356
James Littlefield, 357
James River, 147, 151, 177, 430, 431
James River Flotilla, 409
James River Squadron, 72, 356
Jamestown, 87, 151, 177
Japan, 2, 156n, 363
Japan, 354. See also Georgia; Virginia
Jeffers, William, 129, 176
Jenkins, Thornton, 280, 282, 318
Johnson, John, 392
Johnston, Albert Sidney, 191, 197, 200,
    202
  at Corinth, 203, 205, 210–11, 215
  homestead of, 261, 263
Johnston, James, in Mobile Bay, 308,
    314, 316, 319–24
Johnston, Joseph E., 16
Joint Congressional Committee on the
    Conduct of the War, 304
Jones, Catesby, 308
  ironclad ships and, 140–42, 145–50,
    152–54, 170, 172, 173, 175–77
Joseph Maxwell, 328
Joseph Parke, 328–29
Jouett, James, 317, 319
Juliet, 301, 302
Junkin, Rev. David, 48

Katahdin, 244, 254
Kate Kyer, 337–38
Kate Stewart, 339
Kearsarge, 349–53
Keeler, Anna, 163–68, 178
Keeler, William Frederick, Monitor and,
    163–68, 170–71, 176, 178
Kell, John McIntosh, 343, 350–53
Kennebec, 239–40, 244, 314, 320
Kennon, Beverly, 231
Kentucky, 186–89. See also Fort Donel-
    son, Kentucky; Fort Henry, Ken-
    tucky; and specific towns
Keokuk, in Charleston attack, 376, 377,
    387, 390, 391, 394, 399, 401
Keystone State, 35, 39

in Charleston attack, 380–82
Key West, Florida, 62
Kineo, 254, 281, 283
Kinney, John Coddington, 313–16, 323

Lackawanna, 314, 321–23
Lafayette, 286
Laird & Company, 359–60
Lamb, Colonel, 424, 425, 429
Lancaster, 285
Laning, James, 193–95
Lapwing, 337–38, 340
Laurel, 365
Lee, Robert E., 40, 257, 263, 411, 415
  at Gettysburg, 290
  surrender of, 324, 358, 363, 366
Lee, Sam Phillips (Old Triplicate),
    230–31, 409, 410, 412, 419
  in Vicksburg campaign, 237–40
  Wilmington and, 417, 418
Lehigh, 402, 403
Lena, 158, 160
Leonidas, 106
Leroy, John, 136
Le Roy, William, 323, 381–82
Letcher, Governor, 34
Lewis, 105
Lexington, 181–83, 185–91, 210, 266
  in Red River campaign, 295, 298–300,
    303, 304
Lincoln, Abraham, 3–6, 17–21, 57–61, 63,
    70, 78, 108, 258n, 311, 373, 375,
    430–32, 432
  assassination of, 366, 431
  blockade and, 26, 34, 50–53, 60, 70, 86,
    326
  blockade runners and, 335–36
  Charleston attack, 383–84, 386, 393,
    394
  in election of 1860, 4, 6, 46
  Emancipation Proclamation and, 258
  Fort Pickens relief and, 17–20
  Fort Sumter relief and, 12–15, 18,
    19–21
  in Hampton Roads, 430–31
  Hatteras Inlet action and, 85
  ironclad ships and, 155–56, 159–60
  Mobile Bay and, 324
  New Orleans campaign and, 220
  Norfolk Navy Yard and, 30
  Peninsula campaign and, 165–66
  political appointments made by, 3, 4,
    91
  sea raiders and, 325
  75,000 volunteers called for by, 26,
    31–32, 36, 41, 44, 50

Seward's view of, 17
Trent affair and, 117, 118, 120–22
war declared by, 26
western strategy and, 179, 188, 197,
    288, 294
    Red River campaign, 305
    Vicksburg campaign, 241, 257, 258,
        286, 291, 306
    Wilmington and, 421
Lincoln, Mary Todd, 431
Liquor ration, 72–73, 186, 246
Littlepage, Midshipman, 150
Little Rebel, 212
Lockwood, 129
Loggy Bayou, Louisiana, 298
Logue, Surgeon, 170–71
London Morning Chronicle, 120
Lords Commissioners of the Admiralty,
    120
Louisa Hatch, 347
Louisiana, 61, 292. *See also* Red River
    campaign
    secession of, 12, 26
Louisiana, 223, 224, 228–30, 234–36,
    422–24
Louisiana Provisional Navy, 224, 231
Louisville, 188, 199, 200, 202, 207, 215
    in Vicksburg campaign, 266
Louisville, Kentucky, 191
Lovell, Mansfield, 212
    in New Orleans campaign, 223, 224,
        235
Low, John, 334
Lowry, Reigert B., 76–77
Loyall, Benjamin, 127
Lynch, William, 125–31
Lynchburg Virginian, 142
Lyons, Lord Richard, 51–52
    Trent affair and, 118–22

McAllister, Captain, 256, 261
McCauley, Charles S., 29–38
    burning of Norfolk Navy Yard and, 38
    Welles' relief of, 34
McClellan, George, 61, 91, 124, 185, 190,
    256–58
    ironclad ships and, 155–56
    New Orleans campaign and, 220
    Peninsula campaign and, 165–66
    Peninsula campaign of, 101, 124, 132,
        144, 156, 176–77
    Rodgers' and, 180–82
    Scott replaced by, 188
Mackinac, 425
McClernand, John A., in Vicksburg cam-
    paign, 258, 261, 265–67, 289

Macedonian, 9
Macfarland, Mr., 114
McGowan, John, 11–12
McIntosh, Charles, 228
Macomb, William, 418–19, 421
McRae, 224
Maffitt, John Newland, 68, 410
    as blockade runner, 334–38, 340
Maffitt's Channel, 107, 110
Magruder, George, 42
Magruder, John, 143–45, 267
Mahan, Alfred Thayer, 164
Mallory, Midshipman, 128
Mallory, Stephen Russell, 65–75, 308,
    391
    background of, 65–67
    Charleston and, 385
    ironclad ships and, 136–39, 141,
        143–44, 157, 358–61
    New Orleans campaign as viewed by,
        223
    nominated as Confederate Secretary
        of Navy, 67
    Provisional Navy of the Confederate
        States created by, 73–74
    sea raiders and, 326–27, 332–34, 341
    western strategy and, 187
Malvern, 423–26, 429, 431
Manassas, 184*n*, 218–19
    in New Orleans campaign, 223, 224,
        230, 232–34
Manhattan, in Mobile Bay, 310, 314,
    321
Margaret Scott, 102
Marine Corps, U.S., 41, 81, 263, 346
Marine Railway and Drydock Company,
    182
Marmora, in Vicksburg campaign, 260,
    262
Marston, John, 32–33, 134, 166, 168–69,
    313, 314
Marthon, Joseph, 320
Martin, William, 80, 82, 83
Mary Alvina, 338
Maryland, secession and, 35, 45, 46,
    48–49
Mason, George, 109
Mason, James Murray, 204
    Trent affair and, 109–22
Massachusetts, 404*n*
Matagorda Bay, 293
Mattabesett, 413–15
Maury, Matthew Fontaine, 68, 109,
    354–55, 364
    resignation of, 42
Maury, William L., 354–55

Meade, George Gordon, 289, 291
Meigs, Montgomery, 185
    Fort Pickens relief and, 16–19, 20,
        26–27
    turtles and, 184
Melville, Herman, 102–3
Memphis, Tennessee, 191, 205, 206, 209,
        210, 215–16, 256, 359
Memphis and Charleston Railroad, 205
Mercedita, 379–81, 383
Mercer, Samuel, 15, 19–21, 24
Merchant service, 56
Merrick and Sons, 158, 160
Merrimack, 29–40, 55n, 308
    burning of, 37, 39
    crew of, 142–43
    destruction of, 177
    Hampton Roads trials of, 133, 135–36,
        144–55, 164, 168–76
    as ironclad, 135–56, 138–57, 163–65,
        168–77
    Isherwood inspection of, 31
    lack of commanding officer on, 143
    lack of crew for, 30
    mission of, 144
    Monitor vs., 171–76, 222
    renaming of, 135n, 142
    repair of, 176
    sinking of, 36–37
    Union fears about, 155–56
Mervine, William, 60
Metacomet, in Mobile Bay, 314, 317–19
Meteor, 105
Mexican War, 1, 3–4, 61
Mexico, 1
    French in, 292, 293, 330
Miami, 412, 413–15
Milliken's Bend, Mississippi, 260,
        263–65, 268
Minnesota, 55n, 59, 93, 125, 134, 148,
        169, 175, 176, 425
    in Hatteras Inlet action, 79–82, 84
    Merrimack and, 151, 153–55, 169–71
Minor, Bob, 149, 150, 152
Mississippi, secession of, 12, 26
Mississippi (ironclad), 223, 224, 235
Mississippi (Union frigate), 222, 224–25,
        227–30, 232–34, 281–85
Mississippi Marine Brigade, 259–60,
        272–76
Mississippi Ram Fleet, 79, 214–16
Mississippi River, 179–81, 185–87, 191,
        218, 265, 269, 272, 273
    in Anaconda plan, 61, 179–80
    Island No. 10 in, 205–10, 222
    strategic importance of, 179

    Vicksburg campaign and, 237–46,
        251–55
Mississippi Squadron, 263–69
    in Red River campaign, 295
    in Vicksburg campaign, 258–60
Mississippi Valley campaign, 186–292.
        See also Vicksburg, Mississippi
    Fort Donelson attack in, 197–206, 222
    Fort Henry attack, 191–96, 204–6, 222
    Fort Pillow attack in, 210–15
    Island No. 10 and, 205–10
Missouri, 296
Missouri Wrecking Company, 180
Mitchell, John K., 223, 227–30, 235–36
Mobile, Alabama, 237, 293, 324
    blockade of, 60, 63, 306–7, 309, 335
Mobile Bay, 237, 238, 241, 306–24, 357,
        358
    battle of (1864), 313–24
    Farragut's General Order No. 10 and,
        311
    Farragut's reconnaisance of, 309–10
Mobile Point, 309, 315, 317
Mobile Register, 142
Moir, Captain, 113, 115
Monarch, 216, 266
Mondamin, 341
Monitor, 135, 156, 157, 160–78, 184n,
        310, 371
    crew of, 163–65
    description of, 161–62
    design mistakes in, 166–67
    at Hampton Roads, 154, 156, 164
    Hampton Roads trials of, 359
    launch date of, 163
    Merrimack vs., 171–76, 222
    ordered to Washington, D.C., 166, 169
    repairs and improvements of, 177–78
    sinking of, 178, 375
    as tourist attraction, 178
    trials of, 164
Monongahela, 281, 283, 314, 320–21
Montauk, 375–76, 384, 386, 387, 389,
        403, 430
Montgomery, James, 212, 214
Monticello, in Hatteras Inlet action,
        79–81, 83, 84
Morehead City, North Carolina, 132, 332
Morgan, 309, 319
Morgan, George, 54, 121–22
Morgan, James, 355
Moro, 273
Morris, Charles Manigault, 341–42
Morris, George U., 148, 150–51
Morris Island, 6, 12, 105, 371, 377, 389,
        391, 392, 395, 398–403

Morrison, Captain, 88
Mosher, 233
Mosquito fleet, 125–32, 143
Mound City, 188, 213
  in Vicksburg campaign, 260
Mound City, Illinois, 259–60
Mound City Marine Railway and Ship
  Yard, 187
Mount Vernon, 135
Mullany, Commander, 318
Mullin, Anthony, 424
Murphey, Lieutenant, 319

Nahant, 386–91, 396, 397, 400
Nantucket, 387, 390
Napoleon III, 159, 340, 360–61
Nashville, 110, 111, 331–32, 375, 386
Nashville, Tennessee, 191, 196–97, 202,
  203
Nassau, 363, 416
  sea raiders and, 334–35, 337
Natchez, Mississippi, 239, 241
Natchez Courier, 60
Nationalism, Southern, 22
Naval Academy (Annapolis), 41, 44,
  46–49
Naval Academy (Newport), 49
Naval Observatory, 42
Navy, Confederate (Navy Department),
  67–75. *See also* Mallory, Stephen
  Russell; Provisional Navy of the
  Confederate States
  blacks in, 74, 131–32
  Chicamicomico Island, 89
  creation of, 2, 67
  in Galveston, 267–68
  in Hatteras Inlet action, 83–84
  ironclad ships of, 163–66, 168–77
  ironclads of, 40, 54, 66, 69, 70–71,
    135–57, 222–23, 307–9, 358–63,
    410–15. See also *Manassas; Mer-
    rimack*
  Charleston, 378–83
  mining and undersea warfare of, 70
  in Mobile Bay, 307–11, 313–24
  Mosquito fleet of, 125–32
  in New Orleans campaign, 223, 224,
    227–36
  at Norfolk Navy Yard, 40, 68, 69
  ocean-raiding cruisers of, 55, 325–67.
    See also Sea raiders
  Office of Medicine and Surgery of,
    71–72
  Office of Orders and Details of, 71, 72
  Office of Ordnance and Hydrography
    of, 72

  Office of Provisions and Clothing of,
    71–73
  officers in, 43, 46, 47
    abundance, 67, 73–74
  political appointments made by,
    97–100
  problems of, 308
    industrial weakness, 68–69, 71, 137
  recruitment of, 74
  River Defense Fleet of, 212–16
  Special Service Detachment of,
    385–86, 391
Navy, Secretary of the, 2. *See also* Mal-
    lory, Stephen Russell; Welles,
    Gideon
Navy, U.S. (Navy Department)
  blacks in, 57
  blockade and. *See* Blockade, Union
  Bureau of Construction, Repair, and
    Engineering of, 58
  Bureau of Medicine and Surgery of,
    58
  Bureau of Naval Personnel of, 71
  Bureau of Navigation of, 71
  Bureau of Ordnance and Hydrogra-
    phy of, 42, 58, 157
  Bureau of Provisions and Clothing of,
    3–4, 58
  Bureau of Yards and Docks of, 53, 58
  Confederate Navy compared with,
    71–73, 143
  construction program of, 54–55, 66
  East India Squadron of, 97
  at end of Civil War, 3
  exploration and diplomatic functions
    of, 2
  flogging in, 66
  Fort Pickens relief and, 16–21, 26–27
  Fort Sumter relief and, 9–27
  Hatteras Inlet action of. *See* Hatteras
    Inlet action
  ironclads of, 190, 259
  lack of sailors in, 57
  Mallory's attempted reform of, 66–67
  in Mexican War, 1, 3–4
  nadir of, 1–3
  Norfolk Navy Yard and, 28–39
  Office of Detail of, 71
  problems of, 307
  recruitment of, 55–58
  resignations from, 16, 17, 29, 32,
    41–49, 56
    Buchanan, 44–46
    Naval Academy, 41, 46–49
  Seward's overriding of, 16–20
  Trent affair and, 117

Navy, U.S. (cont.)
  vessels purchased and chartered by,
    53–54, 102–3
  Welles' mobilization of, 53–60
Navy Register, 2, 3, 24, 73
Neapolitan, 330
Neosho, 298, 302, 303, 304
Neptune, 267–68
Neuse, 411, 413
Neuse River, 86, 88, 413
Neutrality, 357, 359, 367
  of Great Britain, 52, 116, 117, 119, 333,
    340, 359
  of Spain, 330
New Bedford, Massachusetts, 103
New Bedford *Standard,* 103
New Berne, South Carolina, 86, 88
New Bern, North Carolina, 132, 410,
    411, 413–15, 417
New Carthage, Mississippi, 286, 287
New Inlet, 416, 417, 426
New Ironsides, 158, 160
  in Charleston attack, 376–77, 378,
    387–90, 400–402, 405, 406
  Wilmington and, 424–25, 429
New Madrid, Missouri, 185, 205–10
New Orleans, Louisiana, 68, 180, 207,
    217–36, 240–42, 257, 280, 281, 328
  blockade of, 60
  Butler's administration of, 258n
  Charleston compared with, 370–72
  fall of, 214, 235–36, 239, 359
  Porter's plan for, 219–20
Newport News, Virginia, 32, 33, 134–36,
    142, 147, 176
  Merrimack at, 135–36, 144–45, 164
Newton, Isaac, 167
Newton, Virginius, 139, 143, 152
New York, 29
New York City, 68, 345–46. *See also*
    Brooklyn Navy Yard
New York Herald, 66, 209
New York Marine Artillery, 79
New York Stock Exchange, 291
New York Times, 85, 119, 374
New York Tribune, 105, 106
New York World, 163
Niagara, 55n, 309, 355, 362
Nicolay, John, 124, 155–56
Nil, 355
95th Illinois, 300
9th New York Zouaves, 79, 82
Norfolk, Virginia, 77, 86, 123, 130,
    132–33, 142
  earthworks built at, 34–35
  secessionists in, 30, 31, 36

Norfolk Day Book, 142
Norfolk Navy Yard, 10, 15, 28–40, 57,
    133, 144, 176
  assets of, 28–29
  burning of, 37–39
  civilian workers at, 29–31
  Confederate evacuation of, 177
  Confederate taking of, 39–40, 68, 69
  dry dock of, 28–29, 38, 39
  ironclad ships constructed at, 139–43
  lack of security at, 142
  scuttling of ships at, 36–37
  strike at, 141
Norfolk United Artillery, 143
North, James, 359
North Atlantic Blocking Squadron,
    124–30, 134, 136, 347, 409, 418
  creation of, 91
North Atlantic Squadron, 120
North Carolina, 61, 123–34, 409–30
  blockade of, 332
  Hatteras Inlet action in. *See* Hatteras
    Inlet action
  secession of, 50, 77
North Carolina, 164
Novelty Iron Works, 158, 161
"No. 290," 343–44. *See also Alabama*

Oauchita River, 297
Ocmulgee, 344
Ocracoke Inlet, 85, 89
Octorara, 247, 309–10, 314, 318
Ohio River, 181–83, 186, 188, 257
Old Bahama Channel, 108, 116
Old Point Comfort, Virginia, 36, 93, 134,
    144, 148, 151, 168
Olinde, 361. See also *Stonewall*
Olustee, 358. See also *Chameleon*
Onandaga, 430
Oneida, 222, 228, 230, 231, 314, 318, 335
*Ordnance Instructions for the United
    State Navy* (Ordnance Manual),
    188 Oregon (gun), 158
Oreto, 334
Osage, in Red River campaign, 296,
    298–300, 303, 304
Ossabaw Sound, 377, 408
Ossipee, 314, 323
Ottawa, 100, 405
Ozark, 303, 304, 305

Pablo, Joseph, 93
Pacific Squadron, 164
Paducah, Kentucky, 186–88. 191
Page, Thomas Jefferson, 361–63
Palmer, James, 329

in Vicksburg campaign, 240, 242
Palmerston, Lord, *Trent* affair and,
115–17, 120, 121
Palmetto State, in Charleston attack,
378–80, 382, 383
Pamlico, 413
Pamlico River, 89
Pamlico Sound, 85, 86, 89, 123–25, 410,
413
Parker, Foxhall, 47
Parker, William, 41, 43, 47–48, 73, 123,
419, 431
in Charleston attack, 378–80, 382, 387,
392–93
on Hatteras Inlet action, 85
as *Merrimack* escort, 147, 152
Mosquito fleet, 126–30
Parrish, William, 145–46
Partisan Rangers, 269
Pasquotank River, 130
Passaic, 374–75, 386, 387, 389, 400
Passaic class, 371–72, 374–76
Patapsco, 386, 387, 389, 400, 402, 408
Patrick Henry, 151, 169
Paulding, Hiram, 45, 63, 246, 363, 374
ironclad ships and, 158, 166
Norfolk Navy Yard, 31, 34–39
Pawnee, 13, 15, 23–26
in Hatteras Inlet action, 79–81, 83, 84
Norfolk Navy Yard and, 34–38
Pay, 259
of Confederate Navy, 72
Peacemaker (gun), 158–59
Pearl Harbor, Japanese attack on, 156*n*
Pegram, Robert, 331–32
Pemberton, John, in Vicksburg cam-
paign, 260, 268, 277, 280, 288–90
Pendergrast, Austin, 151–52
Pendergrast, Garrett
blockade and, 53
Norfolk Navy Yard and, 29, 32–33
Peninsula campaign, 101, 124, 132, 144,
156, 165–66, 176–77
Pennock, Alex, 259, 291
Pennsylvania, 29
Pensacola, 222, 224–25, 228, 230, 232
Pensacola Navy Yard, 16, 26–27, 60, 68,
238
Perry, Horatio G., 330, 331, 362, 363
Perry, Matthew Calbraith, 2
Petrel, 382
Phelps, Sam, 182–83, 187, 188, 191, 193,
196–97
in Fort Pillow attack, 213–14
in Red River campaign, 295–96, 301–2
in Vicksburg campaign, 252

Philadelphia, 125
Philadelphia Naval Yard, 30, 32, 34, 53
Phillips, Surgeon, 153
Phoenix, 105
Pickens, Francis, 6, 8, 21
Pickett, George, 411
Pillow, Gideon, 197, 200, 202–3
Pilot Town, Louisiana, 225, 229
Pinola, 227
Pittsburgh, 188, 199–201, 210, 262, 288
in Red River campaign, 303, 304
Pleasant Hill, Louisiana, 299
Plymouth, 29, 36
Plymouth, North Carolina, 410–13,
419–21
Pocahontas, 104, 107
Fort Sumter relief and, 15, 22, 24, 25
Polk, James K., 3
Polk, Leonidas, 186, 187, 211
in second battle of Bull Run, 211*n*
Pontoosuc, 358
Pook, Samuel, 54, 181, 183–84
Pook turtles. *See* Turtles
Pope, John, 218–19
at Island No. 10, 206–11
Porcher, Phil, 379
Pork Point, Roanoke Island, 125, 127–30
Porter, Bill, 193–95, 252–53
Porter, David Dixon, 15–21, 56, 57,
217–21, 238, 246, 247, 285–300,
326, 349, 353, 372
Albemarle and, 418–19, 421
blockade and, 53, 60
Fort Pickens relief and, 16–21, 26–27,
30
in Hampton Roads, 430–31
Hatteras Inlet action and, 85
in Mobile Bay, 306
in New Orleans campaign, 218–20,
222, 223, 224–28, 234–36
in Red River campaign, 289, 294–99,
301–5, 418
Trent affair and, 122
Vicksburg campaign and, 241–42, 245,
256–61, 263–73, 275–80, 285–91
Wilmington and, 418, 422–30
Porter, John L., ironclad ships and, 138,
139, 141, 142, 145
Port Hudson, Louisiana, 280–85, 290–92,
294
Port Royal, 314
Port Royal, South Carolina, 90–101, 156,
219, 362, 385, 408
Charleston and, 370–71
delays in capture of, 94–96
failure of follow-up on, 101

Port Royal, South Carolina (cont.)
lack of formal surrender at, 100
Mercedita at, 380, 383
New Ironsides test run at, 376
Port Royal Sound, 105
Portsmouth, Virginia, 142
Potomac River, 144, 159, 165, 166, 257
Powhattan, 15, 17–21, 23–27, 30, 217,
218, 306
blockade and, 60
in Charleston, 385–86
Wilmington and, 425, 427
Preble, 218
Preble, George, blockade runners and,
335, 336
Preston, Sam, 402, 403
Wilmington and, 422, 424
Prince Albert, 334
Princess Royal, 377
Princeton, 158–59, 165
Privateering, Confederate, 50–51, 63,
326
in Hatteras Inlet, 77–78
Hatteras Inlet action and. *See* Hatteras
Inlet action
Provisional Congress, 67, 73, 74
ironclad ships and, 136, 139
Naval Affairs Committee of, 136
Provisional Navy of the Confederate
States, creation of, 73–74
Prussia, 361
Punch, 336
Putnam, 126

Quackenbush, Lieutenant, 131
Quaker City, 380
Quaker guns, 103
Queen of the West, 215–16, 295
in Vicksburg campaign, 247, 249–53,
262, 272–77, 281
Quinby, Isaac, 272

Rachel Hatch, 357
Railroads, 181, 205, 239, 308, 407, 408
bridges for, 196–97
cutting of, 86, 101
Forrest's attack on, 263, 264
Raleigh, 130, 132
as *Merrimack* escort, 147, 148, 152
Ramsay, Ashton, on *Merrimack,* 146–47,
148, 164*n,* 170, 172, 173, 175–76
Randolph, Victor, 143
Rappahannock, 355–56, 361
Rations, 72–73, 92, 246
Rattler, 266
Ravenel, Julian, 404

Read, Charles, 248–50, 254, 338–40
Rebecca Sims, 104, 106
Red River campaign, 286, 289, 292–305,
418
advantages of advance up, 293, 294
Banks' retreat in, 298–99, 302, 305
ironclads trapped in, 303–4
Vicksburg campaign and, 272–77
Red Rover, 259, 260
Renshaw, William, 267, 268
Republicans (Republican Party), in elec-
tion of 1860, 4, 6
Revenue Marine, 13*n,* 68
Reynolds, Lieutenant Colonel, 95, 96
Rhind, Alexander, 387, 390, 391, 393
Wilmington and, 422–24
Rhode Island, 178
Richmond, 106, 218–19, 430
in Mobile Bay, 313, 314, 318
in New Orleans campaign, 222, 224,
229
in Vicksburg campaign, 238, 240, 243,
244, 281, 283, 285
Richmond, Virginia, 71, 72, 77, 123, 130,
366, 418
evacuation of, 431
Peninsula campaign and, 124, 132,
144, 176–77
Wilmington and, 416
Richmond Examiner, 324
Richmond Whig, 426–27
Rio Grande River, 293
Ripley, R. S., 368
River Defense Fleet, 212–16, 215, 239–40
in New Orleans campaign, 224,
227–28
River Queen, 430
Roanoke, 55*n,* 134, 148, 151, 168
Roanoke Island, 123–30
Roanoke River, 410–13, 415, 419–21
Robb, Robert, 33
Robert Gilfillan, 332
Robin Hood, 106
Rochelle, Lieutenant, 169–70
Rodgers, Christopher, 49, 389–91, 398
Rodgers, George, 48, 387, 390–91, 400
Rodgers, John, 38, 39, 99, 100, 180–86
in Charleston attack, 387–89, 394,
396–97
Rodgers, Raymond, 372
Roe, Francis, 414–15
Rolling Fork, 277, 278
Ross, Leonard, 269–71
Rousseau, Lawrence, 137
Rowan, Stephen, 23–25, 34, 36, 39, 123
in Albemarle Sound, 130–32

Hatteras Inlet and, 86, 88
naval division of, 125–27, 130–32
R. R. Cuyler, 336
Russell, Earl, 344, 359
Trent affair and, 116, 119–21
Russia, 359

Sabine, 60, 96, 164
Sabine Cross Roads, Louisiana, 298–300
Sabine Pass, Texas, 293
Sachem, 165, 226
Sacramento, 362
St. Lawrence, 134, 151, 153, 155, 166
Saint Louis, 184*n,* 188, 194, 196, 199,
200, 202, 207, 215. *See also* Baron
De Kalb
St. Louis Democrat, 184
St. Philip, 270
San Jacinto, Trent affair and, 108–9,
111–15, 117–18
Santo Domingo, 330
Sarah A. Boyce, 356
Sassacus, 413–15, 422
Savannah, Georgia, 375–76, 408
blockade of, 102–5, 107
Savannah River, 104
S. Bayard, 269
Sciota, 252
Scorpion, 360
Scott, Winfield, 18, 60–64
Anaconda plan of, 61, 62, 64, 179–80
Fort Sumter relief and, 9–11, 13, 14
Hatteras Inlet action and, 79
political appointments made by, 90
retirement of, 188
Union strategy conceived by, 60–62,
64
Scott's Anaconda. *See* Anaconda plan
Sea Bird, 126, 130–32
Sea King, 364–65. See also *El Majidi;*
Shenandoah
Sea raiders, 325–67
aim of, 325–26
Alabama, 338, 344–54, 357, 358,
363–65, 367
Bulloch's role in procurement of,
332–33, 334, 340, 343, 344, 354
Florida, 307, 335–38, 340–43, 347, 358,
367
Georgia, 354–55
Nashville, 331–32
Rappahannock, 355–56
Shenandoah, 360, 364–67
Sumter, 326–32
Tallahassee, 356–58
whaling industry and, 363–66

Secession, 12, 16, 26, 66
Mallory's view of, 66
Maryland's, 35, 45, 46, 48–49
of North Carolina, 77
of South Carolina, 6, 7, 106
of Virginia, 30–32, 36, 41, 42, 44, 50
Second Anglo-Chinese Opium War, 97
2nd U.S. Artillery, 79
Selfridge, Thomas, 35, 36, 176
cotton acquired by, 296–97
on *Cumberland,* 148–50
in Hatteras Inlet action, 81
in Red River campaign, 296, 298,
299–300, 304–5
in Vicksburg campaign, 262
Selma, 309, 316, 318, 319, 324
Selma, Alabama, 307–8
Selma Foundry Works, 69
Seminole, 138, 314
Semmes, Raphael, 74
resignation of, 42
as sea raider, 326–31, 343–53, 363–64
Senate, Confederate, Naval Affairs Com-
mittee of, 71–72
Senate, U.S., 66
Seneca, 94, 97, 100, 101, 104
Seth Low, 165, 168
Seven-Mile Reach, 384
Seventh New York, 49
7th North Carolina Infantry, 80
Seward, Frederick, 19–21
Seward, William, 6, 16–21, 53
blockade and, 51–52, 383
Fort Sumter relief and, 14
France and, 292, 293
ironclad ships and, 155–56, 159
Machiavellian side of, 17
political appointments made by, 91
presidential ambitions of, 4, 14, 17
sea raiders and, 328
Trent affair and, 117, 118, 120–22
western strategy and, 292, 293, 305
Sewell's Point, Virginia, 36, 94, 147, 153,
175, 177
Shenandoah, 360, 364–67
Shannon, 332
Sherman, Thomas, 101, 105
political appointments made by,
90–94, 97, 100
Sherman, William Tecumseh, 90, 179,
256, 307, 408, 427, 430
in Atlanta, 407
Red River campaign and, 293–95, 297,
298
in Vicksburg campaign, 260, 261,
263–66, 268, 278–79, 287–89

Shiloh, battle of, 104
Ship Island, 63, 222, 223, 238
Shippen, Edward, 135–36
Shirk, Jim, 287
Shreveport, Louisiana, 294, 296–99
Shyrock, George, 229, 355–56
Signal, in Vicksburg campaign, 260, 262
Sinclair, Arthur, 347
Sinclair, Terry, 337–38
Slavery (slaves), 77, 101, 142, 259, 295, 345
    fugitive, 81–82
    Great Britain and, 115–16
    in Red River campaign, 302
    in territories, 3, 66
    Vicksburg campaign and, 262, 277, 278–80
Slemmer, Adam, 16
Slidell, John, 360
    Trent affair and, 109–22
Slidell, Mrs. John, 113–15
Slidell, Matilda, 114
Smith, A. J., 295, 297–99, 301
Smith, Commodore Joseph, 53, 217
    ironclad ships and, 158, 160, 162–63
Smith, Elias, 287
Smith, Lt. Joseph, 135
Smith, Melancton, 229–30, 233–34, 283–85
    in Albemarle Sound, 413–14, 418
Smith, T. Kilby, 298, 301
Smith, Watson, 269–71
Smith, William, 151, 152
Smith's Island, 416
Soda bottle guns, 373
South Atlantic Blocking Squadron, 368, 395, 398
    Charleston and, 371, 372
    creation of, 91
    political appointments made by, 91–101
South Carolina, 6–27, 61, 132. *See also* Charleston, South Carolina; Fort Moultrie, South Carolina; Fort Sumter, South Carolina; Port Royal, South Carolina
    secession of, 6, 7, 106
    tariff nullification and, 14
Southfield, 412–13, 419–20
Spain, 137
    ironclad ships and, 361–63
    sea raiders and, 330
Spanish-American War, 404*n*, 427*n*
Spiking method, 38*n*
Spotswood, Charles, 39
Springfield Landing, Louisiana, 298

Staerkodder, 361. See also *Olinde;
    Stonewall*
Stag, 429–30
Stanton, Edwin, 9, 155–56, 305, 383
Star of Peace, 337
Star of the West, 11–12, 21, 47, 270
State Department, U.S., 157, 188
Steel, 68
Steele's Bayou expedition, 277–80, 285
Stellwagen, Henry
    in Charleston attack, 379–80
    Fanny incident and, 89
    Hatteras Inlet action and, 78–80
Stembel, Roger, 213
Stephens, Tom, 384–85
Stevens, Henry Kennedy, 247, 249, 251, 253–55
Stevens, Thomas, 402–4
Stevenson, Master, 227–28
Stewart, Charles, 2
Stimers, Alban, 393
    Monitor and, 164–65, 167, 172, 174
Stinkpots, 181–93
    conversion of, 182–83
    at Corinth, 210–11
    in Vicksburg campaign, 246–47
Stockston, Robert, 158–59
Stodder, Louis, 171–72, 176
Stone Fleet, The (Melville), 102
Stone ships, blockade and, 102–7
Stonewall, 361–63
Stono, 378–85, 392
Stono River, 377–78
Strategy Board. *See* Commission of Conference
Strike at Norfolk Navy Yard, 141
Stringham, Silas, 59–60, 246
    in Hatteras Inlet action, 98, 393
    Hatteras Inlet action and, 62–64, 77–87, 90, 123
    replacement of, 87
Stumpy Point, North Carolina, 126
Sullivan, Seaman, 405
Sullivan's Island, 6. *See also* Fort Moultrie, South Carolina
Sumner, Charles, 51, 118
Sumter, 109, 345
    as sea raider, 326–32
Supreme Court, U.S., 5
Susan Abigail, 366
Susquehanna, 98–100
Switzerland, 285

Tacony, 338–39
Taliaferro, William, 34–35, 39–40
Tallahassee, 356–58

Tallahatchie River, 268, 270
Taney, Roger B., 5
Tariffs, 14
Tattnall, Josiah (Old Tat), 41
  Merrimack and, 176, 177
  political appointments made by,
    97–100
Taylor, Dick, 299
Taylor, Jesse, 192–95
Teaser, 151
Tecumseh, in Mobile Bay, 310, 312–14,
  316–17, 324
Tenedos, 102–3, 106
Tennessee, 216, 307–11, 313–24
Tennessee Ironworks, 203
Tennessee River, 186, 188, 191–97, 205
Terry, Alfred, 427–29
Texas, 61, 292–94, 305
  secession of, 12, 26
Theodora, 111
3rd Georgia Infantry, 83
Third Massachusetts Regiment, 36, 37
Thistle, 278–79
Thomas, Charles, 288
Thompson, Egbert, 199
Thompson, Jacob, 10
Thompson, James, 274
Thompson, Jeff, 212, 247
Tilghman, Lloyd, 192, 196
Timber, 68
Times (London), 331
Tomb, James, 383, 406
Tombigbee River, 307
Tonawanda, 345
Toronto Leader, 119
Totten, General, 63
Toucy, Isaac, 2, 10, 11
  resignations as viewed by, 41–42
Transportation, Confederate problems
  with, 68, 69, 72
Traver, Lorenzo, 126, 128
Treasury, Confederate, 110
Treasury Department, U.S., 187, 294
  Coast Survey of, 15
  Revenue Marine of, 13*n*
Tredegar Iron Works, 68, 69, 137, 138,
  140, 223
Trenholm, George, 110–11
Trent affair, 108–22, 330, 331, 359
  arrests in, 113–15
  British reaction to, 120
  Cabinet meetings about, 118, 121–22
  giving up of prisoners in, 122
  international law and, 111–12, 115,
    116, 122
  Northern reaction to, 118

Trent's Reach, 430
Tristan da Cunha, 365
Trunnions, 38
Tucker, John (Handsome Jack), 381,
  391–93
Turner, Thomas, 376–77, 387–89
Turtles, 184, 190–202, 212–16
  in Fort Donelson attack, 197–203, 206
  in Fort Henry attack, 191–96, 206
  in Fort Pillow attack, 212–15
  guns of, 187–88
  at Island No. 10, 206–10
  in Vicksburg campaign, 246–47, 252,
    262, 276–79, 286
Tuscaloosa, 347, 348, 367
Tuscarora, 55, 331–32
Tuscumbia, 286–88
20th Indiana Regiment, 88–89
20th New York Volunteers, 79, 82–84
Tybee Island, 104, 105
Tycoon, 348–49
Tyler, 181–83, 185–91, 199, 200, 210
  in Vicksburg campaign, 247, 249–51
Tyler, John, 159
Tyler, Robert, 24

Unadilla class, 55
Underwriter, 129
Uniforms, Confederate, 72
United States, 29

Valley City, 127, 129, 132, 421
Van Brunt, Gershon, 169, 170
Vanderbilt, 94
Van Dorn, Earl, 248, 251, 253
  in Vicksburg campaign, 263
Varuna, 222, 228, 230–31, 233, 234
Vicksburg, battle of, 360
Vicksburg, Mississippi, 215–17, 236–92,
  306, 307
  Arkansas episode in, 246–56
  fall of (1863), 179, 289–92, 294
  first attempt at, 237–40
  Red River expedition and, 272–77
  reorganization of Army and Navy,
    258
  second attempt at, 240–53
  Steele's Bayou expedition and,
    278–80, 285
  surrender of, 186
  Yazoo Pass expedition and, 268–72, 277
Vicksburg, Shreveport & Texas, 239
Vicksburg National Military Park, 262
Victor, 355. See also *Rappahannock*
Victoria, Queen of England, 52, 116, 119,
  333

Vincennes, 218–19
Virginia, 22, 61. *See also* Fort Monroe,
   Virginia
   secession of, 30–32, 36, 41, 42, 44, 50
Virginia, 354. See also *Merrimack*
Virginia II, 430
Vixen, 96
Voruz, J., 360

Wabash, 55*n,* 122, 398, 403, 425
   in Hatteras Inlet action, 79–81
   political appointments made by,
      91–100
Wabash class, 29, 55, 138
Wachusett, 342–43
Waddell, James Iredell, 365–67
Wainwright, Jonathan, 268
Walke, Henry, 189–90, 193–201, 205,
      211, 247
   in Fort Donelson attack, 197–201
   in Fort Pillow attack, 213–15
   at Island No. 10, 207–10
   in Vicksburg campaign, 246, 249, 250,
      259–62, 286
Walker, Baldwin, 348
Walker, Leroy, 21
Walker, William, 11
Wallace, Lew, 199, 202
War Department, Confederate, 74
War Department, U.S., 8, 182, 187, 280
   Anderson's cables to, 7
   Fort Sumter relief and, 15
   Hatteras Inlet action and, 78
Warley, Alexander, 232–34
War of 1812, 1, 121*n*
Washington, D.C., 144, 165–66
   defense of, 37
   fear of fall of, 63
   Monitor in, 178
   Monitor ordered to, 166, 169
Washington Navy Yard, 15, 44–45, 373
Watson, John C., 312, 316–18
Waud, Alfred, 232
Webb, 275
Webb, William A., 385
Weber, Max, 82–84
Weed, Thurlow, 335
Weehawken, in Charleston attack,
      387–90, 396–97, 400–402
Weidman, John, 95, 96
Weitzel, Godfrey, 418, 422–26
Welles, Gideon, 3–5, 14–20, 50, 63, 124,
      188, 217, 398
   appointed Secretary of Navy, 3, 4
   background of, 3
   blockade and, 51, 70, 383

blockade runners and, 332, 335–36,
      346–47
Buchanan's hatred of, 145
Charleston attack and, 371–74,
      383–84, 393–95, 404, 408
Cumberland and, 151
Dahlgren's promotion and, 373, 384
election of 1860 and, 4, 17
Foote's correspondence with, 188–90,
      203, 206, 211
Fort Pickens relief and, 16
Fort Sumter relief and, 14, 15, 19
Hatteras Inlet action and, 76–79, 86,
      89
ironclad ships and, 134–35, 155–60,
      166, 169, 363, 410
Mallory compared with, 70
on McCauley, 29
in Mexican War, 3–4
Mobile Bay and, 309–12, 324
Naval Academy and, 47, 49
naval mobilization of, 53–60
naval reforms and, 246
New Orleans campaign and, 219–21
Norfolk Navy Yard and, 28–32, 34, 35
Peninsula campaign and, 166
political appointments made by, 90
press criticism of, 64
resignations as viewed by, 16, 41–43,
      45–46
sea raiders and, 326, 329, 339, 343*n,*
      349
secession as viewed by, 16
Seward's overriding of, 17–20
Stringham replaced by, 87–88
Trent affair and, 111, 117, 119–22
western strategy and, 180, 182, 185,
      188–89, 216, 237, 296
   Red River campaign, 299
   Vicksburg campaign, 239, 241,
      244–46, 253, 256–58, 267, 286,
      290–91
Wilmington and, 416–18, 421
Welles, William, 412
West African Squadron, 2
Western Bar Channel, 416
Western Gunboat Flotilla, 99, 223, 236,
      246. *See also* Stinkpots; Turtles
   problems of, 182–83, 190
   in Vicksburg campaign, 244–45
Western strategy, 179–236. *See also* Mis-
      sissippi Valley campaign; New
      Orleans, Louisiana; Red River
      campaign; Vicksburg, Mississippi
Westfield, 224, 267, 268
West Gulf Blockading Squadron, 293

in New Orleans campaign, 221–36
West Indian Squadron, 120
W. F. Seaver, 354–55
Whaling Charts of the World (Maury), 364
Whaling industry, 363–66
Wharton, Arthur, 316, 320–21
Whigs (Whig Party), 4, 66
Whistling Wind, 338
White, David, 345, 353
Whitehead, 412
Whitman, Walt, ix
Whittle, Lieutenant, 236
Wide-Awakes, 4
Wilderness, 424
Wilderness campaign, 415
Wilkes, Charles, 342, 359
    Norfolk Navy Yard and, 35–39
    Trent affair and, 108–9, 111–15, 117–22
Wilkinson, John, 408
William Bell, 357
Wm. C. Miller & Sons, 334
Williams, Cort, 276–77
Williams, Peter, 171
Williams, Thomas, in Vicksburg campaign, 237, 239, 240, 243, 253, 254
Williamson, William P., 138, 139
Wilmington, Delaware, blockade of, 356, 358
Wilmington, North Carolina, 416–19, 421–30
    blockade of, 416, 430
    Fort Fisher invasion and, 421–29
Wilmington Daily Journal, 325, 358
Wilson, James Harrison, 270, 271
Wilson, Thomas, 342

Winan, Ross, 404
Winnebago, in Mobile Bay, 310, 314
Winona, 252, 335
Winslow, 83
Winslow, John, 349–53
Wise, Henry, 36–38, 197
Wivern, 360
Wolfe, James, 189
Woman Order, 258
Wood, John Taylor
    Merrimack and, 143, 147, 149, 151, 153, 173–75, 177
    as sea raider, 356–58
Woodbury, Paymaster, 400
Woodford, 297
Worden, John L., 16
    in Charleston attack, 387, 389, 391
    at Fort McAllister, 375–76, 384–85
    Monitor and, 162–65, 167–76
Wormley, William, 93
Wright, Horatio, 35, 38, 39
Wright, Richard, 364
Wyalusing, 413–15
Wyandotte, 27

X Corps, 395

Yalobusha River, 270
Yankee, 18, 22, 38, 58
Yazoo City, Mississippi, 268
Yazoo Pass expedition, 268–72, 277
Yazoo River, 215, 241, 242, 246, 247–51, 260–64, 268, 270, 277, 288, 289
York Peninsula, 144. *See also* Peninsula campaign
Young's Point, 239, 243, 252, 255, 277, 287, 289

973.75
Mus   Musicant, Ivan

                Divided waters

$ 30.00